THE
UNITED STATES
IN THE
TWENTIETH CENTURY

KEY
DOCUMENTS

Edited by Richard Maidment
and Michael Dawson

SECOND EDITION

Hodder & Stoughton
in association with

The Open
University

This text forms part of an Open University course D214 *The United States in the Twentieth Century*. The list of texts that make up the course can be found on the back cover. Details of this and other Open University courses can be obtained from the Course Reservations Centre, PO Box 724, The Open University, Milton Keynes MK7 6ZS, United Kingdom: tel. (00 44) 1908 653231. Alternatively, much useful information can be obtained from the Open University's website http://www.open.ac.uk

Published in Great Britain by Hodder & Stoughton Educational, a division of Hodder Headline Plc, 338 Euston Road, London NW1 3BH; written and produced by The Open University.

Orders: please contact Bookpoint Ltd, 39 Milton Park, Abingdon, Oxon OX14 4TD. Telephone: (44) 01235 400414, Fax: (44) 01235 400454. Lines are open from 9.00 – 6.00, Monday to Saturday, with a 24 hour message answering service. Email address: orders@bookpoint.co.uk

British Library Cataloguing in Publication Data

A catalogue record for this title is available from The British Library

ISBN 0 340 75827 9

First published 1994

Second edition published 1999

Impression number   10 9 8 7 6 5 4 3 2 1

Year   2005 2004 2003 2002 2001 2000 1999

Edited, designed and typeset by the Open University.

Printed in the United Kingdom by Scotprint Ltd, Musselburgh, Scotland.

20914C/d214b5prei2.1.doc

THE
UNITED STATES
IN THE
TWENTIETH CENTURY

KEY

DOCUMENTS

Cover

Jefferson Memorial, Washington, DC

CONTENTS

PREFACE

The five volumes in this series are part of an Open University, Faculty of Social Sciences course *The United States in the Twentieth Century*. In many respects the course has been a new venture — it is the first time that The Open University has entered the field of American Studies and it did so at a time when resources were not abundant. So the development of this course is due, in no small part, to the enthusiasm and support of many colleagues in the Faculty of Social Sciences. There are too many people to thank individually, but my appreciation must be recorded for some of them.

The United States in the Twentieth Century would not have been made without my academic colleagues, Anthony McGrew, Jeremy Mitchell and Grahame Thompson. Their role was central to the conception and planning of the course and their presence made the production of it an intellectually stimulating as well as an enjoyable experience. Mike Dawson, the Course Manager, took all the tension out of a process that is normally fraught and difficult. His calm efficiency, common sense and good humour got the rest of us through the production process with few anxieties. Jeremy Cooper of the BBC not only ensured that the course has an excellent audio-visual component, but made a very important contribution to its overall development. The Course Team owes a substantial debt to the editorial work of Stephen Clift and Tom Hunter who did all that was asked of them plus a great deal more. The designs for the covers, and indeed for the entire course, by Sarah Crompton were immediately and enthusiastically welcomed by everybody. David Wilson of the Book Trade Department was always available and his advice was both appreciated and heeded. Our colleagues in Project Control and in the Operations Division of the university were unfailingly supportive and helpful. However, none of these books would have seen the light of day without Anne Hunt who, along with her colleagues Mary Dicker and Carole Kershaw, typed successive drafts of the manuscripts of all five volumes without complaint and with remarkable accuracy and speed.

These books owe an enormous debt to our Americanist colleagues in institutions other than The Open University. This series has drawn on their scholarship and expertise, and above all on their generosity in being willing to participate in this project. The Course Team owes a particular debt to Professor David Adams, Director of the David Bruce Centre at the University of Keele, the external assessor of *The United States in the Twentieth Century*. His tough advice and wise counsel assisted us greatly. We incurred a similar obligation to Professor Ian Bell, also of the University of Keele, who helped us far beyond the call of duty. Doctor Ronald Clifton, who has done so much for American Studies in Britain, was enormously helpful and supportive in making sure this course came to fruition.

Finally there were moments when it might have been easier for Margaret Kiloh, the Dean of the Faculty of Social Sciences, to have been less than enthusiastic about *The United States in the Twentieth Century* but her support never wavered.

Richard Maidment, Course Chair
Milton Keynes, December 1993

FOREWORD TO THE FIRST EDITION

This is the final volume in the series *The United States in the Twentieth Century* and it contains a collection of documents which reflect the interests and content of the preceding volumes. The documents have been structured around the central organizing themes of the four other books and accordingly there are chapters on Culture, Markets, Democracy and Empire. There is also a chapter of maps and statistical data that will be in our opinion of considerable value. This collection has been designed, in the first instance, to provide documents and other materials that relate to the concerns of the interpretive essays of the other volumes. This has resulted in a very distinctive collection which we hope will be particularly useful to the readers of the series, but will also be of interest to a wider audience.

We owe a very considerable debt to the entire *The United States in the Twentieth Century* Course Team. Their collective support and advice was extremely helpful. We have a particular obligation to Professor Ian Bell of the University of Keele whose wise advice and guidance was invaluable in compiling the documents in the Culture chapter. He always responded immediately and generously to our frequent cries for assistance. We are very grateful. Grahame Thompson and Anthony McGrew made several shrewd suggestions for improving the book. Stephen Clift edited this volume to his usual very high standard, but on this occasion he did it at a speed which was extraordinarily impressive. Anne Hunt, Mary Dicker and Carole Kershaw processed the manuscript with their normal efficiency and good humour despite the difficulties we put in their way.

Richard Maidment
Mike Dawson
Milton Keynes, June 1994

FOREWORD TO THE SECOND EDITION

The second edition of *Key Documents* retains the structure of the first and maintains its links to the revised editions of the rest of the series. We have taken the opportunity to fully review and update the statistical information and include new maps and diagrams. Several new documents have been added, some on the advice of those involved with teaching The Open University course associated with the series, while others bring the collection up to date in certain areas.

We are grateful to all those who contributed ideas and suggestions. Stephen Clift again made an important contribution through his editing work on the book, and we would also like to thank Annabel Caulfield for her support as Course Manager, Celia Hart for her work in obtaining the new photographs, Ray Munns for his work on the maps, Jonathan Davies for updating the cover design, and Mary Dicker for inputting the documents.

DOCUMENTS ON THE INTERNET

In this edition several of the sources of documents are important Internet sites. The Internet gives access to a vast amount of information on the United States and countless public domain documents. The sources used have, in most cases, links to many other related sites. Particularly significant and useful sites include the following:

> The White House Web Site, http://www.whitehouse.gov/
>
> United States Information Agency Web Site, http://www.usia.gov/
>
> US State Department Web Site, http://www.state.gov/
>
> US House of Representatives Web Site, http://www.house.gov/
>
> The National Archives and Records Administration Web Site, http://www.nara.gov/
>
> The Library of Congress Web Site, http://www.loc.gov/

Mike Dawson
Richard Maidment
Milton Keynes, June 1999

CULTURE

1.1 INTRODUCTION

In a society much driven by the search for material prosperity as well as industrial, commercial and technological advancement, art is seen as expensive and unfunctional. At the same time it is allowed significant social meaning, which is one of the great paradoxes of American culture. In 1913, the poet Ezra Pound published 'The Serious Artist' where he proposed an argument for the arts and their relationship with the discourses of science: 'The arts, literature, poesy, are a science, just as chemistry is a science'. Pound's argument incorporates the claim that not only does art share the status of the sciences but that it shapes their ethical functions and hence their most important social meaning. Drawing strongly upon analysis from medicine, art is seen as diagnostic, and the moral burden of both art and medicine is to provide an accurate report on the matter under observation. Hence, 'the bad artist is condemned as we would condemn a negligent physician or a sloppy, inaccurate scientist', and the seriousness or social value of the work produced depends entirely on the precision of that work.

Pound's scientific aesthetic was a response to the machine-like nature of the contemporary world, a world which made fresh demands upon the moral and social function of the arts. For Frank Lloyd Wright, at the beginning of the century, the machine itself was the 'forerunner of the democracy that is our dearest hope', and was not to be disassociated from the more recognizably human aspects of culture and, indeed, was to be seen as integral to those aspects:

> Upon this faith in art as the organic heart of the scientific frame of things, I base a belief that we must look to the artist brain of all brains to grasp the significance to society of this thing we call the machine, which is no more or less than the principle of organic growth working irresistibly the will of life through the medium of man.

This new scientific seriousness for the artist's project helped to cultivate a weightier public arena for the arts and their effectiveness, right up to governmental level. The severity of the Depression experienced during the

1930s was such that private industry became largely impotent in tackling the malaise of unemployment and the slums. Government intervention was necessary, and interestingly the New Deal included the arts within the general programme of economic recovery. The Works Progress Administration (WPA) under Harry Hopkins sought to create work for unemployed artists, most notably in the Federal Theater Project headed by Hallie Flanagan who did not hesitate to view the project as part of Hopkins' wider dream of creating and funding 'a decent life for all the people in this country'. Such integration of art and society was central to the next period of cultural history during the 1960s in which aesthetics were impelled towards a fresh justification of their role.

Susan Sontag underlined the illusion of any separation between the arts and sciences. The imagined conflict of the two in fact produced a new, 'potentially unitary' kind of sensibility that would transform the function of art by producing 'a new kind of instrument, an instrument for modifying consciousness and organizing new modes of sensibility'. This new instrument would challenge the materials and methods of artistic practise by the exploitation of those from the world of 'non-art' from technology and commerce. This would challenge the accepted boundaries — science/art, art/non-art, form/content, frivolous/serious, high/low — of older ideas about art. It was this postmodernist challenge which, more than anything, registered the scientific spirit of the new instrument: 'Today's art, with its insistence on coolness, its refusal of what it considers to be sentimentality, its spirit of exactness, its sense of "research" and "problems", is closer to the spirit of science than of art in the old-fashioned sense.'

Sontag's 'new sensibility', emerging in the early years of postmodernism, also marked the demise of a distinction about art 'in the old-fashioned sense'. This was the distinction between the unique and the mass-produced that had received particular urgency during the Cold War period of the 1950s, and the Depression of the 1930s. American Romanticism became revived in the form of a faith in the individual voice protesting against the abstract and invisible forces destroying the land and human possibilities as in John Steinbeck's *The Grapes of Wrath*. It became the only possible alternative to a world becoming blindly technological and bureaucratic — the colourless grey of the dust-bowl or the Eisenhower Administration where the only means of resistance was to move and keep on moving. The itinerant workers and hobos of the 1930s anticipated the mobility of the Beats in the 1950s as a Romantic gesture against facelessness and conformity. It was entirely appropriate that Allen Ginsberg should invoke the ghost of Walt Whitman, the archetypal American Romantic poet from the nineteenth century, to inveigh against contemporary consumerism in *A Supermarket in California* where the unique, personal speaking voice asserts itself amidst mass packaging.

One theme that continues to be discernible is a consideration of the artist's responsibilities to a rapidly changing society. F. Scott Fitzgerald's 'Echoes of the Jazz Age' has given a justly celebrated portrait of the 1920s — its excesses, hedonism, relaxing of sexual mores, amorality, nervous energy, mobility. These are the features we remember from his account, but what is often neglected is its acknowledgement of a crucial shift in the American psyche — a recognition of the need for radical restructurings of the self. The 1920s began as 'an affair of youth' and Fitzgerald locates 1922 as 'the peak of the younger generation'. By 1923, however, 'their elders, tired of watching the carnival with ill-concealed envy, had discovered that young liquor will take the place of young blood, and with a whoop the orgy began'. Fitzgerald makes literal the activity that would come to dominate American thought throughout the decades following — an alertness to the design and the possibilities for re-design of the world. The reconstruction of blood by liquor might stand as a metaphor for the constructed nature of twentieth-century American experience. It was not accidental that Fitzgerald's essay was published within a year of the establishing of the Hays Code which sought to govern the entry of art into the market-place via mass-production — the cinema. The intimacy, widespread appeal and emotional arousal of films imposed upon them a particular responsibility 'for spiritual or moral progress, for higher types of social life, and for much correct thinking' under the aegis of 'wholesome entertainment'. In short, the Hays Code intended to restructure the 'whole standard of a nation' and to effect its restructuring through market practices. Within a consumer culture, it was inevitable that the design and re-design of things would lie mainly in the hands of the advertising industry or the media: even the political areas could not escape the market-place once technology had advanced sufficiently in 1956 to re-structure the face of Eisenhower in order to 'sell' the President.

Claims for the relationship between the media and society were not necessarily as pious as those of the Hays Code nor as cynical as the marketing of a political leader. The iconoclastic and satirical *American Mercury* of H.L. Mencken and George Jean Nathan wanted 'to keep to common sense as fast as they can, to belabor sham as agreeably as possible, to give civilized entertainment' on behalf of a 'middle ground' between Liberal and Tory, between false utopia and oppressive legislation, in order to address the 'outcasts of democracy', to entertain 'the normal, educated, well-disposed, unfrenzied, enlightened citizen of the middle minority'. The responsibility of the journal was thus to be 'entirely devoid of messianic passion', to refuse 'any sovereign balm' for 'all the sorrows of the world'. In large part, such responsibility would involve a reassessment of a wholly novel area of experience within a technologically advanced society: the area of leisure occasioned by new working habits. Fitzgerald at the end of the period nominated the 1920s as the 'Jazz Age'. But perhaps it could be more accurately viewed in Robert Duffus' phrase as the 'Age of Play'. The liberations of technology struck 'a fatal blow at the ancestral faith in mere hard work', and once the economic value of leisure became evident, the notion of play was allowed to move beyond accusations of idleness and be recognized as a 'right', a right claimed as 'the final clause in the charter of democracy'.

This latter is a large claim, particularly within a culture which has oscillated between prosperity and poverty throughout the century. It becomes one of the ways in which America advertises itself to itself, concealing the less acceptable consequences of advanced industrialization: strikingly, documents such as Duffus' testifying to prosperity, omit issues of employment, as does the celebration of the 'Miracle of America' by US Business during the post-Second World War boom. There, the constructivist thrust of American thought foregrounds American ingenuity and inventiveness as the basis for improvements which 'multiplied each man's work power' and 'made us better and better workers — no matter what our jobs'. The contrast between prosperity and poverty is forcefully made in what Michael Harrington, looking back at the 1950s, called the 'Other America'. Harrington tellingly displays another side of America, the 40–50 million 'poor' excluded from the 'affluent society' by a significant shift in perception: 'the nation's problems were no longer a matter of basic human needs, of food, shelter, and clothing. Now they were seen as qualitative, a question of learning to live decently amid luxury.' This suburbanization of the American mind renders poverty invisible and left 'off the beaten track'. The blindness about poverty encouraged by the middle-class move out of the cities is arguably its most damaging aspect as the poor are not simply neglected or forgotten — they are not even *seen* within this shift away from attention to 'basic human needs' by a concern to 'live decently amid luxury', a shift which displays very clearly the abstract nature of a consumer culture where real productivity and real need are suppressed in the interests of expanding the arena for selling. The abstraction of consumption is well expressed by Fredric Jameson in *Marxism and Form*:

> Little by little, in the commercial age, matter as such has ceased to exist, and has given place to commodities … in the commodity age, need as a purely material and physical impulse (as something 'natural') has given way to a structure of artificial stimuli, artificial longings, such that it is no longer possible to separate the true from the false, the primary from the luxury-satisfaction, in them.

> (Jameson, 1971, p.96)

While these abstractions are more evident by the 1950s and 1960s, they have maintained their effects upon American thought since the late nineteenth century. Prominent amongst those effects is the question of identity itself, and specifically the question of an *American* identity, always a contentious issue for a society characterized by heterogeneity. The issue was given special force during the great waves of immigration around the turn of the century. In 1908, the General Conference of the Methodist Episcopal Church sought to establish a creed for the organization of working life in order to codify distinctively American industrial practices, and the Immigration Act of 1924, following on from the Quota Limit Act of 1921, legislated entries in terms of both number and nationality in an attempt to design what it considered to be an American citizen. Not surprisingly, the 1924 Act marked a significant decrease in numbers over that of 1921 while increasing the areas that were to be subject to quota restrictions. By mid-century, the debate about what constituted an American shifted its terms from issues of nationality to those of ideology. President Truman's address at the dedication of the American Legion headquarters in Washington in 1951 made a claim for 'one hundred percent Americanism' which involved not only the familiar virtues (freedom of speech, religion and opportunity) but a warning about McCarthyism and the 'slander-mongers' who were 'trying to get us to believe that our Government is riddled with communism and corruption'. While the threat of communism itself was containable, more dangerous to the American way of life were those who created a climate of fear in which freedom of speech was becoming increasingly difficult.

If the efforts to sustain a stability of identity in America have always been at best temporary, then the advertisement of the affluent society from the 1950s onwards has, despite its contradictions, maintained its image for many. As the Lynds observed in *Middletown*, 'more and more of the activities of living are coming to be strained through the bars of the dollar sign'. The shift from immediate need to the gratification of variousness in suburbia, rapidly becoming *the* site of American identity, was further enabled by the prolifer-ation of 'channels of increased cultural diffusion' such as large-scale adver-tising, popular magazines, syndicated newspapers, cinema, radio and the car. These channels promoted a standardization of thought and perception that allowed suburban identity to remain secure. While the imperatives for prosperity may have been conflicting (the Lynds note how the exhortations to produce, consume, buy and save are accompanied by those older sustain-ing myths of wealth being derivable from the soil, a spirit of hopefulness and a loyalty to the home town), the uniformity of image protected middle America from its blindness to poverty and minority rights. That security was thrown radically into question in that lengthy process of minority acti-vism which began in the 1960s. The demands for 'truly equal partnership' based upon the belief that 'human rights for all are indivisible' from the National Organization for Women may stand as a rallying cry for the work of all of those up to the present day who have struggled to persuade stan-dardized America that its true identity is to be located in its heterogeneity of race and gender, and that the lesson to be learned is to live with the differ-ence.

There was another lesson Americans had to try and come to terms with both during the 1960s and 1970s and since. A long and hard war ending in defeat was a new and difficult experience for the United States. As with all America's other wars, art was called upon to provide an appropriate public memorial to the conflict and its American dead. No easy task. John D. Bee's discussion of the Vietnam Memorial brings out some of the complex issues and emotions which surround a national tragedy.

REFERENCE

Jameson, F. (1971) *Marxism and Form*, Princeton, Princeton University Press.

1.2 ARTS AND SCIENCES

1.2.1 FRANK LLOYD WRIGHT: 'THE ART AND CRAFT OF THE MACHINE' (1901–4)

Frank Lloyd Wright (1869–1959), one of the founders of modern architecture and a major influence as a social philosopher, first gave the lecture 'The Art and Craft of the Machine' at Hull House, Chicago in 1901. It was rewritten and revised a number of times and the following extract includes a section as first delivered, and a revised section given to the Chicago Chapter of the Daughters of the American Revolution in 1904. The lecture addresses the relationship of the artist to the power and potential of the new Machine Age.

Democracy and Its Forms

I do not believe we will ever again have the uniformity of type which has characterized the so-called great 'styles'. Conditions have changed. Our ideal is democracy; the highest possible expression of the individual as a unit not inconsistent with a harmonious whole. The average human intelligence rises steadily, and as the individual unit grows more and more to be trusted we will have an architecture with richer variety in unity than has ever arisen before. But the forms must be born out of our changed conditions. They must be *true* forms; otherwise the best that tradition has to offer is only an inglorious masquerade, devoid of vital significance or true spiritual value.

Obstacles

The trials of the early days were many and at this distance, picturesque. Workmen seldom like to think, especially if there is financial risk entailed. At your peril do you disturb their established processes mental or technical. To do anything in an unusual, even if in a better and simpler way is to complicate the situation at once. Simple things at that time in any industrial field were nowhere at hand. A piece of wood without a molding was an anomaly; a plain wooden slat instead of a turned baluster, a joke; the omission of the merchantable 'grille', a crime. Plain fabrics for hangings or floor covering were nowhere to be found in stock.

Casement Windows

Single-handed I waged a determined battle for casements swinging out, although it was necessary to have special hardware made for them as there was none to be had this side of England.

Use of the Machine

An artist's limitations are his best friends. The machine is here to stay. It is the forerunner of the democracy that is our dearest hope. There is no more important work before the architect now than to use this normal tool of civilization to the best advantage instead of prostituting it as he has hitherto done in reproducing with murderous ubiquity forms born of other times and other conditions and which it can only serve to destroy.

Dead Forms

The old structural forms which up to the present time have spelled 'architecture' are decayed. Their life went from them long ago and new conditions industrially, steel and concrete and terra cotta in particular, are prophesying a more plastic art wherein as the flesh is to our bones so will the covering be to the structure, but more truly and beautifully expressive than ever.

Individualism

I believe that only when one individual forms the concept of the various projects and also determines the character of every detail in the sum total, even to the size and shape of the pieces of glass in the windows, the arrangement and profile of the most insignificant of the architectural members, will unity be secured which is the soul of the individual work of art.

THE ART AND CRAFT OF THE MACHINE (1904 REVISION)

Challenge of the Machine

In this day and generation we must recognize that this transforming force whose outward sign and symbol is the thing of brass and steel we call a machine, is now grown to the point that the artist must take it up, no longer to protest. Genius must dominate the work of the contrivance it has created. This plain duty is relentlessly marked out for the artist in this, the Machine Age. He cannot set it aside, although there is involved an adjustment to cherished gods, perplexing and painful in the extreme, and though the fires of long-honored ideals shall go down to ashes. They will reappear, phoenix-like, with new life and purposes.

The Machine and the City

Upon this faith in art as the organic heart of the scientific frame of things, I base a belief that we must look to the artist brain of all brains to grasp the significance to society of this thing we call the machine, which is no more or less than the principle of organic growth working irresistibly the will of life through the medium of man. We are drawn helplessly into its mesh as we tread our daily round. It has become commonplace background of modern existence and in too many lives the foreground, middle distance, and the future. At best we are some co-operative part in a vast machinery, seemingly controlled by some great crystallizing principle in nature. If you would see how interwoven it is in the warp and woof of civilization, if indeed it is not the very framework, go at night-fall to the top of one of the down-town steel giants and you may see how in the image of material man, at once his glory and his menace, is this thing we call a city. There beneath you is the monster, stretching acre upon acre into the far distance. High over head hangs the stagnant pall of its fetid breath, reddened with light from myriad eyes endlessly, everywhere blinking. Thousands of acres of cellular tissue, the city's flesh outspreads, layer upon layer, enmeshed by an intricate net-work of veins and arteries radiating into the gloom, and in them, with muf-fled, persistent roar, circulating as the blood circulates in your veins, is the almost ceaseless beat of the activity to whose necessities it all conforms.

The poisonous waste is drawn from the system of this gigantic creature by infinitely ramifying, thread-like ducts, gathering at their sensitive terminals matter destructive to its life, hurrying it to millions of small intestines to be collected in turn by larger, flowing to the great sewers, on to the drainage canal, and finally to the ocean.

This wondrous flesh is again knit and interknit with a nervous system effec-tive and complete, delicate filaments of hearing, knowing, and almost feel-ing the pulse of its organism, acting intelligently upon ligaments and tendons for motive impulse, and in all is flowing the impelling fluid of man's own life.

Its muscles are the Corliss tandems, whirling their hundred-ton fly-wheels, fed by gigantic rows of water tube boilers burning oil, a solitary man slowly pacing here and there regulating the little valves controlling the deafening roar of the flaming gas, while the incessant clicking and shifting of the governor gear controlling these modern Goliaths seems a visible brain in action, as it registers infallibly in the enormous magnets, purring in the giant embrace of great induction coils, generating the vital current meeting on the instant in the rolling cars on elevated tracks ten miles away.

More quietly, whispering down the long low rooms of factory buildings buried in the gloom beyond, range on range of stanch, beautifully perfected automatons murmur contentedly, automatons that would have the American manufacturing industry of five years ago by the throat to-day; manipulating steel as delicately as a mystical shuttle of the modern loom manipulates a silk thread in the shimmering pattern of a dainty gown. Night and day these nervous minions of the machine obediently serve the master mind with sensitive capacities as various as those of man himself. Here reflected in steam, steel, and electrical energy is a creature grown in response to man's needs, and in his image, daily becoming more sensitive and complete.

And the labored breathing, the murmur, the clangor, and the roar! — how the voice of this greatest of machines, a great city, rises to proclaim the mar-vel of its structure; the ghastly warning boom from the deep throats of ves-sels heavily seeking inlet to the waterway below, answered by the echoing clangor of the bridge bells, growing nearer and more ominous, warning the living current from the swinging bridge as the vessel cuts for a moment the flow of the nearer artery, and now closing upon its stately passage just in time to receive, in a rush of steam as a streak of light, the avalanche of blood and metal hurled across it and gone roaring into the night on its glittering bands of steel, faithfully encircled in its flight by slender magic lines tick-tapping its protection.

Nearer, in the building ablaze with midnight activity, a wide, white band streams into the marvel of the multiple press, receiving unerringly the indelible impression of the human hopes, joys, and fears throbbing in the pulse of the modern activity and as infallibly as the gray matter of the human brain receives the impression of the senses, coming forth as millions of neatly folded, perfected news-sheets, teeming with vivid appeals, good and evil passions; weaving a web of inter-communication so far-reaching that distance becomes as nothing, the thought of one man in one corner of the earth one day visible to all men the next day; the doings of all the world reflected as in a glass — so marvelously sensitive this simple band streaming endlessly from day to day becomes in the grasp of the multiple press.

If the pulse of this great activity to which the tremor of the mammoth skeleton beneath your feet is but an awe-inspiring response, is thrilling, what of this prolific silent obedience? Remain to contemplate this wonder until the twinkling lights perish in groups, followed one by one, leaving others to smother in the gloom; until the fires are banked, the tumult slowly dies to an echo here and there. Then the darkened pall is lifted and moonlight outlines the sullen, shadowy masses of structure deeply cut here and there by half-luminous channels; huge patches of shadow, shade, and darkness intermingle mysteriously in block-like plan and sky-line; the broad surface of the lake beside, placid and resplendent with a silver gleam. And there reflect that the texture of the tissue of this great machine, this forerunner of the democracy we hope for, has been deposited, particle by particle, in blind obedience to law — the organic law to which the great solar universe is but an obedient machine, and marvel that this masterful force is as yet untouched by art or artist. A magnificent truth with no guise of beauty disguised by tattered garments long outgrown; the outward sign of an inner plan wherein combinations of capital and great industrial tendencies are but symptoms, government's imperfect manifestations, whereof wear and friction are social injustice and waste is war.

Source: Gutheim, F. (ed.) (1941) *Frank Lloyd Wright on Architecture*, New York, The Universal Library, Gosset & Dunlop, pp.23–8.

1.2.2 ARTS AND ECONOMICS (1936)

In the following extract from Hallie Flanagan's book *Arena* (1940) the focus is put on the arts in the context of the Depression and the efforts of the Works Progress Administration. The WPA, under Harry Hopkins from 1934, included the arts in its programme for economic recovery and part of that programme was the Federal Theater Project. The extract looks back to 1936.

Since Mr Hopkins was anxious from the first to stress the fact that the government enterprise was to be national in scope, he decided that the logical place to announce my appointment was the National Theatre Conference to be held at Iowa City on the occasion of the laying of the cornerstone of Mr Mabie's University Theatre. On July 24, Mr Hopkins telephoned me to meet him in Washington on the following day and go with him to Iowa City.

It was an exciting trip. Mr Hopkins talked about everything — about engineering, about the building of airports, about the cities and countryside through which we were passing; but no matter what we started to talk about, it ended up with what was at that time the core and center of his thinking — the relationship of government to the individual. Hadn't our government always acknowledged direct responsibility to the people? Hadn't it given away the national domain in free land to veterans and other settlers? Hadn't it given away vast lands to railroad companies to help them build their systems? Hadn't the government spent fortunes on internal improvements, subsidizing the building of roads and canals, waterways, and harbors? Hadn't the government subsidized infant industries by a protective tariff? Hadn't the government also given away other intangible parts of the public domain, such as franchises to public utilities, the power to issue currency and create credit to banks, patent rights to inventors? In all of these ways, government enlarged industries, put men to work and increased buying power.

The new work program, Mr Hopkins believed, would accomplish these same ends by giving of the nation's resources in wages to the unemployed, in return for which they would help build and improve America. […]

It was on this trip that Mr Hopkins asked me a searching question. It is a question which is bound to be jeered at by critics of New Deal philosophy, but it is one of the questions at the core of that philosophy. The train through Chicago out to the midwest plains passed through the slums, and Mr Hopkins, looking out over the abscessed gray tenements mercilessly exposed under the blinding sun, suddenly asked:

'Can you spend money?'

I said that inability to spend money was not one of my faults, but Mr Hopkins continued seriously: 'It's not easy. It takes a lot of nerve to put your signature down on a piece of paper when it means that the government of the United States is going to pay out a million dollars to the unemployed in Chicago. It takes decision, because you'll have to decide whether Chicago needs that money more than New York City or Los Angeles. You can't care very much what people are going to say because when you're handling other people's money whatever you do is always wrong. If you try to hold down wages, you'll be accused of union-busting and of grinding down the poor; if you pay a decent wage, you'll be competing with private industry and pampering a lot of no-accounts; if you scrimp on production costs, they'll say your shows are lousy and if you spend enough to get a good show on, they'll say you're wasting the taxpayers' money. Don't forget that whatever happens you'll be wrong.'

With that reassuring preface, Mr Hopkins launched into the reasons why, in spite of jeers, in spite of attacks, in spite of vituperation, we must spend money. These slums through which we were riding, these ramshackle, vermin-infested buildings housing our fellow citizens were one reason. These pale children sitting listlessly on fire-escapes were another. Sullen youths hanging around our street corners were another. Worried-looking men, gathered in silent knots before employment agencies, were still another. Houses for these people to live in, parks and playgrounds, fresh air, fresh milk and medical care for these children, schools and recreation places for youth to go to, jobs for men to do. Above all — jobs for men to do. *Danger: Men Not Working.* These were some of the reasons why we had to be able to spend money.

'It costs money to put a man to work and that's why a lot of people prefer direct relief. These people say that if we make the working conditions decent and give people a reasonable minimum to live on, people will get to like their jobs. They suggest that we make relief as degrading and shameful as possible so that people will want to get 'off'. Well — I've been dealing with unemployed people for years in one way and another and they *do* want to get off — but they can't, apparently, get 'off' into private industry. Well — if they can't get off into private industry, where can they turn if they can't turn to their government? What's a government for? And these people can be useful to America; they can do jobs no one else can afford to do — these slums, for instance. No private concern can afford to make houses for poor people to live in, because any private concern has got to show a profit. Why, we've got enough work to do right here in America, work that needs to be done and that no private concern can afford to touch, to lay out a program for twenty years and to employ every unemployed person in this country to carry it out.'

What part could art play in this program? Could we, through the power of the theatre, spotlight the tenements and thus help in the plan to build decent houses for all people? Could we, through actors and artists who had themselves known privation, carry music and plays to children in city parks, and art galleries to little towns? Were not happy people at work the greatest bulwark of democracy?

That was Harry Hopkins' theme when he spoke the next night before a vast audience of farmers drawn from all over Iowa to the great campus of the State University. He was the boy back in the home state and of course he played that up. He was never above a certain amount of hokum, and on that occasion he pulled a piece of business that would delight any stage manager. It was a hot night and the farmers were in their shirt-sleeves. Harry painted the picture of poverty and desolation before work relief had come along, launched the work theme, built up a thrilling story of what it could do. He came to a climax and at that point someone in the crowd called out, 'Who's going to pay for all that?'

That was the question they had been waiting for. On his answer everything depended. Would he hedge? He did not hedge. He looked out over the crowd. He took off his coat, unfastened his tie and took it off, rolled up his sleeves. The crowd got perfectly still. Then he said, 'You are'. His voice took on urgency. 'And who better? Who can better afford to pay for it? Look at this great university. Look at these fields, these forests and rivers. This is America, the richest country in the world. We can afford to pay for anything we want. And we want a decent life for all the people in this country. And we are going to pay for it.'

Source: Cronon, E.D. (ed.) (1966) *Twentieth Century America, Selected Readings, Vol.2: 1929 to the Present*, Belmont, Calif., Dorsey Press/Wadsworth.

1.2.3 TWO CULTURES? (1965)

Susan Sontag has written a number of essays on the creative arts. The following extract is from her essay 'One Culture and the New Sensibility', written in 1965 it appeared in her collection of essays *Against Interpretation* (1966). The essay addresses the relationship between the arts and sciences and the imagined conflict between them.

[…] The role of the individual artist, in the business of making unique objects for the purpose of giving pleasure and educating conscience and sensibility, has repeatedly been called into question. Some literary intellectuals and artists have gone so far as to prophesy the ultimate demise of the art-making activity of man. Art, in an automated scientific society, would be unfunctional, useless.

But this conclusion, I should argue, is plainly unwarranted. Indeed, the whole issue seems to me crudely put. For the question of 'the two cultures' assumes that science and technology are changing, in motion, while the arts are static, fulfilling some perennial generic human function (consolation? edification? diversion?). Only on the basis of this false assumption would anyone reason that the arts might be in danger of becoming obsolete.

Art does not progress, in the sense that science and technology do. But the arts do develop and change. For instance, in our own time, art is becoming increasingly the terrain of specialists. The most interesting and creative art of our time is *not* open to the generally educated; it demands special effort; it speaks a specialized language. The music of Milton Babbitt and Morton Feldman, the painting of Mark Rothko and Frank Stella, the dance of Merce Cunningham and James Waring demand an education of sensibility whose difficulties and length of apprenticeship are at least comparable to the difficulties of mastering physics or engineering. (Only the novel, among the arts, at least in America, fails to provide similar examples.) The parallel between the abstruseness of contemporary art and that of modern science is too obvious to be missed. Another likeness to the scientific culture is the history-mindedness of contemporary art. The most interesting works of contemporary art are full of references to the history of the medium; so far as they comment on past art, they demand a knowledge of at least the recent past. As Harold Rosenberg has pointed out, contemporary paintings are themselves acts of criticism as much as of creation. The point could be made as well of much recent work in the films, music, the dance, poetry, and (in Europe) literature. Again, a similarity with the style of science — this time, with the accumulative aspect of science — can be discerned.

The conflict between 'the two cultures' is in fact an illusion, a temporary phenomenon born of a period of profound and bewildering historical change. What we are witnessing is not so much a conflict of cultures as the creation of a new (potentially unitary) kind of sensibility. This new sensibility is rooted, as it must be, in *our* experience, experiences which are new in the history of humanity — in extreme social and physical mobility; in the crowdedness of the human scene (both people and material commodities multiplying at a dizzying rate); in the availability of new sensations such as speed (physical speed, as in airplane travel; speed of images, as in the cinema); and in the pan-cultural perspective on the arts that is possible through the mass reproduction of art objects.

What we are getting is not the demise of art, but a transformation of the function of art. Art, which arose in human society as a magical-religious operation, and passed over into a technique for depicting and commenting on secular reality, has in our own time arrogated to itself a new function — neither religious, nor serving a secularized religious function, nor merely secular or profane (a notion which breaks down when its opposite, the 'religious' or 'sacred', becomes obsolescent). Art today is a new kind of instrument, an instrument for modifying consciousness and organizing new modes of sensibility. And the means for practicing art have been radically extended. Indeed, in response to this new function (more felt than clearly articulated), artists have had to become self-conscious aestheticians: continually challenging their means, their materials and methods. Often, the conquest and exploitation of new materials and methods drawn from the world of 'non-art' — for example, from industrial technology, from commercial processes and imagery, from purely private and subjective fantasies and dreams — seems to be the principal effort of many artists. Painters no longer feel themselves confined to canvas and paint, but employ hair, photographs, wax, sand, bicycle tires, their own toothbrushes and socks. Musicians have reached beyond the sounds of the traditional instruments to use tampered instruments and (usually on tape) synthetic sounds and industrial noises.

All kinds of conventionally accepted boundaries have thereby been challenged: not just the one between the 'scientific' and the 'literary-artistic' cultures, or the one between 'art' and 'non-art'; but also many established distinctions within the world of culture itself — that between form and content, the frivolous and the serious, and (a favorite of literary intellectuals) 'high' and 'low' culture.

The distinction between 'high' and 'low' (or 'mass' or 'popular') culture is based partly on an evaluation of the difference between unique and mass-produced objects. In an era of mass technological reproduction, the work of the serious artist had a special value simply because it was unique, because it bore his personal, individual signature. The works of popular culture (and even films were for a long time included in this category) were seen as having little value because they were manufactured objects, bearing no individual stamp — group concoctions made for an undifferentiated audience. But in the light of contemporary practice in the arts, this distinction appears extremely shallow. Many of the serious works of art of recent decades have a decidedly impersonal character. The work of art is reasserting its existence as 'object' (even as manufactured or mass-produced object, drawing on the popular arts) rather than as 'individual personal expression'.

The exploration of the impersonal (and trans-personal) in contemporary art is the new classicism; at least, a reaction against what is understood as the romantic spirit dominates most of the interesting art of today. Today's art, with its insistence on coolness, its refusal of what it considers to be sentimentality, its spirit of exactness, its sense of 'research' and 'problems', is closer to the spirit of science than of art in the old-fashioned sense. Often, the artist's work is only his idea, his concept. This is a familiar practice in architecture, of course. And one remembers that painters in the Renaissance often left parts of their canvases to be worked out by students, and that in the flourishing period of the concerto the cadenza at the end of the first movement was left to the inventiveness and discretion of the performing soloist. But similar practices have a different, more polemical meaning today, in the present post-romantic era of the arts. When painters such as Joseph Albers, Ellsworth Kelly, and Andy Warhol assign portions of the work, say, the painting in of the colors themselves, to a friend or the local gardener; when musicians such as Stockhausen, John Cage, and Luigi Nono invite collaboration from performers by leaving opportunities for random effects, switching around the order of the score, and improvisations — they are changing the ground rules which most of us employ to recognize a work of art. They are saying what art need not be. At least, not necessarily.

The primary feature of the new sensibility is that its model product is not the literary work, above all, the novel. A new non-literary culture exists today, of whose very existence, not to mention significance, most literary intellectuals are entirely unaware. This new establishment includes certain painters, sculptors, architects, social planners, film-makers, TV technicians, neurologists, musicians, electronics engineers, dancers, philosophers, and sociologists. (A few poets and prose writers can be included.) Some of the basic texts for this new cultural alignment are to be found in the writings of Nietzsche, Wittgenstein, Antonin Artaud, C.S. Sherrington, Buckminster Fuller, Marshall McLuhan, John Cage, André Breton, Roland Barthes, Claude Lévi-Strauss, Siegfried Gidieon, Norman O. Brown, and Gyorgy Kepes.

[…]

Source: Sontag, S. (1966) *Against Interpretation and Other Essays*, London, Jonathan Cape.

1.3   LITERATURE AND SOCIETY

1.3.1   F. SCOTT FITZGERALD'S 'ECHOES OF THE JAZZ AGE' (1931)

F. Scott Fitzgerald, ca *1928*

When, as the 1920s drew to a close, one of America's leading twentieth century writers — author of *The Great Gatsby* (1925) and *Tender is the Night* (1934) — reflects on the previous ten years, there is much to be learnt about American culture during that period and the author's view of it and place within it.

It is too soon to write about the Jazz Age with perspective, and without being suspected of premature arteriosclerosis. Many people still succumb to violent retching when they happen upon any of its characteristic words — words which have since yielded in vividness to the coinages of the underworld. It is as dead as were the Yellow Nineties in 1902. Yet the present writer already looks back to it with nostalgia. It bore him up, flattered him and gave him more money than he had dreamed of, simply for telling people that he felt as they did, that something had to be done with all the nervous energy stored up and unexpended in the War.

The ten-year period that, as if reluctant to die outmoded in its bed, leaped to a spectacular death in October, 1929, began about the time of the May Day riots in 1919. When the police rode down the demobilized country boys gaping at the orators in Madison Square, it was the sort of measure bound to alienate the more intelligent young men from the prevailing order. We didn't remember anything about the Bill of Rights until Mencken began plugging it, but we did know that such tyranny belonged in the jittery little countries of South Europe. If goose-livered business men had this effect on the government, then maybe we had gone to war for J.P. Morgan's loans after all. But, because we were tired of Great Causes, there was no more than a short outbreak of moral indignation, typified by Dos Passos' *Three Soldiers*. Presently we began to have slices of the national case, and our idealism only flared up when the newspapers made melodrama out of such stories as Harding and the Ohio Gang or Sacco and Vanzetti. The events of 1919 left us cynical rather than revolutionary, in spite of the fact that now we are all rummaging around in our trunks wondering where in hell we left the liberty cap — 'I know I *had* it' — and the moujik blouse. It was characteristic of the Jazz Age that it had no interest in politics at all.

It was an age of miracles, it was an age of art, it was an age of excess, and it was an age of satire. A Stuffed Shirt, squirming to blackmail in a lifelike way, sat upon the throne of the United States; a stylish young man hurried over to represent to us the throne of England. A world of girls yearned for the young Englishman; the old American groaned in his sleep as he waited to be poisoned by his wife, upon the advice of the female Rasputin who then made the ultimate decision in our national affairs. But such matters apart, we had things our way at last. With Americans ordering suits by the gross in London, the Bond Street tailors perforce agreed to moderate their cut to the American long-waisted figure and loose fitting taste, something subtle passed to America, the style of man. During the Renaissance Francis the First looked to Florence to trim his leg. Seventeenth-century England aped the court of France, and fifty years ago the German Guards officer bought his civilian clothes in London. Gentlemen's clothes — symbol of 'the power that man must hold and that passes from race to race'.

We were the most powerful nation. Who could tell us any longer what was fashionable and what was fun? Isolated during the European War, we had begun combing the unknown South and West for folkways and pastimes, and there were more ready to hand.

The first social revelation created a sensation out of all proportion to its novelty. As far back as 1915 the unchaperoned young people of the smaller cities had discovered the mobile privacy of that automobile given to young Bill at sixteen to make him 'self-reliant'. At first petting was a desperate adventure even under such favourable conditions, but presently confidences were exchanged and the old commandment broke down. As early as 1917 there were references to such sweet and casual dalliance in any number of the *Yale Record* or the *Princeton Tiger*.

But petting in its more audacious manifestations was confined to the wealthier classes — among other young people the old standard prevailed until after the War, and a kiss meant that a proposal was expected, as young officers in strange cities sometimes discovered to their dismay. Only in 1920 did the veil finally fall — the Jazz Age was in flower.

Scarcely had the staider citizens of the republic caught their breaths when the wildest of all generations, the generation which had been adolescent during the confusion of the War, brusquely shouldered my contemporaries out of the way and danced into the limelight. This was the generation whose girls dramatized themselves as flappers, the generation that corrupted its elders and eventually overreached itself less through lack of morals than through lack of taste. May one offer in exhibit the year 1922! That was the peak of the younger generation, for though the Jazz Age continued, it became less and less an affair of youth.

The sequel was like a children's party taken over by the elders, leaving the children puzzled and rather neglected and rather taken aback. By 1923 their elders, tired of watching the carnival with ill-concealed envy, had discovered that young liquor will take the place of young blood, and with a whoop the orgy began. The younger generation was starred no longer.

A whole race going hedonistic, deciding on pleasure. The precocious intimacies of the younger generation would have come about with or without prohibition — they were implicit in the attempt to adapt English customs to American conditions. (Our South, for example, is tropical and early maturing — it has never been part of the wisdom of France and Spain to let young girls go unchaperoned at sixteen and seventeen.) But the general decision to be amused that began with the cocktail parties of 1921 had more complicated origins.

The word jazz in its progress towards respectability has meant first sex, then dancing, then music. It is associated with a state of nervous stimulation, not unlike that of big cities behind the lines of a war. To many English the War still goes on because all the forces that menace them are still active — Wherefore eat, drink and be merry, for tomorrow we die. But different causes had now brought about a corresponding state in America — though there were entire classes (people over fifty, for example) who spent a whole decade denying its existence even when its puckish face peered into the family circle. Never did they dream that they had contributed to it. The honest citizens of every class, who believed in a strict public morality and were powerful enough to enforce the necessary legislation, did not know that they would necessarily be served by criminals and quacks, and do not really believe it today. Rich righteousness had always been able to buy honest and intelligent servants to free the slaves or the Cubans, so when this attempt collapsed our elders stood firm with all the stubbornness of people involved in a weak case, preserving their righteousness and losing their children. Silver-haired women and men with fine old faces, people who never did a consciously dishonest thing in their lives, still assure each other in the apartment hotels of New York and Boston and Washington that 'there's a whole generation growing up that will never know the taste of liquor'. Meanwhile their granddaughters pass the well-thumbed copy of *Lady Chatterley's Lover* around the boarding-school and, if they get about at all, know the taste of gin or corn at sixteen. But the generation who reached maturity between 1875 and 1895 continued to believe what they want to believe.

Even the intervening generations were incredulous. In 1920 Heywood Broun announced that all this hubbub was nonsense, that young men didn't kiss but told anyhow. But very shortly people over twenty-five came in for an intensive education. Let me trace some of the revelations vouchsafed them by reference to a dozen works written for various types of mentality during the decade. We begin with the suggestion that Don Juan leads an interesting life (*Jurgen*, 1919); then we learn that there's a lot of sex around if we only knew it (*Winesburg, Ohio*, 1920), that adolescents lead very amorous lives (*This Side of Paradise*, 1920), that there are a lot of neglected Anglo-Saxon words (*Ulysses*, 1921), that older people don't always resist sudden temptations (*Cytherea*, 1922), that girls are sometimes seduced without being ruined (*Flaming Youth*, 1922), that even rape often turns out well (*The Sheik*, 1922), that glamorous English ladies are often promiscuous (*The Green Hat*, 1924), that in fact they devote most of their time to it (*The Vortex*, 1926), that it's a damn good thing too (*Lady Chatterley's Lover*, 1928), and finally that there are abnormal variations (*The Well of Loneliness*, 1928, and *Sodom and Gomorrah*, 1929).

In my opinion the erotic element in these works, even *The Sheik* written for children in the key of *Peter Rabbit*, did not one particle of harm. Everything they described, and much more, was familiar in our contemporary life. The majority of the theses were honest and elucidating — their effect was to restore some dignity to the male as opposed to the he-man in American life. ('And what is a "He-man"!' demanded Gertrude Stein one day. 'Isn't it a large enough order to fill out to the dimensions of all that "a man" has meant in the past? A "*He*-man"!') The married woman can now discover whether she is being cheated, or whether sex is just something to be endured, and her compensation should be to establish a tyranny of the spirit, as her mother may have hinted. Perhaps many women found that love was meant to be fun. Anyhow the objectors lost their tawdry little case, which is one reason why our literature is now the most living in the world.

Contrary to popular opinion, the movies of the Jazz Age had no effect upon its morals. The social attitude of the producers was timid, behind the times, and banal — for example, no picture mirrored even faintly the younger generation until 1923, when magazines had already been started to celebrate it and it had long ceased to be news. There were a few feeble splutters and then Clara Bow in *Flaming Youth*; promptly the Hollywood hacks ran the theme into its cinematographic grave. Throughout the Jazz Age the movies got no farther than Mrs Jiggs, keeping up with its most blatant superficialities. This was no doubt due to the censorship as well as to innate conditions in the industry. In any case, the Jazz Age now raced along under its own power, served by great filling stations full of money.

The people over thirty, the people all the way up to fifty, had joined the dance. We greybeards (to tread down F.P.A.) remember the uproar when in 1912 grandmothers of forty tossed away their crutches and took lessons in the Tango and the Castle-Walk. A dozen years later a woman might pack the Green Hat with her other affairs as she set off for Europe or New York, but Savonarola was too busy flogging dead horses in Augean stables of his own creation to notice. Society, even in small cities, now dined in separate chambers, and the sober table learned about the gay table only from hear-say. There were very few people left at the sober table. One of its former glories, the less sought-after girls who had become resigned to sublimating a probable celibacy, came across Freud and Jung in seeking their intellectual recompense and came tearing back into the fray.

By 1926 the universal preoccupation with sex had become a nuisance. (I remember a perfectly mated, contented young mother asking my wife's advice about 'having an affair right away', though she had no one especially in mind, 'because don't you think it's sort of undignified when you get much over thirty?') For a while bootleg Negro records with their phallic euphemisms made everything suggestive, and simultaneously came a wave of erotic plays — young girls from finishing-schools packed the galleries to hear about the romance of being a Lesbian and George Jean Nathan protested. Then one young producer lost his head entirely, drank a beauty's alcoholic bath-water and went to the penitentiary. Somehow his pathetic attempt at romance belongs to the Jazz Age, while his contemporary in prison, Ruth Snyder, had to be hoisted into it by the tabloids — she was, as *The Daily News* hinted deliciously to gourmets, about 'to cook, *and sizzle, AND FRY!*' in the electric chair.

The gay elements of society had divided into two main streams, one flowing towards Palm Beach and Deauville, and the other, much smaller, towards the summer Riviera. One could get away with more on the summer Riviera, and whatever happened seemed to have something to do with art. From 1926 to 1929, the great years of the Cap d'Antibes, this corner of France was dominated by a group quite distinct from that American society which is dominated by Europeans. Pretty much of anything went at Antibes — by 1929, at the most gorgeous paradise for swimmers on the Mediterranean no one swam any more, save for a short hang-over dip at noon. There was a picturesque graduation of steep rocks over the sea and somebody's valet and an occasional English girl used to dive from them, but the Americans were content to discuss each other in the bar. This was indicative of something that was taking place in the homeland — Americans were getting soft. There were signs everywhere: we still won the Olympic games but with champions whose names had few vowels in them — teams composed, like the fighting Irish combination of Notre Dame, of fresh overseas blood. Once the French became really interested, the Davis Cup gravitated automatically to their intensity in competition. The vacant lots of the Middle-Western cities were built up now — except for a short period in school, we were not turning out to be an athletic people like the British, after all. The hare and the tortoise. Of course if we wanted to we could be in a minute; we still had all those reserves of ancestral vitality, but one day in 1926 we looked down and found we had flabby arms and a fat pot and couldn't say boop-boop-a-doop to a Sicilian. Shades of Van Bibber! — no Utopian ideal, God knows. Even golf, once considered an effeminate game, had seemed very strenuous of late — an emasculated form appeared and proved just right.

By 1927 a widespread neurosis began to be evident, faintly signalled, like a nervous beating of the feet, by the popularity of crossword puzzles. I remember a fellow expatriate opening a letter from a mutual friend of ours, urging him to come home and be revitalized by the hardy, bracing qualities of the native soil. It was a strong letter and it affected us both deeply, until we noticed that it was headed from a nerve sanatorium in Pennsylvania.

By this time contemporaries of mine had begun to disappear into the dark maw of violence. A classmate killed his wife and himself on Long Island, another tumbled 'accidently' from a skyscraper in Philadelphia, another purposely from a skyscraper in New York. One was killed in a speak-easy in Chicago; another was beaten to death in a speak-easy in New York and crawled home to the Princeton Club to die; still another had his skull crushed by a maniac's axe in an insane asylum where he was confined. These are not catastrophes that I went out of my way to look for — these were my friends; moreover, these things happened not during the depression but during the boom.

In the spring of '27, something bright and alien flashed across the sky. A young Minnesotan who seemed to have had nothing to do with his generation did a heroic thing, and for a moment people set down their glasses in country clubs and speak-easies and thought of their old best dreams. Maybe there was a way out by flying, maybe our restless blood could find frontiers in the illimitable air. But by that time we were all pretty well committed; and the Jazz Age continued; we would all have one more.

Nevertheless, Americans were wandering ever more widely — friends seemed eternally bound for Russia, Persia, Abyssinia, and Central Africa. And by 1928 Paris had grown suffocating. With each new shipment of Americans spewed up by the boom the quality fell off, until towards the end there was something sinister about the crazy boatloads. They were no longer the simple pa and ma and son and daughter, infinitely superior in their qualities of kindness and curiosity to the corresponding class in Europe, but fantastic neanderthals who believed something, something vague, that you remembered from a very cheap novel. I remember an Italian on a steamer who promenaded the deck in an American Reserve Officer's uniform picking quarrels in broken English with Americans who criticized their own institutions in the bar. I remember a fat Jewess, inlaid with diamonds, who sat behind us at the Russian ballet and said as the curtain rose, 'Thad's luffly, dey ought to baint a bicture of it.' This was low comedy, but it was evident that money and power were falling into the hands of people in comparison with whom the leader of a village Soviet would be a gold-mine of judgement and culture. There were citizens travelling luxury in 1928 and 1929, who, in the distortion of their new condition, had the human value of Pekingese, bivalves, cretins, goats. I remember the Judge from some New York district who had taken his daughter to see the Bayeux Tapestries and made a scene in the papers advocating their segregation because one scene was immoral. But in those days life was like the race in *Alice in Wonderland*, there was a prize for every one.

The Jazz Age had had a wild youth and a heady middle age. There was the phase of the necking parties, the Leopold-Loeb murder (I remember the time my wife was arrested on Queensborough Bridge on the suspicion of being the 'Bob-haired Bandit') and the John Held Clothes. In the second phase such phenomena as sex and murder became more mature, if much more conventional. Middle age must be served and pyjamas came to the beach to save fat thighs and flabby calves from competition with the one-piece bathing-suit. Finally skirts came down and everything was concealed. Everybody was at scratch now. Let's go —

But it was not to be. Somebody had blundered and the most expensive orgy in history was over.

It ended two years ago [1929], because the utter confidence which was its essential prop received an enormous jolt, and it didn't take long for the flimsy structure to settle earthward. And after two years the Jazz Age seems as far away as the days before the War. It was borrowed time anyhow — the whole upper tenth of a nation living with the insouciance of grand dukes and the casualness of chorus girls. But moralizing is easy now and it was pleasant to be in one's twenties in such a certain and unworried time. Even when you were broke you didn't worry about money, because it was in such profusion around you. Towards the end one had a struggle to pay one's share; it was almost a favour to accept hospitality that required any travelling. Charm, notoriety, mere good manners weighed more than money as a social asset. This was rather splendid, but things were getting thinner and thinner as the eternal necessary human values tried to spread over all that expansion. Writers were geniuses on the strength of one respectable book or play; just as during the War officers of four months' experience commanded hundreds of men, so there were now many little fish lording it over great big bowls. In the theatrical world extravagant productions were carried by a few second-rate stars, and so on up the scale into politics, where it was difficult to interest good men in positions of the highest importance and responsibility, importance and responsibility far exceeding that of business executives but which paid only five or six thousand a year.

Now once more the belt is tight and we summon the proper expression of horror as we look back at our wasted youth. Sometimes, though, there is a ghostly rumble among the drums, an asthmatic whisper in the trombones that swings me back into the early twenties when we drank wood alcohol and every day in every way grew better and better, and there was a first abortive shortening of the skirts, and girls all looked alike in sweater dresses, and people you didn't want to know said 'Yes, we have no bananas', and it seemed only a question of a few years before the older people would step aside and let the world be run by those who saw things as they were — and it all seems rosy and romantic to us who were young then, because we will never feel quite so intensely about our surroundings any more.

Source: Fitzgerald, F.S. (1965) *The Stories of F. Scott Fitzgerald, Vol. Two: The Crack-Up and Other Pieces and Stories*, Harmondsworth, Penguin.

1.3.2   WALT WHITMAN: *LEAVES OF GRASS* (1855) AND *AMERICA* (1888)

No less than other literary forms, poetry addresses wider society and provides a unique insight into aspects of American culture. Walt Whitman was the most important American Romantic poet of the nineteenth century. The following is an extract from his Preface to the 1855 edition of his collected works, *Leaves of Grass*, and one of his poems, *America* (1888). His romantic view of America is clear in both.

Walt Whitman (1819–1892)

PREFACE, *LEAVES OF GRASS*

[…]

The Americans of all nations at any time upon the earth have probably the fullest poetical nature. The United States themselves are essentially the greatest poem. In the history of the earth hitherto the largest and most stirring appear tame and orderly to their ampler largeness and stir. Here at last is something in the doings of man that corresponds with the broadcast doings of the day and night. Here is not merely a nation but a teeming nation of nations. Here is action untied from strings necessarily blind to particulars and details magnificently moving in vast masses. Here is the hospitality which forever indicates heroes […]. Here are the roughs and beards and space and ruggedness and nonchalance that the soul loves. Here the performance disdaining the trivial unapproached in the tremendous audacity of its crowds and groupings and the push of its perspective spreads with crampless and flowing breadth and showers its prolific and splendid extravagance. One sees it must indeed own the riches of the summer and winter, and need never be bankrupt while corn grows from the ground or the orchards drop apples or the bays contain fish or men beget children upon women.

Other states indicate themselves in their deputies […] but the genius of the United States is not best or most in its executives or legislatures, nor in its ambassadors or authors or colleges or churches or parlors, nor even in its newspapers or inventors […] but always most in the common people. Their manners speech dress friendships — the freshness and candor of their physiognomy — the picturesque looseness of their carriage […] their deathless attachment to freedom — their aversion to anything indecorous or soft or mean — the practical acknowledgement of the citizens of one state by the citizens of all other states — the fierceness of their roused resentment — their curiosity and welcome of novelty — their self-esteem and wonderful sympathy — their susceptibility to a slight — the air they have of persons who never knew how it felt to stand in the presence of superiors — the fluency of their speech — their delight in music, the sure symptom of manly tenderness and native elegance of soul […] their good temper and open-handedness — the terrible significance of their elections — the President's taking off his hat to them not they to him — these too are unrhymed poetry. It awaits the gigantic and generous treatment worthy of it. […]

AMERICA

> Centre of equal daughters, equal sons,
> All, all alike endear'd, grown, ungrown, young or old,
> Strong, ample, fair, enduring, capable, rich,
> Perennial with the Earth, with Freedom, Law and Love,
> A grand, sane, towering, seated Mother,
> Chair'd in the adamant of Time.

Source: Murphy, F. (ed.) (1975) *Walt Whitman, the Complete Poems*, Harmondsworth, Penguin.

1.3.3   ALLEN GINSBERG: *A SUPERMARKET IN CALIFORNIA* (1955)

Allen Ginsberg looks back to the romanticism of Whitman as he reflects on consumerism as it manifests itself in a 1950s' supermarket. The poem, *A Supermarket in California*, is from his *The Howl and Other Poems* (1956).

What thoughts I have of you tonight, Walt Whitman, for I walked down the sidestreets under the trees with a headache self-conscious looking at the full moon.

In my hungry fatigue, and shopping for images, I went into the neon fruit supermarket, dreaming of your enumerations!

What peaches and what penumbras! Whole families shopping at night! Aisles full of husbands! Wives in the avocados, babies in the tomatoes! — and you, Garcia Lorca, what were you doing down by the watermelons?

I saw you, Walt Whitman, childless, lonely old grubber, poking among the meats in the refrigerator and eyeing the grocery boys.

I heard you asking questions of each: Who killed the pork chops? What price bananas? Are you my Angel?

I wandered in and out of the brilliant stacks of cans following you, and followed in my imagination by the store detective.

We strode down the open corridors together in our solitary fancy tasting artichokes, possessing every frozen delicacy, and never passing the cashier.

Where are we going, Walt Whitman? The doors close in an hour. Which way does your beard point tonight?

(I touch your book and dream of our odyssey in the supermarket and feel absurd.)

Will we walk all night through solitary streets? The trees add shade to shade, lights out in the houses, we'll both be lonely.

Will we stroll dreaming of the lost America of love past blue automobiles in driveways, home to our silent cottage?

Ah, dear father, graybeard, lonely old courage-teacher, what America did you have when Charon quit poling his ferry and you got out on a smoking bank and stood watching the boat disappear on the black waters of Lethe?

Source: Ginsberg, A. (1956) *The Howl and Other Poems*, San Francisco, City Lights.

1.4   MEDIA AND SOCIETY

1.4.1 'THE AIM OF THE *AMERICAN MERCURY*' (1924)

The *American Mercury*, a monthly review magazine, was first published in 1924. In the first issue the editors George Jean Nathan and Henry L. Mencken set forth 'The Aim of the *American Mercury*'. American newspapers and periodicals have expressed a variety of social, cultural and political opinions through a wide range of styles. In this example a satirical approach is to the fore. Though eclipsed to some extent by the power of television in the second half of the century, their influence and impact should not be underestimated.

The aim of *The American Mercury* is precisely that of every other monthly review the world has ever seen: to ascertain and tell the truth. So far, nothing new. But the Editors cherish the hope that it may be possible, after all, to introduce some element of novelty into the execution of an enterprise so old, and upon that hope they found the magazine. It comes into being with at least one advantage over all its predecessors in the field of public affairs: it is entirely devoid of messianic passion. The Editors have heard no Voice from the burning bush. They will not cry up and offer for sale any sovereign balm, whether political, economic or aesthetic, for all the sorrows of the world. The fact is, indeed, that they doubt that any such sovereign balm exists, or that it will ever exist hereafter. The world, as they see it, is down with at least a score of painful diseases, all of them chronic and incurable; nevertheless, they cling to the notion that human existence remains predominantly charming. Especially is it charming in this unparalleled Republic of the West, where men are earnest and women are intelligent, and all the historic virtues of Christendom are now concentrated. The Editors propose, before jurisprudence develops to the point of prohibiting skepticism altogether, to give a realistic consideration to certain of these virtues, and to try to save what is exhilarating in them, even when all that is divine must be abandoned. They engage to undertake the business in a polished and aseptic manner, without indignation on the one hand and without too much regard for tender feelings on the other. They have no set program, either destructive or constructive. Sufficient unto each day will be the performance thereof.

As has been hinted, the Editors are not fond enough to believe in their own varieties of truth too violently, or to assume that the truth is ascertainable in all cases, or even in most cases. If they are convinced of anything beyond peradventure, it is, indeed, that many of the great problems of man, and particularly of man as a member of society, are intrinsically insoluble — that insolubility is as much a part of their essence as it is of the essence of squaring the circle. But demonstrating this insolubility thus takes on something of the quality of establishing a truth, and even merely arguing it gathers a sort of austere virtue. For human progress is achieved, it must be manifest, not by wasting effort upon hopeless and exhausting enigmas, but by concentrating effort upon inquiries that are within the poor talents of man. In the field of politics, for example, utopianism is not only useless; it is also dangerous, for it centers attention upon what ought to be at the expense of what might be. Yet in the United States politics remains mainly utopian — an inheritance, no doubt, from the gabby, gaudy days of the Revolution. The ideal realm imagined by an A. Mitchell Palmer, a King Kleagle of the Ku Klux Klan or a Grand Inquisitor of the Anti-Saloon League, with all human curiosity and enterprise brought down to a simple passion for the goose-step, is as idiotically utopian as the ideal of an Alcott, a Marx or a Bryan. *The American Mercury* will devote itself pleasantly to exposing the nonsensicality of all such hallucinations, particularly when they show a certain apparent plausibility. Its own pet hallucination will take the form of an hypothesis that the progress of knowledge is less a matter of accumulating facts than a matter of destroying 'facts'. It will assume constantly that the more ignorant a man is the more he knows, positively and indignantly. Among the great leeches and barber-surgeons who profess to medicate the body politic, it will give its suffrage to those who admit frankly that all the basic diseases are beyond cure, and who consecrate themselves to making the patient as comfortable as possible.

In some of the preliminary notices of *The American Mercury,* kindly published in the newspapers, apprehension has been expressed that the Editors are what is called Radicals, *i.e.,* that they harbor designs upon the Republic, and are bound by a secret oath to put down 100% Americanism. The notion is herewith denounced. Neither is a Radical, or the son of a Radical, or, indeed, the friend of any known Radical. Both view the capitalistic system, if not exactly amorously, then at all events politely. The Radical proposals to destroy it at one blow seem to them to be as full of folly as the Liberal proposals to denaturize it by arousing its better nature. They believe that it is destined to endure in the United States, perhaps long after it has broken up everywhere else, if only because the illusion that any bright boy can make himself a part of it remains a cardinal article of the American national religion — and no sentient man will ever confess himself doomed to life imprisonment in the proletariat so long as the slightest hope remains, in fact or in fancy, of getting out of it. Thus class consciousness is not one of our national diseases; we suffer, indeed, from its opposite — the delusion that class barriers are not real. That delusion reveals itself in many forms, some of them as beautiful as a glass eye. One is the Liberal doctrine that a prairie demagogue promoted to the United States Senate will instantly show all the sagacity of a Metternich and all the high rectitude of a Pierre Bayard. Another is the doctrine that a moron run through a university and decorated with a Ph.D. will cease thereby to be a moron. Another is the doctrine that J.P. Morgan's press-agents and dish-washers make competent Cabinet Ministers and Ambassadors. Yet another, a step further, is the doctrine that the interests of capital and labor are identical — which is to say, that the interests of landlord and tenant, hangman and condemned, cat and rat are identical. Such notions, alas, seem to permeate all American thinking, the shallowness of which has been frequently remarked by foreign observers, particularly in the Motherland. It will be an agreeable duty to track down some of the worst nonsense prevailing and to do execution upon it — not indignantly, of course, but nevertheless with a sufficient play of malice to give the business a Christian and philanthropic air.

|||

That air, of course, will be largely deceptive, as it always is. For the second time the nobility and gentry are cautioned that they are here in the presence of no band of passionate altruists, consecrated to Service as, in the late Mr Harding's poignant phrase, 'the supreme commitment'. The Editors are committed to nothing save this: to keep to common sense as fast as they can, to belabor sham as agreeably as possible, to give a civilized entertainment. The reader they have in their eye, whose prejudices they share and whose woes they hope to soothe, is what William Graham Sumner called the Forgotten Man — that is, the normal, educated, well-disposed, unfrenzied, enlightened citizen of the middle minority. This man, as everyone knows, is fast losing all the rights that he once had, at least in theory, under American law. On the one hand he is beset by a vast mass of oppressive legislation issuing from the nether rabble of cowherds, lodge-joiners and Methodists, with Prohibition as its typical masterpiece. And on the other hand he is beset by increasing invasions of his freedom of opinion, the product of craven nightmares among the usurers, exploiters and other rogues who own and try to run the Republic. If, desiring to entertain a guest in the manner universal among civilized men, he procures a bottle or two of harmless wine, he runs a risk of being dragged to jail by official blackmailers and fined and lectured by some political hack in the robes of a Federal Judge. And if, disgusted by the sordid tyranny and dishonesty of the government he suffers under, he denounces it righteously and demands a return to the Bill of Rights, he runs a grave risk of being posted as a paid agent of the Bolsheviki.

This Forgotten Man, when he is recalled at all, is thus recalled only to be placarded as infamous. The normal agencies for relieving psychic distress all pass him over. The Liberals have no comfort for him because he refuses to believe in their endless series of infallible elixirs; most of these very elixirs, in fact, only help to multiply his difficulties. And the Tories who perform in the great daily newspapers and in the Rotary Club weeklies and in the reviews of high tone — these prophets of normalcy can see in his discontent nothing save subversion and worse. There is no middle ground of consolation for men who believe neither in the Socialist fol-de-rol nor in the principal enemies of the Socialist fol-de-rol — and yet it must be obvious that such men constitute the most intelligent and valuable body of citizens that the nation can boast. The leading men of science and learning are in it. The best artists, in all the arts, are in it. Such men of business as have got any imagination are in it. It will be the design of *The American Mercury* to bring, if not alleviation of their lot, then at least some solace to these outcasts of democracy. That they will ever actually escape from the morass in which they now wander so disconsolately is probably too much to hope. But at all events there is some chance of entertaining them to their taste while they flounder.

III

In the field of the fine arts *The American Mercury* will pursue the course that the Editors have followed for fifteen years past in another place. They are asking various other critics to share their work and they will thus be able to cover a wider area than heretofore, but they will not deviate from their old program — to welcome sound and honest work, whatever its form or lack of form, and to carry on steady artillery practise against every variety of artistic pedant and mountebank. They belong to no coterie and have no aesthetic theory to propagate. They do not believe that a work of art has any purpose beyond that of being charming and stimulating, and they do not believe that there is much difficulty, taking one day with another, about distinguishing clearly between the good and the not good. It is only when theories begin to enter into the matter that counsels are corrupted — and between the transcendental, gibberishy theory of a Greenwich Village aesthete and the harsh, moral, patriotic theory of a university pedagogue there is not much to choose. Good work is always done in the middle ground, between the theories. That middle ground now lies wide open: the young American artist is quite as free as he needs to be. The Editors do not believe that he is helped by nursing and coddling him. If the obscure, inner necessity which moves him is not powerful enough to make him function unassisted, then it is not powerful enough to make a genuine artist of him. All he deserves to have is aid against the obscurantists who occasionally beset him — men whose interest in the fine arts, by some occult Freudian means, seems to be grounded upon an implacable hatred of everything that is free, and honest, and beautiful. It will be a pleasure to pursue such obscurantists to their fastnesses, and to work the *lex talionis* upon them. The business is amusing and now and then it may achieve some by-product of good.

The probable general contents of the magazine are indicated by this first number, but there will be no rigid formula, and a number of changes and improvements, indeed, are already in contemplation. In the department of *belles lettres* an effort will be made to publish one or two short stories in each issue, such occasional short plays as will merit print, some verse (but not much), and maybe a few other things, lying outside the categories. The essays and articles, it is hoped, will cover a wide range; no subject likely to be of interest to the sort of reader before described will be avoided, nor will there be any limitation upon the free play of opinion, so long as it is neither doctrinaire nor sentimental. To the departments already set up others may be added later on, but this is a matter that will have to determine itself. The Editors will welcome communications from readers, and those that seem to be of general interest will be printed, perhaps with editorial glosses. No effort will be made in the book reviews to cover all the multitude of books that come from the publishers every month. The reviews will deal only with such books as happen to attract the staff of reviewers, either by their virtues or by their defects. The dramatic reviews will, however, cover the entire range of the New York theatre.

In general *The American Mercury* will live up to the adjective in its name. It will lay chief stress at all times upon American ideas, American problems and American personalities because it assumes that nine-tenths of its readers will be Americans and that they will be more interested in their own country than in any other. A number of excellent magazines are already devoted to making known the notions of the major and minor seers of Europe; at least half a dozen specialize in the ideas emanating from England alone. This leaves the United States rather neglected. It is, as the judicious have frequently observed, an immense country, and full of people. These people entertain themselves with a vast number of ideas and enterprises, many of them of an unprecedented and astounding nature. There are more political theories on tap in the Republic than anywhere else on earth, and more doctrines in aesthetics, and more religions, and more other schemes for regimenting, harrowing and saving human beings. Our annual production of messiahs is greater than that of all Asia. A single session of Congress produces more utopian legislation than Europe has seen since the first meeting of the English Witenagemot. To explore this great complex of inspirations, to isolate the individual prophets from the herd and examine their proposals, to follow the ponderous revolutions of the mass mind — in brief, to attempt a realistic presentation of the whole gaudy, gorgeous American scene — this will be the principal enterprise of *The American Mercury*.

Source: Friedel, F.B. (1972) *Builders of American Institutions: Readings in United States History*, Chicago, Rand McNally.

1.4.2   THE 'HAYS' CODE (1930)

In the 1920s and early 1930s Hollywood was hit by a number of scandals. These scandals combined with a new explicitness in movies, brought about by sound dialogue and growing conservatism in certain strands of American society, and attracted the attentions of numerous moral reformers. In order to pre-empt potentially damaging legislation the movie industry introduced its own production code.

The Code was actually drawn up by Martin Quigley and Father Daniel J. Lord under the supervision of William Hays, a former US Post Master General, who was appointed first President of the Motion Picture Producers and Distributors of America, Inc. This association included all the major movie companies: MGM, Warner Bros., Columbia, Paramount, Universal, Fox, RKO and others. Though introduced in 1930 the Code did not have much impact until an amendment was added in 1934, thereafter scripts and the negative of the film had to be submitted to be checked for departures from the Code. In addition to movie production these companies dominated the distribution side of the industry, this effectively meant that all main-stream commercial cinema was subject to the provisions of the Code. Its influence was also felt beyond the United States since foreign films had to comply with the Code in order to receive a commercial distribution in America. The Code remained in place for more than 30 years but could not survive the pressure of the 'liberated' 1960s and in 1966 it finally gave way to the system of certification by age group which, though modified, has continued ever since.

CODE TO GOVERN THE MAKING OF TALKING, SYNCHRONIZED AND SILENT MOTION PICTURES

Formulated by Association of Motion Picture Producers, Inc., and the Motion Picture Producers and Distributors of America, Inc.

Motion picture producers recognize the high trust and confidence which have been placed in them by the people of the world and which have made motion pictures a universal form of entertainment.

They recognize their responsibility to the public because of this trust and because entertainment and art are important influences in the life of a nation.

Hence, though regarding motion pictures primarily as entertainment without any explicit purpose of teaching or propaganda, they know that the motion picture within its own field of entertainment may be directly responsible for spiritual or moral progress, for higher types of social life, and for much correct thinking.

During the rapid transition from silent to talking pictures they have realized the necessity and the opportunity of subscribing to a Code to govern the production of talking pictures and of reacknowledging this responsibility.

On their part, they ask from the public and from public leaders a sympathetic understanding of their purposes and problems and a spirit of cooperation that will allow them the freedom and opportunity necessary to bring the motion picture to a still higher level of wholesome entertainment for all the people.

GENERAL PRINCIPLES

1. No picture shall be produced which will lower the moral standards of those who see it. Hence the sympathy of the audience shall never be thrown to the side of crime, wrong-doing, evil or sin.

2. Correct standards of life, subject only to the requirements of drama and entertainment, shall be presented.

3. Law, natural or human, shall not be ridiculed, nor shall sympathy be created for its violation.

PARTICULAR APPLICATIONS

I. Crimes against the law

These shall never be presented in such a way as to throw sympathy with the crime as against law and justice or to inspire others with a desire for imitation.

1. *Murder*
    a. The technique of murder must be presented in a way that will not inspire imitation.
    b. Brutal killings are not to be presented in detail.
    c. Revenge in modern times shall not be justified.

2. *Methods of Crime* should not be explicitly presented.

   a. Theft, robbery, safe-cracking, and dynamiting of trains, mines, buildings, etc., should not be detailed in method.

   b. Arson must be subject to the same safeguards.

   c. The use of firearms should be restricted to essentials.

   d. Methods of smuggling should not be presented.

3. *Illegal drug traffic* must never be presented.

4. *The use of liquor* in American life, when not required by the plot or for proper characterization, will not be shown.

II. Sex

The sanctity of the institution of marriage and the home shall be upheld. Pictures shall not infer that low forms of sex relationship are the accepted or common thing.

1. *Adultery,* sometimes necessary plot material, must not be explicitly treated, or justified, or presented attractively.

2. *Scenes of Passion*

   a. They should not be introduced when not essential to the plot.

   b. Excessive and lustful kissing, lustful embraces, suggestive postures and gestures, are not to be shown.

Red Headed Woman *(1932) starring Jean Harlow and Chester Morris. Between the introduction of the Code in 1930 and the amendment of 1934, the sexual and moral content of the films of stars like Jean Harlow and Mae West continued to be controversial.* Red Headed Woman *portrays a woman social climbing through seduction and entrapment*

   c.   In general passion should so be treated that these scenes do not stimulate the lower and baser element.

3. *Seduction or Rape*

   a.   They should never be more than suggested, and only when essential for the plot, and even then never shown by explicit method.

   b.   They are never the proper subject for comedy.

4. *Sex perversion* or any inference to it is forbidden.

5. *White slavery* shall not be treated.

6. *Miscegenation* (sex relationship between the white and black races) is forbidden.

7. *Sex hygiene* and venereal diseases are not subjects for motion pictures.

8. Scenes of *actual child birth*, in fact or in silhouette, are never to be presented.

9. *Children's sex organs* are never to be exposed.

III. Vulgarity

The treatment of low, disgusting, unpleasant, though not necessarily evil, subjects should be subject always to the dictate of good taste and a regard for the sensibilities of the audience.

IV. Obscenity

Obscenity in word, gesture, reference, song, joke, or by suggestion (even when likely to be understood only by part of the audience) is forbidden.

V. Profanity

Pointed profanity (this includes the words, God, Lord, Jesus, Christ — unless used reverently — Hell, S.O.B., damn, Gawd), or every other profane or vulgar expression however used, is forbidden.

VI. Costume

1. *Complete nudity* is never permitted. This includes nudity in fact or in silhouette, or any lecherous or licentious notice thereof by other characters in the picture.

2. *Undressing scenes* should be avoided, and never used save where essential to the plot.

3. *Indecent or undue exposure* is forbidden.

4. *Dancing costumes* intended to permit undue exposure or indecent movements in the dance are forbidden.

VII. Dances

1. Dances suggesting or representing sexual actions or indecent passion are forbidden.

2. Dances which emphasize indecent movements are to be regarded as obscene.

VIII.   Religion

1. No film or episode may throw *ridicule* on any religious faith.

2. *Ministers of religion* in their character as ministers of religion should not be used as comic characters or as villains.

3. *Ceremonies* of any definite religion should be carefully and respectfully handled.

IX.   Locations

The treatment of bedrooms must be governed by good taste and delicacy.

X.   National feelings

1. *The use of the Flag* shall be consistently respectful.

2. The history, institutions, prominent people and citizenry of other nations shall be represented fairly.

XI.   Titles

Salacious, indecent, or obscene titles shall not be used.

XII.   Repellent subjects

The following subjects must be treated within the careful limits of good taste:

1. *Actual hangings* or electrocutions as legal punishments for crime.

2. *Third Degree* methods.

3. *Brutality* and possible gruesomeness.

4. *Branding* of people or animals.

5. *Apparent cruelty* to children or animals.

6. *The sale of women*, or a woman selling her virtue.

7. Surgical operations.

THE REASONS SUPPORTING PREAMBLE OF CODE

1.   Theatrical motion pictures, that is, pictures intended for the theatre as distinct from pictures intended for churches, schools, lecture halls, educational movements, social reform movements, etc., are primarily to be regarded as ENTERTAINMENT.

Mankind has always recognized the importance of entertainment and its value in rebuilding the bodies and souls of human beings.

But it has always recognized that entertainment can be of a character either HELPFUL or HARMFUL to the human race, and in consequence has clearly distinguished between:

a. *Entertainment which tends to improve* the race, or at least to re-create and rebuild human beings exhausted with the realities of life; and

b.   *Entertainment which tends to degrade* human beings, or to lower their standards of life and living.

Hence the MORAL IMPORTANCE of entertainment is something which has been universally recognized. It enters intimately into the lives of men and women and affects them closely; it occupies their minds and affections during leisure hours; and ultimately touches the whole of their lives. A man may be judged by his standard of entertainment as easily as by the standard of his work.

So *correct entertainment raises* the whole standard of a nation.

Wrong entertainment lowers the whole living conditions and moral ideas of a race.

Note, for example, the healthy reactions to healthful, moral sports, like baseball, golf; the unhealthy reactions to sports like cock-fighting, bull-fighting, bear baiting, etc.

Note, too, the effect on ancient nations of gladiatorial combats, the obscene plays of Roman times, etc.

2.   Motion pictures are very important as ART.

Though a new art, possibly a combination art, it has the same object as the other arts, the presentation of human thought, emotion, and experience, in terms of an appeal to the soul through the senses.

Here, as in entertainment:

Art *enters intimately* into the lives of human beings.

Art can be *morally good*, lifting men to higher levels. This has been done through good music, great painting, authentic fiction, poetry, drama.

Art can be *morally* evil in its effects. This is the case clearly enough with unclean art, indecent books, suggestive drama. The effect on the lives of men and women is obvious.

Note: It is often been argued that art in itself is unmoral, neither good nor bad. This is perhaps true of the THING which is music, painting, poetry, etc. But the thing is the PRODUCT of some person's mind, and the intention of that mind was either good or bad morally when it produced the thing. Besides, the thing has its EFFECT upon those who come into contact with it. In both these ways, that is, as a product of a mind and as the cause of definite effects, it has a deep moral significance and an unmistakable moral quality.

Hence: The motion pictures, which are the most popular of modern arts for the masses, have their moral quality from the intention of the minds which produce them and from their effects on the moral lives and reactions of their audiences. This gives them a most important morality.

1.   They *reproduce* the morality of the men who use the pictures as a medium for the expression of their ideas and ideals.

2.   They *affect* the moral standards of those who through the screen take in these ideas and ideals.

In the case of the motion pictures, this effect may be particularly emphasized because no art has so quick and so widespread an appeal to the masses. It has become in an incredibly short period *the art of the multitudes*.

3.   The motion picture, because of its importance as an entertainment and because of the trust placed in it by the peoples of the world, has special MORAL OBLIGATIONS.

A. Most arts appeal to the mature. This art appeals at once to *every class*, immature, developed, undeveloped, law abiding, criminal. Music has its grades for different classes; so has literature and drama. This art of the motion picture, combining as it does the two fundamental appeals of looking at a *picture* and *listening to a story*, at once reaches every class of society.

B. By reason of the mobility of a film and the ease of picture distribution, and because of the possibility of duplicating positives in large quantities, this art *reaches places* unpenetrated by other forms of art.

C. Because of these two facts, it is difficult to produce films intended for only certain classes of people. The exhibitor's theatres are built for the masses, for the cultivated and the rude, the mature and the immature, the self-respecting and the criminal. Films, unlike books and music, can with difficulty be confined to certain selected groups.

D. The latitude given to film material cannot, in consequence, be as wide as the latitude given to *book material*. In addition:

a.   A book describes; a film vividly presents. One presents on a cold page; the other by apparently living people.

b.   A book reaches the mind through words merely; a film reaches the eyes and ears through the reproduction of actual events.

c.   The reaction of a reader to a book depends largely on the keenness of the reader's imagination; the reaction to a film depends on the vividness of presentation.

Hence many things which might be described or suggested in a book could not possibly be presented in a film.

E. This is also true when comparing the film with the newspaper.

a.   Newspapers present by description, films by actual presentation.

b.   Newspapers are after the fact and present things as having taken place; the film gives the events in the process of enactment and with the apparent reality of life.

F. Everything possible in a *play* is not possible in a film.

a.   Because of the *larger audience of the film*, and its consequential mixed character. Psychologically, the larger the audience, the lower the moral mass resistance to suggestion.

b.   Because through light, enlargement of character, presentation, scenic emphasis, etc., the screen story is *brought closer* to the audience than the play.

c. The enthusiasm for and interest in the film actors and actresses, developed beyond anything of the sort in history, makes the audience largely sympathetic toward the characters they portray and the stories in which they figure. Hence the audience is more ready to confuse actor and actress and the characters they portray, and it is most receptive of the emotions and ideals presented by their favorite stars.

G. *Small communities*, remote from sophistication and from the hardening process which often takes place in the ethical and moral standards of groups in larger cities, are easily and readily reached by any sort of film.

H. The grandeur of mass settings, large action, spectacular features, etc., affects and arouses more intensely the emotional side of the audience.

In general, the mobility, popularity, accessibility, emotional appeal, vividness, straightforward presentation of fact in the film make for more intimate contact with a larger audience and for greater emotional appeal. Hence the larger moral responsibilities of the motion pictures.

REASONS SUPPORTING THE GENERAL PRINCIPLES

1.   No picture shall be produced which will lower the moral standards of those who see it. Hence the sympathy of the audience should never be thrown on the side of crime, wrong-doing, evil or sin.

This is done:

1. When *evil* is made to appear *attractive* or *alluring* and good is made to appear *unattractive*.

2. When the *sympathy* of the audience is thrown on the side of crime, wrong-doing, evil, sin. The same thing is true of a film that would throw sympathy against goodness, honor, innocence, purity or honesty.

Note: Sympathy with a person who sins is not the same as sympathy with the sin or crime of which he is guilty. We may feel sorry for the plight of the murderer or even understand the circumstances which led him to his crime. We may not feel sympathy for the wrong which he has done.

The *presentation of evil* is often essential for art or fiction or drama.

This in itself is not wrong provided:

a. That evil is *not presented alluringly.* Even if later in the film the evil is condemned or punished, it must not be allowed to appear so attractive that the audience's emotions are drawn to desire or approve so strongly that later the condemnation is forgotten and only the apparent joy of the sin remembered.

b. That throughout, the audience feels sure that *evil is wrong* and *good is right.*

2.   Correct standards of life shall, as far as possible, be presented.

A *wide knowledge of life and of living* is made possible through the film. When right standards are consistently presented, the motion picture exercises the most powerful influences. It builds character, develops right ideals, inculcates correct principles, and all this in the attractive story form.

If motion pictures consistently *hold up for admiration high types of characters* and present stories that will affect lives for the better, they can become the most powerful natural force for the improvement of mankind.

3.   Law, natural or human, shall not be ridiculed, nor shall sympathy be created for its violation.

> By *natural law* is understood the law which is written in the hearts of all mankind, the great underlying principles of right and justice dictated by conscience.
>
> By *human law* is understood the law written by civilized nations.
>
> 1. *The presentation of crimes* against the law is *often necessary* for the carrying out of the plot. But the presentation must not throw sympathy with the crime as against the law nor with the criminal as against those who punish him.
>
> 2. *The courts of the land* should not be presented as unjust. This does not mean that a single court may not be represented as unjust, much less that a single court official must not be presented this way. But the court system of the country must not suffer as a result of this presentation.

REASONS UNDERLYING PARTICULAR APPLICATIONS

Preliminary:

1. *Sin and evil* enter into the story of human beings and hence in themselves *are dramatic material.*

2. In the use of this material, it must be distinguished between *sin which repels* by its very nature, and *sins which often attract.*

   a. In the fist class come murder, most theft, many legal crimes, lying, hypocrisy, cruelty, etc.

   b. In the second class come sex sins, sins and crimes of apparent heroism, such as banditry, daring thefts, leadership in evil, organized crime, revenge, etc.

   The first class needs far less care in treatment, as sins and crimes of this class are naturally unattractive. The audience instinctively condemns and is repelled. Hence the important objective must be to avoid the hardening of the audience, especially of those who are young and impressionable, to the thought and fact of crime. People can become accustomed even to murder, cruelty, brutality, and repellent crimes, if these are sufficiently repeated. The second class needs real care in handling, as the response of human natures to their appeal is obvious. This is treated more fully below.

3. A careful distinction can be made between films intended for *general distribution*, and films intended for use in theatres restricted to a *limited audience*. Themes and plots quite appropriate for the latter would be altogether out of place and dangerous in the former.

Note: In general the practice of using a general theatre and limiting its patronage during the showing of a certain film to 'Adults Only' is not completely satisfactory and is only partially effective.

However, maturer minds may easily understand and accept without harm subject matter in plots which do younger people positive harm.

Hence: If there should be created a special type of theatre, catering exclusively to an adult audience, for plays of this character (plays with problem themes, difficult discussions and maturer treatment) it would seem to afford an outlet, which does not now exist, for pictures unsuitable for general distribution but permissible for exhibitions to a restricted audience.

I.   Crimes against the law

Scarface (1932) starring Paul Muni. The popular gangster genre of the early 1930s came into conflict with the Code. None more so than Scarface *in which Paul Muni plays a gangster clearly based on Al Capone*

The treatment of crimes against the law must not:

1. *Teach methods* of crime.

2. *Inspire potential criminals* with a desire for imitation.

3. *Make criminals seem heroic* and justified.

Revenge in modern times shall not be justified. In lands and ages of less developed civilization and moral principles, revenge may sometimes be presented. This would be the case especially in places where no law exists to cover the crime because of which revenge is committed.

Because of its evil consequences, the drug traffic should not be presented in any form. The existence of the trade should not be brought to the attention of audiences.

The use of liquor should never be excessively presented even in picturing countries where its use is legal. In scenes from American life, the necessities of plot and proper characterization alone justify its use. And in this case, it should be shown with moderation.

II. Sex

Out of regard for the sanctity of marriage and the home, the *triangle*, that is, the love of a third party for one already married, needs careful handling. The treatment should not throw sympathy against marriage as an institution. *Scenes of passion* must be treated with an honest acknowledgment of human nature and its normal reactions. Many scenes cannot be presented without arousing dangerous emotions on the part of the immature, the young or the *criminal classes*.

Even within the limits of *pure love*, certain facts have been universally regarded by lawmakers as outside the limits of safe presentation.

In the case of *impure love*, the love which society has always regarded as wrong and which has been banned by divine law, the following are important:

1. Impure love must *not* be presented as *attractive and beautiful*.

2. It must *not* be the subject of *comedy or farce*, or treated as material for *laughter*.

3. It must *not* be presented in such a way as to *arouse passion* or morbid curiosity on the part of the audience.

4. It must *not* be made to seem *right and permissible*.

5. In general, it must *not* be *detailed* in method and manner.

III. Vulgarity; IV. Obscenity; V. Profanity,

hardly need further explanation than is contained in the code.

VI.   Costume

General principles:

1.   The effect of nudity or semi-nudity upon the normal man or woman, and much more upon the young and upon immature persons, has been honestly recognized by all lawmakers and moralists.

2.   Hence the fact that the nude or semi-nude body may be *beautiful* does not make its use in the films moral. For, in addition to its beauty, the effect of the nude or semi-nude body on the normal individual must be taken into consideration.

3.   Nudity or semi-nudity used simply to put a *'punch'* into a picture comes under the head of immoral actions. It is immoral in its effect on the average audience.

4.   Nudity can never be permitted as being *necessary for the plot*. Semi-nudity must not result in undue or indecent exposure.

5.   *Transparent* or *translucent materials* and silhouette are frequently more suggestive than actual exposure.

VII.   Dances

Dancing in general is recognized as an *art* and as a *beautiful* form of expressing human emotions.

But dances which suggest or represent sexual actions, whether performed solo or with two or more, dances intended to excite the emotional reaction of an audience, dances with movement of the breasts, excessive body movements while the feet are stationary, violate decency and are wrong.

VIII.   Religion

The reason why ministers of religion may not be comic characters or villains is simply because the attitude taken toward them may easily become the attitude taken toward religion in general. Religion is lowered in the minds of the audience because of the lowering of the audience's respect for a minister.

IX.   Locations

Certain places are so closely and thoroughly associated with sexual life or with sexual sin that their use must be carefully limited.

X.   National feelings

The just rights, history, and feelings of any nation are entitled to consideration and respectful treatment.

XI.   Titles

As the title of a picture is the brand on that particular type of goods, it must conform to the ethical practices of all such honest business.

XII.   Repellent subjects

Such subjects are occasionally necessary for the plot. Their treatment must never offend good taste nor injure the sensibilities of an audience.

RESOLUTION FOR UNIFORM INTERPRETATION

As amended June 13, 1934

1. When requested by production managers, the Motion Picture Producers & Distributors of America, Incorporated, shall secure any facts, information or suggestions concerning the probable reception of stories or the manner in which in its opinion they may best be treated.

2. That each production manager shall submit in confidence a copy of each or any script to the Production Code Administration of the Motion Picture Producers & Distributors of America, Incorporated, (and of the Association of Motion Picture Producers, Inc., California). Such Production Code Administration will give the production manager for his guidance such confidential advice and suggestions as experience, research, and information indicate, designating wherein in its judgment the script departs from the provisions of the Code, or wherein from experience or knowledge it is believed that exception will be taken to the story or treatment.

3. Each production manager of a company belonging to the Motion Picture Producers & Distributors of America, Incorporated, and any producer proposing to distribute and/or distributing his picture through the facilities of any member of the Motion Picture Producers & Distributors of America, Incorporated, shall submit to such Production Code Administration every picture he produces before the negative goes to the laboratory for printing. Said Production Code Administration, having seen the picture, shall inform the production manager in writing whether in its opinion the picture conforms or does not conform to the Code, stating specifically wherein either by theme, treatment or incident, the picture violates the provisions of the Code. In such latter event, the picture shall not be released until the changes indicated by the Production Code Administration have been made; provided, however, that the production manager may appeal from such opinion of said Production Code Administration, so indicated in writing, to the Board of Directors of the Motion Picture Producers & Distributors of America, Incorporated, whose finding shall be final, and such production manager and company shall be governed accordingly.

Source: Moley, R. (1971) *The Hays Office*, Englewood Cliffs, NJ, Jerome S. Ozer, Appendices E, F and G.

1.4.3 THE POWER OF TELEVISION (1956)

The following transcript is of a television broadcast used in President Eisenhower's successful campaign for second term as President in 1956. It is an early example of how the growing power of television was to be used. Television has been credited with considerable, and sometimes crucial, importance in the conduct of political campaigns. However, politics is only one example, the persuasive power of television has been harnessed to mould opinion, beliefs and patterns of consumption in every facet of American life.

1. (OPEN ON)

    CU [close-up] of Eisenhower's face grinning.

    A CU of him on speaker's platform preferably at convention, waving to roaring crowds.

    NARRATOR: This is the most famous grin in the world.

2. (CUT TO)

    Longer shot of above to include crowd.

    NARRATOR: This is probably the best loved man in all the world. A man elected President of the United States by the largest majority in history.

3. (CUT TO)

    Shot of 'Eisenhower' banner being brought down convention aisle.

    NARRATOR: People in America ... people all over the world ... look to this one man with their hopes for the future.

4. (CUT TO)

    ECU [extreme close-up] of 'I like Ike' button.

    NARRATOR: *Everybody* seems to 'like Ike'.

5. (CUT BACK TO)

    Long shot of Ike waving on platform.

    NARRATOR: Why do people 'like Ike'? The experts say it's because of his integrity ... his basic humility. But it's also because ... people seem to know ... what Ike thinks of *them*.

6. (CUT TO)

    Shot of Eisenhower on platform waving. This is shot from behind the president, looking out on the convention floor.

    NARRATOR: What does President Eisenhower think of all the people in the world who look to him for hope? What does he think of America and its future?

7. (DISSOLVE TO BLACK)

   NARRATOR: What does President Eisenhower think of *you*?

8. (DISSOLVE UP)

   Average looking man in front lawn of average looking house.

   NARRATOR: Well, first he thinks you're an *individual*. There's no such thing as a 'common' man to President Eisenhower. You're an individual with rights, privileges ... and responsibilities. And one of your basic rights is the security that your national government is sincerely and honestly working for your best interests.

9.

   Wife and children come out of door to man.

   NARRATOR: It is your right to bring children into the world [in] the secure knowledge that their future is clear and uncluttered by staggering debt ... overwhelming inflation.

10. (CUT TO)

    Group of school children running up school steps. A couple are colored.

    NARRATOR: President Eisenhower believes that it is your privilege to send your children to the school of their choice.

11. (CUT TO)

    CU of face of colored child.

12. (CUT TO)

    Guided missile launching.

    NARRATOR: President Eisenhower believes that you're willing to assume the responsibility of *strength* ... that prevents wars from happening.

13. (CUT TO)

    Factory workers.

    NARRATOR: He thinks that you're entitled to a steady job ... and that you shouldn't have to surrender the major part of your earnings back to the government in taxes.

14. (CUT TO)

    Farmer driving home down road on tractor.

    NARRATOR: President Eisenhower thinks that *you* have integrity ... basic humility ... and honesty. That *you* as an individual want only the right to make your own way in the world with decency and dignity.

15. (CUT TO)

    Shot of mammoth utilities project (St. Lawrence Seaway).

    NARRATOR: And what does Ike think of your *future*? Well, he's a man who looks toward tomorrow with confidence and excitement. And under Ike, America has begun more projects for tomorrow than ever before. Projects that will make America stronger and greater every single day of *your* lifetime ... and your children's.

16. (CUT BACK TO)

Ike at convention.

NARRATOR: President Eisenhower is an optimist. He believes that all of us can meet the challenges of today and tomorrow with confidence.

17. (CUT TO)

CU of smiling Ike's face.

NARRATOR: And maybe that's part of the reason so many of us like *Ike*. Ike likes *us*.

Source: Griffith, R. (ed.) (1992) *Major Problems in American History Since 1945*, Lexington, Mass., D.C. Heath, pp.164–6.

1.5 PROSPERITY AND POVERTY

1.5.1 'THE AGE OF PLAY' (1924)

> The development of new technologies and the transformation of patterns of production and consumption in the latter part of the nineteenth and early part of the twentieth century produced nothing less than a social revolution. The following article by Robert L. Duffus, published in *The Independent* on 20 December 1924, examined the rise of recreation to a level where it constituted a major component in American culture.

[...] It is difficult to assign an exact date for the beginning of the Age of Play. If we seek the influences which brought it about we may go back half a century or more with profit; if we are looking for its external symptoms, a quarter of a century is nearly enough. Obviously the first prerequisite for play is leisure, although animal spirits and some economic leeway are desirable. Play on anything like the American scale would have been impossible except for the short working day, the Saturday holiday or half holiday, and the annual vacation. These are gifts of a century which also presented us with the World War and the Newer Pessimism.

With a decrease in the amount of human energy actually required for earning a living has gone a prodigious increase in wealth, thus upsetting what was once held to be an ethical as well as a mathematical law. In 1850, the national income per capita was $95, in 1918, $586 — a rate of progress which far outruns any inflation of the currency. In 1900, according to Mr Julius Barnes, the average American family spent sixty per cent of its income for the basic necessities of life, but in 1920 had to devote only fifty per cent to the same purpose. Thus there was not only leisure to devote to play, but money to spend on it. There was also, no doubt, an increasing restlessness, growing out of the uninteresting nature of the mechanical tasks to which larger and larger armies of workers were being assigned. So the stage was amply set for the Age of Play.

The first unmistakable sign of the coming era was the development of interest in games, a phenomenon faintly manifested in the United States for a decade or two prior to the Civil War, and slowly gathering strength thereafter. Baseball first appeared in something like its modern form about 1845, but did not produce its first professionals and thus start on its career as a great national spectacle until 1871. Lawn tennis, first played in America in 1875, and golf, introduced early in the last decade of the century, remained games for the few until very recently. Now there are said to be 2,000,000 golfers and from a quarter to one half as many tennis players. These are conspicuous instances of a general tendency. The playing of outdoor games was formerly either a juvenile or an aristocratic diversion; it has now become practically universal. These are golf links upon which horny-handed men in overalls play creditable games. And the number of onlookers at professional sports is legion. In a single year there are said to have been 17,000,000 admissions to college football games and 27,000,000 to big league baseball games.

A second phase of the development of play in America is the community recreation movement, which arose from the discovery by social workers that training and organization for leisure were becoming as necessary as training and organization for work. In 1895, the city of Boston took the radical step of providing three sand piles for the entertainment of young children; model playgrounds came about ten years later, and the first 'recreation centers' were not established until the middle of the first decade of the budding century. As late as 1903, only eighteen cities had public playgrounds of any description. Then the growth of such facilities began with a rush. Last year [1923] there were 6,601 playgrounds in 680 cities, with an average daily attendance of about a million and a half.

In eighty-nine cities there were municipal golf courses on which any man or woman who could afford clubs, balls, and a small green fee could play. Besides golf courses and tennis courts, upon which many a commoner became proficient in what had been 'gentlemen's' games, there were municipal swimming pools, ball grounds, theatres, and, in forty-five instances, summer camps under municipal auspices. Municipal expenditures for public recreation have nearly trebled since 1913, though they are as yet only about one third of the national chewing-gum bill.

But no spontaneous play and no disinterestedly organized recreation program can for a moment be compared in magnitude with what are commonly known as the commercialized amusements — 'the greatest industry in America', as James Edward Rogers of the Playground and Recreation Association has called them. The motion picture, the phonograph, and the cheap automobile came into existence, like the cheap newspaper, because a public had been created which (consciously or not) wanted them and could pay for them. Each had been the object of experimentation during the last quarter of the Nineteenth Century, but each attained social significance only after the opening of the Twentieth, when multitudes, for the first time in history, had money and leisure they did not know how to use.

The most significant aspect of the Age of Play, however, is not in its inventions, good and bad, but in an alteration of an ancient attitude — a veritable change in one of the most fundamental of folk ways. For uncounted generations man has survived and made progress, in the temperate zones, only by unceasing industry; in tropical and subtropical areas, where climatic conditions did not encourage industry, he survived without progress. At first the industrial revolution did not seem to break down this antique scheme of nature; but in this country, at least, and within this generation, it has become evident that unremitting toil is not necessarily a law of human destiny, and that a thimbleful of brains is worth at any time an ocean of sweat. The mechanical multiplication of labor power by ten, twenty, forty, or a hundred, the replacement of a man by two cents' worth of coal, has struck a fatal blow at the ancestral faith in mere hard work.

Less than a hundred years ago the merchants and shipowners of Boston were able to answer the demand of their employees for a ten-hour day with the argument that 'the habits likely to be generated by this indulgence in idleness … will be very detrimental to the journeymen individually and very costly to us as a community.' Fifty years ago a United States Commissioner of Patents, Mortimer D. Leggett, declared amid the applause of well-meaning persons that 'idleness … stimulates vice in all its forms and throttles every attempt at intellectual, moral, and religious culture.' The first break in this armor of conservatism occurred when it was discovered that play added to the worker's efficiency and was therefore of economic value. Through this chink heresy has crept in, and it is now apparent that play is coming to be looked upon, whether athletic in character or not, whether 'commercialized' or not, as an end justifiable in itself. Blindly, blunderingly, yet with more intense conviction than appears on the surface, the masses of the people are uttering a new moral law. The chains of necessity have been loosened; they are nearer a frank and full enjoyment of life than any people that ever lived.

I do not maintain that all their amusements are wholesome, nor that the excessive standardization and mechanization of work and play alike is without its dangers. I do maintain that such evils as exist are minor in comparison with the great gain for civilization that took place when millions learned to play where only thousands played before. These evils are not to be cured by curbing the spirit of play. Reformers and educators must accept this spirit as more sacred than anything they have to give; they can help by guiding, not by restraining.

The right to play is the final clause in the charter of democracy. The people are king — *et le roi s'amuse*.

Source: Mowry, G.E. (ed.) (1963) *The Twenties, Fords, Flappers and Fanatics*, Englewood Cliffs, NJ, Prentice-Hall.

1.5.2 'THE MIRACLE OF AMERICA' (1948)

The growth of prosperity in the twentieth century was far from unin-
terrupted (see Chapter 2, Documents 2.2.4, 2.2.5 and 2.2.6 on the
Depression), however, it was marked throughout the post-Second
World War era. The following document is an advert 'selling' the
American economic system to the American people. It was part of the
1948 campaign by the Advertising Council, a trade association of
advertising agencies, and its message was accepted in part or in whole
by many if not most Americans.

It all started […] when Junior looked up from his homework:

'It says here America is great and powerful on account of the American
economic system. What's our economic system, Dad?'

Dad put his paper down and appeared to be thinking hard.

'I'd like to know, too,' Mother put in. 'I think in these times *every* American
ought to be informed about what makes up the American way of life.'

'So do I,' Sis added.

'Well, I could give you all sorts of answers,' Dad said. 'But maybe we ought
to get the story straight from the one who knows it best.'

'Who's that?' asked Junior.

'You'll recognize him all right,' Dad said. 'Let's go!'

So they did […]

Junior gasped. 'Gee whiz — I know *him!*'

'Uncle Sam,' Dad began, 'my boy here wants to know what makes America
great. You know — our economic system and all that. Fact is, I guess we all
do.' […]

'In the early days, men and animals did most of our work.

'We even used the wind to run our machines.

'Then we began to use water power to turn millstones and run looms. But in
some places no water power was to be had.

'We needed something better. Our inventors and business men kept testing
and trying. There would be big rewards in our free market for reliable power
that could be used *anywhere*.

'At last we had it — thanks to an ingenious Scotsman — James Watt. He
invented an engine driven by steam made from coal!

'Later still Americans developed engines run by gasoline and electricity.

'Now we're looking for ways to use atomic power. […]

'Americans are known as inventive people. Why? Because we have had the incentive to profit by making improvements — and backing them with our savings.

'When our people realized that they were free to shape their own destinies, they began to devise machines which multiplied each man's work power.

'In 1799, Eli Whitney, inventor of the cotton gin that did 50 men's work, made history with an order for muskets awarded by the U.S. Army. Instead of building each gun separately, he turned out standard parts which could be used interchangeably on *any* gun.

'Hearing of this, the clocksmith Eli Terry started to make clocks on the same principle. With all the laborious fitting eliminated, he found that he could sell clocks for $10 apiece instead of the regular $25. In three years, he and his partner, Seth Thomas sold 5,000.

'Eli Terry saw that if he cut his costs by mass production, and distributed a bigger volume more widely, he would benefit more people and make more money. And it worked out exactly that way!

'Pins had long been made by hand, selling as high as 20 cents each. Then a Connecticut man perfected machines to make *two million pins a week!*

'Down through the years. Americans invented hundreds of thousands of work-saving machines.

'Of course, it takes money to make and install those new, labor-saving machines in factories — more money than any one man could afford. A machine for one worker often costs thousands of dollars. So the owner took in many *partners* — thrifty men and women who received *stock* in exchange for their money. All these *partners* joined to form a *company* which they owned together. In order to make a profit in competition with other companies, they had to turn out better and less expensive products.

'The same new freedoms that made Americans ingenious and inventive made us better and better workers — no matter what our jobs.

'The planners and managers of industry found new and improved ways of designing factories and work flow — so that goods were turned out more quickly and cheaply.

'They found new and better ways to get those goods from the factories to the stores and into the homes. Advertising and selling opened up bigger markets by telling the story to millions.

'And the individual worker became steadily more skillful at his job. He realized that the more he could produce during the hours he worked, the more he would increase his own value. When many workers did that, it added up to national prosperity!

'Labor unions and collective bargaining strengthened the worker's sense of security and improved working conditions. The result is that America gradually developed the greatest group of skilled workers and technicians the world has ever seen. […]

'It is because we Americans *produce* so much better for every hour we work that we *earn* more and can *buy* more. […]

'[…] and the end is not yet. We have learned that *in the long run*

'*When output per hour goes up, prices drop, so more people can buy and all of us* gain.

'*But when output per hour goes down, prices rise, so fewer people can buy and all of us* lose.

'Of course, there are unusual periods when these principles don't seem to work — times when business is far above or far below normal. But over the long pull you'll find that these rules of productivity *do* apply.

'On the average, productivity has increased in the United States almost one-fifth every 10 years since 1850. We topped this in the 20 years 1920–1940, and we can do it again!'

'Can we keep right on doing it?' Dad asked.

'We certainly can!' Uncle Sam replied. 'If everybody who plays a part in making things will team up to do it, we can raise productivity so far and so fast that we can share the benefits and have real security for *all* our people.'

Source: Griffith, R. (ed.) (1992) *Major Problems in American History Since 1945*, Lexington, Mass., D.C. Heath, pp.200–2.

1.5.3 EXTRACT FROM *THE OTHER AMERICA* BY MICHAEL HARRINGTON (1962)

In the post-war era the United States experienced rapid economic growth and a level of prosperity never seen before. However, millions of Americans still lived in poverty. The following extract from Michael Harrington's 1962 book *The Other America: Poverty in the United States* describes the invisibility of the poor.

CHAPTER 1 THE INVISIBLE LAND

There is a familiar America. It is celebrated in speeches and advertised on television and in the magazines. It has the highest mass standard of living the world has ever known.

In the 1950s this America worried about itself, yet even its anxieties were products of abundance. The title of a brilliant book was widely misinterpreted, and the familiar America began to call itself 'the affluent society'. There was introspection about Madison Avenue and tail fins; there was discussion of the emotional suffering taking place in the suburbs. In all this, there was an implicit assumption that the basic grinding economic problems had been solved in the United States. In this theory the nation's problems were no longer a matter of basic human needs, of food, shelter, and clothing.

Now they were seen as qualitative, a question of learning to live decently amid luxury.

While this discussion was carried on, there existed another America. In it dwelt somewhere between 40,000,000 and 50,000,000 citizens of this land. They were poor. They still are.

To be sure, the other America is not impoverished in the same sense as those poor nations where millions cling to hunger as a defense against starvation. This country has escaped such extremes. That does not change the fact that tens of millions of Americans are, at this very moment, maimed in body and spirit, existing at levels beneath those necessary for human decency. If these people are not starving, they are hungry, and sometimes fat with hunger, for that is what cheap foods do. They are without adequate housing and education and medical care.

The Government has documented what this means to the bodies of the poor, and the figures will be cited throughout this book. But even more basic, this poverty twists and deforms the spirit. The American poor are pessimistic and defeated, and they are victimized by mental suffering to a degree unknown in Suburbia.

This book is a description of the world in which these people live; it is about the other America. Here are the unskilled workers, the migrant farm workers, the aged, the minorities, and all the others who live in the economic underworld of American life. In all this, there will be statistics, and that offers the opportunity for disagreement among honest and sincere men. I would ask the reader to respond critically to every assertion, but not to allow statistical quibbling to obscure the huge, enormous, and intolerable fact of poverty in America. For, when all is said and done, that fact is unmistakable, whatever its exact dimensions, and the truly human reaction can only be outrage. As W.H. Auden wrote:

> Hunger allows no choice
> To the citizen or the police;
> We must love one another or die.

I

The millions who are poor in the United States tend to become increasingly invisible. Here is a great mass of people, yet it takes an effort of the intellect and will even to see them.

I discovered this personally in a curious way. After I wrote my first article on poverty in America, I had all the statistics down on paper. I had proved to my satisfaction that there were around 50,000,000 poor in this country. Yet, I realized I did not believe my own figures. The poor existed in the Government reports; they were percentages and numbers in long, close columns, but they were not part of my experience. I could prove that the other America existed, but I had never been there.

My response was not accidental. It was typical of what is happening to an entire society, and it reflects profound social changes in this nation. The other

America, the America of poverty, is hidden today in a way that it never was before. Its millions are socially invisible to the rest of us. No wonder that so many misinterpreted [John K.] Galbraith's title and assumed that 'the affluent society' meant that everyone had a decent standard of life. The misinterpretation was true as far as the actual day-to-day lives of two-thirds of the nation were concerned. Thus, one must begin a description of the other America by understanding why we do not see it.

There are perennial reasons that make the other America an invisible land.

Poverty is often off the beaten track. It always has been. The ordinary tourist never left the main highway, and today he rides interstate turnpikes. He does not go into the valleys of Pennsylvania where the towns look like movie sets of Wales in the thirties. He does not see the company houses in rows, the rutted roads (the poor always have bad roads whether they live in the city, in towns, or on farms), and everything is black and dirty. And even if he were to pass through such a place by accident, the tourist would not meet the unemployed men in the bar or the women coming home from a runaway sweatshop.

Then, too, beauty and myths are perennial masks of poverty. The traveler comes to the Appalachians in the lovely season. He sees the hills, the streams, the foliage — but not the poor. Or perhaps he looks at a run-down mountain house and, remembering [French enlightenment philosopher Jean-Jacques] Rousseau rather than seeing with his eyes, decides that 'those people' are truly fortunate to be living the way they are and that they are lucky to be exempt from the strains and tensions of the middle class. The only problem is that 'those people', the quaint inhabitants of those hills, are undereducated, underprivileged, lack medical care, and are in the process of being forced from the land into a life in the cities, where they are misfits.

These are normal and obvious causes of the invisibility of the poor. They operated a generation ago; they will be functioning a generation hence. It is more important to understand that the very development of American society is creating a new kind of blindness about poverty. The poor are increasingly slipping out of the very experience and consciousness of the nation.

If the middle class never did like ugliness and poverty, it was at least aware of them. 'Across the tracks' was not a very long way to go. There were forays into the slums at Christmas time; there were charitable organizations that brought contact with the poor. Occasionally, almost everyone passed through the Negro ghetto or the blocks of tenements, if only to get downtown to work or to entertainment.

Now the American city has been transformed. The poor still inhabit the miserable housing in the central area, but they are increasingly isolated from contact with, or sight of, anybody else. Middle-class women coming in from Suburbia on a rare trip may catch the merest glimpse of the other America on the way to an evening at the theater, but their children are segregated in suburban schools. The business or professional man may drive along the fringes of slums in a car or bus, but it is not an important experience to him.

The failures, the unskilled, the disabled, the aged, and the minorities are right there, across the tracks, where they have always been. But hardly anyone else is.

In short, the very development of the American city has removed poverty from the living, emotional experience of millions upon millions of middle-class Americans. Living out in the suburbs, it is easy to assume that ours is, indeed, an affluent society.

This new segregation of poverty is compounded by a well-meaning ignorance. A good many concerned and sympathetic Americans are aware that there is much discussion of urban renewal. Suddenly, driving through the city, they notice that a familiar slum has been torn down and that there are towering, modern buildings where once there had been tenements or hovels. There is a warm feeling of satisfaction, of pride in the way things are working out: the poor, it is obvious, are being taken care of.

The irony in this […] is that the truth is nearly the exact opposite to the impression. The total impact of the various housing programs in postwar America has been to squeeze more and more people into existing slums. More often than not, the modern apartment in a towering building rents at $40 a room or more. For, during the past decade and a half, there has been more subsidization of middle- and upper-income housing than there has been of housing for the poor.

Clothes make the poor invisible too: America has the best-dressed poverty the world has ever known. For a variety of reasons, the benefits of mass production have been spread much more evenly in this area than in many others. It is much easier in the United States to be decently dressed than it is to be decently housed, fed, or doctored. Even people with terribly depressed incomes can look prosperous.

This is an extremely important factor in defining our emotional and existential ignorance of poverty. In Detroit the existence of social classes became much more difficult to discern the day the companies put lockers in the plants. From that moment on, one did not see men in work clothes on the way to the factory, but citizens in slacks and white shirts. This process has been magnified with the poor throughout the country. There are tens of thousands of Americans in the big cities who are wearing shoes, perhaps even a stylishly cut suit or dress, and yet are hungry. It is not a matter of planning, though it almost seems as if the affluent society had given out costumes to the poor so that they would not offend the rest of society with the sight of rags.

Then, many of the poor are the wrong age to be seen. A good number of them (over 8,000,000) are sixty-five years of age or better; an even larger number are under eighteen. The aged members of the other America are often sick, and they cannot move. Another group of them live out their lives in loneliness and frustration: they sit in rented rooms, or else they stay close to a house in a neighborhood that has completely changed from the old days. Indeed, one of the worst aspects of poverty among the aged is that these people are out of sight and out of mind, and alone.

☆

The young are somewhat more visible, yet they too stay close to their neighborhoods. Sometimes they advertise their poverty through a lurid tabloid story about a gang killing. But generally they do not disturb the quiet streets of the middle class.

And finally, the poor are politically invisible. It is one of the cruelest ironies of social life in advanced countries that the dispossessed at the bottom of society are unable to speak for themselves. The people of the other America do not, by far and large, belong to unions, to fraternal organizations, or to political parties. They are without lobbies of their own; they put forward no legislative program. As a group, they are atomized. They have no face; they have no voice.

Thus, there is not even a cynical political motive for caring about the poor, as in the old days. Because the slums are no longer centers of powerful political organizations, the politicians need not really care about their inhabitants. The slums are no longer visible to the middle class, so much of the idealistic urge to fight for those who need help is gone. Only the social agencies have a really direct involvement with the other America, and they are without any great political power.

To the extent that the poor have a spokesman in American life, that role is played by the labor movement. The unions have their own particular idealism, an ideology of concern. More than that, they realize that the existence of a reservoir of cheap, unorganized labor is a menace to wages and working conditions throughout the entire economy. Thus, many union legislative proposals — to extend the coverage of minimum wage and social security, to organize migrant farm laborers — articulate the needs of the poor.

That the poor are invisible is one of the most important things about them. They are not simply neglected and forgotten as in the old rhetoric of reform; what is much worse, they are not seen.

[...]

Source: Griffith, R. (ed.) (1992) *Major Problems in American History Since 1945*, Lexington, Mass., D.C. Heath, pp.305–9.

1.6 IDENTITY AND THE 'TRUE AMERICAN'

1.6.1 THE SOCIAL CREED OF THE CHURCHES (1908)

Christianity in its numerous denominations has been a major element in American society since its foundation. In the early years of the twentieth century the movement for the socialization of Christianity reached its peak. The following statement is a significant example of a Christian perspective on wider social issues which this movement encouraged. The statement was adopted by the General Conference of the Methodist Episcopal Church in May 1908.

The Methodist Episcopal Church stands:

For equal rights and complete justice for all men in all stations of life.

For the principle of conciliation and arbitration in industrial dissensions.

For the protection of the worker from dangerous machinery, occupational disease, injuries and mortality.

For the abolition of child labor.

For such regulation of the conditions of labor for women as shall safeguard the physical and moral health of the community.

For the suppression of the 'sweating system'.

For the gradual and reasonable reduction of the hours of labor to the lowest practical point, with work for all; and for that degree of leisure for all which is the condition of the highest human life.

For a release from employment one day in seven.

For a living wage in every industry.

For the highest wage that each industry can afford, and for the most equitable division of the products in industry that can ultimately be devised.

For the recognition of the Golden Rule, and the mind of Christ as the supreme law of society and the sure remedy for all social ills.

Source: Commager, H.S. (ed.) (1963) *Documents of American History* (7th edn), New York, Appleton Century Crofts, vol.2, p.52.

1.6.2 THE IMMIGRATION ACT (1924)

American identity has been moulded by the process of immigration that created its society. During the twentieth century American society, or rather its government, has attempted to mould the pattern of future immigration. The 1924 Immigration Act, following earlier legislation, sought a pattern of immigration which reflected the ethnic and national groups already resident in the United States, using 1890 as the base line. The bias towards Northern and Western Europe is very evident. A summary of the Act is given with President Coolidge's Proclamation listing the quota for each nation.

ANNUAL REPORT OF THE COMMISSIONER-GENERAL OF IMMIGRATION

[...] The 'Immigration act of 1924' [...] which supplants the so-called quota limit act of May 19, 1921, the latter having expired by limitation at the close of the fiscal year just ended, makes several very important changes not only in our immigration policy but also in the administrative machinery of the Immigration Service. Some of the more important changes in these respects will be briefly referred to.

It will be remembered that the quota limit act of May, 1921, provided that the number of aliens of any nationality admissible to the United States in any fiscal year should be limited to 3 per cent of the number of persons of such nationality who were resident in the United States according to the census of 1910, it being also provided that not more than 20 per cent of any annual quota could be admitted in any one month. Under the act of 1924 the number of each nationality who may be admitted annually is limited to 2 per cent of the population of such nationality resident in the United States according to the census of 1890, and not more than 10 per cent of any annual quota may be admitted in any month except in cases where such quota is less than 300 for the entire year.

Under the act of May, 1921, the quota area was limited to Europe, the Near East, Africa, and Australasia. The countries of North and South America, with adjacent islands, and countries immigration from which was otherwise regulated, such as China, Japan, and countries within the Asiatic barred zone, were not within the scope of the quota law. Under the new act, however, immigration from the entire world, with the exception of the Dominion of Canada, Newfoundland, the Republic of Mexico, the Republic of Cuba, the Republic of Haiti, the Dominican Republic, the Canal Zone, and independent countries of Central and South America, is subject to quota limitations. The various quotas established under the new law are shown in the following proclamation of the President, issued on the last day of the present fiscal year:

By the President of the United States of America
A Proclamation

Whereas it is provided in the act of Congress approved May 26, 1924, entitled 'An act to limit the immigration of aliens into the United States, and for other purposes' that —

'The annual quota of any nationality shall be two per centum of the number of foreign-born individuals of such nationality resident in continental United States as determined by the United States census of 1890, but the minimum quota of any nationality shall be 100 (Sec. 11 (a)). […]

'The Secretary of State, the Secretary of Commerce, and the Secretary of Labor, jointly, shall, as soon as feasible after the enactment of this act, prepare a statement showing the number of individuals of the various nationalities resident in continental United States as determined by the United States census of 1890, which statement shall be the population basis for the purposes of subdivision (a) of section 11 (Sec. 12 (b)).

'Such officials shall, jointly, report annually to the President the quota of each nationality under subdivision (a) of section 11, together with the statements, estimates, and revisions provided for in this section. The President shall proclaim and make known the quotas so reported.' (Sec. 12 (e)).

Now, therefore, I, Calvin Coolidge, President of the United States of America acting under and by virtue of the power in me vested by the aforesaid act of Congress, do hereby proclaim and make known that on and after July 1, 1924, and throughout the fiscal year 1924–1925, the quota of each nationality provided in said Act shall be as follows:

Country or area of birth	Quota 1924–1925	Country or area of birth	Quota 1924–1925	Country or area of birth	Quota 1924–1925
Afghanistan	100	Greece	100	Palestine (with Trans-Jordan, proposed British mandate)	100
Albania	100	Hungary	473	Persia (1)	100
Andorra	100	Iceland	100	Poland	5,982
Arabian peninsula (1, 2)	100	India (3)	100	Portugal (1, 5)	503
Armenia	124	Iraq (Mesopotamia)	100	Ruanda and Urundi (Belgium mandate)	100
Australia, including Papua, Tasmania, and all islands appertaining to Australia (3, 4)	121	Irish Free State (3)	28,567	Rumania	603
Austria	785	Italy, including Rhodes, Dodekanesia, and Castellorizzo (5)	3,845	Russia, European and Asiatic (1)	2,248
Belgium (5)	512	Japan	100	Samoa, Western (4) (proposed mandate of New Zealand)	100
Bhutan	100	Latvia	142	San Marino	100
Bulgaria	100	Liberia	100	Siam	100
Cameroon (proposed British mandate)	100	Liechtenstein	100	South Africa, Union of (3)	100
Cameroon (French mandate)	100	Lithuania	344	South West Africa (proposed mandate of Union of South Africa)	100
China	100	Luxemburg	100	Spain (5)	131
Czechoslovakia	3,073	Monaco	100	Sweden	9,561
Danzig, Free City of	228	Morocco (French and Spanish Zones and Tangier)	100	Switzerland	2,081
Denmark (5, 6)	2,789	Muscat (Oman)	100	Syria and The Lebanon (French mandate)	100
Egypt	100	Nauru (proposed British mandate) (4)	100	Tanganyika (proposed British mandate)	100
Esthonia	124	Nepal	100	Togoland (proposed British mandate)	100

Country or area of birth	Quota 1924–1925	Country or area of birth	Quota 1924–1925	Country or area of birth	Quota 1924–1925
Ethiopia (Abyssinia)	100	Netherlands (1, 5, 6)	1,648	Togoland (French mandate)	100
Finland	170	New Zealand (including appertaining islands) (3, 4)	100	Turkey	100
France (1, 5, 6)	3,954	Norway (5)	6,453	Yap and other Pacific islands (under Japanese mandate) (4)	100
Germany	51,227	New Guinea, and other Pacific Islands under proposed Australian mandate (4)	100	Yugoslavia	671
Great Britain and Northern Ireland (1, 3, 5, 6)	34,007				

1. (a) Persons born in the portions of Persia, Russia, or the Arabian peninsula situated within the barred zone, and who are admissible under the immigration laws of the United States as quota immigrants, will be charged to the quotas of these countries; and (b) persons born in the colonies, dependencies, or protectorates, or portions thereof, within the barred zone, of France, Great Britain, the Netherlands, or Portugal, who are admissible under the immigration laws of the United States as quota immigrants, will be charged to the quota of the country to which such colony or dependency belongs or by which it is administered as a protectorate.

2. The quota-area denominated 'Arabian peninsula' consists of all territory except Muscat and Aden, situated in the portion of that peninsula and adjacent islands, to the southeast of Iraq, of Palestine with Trans-Jordan, and of Egypt.

3. Quota immigrants born in the British self-governing dominions or in the Empire of India, will be charged to the appropriate quota rather than to that of Great Britain and Northern Ireland. There are no quota restrictions for Canada and Newfoundland. […]

4. Quota immigrants eligible to citizenship in the United States, born in a colony, dependency, or protectorate of any country to which a quota applies will be charged to the quota of that country.

5. In contrast with the law of 1921, the immigration act of 1924 provides that persons born in the colonies or dependencies of European countries situated in Central America, South America, or the islands adjacent to the American continents (except Newfoundland and islands pertaining to Newfoundland, Labrador and Canada), will be charged to the quota of the country to which such colony or dependency belongs.

General note. — The immigration quotas assigned to the various countries and quota-areas should not be regarded as having any political significance whatever, or as involving recognition of new governments, or of new boundaries, or of transfers of territory except as the United States Government has already made such recognition in a formal and official manner. […]

Source: Commager, H.S. (ed.) (1963) *Documents of American History* (7th edn), New York, Appleton Century Crofts, vol.2, pp.192–4.

1.6.3 THE NEW ERA IN MIDDLETOWN (1929)

The following extracts are from the classic 1929 sociological study of Muncie, Indiana by Robert S. Lynd and Helen Merrell Lynd. Muncie was seen as an average American city. The city in the account was given the name 'Middletown' and the sections reproduced here deal with work and leisure.

The business district in Muncie, Indiana, ca 1928. *(Courtesy: Ball State University)*

GETTING A LIVING

For both working and business class no other accompaniment of getting a living approaches in importance the money received for their work. It is more this future, instrumental aspect of work, rather than the intrinsic satisfactions involved, that keeps Middletown working so hard as more and more of the activities of living are coming to be strained through the bars of the dollar sign. Among the business group, such things as one's circle of friends, the kind of car one drives, playing golf, joining Rotary, the church to which one belongs, one's political principles, the social position of one's wife apparently tend to be scrutinized somewhat more than formerly in Middletown for their instrumental bearing upon the main business of getting a living, while, conversely, one's status in these various other activities tends to be much influenced by one's financial position. As vicinage has decreased in its influence upon the ordinary social contacts of this group, there appears to be a constantly closer relation between the solitary factor of financial status and one's social status. A leading citizen presented this matter in a nutshell to a member of the research staff in discussing the almost universal local custom of 'placing' newcomers in terms of where they live, how they live, the kind of car they drive, and similar externals: 'It's perfectly natural. You see, they know money, and they don't know you.'

This dominance of the dollar appears in the apparently growing tendency among younger working class men to swap a problematic future for immediate 'big money'. Foremen complain that Middletown boys entering the shops today are increasingly less interested in being moved from job to job until they have become all-round skilled workers, but want to stay on one machine and run up their production so that they may quickly reach a maximum wage scale.

The rise of large-scale advertising, popular magazines, movies, radio, and other channels of increased cultural diffusion from without are rapidly changing habits of thought as to what things are essential to living and multiplying optional occasions for spending money. Installment buying, which turns wishes into horses overnight, and the heavy increase in the number of children receiving higher education, with its occasions for breaking with home traditions, are facilitating this rise to new standards of living. In 1890 Middletown appears to have lived on a series of plateaus as regards standard of living; old citizens say there was more contentment with relative arrival; it was a common thing to hear a remark that so and so 'is pretty good for people in our circumstances'. Today the edges of the plateaus have been shaved off, and every one lives on a slope from any point of which desirable things belonging to people all the way to the top are in view.

This diffusion of new urgent occasions for spending money in every sector of living is exhibited by such new tools and services commonly used in Middletown today, but either unknown or little used in the nineties, as the following:

In the home furnace, running hot and cold water, modern sanitation, electric appliances ranging from toasters to washing machines, telephone, refrigeration, green vegetables and fresh fruit all the year round, greater variety of clothing, silk hose and underwear, commercial pressing and cleaning of clothes, commercial laundering or use of expensive electrical equipment in the home, cosmetics, manicuring, and commercial hair-dressing.

In spending leisure time movies (attendance far more frequent than at earlier occasional 'shows'), automobile (gas, tires, depreciation, cost of trips), phonograph, radio, more elaborate children's playthings, more club dues for more members of the family, Y.M.C.A. and Y.W.C.A., more formal dances and banquets, including a highly competitive series of 'smartly appointed affairs' by high school clubs; cigarette smoking and expensive cigars.

In education high school and college (involving longer dependence of children), many new incidental costs such as entrance to constant school athletic contests.

In the face of these rapidly multiplying accessories to living, the 'social problem' of 'the high cost of living' is apparently envisaged by most people in Middletown as soluble if they can only inch themselves up a notch higher in the amount of money received for their work. Under these circumstances, why shouldn't money be important to people in Middletown? 'The Bible never spoke a truer word', says the local paper in an editorial headed 'Your Bank Account Your Best Friend', 'than when it said: "But money answereth all things." … If it doesn't answer all things, it at least answers more than 50 per cent of them.' And again, 'Of our happy position in world affairs there need be no … further proof than the stability of our money system.' One leading Middletown business man summed up this trend toward a monetary approach to the satisfactions of life in addressing a local civic club when he said, 'Next to the doctor we think of the banker to help us and to guide us in our wants and worries today.'

Money being, then, so crucial, how much money do Middletown people actually receive? The minimum cost of living for a 'standard family of five' in Middletown in 1924 was $1,920.87. A complete distribution of the earnings of Middletown is not available. Twelve to 15 per cent of those getting the city's living reported a large enough income for 1923 to make the filing of a Federal income tax return necessary. Of the 16,000–17,000 people gainfully employed in 1923 — including, however, somewhere in the neighborhood of a thousand married women, some of whom undoubtedly made joint returns with their husbands — 210 reported net incomes (i.e., minus interest, contributions, etc.) of $5,000 or over, 999 more net incomes less than $5,000 but large enough to be taxable after subtracting allowed exemptions ($1,000 if single, $2,500 if married, and $400 per dependent), while 1,036 more filed returns but were not taxable after subtracting allowed deductions and exemptions. The other 85–88 per cent of those earning the city's living presumably received either less than $1,000 if single or less than $2,000 if married, or failed to make income tax returns. […]

Thus this crucial activity of spending one's best energies year in and year out in doing things remote from the immediate concerns of living eventuates apparently in the ability to buy somewhat more than formerly, but both business men and working men seem to be running for dear life in this business of making the money they earn keep pace with the even more rapid growth of their subjective wants. A Rip Van Winkle who fell asleep in the Middletown of 1885 to awake today would marvel at the change as did the French economist say when he revisited England at the close of the Napoleonic Wars; every one seemed to run intent upon his own business as though fearing to stop lest those behind trample him down. In the quiet county-seat of the middle eighties men lived relatively close to the earth and its products. In less than four decades, business class and working class, bosses and bossed, have been caught up by Industry, this new trait in the city's culture that is shaping the pattern of the whole of living. According to its needs, large numbers of people anxious to get their living are periodically stopped by the recurrent phenomenon of 'bad times' when the machines stop running, workers are 'laid off' by the hundreds, salesmen sell less, bankers call in loans, 'credit freezes', and many Middletown families may take their children from school, move into cheaper homes, cut down on food, and do without many of the countless things they desire.

The working class is mystified by the whole fateful business. Many of them say, for instance, that they went to the polls and voted for Coolidge in November, 1924, after being assured daily by the local papers that 'A vote for Coolidge is a vote for prosperity and your job'; puzzled as to why 'times' did not improve after the overwhelming victory of Coolidge, a number of them asked the interviewers if the latter thought times would be better 'after the first of the year'; the first of the year having come and gone, their question was changed to 'Will business pick up in the spring?'

The attitude of the business men, as fairly reflected by the editorial pages of the press which today echo the sentiments heard at Rotary and the Chamber of Commerce, is more confident but confusing. Within a year the leading paper offered the following prescriptions for local prosperity: 'The first duty of a citizen is to produce'; and later, 'The American citizen's first importance to his country is no longer that of citizen but that of consumer. Consumption is a new necessity.' 'The way to make business boom is to buy.' At the same time that the citizen is told to 'consume' he is told, 'Better start saving late than never. If you haven't opened your weekly savings account with some local bank, trust company, or building and loan, today's the day.' Still within the same year the people of Middletown are told: 'The only true prosperity is that for which can be assigned natural reasons such as good crops, a demand for building materials, … increased need for transportation', and ' … advancing prices are due to natural causes which are always responsible for prices. … As all wealth comes from the soil, so does all prosperity, which is only another way of saying so does all business.' But again, 'natural causes' are apparently not the chief essential: 'There can be no greater single contribution to the welfare of the nation than the spirit of hopefulness. … '[This] will be a banner year because the people believe it will be, which amounts to the determination that it shall be … ' Still another solution for securing 'good times' appears: 'The most prosperous town is that in which the citizens are bound most closely together. … Loyalty to the home town … is intensely practical. … The thing we must get into our heads about this out-of-town buying business is that it hurts the individual who does it and his friends who live here. Spending your money at home in the long run amounts practically to spending it upon yourself, and buying away from home means buying the comforts and luxuries for the other fellow.' 'A dollar that is spent out of town never returns.' One looking on at this procedure may begin to wonder if the business men, too, are not some-what bewildered.

Although neither business men nor working men like the recurring 'hard times', members of both groups urge the maintenance of the present indus-trial system. The former laud the group leaders who urge 'normalcy' and 'more business in government and less government in business', while the following sentences from an address by a leading worker, the president of the Trades Council, during the 1924 political campaign, sets forth the same faith in 'free competition' on the part of the working class: 'The important issue is the economic issue. We can all unite on that. We want a return to active free competition, so that prices will be lower and a man can buy enough for himself and his family with the money he makes.' Both groups, as they order a lay-off, cut wages to meet outside competition, or, on the other hand, vote for La Follette in the hope of his being able to 'do some-thing to help the working man', appear to be fumbling earnestly to make their appropriate moves in the situation according to the rules of the game as far as they see them; but both appear to be bound on the wheel of this modern game of corner-clipping production. The puzzled observer may wonder how far any of them realizes the relation of his particular move to the whole function of getting a living. […]

INVENTIONS RE-MAKING LEISURE

Although lectures, reading, music, and art are strongly intrenched in Middletown's traditions, it is none of these that would first attract the attention of a newcomer watching Middletown at play.

'Why on earth do you need to study what's changing this country?' said a lifelong resident and shrewd observer of the Middle West. 'I can tell you what's happening in just four letters: A-U-T-O!'

In 1890 the possession of a pony was the wildest flight of a Middletown boy's dreams. In 1924 a Bible class teacher in a Middletown school con-cluded her teaching of the Creation: 'And now, children, is there any of these animals that God created that man could have got along without?' One after another of the animals from goat to mosquito was mentioned and for some reason rejected; finally, 'The horse!' said one boy triumphantly, and the rest of the class agreed. Ten or twelve years ago a new horse fountain was installed at the corner of the Courthouse square; now it remains dry during most of the blazing heat of a Mid-Western summer, and no one cares. The 'horse culture' of Middletown has almost disappeared. […]

The first real automobile appeared in Middletown in 1900. About 1906 it was estimated that 'there are probably 200 in the city and county'. At the close of 1923 there were 6,221 passenger cars in the city, one for every 6.1 persons, or roughly two for every three families. Of these 6,221 cars, 41 per cent were Fords; 54 per cent of the total were cars of models of 1920 or later, and 17 per cent models earlier than 1917. These cars average a bit over 5,000 miles a year. For some of the workers and some of the business class, use of the automobile is a seasonal matter, but the increase in surfaced roads and in closed cars is rapidly making the car a year-round tool for leisure-time as well as getting-a-living activities. As, at the turn of the century, business class people began to feel apologetic if they did not have a telephone, so ownership of an automobile has now reached the point of being an accepted essential of normal living.

Into the equilibrium of habits which constitutes for each individual some integration in living has come this new habit, upsetting old adjustments, and blasting its way through such accustomed and unquestioned dicta as 'Rain or shine, I never miss a Sunday morning at church'; 'A high school boy does not need much spending money'; 'I don't need exercise, walking to the office keeps me fit'; 'I wouldn't think of moving out of town and being so far from my friends'; 'Parents ought always to know where their children are.' The newcomer is most quickly and amicably incorporated into those regions of behavior in which men are engaged in doing impersonal, matter-of-fact things; much more contested is its advent where emotionally charged sanctions and taboos are concerned. No one questions the use of the auto for transporting groceries, getting to one's place of work or to the golf course, or in place of the porch for 'cooling off after supper' on a hot summer evening; however much the activities concerned with getting a living may be altered by the fact that a factory can draw from workmen within a radius of forty-five miles, or however much old labor union men resent the intrusion of this new alternate way of spending an evening, these things are hardly major issues. But when auto riding tends to replace the traditional call in the family parlor as a way of approach between the unmarried, 'the home is endangered', and all-day Sunday motor trips are a 'threat against the church'; it is in the activities concerned with the home and religion that the automobile occasions the greatest emotional conflicts. […]

Today a few plants close for one or two weeks each summer, allowing their workers an annual 'vacation' without pay. Others do not close down, but workers 'can usually take not over two weeks off without pay and have their jobs back when they return.' Foremen in many plants get one or two weeks with pay. Of the 122 working class families giving information on this point, five families took one week off in 1923 and again in 1924, seven others took something over a week in each year, twelve took a week or more in only one of the two years. No others had as extensive vacations as these twenty-four, although other entire families took less than a week in one or both years, and in other cases some members of the families took vacations of varying lengths. Of the 100 families for whom income distribution was secured, thirty-four reported money spent on vacations; the amounts ranged from $1.49 to $175.00, averaging $24.12.

But even short trips are still beyond the horizon of many workers' families, as such comments as the following show: 'We haven't had a vacation in five years. He got a day off to paint the house, and another year they gave him two hours off to get the deed to the house signed.' 'Never had a vacation in my life, honey!' 'Can't afford one this year because we're repairing the house.' 'I don't know what a vacation is — I haven't had one for so long.'

'We like to get out in the car each week for half a day but can't afford a longer vacation.'

But the automobile is extending the radius of those who are allowed vacations with pay and is putting short trips within the reach of some for whom such vacations are still 'not in the dictionary'. 'The only vacation we've had in twenty years was three days we took off last year to go to Benton Harbor with my brother-in-law', said one woman, proudly recounting her trip. 'We had two Fords. The women slept in the cars, the men on boards between the two running boards. Here's a picture of the two cars, taken just as the sun was coming up. See the shadows? And there's a *hill* back of them.'

Like the automobile, the motion picture is more to Middletown than simply a new way of doing an old thing; it has added new dimensions to the city's leisure. To be sure, the spectacle-watching habit was strong upon Middletown in the nineties. Whenever they had a chance people turned out to a 'show', but chances were relatively fewer. Fourteen times during January, 1890, for instance, the Opera House was opened for performances ranging from *Uncle Tom's Cabin* to *The Black Crook*, before the paper announced that 'there will not be any more attractions at the Opera House for nearly two weeks'. In July there were no 'attractions'; a half dozen were scattered through August and September; there were twelve in October.

Today nine motion picture theaters operate from 1 to 11 p.m. seven days a week summer and winter; four of the nine give three different programs a week, the other five having two a week; thus twenty-two different programs with a total of over 300 performances are available to Middletown every week in the year. In addition, during January, 1923, there were three plays in Middletown and four motion pictures in other places than the regular theaters, in July three plays and one additional movie, in October two plays and one movie. […]

The program of the five cheaper houses is usually a 'Wild West' feature, and a comedy; of the four better houses, one feature film, usually a 'society' film but frequently Wild West or comedy, one short comedy, or if the feature is a comedy, an educational film (e.g., *Laying an Ocean Cable* or *Making a Telephone*), and a news film. In general, people do not go to the movies to be instructed; the Yale Press series of historical films, as noted earlier, were a flat failure and the local exhibitor discontinued them after the second picture. As in the case of the books it reads, comedy, heart interest, and adventure compose the great bulk of what Middletown enjoys in the movies. Its heroes, according to the manager of the leading theater, are, in the order named, Harold Lloyd, comedian; Gloria Swanson, heroine in modern society films; Thomas Meighan, hero in modern society films; Colleen Moore, ingénue; Douglas Fairbanks, comedian and adventurer; Mary Pickford, ingénue; and Norma Talmadge, heroine in modern society films. Harold Lloyd comedies draw the largest crowds. 'Middletown is amusement hungry', says the opening sentence in a local editorial; at the comedies Middletown lives for an hour in a happy sophisticated make-believe world that leaves it, according to the advertisement of one film, 'happily convinced that Life is very well worth living'.

Next largest are the crowds which come to see the sensational society films. The kind of vicarious living brought to Middletown by these films may be inferred from such titles as: '*Alimony* — brilliant men, beautiful jazz babies, champagne baths, midnight revels, petting parties in the purple dawn, all ending in one terrific smashing climax that makes you gasp'; '*Married Flirts* — *Husbands*: Do you flirt? Does your wife always know where you are? Are you faithful to your vows? *Wives*: What's your hubby doing? Do you know? Do you worry? Watch out for *Married Flirts*.' So fast do these flow across the silver screen that, e.g., at one time *The Daring Years, Sinners in Silk, Women Who Give*, and *The Price She Paid* were all running synchronously, and at another '*Name the Man* — a story of betrayed womanhood', *Rouged Lips*, and *The Queen of Sin*. While Western 'action' films and a million-dollar spectacle like *The Covered Wagon* or *The Hunchback of Notre Dame* draw heavy houses, and while managers lament that there are too few of the popular comedy films, it is the film with burning 'heart interest', that packs Middletown's motion picture houses week after week. Young Middletown enters eagerly into the vivid experience of *Flaming Youth*: 'neckers, petters, white kisses, red kisses, pleasure-mad daughters, sensation-craving mothers, by an author who didn't dare sign his name; the truth bold, naked, sensational' — so ran the press advertisement — under the spell of the powerful conditioning medium of pictures presented with music and all possible heightening of the emotional content, and the added factor of sharing this experience with a 'date' in a darkened room. Meanwhile, *Down to the Sea in Ships*, a costly spectacle of whaling adventure, failed at the leading theater 'because', the exhibitor explained, 'the whale is really the hero in the film and there wasn't enough "heart interest" for the women.' […]

Actual changes of habits resulting from the week-after-week witnessing of these films can only be inferred. Young Middletown is finding discussion of problems of mating in this new agency that boasts in large illustrated advertisements, 'Girls! You will learn how to handle 'em!' and 'Is it true that marriage kills love? If you want to know what love really means, its exquisite torture, its overwhelming raptures, see —.' 'Sheiks and their "shebas"', according to the press account of the Sunday opening of one film, ' … sat without a movement or a whisper through the presentation. … It was a real exhibition of love-making and the youths and maidens of [Middletown] who thought that they knew something about the art found that they still had a great deal to learn.' Some high school teachers are convinced that the movies are a powerful factor in bringing about the 'early sophistication' of the young and the relaxing of social taboos. One working class mother frankly welcomes the movies as an aid of childrearing, saying, 'I will send my daughter because a girl has to learn the ways of the world somehow and the movies are a good safe way.' The judge of the juvenile court lists the movies as one of the 'big four' causes of local juvenile delinquency, believing that the disregard of group mores by the young is definitely related to the witnessing week after week of fictitious behavior sequences that habitually link the taking of long chances and the happy ending. While the community attempts to safeguard its schools from commercially intent private hands, this powerful new educational instrument, which has taken Middletown unawares, remains in the hands of a group of men — an ex-peanut-stand proprietor, an ex-bicycle racer and race promoter, and so on — whose primary concern is making money. […]

Though less widely diffused as yet than automobile owning or movie attendance, the radio nevertheless is rapidly crowding its way in among the necessities in the family standard of living. Not the least remarkable feature of this new invention is its accessibility. Here skill and ingenuity can in part offset money as an open sesame to swift sharing of the enjoyments of the wealthy. With but little equipment one can call the life of the rest of the world from the air, and this equipment can be purchased piecemeal at the ten-cent store. Far from being simply one more means of passive enjoyment, the radio has given rise to much ingenious manipulative activity. In a count of representative sections of Middletown, it was found that, of 303 homes in twenty-eight blocks in the 'best section' of town, inhabited almost entirely by the business class, 12 per cent had radios; of 518 workers' homes in sixty-four blocks, 6 per cent had radios.

As this new tool is rolling back the horizons of Middletown for the bank clerk or the mechanic sitting at home and listening to a Philharmonic concert or a sermon by Dr Fosdick, or to President Coolidge bidding his father good night on the eve of election, and as it is wedging its way with the movie, the automobile, and other new tools into the twisted mass of habits that are living for the 38,000 people of Middletown, readjustments necessarily occur. Such comments as the following suggest their nature:

'I use time evenings listening in that I used to spend in reading.'

'The radio is hurting movie going, especially Sunday evening.' (From a leading movie exhibitor.)

'I don't use my car so much any more. The heavy traffic makes it less fun. But I spend seven nights a week on my radio. We hear fine music from Boston.' (From a shabby man of fifty.)

'Sundays I take the boy to Sunday School and come straight home and tune in. I get first an eastern service, then a Cincinnati one. Then there's nothing doing till about two-thirty, when I pick up an eastern service again and follow 'em across the country till I wind up with California about ten-thirty. Last night I heard a ripping sermon from Westminster Church somewhere in California. We've no preachers here that can compare with any of them.'

'One of the bad features of radio', according to a teacher, 'is that children stay up late at night and are not fit for school next day.'

'We've spent close on to $100 on our radio, and we built it ourselves at that', commented one of the worker's wives. 'Where'd we get the money? Oh, out of our savings, like everybody else.'

In the flux of competing habits that are oscillating the members of the family now towards and now away from the home, radio occupies an intermediate position. Twenty-five per cent of 337 high school boys and 22 per cent of 423 high school girls said that they listen more often to the radio with their parents than without them, and, as pointed out above, 20 per cent of 274 boys in the three upper years of the high school answered 'radio' to the question, 'In what thing that you are doing at home this fall are you most interested?' — more than gave any other answer. More than one mother said that her family used to scatter in the evening — 'but now we all sit around and listen to the radio.'

Likewise the place of the radio in relation to Middletown's other leisure habits is not wholly clear. As it becomes more perfected, cheaper, and a more accepted part of life, it may cease to call forth so much active, constructive ingenuity and become one more form of passive enjoyment. Doubtless it will continue to play a mighty role in lifting Middletown out of the humdrum of every day; it is beginning to take over that function of the great political rallies or the trips by the trainload to the state capital to hear a noted speaker or to see a monument dedicated that a generation ago helped to set the average man in a wide place. But it seems not unlikely that, while furnishing a new means of diversified enjoyment, it will at the same time operate, with national advertising, syndicated newspapers, and other means of large-scale diffusion, as yet another means of standardizing many of Middletown's habits. Indeed, at no point is one brought up more sharply against the impossibility of studying Middletown as a self-contained, self-starting community than when one watches these space-binding leisure-time inventions imported from without — automobile, motion picture, and radio — reshaping the city.

Source: Friedel, F.B. (1972) *Builders of American Institutions: Readings in United States History*, Chicago, Rand McNally.

1.6.4 PRESIDENT TRUMAN CALLS FOR 'REAL AMERICANISM' (1951)

In his speech to the American Legion on 14 August 1951 President Truman strikes at the climate of fear and suspicion unleashed by Senator Joseph McCarthy and his supporters in their campaign to root out supposed communists and others engaged in 'un-American activities' from positions of power and influence. Truman fears the threat to 'real Americanism' from McCarthy's brand of patriotism. The tide of opinion was soon to turn against McCarthy, but not before many careers and reputations had been damaged or destroyed.

In the preamble to the Legion's constitution, its members pledged themselves — among other things — to 'uphold and defend the Constitution of the United States ... to foster and perpetuate a one hundred percent

Americanism ... to safeguard and transmit to posterity the principles of justice, freedom and democracy.'

At the present time, it is especially important for us to understand what these words mean and to live up to them.

The keystone of our form of government is the liberty of the individual. The Bill of Rights, which protects our individual liberties, is the most fundamental part of our Constitution.

When the Legion pledged itself to uphold the Constitution and to foster 100 percent Americanism, it pledged itself to protect the rights and liberties of all our citizens.

Real Americanism means that we will protect freedom of speech — we will defend the right of people to say what they think, regardless of how much we may disagree with them.

Real Americanism means freedom of religion. It means that we will not discriminate against a man because of his religious faith.

Real Americanism means fair opportunities for all our citizens. It means that none of our citizens should be held back by unfair discrimination and prejudice.

Real Americanism means fair play. It means that a man who is accused of a crime shall be considered innocent until he has been proved guilty. It means that people are not to be penalized and persecuted for exercising their constitutional liberties.

Real Americanism means also that liberty is not license. There is no freedom to injure others. The Constitution does not protect free speech to the extent of permitting conspiracies to overthrow the Government. Neither does the right of free speech authorize slander or character assassination. These limitations are essential to keep us working together in one great community.

Real Americanism includes all these things. And it takes all of them together to make 100 percent Americanism — the kind the Legion is pledged to support.

I'm glad the Legion has made that pledge. For true Americanism is under terrible attack today. True Americanism needs defending — here and now. It needs defending by every decent human being in this country.

Americanism is under attack by communism, at home and abroad. We are defending it against that attack. We are protecting our country from spies and saboteurs. We are breaking up the communist conspiracy in the United States. We are building our defenses, and making our country strong, and helping our allies to help themselves.

If we keep on doing these things — if we put our best into the job — we can protect ourselves from the attack of communism.

But Americanism is also under another kind of attack. It is being undermined by some people in this country who are loudly proclaiming that they are its chief defenders. These people claim to be against communism. But they are chipping away at our basic freedoms just as insidiously and far more effectively than the communists have ever been able to do.

These people have attacked the basic principle of fair play that underlies our Constitution. They are trying to create fear and suspicion among us by the use of slander, unproved accusations, and just plain lies.

They are filling the air with the most irresponsible kinds of accusations against other people. They are trying to get us to believe that our Government is riddled with communism and corruption — when the fact is that we have the finest and most loyal body of civil servants in the world. These slander-mongers are trying to get us so hysterical that no one will stand up to them for fear of being called a communist.

Now, this is an old communist trick in reverse. Everybody in Russia lives in terror of being called an anti-communist. For once that charge is made against anybody in Russia — no matter what the facts are — he is on the way out.

In a dictatorship, everybody lives in fear and terror of being denounced and slandered. Nobody dares stand up for his rights.

We must never let such a condition come to pass in this country.

Yet this is exactly what the scaremongers and hatemongers are trying to bring about. Character assassination is their stock in trade. Guilt by association is their motto. They have created such a wave of fear and uncertainty that their attacks upon our liberties go almost unchallenged. Many people are growing frightened — and frightened people don't protest.

Stop and think. Stop and think where this is leading us.

The growing practice of character assassination is already curbing free speech and it is threatening all our other freedoms. I daresay there are people here today who have reached the point where they are afraid to explore a new idea. How many of you are afraid to come right out in public and say what you think about a controversial issue? How many of you feel that you must 'play it safe' in all things — and on all occasions?

I hope there are not many, but from all that I have seen and heard, I am afraid of what your answers might be.

For I know you have no way of telling when some unfounded accusation may be hurled at you, perhaps straight from the Halls of Congress.

Some of you have friends or neighbors who have been singled out for the pitiless publicity that follows accusations of this kind — accusations that are made without any regard for the actual guilt or innocence of the victim.

That is not playing fair. That is not Americanism. It is not the American way to slur the loyalty and besmirch the character of the innocent and the guilty alike. We have always considered it just as important to protect the innocent as it is to punish the guilty.

We want to protect the country against disloyalty — of course we do. We have been punishing people for disloyal acts, and we are going to keep on punishing the guilty whenever we have a case against them. But we don't want to destroy our whole system of justice in the process. We don't want to injure innocent people. And yet the scurrilous work of the scandal mongers gravely threatens the whole idea of protection for the innocent in our country today.

Perhaps the Americans who live outside of Washington are less aware of this than you and I. If that is so, I want to warn them all. Slander, lies, character assassination — these things are a threat to every single citizen everywhere in this country. When even one American — who has done nothing wrong — is forced by fear to shut his mind and close his mouth, then all Americans are in peril.

It is the job of all of us — of every American who loves his country and his freedom — to rise up and put a stop to this terrible business. This is one of the greatest challenges we face today. We have got to make a fight for real 100 percent Americanism.

You Legionnaires, living up to your constitution as I know you want to do, can help lead the way. You can set an example of fair play. You can raise your voices against hysteria. You can expose the rotten motives of those people who are trying to divide us and confuse us and tear up the Bill of Rights.

No organization ever had the opportunity to do a greater service for America. No organization was ever better suited or better equipped to do the job.

I know the Legion. I know what a tremendous force for good it can be.

Now go to it.

And God bless you.

Source: Cronon, E.D. (ed.) (1966) *Twentieth Century America, Selected Readings, Vol.2: 1929 to the Present*, Belmont, Calif., Dorsey Press/Wadsworth.

1.6.5 THE NATIONAL ORGANIZATION FOR WOMEN: STATEMENT OF PURPOSE (1966)

The role of women had undergone a transformation along with, and as part of, the social and economic revolution that transformed America from the late nineteenth century. Nevertheless, discrimination and inequality had hardly been addressed. The women's movement of the 1960s and beyond had many strands. NOW formed in 1966 was less radical than some, being largely liberal and middle class, but its Statement of Purpose does provide another perspective on American identity.

We, men and women who hereby constitute ourselves as the National Organization for Women, believe that the time has come for a new movement toward true equality for all women in America, and toward a fully equal partnership of the sexes, as part of the world-wide revolution of human rights now taking place within and beyond our national borders.

The purpose of NOW is to take action to bring women into full participation in the mainstream of American society now, exercising all the privileges and responsibilities thereof in truly equal partnership with men.

We believe the time has come to move beyond the abstract argument, discussion and symposia over the status and special nature of women which has raged in America in recent years; the time has come to confront, with concrete action, the conditions that now prevent women from enjoying the equality of opportunity and freedom of choice which is their right as individual Americans, and as human beings.

NOW is dedicated to the proposition that women first and foremost are human beings, who, like all other people in our society, must have the chance to develop their fullest human potential. We believe that women can achieve such equality only by accepting to the full the challenges and responsibilities they share with all other people in our society, as part of the decision-making mainstream of American political, economic and social life.

We organize to initiate or support action, nationally or in any part of this nation, by individuals or organizations, to break through the silken curtain of prejudice and discrimination against women in government, industry, the professions, the churches, the political parties, the judiciary, the labor unions, in education, science, medicine, law, religion and every other field of importance in American society. […]

There is no civil rights movement to speak for women, as there has been for Negroes and other victims of discrimination. The National Organization for Women must therefore begin to speak.

WE BELIEVE that the power of American law, and the protection guaranteed by the U.S. Constitution to the civil rights of all individuals, must be effectively applied and enforced to isolate and remove patterns of sex discrimination, to ensure equality of opportunity in employment and education, and equality of civil and political rights and responsibilities on behalf of women, as well as for Negroes and other deprived groups.

We realize that women's problems are linked to many broader questions of social justice; their solution will require concerted action by many groups. Therefore, convinced that human rights for all are indivisible, we expect to give active support to the common cause of equal rights for all those who suffer discrimination and deprivation, and we call upon other organizations committed to such goals to support our efforts toward equality for women.

WE DO NOT ACCEPT the token appointment of a few women to high-level positions in government and industry as a substitute for a serious continuing effort to recruit and advance women according to their individual

abilities. To this end, we urge American government and industry to mobilize the same resources of ingenuity and command with which they have
solved problems of far greater difficulty than those now impeding the
progress of women.

WE BELIEVE that this nation has a capacity at least as great as other
nations, to innovate new social institutions which will enable women to
enjoy true equality of opportunity and responsibility in society, without conflict with their responsibilities as mothers and homemakers. In such innovations, America does not lead the Western world, but lags by decades
behind many European countries. We do not accept the traditional assumption that a woman has to choose between marriage and motherhood, on the
one hand, and serious participation in industry or the professions on the
other. We question the present expectation that all normal women will retire
from job or profession for ten or fifteen years, to devote their full time to
raising children, only to reenter the job market at a relatively minor level.
This in itself is a deterrent to the aspirations of women, to their acceptance
into management or professional training courses, and to the very possibility of equality of opportunity or real choice, for all but a few women.
Above all, we reject the assumption that these problems are the unique
responsibility of each individual woman, rather than a basic social dilemma
which society must solve. True equality of opportunity and freedom of
choice for women requires such practical and possible innovations as a
nationwide network of child-care centers, which will make it unnecessary
for women to retire completely from society until their children are grown,
and national programs to provide retraining for women who have chosen to
care for their own children full time.

WE BELIEVE that it is as essential for every girl to be educated to her full
potential of human ability as it is for every boy — with the knowledge that
such education is the key to effective participation in today's economy and
that, for a girl as for a boy, education can only be serious where there is
expectation that it will be used in society. We believe that American educators are capable of devising means of imparting such expectations to girl
students. Moreover, we consider the decline in the proportion of women
receiving higher and professional education to be evidence of discrimination. This discrimination may take the form of quotas against the
admission of women to colleges and professional schools; lack of encourage-
ment by parents, counsellors and educators; denial of loans or fellowships;
or the traditional or arbitrary procedures in graduate and professional training geared in terms of men, which inadvertently discriminate against
women. We believe that the same serious attention must be given to high
school dropouts who are girls as to boys.

WE REJECT the current assumptions that a man must carry the sole burden
of supporting himself, his wife, and family, and that a woman is automatically entitled to lifelong support by a man upon her marriage, or that marriage, home and family are primarily woman's world and responsibility —
hers, to dominate, his to support. We believe that a true partnership
between the sexes demands a different concept of marriage, an equitable

sharing of the responsibilities of home and children and of the economic burdens of their support. We believe that proper recognition should be given to the economic and social value of homemaking and child care. To these ends, we will seek to open a reexamination of laws and mores governing marriage and divorce, for we believe that the current sate of 'half-equality' between the sexes discriminates against both men and women, and is the cause of much unnecessary hostility between the sexes.

WE BELIEVE that women must now exercise their political rights and responsibilities as American citizens. They must refuse to be segregated on the basis of sex into separate-and-not-equal ladies' auxiliaries in the political parties, and they must demand representation according to their numbers in the regularly constituted party committees — at local, state, and national levels — and in the informal power structure, participating fully in the selection of candidates and political decision-making, and running for office themselves.

IN THE INTERESTS OF THE HUMAN DIGNITY OF WOMEN, we will protest and endeavor to change the false image of women now prevalent in the mass media, and in the texts, ceremonies, laws, and practices of our major social institutions. Such images perpetuate contempt for women by society and by women for themselves. We are similarly opposed to all policies and practices — in church, state, college, factory, or office — which, in the guise of protectiveness, not only deny opportunities but also foster in women self-denigration, dependence, and evasion of responsibility, undermine their confidence in their own abilities and foster contempt for women.

NOW WILL HOLD ITSELF INDEPENDENT OF ANY POLITICAL PARTY in order to mobilize the political power of all women and men intent on our goals. We will strive to ensure that no party, candidate, President, senator, governor, congressman, or any public official who betrays or ignores the principle of full equality between the sexes is elected or appointed to office. If it is necessary to mobilize the votes of men and women who believe in our cause, in order to win for women the final right to be fully free and equal human beings, we so commit ourselves.

WE BELIEVE THAT women will do most to create a new image of women by *acting* now, and by speaking out in behalf of their own equality, freedom, and human dignity — not in pleas for special privilege, nor in enmity toward men, who are also victims of the current half equality between the sexes — but in an active, self-respecting partnership with men. By so doing, women will develop confidence in their own ability to determine actively, in partnership with men, the conditions of their life, their choices, their future and their society.

Source: Griffith, R. (ed.) (1992) *Major Problems in American History Since 1945,* Lexington, Mass., D.C. Heath, pp.507–9.

1.6.6 AN ANALYSIS OF THE VIETNAM MEMORIAL (1989)

The trauma of the Vietnam War (see Chapter 4, Documents 4.4.8, 4.4.9 and 4.4.10) has impacted on every aspect of American society and culture. The following extract from John D. Bee's *Eros and Thanatos: an Analysis of the Vietnam Memorial* analyses the memorial looking at some of the emotions and tensions which surrounded its construction and reception, and which reflect on wider concerns about the war and its impact on American society.

The Vietnam Memorial, consisting of a wall and the group statue, has been completed with remarkable speed. Veteran Jan Scruggs formed the Vietnam Veterans' Memorial Fund in May 1979. The Maya Lin wall was dedicated in November 1982 and the Frederick Hart statue was dedicated on 11 November 1984, as an official addition to Lin's work. Since it was built the memorial has attracted millions of visitors — veterans, their relatives and others — who have taken the occasion to contemplate America's Vietnam experience and by so doing have shown the importance of monuments and memorials as public symbols.

[…] public symbols are complex rhetorical events. To create them, we notice a set of events, classify those events and make a set of judgements on how the events do or should fit with the social values and structures to which they pertain. Viewed in this light, a public symbol or monument is a rhetorical statement interpreting the connection between events and the social order. This is the perspective from which I propose to comment on the Vietnam Memorial.

Maya Lin's memorial design was selected from among 1421 competing entries. Though commonly described as a wall, the memorial actually consists of two intersecting walls, with both ends of the memorial starting at ground level and descending to a depth of about ten feet, where the walls meet. The walls are polished black granite, bearing the names of all the casualties listed chronologically in the order of their death. The two walls meet at an angle on lines pointing to the Lincoln and Washington monuments. There is a brief dedicatory statement before the first and after the last name. There is no flag.

When Maya Lin's design was exhibited, some believed it was too stark and unheroic. One dissenting voice was that of Tom Carhart, who appeared before the government committee and described Lin's piece as 'a degrading black ditch' and 'an open urinal'. Carhart found an ally in the wealthy and eccentric H. Ross Perrot, who financed and organized a campaign to modify the design. Their efforts resulted in an agreement to make an addition to the memorial. Sculptor Frederick Hart designed and executed the piece, consisting of three soldiers — one black and two white — dressed in authentic

Vietnam gear and situated by a grove of trees approximately seventy yards from the apex of the walls. Hart describes his contribution as follows: 'One senses the figures as passing by the tree line and caught by the presence of the wall, turning their gaze upon it almost as a vision […] the contrast between the innocence of their youth and the weapons of war underscores the poignancy of their sacrifice.'

If the Maya Lin and Frederick Hart memorials constitute an interpretation of the Vietnam experience, it will be helpful to outline the core meanings of such events — meanings that inform our expectations for such a memorial and underscore the unique, unexpected message that now stands on the Mall.

The Vietnam Memorial is a public symbol intended to complete or round out the material events of an armed conflict. Implicit in conflicts is the assumption that they are efforts to establish or defend social principles and the accompanying political and social order. The memorial to a conflict, then, stands as an assessment of success or failure. But success or failure is reckoned as more than simply the preservation or loss of life. A battle acts out a wish or desire to defend or establish certain values, and the outcome may be stated in terms either of the fulfilment or the frustration of that wish. Having traced the origins and developments of the combat myth, Joseph Fontenrose finds the meaning reducible to two ideas. 'We may', he says, 'look upon the combat myth in all its forms as the conflict between Eros and Thanatos.' Commenting on Fontenrose, Burke says, 'reduction [of the combat myth] to terms of Eros and Thanatos is in effect reduction to these three categories: purpose, fulfilment of purpose, frustration of purpose'. We expect the combat memorial to interpret events in terms of the larger purpose, that of defending or establishing the national goals and values. The balance of this discussion presents the view that the memorial interprets our experience in Vietnam on the side of Thanatos: death and the frustration of purpose. Specifically, I shall suggest that it marks the human loss of life and the national frustration and loss of purpose in that effort.

The wall's funerary design immediately calls to mind the theme of death, Thanatos. Lin's entry in the contest was an assignment for a class of funerary design and she admits to an interest and fascination with death. 'We are supposedly the only creature that realizes its mortality […] We don't tell children about it. We say someone "went away, passed away". We can't admit it to ourselves. That's always disturbed me.' Lin is quite clear that in her memorial she wished to impress on visitors the reality of the death of the 58,000 casualties.

> These [American troops in Vietnam] died. You have to accept that fact before you can really truly recognize and remember them. I just wanted to be honest with people. I didn't want to make something that would just simply say, 'They've gone away for a while.' I wanted something that would just simply say, 'They can never come back. They should be remembered.'

For Lin, the inspiration for the memorial and the summary statement about the conflict is the fact of death.

The Frederick Hart addition was instigated by those who believed the memorial should look beyond the facts of death and pay tribute to the cause. Hart was to provide a more realistic, more heroic monument, with a flag and real soldiers. Hart's work met the material conditions, but Lin's thesis was powerful enough and Hart's artistic sensibilities strong enough to ensure that the addition became a complement to the walls, reinforcing the funerary, death motif. Hart's soldiers stand trance-like as permanent visitors to their own memorial, drawn into Lin's theme of death.

Of the wall's various features, visiting columnists and commentators remark the powerful effect of the names, in driving home the magnitude of personal loss in the conflict. The *Washington Post* commented, 'We are not sure where the idea came from that wars should be remembered through the representation of an unknown soldier. This memorial makes the soldiers known, and the effect is strong and clear, like the morning sunlight.' Lin's list works the awareness of death into the visitor's sensibilities.

But, beyond asserting the fact of death, Lin wished to create an atmosphere for the visitor to contemplate and reflect on that stark reality. 'I wanted people to honestly accept that these people served and some of them died. And I think I wanted to create a very serene, tranquil place after I brought them to this sharp awareness.' The face of the wall is a scene for personal rituals and liturgies. Touching, shielding, making rubbings of names, leaving letters and personal mementos — all these are common observances. To those without a relative or friend's name on the wall, the names prompt the personal reflection Lin intended. One commentator wrote, 'Gradually, the enormous extent of this register of death and loss made its impression, humbling the visitor; revealing to him his own frailty, his own vulnerability, his own mortality'.

The millions of visitors to the wall and the experiences they report serve to validate Lin's focus on death and the theme of Thanatos as the central message of the Vietnam Memorial. But one still asks why visitors are so responsive to this theme for this conflict. Every conflict exacts a toll in lives, but other monuments commemorate more than death. We find affirmations of heroism, patriotic sacrifice and victory for the cause as themes that go beyond the killing. For Lin's reading to be valid and appropriate, there must be something different or unique about the Vietnam conflict.

The question prompts us to consider the broader meaning of Eros and Thanatos in the combat myth. These terms refer not just to the individual's death or survival, but to the larger outcome. Battles are undertaken to establish or defend a cause. When the victory is won, Eros triumphs. When defeat comes, Thanatos remains. Combats are quests and contests between ideals and systems as well as people.

At this level, the events of Vietnam once again register on the side of Thanatos. Whatever the United States' goals in Vietnam may have been, they were not achieved. Pieces in the press commemorating the tenth anniversary of the fall of Saigon note that Vietnam was the first war the United States lost. Painting the departure of Marines from the embassy roof as a summarizing event *Newsweek* commented, 'After 58,000 men had died, after billions of dollars had been squandered, America's crusade in Vietnam dwindled down to the rooftop rescue of a few Marines with a mob of abandoned allies howling at their heels'.

The United States' failure to effect an orderly withdrawal from Vietnam is a synecdoche for the failure in its larger purpose. The larger failure remains vivid in the public mind, as reflected in the comments of a columnist for *Commonweal*: 'Vietnam is not a metaphor for arrogant national ambition, nor a key-word for misplaced national generosity, nor a code-name for national trauma. It is simply a name for loss.' There is still considerable debate on why the United States lost. Whatever the reason, Vietnam become the first American defeat and this sad ending is expressed in the memorial.

Both the Maya Lin and Hart pieces lack the character of triumphant assertion that marks pieces as diverse in mood and character as the Washington Monument, the Lincoln Memorial and the Iwo Jima Memorial. All these proclaim the establishment or preservation of the national values. By contrast, the Lin memorial purposely excludes any such statement. It acknowledges that soldiers served and died. The Hart figures are standing beneath the American flag, but they and the flag are oriented towards the wall. They are apprehensive. They are reflective. There is certainly no hint of triumph.

To the theme of loss in battle we may add the theme of internal conflict and dissent, the loss of purpose. There never was unanimous domestic support for the US involvement in Vietnam. The reasons for being in the war were murky, the objectives of staying in were often doubted, and the best policy to pursue was never clear either to hawks or to doves. Beyond national loss, the Vietnam conflict produced an element of self-doubt and internal dissent that caused many to question the fundamental validity of the cause. From the time US involvement increased, public support for it decreased. Gallup results show that the number of Americans believing that involvement in the war was a mistake went from some 24 per cent in 1964 to 64 per cent in 1975. As the conflict ended, two-thirds of the public felt that involvement had been a mistake.

[...]

Source: The Open University (1997) *A103, An Introduction to the Humanities, Preparatory Material*, Milton Keynes, The Open University, pp.92–7.

MARKETS

2.1 INTRODUCTION

The documents and statistical data in this chapter offer a wide selection of material that provides a portrait, in part, of the US economy. The documents touch some of the key themes about the operation and management of the economy, while the tables offer a wealth of information not only about the economy but also about the way that Americans have lived and the manner in which they continue to conduct their lives.

Americans have always placed a great deal of importance on private property. The importance of owning property and then protecting that property, either from the government or individuals, has been high on the list of American values since the foundation of the Republic. There have been some who believed that this national affection for private property has led to a distinctively American economic policy which was characterized by the absence of governmental intervention. Americans and their government, it is suggested, were wedded to a notion of *laissez-faire*. There is a degree of truth in this view. Certainly the level of intervention by the US government is less than in most other liberal democracies. For instance, expenditure by the federal government, as measured by a percentage of Gross National Product is just over 25%, which is lower than virtually every Western European nation. Similarly the welfare net provided by government is considerably less elaborate than those available in Europe. So the profile of government in the US has been and continues to be less prominent than in those nations where private property and private economic arrangements are less valued. However, it would be a mistake to assume that the conduct of economic policy in the United States has consistently eschewed governmental intervention. There are two main reasons why there has been no consistency of principle in the formation of economic policy. Firstly, policy is made by politicians and they pay homage to the desires of their constituents and not to the doctrinal consistency of *laissez-faire*. Political survival and advantage has been the only doctrine that American politicians have obeyed with any rigour. Secondly, the interplay of private economic arrangements, or the market, has not always provided outcomes that have been attractive to a significant number of Americans. In turn those who have been displeased have turned to their political representatives for redress, and the politicians have been more than willing to attempt to modify the position. As a consequence the history of economic policy in the United States is relatively incoherent or eclectic rather than consistent, with influences drawn from all shades of political opinion. But it is important to note that within the tradition of incoherence there is a long and substantial history of government intervention and a multitude of attempts to regulate the economy.

The Sherman Antitrust Act is one instance of economic regulation. It is a very important example of government policy which seeks to modify the outcome of the market. The Sherman Act was to a large extent passed as a result of public demand. The American electorate at the end of the nineteenth century had developed a growing and vocal hostility to the development of the trusts. For a number of Americans the trusts were synonymous with monopoly and there was an American tradition of hostility to monopoly. Of course, the monopolies that most Americans historically had objected to were those that had been granted by the British Crown in the colonies. These were monopolies created by government and were the beneficiaries of legal privilege. However, the issue raised by the emergence of the trusts was very different. In the late nineteenth century, the economic circumstances of certain industries and services may well have encouraged a concentration of providers. The concentration of power within these industries, like oil or the railroads, might well be a consequence of the market that operated for these industries and services. In other words there was no issue of privilege but the response to the market. Interestingly the American public was not persuaded. They did not want to see monopoly or near monopoly whatever the reason. If necessary they wanted their representatives in the Congress to ensure that this did not occur. The Sherman Act was the first of several attempts by the federal government to implement a notion of fair competition and to prevent the forces of the market from subverting it.

The National Industrial Recovery Act sought to reverse this general direction of hostility toward monopoly. This was a sharp change in policy and undoubtedly would not have been considered but for the circumstances that the nation found itself. The financial collapse of 1929 and the severe economic depression that followed was one of the key watersheds in American political and economic history. In the election of 1932, Herbert Hoover, the incumbent President, undoubtedly lost because he was identified with the Depression. By contrast his opponent Franklin D. Roosevelt had promised the electorate a 'New Deal'. On taking office in March 1933, President Roosevelt and the Congress enacted fifteen major bills within a hundred days. This was an unprecedented achievement almost regardless of the merits of the legislation. The sheer speed and response of the Roosevelt Administration went some considerable way to removing the sense of gloom that had enveloped the nation in the preceding three years. The National Industrial Recovery Act (NIRA) was one of the key elements of the New Deal. It is difficult to establish the rationale behind the NIRA because it was created so rapidly and was the result of a host of compromises within the Congress. However, it is possible to detect a guiding belief in the Act that viewed competition as potentially destructive at least during the Depression. The NIRA sought to use the agency of government to promote collaboration in industry rather than enforcing a regime of competition. The NIRA, however, was unsuccessful. It was held unconstitutional by the US Supreme Court in 1935 but perhaps even more importantly it was ineffective and had lost public support. Soon after the demise of the NIRA, the Roosevelt Administration returned to the traditions of the Sherman Act and sought to maintain competition.

The New Deal radically altered the landscape of American society. Even when legislation was unsuccessful, it changed the terrain of both the polity and the economy. The balance of power, for example, between the states and the federal government was irrevocably altered. But perhaps the most significant development was the assumption by the federal government of responsibility for a vast range of economic and social policies. The Employment Act of 1946 and the documents concerning the state of the economy in the 1950s and 1961, and most recently President Clinton's International Economic Program are all indications that the federal government has assumed responsibilities in this area. Prior to the New Deal this would have been unthinkable, now it is commonplace and does not raise an eyebrow.

It is interesting to note the concerns of these documents. The Employment Act of 1946 and the documents describing the economy in the 1950s and in 1961 were all written during the great post-war expansion, one of the most remarkable periods of economic growth this century. They were also produced at a time of American global economic dominance. This is particularly true of the report on the economy in the 1950s. Certainly the years of the Eisenhower Administration (1953–61) were characterized by a sense of prosperity and well-being. The nation appeared to be more at ease with itself after having emerged from the Great Depression, the Second World War and the Korean War without a moment to catch its breath. Of course there were major problems that had to be dealt with, above all the Cold War and all the internal consequences from it. Nevertheless the steady and growing prosperity of the nation during the 1950s makes it appear a decade of calm sandwiched between two turbulent decades.

The Employment Act of 1946, by contrast, was driven by the memories of the Depression. The great fear was that the conditions of the 1930s would return after the end of the war. There was considerable concern that the return to a peacetime economy would see a resumption of mass unemployment. This Act was a clear statement by the Congress and the administration of President Harry S. Truman that such unemployment was unacceptable, even if at the point when the Act was passed there was no particular set of measures that would guarantee such an outcome. The Employment Act was nevertheless an indication of the responsibilities and attitudes of government towards economic management in the immediate post-war years.

The report on the economy in 1961 in its own way suggests that concerns about the economy were beginning to develop. In part these concerns were the result of a recession at the end of the 1950s and a growing awareness that despite the unprecedented prosperity of the United States, the American economy had not been performing comparatively well. Similar concerns are also evident in President Clinton's International Economic Program — by the 1990s the relatively poor performance of the American economy had become a major political concern. The difference in the perceptions between 1961 and the early 1990s is striking. Improving the global competitiveness of the economy had moved to the centre of the American political stage. In the 1992 presidential campaign Bill Clinton made the economy the central theme of his candidacy. 'The Economy stupid' was the slogan which captured the strategy of the campaign. Interestingly, the fears over the economy have diminished. The long economic expansion which began in 1991 has restored a substantial degree of confidence in the American economy. It has encouraged the United States to develop new trading relationships which are evident from the North American Free Trade Agreement (NAFTA) and Asia-Pacific Economic Co-operation (APEC) treaties.

2.2   PRE-1950

2.2.1   THE SHERMAN ANTITRUST ACT (1890)

The Sherman Act was an attempt to counter the perceived anti-competitiveness of trusts, that is the combination of business enterprises into powerful and sometimes dominant forces in certain markets. The latter part of the nineteenth century saw the development of many large corporations and trusts. Public opinion and political consensus was, and has continued to be, largely opposed to the presumed monopolistic nature of a small number of large enterprises, and supportive of a large number of competing smaller businesses. The implementation of the Act and its interpretation by the courts proved to be problematic. In 1911 a Supreme Court ruling emphasized the illegality of anti-competitive behaviour rather than the mere size and/or dominant position of an enterprise.

— An act to protect trade and commerce against unlawful restraints and monopolies.

Be it enacted by the Senate and House of Representatives of the United States of America in Congress assembled,

Sec. 1. Every contract, combination in the form of trust or otherwise, or conspiracy, in restraint of trade or commerce among the several States, or with foreign nations, is hereby declared to be illegal. Every person who shall make any such contract or engage in any such combination or conspiracy, shall be deemed guilty of a misdemeanor, and, on conviction thereof, shall be punished by fine not exceeding five thousand dollars, or by imprisonment not exceeding one year, or by both said punishments, in the discretion of the court.

Sec. 2. Every person who shall monopolize, or attempt to monopolize, or combine or conspire with any other person or persons, to monopolize any part of the trade or commerce among the several States, or with foreign nations, shall be deemed guilty of a misdemeanor, and, on conviction thereof, shall be punished by fine not exceeding five thousand dollars, or by imprisonment not exceeding one year, or by both said punishments, in the discretion of the court.

Sec. 3. Every contract, combination in form of trust or otherwise, or conspiracy, in restraint of trade or commerce in any Territory of the United States or of the District of Columbia, or in restraint of trade or commerce between any such Territory and another, or between any such Territory or Territories and any State or States or the District of Columbia, or with any foreign nations, or between the District of Columbia and any State or States or foreign nations, is hereby declared illegal. Every person who shall make any such contract or engage in any such combination or conspiracy, shall be deemed guilty of a misdemeanor, and, on conviction thereof, shall be punished by fine not exceeding five thousand dollars, or by imprisonment not exceeding one year, or by both said punishments, in the discretion of the court.

Sec. 4. The several circuit courts of the United States are hereby invested with jurisdiction to prevent and restrain violations of this act; and it shall be the duty of the several district attorneys of the United States, in their respective districts, under the direction of the Attorney-General, to institute proceedings in equity to prevent and restrain such violations. Such proceedings may be by way of petition setting forth the case and praying that such violation shall be enjoined or otherwise prohibited. When the parties complained of shall have been duly notified of such petition the court shall proceed, as soon as may be, to the hearing and determination of the case; and pending such petition and before the final decree, the court may at any time make such temporary restraining order or prohibition as shall be deemed just in the premises.

Sec. 5. Whenever it shall appear to the court before which any proceeding under section four of this act may be pending, that the ends of justice require that other parties should be brought before the court, the court may cause them to be summoned, whether they reside in the district in which the court is held or not; and subpoenas to that end may be served in any district by the marshal thereof.

Sec. 6. Any property owned under any contract or by any combination, or pursuant to any conspiracy (and being the subject thereof) mentioned in section one of this act, and being in the course of transportation from one State to another, or to a foreign country, shall be forfeited to the United States, and may be seized and condemned by like proceedings as those provided by law for the forfeiture, seizure, and condemnation of property imported into the United States contrary to law.

Sec. 7. Any person who shall be injured in his business or property by any other person or corporation by reason of anything forbidden or declared to be unlawful by this act, may sue therefor in any circuit court of the United States in the district in which the defendant resides or is found, without respect to the amount in controversy, and shall recover three fold the damages by him sustained, and the costs of suit, including a reasonable attorney's fee.

Sec. 8. That the word 'person', or 'persons', wherever used in this act shall be deemed to include corporations and associations existing under or authorized by the laws of either the United States, the laws of any of the Territories, the laws of any State, or the laws of any foreign country.

Source: Hacker, L.M. (ed.) (1961) *Major Documents in American Economic History, Vol.I*, Princeton, NJ, Van Nostrand, pp.124–6.

2.2.2 'CONFESSIONS OF AN AUTOMOBILIST' BY WILLIAM ASHDOWN (1925)

New values and attitudes towards consumption developed along with the processes of mass production and distribution. The consumer product as status symbol was a powerful force, and no product had more status than the motor car. William Ashdown described the effects on him, and some of those around him, in an article for the *Atlantic Monthly* in June 1925.

I am a small-town banker, and I am expected to act the part, living well, dressing well, and patronizing all our local affairs, as a banker should.

As a dispenser of credit, I have many opportunities to study human nature and to observe how men get ahead and how they fall behind. I believe my bank has handled more automobile propositions than any bank of its size in the country. We have made a specialty of loans on automobiles and have watched the agencies as they have grown from nothing to substantial business concerns. In this connection we have acquired a large amount of experience, suffered no losses, and learned not a little of the weaknesses of human nature as reflected in the automobile.

I am not a 'tightwad'. I am careful and I am thrifty — at least I was until I become a motorist. I am not a good spender. I have always worked for my money and I part with it only for value received. I have always saved part of my earnings, from habit rather than from necessity. I have never earned 'big money', but I have always had enough. I have never celebrated a stroke of good fortune more riotously than by buying a new suit of clothes and a necktie. But several years ago, when I was getting into my stride, I was told by my friends that I had arrived; and I wanted to believe them. Perhaps the moment had come to paraphrase General Pershing and tell the world

'Ashdown's here!' How could I tell it more effectively than by the purchase of a car?

At that time the automobile had not yet become a popular fad. The streetcar was still the common method of local conveyance and the railroad still the common medium of long-distance transportation. There were no finance companies especially equipped to handle time-payments on cars. The banks were highly skeptical of the automobile as a credit-risk, and the man who borrowed in order to buy a car was looked upon as dangerous. Even the humble Ford had to be sold, instead of selling itself as it now does. The dealers were inexperienced and without adequate resources. A car was considered distinctly a luxury, not, as at present, a rudimentary necessity.

After a severe battle with my thrifty conscience, I persuaded myself that I could afford a car. Absolutely ignorant of cars and car values, I finally decided upon a modest secondhand machine, of a make that was neither standard nor popular. The price represented about one tenth of my yearly income, and I had never before spent half so much on a luxury. Theretofore my greatest single extravagance had been a bicycle, which, while bearing at the time about the same relation in cost to my earnings, carried with it no upkeep or heavy depreciation, no social obligations or incidental expenditures; its first cost was its last.

It is a rigid rule with me not to buy what I cannot pay for, and whenever I drive a new car out of the salesroom it has no lien upon it; but it was not without trepidation that I drew my check in payment for that first automobile. [...]

At first I carefully set down all expenses connected with my car. I was curious to see if my budget was working out, but the figures mounted up so fast that I dared not look the facts in the face and so closed my books. Ignorance is bliss and bliss is expensive.

Having a quick method of locomotion, it was easy to run out into the country of a Sunday for dinner, or of an evening for a drive and a 'bite'. Then, too, my friends expected me to do the honors, as chauffeur and host, and this added to the mounting costs. But I had started something that I could not stop gracefully or consistently. My thrift habits were steadily giving way to spendthrift habits.

After eight years of experience I find that the psychological processes of car-owners are much alike. First you want a car; then you conclude to buy it. Once bought, you must keep it running, for cars are useless standing in a garage. Therefore you spend and keep on spending, be the consequences what they may. You have only one alternative — to sell out; and this pride forbids.

The result upon the individual is to break down his sense of values. Whether he will or no, he must spend money at every turn. Having succumbed to the lure of the car, he is quite helpless thereafter. If a new device will make his automobile run smoother or look better, he attaches that device. If a new polish will make it shine brighter, he buys that polish. If a new idea will give more mileage, or remove carbon, he adopts that new idea. These little costs quickly mount up and in many instances represent the margin of safety between income and outgo. The overplus in the pay envelope, instead of going into the bank as a reserve-fund, goes into automobile expense. Many families live on the brink of danger all the time. They are car-poor. Saving is impossible. The joy of security in the future is sacrificed for the pleasure of the moment. And with the pleasure of the moment is mingled the constant anxiety entailed by living beyond one's means.

Time was when the leading men of the community vied with one another as owners of houses. The mansions of an earlier day, with their mansard roofs and spacious outbuildings, are mute evidence of the race for prestige years ago. A man expressed himself and his tastes through his home and its surroundings. If he owned a span of horses and a few carriages and hired a coachman, his entire investment was not half that often covered by one car today. The upkeep was small and could be figured with reasonable certainty. The coachman got board and lodging and perhaps two dollars a day; now a chauffeur gets five dollars a day and meals wherever he happens to be.

The paramount ambition of the average man a few years ago was to own a home and have a bank account. The ambition of the same man today is to own a car. While the desire for home-ownership is still strong, I believe people are giving less thought to the home and more to the car as an indicator of social position. The house stands still; only a chosen few can see the inside. But the car goes about; everybody sees is, and many observers know what it cost.

Given the choice of a fine home without a car and a modest one with a car, the latter will win. Real-estate men testify that the first question asked by the prospective buyer is about the garage. The house without a garage is a slow seller. While the country makes an appeal of its own, it has an added lure if it can be enjoyed through the medium of the car, and many a man has moved from city to country in order to get away from the high cost of maintaining an automobile in the city. The whole scheme of domestic life centers about the motor-car.

Dangerous rivalries among friends and in families are created by the motor. If one member of a family makes a bit of money he must advertise it to the rest of the family and to the world by the purchase of a car. Or, if his social scale seems a bit below that of the rest of the family, he seeks to lift himself higher through the medium of a car. The result is a costly rivalry that brings the whole group into debt.

Not only is the car a symbol of the social and business status of the owner, but its loss is a calamity. I have never known a man to give up an automobile once owned, except to buy a better one. The experience of the finance companies is that only an insignificant percentage of the cars financed by them are ever repossessed. In other words, the car stays sold, no matter what hardships may attend its keeping. It takes courage of no mean order to confess to the world that you have had a motor and have lost it. Therefore the car is the last sacrifice to be offered on the altar of reverses. I know a man who did not have the price of his next month's commutation ticket and yet he kept his automobile.

The ambition to own an automobile does not confine itself to the upper classes and those with substantial incomes, but reaches down into the 'white-collar workers' — the clerks and salaried men on limited incomes. In my own bank fifty per cent of the force own cars and drive to work in them. I do not believe the middle classes are getting ahead as they once were. What formerly went into the bank now goes into the motor-car. The thought in the minds of many workers is not how much they can save, but how long it will be before they can have a motor. I had occasion not long ago to check up a number of automobiles on the time-payment plan with a New York company. We found that the owners were carpenters, masons, bricklayers, and so on, living in inaccessible suburban places, who used their cars — all new ones — to go to and from their work. Perhaps their investment is justified by the high wages they now earn, but time was when the humble bicycle or the trolley-car was good enough for them. Walking today is a lost art. Even my laundress comes to work in a taxi and goes home by the same route. No doubt I pay the bill. To go to the village shopping on foot is now a social error, even though the distance be but a few blocks.

True, many automobiles are now sold to those who can afford them, but the competition is so keen and the driving force behind the dealers is so insistent that many who would not ordinarily buy are persuaded that they should do so. I use our own town as typical of many others. During a period of about four weeks I saw the following sales made: (a) a $1500 touring car to a small tailor, who had no place to keep it, had nothing to pay down on it, — except an old Ford in exchange, — and who could not in the course of two years pay a note of seventy-five dollars at his bank; (b) a similar car to the policeman on the post, who went in debt for half his monthly salary for a year in order to pay for it; (c) a sedan selling for about $2000 to a restaurant keeper who had just gone into business for himself. He had saved $1000, purchased a place for $5000, borrowed $2500 from the bank, and gave notes for the balance in order to take possession. After the first season, with a hard winter before him, this man deliberately — or through the efforts of a good salesman — plunged into debt for $1200. The result is that all he earns must be applied to his debts, and he now has no margin of safety at all. Before, he was sure of his ground and free from anxiety. Now, he must not only work, but he must also worry.

Some will blame the dealers for sharp selling practices; others will blame the finance companies for accepting any risk that is offered; still others will blame the buyer for being an easy mark. But, whatever the reason, the result is the same — debt, debt, debt, for a costly article that depreciates very rapidly and has an insatiable appetite for money. To be sure, the money goes out in small lots, but the toll is large if it be reckoned for a year, and this the average man has not the courage to face; or, facing it, he has not the courage to quit. He must keep his car.

The avalanche of automobile-owners is not a good omen. It signifies that the people are living either up to their means or beyond them; that the old margin of safety no longer obtains; that the expense account must constantly increase. The race to outdo the other fellow is a mad race indeed. The ease with which a car can be purchased on the time-payment plan is all too easy a road to ruin. The habit of thrift can never be acquired through so wasteful a medium as an automobile. Instead, the habit of spending must be acquired, for with the constant demand for fuel, oil, and repairs, together with the heavy depreciation, the automobile stands unique as the most extravagant piece of machinery ever devised for the pleasure of man.

But —

I still drive one myself. I must keep up with the procession, even though it has taken four cars to do so.

Source: Mowry, G.E. (ed.) (1963) *The Twenties, Fords, Flappers and Fanatics*, Englewood Cliffs, NJ, Prentice-Hall.

2.2.3 'CONFESSIONS OF A FORD DEALER' AS TOLD TO JESSE RAINSFORD SPRAGUE (1927)

The drive to sell was no less potent than the desire to buy, and in the 1920s manufacturers like Ford and their agents were happy to sell on virtually any terms. The following 'confessions' by a Ford dealer to Jesse Rainsford Sprague writing for *Harper's Monthly Magazine* in June 1927, indicates the vital importance of credit in the process. Some of the resulting pressures and risks, both economic and social, are very evident.

The former Ford dealer said: Things have changed a lot around here since 1912, when I bought out the man who had the Ford agency and paid him inventory price for his stock, plus a bonus of five hundred dollars for good will. A dealer didn't have to hustle so hard then to make both ends meet. You kept a few cars on your floor and when you needed more you bought them. You were your own boss. There weren't any iron-clad rules laid down for you saying how you had to run your business.

Sometimes I wonder if Mr Ford knows how things have changed. I have just finished reading his book, and in one place he says: 'Business grows big by public demand. But it never gets bigger than the demand. It cannot control or force the demand.'

Understand me, I think Mr Ford is a wonderful man. They say he is worth a billion dollars; and no one can make that much money unless he has plenty of brains. Still and all, when Mr Ford says business cannot control or force the demand I can't quite think he means it. Or maybe it's his little joke. You *can* force demand if you ride people hard enough. And, believe me, you have only to get on the inside of a Ford agency to learn how.

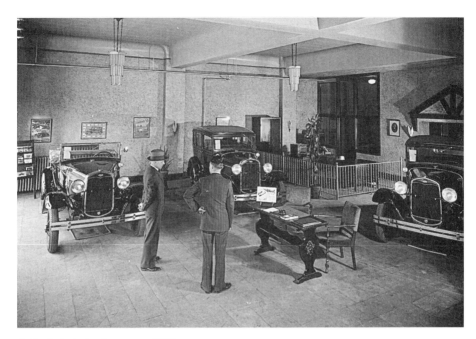

A Ford dealer's showroom, 1931

Take my own case, for instance. Like I say, when I first took the agency I was my own boss like any other business man, selling as many cars as I could and buying more when I needed them. I didn't have to make many sales on installments, because people who wanted cars usually saved up in advance and had the cash in hand when they got ready to buy. Occasionally some man that I knew would want a little time, in which case I just charged it the same as if it was a bill of dry goods or groceries, and when the account fell due he paid me. There was no such thing then as putting a mortgage on the car and taking it away from him if he didn't pay up. If I didn't believe a man was honest I simply didn't give him credit.

I did a pretty good business this way and by 1916 was selling an average of about ten cars a month. Then one day a representative of the Company came to see me. I'll call him by the name of Benson, though that was not his real name. In fact wherever I mention a man's name in giving my experiences I shall call him something different because some of them probably would not like to be identified. Well, anyway, this man that I call Benson came into my place at the time I speak of and said ten cars a month was not enough for a dealer like me to sell. It seems the Company had made a survey of my territory and decided that the sales possibilities were much greater. Benson said my quota had been fixed at twenty cars a month, and from then on that number would be shipped me. […]

Well, I finally decided to take a chance on twenty cars a month rather than lose the agency. I had read a lot of nice things about Mr Ford in the newspapers and I felt sure he wouldn't ask me to do anything he wouldn't be willing to do himself. Benson said he was glad I looked at things in a businesslike way and promised me plenty of assistance in moving my twenty cars a month. He called it 'breaking down sales resistance'.

I guess I should explain that out West here an ordinary Ford dealer doesn't do business direct from the factory in Detroit, but works under a general agency. The agency that I worked under was located in the city about a hundred and fifty miles from here, and I suppose the manager there took his orders from the factory. During the fourteen years I was in business there were eight different managers, and some of them rode us local agents pretty hard. I always thought I wouldn't have so many troubles if I could have done business direct with Mr Ford, but I can realize how busy a big man like him must be, and I guess it is necessary for him to leave things pretty much in the hands of his managers that way. A few times when I thought they were riding me too hard I wrote in to the factory and complained about certain things, but I never got any answer. My letters were sent on to the branch manager and of course that got me in bad with him. I found that if I wanted to hold my agency I had better do what I was told. Out of the eight managers six were transferred to other branches and two threw up their jobs to go into other lines of business. I met one of these fellows after he had quit and asked him why there were so many changes. He said he guessed it was because the Company believed a man had a tendency to get too friendly with the local agents if he stayed too long in one territory, and to see things too much from the agents' viewpoint. Personally, he said he quit the Company's service altogether because he couldn't stand the pace. […]

I sure got it in the neck when the slump of 1920 came on. If anyone wants to know what hard times are he ought to try to do business in a Western farming community during a panic. Almost overnight half of our sheep men went bankrupt when wool dropped from sixty cents a pound to twenty cents, and hardly any buyers at that price. The potato growers couldn't get enough for their stuff to pay freight to the Chicago market, and most of them let their crop rot in the ground. Of our four banks in town two went into the hands of receivers and the other two had to call in every possible loan in order to save their own necks. A lot of our Main Street retailers fell into the hands of their creditors that year, too.

I was in about as bad a fix as anyone else. By then I had agreed to take thirty Fords a month, which was a pretty heavy job to get away with in good times, to say nothing of the sort of a situation we were going through. These cars came in each month, regular as clock work, and I had stretched my credit at the bank about as far as it would go in paying for them as they arrived. The bank kept hounding me all the time to cut down my loan, which I couldn't do with my expenses running on all the time and hardly any business going on. From September to January that year I sold exactly four cars.

Pretty bad? I'll say it was. But the worst was yet to come. Altogether I had more than one hundred and forty new cars on hand, besides a lot of trade-ins, and no immediate prospect of selling any. Then all of a sudden came notice that a shipment of fifteen Fords was on the way to me, and that I would be expected to pay for them on arrival. I thought there must be some mistake, and got the branch manager in the city on the long distance. He was a pretty hard-boiled egg named Blassingham.

'What's the meaning of these fifteen cars that are being shipped me?' I asked. 'I've already taken my quota for the month.'

'It don't mean anything', Blassingham answered, 'except that you're going to buy fifteen extra cars this month.'

I tried to explain to him that I was in no position to get hold of the cash for such a purchase, and even if I was I wanted to know the whys and where-fores.

'You know as much about it as I do', he snapped. 'Those are the orders, and my advice to you is to pay for those cars when they arrive.'

Of course I sensed the reason later on, when it came out in the newspapers about Mr Ford's little tilt with the money sharks down in New York, how they tried to get a hold on his business and how he fooled them by getting the cash without their help and then told them to go chase themselves. […]

I am willing to confess that we rode the public a little ourselves while we were getting rid of our big surplus of cars. There are always some people that you can sell anything to if you hammer them hard enough. We had a salesman named Nichols who was a humdinger at running down prospects, and one day he told me he had a fellow on the string with a couple of hundred dollars who would buy a car if we would give him a little extra time on the balance. This prospect was a young fellow that had come out West on account of his health and was trying to make a living for his family as an expert accountant. Just at that time the referee in bankruptcy was doing most of the accounting business around town, and I knew the young fellow wasn't getting on at all. He had about as much use for a car as a jack rabbit. I told Nichols this, but you know how plausible these go-getter sales-men are; he told me it wasn't our business whether the young fellow had any use for a Ford or not; the main thing was he had two hundred dollars in cash.

Well, we went ahead and made the sale, but we never got any more pay-ments. The young fellow took to his bed just after that, and the church peo-ple had to look out for him and his family until he died. In the final showdown it turned out that the two-hundred dollar equity in the car was everything they had on earth, and by the time we replevined it and sold it as a trade-in there wasn't anything at all. I gave twenty dollars toward his funeral expenses. I know this sounds pretty tough; but when it's a case of your own scalp or some other fellow's you can't afford to be too particular. […]

About the most nagging thing to me were the visits of the expert salesmen who came around every so often to show us how to sell cars. It seemed to me that so long as I was taking my quota every month I ought to be the best judge of how and who to sell. There was one expert I specially remember by the name of Burke. Among other things I had to do was to keep a card file of people in the territory who had not bought cars, and usually on these cards we wrote items like 'says maybe will be in market this fall', or 'not ready to buy yet'. Burke was always raising Cain because we didn't make people give more explicit reasons for not buying. I remember once he laid me out because a card said only 'Can't sell him'. The man was a poor devil of a renter seven or eight miles out of town who never had enough cash ahead to buy a wheelbarrow, but Burke insisted that one of my salesmen go out there with him to try and land a sale. When they got there a couple of the children were down with whooping cough and a hailstorm had laid out his bean crop, but Burke came back and told me he would expect me to put over a Ford on the fellow before he came on his next trip. […]

You do a lot of things when someone is riding you all the time that you wouldn't do under ordinary circumstances. Beans and clover seed are the farmers' principal money crops around here, and one fall in September and October we had one heavy rain after the other that practically ruined everything. Business was terrible because the farmers hadn't recovered yet from the bank failures and the slump of 1920; and one day I wrote in to the Company, telling what bad shape the farmers were in and asking if my quota couldn't be reduced for a few months until things picked up. All I got for my trouble was a letter stating that 'such farmers are not the people to sell to'.

Of course it was easy enough for them to write such a letter, but I always thought Mr Ford ought to realize that in a country community when the farmers are broke the doctors and dentists and storekeepers are in about the same fix. Not being able to get my quota reduced, I had to take business wherever I could find it, and it was about this time that I had my experience with the army captain. It seems this captain had been kicked by a horse in the course of his duties and came to our town for treatment in the hospital. He showed up at my place one day and said he wanted to buy a Ford coupe. He had a dented-in place on the side of his head from the accident, which I suppose was the reason for his acting so queer. There were some big used cars in the place that belonged to customers, and while the salesman was showing him Fords he would hop into these cars and start the engines and then say he wanted to buy one of them instead of a Ford. It didn't make any difference when the salesman told him the cars belonged to other people. Finally the salesman came to me and asked what to do. I had a talk with the captain and at first was inclined not to sell him, especially when he said he only had fifty dollars to lay down as a first payment. We are supposed to get a third down on a new car, but of course when the branch manager is riding you all the time you sometimes make deals that are not strictly according to Hoyle, and with my quota of thirty cars coming in every month and no farmer trade in sight I was inclined to take chances. The upshot was that I took the captain's fifty dollars and off he drove.

He had promised to bring in another hundred dollars when he got his salary check, but the first of the month rolled around and no captain. We wrote him letters but he didn't answer, and the collector never could catch him in at the place where he was staying. When it strung along for another month I set a private detective on his trail and found the captain went three times a week to the hospital for treatment, from ten to twelve in the morning. We have duplicate keys for all the cars we sell, so one morning I sent one of my mechanics out to the hospital and when the captain parked his car at the curb and went inside the building this mechanic just unlocked the car and drove it back to the garage. Of course I didn't have any right to do this but possession is nine points of the law, and when the captain threatened to make trouble I reported him to the army authorities as a deadbeat. I guess he was a little daffy anyhow, from the dent in his head, because it turned out he had been buying a lot of other things on installments. People said he was a real nice fellow before his accident, but in the investigation that followed he lost his commission and was fired out of the army. The last I heard of him he was bootlegging.

If Mr Ford knew personally some of the things that go on I am sure he would call a halt to his branch managers riding the local agents the way they do. Like I say, when you are crowded all the time to make your quota under all sorts of business conditions, you do things you don't like to. There are some pretty tough characters in this town just as there are everywhere else; but a quota is a quota and you can't stop to pick your customers. One thing I have noticed is that the hardest boiled eggs are most likely to come up with their time payments. Only last year I sold a car to a big colored fellow and of course as he had no visible means of support I took a mortgage on it so I could replevine it in case he didn't pay, but every month he came in right on the dot with the cash. Naturally I'm not bragging about it, and I'm not saying anything was wrong; but during that time a street car conductor was held up at the end of the line a couple of times and there were some other bits of devilment of a like character.

Source: Mowry, G.E. (ed.) (1963) *The Twenties, Fords, Flappers and Fanatics*, Englewood Cliffs, NJ, Prentice-Hall.

2.2.4 'BROKERS AND SUCKERS' BY ROBERT RYAN (1928)

The causes of the Great Depression were numerous, complex, and still vigorously debated, but the Wall Street Crash on Thursday 24 October 1929 marked its beginning for many. The panic in the financial system which followed ruined countless investors large and small and badly undermined consumer and business confidence. In the lead up to the crash, optimistic investors indulged in mounting speculation on the stock market. The following account by business man Robert Ryan, who spent two months in a Wall Street brokers office in 1928, gives an interesting insight into how the stock market conducted itself as it headed towards the crash just over a year later. The account was published in *The Nation* on 15 August 1928.

Wall Street, 1926

During the spring months of this year the customers' rooms of Wall Street's brokerage houses were overflowing with a new type of speculator. In these broad rooms you could see feverish young men and heated elders, eyes intent upon the ticker tape. The ranks of the inexperienced — the 'suckers' — were swelled by numbers of men who had been attracted by newspaper stories of the big, easy profits to be made in a tremendous bull market, of millions captured overnight by the Fisher Brothers, Arthur Cutten, and Durant. At first these newcomers risked a few hundred dollars with some broker they knew, discovered that it was easy to make money this way, and finally made their headquarters in the broker's large customer's room, bringing with them their entire checking and savings accounts.

These amateurs were not schooled in markets that had seen stringent, panicky drops in prices. They came in on a rising tide. They speculated on tips, on hunches, on 'follow-the-leader' principles. When a stock rose sharply they all jumped for it — and frequently were left holding the bag of higher prices. They would sell or buy on the slightest notice, usually obeying implicitly the advice of their broker.

Out of this combustible desire to trade in and out of the market, abuses have arisen. Some brokers, none too scrupulous, have taken advantage of the helplessness of the small customer. The broker can make more commissions by rapid trading than by holding stocks for real appreciation in value, and he knows that this particular type of customer is here today and gone tomorrow. He must make commissions while the money shines.

Sometime ago I spent about two months in a busy broker's office. I had been offered a position as customer's man (to get new accounts and keep them posted on the market's doings). As I wanted to see whether I would like this work, I asked for a two months' period in which to learn the business. The broker with whom I became associated is considered reliable and honest, and the offer was supposedly an attractive one. I sat in the private office of the president and was thus able to follow quite minutely the methods by which he conducted his business. Years of experience with ordinary business had given me no hint of the practices I saw occur as everyday procedure — in the main practices highly prejudicial to the average customer's interest. So astonished was I that I questioned several other Wall Street brokers, only to find that the practices I saw were common enough on the Street, indulged in more or less generally by large and small firms. […]

I shall list here a few of the incidents I witnessed while in the office. On Thursday the partner of Mr X, whose name I shall conceal, had bought some shares of Arabian bank stock at $440 a share. This stock was not listed on the Stock Exchange but was dealt in by over-the-counter houses (houses which deal in unlisted securities). These firms make their own prices, determined solely by the demand for the stock. There is usually a marked difference in quotations by these houses, and the practice is to call several of them before buying in order to get the best price. On Friday morning a customer of Mr X telephoned an order to sell 50 shares of Arabian bank stock. Mr X obtained his permission to sell 'at the best price'. He called to his partner, 'Want any more of that Arabian bank stock?'

'At what price?' answered Mr Y. 'I paid $440 a share yesterday.'

'You can have this for less', said Mr X. 'I've got a market order. The market is 415 bid, 445 offered. Want it at 415?'

'Sure', said Mr Y. And the customer was informed that it was too bad he got such a low price — but after all, 'we sold it at the market'.

The dishonesty of this transaction lies in the fact that if several firms had been called and the stock offered for sale, a better price could have been obtained, for this was an active stock in good demand with a wide difference between the bid-and-ask prices.

Incident No. 2: This firm was 'bullish' on a certain stock — they believed its price would go higher. Suddenly a panic developed in the stock and it began to decline at a rapid rate. The large and small customers who owned the stock all began selling at once. When the selling confirmations came in, Mr X announced that no selling prices could be given out until all the orders were checked. In the next half hour Mr X and his partners selected those sales which had brought the best prices, allotted these best prices to their larger customers, and allowed the small fry to get what was left. This is obviously unfair discrimination. A record is kept by the order clerk of the sequence in which the selling orders are placed. Consequently, the prices of the sales should have been allotted in that order. 'Of course', Mr X remarked, 'we make most money from our large customers, and we must keep them satisfied'.

Incident No. 3: The broker charges a standard — and substantial — commission on the orders he executes, yet it is common practice among all firms to borrow money at, let us say, 5 per cent and charge 6 per cent to their customers who buy on margin. The Stock Exchange has ruled that brokers may charge their customers the exact amount of interest, or more than the exact amount, that they themselves have to pay when they borrow the money in the open market or from banks; but in no case may brokers charge the customers *less* than the brokers pay in borrowing the money. This rule has been promulgated in order that brokers may not offer the extra inducement of a reduced interest rate to large speculators in order to acquire them as customers. This rule does away with a great deal of cut-throat competition; but in practice the large customer is actually charged the same amount of interest as the broker pays or very little more, while the small customer pays an average of $\frac{3}{4}$ of one per cent additional on all money which he uses when buying on margin. This $\frac{3}{4}$ of one per cent, various brokers have told me, is intended to cover the entire overhead cost of their business. This means that the commissions which are paid for buying or selling the stock are net income to the brokerage house. It is easy to understand why brokerage houses insist that they are justified in charging this so-called 'service fee' for negotiating a loan for a client.

Incident No. 4: Mr X stepped into the customers' room and announced with a great show of sagacity that 'Pomegranate A' was a purchase at current prices, and that he advised immediate purchase. His advice was quickly followed; there was general buying by the customers who thought they saw an opportunity to make some quick money. A few minutes later Mr X notified one of his large customers that he had sold 1,500 shares of 'Pomegranate A' at excellent prices, and received the client's congratulations for a good 'execution'. Those customers in the big room who bought on Mr X's advice paid 6 per cent or more on their money, and watched the stock drop in value. The story behind this transaction was enlightening. Mr X's large customer had heard from a director of 'Pomegranate A' that the quarterly dividend would not be paid and that this fact would be announced in a few days. Knowing that the stock would drop in price after such an announcement, Mr X's customer gave immediate orders to sell at the current prices. Mr X knew that 'Pomegranate A' was a volatile stock and that if he dumped 1,500 shares on the market it would break the price of the stock. So, by getting his small customers to buy these shares, he placed a cushion under the stock to absorb the 1,500 shares he was selling. He sold at no sacrifice and induced his smaller customers to buy stock which he knew would decline in value.

Incident No. 5: A 'pool' is made to maintain current prices in a certain stock or push those prices higher. Mr X was in a pool to raise the price on 'New York Rug'. This pool had made a substantial profit by the time its price had been shoved up to $212 a share. Thereupon the members of the pool decided to liquidate their holdings and take their profits. Mr X knew that this stock was not worth $212 a share and that when the pool had distributed its holdings the stock would drop in value. Mr X had put a large number of his customers into this stock at high prices. When any of them called to inquire about it he answered cheerfully, 'It's good for $250 a share. Yes, I'm holding mine.' So his customers held on.

When Mr X and his friends had finished taking their profits by selling the stock and the news had come out on the floor that the pool had disbanded there was a great deal of 'short selling'. (If you believe a stock is selling at a price above its real value, you sell it and buy it back at a lower price — if you are lucky.) These 'short sales' forced the stock down, and it was only then that Mr X telephoned his customers that he understood the stock was a sale at once, and watched his customers receive much lower prices.

Incident No. 6: Mr X advised all his customers to buy 'Rotten Apples Common'. Since Mr X's firm helped to finance the stock issue their interest in selling this stock could hardly be wholly disinterested.

It would be simple to multiply these incidents and cite other practices, but what I suggested in the first part of this article has, I believe, been amply shown: in every case under my observation the broker felt that he must give the advantage, even though it were a dishonest advantage, to his large customer, for the large customer is his bread and butter and his profits. The small investor or speculator remains completely unaware of these practices. In a rising market such methods may be employed without losing the customer's business, for a speculator will overlook small irregularities as long as he continues to make money; while in a declining market the broker gets away with an equal amount of dishonesty, the customer blames the results on market drops. If a customer loses all his money, or so dislikes the actions of Mr X's firm that he withdraws his business, Mr X is completely unconcerned. As he remarked to me: 'Suckers are born every minute; the glamor of easy money gets them all. One goes, two come in. Win or lose, we get our commissions.' It is an easy-going philosophy which has been so completely proved true by many Wall Street brokers that they have no reason to revise it.

How such practices can be stopped I do not know; nor do I imagine that it is within the power of the Stock Exchange authorities to prevent them. I do believe that one step ahead would be to forbid all brokerage houses or their employees to transact business for themselves, to compel them to act solely as customers' agents. Surely this would make them a trifle more disinterested in the advice they give their clients.

In the meantime Mr X's firm is making money hand over fist. In another month they will move to quarters three times their present space.

Source: Mowry, G.E. (ed.) (1963) *The Twenties, Fords, Flappers and Fanatics*, Englewood Cliffs, NJ, Prentice-Hall.

2.2.5   THE NATIONAL INDUSTRIAL RECOVERY ACT (1933)

The National Industrial Recovery Act of June 1933 was a key piece of legislation in the early part of President Roosevelt's New Deal designed to combat the Depression. This framework of regulations and attempt to instil co-operation and recovery in the American economy was not a success. In May 1935 the Supreme Court declared the delegation of legislative power in the Act, and therefore the Act as a whole, to be unconstitutional. However, the Act does emphasize the notion of 'fair competition' and its history illustrates some of the tensions between competition and regulation in the United States.

AN ACT

To encourage national industrial recovery, to foster fair competition, and to provide for the construction of certain useful public works, and for other purposes.

Be it enacted by the Senate and House of Representatives of the United States of America in Congress assembled,

TITLE I — INDUSTRIAL RECOVERY

Declaration of policy

Section 1. A national emergency productive of wide-spread unemployment and disorganization of industry, which burdens interstate and foreign commerce, affects the public welfare, and undermines the standards of living of the American people, is hereby declared to exist. It is hereby declared to be the policy of Congress to remove obstructions to the free flow of interstate and foreign commerce which tend to diminish the amount thereof; and to provide for the general welfare by promoting the organization of industry for the purpose of cooperative action among trade groups, to induce and maintain united action of labor and management under adequate governmental sanctions and supervision, to eliminate unfair competitive practices, to promote the fullest possible utilization of the present productive capacity of industries, to avoid undue restriction of production (except as may be temporarily required), to increase the consumption of industrial and agricultural products by increasing purchasing power, to reduce and relieve unemployment, to improve standards of labor, and otherwise to rehabilitate industry and to conserve natural resources.

Administrative agencies

[…] Sec. 2. (b) The President may delegate any of his functions and powers under this title to such officers, agents, and employees as he may designate or appoint, and may establish an industrial planning and research agency to aid in carrying out his functions under this title. [...]

Codes of fair competition

Sec. 3. (a) Upon the application to the President by one or more trade or industrial associations or groups, the President may approve a code or codes of fair competition for the trade or industry or subdivision thereof, represented by the applicant or applicants, if the President finds (1) that such associations or groups impose no inequitable restrictions on admission to membership therein and are truly representative of such trades or industries or subdivisions thereof, and (2) that such code or codes are not designed to promote monopolies or to eliminate or oppress small enterprises and will not operate to discriminate against them, and will tend to effectuate the policy of this title: [...]

(b) After the President shall have approved any such code, the provisions of such code shall be the standards of fair competition for such trade or industry or subdivision thereof. Any violation of such standards in any transaction in or affecting interstate or foreign commerce shall be deemed an unfair method of competition in commerce within the meaning of the Federal Trade Commission Act, as amended; but nothing in this title shall be construed to impair the powers of the Federal Trade Commission under such Act, as amended. [...]

(d) Upon his own motion, or if complaint is made to the President that abuses inimical to the public interest and contrary to the policy herein declared are prevalent in any trade or industry or subdivision thereof, and if no code of fair competition therefor has theretofore been approved by the President, the President, after such public notice and hearing as he shall specify, may prescribe and approve a code of fair competition for such trade or industry or subdivision thereof, which shall have the same effect as a code of fair competition approved by the President under subsection (a) of this section. [...]

(f) When a code of fair competition has been approved or prescribed by the President under this title, any violation of any provision thereof in any transaction in or affecting interstate or foreign commerce shall be a misdemeanor and upon conviction thereof an offender shall be fined not more than $500 for each offense, and each day such violation continues shall be deemed a separate offense.

Agreements and licenses

Sec. 4. (a) The President is authorized to enter into agreements with, and to approve voluntary agreements between and among, persons engaged in a trade or industry, labor organizations, and trade or industrial organizations, associations, or groups, relating to any trade or industry, if in his judgment such agreements will aid in effectuating the policy of this title with respect to transactions in or affecting interstate or foreign commerce, and will be consistent with the requirements of clause (2) of subsection (a) of section 3 for a code of fair competition.

(b) Whenever the President shall find that destructive wage or price cutting or other activities contrary to the policy of this title are being practiced in any trade or industry or any subdivision thereof, and, after such public notice and hearing as he shall specify, shall find it essential to license business enterprises in order to make effective a code of fair competition or an agreement under this title or otherwise to effectuate the policy of this title, and shall publicly so announce, no person shall, after a date fixed in such announcement, engage in or carry on any business, in or affecting interstate or foreign commerce, specified in such announcement, unless he shall have first obtained a license issued pursuant to such regulations as the President shall prescribe. The President may suspend or revoke any such license, after due notice and opportunity for hearing, for violations of the terms or conditions thereof. Any order of the President suspending or revoking any such license shall be final if in accordance with law. Any person who, without such a license or in violation of any condition thereof, carries on any such business for which a license is so required, shall, upon conviction thereof, be fined not more than $500, or imprisoned not more than six months, or both, and each day such violation continues shall be deemed a separate offense. Notwithstanding the provisions of section 2 (c), this subsection shall cease to be in effect at the expiration of one year after the date of enactment of this Act or sooner if the President shall by proclamation or the Congress shall by joint resolution declare that the emergency recognized by section 1 has ended.

Sec. 5. While this title is in effect (or in the case of a license, while section 4 (a) is in effect) and for sixty days thereafter, any code, agreement, or license approved, prescribed, or issued and in effect under this title, and any action complying with the provisions thereof taken during such period, shall be exempt from the provisions of the antitrust laws of the United States. [...]

Sec. 7. (a) Every code of fair competition, agreement, and license approved, prescribed, or issued under this title shall contain the following conditions: (1) That employees shall have the right to organize and bargain collectively through representatives of their own choosing, and shall be free from the interference, restraint, or coercion of employers of labor, or their agents, in the designation of such representatives or in self-organization or in other concerted activities for the purpose of collective bargaining or other mutual aid or protection: (2) that no employee and no one seeking employment shall be required as a condition of employment to join any company union or to refrain from joining, organizing, or assisting a labor organization of his own choosing; and (3) that employers shall comply with the maximum hours of labor, minimum rates of pay, and other conditions of employment, approved or prescribed by the President. [...]

Source: Hacker, L.M. (ed.) (1961) *Major Documents in American Economic History, Vol.II*, Princeton, NJ, Van Nostrand, pp.72–6.

2.2.6   A DEPRESSION FAMILY (1938)

The Depression of the 1930s impacted on millions of Americans. In an effort to assess its effects the Federal Works Progress Administration, Division of Research, surveyed 103 families in Dubuque, Iowa in 1938–9. 45 case histories including the Parks were later published in *The Personal Side* edited by Jessie A. Bloodworth in 1939. There is nothing particularly unusual about the experiences of the Park family who were interviewed in January 1938.

The Park family: Mr Park, 32; Mrs Park, 31; Claud, Jr., 11; Mary, 9; Dorothy, 4.

When Claud Park was granted a pay raise a year ago at the Mississippi Milling Company, where he had been hired in August 1935 after 4 years of unemployment, the Parks thought the depression was ended for them. Now, however, with working hours reduced to 25 a week, the Park family fear that they are 'getting right back' where they were 5 or 6 years ago.

At 32 Claud is weatherbeaten in appearance and shows the effects of worry and anxiety. Though frank and spontaneous, he is slow of speech and drawls out his words as he discusses the family's depression experiences. After the long siege of unemployment and dependency on either direct relief or work projects, Claud considers himself an 'authority on the depression'.

The Parks live in a rented five-room brick house in a neighborhood of small homes in the north end of town. Martha Park, the mother of three children, has found time to take an active part in the Parent Teachers Association and the Mothers Club of the church, despite her desperate struggle to make ends meet on a limited budget. She considers that her high school courses, especially home economics, have stood her in good stead in managing her household on a limited budget. Believing that the family's depressed circumstances should not be permitted to interfere with the proper rearing of the children, she has always taken advantage of anything that would help her to become a more understanding mother and homemaker. Claud Jr., 11 years old, is in the sixth grade and Mary, 9, is a fourth-grader. Dorothy, 4, a 'depression baby' is the pet of the family.

Claud and Martha Park 'grew up' in a small town in southern Minnesota, but have lived in Dubuque during most of the 13 years of their marriage. Claud's education was cut short when he had to leave school after completing the eighth grade to help his father support a large family.

The Parks moved to Dubuque immediately after their marriage in 1924, when Claud, through a relative, got a job as a spray painter at the Iowa Foundry. His entrance rate was 45¢ an hour and he worked 54 hours a week. After 2 years, Claud was advanced to the position of foreman of the paint department; his rate of pay was increased to 50¢ an hour. The paint did not agree with him, however, and after he had lost considerable weight and suffered from ulcers of the throat, he decided to quit early in 1927 and go to Chicago where he had heard of a chance to 'get on' as a janitor in a new building at $200 a month. Soon after the Parks arrived in Chicago, they both came down with typhoid fever; by the time Claud had recovered, all jobs in the new building had been filled. He found a janitorial job in another building, but it paid only $100 a month. After having worked at this job for about 2 years, he decided that with the higher cost of living in Chicago, he would be better off working at the foundry in Dubuque.

On his return to Dubuque, he worked at the Iowa Foundry for a year before he was laid off during the general reduction in force in February 1931. From February 1931 to the fall of 1932 he worked irregularly for a barge line and at an insulating plant, averaging from $5 to $25 a week, depending on the amount of work available. The family began running in debt and it was necessary for Claud to borrow $200 from his 'folks'. When this was exhausted, $80 was borrowed on a $1,000 insurance policy, which was later allowed to lapse. Claud regrets very much losing his only insurance policy. On their return from Chicago, the Parks lived in a five-room house for which the rent was $18 a month, but as circumstances became more strained, they moved to a small four-room house for which they paid only $10.

By December 1932 the situation had become desperate. The temperature was below zero, and there was little fuel or food left. As the Parks owed a coal bill of $40 and a grocery bill of $25, they expected credit to be discontinued at any time. To add to the seriousness of their plight, Mrs Park was pregnant. After talking things over one night they could see no alternative except to apply for relief; yet they both felt that they would be 'disgraced'. Mrs Park bitterly opposed going on relief, but during the night Claud got 'scared about the kids', and thought 'we can't let the kids starve just because we are proud'. The next morning, without telling his wife his intentions, he went to the courthouse to make application for relief. When he arrived at the courthouse he couldn't go in. 'I must have walked around the block over a dozen times — it was 10 below zero, but I didn't know it.' Finally he got up sufficient courage to make his application.

The family was 'investigated' and after about 2 weeks 'a lady brought out a grocery and coal order'. This was just in the 'nick of time' as they were completely out of provisions. Mr Park considered that they got along very nicely on the weekly grocery order. Part of the time they were also allowed milk from the milk fund and 'this helped a lot'. The Parks feel that they were well treated by the relief office and did not find the routine investigations obnoxious. 'It's part of the system and when you ask for relief, of course you have to cooperate.' 'The questions didn't bother us so much as the idea of being on charity.'

Mrs Park's confinement created less hardship than the Parks expected, as Mr Park did all of the housework and a visiting nurse came in once a day to care for Mrs Park.

Claud Park 'never felt right about accepting the relief slip'. He says, 'Later, when they let me do some work for it, I felt better.' The relief office allowed only $7.50 a month for rent and Claud did odd jobs for the landlord to make up the difference. In the fall of 1933 he was placed on a CWA road construction project at $80 a month. He was delighted to be paid in cash and didn't feel that he was 'getting something for nothing'. At the close of CWA in the spring of 1934, he was placed by the public employment office on the lock and dam project, and his wages were cut to $50 a month and later to $48. He was intermittently employed on emergency work projects until August 31, 1936, when he got a job as a benchman finishing sashes at the Mississippi Milling Company. Claud had made application at all the factories in town, but he feels that he would never have been taken on at the Mississippi Milling Company had not an old employee there spoken for him.

The Parks kept a detailed monthly account of their income from all sources, including work relief, direct relief, and odd jobs, from 1933 through 1935. The total income in 1933 was $450.96, and for 1935 it was $698.64. Included in these amounts is work for back rent totaling $85.15 in 1933 and $107.25 in 1935. The Parks feel that 1932 and 1933 were their 'hardest years'. After Claud started to work on emergency projects, the family had 'a little more to live on'.

During the lean years of the depression the Parks barely 'subsisted', and Claud feels that it would be impossible 'even to subsist' on this low income over an extended period as clothing and furniture would have to be replaced. The Parks thought they were very economical in 1926, when their total expenditures were $1,095.15, including payments on furniture, medical bills, insurance, and a move to Chicago. At that time, there were only three in the family, but in 1933 there were five. The Parks are keeping the calendars on which they marked every item of income for the depression years as 'relics' to look at when they are old, and, Claud hopes, 'better off'.

At the Mississippi Milling Company, Claud had worked 9 hours a day, $5\frac{1}{2}$ days a week, for about 7 months. The time was then reduced to 35 hours a week, and about 2 months ago, a 25-hour week went into effect. His entrance rate was 45¢ an hour, but when he requested a raise a few months after starting work, his rate was increased to 47¢ an hour. At present, the weekly pay check amounts to only $11.75, and the family is again getting behind with bills. Because of the uncertainty of the working hours at the mill, it is impossible for Claud to 'fill in' with odd jobs. He feels that there is no use to look for more regular work in other factories, for in most of them work in just as irregular as at the Mississippi Milling Company. Then, too, if he quits to take another job, he might never be able to get on again at the Mississippi Milling Company.

After Claud's pay rise, 'things began to look bright again', and the family moved to their present home where the rent is $17 a month. Mrs Park felt that the overcrowding in the other house was bad for the children. After paying up back bills, she had even started some long-needed dental work, which she discontinued before completion when Claud went on short hours. She told the dentist he could keep the bridge he had finished in his safe, but he said that it was of no use to him and he was willing to trust the Parks.

In an attempt to make ends meet with the reduced income, the Parks now take 1 quart of milk for the children instead of 2, and buy meat only once a week. They have enough canned and dried vegetables from their garden on 'the island' to last through the winter. The biggest problem is warm clothing for the children. Claud Jr. and Mary both need shoes, overshoes, and winter underwear, but so far it has been impossible for the Parks to do more than buy food and pay the rent, gas, and electric bills. In bad weather 'the children will have to be kept home from school', and Mrs Park 'feels terrible' about that. She thinks 'employers don't begin to realize how much hardship they cause by reducing the pay checks of the workers.'

Source: Cronon, E.D. (ed.) (1966) *Twentieth Century America, Selected Readings, Vol.2: 1929 to the Present*, Belmont, Calif., Dorsey Press/Wadsworth.

2.2.7   THE EMPLOYMENT ACT (1946)

The Council of Economic Advisers and the Joint Committee on the Economic Report, both set up by the Employment Act of 1946, were intended to 'gather timely and authoritative information concerning economic developments and economic trends'. Such information was to be used by the President and Congress in order to formulate appropriate policy, and there is little doubt that measures taken under the Act have helped in addressing some of the worst effects of post-war recessions.

AN ACT

To declare a national policy on employment, production, and purchasing power, and for other purposes.

Be it enacted by the Senate and House of Representatives of the United States of America in Congress assembled,

Short title

Section 1. This Act may be cited as the 'Employment Act of 1946'.

Declaration of policy

Sec. 2. The Congress hereby declares that it is the continuing policy and responsibility of the Federal Government to use all practicable means consisting with its needs and obligations and other essential considerations of national policy, with the assistance and cooperation of industry, agriculture, labor, and State and local governments, to coordinate and utilize all its plans, functions, and resources for the purposes of creating and maintaining, in a manner calculated to foster and promote free competitive enterprise and the general welfare, conditions under which there will be afforded useful employment opportunities, including self-employment, for those able, willing, and seeking to work, and to promote maximum employment, production, and purchasing power.

Economic Report of the President

Sec. 3. (a) The President shall transmit to the Congress within sixty days after the beginning of each regular session (commencing with the year 1947) an economic report (hereinafter called the 'Economic Report') setting forth (1) the levels of employment, production, and purchasing power obtaining in the United States and such levels needed to carry out the policy declared in section 2; (2) current and foreseeable trends in the levels of employment, production, and purchasing power; (3) a review of the economic program of the Federal Government and a review of economic conditions affecting employment in the United States or any considerable portion thereof during the preceding year and of their effect upon employment, production, and purchasing power; and (4) a program for carrying out the policy declared in section 2, together with such recommendations for legislation as he may deem necessary or desirable. […]

Council of Economic Advisers to the President

Sec. 4. (a) There is hereby created in the Executive Office of the President a Council of Economic Advisers (hereinafter called the 'Council'). The Council shall be composed of three members who shall be appointed by the President, by and with the advice and consent of the Senate, and each of whom shall be a person who, as a result of his training, experience, and attainments, is exceptionally qualified to analyze and interpret economic developments, to appraise programs and activities of the Government in the light of the policy declared in section 2, and to formulate and recommend national economic policy to promote employment, production, and purchasing power under free competitive enterprise. Each member of the Council shall receive compensation at the rate of $15,000 per annum. The President shall designate one of the members of the Council as chairman and one as vice chairman, who shall act as chairman in the absence of the chairman. […]

(c) It shall be the duty and function of the Council —

(1) to assist and advise the President in the preparation of the Economic Report;

(2) to gather timely and authoritative information concerning economic developments and economic trends, both current and prospective, to analyze and interpret such information in the light of the policy declared in section 2 for the purpose of determining whether such

developments and trends are interfering, or are likely to interfere, with the achievement of such policy, and to compile and submit to the President studies relating to such developments and trends;

(3) to appraise the various programs and activities of the Federal Government in the light of the policy declared in section 2 for the purpose of determining the extent to which such programs and activities are contributing, and the extent to which they are not contributing, to the achievement of such policy, and to make recommendations to the President with respect thereto;

(4) to develop and recommend to the President national economic policies to foster and promote free competitive enterprise, to avoid economic fluctuations or to diminish the effects thereof, and to maintain employment, production, and purchasing power;

(5) to make and furnish such studies, reports thereon, and recommendations with respect to matters of Federal economic policy and legislation as the President may request. [...]

Joint Committee of the Economic Report

Sec. 5. (a) There is hereby established a Joint Committee on the Economic Report, to be composed of seven Members of the Senate, to be appointed by the President of the Senate, and seven Members of the House of Representatives, to be appointed by the Speaker of the House of Representatives. The party representation on the joint committee shall as nearly as may be feasible reflect the relative membership of the majority and minority parties in the Senate and House of Representatives.

(b) It shall be the function of the joint committee —

(1) to make a continuing study of matters relating to the Economic Report;

(2) to study means of coordinating programs in order to further the policy of this Act; and

(3) as a guide to the several committees of the Congress dealing with legislation relating to the Economic Report, not later than May 1 of each year (beginning with the year 1947) to file a report with the Senate and the House of Representatives containing its findings and recommendations with respect to each of the main recommendations made by the President in the Economic Report, and from time to time to make such other reports and recommendations to the Senate and House of Representatives as it deems advisable. [...]

Source: Hacker, L.M. (ed.) (1961) *Major Documents in American Economic History, Vol.II*, Princeton, NJ, Van Nostrand, pp.108–11.

2.3 THE 1950s AND 1960s

2.3.1 THE ECONOMY IN THE 1950s (1958)

The following document is an extract from a 1958 report on the economy from the US Department of Commerce. The Department periodically issues such reports for Congress and the public. The confident tone in the report reflects a period of considerable economic growth and prosperity.

GENERAL CONSIDERATIONS

Growth and progress have constituted the outstanding feature of the American economy in the postwar period. The physical volume of total output in 1957 was more than two-fifths above that of 10 years earlier; on a per capita basis, output was up more than one-fifth.

The postwar economic expansion has been a continuation of the longer-term course of developments in this country. […]

While growth in the past decade has not been a steady process, the postwar setbacks to business have been mild. With a concatenation of forceful influences — some temporary and some of a longer-term character — conducive to expansion, prosperous conditions have prevailed throughout most of the past decade. The standard of living has improved substantially.

Postwar developments have reflected primarily continued operation of the same basic forces that have characterized our economic life in the past. However, new factors have also been at work. Government has played an increasing role, in the main to meet the defense requirements of the cold war but also to discharge added responsibilities in the civilian sphere through a broad range of social and economic programs.

Another set of factors influencing the postwar scene was the abnormality of demand and supply conditions immediately after the war. On the one hand, there was a translation into effective demand of consumption and investment that had been postponed during World War II and the 1930s. On the other, capacity to produce civilian goods was limited pending the completion of economic reconversion. Because of these circumstances, the rate of economic advance was above average in the first half of the decade.

In these years, technological progress that had been latent during the depression and unusually rapid under the exigencies of war, became embodied in civilian production on a large scale. However, continuous improvements in the techniques and organization of production were an outstanding feature of the entire postwar period, and were both a cause and an effect of the generally high rate of business investment.

It seems appropriate at this point to review our progress — to establish its dimensions and characteristics, and to assay our current status not only in the light of the more recent past but in broader historical perspective. […]

EXPANSION OF THE POSTWAR ECONOMY

Gross national product in 1957 was valued at $440 billion, as compared with $234 billion 10 years earlier. Over this period, prices rose 30 per cent. Much of the advance reflected the aftermath of World War II, and another spurt came with the Korean conflict, but pressures on the price level were characteristic of the entire period. After adjustment for the price factor, aggregate output expanded, as already indicated, by more than two-fifths over the decade. […]

The decade started from a relatively low base. Investment had lagged in the 1930s; and during the war the stock of capital available for peacetime use had been depleted by heavy wear-and-tear and by the need to channel resources into the production of facilities and munitions required directly for the war effort. Moreover, employment and real output immediately after the war were affected by the technical and organizational bottlenecks associated with the transition to peacetime production.

Productive capacity was thus capable of very rapid expansion from the early postwar base. Demand factors were also conducive to a swift rise of output. Consumers had had to defer demand on a large scale during the war, and correspondingly had accumulated financial resources which greatly improved their liquidity positions. Backlog demands made themselves felt extensively in consumer markets once wartime restrictions had been removed.

Another factor affecting the consumer market was rapid population growth. Population had not sustained its earlier expansion during the 1930s, when the increase was roughly half that of the preceding decade. The birthrate began to rise during the war and this rise was further accentuated after the termination of hostilities. Similarly, the rate of new family formation was particularly high during the early postwar period. These demographic developments reinforced the buoyancy of consumer demand.

Incentives to invest were also powerful. Against the background of a receptive consumer market, the business community was eager to make up for capital depletion in the prior span of years, to incorporate in productive facilities past advances in technology, and to lay the basis for further expansion on a broad scale. As in the case of consumers, liquid resources accumulated during the war helped to finance postwar expenditures. After-tax profits, which had been restrained during the war, assumed a more normal relationship to sales as taxes were lowered and other wartime controls removed.

Foreign markets also had an influence on United States production that was special to this period. Some of our customers abroad were in a backlog-demand and liquid-asset position analogous to that of domestic buyer groups. Other foreign countries, whose productive operations had been seriously damaged and disorganized by the war, needed to supplement their current output, both in order to maintain minimum living standards and to initiate programs designed to rebuild their capital facilities. Crop failures further added to foreign requirements in the short run. With the U.S. Government financing these requirements on a large scale, the demand for our exports soon rose to a postwar peak not approached in earlier or later peacetime years. [...]

The salient features of this long-term record may be summarized as follows. The $440 billion of gross national output in 1957 compares with an aggregate of $196 billion at the end of the 1920s — the last prewar period of generally prosperous conditions — and with the $112 billion in 1909, these earlier figures also being stated in 1957 prices. Thus, total real output has quadrupled over the last 50 years. This rise represents an average annual growth of about 3 per cent — a rate which held approximately both in the 1909–29 period and in the subsequent 3-decade interval.

With population doubling, per capita output in real terms in 1957 was twice that in 1909.

In a basic sense, the increase in real output was even more pronounced. The available statistical techniques make only partial allowance for changes in the quality — as distinguished from the quantity — of real output. Inasmuch as improvements in product quality have constituted a major avenue of economic progress, the quantitative measures that can be calculated do not reflect the full extent of our economic growth.

The increase in the number of man-hours worked — an average of about 1 per cent per year since 1909 — has been a clear-cut factor in the long-term growth of real output. Employment, it may be noted, expanded substantially more over this period — $1\frac{1}{2}$ per cent per year. But the average length of the workweek declined sharply, as employees and entrepreneurs chose to take some of the improvement in their living standards in the form of shorter working hours.

All of the other factors that — in addition to man-hours worked — have contributed to the growth of real output are summed up in a conventional statistical calculation — 'out-put per man-hour worked'. This measure has increased at an average annual rate of about 2 per cent over the last half century, thus accounting for the larger part of real output expansion.

Most of this gain has come from technological and managerial progress, a high rate of capital formation including the development of natural resources, and constant advances in the education and skills of the working population. Shifting of the work force into activities in which productivity is relatively high has also contributed. So have the economies of large-scale production and increased division of labor associated with the growth of population and of the market economy.

It is not possible to quantify in a comprehensive manner these manifold factors which have contributed to economic growth. However, significant measures are available of one of them — the stock of tangible capital assets used in the Nation's productive establishments. These show a striking secular growth in the amount of plant and equipment used per unit of labor engaged in production, and corroborate the view that this growth is one of the major factors explaining the rise in the productivity of American business. [...]

From the standpoint of the present discussion, the most important facts brought out by this study are those relating to the relative use of labor and capital in manufacturing. Over the last 30 years, the physical amount of capital applied in manufacturing production virtually doubled, whereas the number of man-hours worked increased by two-fifths. In other words, over this period the amount of capital per man-hour increased more than one-third. This increased application of capital of improved efficiency undoubtedly has been a big factor in the growth of manufacturing production, which in 1957 had risen to $2\frac{1}{2}$ times its 1929 volume.

The fact that the expansion of output in manufacturing significantly outstripped that in either labor or capital input underscores the importance of the other factors, noted above, making for production growth — factors which cannot be quantified. [...]

CHANGING INCOME STRUCTURE

The expansion of gross national product has been accompanied by a corresponding rise in the national income — a comprehensive alternative measure of national output expressed in terms of the earnings derived from production. From 1947 to 1957, the national income increased from $198 billion to $364 billion, or four-fifths. This rise, of course, reflected not only the expansion in physical volume of production but also the sharp advance in prices over the period.

Interest attaches to the national income mainly because it lends itself to breakdowns which differ from those of the gross national product, and hence throw additional light on the functioning of the economy.

In this section, the broad effects of changes in the product composition of output on the industrial income structure are traced, and it is shown how changes in that structure, in turn, influenced the forms — such as wages and profits — in which income has accrued. Industrial shifts affect the forms of income mainly because the various industries differ widely as to their predominant type of legal organization — e.g., corporate vs. noncorporate business — and hence as to the income type patterns they generate.

Analysis of these basic distributions of income — by industry, by type, and by legal form of organization — is of interest primarily because they provide essential links in explaining the circular flow of income and purchasing power through the economy as this is affected by, and in turn affects, final demand as registered in the GNP. [...]

In the conventional breakdown of gross national product by type of expenditures, the goods-services classification is provided only for the consumer market, and, in the case of construction, only the private component is shown. The new table extends the goods-services-construction breakdown to the entire GNP. It provides a superior basis for studying the link between product demand and industrial activity, since the industrial structure of national income is closely related to this comprehensive product classification of total output. […]

Over the past decade, the principal change in composition of gross national product was a relative decline in the goods portion and a rise in the services portion. This is evident from the following data:

	Per cent of GNP		
	1929	1947	1957
Goods	54	61	53
Services	35	31	35
Construction	11	8	12

This shift from 1947 to 1957 does not appear to have been part of a long-run trend. When the figures are considered in historical perspective, and interpreted in light of the particular economic forces at work in the early postwar period, the goods-services-construction breakdown of GNP for 1947 appears out of line. Specifically, the goods component seems relatively high, and services and construction correspondingly low. From this vantage point, the postwar shifts in broad product composition are seen to have represented a return toward earlier, more normal patterns, rather than the establishment of new basic movements and relationships. This generalization is similar to that already made in the case of personal consumption, which, of course, is a major determinant of the product composition of GNP.

When durable goods and nondurable goods are looked at separately, it is clear that the up-then-down pattern of the total goods percentage reflects the movement of non-durable goods, which are the larger part of the total. The durable goods percentage for 1947 did not differ substantially from what would have been expected on the basis of the apparent long-term upward trend in the relative importance of durable goods in the gross national product. […]

The effect of this pattern on the industrial origin of national income is clearly evident when the separate industry divisions are grouped according to whether their output is mainly dependent, directly or indirectly, on final demand for goods and construction, on the one hand, or for services, on the other. Needless to say, such a grouping of industries must be somewhat arbitrary. Many industries contribute to the final value of both goods and services. The transportation industry is an example. Transportation services enter the value of goods output in the GNP and are also represented directly as services when bought separately by final users, as in the case of the transportation of passengers.

For purpose of the present analysis, the goods-associated industries are considered to be agriculture, manufacturing, mining, contract construction, trade, and transportation; the services-associated industries consist of finance, communications and public utilities, services proper, and government.

The contract construction industry is not classified separately by reason of the fact that there is only tenuous correspondence in movement between this industry on the income side and construction activity as included in the GNP. Among the several differences in coverage between the two measures, most important are these: That the GNP construction component — unlike the contract construction industry — includes force-account work and excludes altogether the value of maintenance and repair. In the text table below, construction is included with goods in both the GNP and national income [NI] breakdowns:

	1929	1947	1957
Goods (including construction) as per cent of GNP	65	69	65
Goods-associated industries as per cent of NI	64	70	64
Services as per cent of GNP	35	31	35
Services-associated industries as per cent of NI	36	30	36

As may be seen, there is a remarkable correspondence between the goods and services breakdowns of the gross national product and national income. While this may have stemmed in part from offsetting errors in the income allocations, the tabulation establishes beyond doubt the pervasive influence of shifts in the composition of final demand on the postwar industrial income structure. This influence, it may be added, is evident not only in the above comparison involving the years 1947 and 1957, but on an annual basis as well. Clearly depicted by the annual data is a more or less steady rise in the services share of both GNP and national income, and a corresponding reduction in the share of these aggregates accounted for by goods.

Since the postwar shifts in product composition of GNP reflected in the main relatively short-term adjustments, rather than basic trends, the same generalization applies to the income changes which they produced. This central finding should serve as a background in more detailed studies of the postwar industrial origin of national income.

The breakdowns of GNP shown above are based on the current-dollar values of goods and services. If analogous breakdowns of constant-dollar GNP are prepared, the relative shares of goods and services in 1947 appear to be fairly well in line with long-run developments. In other words, the postwar shifts in product composition of GNP were due mainly to the price factor — to relatively high prices for goods and low prices for services in 1947, and to their subsequent readjustment. Therefore, it seems evident that measures of real income or output by industry would show developments for the postwar period much more in conformity with long-term trends than those displayed by the current-dollar data analyzed above.

While any detailed examination of individual industries is precluded, it will be of interest to highlight the main developments which occurred in farming, manufacturing, trade, and government. The first three account for the bulk of the goods-associated industry group. Government forms a significant part of the services-associated group, and is of independent interest. With respect to the private-industry components of the latter group, it may be noted that their rate of increase over the postwar period generally exceeded that of total national income. This uniformity of developments reflected the broad supply and demand conditions which in the past decade affected the services area of the economy as a whole.

Income originating in farming has had a long-term downtrend relative to total national income. In the early postwar period, however, farming temporarily regained a share of the income total — nearly 10 per cent — matching that of the late 1920s. This experience was due to the prevailing relatively high prices for farm products which reflected a strong domestic market reinforced by exceptional foreign demand. The latter, as noted earlier, was an outcome of the damaged state of world agriculture and of the poor growing conditions abroad which characterized the early postwar years.

As world crop and livestock conditions improved, farm prices began to recede, and the longer-term trends affecting United States farm income reappeared. Beginning with 1949, income from farming declined steadily as a proportion of the national income, to a figure of 4 per cent in 1957.

Though the farm share of total national income has fallen sharply, per capita income originating in farming has been well maintained over the past quarter-century in relation to the all-industry average. Underlying this development is a strong shift of labor away from farming; the number of persons engaged in this industry declined from 19 per cent of all persons engaged in production in 1929 to 8 per cent in 1957.

Manufacturing, the largest of the goods-associated industries, increased greatly in relative importance from 1929 to 1957 — from 25 per cent to 31 per cent of the national income. A figure similar to that for 1957 had been established by 1947 and, with irregular variations, was characteristic of the entire postwar decade.

The trend significance of this stability — its meaning for the longer run — is quite uncertain because of the many special factors that were operative in this comparatively brief period. Important among them were the abnormally high output of goods in the early postwar years, to which manufacturing was the major contributor; the particular impact of the Korean conflict upon this industry; and the three postwar recessions which, although mild for the economy as a whole, significantly affected the course of production in manufacturing. While measurement is not possible, it would seem that up through the Korean conflict the net balance of economic forces was especially favorable for the manufacturing industry; one should therefore not conclude that the postwar stability in the ratio of manufacturing to total national income rules out the presence of an underlying upward trend.

Income originating in trade is strongly correlated with demand for goods, and followed quite closely the post-1947 decline in the ratio of goods output to total production. Trade income rose from 15 per cent of the national income total in 1929 to 19 per cent in 1947 — then declined to 16 per cent in 1957. This postwar decline was broken only by slight rises in 1949 and 1954 as income from trade in those years weakened less than income from manufacturing and certain other industries particularly affected by the recessions.

Income originating in government — the compensation of government employees (including military personnel) — accounted for 9 per cent of the national income in 1947. It moved up irregularly to 12 per cent of the total by 1952, and held approximately at that figure though 1957. […]

POSTWAR CYCLICAL DEVELOPMENTS

While one of the outstanding features of the postwar period has been the vigorous uptrend in business activity, the economy has been subject to periods of cyclical fluctuations with recessions occurring in 1948–49, 1953–54, and 1957–58.

These recessions were mild. There was no repetition of the serious cyclical disturbance which ensued shortly after World War I, when total output dropped by 9 per cent from 1920 to 1921, manufacturing activity was off by 25 per cent in the same period, and unemployment in the latter year averaged over 10 per cent of the labor force. The postwar recessions were rather of the same order as the more moderate contractions of the 1910s and 1920s, and substantially milder than the downturn in 1937–38 when the economy moved sharply lower despite the incomplete nature of the previous recovery from the deep 1930–32 depression. […]

The spread between the current-dollar and constant-dollar values of gross national product reflects, of course, the advance in prices which prevailed over much of the postwar period, and which made for a generally more pronounced upward movement in the current-dollar line. The impact of inflation was largest in the years immediately after the war, when controls were lifted and costs and prices were brought into a new alignment. More than one-half of the entire postwar price increase occurred in the 1946–48 period, when extraordinary demands placed a severe strain on productive capacity.

The postwar period featured two other pronounced upward movements in prices. One was associated with the Korean conflict; the other occurred during 1956 and 1957 […] comparative stability prevailed in the period 1952–55, although the general average of GNP prices edged upward. This experience reflected the better adaptation of supply to demand after the Korean buildup […]; the dampening effects of the 1953–54 downturn; and the offsetting movements during the period in the agricultural and industrial components entering the final price structure. By early 1956, agricultural as well as other prices were on the upgrade in a general setting of buoyant demand, high output, and rising production costs.

It is noteworthy that in the past decade there was an almost total absence of downward pressures on the general price level. Even in the two most recent recessions, prices edged forward. A moderate downward movement was registered in the 1948–49 period concurrent with the break in agricultural prices in early 1948.

[…]

Source: Hacker, L.M. (ed.) (1961) *Major Documents in American Economic History, Vol.II*, Princeton, NJ, Van Nostrand, pp.133–65.

2.3.2   THE NEW TEENAGE MARKET (1959)

One consequence of the economic prosperity of the 1950s was the growth of teenage spending power, and business soon responded to this rapidly developing market. In August 1959 *Life* magazine printed the following item entitled 'A young $10 billion power: the US teen-age consumer has become a major factor in the nation's economy'. The importance of this market has remained considerable ever since.

To some people the vision of a leggy adolescent happily squealing over the latest fancy present from Daddy is just another example of the way teen-agers are spoiled to death these days. But to a growing number of business-men the picture spells out the profitable fact that the American teen-agers have emerged as a big-time consumer in the US economy. They are multi-plying in numbers. They spend more and have more spent on them. And they have minds of their own about what they want.

The time is past when a boy's chief possession was his bike and a girl's party wardrobe consisted of a fancy dress worn with a string of dime-store pearls. What Depression-bred parents may still think of as luxuries are looked on as necessities by their offspring. Today teen-agers surround them-selves with a fantastic array of garish and often expensive baubles and amusements. They own 10 million phonographs, over a million TV sets, 13 million cameras. Nobody knows how much parents spend on them for actual necessities nor to what extent teen-agers act as hidden persuaders on their parents' other buying habits. Counting only what is spent to satisfy their special teen-age demands, the youngsters and their parents will shell out about $10 billion this year, a billion more than the total sales of GM.

Until recently businessmen have largely ignored the teen-age market. But now they are spending millions on advertising and razzle-dazzle promo-tional stunts. Their efforts so far seem only to have scratched the surface of a rich lode. In 1970, when the teen-age population expands from its present

18 million to 28 million, the market may be worth $20 billion. If parents have any idea of organized revolt, it is already too late. Teen-age spending is so important that such action would send quivers through the entire national economy. […]

At 17 Suzie Slattery of Van Nuys, Calif. fits any businessman's dream of the ideal teen-age consumer. The daughter of a reasonably well-to-do TV announcer, Suzie costs her parents close to $4,000 a year, far more than average for the country but not much more than many of the upper middle income families of her town. In an expanding economy more and more teenagers will be moving up into Suzie's bracket or be influenced as consumers by her example.

Last year $1,500 was spent on Suzie's clothes and $550 for her entertainment. Her annual food bill comes to $900. She pays $4 every two weeks at the beauty parlor. She has her own telephone and even has her own soda fountain in the house. On summer vacation days she loves to wander with her mother through fashionable department stores, picking out frocks or furnishings for her room or silver and expensive crockery for the hope chest she has already started.

As a high school graduation present, Suzie was given a holiday cruise to Hawaii and is now in the midst of a new clothes-buying spree for college. Her parents' constant indulgence has not spoiled Suzie. She takes for granted all the luxuries that surround her because she has had them all her life. But she also has a good mind and some serious interests. A top student in her school, she is entering Occidental College this fall and will major in political science. […]

SOME FASCINATING FACTS ABOUT A BOOMING MARKET

FOOD: Teen-agers eat 20% more than adults. They down $3\frac{1}{2}$ billion quarts of milk every year, almost four times as much as is drunk by infant population under 1. Teen-agers are a main prop of the ice cream industry, gobble 145 million gallons a year.

BEAUTY CARE: Teen-agers spent $20 million on lipstick last year, $25 million on deodorants (a fifth of total sold), $9 million on home permanents. Male teen-agers own 2 million electric razors.

ENTERTAINMENT: Teen-agers lay out more than $1.5 billion a year for entertainment. They spend about $75 million on single pop records. Although they create new musical idols, they are staunchly faithful to the old. Elvis Presley, still their favorite, has sold 25 million copies of single records in four years, an all-time high.

HOMEMAKERS: Major items like furniture and silver are moving into the teen-age market because of growing number of teen-age marriages. One third of all 18- and 19-year-old girls are already married. More than 600,000 teen-agers will be married this year. Teen-agers are now starting hope chests at 15.

CREDIT RISKS: Some 800,000 teen-agers work at full-time jobs and can buy major items on credit.

Source: Griffith, R. (ed.) (1992) *Major Problems in American History Since 1945*, Lexington, Mass., D.C. Heath, p.203.

2.3.3 THE ECONOMY IN 1961

Some of the economic optimism evident in the 1950s had gone by the early 1960s. The following extract is from 'Prospects and Policies for the 1961 American Economy', a report written by Professor Paul A. Samuelson of the Massachusetts Institute of Technology. The report was released on 5 January 1961 and reprinted in newspapers the following day.

I. THE ECONOMIC OUTLOOK

1. Recession

Economic experts are generally agreed that the nation's economy is now in a 'recession'. The slide since mid-1960 cannot be termed a 'depression' like that after 1929, but so widespread a decline in production deserves more than the euphemism of a 'rolling readjustment'.

Prudent economic policy must face the fact that we go into 1961 with business still moving downward. This means that unemployment, now above 6 per cent of the labor force, may this winter rise more than seasonally. It means still lower profits ahead.

The fact of recession also has significant implications for the prospective budget. It means a falling off of tax receipts from earlier estimated levels. This recession is wiping out the previously estimated budget surplus for the fiscal year ending June 30. Many experts now believe that, as of today, it is reasonable to forecast a deficit for this fiscal year, assuming only expenditures already authorized and in the absence of desirable new expenditures from an accelerated effort. Recalling the experience of the 1957–58 recession may be useful: Due largely to the impact of a recession that everyone but the authorities admitted was then taking place, the announcement in early 1958 of a small fiscal 1959 budget surplus was actually followed by a final fiscal 1959 budget deficit of more than $12,000,000,000! Not even the ostrich can avert the economic facts of life. He misreads the role of confidence in economic life who thinks that denying the obvious will cure the ailments of a modern economy.

No one can know exactly when this fourth postwar recession will come to an end. A careful canvass of expert opinion and analysis of the economic forces making for further contraction suggest this probability.

With proper actions by the Government, the contraction in business can be brought to a halt within 1961 itself and converted into an upturn. Recognizing that many analysts hope the upturn may come by the middle of the year but recalling how subject to error were their rosy forecasts for 1960, policy makers realize the necessity for preparing to take actions that might be needed if this fourth recession turns out to be a more serious one than its predecessors.

2. Chronic slackness

In economics, the striking event drives out attention from the less-dramatic but truly more fundamental processes. More fraught with significance for public policy than the recession itself is the vital fact that it has been superimposed upon an economy which, in the last few years, has been sluggish and tired.

Thus, anyone who thought in 1958 that all was well with the American economy just because the recession of that year bottomed out early was proved to be wrong by the sad fact that our last recovery was an anemic one: 1959 and 1960 have been grievously disappointing years, as the period of expansion proved both to be shorter than earlier postwar recoveries and to have been abortive in the sense of never carrying us back anywhere near to high employment and high capacity levels of operations.

This is illustrated by the striking fact that unemployment has remained above 5 per cent of the labor force, a most disappointing performance in comparison with earlier postwar recoveries and desirable social goals.

If what we now faced were only the case of a short recession that was imposed on an economy showing healthy growth and desirable high employment patterns, then governmental policies would have to be vastly different from those called for by the present outlook. But this is not 1949, nor 1954.

Prudent policy now requires that we also combat the basic sluggishness which underlies the more dramatic recession. In some ways a recession imposed on top of a disappointingly slack economy simplifies prudent decision-making.

Thus, certain expenditure programs that are worthwhile for their own sake, but that inevitably involve a lag of some months before they can get going, can be pushed more vigorously in the current situation because of the knowledge that the extra stimulus they later bring is unlikely to impinge upon a recovery that has already led us back to full employment.

The following recommendations try to take careful account of the fact that the recession slide is only the most dramatic manifestation of the grave economic challenge confronting our economic system.

II. FEASIBLE ECONOMIC GOALS

3. Our economic potential

Had our economy progressed since 1956 — not at the dramatic sprint of the Western European and Japanese economies or at the rush of the controlled totalitarian systems, but simply at the modest pace made possible by our labor force and productivity trends — we could have expected 1961 to bring a Gross National Product some 10 per cent above the $500,000,000,000 level we are now experiencing.

With unemployment below 4 per cent, with overcapacity put to work, and with productivity unleashed by economic opportunity, such a level of activity would mean higher private consumption, higher corporate profits, higher capital formation for the future, and higher resources for much-needed public programs.

Instead of our having now to debate about the size of the budget deficit to be associated with a recession, such an outcome would have produced tax revenues under our present tax structure sufficient to lead to a surplus of around $10,000,000,000; and the authorities might be facing the not unpleasant task of deciding how to deal with such a surplus.

4. The targets ahead

Looking forward, one cannot realistically expect to undo in 1961 the inad-equacies of several years. It is not realistic to aim for the restoration of high employment within a single calendar year. The goal for 1961 must be to bring the recession to an end, to reinstate a condition of expansion and recovery and to adopt measures likely to make that expansion one that will not after a year or two peter out at levels of activity far below our true potential.

Indeed, policy for 1961 should be directed against the background of the whole decade ahead. Specifically, if the American economy is to show healthy growth during this period and to average out at satisfactory levels of employment, we must learn not to be misled by statements that this or that is now at an all-time peak; in an economy like ours, with more than 1,000,000 people coming into the labor force each year and with continuing technological change, the most shocking frittering away of our economic opportunities is fully compatible with statistical reports that employment and national product are 'setting new records every year'.

5. Prudent budget goals

A healthy decade of the Nineteen Sixties will not call for a budget that is exactly balanced in every fiscal year. For the period as a whole, if the forces making for expansion are strong and vigorous, there should be many years of budgetary surpluses and these may well have to exceed the deficits of other years. Economic forecasting of the far future is too difficult to make possible any positive statements concerning the desirable decade average of such surpluses and deficits. But careful students of sound economic fiscal policy will perhaps agree on the following:

(i) The first years of such a decade, characterized as they are by stubborn unemployment and excess capacity and following on a period of disappointing slackness, are the more appropriate periods for programs of economic stimulation by well-thought-out fiscal policy.

(ii) The unplanned deficits that result from recession-induced declines in tax receipts levied on corporate profits and individual incomes and also those that come from a carefully designed anti-recession program must be sharply distinguished from deficits that take place in times of zooming demand inflation. This last kind of deficit would represent Government spending out of control and be indeed deserving of grave concern. The deficits that come automatically from recession or which are a necessary part of a determined effort to restore the economic system to health are quite different phenomena: They are signs that our automatic built-in stabilizers are working, and that we no longer will run the risk of going into one of the great depressions that characterized our economic history before the war.

III. THE CONSTRAINTS WITHIN WHICH POLICY MUST WORK

6. Gold and the international payments

Granted that the new Administration is preparing a whole series of measures to correct our balance of payments position, the days are gone when America could shape her domestic stabilization policies taking no thought for their international repercussions. The fact that we have been losing gold for many years will, without question, have to affect our choice among activist policies to restore production and employment. The art of statecraft for the new Administration will be to innovate, within this recognized constraint, new programs that promote healthy recovery.

It would be unthinkable for a present-day American government to deliberately countenance high unemployment as a mechanism for adjusting to the balance of payments deficit.

Such a policy would be largely ineffective anyway; but even were it highly effective, only a cynic would counsel its acceptance. It is equally unthinkable that a responsible Administration can give up its militant efforts toward domestic recovery because of the limitations imposed on it by the international situation. What is needed is realistic taking into account of the international aspects of vigorous domestic policy.

7. The problem of inflation

Various experts, here and abroad, believe that the immediate postwar inflationary climate has now been converted into an epoch of price stability. One hopes this cheerful diagnosis is correct.

However, a careful survey of the behavior of prices and costs shows that our recent stability in the wholesale price index has come in a period of admittedly high unemployment and slackness in our economy. For this reason it is premature to believe that the restoration of high employment will no longer involve problems concerning the stability of prices.

Postwar experience, here and abroad, suggests that a mixed economy like ours may tend to generate an upward creep of prices before it arrives at high employment. Such a price creep, which has to be distinguished from the ancient inflations brought about by the upward pull on prices and wages that comes from excessive dollars of demand spending, has been given many names: 'cost-push' inflation, 'sellers' (rather than demanders) inflation, 'market-power' inflation — these are all variants of the same stubborn phenomenon.

Economists are not yet agreed how serious this new malady of inflation really is. Many feel that new institutional programs, other than conventional fiscal and monetary policies, must be devised to meet this new challenge. But whatever be the merits of the varying views on this subject, it should be manifest that the goal of high employment and effective real growth cannot be abandoned because of the problematical fear that re-attaining of prosperity in America may bring with it some difficulties; if recovery means a reopening of the cost-push problem, then we have no choice but to move closer to the day when that problem has to be successfully grappled with. Economic statesmanship does involve difficult compromises, but not capitulation to any one of the pluralistic goals of modern society.

Running a deliberately slack economy in order to put off the day when such doubts about inflation can be tested is not a policy open to a responsible democratic government in this decade of perilous world crisis. A policy of inaction can be as truly a policy of living dangerously as one of overaction. Far from averting deterioration of our international position, a program that tolerates stagnation in the American economy can prevent us from making those improvements in our industrial productivity that are so desperately needed if we are to remain competitive in the international markets of the world.

History reminds us that even in the worst days of the Great Depression there was never a shortage of experts to warn against all curative public actions, on the ground that they were likely to create a problem of inflation. Had this counsel prevailed here, as it did in pre-Hitler Germany, the very existence of our form of government could be at stake. No modern government will make that mistake again.

[…]

Source: Hacker, L.M. (ed.) (1961) *Major Documents in American Economic History*, *Vol.II*, Princeton, NJ, Van Nostrand, pp.170–87.

2.4   THE INTERNATIONAL CONTEXT

2.4.1   APEC: FIRST MINISTERIAL MEETING (1989)

The United States has long been a Pacific as well as an Atlantic political and economic power and the dynamic growth in the Asia-Pacific in the last few decades has given the region a significantly increased prominence in US economic affairs. Asia-Pacific Economic Co-operation (APEC) is one of the region's most important international forums. APEC was founded in 1989 following an Australian initiative at a time of concern over the difficulties in the General Agreement on Tariffs and Trade (GATT) 'Uruguay Round' of negotiations which would eventually lead to the establishment of the World Trade Organization in 1994. Reproduced below is the Joint Statement and also the Chairman's Summary Statement from the first ministerial meeting of APEC in November 1989. The founding members are listed in the opening paragraph.

First APEC Ministerial Meeting, Canberra, November 1989

JOINT STATEMENT

Ministers from Australia, Brunei Darussalam, Canada, Indonesia, Japan, Republic of Korea [South], Malaysia, New Zealand, The Philippines, Singapore, Thailand, and the United States gathered in Canberra, Australia on 6–7 November 1989 to discuss how to advance the process of Asia Pacific Economic Co-operation. […]

Discussions covered a variety of topics under four agenda items:

- World and Regional Economic Developments

- Global Trade Liberalization — The Role of the Asia Pacific Region

- Opportunity for Regional Co-operation in Specific Areas, and

- Future Steps for Asia Pacific Economic Co-operation

At the conclusion of this first meeting, Ministers expressed satisfaction with the discussions, which demonstrated the value of closer regional consultation and economic co-operation on matters of mutual interest.

Ministers also expressed their recognition of the important contribution ASEAN [Association of South-East Asian Nations] and its dialogue relationships have played in the development to date of APEC, and noted the significant role ASEAN institutional mechanisms can continue to play in supporting the present effort to broaden and strengthen regional economic co-operation.

Multilateral Trade Negotiations

The discussions on world and regional developments, and on global trade liberalization, focused particularly on the need to advance the present round of Multilateral Trade Negotiations [MTN]. Every economy represented in Canberra relies heavily on a strong and open multilateral trading system, and none believes that Asia Pacific Economic Co-operation should be directed to the formation of a trading bloc.

Ministers agreed that the further opening of the multilateral trading system was of substantial and common interest for all countries in the region, and that the Uruguay Round represents the most immediate and practical opportunity to pursue this objective on a broad basis. In particular, Ministers reaffirmed their commitment to open markets and to expand trade through the successful conclusion of the Round by December 1990.

Ministers agreed that continued close consultation within the region should be used wherever possible to promote a positive conclusion to the Round. In this respect, it was agreed that Ministers concerned with trade policy should meet in early September 1990 to discuss the emerging results and consider how to unblock any obstacles to a comprehensive and ambitious MTN result. Ministers would then meet again in Brussels in early December on the eve of the concluding session. In the meantime, senior officials should consult regularly in Geneva to exchange views on MTN progress.

Ministers expressed strong support for the timely and successful completion of the Uruguay Round. They noted that much remained to be done if the December 1990 conclusion was to be achieved. They called on all Contracting Parties to work with them more vigorously to that end.

Future Steps

Ministers agreed that it was premature at this stage to decide upon any particular structure either for a Ministerial-level forum or its necessary support mechanism, but that — while ideas were evolving — it was appropriate for further consultative meetings to take place and for work to be undertaken on matters of common interest and concern.

Accordingly, Ministers welcomed the invitation of Singapore to host a second Ministerial-level Consultative meeting in mid 1990, and they also welcomed the Republic of Korea's offer to host a third such meeting in Seoul during 1991.

Ministers asked their respective senior officials, together with representation from the ASEAN Secretariat, to meet early in 1990 to begin preparations for the next Ministerial-level consultative meeting.

They asked senior officials to undertake or set in train further work on a number of possible topics for regional economic co-operation, on the possible participation of other economies in future meetings, and on other issues related to the future of such co-operation, for consideration by Ministers at their next meeting.

Summary Statement

Attached to this joint statement is Chairman Evans's concluding summary statement which records the substance of discussions during this meeting.

Visiting participating Ministers and their Delegations expressed their deep appreciation to the Government and people of Australia for organizing the meeting and for the excellent arrangements made for it, as well as for the warm hospitality extended to them.

CHAIRMAN'S SUMMARY STATEMENT

Introduction

1. This meeting has brought together in an unprecedented way key decisions makers from twelve dynamic economies in the Asia Pacific Region: Brunei Darussalam, Canada, Indonesia, Japan, the Republic of Korea, Malaysia, New Zealand, Philippines, Singapore, Thailand, the United States and Australia. The presence here of ministers from across this vast region, addressing constructively and with great goodwill and commitment our common economic concerns, has shown that the time is indeed right to advance the process of Asia Pacific Economic Co-operation.

2. The stimulus for this meeting was Australian Prime Minister Hawke's call, in January 1989, for more effective Asia Pacific Economic Co-operation. That proposal stemmed from a recognition that the increasingly interdependence of regional economies indicated a need for effective consultations among regional decision-makers to:

- help strengthen the multilateral trading system and enhance the prospects for success in the Uruguay round;

- provide an opportunity to assess prospects for, and obstacles to, increased trade and investment flows within the Asia Pacific region; and

- identify the range of practical common economic interests.

3. In making and following up this proposal Australia, working closely with ASEAN and other participants, sought to give a sense of direction to a range of earlier proposals for closer regional economic co-operation. The intense process of consultation which has taken place since January, and culminated in this meeting, has succeeded in those terms: for the first time we have had the opportunity to assess collectively, and in some depth, the economic prospect of the region, the factors which can help us to maintain the impressive momentum of growth of recent years as well as the problems which, if not anticipated, could impede future development.

4. A key theme which has run through all our deliberations in the last two days is that the continuing economic success of the region, with all its implications for improved living standards for our people, depends on preserving and improving the multilateral trading system through progressive enhancement of, and adherence to, the GATT framework. By contributing to that effort through the Uruguay Round and beyond, this region can not only help assure its own economic future but improve economic prospects globally. We are all agreed that an open multilateral trading system has been, and remains, critical to rapid regional growth. None of us support the creation of trading blocs.

World and Regional Economic Developments

5. Our exchanges on world and regional economic developments have underlined the extent to which the economic prospects of regional economies are interconnected. Our discussions have highlighted the pace of structural change which has occurred in the region in recent years, and to the opportunities provided by emerging new patterns of regional and international specialization. They have also underlined the strong contribution which sound macro- and micro-economic policies and market oriented reforms have played in the region's growth, and provided a useful opportunity for us to compare experiences on these matters.

6. Participants noted the changing relative strengths and the growing inter-dependence of regional economies. Participants noted that the non-inflationary economic expansion of the United States, now nearly 7 years in duration, has played a key role in the economic performance of the region. They also welcomed the extent to which Japan and other Western Pacific economies are acting increasingly as engines of growth for the region as a whole. The increase in living standards in all parts of the region in recent decades was particularly welcome. It was agreed

that an important aspect of Asia Pacific Economic Co-operation is to maintain conditions which will lead to accelerated development in the currently less developed parts of the region, including the Pacific Island countries, and that open access to developed country markets is essential for such development.

7. Ministers also noted some potential threats to further growth and to the further productive interdependence of Asia Pacific economies. The positive trends of recent years could be disrupted if, instead of continued willingness to undertake structural change, there were to be increased resort to protectionism and if instead of positive joint international action to further liberalize trade, there were to be increased resort to retaliatory or defensive measures.

Trade Liberalization and The Role of the Asia Pacific Region

8. There was general recognition that the Uruguay Round represents the principal, and most immediate and practical, opportunity before us to strengthen and further liberalize the multilateral trading system. All Ministers emphasized the importance, both for the region and for the world economy, of a timely and successful outcome to the Uruguay Round. In this regard, Ministers agreed that continued close consultation, and where possible, support for each others' Uruguay Round objectives could contribute significantly to achieving such an outcome.

9. In this respect, it was agreed that Ministers concerned with trade policy should meet in early September 1990 to discuss the emerging results and consider how to unblock any obstacles to a comprehensive and ambitious MTN result. Ministers would then meet again in Brussels in early December on the eve of the concluding session. In the meantime, senior officials should consult regularly in Geneva to exchange views on MTN progress.

10. Ministers expressed strong support for the timely and successful completion of the GATT Round. Ministers noted that much remained to be done if the December 1990 conclusion was to be achieved. They called on all Contracting Parties to work with them more vigorously to that end.

11. Ministers agreed that the Asia Pacific region has a long-term common interest in promoting world-wide trade liberalization. By working together, the region can inject positive views into a range of important international economic forums, including not only the GATT but the OECD, and sectoral bodies (e.g. the International Telecommunications Union). It was acknowledged that our regional economies would be better placed to show such leadership if we can continue the recent trend of reducing impediments to trade among ourselves, without discriminating against others. It was further agreed that the prospects for such further liberalization of trade in the region would

need to be based on better information about emerging regional trade patterns and developments, as well as the economic impact of such developments.

Regional Co-operation in Specific Areas

12. Rapid growth and increasingly interdependence in the Asia Pacific are giving rise to both challenges and opportunities at the sectoral level.

13. It was agreed that it would be useful to focus further on the scope for co-operation in the area of investment, technology transfer and associated areas of human resources development. Areas which warrant consideration include:

    - co-operative programmes for human resource development;
    - the scope to enhance exchange of information on scientific, technological and industrial indicators, policies and developments;
    - the scope to enhance the comparability of foreign direct investment statistics; and
    - the scope for collaborative research and development projects.

14. In discussing the adequacy of regional infrastructure, Ministers concluded that there would be merit in seeking to develop techniques which might help countries in the region to better anticipate the kind of bottlenecks which might occur as a result of rapid growth. There was general support for work to explore further co-operation in specific areas relating to infrastructure, including telecommunications, maritime transport and aviation.

15. Ministers also noted the need to identify more clearly the scope to extend co-operation in other areas, including energy, resources, fisheries, the environment, trade promotion and tourism and it was agreed that officials should carry forward preliminary work in other areas for consideration at future meetings.

General Principles of Asia Pacific Economic Co-operation

16. The discussion of all these areas has served to underline the broad areas of economic interest participants have in common. In particular, a consensus emerged in the following principles of Asia Pacific Economic Co-operation:

    - the objective of enhanced Asia Pacific Economic Co-operation is to sustain the growth and development of the region, and in this way, to contribute to the growth and development of the world economy;
    - co-operation should recognize the diversity of the region, including differing social and economic systems and current levels of development;
    - co-operation should involve a commitment to open dialogue and consensus, with equal respect for the views of all participants;

- co-operation should be based on non-formal consultative exchanges of views among Asia Pacific economies;

- co-operation should focus on those economic areas where there is scope to advance common interests and achieve mutual benefits;

- consistent with the interests of Asia Pacific economies, co-operation should be directed at strengthening the open multilateral trading system; it should not involve the formation of a trading bloc;

- co-operation should aim to strengthen the gains from interdependence, both for the region and the world economy, including by encouraging the flow of goods, services, capital and technology;

- co-operation should complement and draw upon, rather than detract from, existing organizations in the region, including formal intergovernmental bodies such as ASEAN and less formal consultative bodies like the Pacific Economic Co-operation Conference [subsequently Council] (PECC); and

- participation by Asia Pacific economies should be assessed in the light of the strength of economic linkages with the region, and may be extended in future on the basis of consensus on the part of all participants.

Carrying Forward Regional Economic Co-operation

17. Further Consultative Meetings. It is evident that there is a large range of significant issues confronting the region, and affecting each participant's fundamental economic interests. Ministers agreed that it was premature at this stage to decide upon any particular structure for a Ministerial-level forum (or its necessary support mechanism), but that while ideas were evolving it was both appropriate and valuable for further consultative meetings to take place and for work to be undertaken on matters of common interest and concern. Accordingly, Ministers welcomed the invitation of Singapore to host a second Ministerial-level Consultative meeting in mid 1990, and they also welcomed the Republic of Korea's offer to host a third such meeting during 1991. It was further agreed that it would be appropriate, in the case of any future such meetings, for at least every other such meeting to be held in an ASEAN member country.

18. Work Programme. Ministers agreed that if co-operation is to lead to increasingly tangible benefits, the process of co-operation needs to progress beyond agreements on general principles. This will involve the identification and implementation of specific projects as well as enhancing the capacity for objective professional analysis to allow a more systematic identification of our common interests. In this context, Ministers identified the following broad areas as the basis for the development of a work programme:

- Economic studies: including the review and analysis of the economic outlook for the region and its implications for policy, and the improvement of regional economic and trade data;

- Trade liberalization: with an initial focus on consultations among participants at Ministerial as well as official level to pursue a timely and comprehensive outcome for the Uruguay Round of multilateral trade negotiations;

- Investment, technology transfer and human resource development: including programmes for information exchange and training; and

- Sectoral co-operation: in fields such as tourism, energy, trade promotion, environment matters and infrastructure development.

19. Within these categories, Ministers further identified a wide range of specific activities or projects which has significant potential for enhancing the process of regional economic co-operation; these are listed in the Attachment to this Summary Statement. It was agreed that these subjects should be closely considered by senior officials, together with any other proposals that may be made by participants, with a view to setting in train a viable short- to medium-term work programme. Progress in the implementation of that work programme would be reviewed at the next Ministerial-level meeting.

20. Ministers agreed that two particular projects should proceed as soon as possible, viz.:

(a) Review of data on regional trade flows and developments (covering trade in goods and services) and on capital flows (including direct investment) in order to:

- identify areas where there is a need to improve the comparability of regional data;

- identify gaps in data and improve country and industry sector coverage; and

- develop new data bases as necessary.

(b) Examination of mechanisms to facilitate the identification of trade, investment and technology transfer opportunities in regional countries, which might include:

- the establishment of joint sectoral industry groups to identify specific projects, particular the small and medium scale industry;

- a data base on commercial opportunities;

- the promotion of regional confederations of chambers of industry;

- specific joint project investment studies; and

- enterprise to enterprise linkages.

It was agreed that senior officials would settle the detailed arrangements for implementation of these projects at their next meeting.

21. Support Mechanism. While some Ministers expressed a preference for moving as soon as possible to servicing the future needs of the APEC process through specifically identified structural arrangements of one kind or another, it was agreed that consideration of the support mechanism would benefit from a further period of reflection and evolution of

the co-operation process. Accordingly, Ministers agreed that arrangements for the next one or two Ministerial-level Meetings should be overseen by senior officials from participating economies, joined by representation from the ASEAN Secretariat.

22. It was agreed that this group of Senior Officials should convene at an early date, preferably no later than January 1990, in the first instance to advance a work programme in the way outlined above.

23. It was agreed that follow-up work should draw on existing resources for analysis in the Asia Pacific region, including the work of PECC task forces. The Chairman of the Standing Committee of PECC indicated PECC's willingness to assist in this regard.

24. Participation. Ministers have noted the importance of the People's Republic of China and the economies of Hong Kong and Taiwan to future prosperity of the Asia Pacific region. Taking into account the general principles of co-operation identified above, and recognizing that APEC is a non-formal forum for consultations among high-level representatives of significant economies in the Asia Pacific region, it has been agreed that it would be desirable to consider further the involvement of these three economies in the process of Asia Pacific Economic Co-operation.

25. It has been agreed that it would be appropriate for senior officials to undertake further consultations and consider issues related to future participation in the APEC process by these and other economies, including those of the Pacific Islands, and to report back to the next APEC Ministerial-level Meeting.

Conclusion

26. I believe we have made very worthwhile progress during our two days of discussions. We have been able to build on the efforts of those who have sought to promote Asia Pacific Economic Co-operation in the past and are able to look forward to a further positive process of evolution. Such evolution will take place on the basis of further careful consensus building, drawing constructively on existing mechanisms, such as the valuable institutions and processes of ASEAN as well as the analytical capacity of the PECC.

27. We have all been pleased with the way in which leaders from this diverse and dynamic region have been able to reach consensus on a range of important issues. There is good reason for confidence that, by sustaining the spirit of goodwill and flexibility which has been shown at this meeting, we can develop Asia Pacific Economic Co-operation to benefit not only the region, but to enhance world wide economic prospects.

Source: APEC Net Site, Singapore, APEC Secretariat. Available from:
http://www.apecsec.org.s

2.4.2 PRESIDENT CLINTON'S INTERNATIONAL ECONOMIC PROGRAM (1993)

President Clinton came to power after a successful campaign which emphasized the need to address America's domestic economic problems, in contrast to the perceived preoccupation with foreign policy which characterized the Bush Administration. At the American University in Washington, DC on 26 February 1993 President Clinton outlined an economic programme which placed domestic economic well-being and security in its international context. The speech proposes a five-point plan of action in relation to the domestic and global economy.

[...]

Over the past year, I have tried to speak at some length about what we must do to update our definition of national security and to promote it and to protect it — and to foster democracy and human rights around the world. Today, I want to allude to those matters, but to focus on the economic leadership we must exert at home and aboard as a new global economy unfolds before our eyes.

Twice before in this century, history has asked the United States and other great powers to provide leadership for a world ravaged by war. After World War I, that call went unheeded. Britain was too weakened to lead the world to reconstruction. The United States was too unwilling. The great powers together turned inward as violent, totalitarian power emerged. We raised trade barriers. We sought to humiliate rather than rehabilitate the vanquished. And the result was instability, inflation, then depression and ultimately a second World War.

After the second war, we refused to let history repeat itself. Led by a great American President, Harry Truman, a man of very common roots but uncommon vision, we drew together with other Western powers to reshape a new era. We established NATO to oppose the aggression of communism. We rebuilt the American economy with investments like the GI Bill and a national highway system. We carried out the Marshall Plan to rebuild war-ravaged nations abroad. General MacArthur's vision prevailed in Japan, which built a massive economy and a remarkable democracy. We built new institutions to foster peace and prosperity — the United Nations, the International Monetary Fund, the World Bank, the General Agreement on Tariffs and Trade, and more.

These actions helped to usher in four decades of robust economic growth and collective security. Yet the Cold War was a draining time. We devoted trillions of dollars to it, much more than many of our more visionary leaders thought we should have. We posted our sons and daughters around the world. We lost tens of thousands of them in the defense of freedom and in the pursuit of a containment of communism.

We, my generation, grew up going to school assemblies, learning about what we would do in the event a nuclear war broke out. We were taught to practice ducking under our desks and praying that somehow they might shield us from nuclear radiation. We all learned about whether we needed a bomb shelter in our neighborhood to which we could run in the event that two great superpowers rained nuclear weapons on one another. And that fate, frankly, seemed still frighteningly possible just months before President Kennedy came here to speak in 1963. Now, thanks to his leadership and that of every American president since the Second World War from Harry Truman to George Bush, the Cold War is over.

The Soviet Union itself has disintegrated. The nuclear shadow is receding in the face of the START I and START II agreements, and others that we have made and others yet to come. Democracy is on the march everywhere in the world. It is a new day and a great moment for America.

Yet, across America I hear people raising central questions about our place and our prospects in this new world we have done so much to make. They ask: Will we and our children really have good jobs, first-class opportunities, world-class education, quality affordable health care, safe streets? After having fully defended freedom's ramparts, they want to know if we will share in freedom's bounty.

One of the young public school students President Duffey just introduced was part of the children's program that I did last Saturday with children from around America. If you saw their stories, so many of them raised troubling questions about our capacity to guarantee the fruits of the American Dream to all of our own people.

I believe we can do that, and I believe we must. For in a new global economy, still recovering from the after-effects of the Cold War, a prosperous America is not only good for Americans, as the prime minister of Great Britain reminded me just a couple of days ago, it is absolutely essential for the prosperity of the rest of the world.

Washington can no longer remain caught in the death grip of gridlock, governed by an outmoded ideology that says change is to be resisted, the status quo is to be preserved like King Canute ordering the tide to recede. We cannot do that. And so, my fellow Americans, I submit to you that we stand at the third great moment of decision in the 20th century. Will we repeat the mistakes of the 1920s or the 1930s by turning inward, or will we repeat the successes of the 1940s and the 1950s by reaching outward and improving ourselves as well? I say that if we set a new direction at home, we can set a new direction for the world as well.

The change confronting us in the 1990s is in some ways more difficult than previous times because it is less distinct. It is more complex and in some ways the path is less clear to most of our people still today, even after

20 years of declining relative productivity and a decade or more of stagnant wages and greater effort.

The world clearly remains a dangerous place. Ethnic hatreds, religious strife, the proliferation of weapons of mass destruction, the violation of human rights flagrantly in altogether too many places around the world still call on us to have a sense of national security in which our national defense is an integral part. And the world still calls on us to promote democracy, for even though democracy is on the march in many places in the world, you and I know that it has been thwarted in many places, too. And yet we still face, overarching everything else, this amorphous but profound challenge in the way humankind conducts its commerce.

We cannot let these changes in the global economy carry us passively toward a future of insecurity and instability. For change is the law of life. Whether you like it or not, the world will change much more rapidly in your lifetime than it has in mine.

It is absolutely astonishing the speed with which the sheer volume of knowledge in the world is doubling every few years. And a critical issue before us, and especially before the young people here in this audience, is whether you will grow up in a world where change is your friend or your enemy.

We must challenge the changes now engulfing our world toward America's enduring objectives of peace and prosperity, of democracy and human dignity. And we must work to do it at home and abroad. It is important to understand the monumental scope of these changes. When I was growing up, business was mostly a local affair. Most farms and firms were owned locally, they borrowed locally, they hired locally, they shipped most of their products to neighboring communities or states within the United States. It was the same for the country as a whole. By and large, we had a domestic economy.

But now we are woven inextricably into the fabric of a global economy. Imports and exports, which accounted for about one in ten dollars when I was growing up, now represent one dollar in every five. Nearly three-quarters of the things that we make in America are subject to competition at home or abroad from foreign producers and foreign providers of services. Whether we see it or not, our daily lives are touched everywhere by the flows of commerce that cross national borders as inexorably as the weather.

Capital clearly has become global. Some 3,000,000 million dollars of capital race around the world every day. And when a firm wants to build a new factory, it can turn to financial markets now open 24 hours a day, from London to Tokyo, from New York to Singapore. Products have clearly become more global. Now, if you buy an American car, it may be an American car built with some parts from Taiwan, designed by Germans, sold with British-made advertisements, or a combination of others in a different mix.

Services have become global. The accounting firm that keeps the books for a small business in Wichita may also be helping new entrepreneurs in

Warsaw. And the same fast food restaurant that your family goes to — or at least that I go to — also may well be serving families from Manila to Moscow, and managing its business globally with information, technologies, and satellites.

And most important of all, information has become global and has become king of the global economy. In earlier history, wealth was measured in land, in gold, in oil, in machines. Today, the principal measure of our wealth is information — its quality, its quantity, and the speed with which we acquire it and adapt to it. We need, more than anything else to measure our wealth and our potential by what we know and what we can learn, and what we can do with it. The value and volume of information has soared; the half-life of new ideas has trumped.

Just a few days ago, I was out in Silicon Valley at a remarkable company called Silicon Graphics that has expanded exponentially, partly by developing computer software with a life of 12 months to 18 months, knowing that it will be obsolete after that, and always being ready with a new product to replace it.

We are in a constant race toward innovation that will not end in the lifetime of anyone in this room. What all this means is that the best investment we can make today is in the one resource firmly rooted in our own borders. That is, in the education, the skills, the reasoning capacity and the creativity of our own people.

For all the adventure and opportunity in this global economy, an American cannot approach it without mixed feelings. We still sometimes wish wistfully that everything we really want, particularly those things that produce good wages, could be made in America. We recall simpler times when one product line would be made to endure and last for years. We're angry when we see jobs and factories moving overseas or across the borders or depressing wages here at home when we think there is nothing we can do about it. We worry about our own prosperity being so dependent on events and forces beyond our shores. Could it be that the world's most powerful nation has also given up a significant measure of its sovereignty in the quest to lift the fortunes of people throughout the world?

It is ironic and even painful that the global village we have worked so hard to create has done so much to be the source of higher unemployment and lower wages for some of our people. But that is no wonder. For years our leaders have failed to take the steps that would harness the global economy to the benefit of all of our people. Steps such as investing in our people and their skills, enforcing our trade laws, helping communities hurt by change — in short, putting the American people first without withdrawing from the world and people beyond our borders.

The truth of our age is this — and must be this: Open and competitive commerce will enrich us as a nation. It spurs us to innovate. It forces us to compete. It connects us with new customers. It promotes global growth without which no rich country can hope to grow wealthier. It enables our producers, who are themselves consumers of services and raw materials, to prosper.

And so I say to you in the face of all the pressures to do the reverse, we must compete, not retreat.

Our exports are especially important to us. As bad as the recent recession was, it would have gone on for twice as long had it not been for what we were able to sell to other nations. Every billion dollars of our exports creates nearly 20,000 jobs here, and we now have over seven million export-related jobs in America. They tend to involve better work and better pay. Most are in manufacturing and, on average, they pay almost $3,500 more per year than the average American job. They are exactly the kind of jobs we need for a new generation of Americans.

American jobs and prosperity are reason enough for us to be working at mastering the essentials of the global economy. But far more is at stake. For this new fabric of commerce will also shape global prosperity or the lack of it, and with it, the prospects of people around the world for democracy, freedom and peace.

We must remember that even with all our problems today, the United States is still the world's strongest engine of growth and progress. We remain the world's largest producer and its largest and most open market. Other nations, such as Germany and Japan, are moving rapidly. They have done better than we have in certain areas. We should respect them for it, and where appropriate, we should learn from that. But we must also say to them, you, too, must act as engines of global prosperity.

Nonetheless, the fact is that for now and for the foreseeable future, the world looks to us to be the engine of global growth and to be the leaders.

Our leadership is especially important for the world's new and emerging democracies. To grow and deepen their legitimacy, to foster a middle class and a civic culture, they need the ability to tap into a growing global economy. And our security and our prosperity will be greatly affected in the years ahead by how many of these nations can become and stay democracies.

All you have to do to know that is to look at the problems in Somalia, to look at Bosnia, to look at the other trouble spots in the world. If we could make a garden of democracy and prosperity and free enterprise in every part of this globe, the world would be a safer and a better and a more prosperous place for the United States and for all of you to raise your children in.

Let us not minimize the difficulty of this task. Democracy's prospects are dimmed, especially in the developing world by trade barriers and slow global growth. Even though 60 developing nations have reduced their trade barriers in recent years, when you add up the sum of their collective actions, 20 of the 24 developed nations have actually increased their trade barriers in recent years. This is a powerful testament to the painful difficulty of trying to maintain a high-wage economy in a global economy where production is mobile and can quickly fly to a place with low wages.

We have got to focus on how to help our people adapt to these changes, how to maintain a high-wage economy in the United States without ourselves adding to the protectionist direction that so many of the developed nations have taken in the last few years. These barriers in the end will cost the developing world more in lost exports and incomes than all the foreign assistance that developed nations provide, but after that they will begin to undermine our economic prosperity as well.

It's more than a matter of incomes, I remind you — it's a matter of culture and stability. Trade, of course, cannot ensure the survival of new democracies, and we have seen the enduring power of ethnic hatred, the incredible power of ethnic divisions — even among people literate and allegedly understanding — to splinter democracy and to savage the nation state.

But, as philosophers from Thucydides to Adam Smith have noted, the habits of commerce run counter to the habits of war. Just as neighbors who raise each other's barns are less likely to become arsonists, people who raise each other's living standards through commerce are less likely to become combatants. So if we believe in the bonds of democracy, we must resolve to strengthen the bonds of commerce.

Our own nation has the greatest potential to benefit from the emerging economy, but to do so we have to confront the obstacles that stand in our way. Many of our trading partners cling to unfair practices. Protectionist voices here at home and abroad call for new barriers. Indifferent policies have left too many of our workers and communities exposed to the harsh winds of trade without letting them share in the sheltering prosperity trade has also brought, and without helping them in any way to build new ways to work so they can be rewarded for their efforts in global commerce.

Cooperation among the major powers toward world growth is not working well at all today. And most of all, we simply haven't done enough to prepare our own people and to produce our own resources so that we can face with success the rigors of the new world. We can change all that if we have the will to do it. Leonardo da Vinci said that God sells all things at the price of labor. Our labor must be to make this change.

I believe there are five steps we can and must take to set a new direction at home and to help create a new direction for the world. First, we simply have to get our own economic house in order. I have outlined a new national economic strategy that will give America the new direction we require to meet our challenges. It seeks to do what no generation of Americans has ever been called upon to do before: to increase investment in our productive future, and to reduce our deficit at the same time.

We must do both. A plan that only plays down the deficit without investing in those things that make us more productive will not make us stronger. A plan that only invests more money without bringing down the deficit will weaken the fabric of our overall economy such that even educated and productive people cannot succeed in it.

It is more difficult to do both. The challenges are more abrasive — you have to cut more other spending and raise more other taxes. But it is essential that we do both — invest so that we can compete; bring down the debt so that we can compete. The future of the American dream and the fate of our economy and much of the world's economy hangs in the balance on what happens in this city in the next few months.

Already the voices of inertia and self-interest have said, well, we shouldn't do this or this or that detail is wrong with that plan. But almost no one has taken up my original challenge that anyone who has any specific ideas about how we can cut more should simply come forward with them. I am genuinely open to new ideas to cut inessential spending and to make the kinds of dramatic changes in the way government works that all of us know we have to make. I don't care whether they come from Republicans or Democrats or I don't even care whether they come from home or abroad. I don't care who gets the credit, but I do care that we not vary from our determination to pass a plan that increases investment and reduces the deficit.

I think every one of you who is a student at this university has a far bigger stake in the future than I do. I have lived in all probability more than half my life with benefits far beyond anything I ever dreamed or deserve because my country worked. And I want my country to work for you.

The plan I have offered is assuredly not perfect, but it is an honest and bold attempt to honestly confront the challenges before us, to secure the foundations of our economic growth, to expand the resources, the confidence and the moral suasion we need to continue our global leadership into the next century.

And I plead with all of you to do everything you can to replace the blame game that has dominated this city too long with the bigger game of competing and winning in the global economy.

Second, it is time for us to make trade a priority element of American security. For too long, debates over trade have been dominated by voices from the extremes. One says government should build walls to protect firms from competition. Another says government should do nothing in the face of foreign competition, no matter what the dimension and shape of that competition is, no matter what the consequences are in terms of job losses, trade dislocations, or crushed incomes.

Neither view takes on the hard work of creating a more open trading system that enables us and our trading partners to prosper. Neither steps up to the task of empowering our workers to compete or of ensuring that there is some compact of shared responsibility regarding trade's impact on our people, or of guaranteeing a continuous flow of investment into emerging areas of new technology which will create the high-wage jobs of the 21st century.

Our administration is now developing a comprehensive trade policy that will step up to those challenges. And I want to describe the principles upon which it will rest. It will not be a policy of blame, but one of responsibility. It will say to our trading partners that we value their business, but none of us should expect something for nothing.

We will continue to welcome foreign products and services into our markets, but insist that our products and services be able to enter theirs on equal terms. We will welcome foreign investment in our businesses knowing that with it come new ideas as well as capital — new technologies, new management techniques and new opportunities for us to learn from one another and grow. But as we welcome that investment, we insist that our investors should be equally welcome in other countries.

We welcome the subsidiaries of foreign companies on our soil. We appreciate the jobs they create and the products and services they bring. But we do insist simply that they pay the same taxes on the same income that our companies do for doing the same business.

Our trade policy will be part of an integrated economic program, not just something we use to compensate for the lack of a domestic agenda. We must enforce our trade laws and our agreements with all the tools and energy at our disposal. But there is much about our competitive posture that simply cannot be straightened out by trade retaliation. Better-educated and trained workers, a lower deficit, stable, low interest rates, a reformed health care system, world-class technologies, revived cities: these must be the steel of our competitive edge. And there must be a continuing quest by business and labor and, yes, by government for higher and higher and higher levels of productivity.

Too many of the chains that have hobbled us in world trade have been made in America. Our trade policy will also bypass the distracting debates over whether efforts should be multilateral, regional, bilateral, unilateral. The fact is that each of these efforts has its place. Certainly we need to seek to open other nations' markets and to establish clear and enforceable rules on which to expand trade.

That is why I'm committed to a prompt and successful completion of the Uruguay Round of the GATT talks. That round has dragged on entirely too long. But it still holds the potential, if other nations do their share and we do ours to boost American wages and living standards significantly and to do the same for other nations around the world.

We also know that regional and bilateral agreements provide opportunities to explore new kinds of trade concerns, such as how trade relates to policies affecting the environment and labor standards and the antitrust laws. And these agreements, once concluded, can act as a magnet including other countries to drop barriers and to open their trading systems.

The North American Free Trade Agreement is a good example. It began as an agreement with Canada, which I strongly supported, which has now led to a pact with Mexico as well. That agreement holds the potential to create many, many jobs in America over the next decade if it is joined with others to ensure that the environment, that living standards, that working conditions, are honored — that we can literally know that we are going to raise the condition of people in America and in Mexico. We have a vested interest in a wealthier, stronger Mexico, but we need to do it on terms that are good for our people.

And we should work with organizations, such as the Asian-Pacific Economic Cooperation Forum, to liberalize our trade across the Pacific as well.

And let me say just a moment about this. I am proud of the contribution America has made to prosperity in Asia and to the march of democracy. I have seen it in Japan after World War II. I have seen it, then, in Taiwan as a country became more progressive and less repressive at the same time. I have seen it in Korea as a country has become more progressive and more open. And we are now making a major contribution to the astonishing revitalization of the Chinese economy, now growing at 10 percent a year, with the United States buying a huge percentage of those imports. And I say, I want to continue that partnership, but I also think we have a right to expect progress in human rights and democracy and should support that progress.

Third, it is time for us to do our best to exercise leadership among the major financial powers to improve our coordination on behalf of global economic growth. At a time when capital is mobile and highly fungible, we simply cannot afford to work at cross-purposes with the other major industrial democracies. Our major partners must work harder and more closely with us to reduce interest rates, stimulate investment, reduce structural barriers to trade and to restore robust global growth. And we must look anew at institutions we use to chart our way in the global economy and ask whether they are serving our interests in this new world, or whether we need to modify them or create others.

Tomorrow, our Treasury secretary, Secretary Bentsen, and the Federal Reserve Board chairman, Alan Greenspan, will meet with their counterparts from these Group of Seven nations to begin that work. And I look forward to meeting with the G-7 heads of state and the representatives of the European Community at our Tokyo Summit in July. I am especially hopeful that by then our economic package here at home will have been substantially enacted by the Congress. And if that is so, I will be able to say to my counterparts, you have been telling us for years that America must reduce its debt and put its own house in order. You have been saying to us for years we must increase investment in our own education and technology to improve productivity. We have done it. We have done it for ourselves, we have done it for you, now you must work with us in Germany and Japan and other nations to promote global growth.

We have to work with these nations. None of us are very good at it. America doesn't want to give up its prerogatives. The Japanese don't want to give up theirs. The Germans don't want to give up theirs. There are deep and ingrained traditions in all these nations. But the fact is that the world can't grow if America is in recession, but it will be difficult for us to grow coming out of this recovery unless we can spark a renewed round of growth in Europe and in Japan. We have got to try to work more closely together.

Fourthly, we need to promote the steady expansion of growth in the developing world, not only because it's in our interests, but because it will help them as well. These nations are a rapidly expanding market for our products — some three million American jobs flow from exports to the developing world. Indeed, because of unilateral actions taken by Mexico over the last few years, the volume of our trade has increased dramatically, and our trade deficit has disappeared.

Our ability to protect the global environment and our ability to combat the flow of illegal narcotics also rests in large measure on the relationships we develop commercially with the developing world.

There is a great deal that we can do to open the flow of goods and services. Our aid policies must do more to address population pressures; to support environmentally responsible, sustainable development; to promote more accountable government — and to foster a fair distribution of the fruits of growth among an increasingly restive world population — where over 1,000 million people still exist on barely a dollar a day. These efforts will reap us dividends of trade, of friendship and peace.

The final step we must take, my fellow Americans, is toward the success of democracy in Russia and in the world's other new democracies. The perils facing Russia and other former Soviet republics are especially acute and especially important to our future. For the reductions in our defense spending that are an important part of our economic program over the long run here at home are only tenable as long as Russia and the other nuclear republics pose a diminishing threat to our security and to the security of our allies and the democracies throughout the world. Most worrisome is Russia's precarious economic condition. If the economic reforms begun by President Yeltsin are abandoned, if hyperinflation cannot be stemmed, the world will suffer.

Consider the implications for Europe if millions of Russian citizens decide they have no alternative but to flee to the West where wages are 50 times higher. Consider the implication for the global environment if all the Chernobyl-style nuclear plants are forced to start operating there without spare parts, when we should be in phased stage of building them and shutting them down — building them down, closing them up, cleaning them up. If we are willing to spend trillions of dollars to ensure communism's defeat in the Cold War, surely we should be willing to invest a tiny fraction of that to support democracy's success where communism failed.

To be sure, the former Soviet republics and especially Russia, must be willing to assume most of the hard work and high cost of the reconstruction process. But then again, remember that the Marshall Plan itself financed only a small fraction of postwar investments in Europe. It was a magnet, a beginning, a confidence-building measure, a way of starting a process that turned out to produce an economic miracle.

Like Europe then, these republics now have a wealth of resources and talent and potential. And with carefully targeted assistance, conditioned on progress toward reform and arms control and non-proliferation, we can improve our own security and our future prosperity at the same time we extend democracy's reach.

These five steps constitute an agenda for American action in a global economy. As such, they constitute an agenda for our own prosperity as well. Some may wish we could pursue our own domestic effort strictly through domestic policies, as we have understood them in the past. But in this global economy, there is no such thing as a purely domestic policy. This thing we call the global economy is unruly; it's a bucking bronco that often lands with its feet on different sides of old lines, and sometimes with its whole body on us. But if we are to ride the bronco into the next century, we must harness the whole horse, not just part of it.

I know there are those in this country, in both political parties and all across the land, who say that we should not try to take this ride, that these goals are too ambitious, that we should withdraw and focus only on those things which we have to do at home. But I believe that would be a sad mistake and a great loss. For the new world toward which we are moving actually favors us. We are better equipped than any other people on earth by reason of our history, our culture and our disposition, to change, to lead and to prosper. The experience of the last few years where we have stubbornly refused to make the adjustment we need to compete and win are actually atypical and unusual seen against the backdrop of our nation's history.

Look now at our immigrant nation and think of the world toward which we are tending. Look at how diverse and multi-ethnic and multi-lingual we are — in a world in which the ability to communicate with all kinds of people from all over the world and to understand them will be critical. Look at our civic habits of tolerance and respect. They are not perfect in our own eyes. It grieved us all when there was so much trouble a year ago in Los Angeles. But Los Angeles is a country (sic) with 150 different ethnic groups of widely differing levels of education and access to capital and income. It is a miracle that we get along as well as we do. And all you have to do is to look at Bosnia, where the differences were not so great, to see how well we have done in spite of all of our difficulties.

And look at the way our culture has merged technology and values. This is an expressive land that produced CNN and MTV. We were all born for the information age. This is a jazzy nation, thank goodness, for my sake. It created be-bop and hip-hop and all those other things. We are wired for real time. And we have always been a nation of pioneers. Consider the astonishing outpouring of support for the challenges I laid down last week in an economic program that violates every American's narrow special interest if you just take part of it out and look at it.

And, yet, here we are again, ready to accept a new challenge, ready to seek new change because we're curious and restless and bold. It flows out of our heritage. It's ingrained in the soul of Americans. It's no accident that our nation has steadily expanded the frontiers of democracy, of religious tolerance, of racial justice, of equality for all people, of environmental protection and technology and, indeed, the cosmos itself. For it is our nature to reach out, and reaching out has served not only ourselves, but the world as well.

Now, together, it is time for us to reach out again. Toward tomorrow's economy. Toward a better future. Toward a new direction. Toward securing for you, the students at American University, the American Dream.

Source: White House Web Site, Electronic Publications. Available from: http://www.pub.whitehouse.gov/WH/Publications/html/Publications.html

2.4.3 NORTH AMERICAN FREE TRADE AGREEMENT (1994)

The North American Free Trade Agreement, mentioned in President Clinton's International Economic Program (previous document), came into effect from the beginning of 1994. It established a formal and legally binding free trade area covering the United States, Canada and Mexico. The opening articles are reproduced below.

Preamble

The Government of Canada, the Government of the United Mexican States and the Government of the United States of America, resolved to:

STRENGTHEN the special bonds of friendship and co-operation among their nations;

CONTRIBUTE to the harmonious development and expansion of world trade and provide a catalyst to broader international co-operation;

CREATE an expanded and secure market for the goods and services produced in their territories;

REDUCE distortions to trade;

ESTABLISH clear and mutually advantageous rules governing their trade;

ENSURE a predictable commercial framework for business planning and investment;

BUILD on their respective rights and obligations under the General Agreement on Tariffs and Trade and other multilateral and bilateral instruments of co-operation;

ENHANCE the competitiveness of their firms in global markets;

FOSTER creativity and innovation, and promote trade in goods and services that are the subject of intellectual property rights;

CREATE new employment opportunities and improve working conditions and living standards in their respective territories;

UNDERTAKE each of the preceding in a manner consistent with environmental protection and conservation;

PRESERVE their flexibility to safeguard the public welfare;

PROMOTE sustainable development;

STRENGTHEN the development and enforcement of environmental laws and regulations; and

PROTECT, enhance and enforce basic workers' rights;

HAVE AGREED as follows:

PART ONE — GENERAL PART

Chapter One — Objectives

Article 101: Establishment of the Free Trade Area

The Parties to this Agreement, consistent with Article XXIV of the General Agreement on Tariffs and Trade, hereby establish a free trade area.

Article 102: Objectives

1. The objectives of this Agreement, as elaborated more specifically through its principles and rules, including national treatment, most-favored-nation treatment and transparency are to:

    (a) eliminate barriers to trade in, and facilitate the cross border movement of, goods and services between the territories of the Parties;

    (b) promote conditions of fair competition in the free trade area;

    (c) increase substantially investment opportunities in their territories;

    (d) provide adequate and effective protection and enforcement of intellectual property rights in each Party's territory;

    (e) create effective procedures for the implementation and application of this Agreement, and for its joint administration and the resolution of disputes; and

    (f) establish a framework for further trilateral, regional and multilateral co-operation to expand and enhance the benefits of this Agreement.

2. The Parties shall interpret and apply the provisions of this Agreement in the light of its objectives set out in paragraph 1 and in accordance with applicable rules of international law.

Article 103: Relation to Other Agreements

1. The Parties affirm their existing rights and obligations with respect to each other under the General Agreement on Tariffs and Trade and other agreements to which such Parties are party.

2. In the event of any inconsistency between the provisions of this Agreement and such other agreements, the provisions of this Agreement shall prevail to the extent of the inconsistency, except as otherwise provided in this Agreement.

Article 104: Relation to Environmental and Conservation Agreements

1. In the event of any inconsistency between this Agreement and the specific trade obligations set out in:

   (a) Convention on the International Trade in Endangered Species of Wild Fauna and Flora, done at Washington, March 3, 1973;

   (b) the Montreal Protocol on Substances that Deplete the Ozone Layer, done at Montreal, September 16, 1987, as amended June 29, 1990;

   (c) Basel Convention on the Control of Transboundary Movements of Hazardous Wastes and Their Disposal, done at Basel, March 22, 1989, upon its entry into force for Canada, Mexico and the United States; or

   (d) the agreements set out in Annex 104.1, such obligations shall prevail to the extent of the inconsistency, provided that where a Party has a choice among equally effective and reasonably available means of complying with such obligations, the Party chooses the alternative that is the least inconsistent with the other provisions of this Agreement.

2. The Parties may agree in writing to modify Annex 104.1 to include any amendment to the agreements listed in paragraph 1, and any other environmental or conservation agreement.

Article 105: Extent of Obligations

The Parties shall ensure that all necessary measures are taken in order to give effect to the provisions of this Agreement, including their observance, except as otherwise provided in this Agreement, by state and provincial governments.

[...]

Annex 104

Bilateral and Other Environmental and Conservation Agreements

1. The Agreement Between the Government of Canada and the Government of the United States of America Concerning the Transboundary Movement of Hazardous Waste, signed at Ottawa, October 28, 1986.

2. The Agreement between the United States of America and the United Mexican States on Co-operation for the Protection and Improvement of

the Environment in the Border Area, signed at La Paz, Baja California Sur, August 14, 1983.

[...]

Source: NAFTANET, Austin, Tex., NAFTAnet, Inc. Available from: http://www.nafta.net

2.4.4 APEC: DECLARATION (1996)

The first meeting of APEC in 1989 had agreed that the organization should continue to evolve, and it has done so. In Manila in November 1996, building on earlier meetings, the ministers made the following declaration on a 'Framework for Strengthening Economic Co-operation and Development'. By the end of 1996 membership had expanded to eighteen countries with new members including China, Mexico and Chile. However, for all its evolution APEC does not involve any legally binding commitments or sanctions.

[...] Ministers jointly resolve to:

Adopt the following Framework for Strengthening Economic Co-operation and Development to guide member economies in the implementation of Part II of the Osaka Action Agenda, entitled Economic and Technical Co-operation.

I GOALS

We agree that the goals of economic and technical co-operation and development in APEC are:

- to attain sustainable growth and equitable development in the Asia-Pacific region;

- to reduce economic disparities among APEC economies;

- to improve the economic and social well-being of the people; and

- to deepen the spirit of community in the Asia Pacific.

II GUIDING PRINCIPLES

1. In line with APEC's fundamental principles, we will pursue economic co-operation and development in the region on the basis of:
   - *mutual respect and equality* including respect for diversity and the different situations of members, focusing on members economies' strengths;
   - *mutual benefit and assistance*, with a firm commitment to making genuine contributions toward the goals of sustainable growth and equitable development and reducing disparities in the region, based

on the APEC member economies' diverse and complementary capabilities;

- *constructive and genuine partnership*, creating opportunities for mutually beneficial exchange between and among industrialized and developing economies, thus promoting the development and dynamism of the economies in the region. This will include a working partnership with the private/business sector, other pertinent institutions, and the community in general, to ensure that co-operation is consistent with market principles. This partnership will engender co-operative undertakings toward the efficient allocation of resources and reduction of economic disparities within an increasingly integrated Asia Pacific Community; and

- *consensus building*, in line with the consultative, consensual approach nurtured through the development of APEC, while respecting the autonomy of each economy through their voluntary participation.

2. We emphasize the need to jointly undertake economic and technical co-operation activities that will promote the full participation of all men and women in the benefits of economic growth. In pursuing these activities, we shall be guided by our responsibility in making economic growth consistent with environmental quality.

III CHARACTER OF APEC ECONOMIC AND TECHNICAL CO-OPERATION

1. To achieve our goals, we agree that economic and technical co-operation in APEC must be goal-oriented with explicit objectives, milestones, and performance criteria.

2. Considering the increasing role of the private/business sectors in APEC, we encourage them not only to participate but also initiate economic and technical co-operation activities in line with APEC goals. Thus, economic and technical activities can combine government actions, private sector projects and joint public–private activities with the public sector playing a direct or indirect role in creating an enabling environment for private sector initiative.

3. To help build a growing sense of community and promote a spirit of enterprise that leads our people to work with and learn from each other in a co-operative spirit, economic and technical co-operation activities should draw on voluntary contributions commensurate with member economies' capabilities and generate direct and broadly shared benefits among APEC member economies to reduce economic disparities in the region.

IV ORGANIZING THEMES AND PRIORITIES

1. To achieve sustainable growth and equitable development, and benefit from the move towards free and open trade and investment, and to promote the welfare of economies of the region, we give priority to joint co-operative activities which:

- *Develop Human Capital*, the region's main asset in economic development, to broaden the benefits of economic growth, deepen the basis for sustainable growth, and strengthen social cohesion domestically and regionally;

- *Develop Stable, Safe and Efficient Capital Markets* to promote capital flows that generate real economic returns, to mobilize domestic savings through broad, deep capital and financial markets, as discussed by the Finance Ministers Meeting and to enhance the environment for private investment in infrastructure;

- *Strengthen Economic Infrastructure* to eliminate bottlenecks to economic growth, especially in such areas as telecommunications, transportation, and energy in order to further integrate members into the regional economy, and the region into the global economy;

- *Harness Technologies for the Future* to ensure that APEC joint activities promote the flow and expand the capacities of its members to absorb existing industrial science and technology as well as develop new technologies for the future, thus promoting a free flow of information and technology;

- *Safeguard the Quality of Life Through Environmentally Sound Growth* by promoting sound policies and practices, taking into account concerns about sustainable development.

- *Develop and Strengthen the Dynamism of Small and Medium Enterprises* so that they may respond more efficiently and effectively to market developments in a more open and liberal economic development.

2. We will support new themes that may emerge in the co-operation process that are consistent with the goals and guiding principles defined in this framework.

3. In consonance with the goals, principles, and themes laid out in this Declaration, we hereby urge Working Groups and other relevant APEC fora to co-ordinate with each other and integrate their work on cross-cutting issues to achieve focused outcomes and demonstrate breakthroughs in advancing the goals of APEC in the light of Part II of the Osaka Action Agenda and the themes mentioned in paragraph 1 of this section.

4. We are confident that, by giving further coherence and direction to our economic and technical co-operation, we will contribute substantially to the goal of a prosperous Asia Pacific community as we move towards the twenty-first century.

Source: APEC Net Site, Singapore, APEC Secretariat. Available from:
http://www.apecsec.org.s

2.5 SELECTED ECONOMIC STATISTICS

This section is devoted to a selection of economic statistical information taken from the mass of data made available by the federal government. There is no attempt to be comprehensive, the intention is to illustrate some of the economic trends and supply some figures which indicate the characteristics of certain markets. Tables include historical information, however, there has been a deliberate emphasis on more recent data and trends.

The tables have been reproduced from *The American Almanac* and references in some of the footnotes refer to this publication. *The Almanac* is published by The Reference Press and based on the *Statistical Abstract of the United States*; the 1997 version of which is also used. The *Statistical Abstract* is compiled by the US Bureau of the Census and has been published annually since 1880 by the Government Printing Office.

In several of the tables data are broken down by region and/or sub-regions, the composition of these regions is shown in the map at the end of Chapter 5.

2.5.1 PRODUCTION AND CONSUMPTION

The first two tables give an overview of the economy, the first shows the Gross Domestic Product from 1960 to 1996, that is the value of the output of all goods and services produced within the nation's borders, including foreign owned firms within the country but excluding income of domestically owned firms located abroad. The second, Gross National Product from 1980 to 1989, is the total value of all goods and services produced by firms owned by the country including those located abroad. GNP excludes foreign owned firms within the country. The third table summarizes what Americans have spent their money on between 1970 and 1990. Each of these tables is expressed in current and constant dollars for comparison. The current dollar represents the value in dollars at any given time, i.e. how many dollars in that year, while the constant dollar pegs the dollar's value at a particular time or base line, removing factors such as inflation and allowing a better comparison in real terms. The constant dollar columns will more readily indicate changing trends.

Table 2.1 GDP in current and real (1992) dollars: 1960–96. (In billions of dollars)

ITEM	1960	1970	1980	1982	1983	1984	1985	1986	1987
CURRENT DOLLARS									
Gross domestic product (GDP)	**526.6**	**1,035.6**	**2,784.2**	**3,242.1**	**3,514.5**	**3,902.4**	**4,180.7**	**4,422.2**	**4,692.3**
Personal consumption expenditures . .	332.2	648.1	1,760.4	2,076.8	2,283.4	2,492.3	2,704.8	2,892.7	3,094.5
Durable goods	43.3	85.0	213.5	239.3	279.8	325.1	361.1	398.7	416.7
Nondurable goods	152.9	272.0	695.5	786.8	830.3	883.6	927.6	957.2	1,014.0
Services	136.0	291.1	851.4	1,050.7	1,173.3	1,283.6	1,416.1	1,536.8	1,663.8
Gross private domestic investment. . .	78.8	150.2	465.9	501.1	547.1	715.6	715.1	722.5	747.2
Fixed investment	75.5	148.1	473.5	515.6	552.0	648.1	688.9	712.9	722.9
Nonresidential	49.2	106.7	350.3	409.9	399.4	468.3	502.0	494.8	495.4
Residential	26.3	41.4	123.2	105.7	152.5	179.8	186.9	218.1	227.6
Change in business inventories . . .	3.2	2.2	-7.6	-14.5	-4.9	67.5	26.2	9.6	24.2
Net exports of goods and services . . .	2.4	1.2	-14.9	-20.5	-51.7	-102.0	-114.2	-131.5	-142.1
Exports	25.3	57.0	278.9	282.6	277.0	303.1	303.0	320.7	365.7
Imports	22.8	55.8	293.8	303.2	328.6	405.1	417.2	452.2	507.9
Government consumption expenditures and gross investment.	113.2	236.1	572.8	684.8	735.7	796.6	875.0	938.5	992.8
Federal	65.6	115.9	248.4	313.2	344.5	372.6	410.1	435.2	455.7
National defense	54.9	90.6	174.2	230.9	255.0	282.7	312.4	332.4	350.4
State and local	47.6	120.2	324.4	371.6	391.2	424.0	464.9	503.3	537.2
CHAINED (1992) DOLLARS									
Gross domestic product (GDP)	**2,262.9**	**3,397.6**	**4,615.0**	**4,620.3**	**4,803.7**	**5,140.1**	**5,323.5**	**5,487.7**	**5,649.5**
Personal consumption expenditures . .	1,432.6	2,197.8	3,009.7	3,081.5	3,240.6	3,407.6	3,566.5	3,708.7	3,822.3
Gross private domestic investment. . .	270.5	426.1	628.3	587.2	642.1	833.4	823.8	811.8	821.5
Net exports of goods and services . . .	-21.3	-65.0	10.1	-14.1	-63.3	-127.3	-147.9	-163.9	-156.2
Exports	86.8	158.1	331.4	311.4	303.3	328.4	337.3	362.2	402.0
Imports	108.1	223.1	321.3	325.5	366.6	455.7	485.2	526.1	558.2
Government consumption expenditures and gross investment.	617.2	866.8	941.4	960.1	987.3	1,018.4	1,080.1	1,135.0	1,165.9

ITEM	1988	1989	1990	1991	1992	1993	1994	1995	1996
CURRENT DOLLARS									
Gross domestic product (GDP)	**5,049.6**	**5,438.7**	**5,743.8**	**5,916.7**	**6,244.4**	**6,553.0**	**6,935.7**	**7,253.8**	**7,576.1**
Personal consumption expenditures . .	3,349.7	3,594.8	3,839.3	3,975.1	4,219.8	4,454.1	4,700.9	4924.9	5,151.4
Durable goods	451.0	472.8	476.5	455.2	488.5	530.7	580.9	606.4	632.1
Nondurable goods	1,081.1	1,163.8	1,245.3	1,277.6	1,321.8	1,368.9	1,429.7	1,485.9	1,545.1
Services	1,817.6	1,958.1	2,117.5	2,242.3	2,409.4	2,554.6	2,690.3	2,832.6	2,974.3
Gross private domestic investment. . .	773.9	829.2	799.7	736.2	790.4	871.1	1,014.4	1,065.3	1,117.0
Fixed investment	763.1	797.5	791.6	738.5	783.4	850.5	954.9	1,028.2	1,101.5
Nonresidential	530.6	566.2	575.9	547.3	557.9	598.8	667.2	738.5	791.1
Residential	232.5	231.3	215.7	191.2	225.6	251.7	287.7	289.8	310.5
Change in business inventories . . .	10.9	31.7	8.0	-2.3	7.0	20.6	59.5	37.0	15.4
Net exports of goods and services . . .	-106.1	-80.4	-71.3	-20.5	-29.5	-62.7	-94.4	-94.7	-98.7
Exports	447.2	509.3	557.3	601.8	639.4	657.8	719.1	807.4	855.2
Imports	553.2	589.7	628.6	622.3	669.0	720.5	813.5	902.0	953.9
Government consumption expenditures and gross investment.	1,032.0	1,095.1	1,176.1	1,225.9	1,263.8	1,290.4	1,314.7	1,358.3	1,406.4
Federal	457.3	477.2	503.6	522.6	528.0	522.6	516.4	516.6	523.1
National defense	354.0	360.6	373.1	383.5	375.8	362.2	352.0	345.7	(NA)
State and local	574.7	617.9	672.6	703.4	735.8	767.8	798.4	841.7	883.3
CHAINED (1992) DOLLARS									
Gross domestic product (GDP)	**5,865.2**	**6,062.0**	**6,136.3**	**6,079.4**	**6,244.4**	**6,386.1**	**6,608.4**	**6,742.2**	**6,906.8**
Personal consumption expenditures . .	3,972.7	4,064.6	4,132.2	4,105.8	4,219.8	4,339.5	4,473.2	4,577.8	4,690.7
Gross private domestic investment. . .	828.2	863.5	815.0	738.1	790.4	857.0	979.3	1,009.4	1,056.6
Net exports of goods and services . . .	-114.4	-82.7	-61.9	-22.3	-29.5	-74.4	-108.1	-114.2	-113.6
Exports	465.8	520.2	564.4	599.9	639.4	658.2	712.0	775.4	825.9
Imports	580.2	603.0	626.3	622.2	669.0	730.2	817.6	883.0	939.5
Government consumption expenditures and gross investment.	1,180.9	1,213.9	1,250.4	1,258.0	1,263.8	1,261.0	1,260.0	1,260.2	1,270.6

NA Not available.
Source: U.S. Bureau of Economic Analysis, *National Income and Product Accounts of the United States, 1929-94*, forthcoming; and *Survey of Current Business*, May 1997.

Table 2.2   GNP, by industry, in current and constant (1982) dollars: 1980–89.
(In billions of dollars, except per cent. Based on the *1972 Standard Industrial Classification Manual.* Data include non-factor charges (capital consumption allowances and indirect business taxes, etc.) as well as factor charges against gross product corporate profits and capital consumption allowances have been shifted from a company to an establishment basis. These data are not fully consistent with other gross domestic product tables because they do not yet reflect the results of the comprehensive National Income and Product Accounts revision)

INDUSTRY	CURRENT DOLLARS				CONSTANT (1982) DOLLARS			
	1980	1985	1988	1989	1980	1985	1988	1989
Gross national product	2,732	4,015	4,874	5,201	3,187	3,619	4,017	4,118
Domestic industries (gross domestic product)	2,684	3,974	4,840	5,163	3,132	3,582	3,989	4,088
Private industries	2,357	3,502	4,296	4,561	2,743	3,200	3,620	3,711
Agriculture, forestry, and fisheries	77	92	104	113	76	96	97	100
Mining	107	114	80	80	144	139	130	127
Construction	138	187	237	248	153	166	178	179
Manufacturing [1]	581	790	941	966	674	779	917	929
Durable goods [1]	352	459	527	541	408	472	571	584
Lumber and wood products	19	22	31	32	21	20	26	26
Furniture and fixtures	9	14	15	16	10	12	12	12
Stone, clay, and glass products	19	25	26	26	21	22	23	24
Primary metal industries	44	35	43	44	48	33	38	37
Fabricated metal products	46	58	65	68	54	56	66	66
Machinery, except electrical	77	83	96	97	86	124	164	175
Electric and electronic equipment	55	82	90	97	63	74	88	91
Motor vehicles and equipment	27	54	53	50	35	50	50	47
Instruments and related products	19	26	30	31	22	24	28	27
Nondurable goods	229	331	414	425	265	308	347	345
Food and kindred products	52	70	81	81	60	65	68	70
Tobacco manufactures	7	12	14	16	10	6	4	3
Textile mill products	15	17	20	21	16	16	17	17
Apparel and other textile products	17	21	24	25	21	20	22	22
Paper and allied products	23	33	46	47	26	30	35	33
Printing and publishing	32	53	66	68	37	43	47	45
Chemicals and allied products	45	64	96	99	50	59	78	76
Petroleum and coal products	17	32	35	34	23	39	44	45
Rubber and misc. plastic products	17	26	30	31	19	27	30	31
Leather and leather products	4	3	3	3	4	3	3	3
Transportation and public utilities	241	374	444	461	294	331	395	402
Transportation	106	138	165	172	117	132	154	156
Railroad transportation	21	22	22	21	23	23	27	28
Local and interurban passenger transit	5	7	9	10	6	7	6	6
Trucking and warehousing	44	59	70	73	50	61	67	69
Water transportation	7	8	8	8	8	4	4	4
Transportation by air	18	27	38	40	17	23	32	32
Pipelines, except natural gas	5	5	4	4	5	5	5	6
Transportation services	6	10	14	15	7	10	12	12
Communications	67	110	129	134	80	90	108	109
Telephone and telegraph	60	98	114	117	71	82	98	99
Radio and television broadcasting	6	11	15	16	8	8	10	11
Electric, gas, and sanitary services	68	127	150	156	97	109	134	137
Wholesale trade	194	281	317	339	200	267	291	305
Retail trade	245	377	460	486	282	354	399	412
Finance, insurance, and real estate	401	640	827	897	469	528	590	604
Banking	51	79	100	119	57	62	62	63
Credit agencies other than banks	6	12	16	20	5	7	8	8
Security and commodity brokers	10	24	42	44	11	19	36	38
Insurance carriers	37	41	62	60	39	39	37	37
Insurance agents and brokers	14	22	35	37	16	18	21	22
Real estate	282	449	562	607	335	374	413	424
Holding and other investment companies	1	12	10	8	6	9	11	11
Services [1]	374	648	885	971	451	539	623	652
Hotels and other lodging places	19	30	41	44	22	26	31	32
Personal services	19	30	39	43	22	25	29	30
Business services	69	146	202	223	84	121	148	159
Auto repair, services, and garages	21	33	41	44	25	29	28	29
Motion pictures	5	9	14	15	6	7	9	10
Amusement and recreation services	12	20	27	30	13	18	22	23
Health services	108	185	250	273	134	149	161	164
Legal services	23	46	69	75	31	34	41	42
Educational services	16	26	32	36	19	22	23	24
Social services and membership organizations	26	38	51	56	30	33	39	41
Private households	7	9	10	10	7	9	9	10
Government and government enterprises	322	477	573	619	383	401	423	431
Federal	115	171	192	208	138	146	152	152
State and local	207	306	380	411	245	254	272	278
Statistical discrepancy	*5*	*-5*	*-28*	*-17*	*6*	*-4*	*-24*	*-14*
Rest of the world	48	41	33	38	56	37	28	30

[1] Includes items not shown separately.

Source: U.S. Bureau of Economic Analysis, *Survey of Current Business,* April, 1991.

Table 2.3   Personal consumption expenditures, by type of expenditure in current and constant (1987) dollars: 1970–90. (In billions of dollars)

TYPE OF EXPENDITURE	CURRENT DOLLARS				CONSTANT (1987) DOLLARS			
	1970	1980	1985	1990	1970	1980	1985	1990
Personal consumption expenditures	**646.5**	**1,748.1**	**2,667.4**	**3,742.6**	**1,813.5**	**2,447.1**	**2,865.8**	**3,262.6**
Food and tobacco [1]	152.9	362.6	482.8	639.8	431.0	487.5	519.4	548.2
Food purchased for off-premise consumption	104.4	241.7	309.5	396.8	283.6	307.5	329.5	341.8
Purchased meals and beverages [2]	34.9	93.4	132.9	187.5	105.8	132.3	144.1	163.9
Tobacco products	10.8	20.9	31.7	43.9	33.5	38.7	36.4	32.4
Clothing, accessories, and jewelry [1]	57.6	131.8	185.9	259.7	107.8	157.1	195.5	230.0
Shoes	7.8	17.4	22.8	31.5	14.4	19.9	23.4	28.2
Clothing	39.8	89.8	129.3	177.1	66.3	106.0	135.3	159.1
Jewelry and watches	4.1	15.0	21.4	30.7	8.4	16.8	23.2	25.0
Personal care	11.8	26.9	39.9	59.1	34.0	38.0	42.4	52.2
Housing [1]	94.0	255.2	392.5	547.1	269.3	399.4	435.9	474.5
Owner-occupied nonfarm dwellings-space rent	61.3	178.4	271.0	379.7	174.4	278.7	301.3	326.8
Tenant-occupied nonfarm dwellings-rent	26.0	61.8	101.0	140.8	75.1	98.2	112.2	125.2
Household operation [1]	84.8	233.6	342.3	434.2	239.2	315.3	348.4	406.4
Furniture [3]	8.6	20.7	28.6	37.6	17.8	25.8	29.9	35.6
Semidurable house furnishings [4]	4.9	10.6	15.7	21.1	12.2	14.9	16.7	19.7
Cleaning and polishing preparations	8.2	22.9	36.7	51.4	26.4	31.2	38.8	45.4
Household utilities	22.7	81.1	119.3	135.9	92.3	111.7	116.5	123.8
Electricity	9.6	37.2	59.3	70.6	33.3	54.0	59.9	66.2
Gas	5.6	19.1	29.4	26.6	27.0	27.6	26.7	26.0
Water and other sanitary services	3.2	9.4	16.5	26.2	11.7	16.2	18.4	21.7
Fuel oil and coal	4.4	15.4	14.1	12.5	20.2	14.0	11.5	10.0
Telephone and telegraph	10.1	27.6	42.8	52.7	19.9	41.1	43.4	54.1
Medical care [1]	60.0	207.2	364.7	593.0	208.7	346.5	404.3	482.0
Drug preparations and sundries [5]	8.1	21.8	38.9	59.9	23.5	38.8	44.3	48.9
Physicians	14.0	42.8	76.3	133.5	52.7	72.9	87.9	108.3
Dentists	4.9	13.7	22.1	32.2	16.0	22.4	24.9	26.7
Hospitals and nursing homes [6]	23.4	98.7	170.4	269.2	87.1	164.0	187.4	217.8
Health insurance	4.4	12.8	22.7	34.2	13.9	23.0	22.6	25.6
Medical care [7]	2.1	7.6	19.1	28.6	10.0	17.7	18.4	20.3
Personal business [1]	32.0	101.6	184.9	289.2	119.5	175.5	216.3	248.3
Expense of handling life insurance [8]	7.1	23.4	38.8	55.1	22.6	37.8	45.0	47.5
Legal services	4.9	13.6	28.6	49.2	21.7	26.6	32.8	41.6
Funeral and burial expenses	2.3	4.6	6.6	8.2	8.2	8.8	7.5	7.2
Transportation	81.1	235.7	363.3	458.1	219.5	274.8	368.6	405.4
User-operated transportation [1]	74.2	214.9	333.5	419.3	198.8	247.4	338.8	372.2
New autos	21.9	46.4	87.4	96.6	47.4	60.2	94.5	91.5
Net purchases of used autos	4.8	10.8	24.3	35.8	20.9	20.8	27.9	33.4
Tires, tubes, accessories, etc.	6.1	14.9	18.1	22.4	10.8	15.3	18.3	21.3
Repair, greasing, washing, parking, storage, rental, and leasing	12.3	33.7	57.7	88.6	39.3	48.3	63.0	77.9
Gasoline and oil	21.9	86.7	96.9	106.8	62.9	72.0	79.2	85.0
Purchased local transportation	3.0	4.8	7.4	8.7	8.8	7.8	8.1	7.7
Mass transit systems	1.8	2.9	4.4	5.7	5.3	5.3	4.9	5.1
Taxicab	1.2	1.9	2.9	3.0	3.5	2.5	3.2	2.6
Purchased intercity transportation [1]	4.0	16.1	22.4	30.0	11.9	19.7	21.6	25.5
Railway (commutation)	0.2	0.3	0.4	0.7	0.8	0.5	0.5	0.6
Bus	0.5	1.4	1.6	1.5	2.3	2.4	1.8	1.3
Airline	3.1	13.5	18.7	25.2	8.1	15.2	17.6	21.3
Recreation [1] [9]	43.1	117.6	187.9	280.2	91.3	149.1	195.5	256.6
Magazines, newspapers, and sheet music	4.1	12.0	16.6	23.7	13.2	18.4	17.9	20.8
Nondurable toys and sport supplies	5.5	14.6	21.5	31.6	9.5	17.4	22.3	28.3
Radio and television receivers, records, and musical instruments	8.5	19.9	32.1	48.8	8.8	17.6	29.7	52.5
Education and research	12.5	33.6	54.5	86.7	41.6	51.7	59.6	74.5
Religious and welfare activities	12.1	38.6	63.3	103.8	35.4	51.3	67.7	92.0

[1] Includes other expenditures not shown separately.   [2] Consists of purchases (including tips) of meals and beverages from retail, service, and amusement establishments, hotels, dining and buffet cars, schools, school fraternities, institutions, clubs, and industrial lunch rooms. Includes meals and beverages consumed both on and off-premise.   [3] Includes mattresses and bedsprings.   [4] Consist largely of textile house furnishings including piece goods allocated to house furnishing use. Also includes lamp shades, brooms, and brushes.   [5] Excludes drug preparations and related products dispensed by physicians, hospitals, and other medical services.   [6] Consists of (1) current expenditures (including consumption of fixed capital) of nonprofit hospitals and nursing homes, and (2) payments by patients to proprietary and government hospitals and nursing homes.   [7] Consist of (1) premiums, less benefits and dividends, for health, hospitalization and accidental death and dismemberment insurance provided by commercial insurance carriers, and (2) administrative expenses (including consumption of fixed capital) of Blue Cross and Blue Shield plans and of other independent prepaid and self-insured health plans.   [8] Consist of (1) operating expenses of life insurance carriers and private noninsured pension plans, and (2) premiums, less benefits and dividends, of fraternal benefit societies. Excludes expenses allocated by commercial carriers to accident and health insurance.   [9] For additional details, see table 383.

Source: U.S. Bureau of Economic Analysis, *Survey of Current Business*, January 1992; and unpublished data.

2.5.2   EMPLOYMENT

The following tables provide a wealth of information on occupations, the changing levels of employment since 1983, and projections of employment patterns of growth and decline to 2005. It is noteworthy how women, black and Hispanic Americans fare in different occupations.

Table 2.4 Employed civilians, by occupation, sex, race, and Hispanic origin: 1983 and 1996. (For civilian non-institutional population 16 years old and over. Annual average of monthly figures. Based on Current Population Survey. Persons of Hispanic origin may be of any race)

OCCUPATION	1983				1996 [1]			
	Total employed (1,000)	Percent of total			Total employed (1,000)	Percent of total		
		Female	Black	Hispanic		Female	Black	Hispanic
Total.	100,834	43.7	9.3	5.3	126,708	46.2	10.7	9.2
Managerial and professional specialty	23,592	40.9	5.6	2.6	36,497	48.6	7.4	4.5
Executive, administrative, and managerial [2]	10,772	32.4	4.7	2.8	17,746	43.8	6.9	4.8
Officials and administrators, public	417	38.5	8.3	3.8	636	47.7	12.9	4.9
Financial managers	357	38.6	3.5	3.1	621	54.0	6.5	5.1
Personnel and labor relations managers	106	43.9	4.9	2.6	122	51.6	12.9	4.3
Purchasing managers.	82	23.6	5.1	1.4	121	45.7	4.6	6.5
Managers, marketing, advertising and public relations . .	396	21.8	2.7	1.7	655	37.8	2.9	2.8
Administrators, education and related fields	415	41.4	11.3	2.4	668	56.9	10.2	5.6
Managers, medicine and health	91	57.0	5.0	2.0	713	75.3	8.5	4.1
Managers, properties and real estate	305	42.8	5.5	5.2	530	48.0	7.7	8.1
Management-related occupations [2]	2,966	40.3	5.8	3.5	4,374	56.7	9.2	5.1
Accountants and auditors	1,105	38.7	5.5	3.3	1,538	56.0	8.8	4.8
Professional specialty [2]	12,820	48.1	6.4	2.5	18,752	53.3	7.9	4.3
Architects.	103	12.7	1.6	1.5	160	16.7	2.7	4.3
Engineers [2]	1,572	5.8	2.7	2.2	1,960	8.5	4.2	3.8
Aerospace engineers	80	6.9	1.5	2.1	80	4.8	2.7	3.5
Chemical engineers	67	6.1	3.0	1.4	95	15.2	8.7	2.4
Civil engineers.	211	4.0	1.9	3.2	243	7.2	4.7	4.3
Electrical and electronic.	450	6.1	3.4	3.1	601	8.0	4.4	3.9
Industrial engineers	210	11.0	3.3	2.4	257	13.2	2.8	5.9
Mechanical	259	2.8	3.2	1.1	350	6.9	3.9	2.4
Mathematical and computer scientists [2]	463	29.6	5.4	2.6	1,345	30.6	7.2	2.6
Computer systems analysts, scientists	276	27.8	6.2	2.7	1,093	28.1	7.2	2.5
Operations and systems researchers and analysts	142	31.3	4.9	2.2	209	42.8	8.0	3.4
Natural scientists [2].	357	20.5	2.6	2.1	536	29.3	3.3	1.9
Chemists, except biochemists.	98	23.3	4.3	1.2	149	28.6	3.7	2.1
Biological and life scientists	55	40.8	2.4	1.8	116	39.0	4.7	3.0
Medical scientists	(3)	(3)	(3)	(3)	73	48.5	4.8	3.5
Health diagnosing occupations [2]	735	13.3	2.7	3.3	960	25.5	3.7	4.3
Physicians	519	15.8	3.2	4.5	667	26.4	4.5	5.1
Dentists	126	6.7	2.4	1.0	137	13.7	1.2	0.9
Health assessment and treating occupations	1,900	85.8	7.1	2.2	2,812	85.7	8.7	3.1
Registered nurses	1,372	95.8	6.7	1.8	1,986	93.3	8.6	2.6
Pharmacists	158	26.7	3.8	2.6	184	42.6	6.8	1.3
Dietitians	71	90.8	21.0	3.7	105	90.2	29.3	7.4
Therapists [2]	247	76.3	7.6	2.7	474	73.3	6.6	4.4
Respiratory therapists	69	69.4	6.5	3.7	96	58.4	8.5	6.8
Physical therapists	55	77.0	9.7	1.5	118	61.9	3.8	4.3
Speech therapists	51	90.5	1.5	-	97	93.3	2.2	2.9
Physicians' assistants	51	36.3	7.7	4.4	63	55.9	1.8	5.2
Teachers, college and university.	606	36.3	4.4	1.8	889	43.5	6.5	4.1
Teachers, except college and university [2]	3,365	70.9	9.1	2.7	4,724	74.4	9.8	4.8
Prekindergarten and kindergarten	299	98.2	11.8	3.4	543	98.1	13.6	5.8
Elementary school	1,350	83.3	11.1	3.1	1,846	83.3	9.9	4.8
Secondary school.	1,209	51.8	7.2	2.3	1,228	55.9	7.9	5.0
Special education.	81	82.2	10.2	2.3	340	84.8	12.5	2.1
Counselors, educational and vocational	184	53.1	13.9	3.2	275	69.8	15.0	5.9
Librarians, archivists, and curators	213	84.4	7.8	1.6	202	79.8	8.0	2.9
Librarians	193	87.3	7.9	1.8	180	82.7	7.9	3.2
Social scientists and urban planners [2]	261	46.8	7.1	2.1	438	56.9	9.0	3.7
Economists.	98	37.9	6.3	2.7	148	54.4	3.9	5.4
Psychologists	135	57.1	8.6	1.1	245	61.4	12.2	3.1
Social, recreation, and religious workers [2]	831	43.1	12.1	3.8	1,332	53.8	17.1	6.4
Social workers.	407	64.3	18.2	6.3	745	68.5	22.6	7.7
Recreation workers.	65	71.9	15.7	2.0	106	74.0	13.8	5.0
Clergy	293	5.6	4.9	1.4	354	12.3	11.2	4.9
Lawyers and judges.	651	15.8	2.7	1.0	911	29.0	3.4	2.9
Lawyers	612	15.3	2.6	0.9	880	29.5	3.5	2.8
Writers, artists, entertainers, and athletes [2]	1,544	42.7	4.8	2.9	2,188	49.4	6.0	6.0
Authors	62	46.7	2.1	0.9	114	54.1	5.4	0.9
Technical writers	(3)	(3)	(3)	(3)	63	40.2	7.4	2.6
Designers	393	52.7	3.1	2.7	603	57.5	2.1	5.9
Musicians and composers	155	28.0	7.9	4.4	175	34.2	12.8	10.4
Actors and directors	60	30.8	6.6	3.4	136	41.3	10.2	7.8
Painters, sculptors, craft-artists, and artist printmakers.	186	47.4	2.1	2.3	235	50.4	1.7	5.2
Photographers.	113	20.7	4.0	3.4	141	28.6	6.8	5.5
Editors and reporters	204	48.4	2.9	2.1	280	55.7	6.5	3.3
Public relations specialists	157	50.1	6.2	1.9	150	62.0	13.0	4.6
Announcers.	(3)	(3)	(3)	(3)	62	17.4	13.1	5.6
Athletes	58	17.6	9.4	1.7	85	30.9	5.6	5.7

See footnotes at end of table.

Table 2.4 (continued)

OCCUPATION	1983				1996 [1]			
	Total employed (1,000)	Percent of total			Total employed (1,000)	Percent of total		
		Female	Black	Hispanic		Female	Black	Hispanic
Technical, sales, and administrative support	**31,265**	**64.6**	**7.6**	**4.3**	**37,683**	**64.2**	**10.3**	**7.6**
Technicians and related support	3,053	48.2	8.2	3.1	3,926	52.5	9.4	6.3
Health technologists and technicians [2]	1,111	84.3	12.7	3.1	1,605	80.6	12.2	6.7
Clinical laboratory technologists and technicians	255	76.2	10.5	2.9	376	73.3	16.1	8.7
Dental hygienists	66	98.6	1.6	-	94	98.2	-	2.9
Radiologic technicians	101	71.7	8.6	4.5	135	69.6	8.7	3.8
Licensed practical nurses	443	97.0	17.7	3.1	395	95.3	14.0	3.8
Engineering and related technologists and technicians [2]	822	18.4	6.1	3.5	919	19.9	8.5	6.1
Electrical and electronic technicians	260	12.5	8.2	4.6	361	12.7	8.2	6.5
Drafting occupations	273	17.5	5.5	2.3	233	20.9	5.6	4.5
Surveying and mapping technicians	(3)	(3)	(3)	(3)	73	12.6	10.8	4.4
Science technicians [2]	202	29.1	6.6	2.8	245	37.4	10.6	6.2
Biological technicians	52	37.7	2.9	2.0	79	57.6	9.3	4.0
Chemical technicians	82	26.9	9.5	3.5	78	26.7	14.5	7.3
Technicians, except health, engineering, and science [2]	917	35.3	5.0	2.7	1,157	42.6	5.8	6.0
Airplane pilots and navigators	69	2.1	-	1.6	114	1.4	1.4	3.5
Computer programmers	443	32.5	4.4	2.1	561	30.8	5.3	4.7
Legal assistants	128	74.0	4.3	3.6	307	82.9	7.5	8.3
Sales occupations	11,818	47.5	4.7	3.7	15,404	49.5	7.9	7.0
Supervisors and proprietors	2,958	28.4	3.6	3.4	4,501	37.5	5.4	5.9
Sales representatives, finance and business services [2]	1,853	37.2	2.7	2.2	2,529	42.9	6.1	4.8
Insurance sales	551	25.1	3.8	2.5	625	40.4	7.2	5.5
Real estate sales	570	48.9	1.3	1.5	737	49.2	3.3	4.5
Securities and financial services sales	212	23.6	3.1	1.1	406	30.4	4.5	3.5
Advertising and related sales	124	47.9	4.5	3.3	158	61.1	9.8	4.3
Sales representatives, commodities, except retail	1,442	15.1	2.1	2.2	1,559	25.0	3.1	5.0
Sales workers, retail and personal services	5,511	69.7	6.7	4.8	6,728	65.3	11.4	9.2
Cashiers	2,009	84.4	10.1	5.4	2,856	78.1	15.6	10.6
Sales-related occupations	54	58.7	2.8	1.3	87	75.8	5.3	4.8
Administrative support, including clerical	16,395	79.9	9.6	5.0	18,353	79.1	12.5	8.3
Supervisors	676	53.4	9.3	5.0	670	60.2	13.6	8.3
Computer equipment operators	605	63.9	12.5	6.0	402	60.5	13.8	7.8
Computer operators	597	63.7	12.1	6.0	398	60.2	13.3	7.9
Secretaries, stenographers, and typists [2]	4,861	98.2	7.3	4.5	3,868	97.8	10.3	6.4
Secretaries	3,891	99.0	5.8	4.0	3,164	98.6	9.3	6.2
Typists	906	95.6	13.8	6.4	595	94.8	16.9	8.1
Information clerks	1,174	88.9	8.5	5.5	1,927	89.0	10.2	8.7
Receptionists	602	96.8	7.5	6.6	960	96.9	9.8	8.3
Records processing occupations, except financial [2]	866	82.4	13.9	4.8	911	77.8	16.0	9.1
Order clerks	188	78.1	10.6	4.4	220	73.7	18.7	12.5
Personnel clerks, except payroll and time keeping	64	91.1	14.9	4.6	66	83.2	12.4	4.5
Library clerks	147	81.9	15.4	2.5	145	74.6	11.6	3.5
File clerks	287	83.5	16.7	6.1	309	77.6	18.3	11.3
Records clerks	157	82.8	11.6	5.6	163	85.2	13.7	7.5
Financial records processing [2]	2,457	89.4	4.6	3.7	2,272	91.1	6.8	6.1
Bookkeepers, accounting, and auditing clerks	1,970	91.0	4.3	3.3	1,774	91.9	5.6	5.6
Payroll and time keeping clerks	192	82.2	5.9	5.0	167	90.7	13.5	8.3
Billing clerks	146	88.4	6.2	3.9	169	88.5	12.1	8.0
Cost and rate clerks	96	75.6	5.9	5.3	57	78.7	6.1	4.4
Billing, posting, and calculating machine operators	(3)	(3)	(3)	(3)	104	89.6	7.5	9.2
Duplicating, mail and other office machine operators	68	62.6	16.0	6.1	75	63.6	13.2	13.1
Communications equipment operators	256	89.1	17.0	4.4	177	88.8	21.8	8.0
Telephone operators	244	90.4	17.0	4.3	164	90.5	21.4	7.2
Mail and message distributing occupations	799	31.6	18.1	4.5	998	37.2	21.3	9.1
Postal clerks, except mail carriers	248	36.7	26.2	5.2	310	46.8	28.3	7.9
Mail carrier, postal service	259	17.1	12.5	2.7	325	28.3	14.1	8.1
Mail clerks, except postal service	170	50.0	15.8	5.9	188	49.3	29.8	11.1
Messengers	122	26.2	16.7	5.2	175	23.7	13.1	11.1
Material recording, scheduling, and distributing [2]	1,562	37.5	10.9	6.6	1,922	44.6	14.7	9.5
Dispatchers	157	45.7	11.4	4.3	249	50.6	12.2	5.7
Production coordinators	182	44.0	6.1	2.2	214	53.3	8.6	5.0
Traffic, shipping, and receiving clerks	421	22.6	9.1	11.1	616	30.4	16.1	13.4
Stock and inventory clerks	532	38.7	13.3	5.5	497	44.2	16.4	10.5
Weighers, measurers, and checkers	79	47.2	16.9	5.8	55	54.0	18.1	9.5
Expediters	112	57.5	8.4	4.3	220	69.2	13.6	5.1
Adjusters and investigators	675	69.9	11.1	5.1	1,598	74.3	13.4	8.6
Insurance adjusters, examiners, and investigators	199	65.0	11.5	3.3	410	68.7	11.8	7.5
Investigators and adjusters, except insurance	301	70.1	11.3	4.8	907	76.3	13.5	8.1
Eligibility clerks, social welfare	69	88.7	12.9	9.4	114	87.2	12.7	16.0
Bill and account collectors	106	66.4	8.5	6.5	166	68.7	17.4	8.6
Miscellaneous administrative support [2]	2,397	85.2	12.5	5.9	3,533	84.0	13.8	10.1
General office clerks	648	80.6	12.7	5.2	762	80.8	12.1	9.9
Bank tellers	480	91.0	7.5	4.3	431	90.1	9.7	10.0
Data entry keyers	311	93.6	18.6	5.6	693	84.5	17.0	10.8
Statistical clerks	96	75.7	7.5	3.4	96	90.3	20.2	5.8
Teachers' aides	348	93.7	17.8	12.6	623	92.1	15.9	14.4

See footnotes at end of table.

Table 2.4 (continued)

OCCUPATION	1983 Total employed (1,000)	1983 Fe-male	1983 Black	1983 His-panic	1996 [1] Total employed (1,000)	1996 Fe-male	1996 Black	1996 His-panic
Service occupations	**13,857**	**60.1**	**16.6**	**6.8**	**17,177**	**59.4**	**17.2**	**13.7**
Private household [2]	980	96.1	27.8	8.5	804	94.9	17.2	26.2
Child care workers	408	96.9	7.9	3.6	276	97.1	13.1	15.2
Cleaners and servants	512	95.8	42.4	11.8	504	93.6	18.5	32.4
Protective service	1,672	12.8	13.6	4.6	2,187	17.2	17.8	8.0
Supervisors, protective service	127	4.7	7.7	3.1	184	10.5	13.1	6.0
Supervisors, police and detectives	58	4.2	9.3	1.2	97	13.6	9.2	7.2
Firefighting and fire prevention	189	1.0	6.7	4.1	231	2.1	13.5	5.6
Firefighting occupations	170	1.0	7.3	3.8	217	1.8	13.8	5.0
Police and detectives	645	9.4	13.1	4.0	960	15.8	16.0	8.2
Police and detectives, public service	412	5.7	9.5	4.4	566	12.9	12.6	8.2
Sheriffs, bailiffs, and other law enforcement officers	87	13.2	11.5	4.0	126	15.8	18.7	7.9
Correctional institution officers	146	17.8	24.0	2.8	267	21.7	22.1	8.4
Guards	711	20.6	17.0	5.6	811	24.6	22.1	8.9
Guards and police, except public service	602	13.0	18.9	6.2	686	17.3	24.1	9.2
Service except private household and protective	11,205	64.0	16.0	6.9	14,186	63.9	17.2	13.8
Food preparation and service occupations [2]	4,860	63.3	10.5	6.8	5,906	56.6	11.4	15.1
Bartenders	338	48.4	2.7	4.4	314	53.8	2.4	7.0
Waiters and waitresses	1,357	87.8	4.1	3.6	1,375	77.9	4.8	9.6
Cooks	1,452	50.0	15.8	6.5	2,061	42.2	16.4	18.5
Food counter, fountain, and related occupations	326	76.0	9.1	6.7	311	67.2	12.8	10.4
Kitchen workers, food preparation	138	77.0	13.7	8.1	257	71.3	11.0	13.0
Waiters' and waitresses' assistants	364	38.8	12.6	14.2	523	46.9	10.6	19.6
Health service occupations	1,739	89.2	23.5	4.8	2,398	88.2	29.4	8.2
Dental assistants	154	98.1	6.1	5.7	212	99.1	6.2	11.2
Health aides, except nursing	316	86.8	16.5	4.8	336	79.8	23.3	6.8
Nursing aides, orderlies, and attendants	1,269	88.7	27.3	4.7	1,850	88.4	33.2	8.1
Cleaning and building service occupations [2]	2,736	38.8	24.4	9.2	3,125	44.4	22.8	19.6
Maids and housemen	531	81.2	32.3	10.1	683	81.8	29.6	21.1
Janitors and cleaners	2,031	28.6	22.6	8.9	2,205	34.9	21.1	19.7
Personal service occupations [2]	1,870	79.2	11.1	6.0	2,756	80.7	12.4	9.5
Barbers	92	12.9	8.4	12.1	85	25.2	30.3	8.0
Hairdressers and cosmetologists	622	88.7	7.0	5.7	737	91.1	10.2	8.2
Attendants, amusement and recreation facilities	131	40.2	7.1	4.3	197	38.4	6.3	7.6
Public transportation attendants	63	74.3	11.3	5.9	95	81.2	10.3	6.7
Welfare service aides	77	92.5	24.2	10.5	96	87.3	28.4	14.0
Family child care providers	(NA)	(NA)	(NA)	(NA)	479	98.5	8.8	10.2
Early childhood teachers' assistants	(NA)	(NA)	(NA)	(NA)	387	95.4	15.3	10.3
Precision production, craft, and repair	**12,328**	**8.1**	**6.8**	**6.2**	**13,587**	**9.0**	**7.9**	**11.0**
Mechanics and repairers	4,158	3.0	6.8	5.3	4,521	4.1	7.4	9.6
Mechanics and repairers, except supervisors [2]	3,906	2.8	7.0	5.5	4,296	3.9	7.6	9.8
Vehicle and mobile equipment mechanics/repairers [2]	1,683	0.8	6.9	6.0	1,831	1.0	7.9	11.2
Automobile mechanics	800	0.5	7.8	6.0	889	1.2	7.6	13.9
Aircraft engine mechanics	95	2.5	4.0	7.6	137	1.1	11.3	6.0
Electrical and electronic equipment repairers [2]	674	7.4	7.3	4.5	662	11.0	9.7	8.7
Data processing equipment repairers	98	9.3	6.1	4.5	188	18.3	9.9	7.9
Telephone installers and repairers	247	9.9	7.8	3.7	176	13.9	11.9	5.2
Construction trades	4,289	1.8	6.6	6.0	5,108	2.5	7.5	11.7
Construction trades, except supervisors	3,784	1.9	7.1	6.1	4,443	2.5	7.9	12.2
Carpenters	1,160	1.4	5.0	5.0	1,220	1.3	6.2	9.9
Extractive occupations	196	2.3	3.3	6.0	130	2.5	6.0	7.8
Precision production occupations	3,685	21.5	7.3	7.4	3,828	23.6	9.0	11.9
Operators, fabricators, and laborers	**16,091**	**26.6**	**14.0**	**8.3**	**18,197**	**24.4**	**15.3**	**14.3**
Machine operators, assemblers, and inspectors [2]	7,744	42.1	14.0	9.4	7,874	37.7	15.2	16.4
Textile, apparel, and furnishings machine operators [2]	1,414	82.1	18.7	13.1	1,071	74.1	19.7	24.4
Textile sewing machine operators	806	94.0	15.5	14.5	595	83.3	16.7	28.1
Pressing machine operators	141	66.4	27.1	14.2	100	76.3	22.7	38.4
Fabricators, assemblers, and hand working occupations	1,715	33.7	11.3	8.7	2,071	32.4	14.3	13.6
Production inspectors, testers, samplers, and weighers	794	53.8	13.0	7.7	771	50.7	12.6	17.3
Transportation and material moving occupations	4,201	7.8	13.0	5.9	5,302	9.5	14.6	10.3
Motor vehicle operators	2,978	9.2	13.5	6.0	4,025	11.2	14.8	10.4
Trucks drivers	2,195	3.1	12.3	5.7	3,019	5.3	12.4	10.3
Transportation occupations, except motor vehicles	212	2.4	6.7	3.0	184	2.0	11.4	4.5
Material moving equipment operators	1,011	4.8	12.9	6.3	1,093	4.6	14.4	11.1
Industrial truck and tractor operators	369	5.6	19.6	8.2	512	6.2	18.5	16.1
Handlers, equipment cleaners, helpers, and laborers [2]	4,147	16.8	15.1	8.6	5,021	19.3	16.4	15.2
Freight, stock, and material handlers	1,488	15.4	15.3	7.1	1,929	23.0	16.4	12.6
Laborers, except construction	1,024	19.4	16.0	8.6	1,334	20.2	17.8	13.5
Farming, forestry, and fishing [2]	**3,700**	**16.0**	**7.5**	**8.2**	**3,566**	**19.0**	**3.9**	**19.2**
Farm operators and managers	1,450	12.1	1.3	0.7	1,314	23.1	0.5	2.7
Other agricultural and related occupations	2,072	19.9	11.7	14.0	2,096	17.5	6.0	30.5
Farm workers	1,149	24.8	11.6	15.9	840	18.8	3.4	37.3
Forestry and logging occupations	126	1.4	12.8	2.1	108	3.5	5.2	6.9

- Represents or rounds to zero.   NA Not available.   [1] See footnote 2, table 614.   [2] Includes other occupations, not shown separately.   [3] Level of total employment below 50,000.   [4] Includes clerks.

Source: U.S. Bureau of Labor Statistics, *Employment and Earnings*, monthly, January issues; and unpublished data.

Table 2.5   Civilian employment in the fastest growing and fastest declining occupations: 1994–2005. Occupations are in order of employment per cent change 1994–2005 (moderate growth). Includes wage and salary jobs, self-employed and unpaid family members. Estimates based on the Current Employment Statistics estimates and the Occupational Employment Statistics estimates. Minus sign indicates decrease)

OCCUPATION	EMPLOYMENT (1,000)				PERCENT CHANGE 1994-2005		
	1994	2005 [1]			Low	Mod-erate	High
		Low	Mod-erate	High			
Total, all occupations [2]	127,014	140,261	144,708	150,212	10.4	13.9	18.3
FASTEST GROWING							
Personal and home care aides.	179	382	391	397	114.0	118.7	122.3
Home health aides.	420	832	848	863	98.3	102.0	105.7
Systems analysts.	483	893	928	972	84.9	92.1	101.3
Computer engineers.	195	355	372	394	81.8	90.4	101.9
Physical and corrective therapy assistants and aides	78	141	142	143	82.3	83.1	84.5
Electronic pagination systems workers.	18	32	33	34	77.2	82.8	88.2
Occupational therapy assistants and aides	16	28	29	29	80.0	82.1	86.5
Physical therapists.	102	182	183	185	78.9	80.0	81.9
Residential counselors	165	284	290	295	72.7	76.5	79.5
Human services workers.	168	284	293	303	68.8	74.5	80.0
Occupational therapists.	54	91	93	95	68.7	72.2	77.3
Manicurists.	38	63	64	64	68.7	69.5	69.9
Medical assistants	206	329	327	324	59.9	59.0	57.9
Paralegals	110	170	175	179	54.3	58.3	62.4
Medical records technicians.	81	125	126	130	53.5	55.8	59.8
Teachers, special education.	388	545	593	648	40.6	53.0	67.2
Amusement and recreation attendants.	267	398	406	414	49.2	52.0	55.2
Correction officers	310	430	468	513	38.5	50.9	65.2
Operations research analysts.	44	65	67	69	45.5	50.0	55.8
Guards	867	1,248	1,282	1,322	44.0	47.9	52.5
Speech-language pathologists and audiologists.	85	120	125	130	40.3	46.0	52.8
Detectives, except public.	55	77	79	80	41.7	44.3	47.2
Surgical technologists.	46	64	65	68	39.3	42.5	48.6
Dental hygienists.	127	182	180	178	43.3	42.1	40.1
Dental assistants	190	271	269	266	43.1	41.9	40.0
Adjustment clerks	373	505	521	540	35.1	39.6	44.6
Teacher aides and educational assistants.	932	1,211	1,296	1,393	29.9	39.0	49.5
Data processing equipment repairers.	75	100	104	108	33.3	38.2	44.1
Nursery and greenhouse managers	19	26	26	26	38.3	37.5	37.3
Securities and financial services sales workers	246	328	335	343	33.6	36.6	39.5
Bill and account collectors	250	334	342	351	33.3	36.5	40.1
Respiratory therapists.	73	96	99	104	32.3	36.4	43.8
Pest controllers and assistants.	56	75	76	78	33.2	35.6	38.6
Emergency medical technicians	138	178	187	197	29.0	35.6	42.6
FASTEST DECLINING							
Letterpress operators	14	4	4	4	-72.2	-71.3	-70.5
Typesetting and composing machine operators [3]	20	6	6	6	-72.0	-71.1	-70.2
Directory assistance operators	33	10	10	10	-71.5	-70.4	-69.4
Station installers and repairers, telephone	37	10	11	11	-71.5	-70.4	-69.4
Central office operators.	48	14	14	15	-71.4	-70.3	-69.2
Billing, posting, and calculating machine operators.	96	32	32	33	-67.2	-66.7	-66.1
Data entry keyers, composing	19	6	6	7	-67.7	-66.6	-65.5
Shoe sewing machine operators and tenders	14	4	5	7	-70.9	-63.6	-53.8
Roustabouts	28	13	13	16	-54.2	-55.0	-43.5
Peripheral EDP equipment operators.	30	13	13	14	-56.9	-54.8	-52.3
Cooks, private household	9	5	5	4	-48.1	-49.2	-50.5
Motion picture projectionists.	8	4	4	4	-46.4	-47.3	-48.0
Rail yard engineers, dinkey operators, and hostlers	6	3	4	4	-44.3	-40.4	-36.5
Central office and PBX installers and repairers	84	50	51	53	-41.0	-39.1	-37.1
Computer operators, except peripheral equipment	259	157	162	168	-39.6	-37.7	-35.3
Statement clerks	25	15	16	16	-39.8	-37.7	-35.5
Housekeepers and butlers.	20	13	12	12	-36.1	-37.5	-39.1
Drilling/boring machine tool setters and set-up operators [4] . . .	45	28	30	32	-38.1	-34.9	-29.6
Fitters, structural metal, precision	14	9	9	10	-38.3	-34.6	-29.4
Mining, quarrying, and tunneling occupations	18	11	12	13	-39.5	-33.9	-27.8
Typists and word processors	646	418	434	452	-35.2	-32.8	-30.0
Photoengraving and lithographic machine operators [3].	5	3	3	3	-33.7	-32.1	-30.5
Boiler operators and tenders, low pressure.	18	12	12	13	-34.5	-31.9	-29.1
Railroad brake, signal, and switch operators	19	12	13	14	-35.8	-30.8	-26.1
Lathe and turning machine tool setters and set-up operators [4]	71	47	50	54	-34.2	-30.6	-24.9
Cement and gluing machine operators and tenders	36	24	25	27	-34.0	-30.1	-25.3
EKG technicians	16	11	11	12	-31.5	-29.7	-26.6
Machine tool cutting operators and tenders, metal and plastic .	119	80	85	92	-32.8	-28.9	-22.8
Paste-up workers.	22	16	16	17	-30.1	-27.8	-25.7
Shoe and leather workers and repairers, precision.	24	16	17	19	-33.8	-27.6	-19.4
Bank tellers	559	391	407	423	-30.1	-27.3	-24.4

[1] Based on low, moderate, or high trend assumptions.   [2] Includes other occupations, not shown separately.   [3] Includes tenders.   [4] Includes metal and plastic.

Source: U.S. Bureau of Labor Statistics, *Monthly Labor Review*, November 1995.

2.5.3 WEALTH AND POVERTY

Many of the tables reproduced here have clear links to documents and the issues they explore, which are reproduced elsewhere in this book, and that includes the following tables on wealth and poverty. The recent economic data they provide clearly shows which sections of society poverty mainly impacts upon.

Table 2.6 Money income of families — per cent distribution by income quintile and top 5 per cent: 1994

CHARACTERISTIC	Number (1,000)	PERCENT DISTRIBUTION						
		Total	Lowest fifth	Second fifth	Third fifth	Fourth fifth	Highest fifth	Top 5 percent
All families	69,313	100.0	20.0	20.0	20.0	20.0	20.0	5.0
Age of householder:								
15 to 24 years old	3,079	100.0	50.0	27.3	14.7	5.9	2.1	0.2
25 to 34 years old	14,082	100.0	24.4	21.9	21.9	20.0	11.8	2.0
35 to 44 years old	18,274	100.0	16.0	15.7	20.9	24.1	23.3	5.8
45 to 54 years old	13,746	100.0	10.7	12.7	18.7	24.1	33.9	8.7
55 to 64 years old	8,895	100.0	15.6	18.8	20.3	21.4	23.8	7.1
65 years old and over	11,236	100.0	27.6	32.5	19.0	11.2	9.7	2.5
White	58,444	100.0	17.2	19.8	20.6	20.9	21.5	5.4
Black	8,093	100.0	38.5	21.7	16.2	14.1	9.5	1.7
Hispanic origin [1]	6,202	100.0	37.2	24.3	17.5	12.3	8.7	1.7
Type of family:								
Married-couple families	53,865	100.0	12.7	18.9	21.0	23.0	24.4	6.2
Male householder, wife absent	3,228	100.0	31.0	25.6	19.1	15.2	9.1	1.8
Female householder, husband absent .	12,220	100.0	49.3	23.5	15.8	8.0	3.3	0.4
Presence of related children under 18 years old:								
No related children	32,531	100.0	16.8	21.8	20.2	19.8	21.4	5.5
One or more related children	36,782	100.0	22.9	18.4	19.8	20.2	18.8	4.6
One child	15,084	100.0	22.4	19.5	19.6	19.8	18.7	4.2
Two children or more	21,698	100.0	23.2	17.6	19.9	20.5	18.9	4.9
Education attainment of householder: [2]								
Total	66,234	100.0	18.6	19.7	20.2	20.7	20.8	5.2
Less than 9th grade	5,223	100.0	46.2	29.3	14.4	6.8	3.3	0.6
9th to 12th grade (no diploma)	6,618	100.0	39.2	26.6	18.6	10.6	5.0	0.4
High school graduate (includes equiva-lency)	21,358	100.0	19.6	23.8	24.2	20.5	11.9	1.8
Some college, no degree	12,136	100.0	14.6	19.9	23.6	24.0	18.0	3.3
Associate degree	4,669	100.0	10.7	16.8	22.8	27.3	22.4	4.1
Bachelor's degree or more	16,230	100.0	5.2	8.9	14.4	25.0	46.4	15.0
Bachelor's degree	10,101	100.0	6.2	10.5	15.8	26.8	40.7	10.9
Master's degree	3,864	100.0	3.3	6.9	14.6	24.6	50.7	15.1
Professional degree	1,302	100.0	4.1	5.3	9.4	18.3	62.9	35.7
Doctorate degree	964	100.0	3.7	5.2	6.7	18.0	66.4	30.1

[1] Persons of Hispanic origin may be of any race.   [2] 25 years old and over.

Source: U.S. Bureau of the Census, Current Population Survey, unpublished data.

Table 2.7 Money income of families — per cent distribution by income level and selected characteristics: 1993

ITEM	Number of families (1,000)	PERCENT DISTRIBUTION							Median income (dollars)
		Under $10,000	$10,000 to $14,999	$15,000 to $24,999	$25,000 to $34,999	$35,000 to $49,999	$50,000 to $74,999	$75,000 and over	
All families [1]	**68,506**	**9.6**	**7.2**	**15.5**	**14.8**	**17.9**	**19.4**	**15.5**	**36,959**
White, total.	57,881	7.3	6.6	15.1	15.1	18.8	20.6	16.6	39,300
Northeast	11,690	7.2	5.7	13.5	13.5	18.3	21.5	20.3	42,526
Midwest	14,258	6.4	5.8	14.9	15.6	20.7	21.8	14.8	40,158
South	19,461	7.8	7.6	16.4	16.0	18.4	19.0	14.9	36,504
West	12,472	7.5	6.7	14.9	14.5	17.7	20.8	17.8	39,614
Black, total	7,993	25.8	11.4	18.6	13.7	12.9	10.9	6.6	21,542
Northeast	1,298	25.1	9.6	15.3	14.1	14.0	13.4	8.5	25,002
Midwest	1,643	30.7	10.0	17.3	13.1	12.2	9.7	6.8	20,794
South	4,461	25.2	12.6	20.2	13.3	13.2	10.2	5.4	20,372
West	591	18.8	10.0	17.6	17.1	10.8	15.1	11.2	26,182
Hispanic, [2] total	5,946	17.9	12.5	22.2	16.6	14.0	11.4	5.4	23,654
Northeast	1,001	28.4	11.9	19.5	13.6	12.7	8.5	5.5	19,580
Midwest	405	15.1	10.6	20.2	17.5	18.0	13.6	5.2	27,501
South	1,915	17.0	13.3	23.1	16.9	12.4	11.1	6.2	23,651
West	2,624	15.0	12.3	22.9	17.3	14.9	12.4	4.9	24,781
Presence of related children under 18 years old:									
All families	68,506	9.6	7.2	15.5	14.8	17.9	19.4	15.5	36,959
No children	32,050	5.5	7.4	17.1	15.9	17.7	19.7	16.6	37,849
One or more children	36,456	13.2	7.1	14.2	13.9	18.1	19.1	14.5	36,200
Married-couple families	53,181	4.4	5.5	14.1	14.9	19.5	22.7	18.9	43,005
No children	27,060	4.7	6.7	16.2	15.6	17.6	20.8	18.5	40,293
One or more children	26,121	4.2	4.2	11.8	14.2	21.6	24.7	19.4	45,548
Female householder, no husband present	12,411	30.8	14.0	20.3	14.0	11.2	7.1	2.7	17,443
No children	3,653	10.9	11.8	22.5	18.0	18.0	13.1	5.6	27,184
One or more children	8,758	39.1	15.0	19.4	12.3	8.3	4.5	1.5	13,472

[1] Includes other races not shown separately.   [2] Persons of Hispanic origin may be of any race.

Source of tables 721 and 722: U.S. Bureau of the Census, *Current Population Reports*, P60-188; and unpublished data.

Table 2.8 Money income of persons — per cent distribution, by income level in constant (1993) dollars: 1970–93. (As of March of following year. For 1970, persons 14 years old and over; thereafter, 15 years old and over)

ITEM	All persons (mil.)	PERSONS WITH INCOME									Median income (dollars)
		Total (mil.)	Percent distribution								
			$1 to $2,499 or loss [1]	$2,500 to $4,999	$5,000 to $9,999	$10,000 to $14,999	$15,000 to $24,999	$25,000 to $49,999	$50,000 to $74,999	$75,000 and over	
MALE											
1970	70.6	65.0	8.3	5.9	10.8	9.8	19.5	35.6	7.1	3.1	23,337
1980	82.9	78.7	7.2	5.1	11.9	11.1	20.0	32.9	8.1	3.6	22,000
1981	84.0	79.7	7.6	5.8	12.1	10.9	20.1	32.1	7.8	3.6	21,608
1982 [2]	85.0	79.7	8.2	5.6	12.2	10.6	21.1	30.6	7.6	4.0	21,086
1983 [2]	86.0	80.8	8.3	5.6	12.1	11.7	20.1	30.1	8.4	3.8	21,220
1984	87.3	82.2	7.6	5.5	12.6	11.1	19.0	31.3	8.7	4.1	21,696
1985	88.5	83.6	7.3	5.5	12.0	11.6	19.8	30.6	8.9	4.3	21,905
1986	89.4	84.5	7.0	5.1	11.8	11.1	19.3	31.3	9.6	4.8	22,564
1987 [3]	90.3	85.7	6.7	5.1	11.6	11.1	19.7	31.0	9.8	5.0	22,624
1988	91.0	86.6	6.7	4.9	11.7	11.0	20.1	31.1	9.5	5.0	23,096
1989	92.0	87.5	6.3	4.7	11.6	11.2	20.5	30.7	9.4	5.5	23,182
1990	92.8	88.2	6.4	4.7	12.3	11.5	20.9	30.4	9.0	5.0	22,436
1991	93.8	88.7	6.4	5.1	12.5	12.4	20.3	30.2	8.4	4.8	21,716
1992 [4]	94.9	89.6	6.9	5.1	12.9	12.3	20.6	29.0	8.4	4.8	21,067
1993	**96.8**	**90.2**	**7.0**	**4.9**	**12.1**	**12.4**	**20.8**	**28.8**	**8.7**	**5.2**	**21,102**
15 to 24 years old	18.2	13.8	27.7	15.0	21.0	14.9	15.2	5.6	0.5	0.2	6,429
25 to 34 years old	20.9	20.2	3.7	3.7	9.5	12.8	27.8	33.8	6.3	2.4	21,927
35 to 44 years old	20.5	19.9	3.7	2.2	6.9	8.1	18.9	39.3	13.3	7.6	30,342
45 to 54 years old	14.5	14.1	3.6	1.9	7.0	7.1	15.4	37.2	16.5	11.2	33,154
55 to 64 years old	9.9	9.6	3.8	3.1	11.0	11.7	20.1	31.6	10.7	7.9	25,139
65 yr. old and over	12.7	12.6	1.4	4.6	21.6	22.5	25.2	18.1	4.0	2.6	14,983
White	82.0	77.7	6.5	4.5	11.3	12.2	20.7	29.8	9.3	5.7	21,981
Black	10.6	8.9	11.1	7.5	18.0	14.1	21.8	22.2	4.1	1.2	14,605
Hispanic [5]	9.3	8.2	7.8	7.1	20.1	18.5	23.1	18.4	3.5	1.4	13,689
Northeast	19.3	17.9	6.4	4.8	11.3	11.8	19.9	29.5	10.0	6.3	22,283
Midwest	22.5	21.4	7.0	4.9	10.7	12.4	21.2	31.2	8.7	4.1	21,696
South	33.5	31.0	7.4	5.2	13.7	13.0	21.4	26.6	7.8	4.8	19,714
West	21.4	19.9	7.0	4.3	12.2	12.1	20.1	29.1	9.0	6.1	21,536
FEMALE											
1970	77.6	51.6	20.8	16.3	20.4	15.0	18.0	8.9	0.5	0.2	7,827
1980	91.1	80.8	20.3	12.8	22.3	14.4	18.3	10.8	0.8	0.3	8,638
1981	92.2	82.1	19.9	12.6	22.8	14.1	18.6	11.0	0.8	0.2	8,753
1982 [2]	93.1	82.5	19.8	12.2	22.4	13.6	18.9	11.7	1.0	0.4	8,898
1983 [2]	94.3	83.8	18.9	12.1	21.7	14.6	18.4	12.7	1.2	0.4	9,292
1984	95.3	85.6	18.1	11.9	22.0	14.1	18.2	13.9	1.4	0.5	9,552
1985	96.4	86.5	17.7	12.0	21.7	14.0	18.1	14.4	1.5	0.5	9,692
1986	97.3	87.8	17.1	11.6	21.6	13.7	18.4	15.2	1.7	0.6	10,033
1987 [3]	98.2	89.7	16.0	11.4	21.2	13.8	19.1	15.8	1.9	0.7	10,551
1988	99.0	90.6	15.9	11.1	21.3	14.0	18.9	16.1	2.1	0.7	10,852
1989	99.8	91.4	15.1	11.1	20.6	13.9	19.6	16.6	2.2	0.8	11,215
1990	100.7	92.2	14.9	11.2	20.9	14.4	19.1	16.4	2.3	0.8	11,133
1991	101.5	92.6	14.3	10.8	21.7	14.9	19.0	16.3	2.2	0.8	11,114
1992 [4]	102.4	93.2	14.6	10.9	21.3	14.7	18.7	16.7	2.2	0.8	11,035
1993	**104.0**	**94.4**	**14.1**	**10.9**	**21.4**	**14.4**	**19.1**	**16.5**	**2.6**	**0.9**	**11,046**
15 to 24 years old	18.1	13.5	30.5	17.4	23.5	13.2	12.2	3.0	0.1	0.1	5,351
25 to 34 years old	21.1	19.6	13.2	8.4	16.3	14.5	24.1	20.6	2.3	0.6	13,988
35 to 44 years old	21.0	19.7	13.0	7.1	14.6	13.3	21.5	25.0	4.0	1.7	15,844
45 to 54 years old	15.1	14.0	12.8	5.9	14.7	13.2	22.5	24.7	4.9	1.5	16,324
55 to 64 years old	10.8	10.0	15.8	11.2	20.3	14.1	18.4	16.1	3.0	1.1	10,829
65 yr. old and over	18.0	17.7	4.0	16.7	38.9	17.9	14.2	6.7	1.2	0.5	8,499
White	86.8	79.5	14.2	10.4	21.0	14.5	19.3	16.9	2.7	1.0	11,266
Black	12.9	11.3	11.8	14.7	25.3	14.7	17.7	13.8	1.5	0.5	9,508
Hispanic [5]	9.1	7.1	16.3	14.5	27.1	15.3	15.7	9.8	1.0	0.4	8,100
Northeast	21.3	19.5	13.3	10.6	21.8	13.1	18.4	17.8	3.5	1.4	11,375
Midwest	24.5	22.9	14.0	11.0	21.4	14.8	20.3	16.0	2.0	0.6	11,031
South	36.4	32.4	14.4	11.7	22.0	14.9	19.2	15.1	2.1	0.7	10,557
West	21.9	19.6	14.6	9.8	19.9	14.6	18.3	18.2	3.2	1.3	11,568

[1] Includes persons with income deficit.　[2] Beginning 1983, data based on revised Hispanic population controls and not directly comparable with prior years.　[3] Beginning 1987, data based on revised processing procedures and not directly comparable with prior years.　[4] Based on 1990 populations controls.　[5] Persons of Hispanic origin may be of any race.

Source: U.S. Bureau of the Census, *Current Population Reports*, P60-188; and unpublished data.

Table 2.9 Families below poverty level and below 125 per cent of poverty level: 1960–95. (Families as of March of the following year)

YEAR	NUMBER BELOW POVERTY LEVEL (1,000)				PERCENT BELOW POVERTY LEVEL				BELOW 125 PERCENT OF POVERTY LEVEL	
	All races [1]	White	Black	His-panic [2]	All races [1]	White	Black	His-panic [2]	Number (1,000)	Percent
1960	8,243	6,115	(NA)	(NA)	18.1	14.9	(NA)	(NA)	11,525	25.4
1970	5,260	3,708	1,481	(NA)	10.1	8.0	29.5	(NA)	7,516	14.4
1971	5,303	3,751	1,484	(NA)	10.0	7.9	28.8	(NA)	(NA)	(NA)
1972	5,075	3,441	1,529	477	9.3	7.1	29.0	20.6	7,347	13.5
1973	4,828	3,219	1,527	468	8.8	6.6	28.1	19.8	7,044	12.8
1974	4,922	3,352	1,479	526	8.8	6.8	26.9	21.2	7,195	12.9
1975	5,450	3,838	1,513	627	9.7	7.7	27.1	25.1	7,974	14.2
1976	5,311	3,560	1,617	598	9.4	7.1	27.9	23.1	7,647	13.5
1977	5,311	3,540	1,637	591	9.3	7.0	28.2	21.4	7,713	13.5
1978	5,280	3,523	1,622	559	9.1	6.9	27.5	20.4	7,417	12.8
1979 [3]	5,461	3,581	1,722	614	9.2	6.9	27.8	20.3	7,784	13.1
1980	6,217	4,195	1,826	751	10.3	8.0	28.9	23.2	8,764	14.5
1981	6,851	4,670	1,972	792	11.2	8.8	30.8	24.0	9,568	15.7
1982	7,512	5,118	2,158	916	12.2	9.6	33.0	27.2	10,279	16.7
1983 [4]	7,647	5,220	2,161	981	12.3	9.7	32.3	25.9	10,358	16.7
1984	7,277	4,925	2,094	991	11.6	9.1	30.9	25.2	9,901	15.8
1985	7,223	4,983	1,983	1,074	11.4	9.1	28.7	25.5	9,753	15.3
1986	7,023	4,811	1,987	1,085	10.9	8.6	28.0	24.7	9,476	14.7
1987 [5]	7,005	4,567	2,117	1,168	10.7	8.1	29.4	25.5	9,338	14.3
1988	6,874	4,471	2,089	1,141	10.4	7.9	28.2	23.7	9,284	14.1
1989	6,784	4,409	2,077	1,133	10.3	7.8	27.8	23.4	9,267	14.0
1990	7,098	4,622	2,193	1,244	10.7	8.1	29.3	25.0	9,564	14.4
1991	7,712	5,022	2,343	1,372	11.5	8.8	30.4	26.5	10,244	15.3
1992 [6]	8,144	5,255	2,484	1,529	11.9	9.1	31.1	26.7	10,959	16.1
1993	8,393	5,452	2,499	1,625	12.3	9.4	31.3	27.3	11,203	16.4
1994	8,053	5,312	2,212	1,724	11.6	9.1	27.3	27.8	10,771	15.5
1995	7,532	4,994	2,127	1,695	10.8	8.5	26.4	27.0	10,223	14.7

NA Not available.   [1] Includes other races not shown separately.   [2] Persons of Hispanic origin may be of any race.
[3] Population controls based on 1980 census; see text, section 14.   [4] Beginning 1983, data based on revised Hispanic population controls and not directly comparable with prior years.   [5] Beginning 1987, data based on revised processing procedures and not directly comparable with prior years.   [6] Beginning 1992, based on 1990 population controls.

Source: U.S. Bureau of the Census, *Current Population Reports*, P60-194.

Table 2.10 Families below poverty level — selected characteristics, by race and Hispanic origin: 1990. (Families as of March 1991)

CHARACTERISTIC	NUMBER BELOW POVERTY LEVEL (1,000)				PERCENT BELOW POVERTY LEVEL			
	All races [1]	White	Black	His-panic [2]	All races [1]	White	Black	His-panic [2]
Total	**7,098**	**4,622**	**2,193**	**1,244**	**10.7**	**8.1**	**29.3**	**25.0**
Age of householder:								
15 to 24 years old	955	617	311	182	35.0	28.5	65.3	43.0
25 to 34 years old	2,377	1,568	734	441	16.3	12.9	37.8	29.5
35 to 44 years old	1,648	1,063	482	322	9.6	7.4	23.8	24.4
45 to 54 years old	806	508	263	161	6.9	5.1	21.0	20.0
55 to 64 years old	627	422	180	67	6.7	5.1	21.0	12.7
65 years old and over	686	443	224	69	6.3	4.5	24.2	17.0
Northeast	1,234	839	360	297	9.2	7.1	27.4	33.8
Midwest	1,583	1,050	479	73	9.8	7.3	33.3	22.5
South	2,942	1,661	1,231	385	12.6	8.9	29.5	23.8
West	1,339	1,072	123	488	9.9	9.1	22.4	22.6
Size of family:								
Two persons	2,234	1,587	566	235	8.1	6.5	22.7	19.1
Three persons	1,698	1,053	587	285	11.1	8.1	30.3	24.0
Four persons	1,507	954	488	295	10.7	8.0	30.5	25.8
Five persons	876	570	284	214	14.7	11.6	36.0	27.5
Six persons	415	275	108	117	20.2	17.1	33.0	34.2
Seven persons or more	368	183	160	98	28.6	21.3	50.0	32.9
Mean size	3.55	3.45	3.71	4.09	(X)	(X)	(X)	(X)
Mean number of children per family with children .	2.24	2.17	2.34	2.53	(X)	(X)	(X)	(X)
Education of householder: [3]								
Elementary: Less than 8 years	910	595	268	344	26.3	22.6	38.7	31.6
8 years	479	365	107	104	17.0	14.6	39.5	34.5
High school: 1 to 3 years	1,460	889	540	270	20.7	15.9	41.5	35.9
4 years	2,188	1,411	703	190	9.3	6.9	26.2	15.0
College: 1 year or more	996	675	238	93	3.8	2.9	11.9	9.3
Work experience of householder in 1989: [4]								
Total [5]	7,098	4,622	2,193	1,244	10.7	8.1	29.3	25.0
Worked	3,533	2,481	931	626	7.0	5.6	18.1	16.7
50 to 52 weeks	1,442	1,029	360	291	3.6	2.9	9.6	10.7
49 weeks or less	2,091	1,452	571	335	19.5	16.1	40.8	32.5
Did not work	3,527	2,114	1,252	614	23.7	17.2	56.7	51.8

X Not applicable.   [1] Includes other races not shown separately.   [2] Hispanic persons may be of any race.   [3] Householder 25 years old and over.   [4] Restricted to families with civilian workers.   [5] Includes Armed Forces not shown separately.
Source: U.S. Bureau of the Census, *Current Population Reports*, series P-60, No. 175.

Table 2.11 Social and economic characteristics of the white and black populations: 1990–96. (As of March, except labor force status, annual average. Excludes members of the Armed Forces except those living off post or with their families on post. Data for 1990 are based on 1980 census population controls; 1995 and 1996 data based on 1990 census population controls. Based on Current Population Survey)

CHARACTERISTIC	NUMBER (1,000)						PERCENT DISTRIBUTION			
	White			Black			White		Black	
	1990	1995	1996	1990	1995	1996	1990	1996	1990	1996
Total persons	206,983	216,751	218,442	30,392	33,531	33,889	100.0	100.0	100.0	100.0
Under 5 years old	15,161	15,915	15,736	2,932	3,342	3,243	7.3	7.2	9.6	9.6
5 to 14 years old	28,405	30,786	31,110	5,546	6,268	6,432	13.7	14.2	18.2	19.0
15 to 44 years old	96,656	97,876	98,146	14,660	16,101	16,154	46.6	44.9	48.2	47.7
45 to 64 years old	40,282	44,189	45,016	4,766	5,264	5,582	19.5	20.6	15.7	16.5
65 years old and over.	26,479	27,985	28,436	2,487	2,557	2,478	12.8	13.0	8.2	7.3
EDUCATIONAL ATTAINMENT										
Persons 25 years old and over	134,687	141,113	142,733	16,751	18,457	18,715	100.0	100.0	100.0	100.0
Elementary: 0 to 8 years	14,131	11,101	11,141	2,701	1,800	1,734	10.5	7.8	16.1	9.3
High school: 1 to 3 years	14,080	[1]12,882	[1]13,461	2,969	[1]3,041	[1]3,085	10.5	[1]9.4	17.7	[1]16.5
4 years	52,449	[2]47,986	[2]48,356	6,239	[2]6,686	[2]6,576	38.9	[2]33.9	37.2	[2]35.1
College: 1 to 3 years	24,350	[3]35,321	[3]35,161	2,952	[3]4,486	[3]4,769	18.1	[3]24.6	17.6	[3]25.5
4 years or more.	29,677	[4]33,824	[4]34,614	1,890	[4]2,444	[4]2,551	22.0	[4]24.3	11.3	[4]13.6
LABOR FORCE STATUS [5]										
Civilians 16 years old and over	160,625	166,914	168,317	21,477	23,246	23,604	100.0	100.0	100.0	100.0
Civilian labor force	107,447	111,950	113,108	13,740	14,817	15,134	66.9	67.2	64.0	64.1
Employed	102,261	106,490	107,808	12,175	13,279	13,542	63.7	64.1	56.7	57.4
Unemployed	5,186	5,459	5,300	1,565	1,538	1,592	3.2	3.1	7.3	6.7
Unemployment rate [6]	4.8	4.9	4.7	11.4	10.4	10.5	(X)	(X)	(X)	(X)
Not in labor force.	53,178	54,965	55,209	7,737	8,429	8,470	33.1	32.8	36.0	35.9
FAMILY TYPE										
Total families . . . . . [7] . . .	56,590	58,437	58,869	7,470	8,093	8,055	100.0	100.0	100.0	100.0
With own children [7]	26,718	27,951	28,086	4,378	4,682	4,583	47.2	47.7	58.6	56.9
Married couple	46,981	47,899	47,873	3,750	3,842	3,713	83.0	81.3	50.2	46.1
With own children [7]	21,579	22,005	21,835	1,972	1,926	1,901	38.1	37.1	26.4	23.6
Female householder, no spouse present	7,306	8,031	8,284	3,275	3,716	3,769	12.9	14.1	43.8	46.8
With own children [7].	4,199	4,841	4,975	2,232	2,489	2,404	7.4	8.5	29.9	29.8
Male householder, no spouse present . . . [7] . . .	2,303	2,507	2,712	446	536	573	4.1	4.6	6.0	7.1
With own children [7].	939	1,105	1,276	173	267	278	1.7	2.2	2.3	3.4
FAMILY INCOME IN PREVIOUS YEAR IN CONSTANT (1995) DOLLARS										
Total families	56,590	58,437	58,869	7,470	8,093	8,055	100.0	100.0	100.0	100.0
Less than $5,000.	1,132	1,286	1,163	627	647	632	2.0	2.0	8.4	7.9
$5,000 to $9,999	2,037	2,572	2,228	934	1,028	926	3.6	3.8	12.5	11.5
$10,000 to $14,999	3,056	3,507	3,425	837	882	881	5.4	5.8	11.2	10.9
$15,000 to $24,999	7,413	8,299	8,204	1,374	1,449	1,478	13.1	13.9	18.4	18.3
$25,000 to $34,999	7,696	8,299	8,372	956	1,117	1,149	13.6	14.2	12.8	14.3
$35,000-$49,999	11,148	10,754	11,095	1,173	1,198	1,279	19.7	18.8	15.7	15.9
$50,000 or more	24,051	23,728	24,385	1,569	1,772	1,710	42.5	41.4	21.0	21.3
Median income (dol.) [8]	44,214	42,043	42,646	24,838	25,398	25,970	(X)	(X)	(X)	(X)
Families below poverty level [9] .	4,409	5,312	4,994	2,077	2,212	2,127	7.8	8.5	27.8	26.4
Persons below poverty level [9] .	20,785	25,379	24,423	9,302	10,196	9,872	10.0	11.2	30.7	29.3
HOUSING TENURE										
Total occupied units	80,163	83,737	84,511	10,486	11,655	11,577	100.0	100.0	100.0	100.0
Owner-occupied	54,094	57,449	58,282	4,445	4,888	5,085	67.5	69.0	42.4	43.9
Renter-occupied	24,685	24,793	24,798	5,862	6,547	6,290	30.8	29.3	55.9	54.3
No cash rent.	1,384	1,494	1,430	178	220	201	1.7	1.7	1.7	1.7

X Not applicable. [1] Represents those who completed ninth to twelfth grade, but have no high school diploma. [2] High school graduate. [3] Some college or associate degree. [4] Bachelor's or advanced degree. [5] Source: U.S. Bureau of Labor Statistics, *Employment and Earnings*, January issues. [6] Total unemployment as percent of civilian labor force. [7] Children under 18 years old. [8] For definition of median, see Guide to Tabular Presentation. [9] For explanation of poverty level, see text, section 14.

Source: Except as noted, U.S. Bureau of the Census, *Current Population Reports*, P20-448, and earlier reports; P60-193; and unpublished data.

Table 2.12 Social and economic characteristics of the Hispanic population: 1995. (As of March, except labor force status, annual average. Excludes members of the Armed Forces except those living off post or with their families on post. Based on Current Population Survey)

CHARACTERISTIC	NUMBER (1,000)						PERCENT DISTRIBUTION					
	Hispanic, total	Mexican	Puerto Rican	Cuban	Central and South American	Other Hispanic	Hispanic, total	Mexican	Puerto Rican	Cuban	Central and South American	Other Hispanic
Total persons	27,521	17,982	2,730	1,156	3,686	1,967	100.0	100.0	100.0	100.0	100.0	100.0
Under 5 years old	3,318	2,413	272	68	360	205	12.1	13.4	10.0	5.9	9.8	10.4
5 to 14 years old	5,215	3,611	539	131	577	356	18.9	20.1	19.7	11.3	15.7	18.1
15 to 44 years old	13,894	9,049	1,323	486	2,102	933	50.5	50.3	48.5	42.0	57.0	47.4
45 to 64 years old	3,666	2,127	466	265	489	320	13.3	11.8	17.1	22.9	13.3	16.3
65 years old and over	1,428	781	130	207	159	154	5.2	4.3	4.8	17.9	4.3	7.8
EDUCATIONAL ATTAINMENT												
Persons 25 years old and over	14,171	8,737	1,437	820	2,082	1,095	100.0	100.0	100.0	100.0	100.0	100.0
High school graduate or higher	7,563	4,067	880	531	1,337	749	53.4	46.5	61.3	64.7	64.2	68.4
Bachelor's degree or higher	1,312	572	153	158	272	156	9.3	6.5	10.7	19.3	13.1	14.2
LABOR FORCE STATUS [1]												
Civilians 16 years old and over	18,629	11,609	1,896	1,019	2,686	1,419	100.0	100.0	100.0	100.0	100.0	100.0
Civilian labor force	12,267	7,765	1,098	613	1,885	906	65.8	66.9	57.9	60.2	70.2	63.8
Employed	11,127	7,016	974	568	1,734	835	59.7	60.4	51.4	55.7	64.6	58.8
Unemployed	1,140	750	123	45	150	72	6.1	6.5	6.5	4.4	5.6	5.1
Unemployment rate [2]	9.3	9.7	11.2	7.4	8.0	7.9	(X)	(X)	(X)	(X)	(X)	(X)
Not in labor force	6,362	3,844	798	406	802	512	34.2	33.1	42.1	39.8	29.9	36.1
FAMILY TYPE												
Total families	6,200	3,847	729	315	817	491	100.0	100.0	100.0	100.0	100.0	100.0
Married couple	4,235	2,745	386	235	541	328	68.3	71.4	52.9	74.6	66.1	66.8
Female householder, no spouse present	1,485	766	300	67	208	145	24.0	19.9	41.2	21.3	25.4	29.5
Male householder, no spouse present	479	336	43	13	69	18	7.7	8.7	5.9	4.0	8.5	3.7
FAMILY INCOME IN 1994												
Total families	6,200	3,847	729	315	817	491	100.0	100.0	100.0	100.0	100.0	100.0
Less than $5,000	375	232	54	14	45	30	6.0	6.0	7.4	4.4	5.6	6.0
$5,000 to $9,999	730	446	136	27	73	49	11.8	11.6	18.6	8.5	8.9	9.9
$10,000 to $14,999	779	517	97	24	92	50	12.6	13.4	13.3	7.5	11.3	10.1
$15,000 to $24,999	1,301	844	122	68	180	88	21.0	21.9	16.7	21.5	22.0	17.9
$25,000 to $34,999	923	583	92	46	133	68	14.9	15.2	12.6	14.5	16.3	13.9
$35,000 to $49,999	924	575	80	38	139	92	14.9	14.9	10.9	12.0	17.1	18.7
$50,000 or more	1,168	650	149	100	154	115	18.8	16.9	20.4	31.7	18.8	23.4
Median income (dol.) [3]	24,313	23,609	20,929	30,584	26,558	28,658	(X)	(X)	(X)	(X)	(X)	(X)
Families below poverty level [4]	1,724	1,138	242	43	196	105	27.8	29.6	33.2	13.6	23.9	21.4
Persons below poverty level [4]	8,416	5,781	981	205	949	500	30.7	32.3	36.0	17.8	25.8	25.5
HOUSING TENURE												
Total occupied units	7,735	4,653	935	451	1,040	656	100.0	100.0	100.0	100.0	100.0	100.0
Owner-occupied [5]	3,278	2,145	268	236	304	325	42.4	46.1	28.7	52.3	29.2	49.6
Renter-occupied [5]	4,457	2,508	667	215	736	331	57.6	53.9	71.3	47.7	70.8	50.4

X Not applicable.   [1] Source: U.S. Bureau of Labor Statistics, *Employment and Earnings*, January 1996.   [2] Total unemployment as percent of civilian labor force.   [3] For definition of median, see Guide to Tabular Presentation.   [4] For explanation of poverty level, see text, section 14.   [5] Includes no cash rent.

Source: Except as noted, U.S. Bureau of the Census, unpublished data.

2.5.4   HEALTH EXPENDITURE AND INSURANCE

Health care is one of the most important political and economic issues in the United States today. America spends a vast amount of money on health and at their best American medical services are second to none. However, the debate over public and private expenditure continues and the key issue of millions of Americans with little or no health insurance coverage (the principal method of paying for the almost inevitably high cost of medical treatment) remains and is likely to do so for some time.

Table 2.13   National health expenditures: 1960–94. (Includes Puerto Rico and outlying areas)

YEAR	TOTAL[1] Total (bil.dol.)	Per capita (dol.)	Percent of GDP[2]	HEALTH SERVICES AND SUPPLIES — Private — Total[3] (bil.dol.)	Out-of-pocket payments Total (bil.dol.)	Percent of total private	Insurance premiums[4] (bil.dol.)	Public Total (bil.dol.)	Medical payments Medicare (bil.dol.)	Public assistance (bil.dol.)
1960	26.9	141	5.1	19.5	13.1	67.2	5.9	5.7	(X)	0.5
1965	41.1	202	5.7	29.4	18.5	62.9	10.0	8.3	(X)	1.7
1970	73.2	341	7.1	43.0	24.9	57.9	16.3	24.9	7.7	6.3
1971	81.0	373	7.2	46.9	26.4	56.3	18.6	28.1	8.5	7.7
1972	90.9	415	7.4	52.5	29.0	55.2	21.3	31.8	9.4	8.9
1973	100.8	456	7.3	58.2	32.0	55.0	23.9	35.9	10.8	10.2
1974	114.3	513	7.6	64.3	34.8	54.1	26.8	42.7	13.5	11.9
1975	130.7	582	8.0	72.3	38.1	52.7	31.3	50.1	16.4	14.5
1976	149.9	662	8.2	83.8	41.9	50.0	37.9	56.7	19.8	16.4
1977	170.4	746	8.4	96.6	46.4	48.0	45.9	64.5	23.0	18.8
1978	190.6	827	8.3	107.4	49.7	46.3	52.5	73.3	26.8	20.9
1979	215.2	924	8.4	121.2	54.3	44.8	60.9	83.7	31.0	24.0
1980	247.2	1,052	8.9	138.0	60.3	43.7	69.7	97.6	37.5	28.0
1981	286.9	1,208	9.2	160.3	68.5	42.7	82.1	113.4	44.9	32.6
1982	322.9	1,346	10.0	181.8	75.5	41.5	95.3	126.4	52.5	34.6
1983	355.2	1,467	10.1	200.3	82.3	41.1	106.1	138.9	59.8	38.0
1984	389.7	1,594	10.0	222.4	90.8	40.8	118.8	150.9	66.5	41.1
1985	428.2	1,735	10.2	247.4	100.6	40.7	132.3	164.4	72.2	44.4
1986	460.9	1,849	10.4	264.4	108.0	40.8	140.1	179.7	76.9	49.0
1987	500.1	1,987	10.7	285.7	116.0	40.6	152.1	196.1	82.6	54.0
1988	559.6	2,201	11.1	324.5	129.2	39.8	175.1	213.9	90.4	58.9
1989	622.0	2,422	11.4	360.8	136.2	37.7	203.8	239.0	102.5	66.4
1990	697.5	2,688	12.1	402.9	148.4	36.8	232.4	270.0	112.1	80.4
1991	761.3	2,902	12.9	430.9	155.1	36.0	251.9	305.5	123.0	99.2
1992	833.6	3,144	13.3	465.9	164.4	35.3	276.6	340.1	138.7	112.4
1993	892.3	3,331	13.6	493.1	169.4	34.4	296.5	370.0	151.7	124.4
1994	949.4	3,510	13.7	517.1	174.9	33.8	313.3	402.2	169.2	134.8

X Not applicable. [1] Includes medical research and medical facilities construction. [2] GDP=Gross domestic product; see table 687. [3] Includes other sources of funds not shown separately. [4] See footnote 2, table 155.

Source: U. S. Health Care Financing Administration, *Health Care Financing Review*, spring 1996.

☆☆

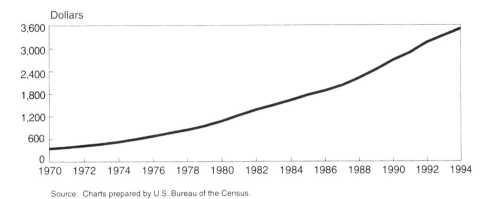

Source: Charts prepared by U.S. Bureau of the Census.

Figure 2.1   *Personal health care expenditures per capita: 1970–94*

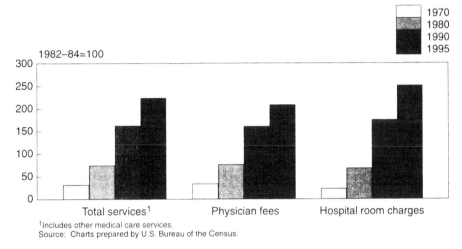

1Includes other medical care services.
Source: Charts prepared by U.S. Bureau of the Census.

Figure 2.2   *Consumer price indexes — medical services: 1970–95*

Table 2.14 National health expenditures, by type: 1980–95. (In millions of dollars, except per cent. Includes Puerto Rico and outlying areas)

TYPE OF EXPENDITURE	1980	1985	1990	1991	1992	1993	1994	1995
Total	**247,245**	**428,204**	**697,453**	**761,704**	**834,226**	**892,074**	**937,139**	**988,489**
Annual percent change [1]	14.9	9.5	12.1	9.2	9.5	6.9	5.1	5.5
Private expenditures	**142,463**	**253,903**	**413,145**	**441,409**	**478,780**	**505,548**	**517,250**	**532,089**
Health services and supplies	138,010	247,403	402,896	431,286	467,774	493,651	505,478	521,152
Out-of-pocket payments	60,254	100,595	148,390	154,984	165,763	171,590	175,972	182,563
Insurance premiums [2]	69,728	132,254	232,436	252,312	277,015	295,413	302,691	310,616
Other	8,028	14,554	22,071	23,990	24,996	26,647	26,815	27,972
Medical research	292	538	960	1,090	1,183	1,215	1,276	1,372
Medical facilities construction	4,161	5,962	9,288	9,033	9,824	10,682	10,496	9,566
Public expenditures	**104,782**	**174,301**	**284,309**	**320,295**	**355,446**	**386,526**	**419,889**	**456,400**
Percent Federal of public	68.7	70.7	68.9	70.1	71.4	71.8	71.9	72.0
Health services and supplies	97,599	164,430	270,033	305,486	338,910	369,415	401,234	436,678
Medicare [3]	37,519	72,186	112,091	123,017	138,280	150,927	167,602	187,024
Public assistance medical payments [4]	28,033	44,439	80,395	99,235	111,917	124,833	135,440	146,411
Temporary disability insurance [5]	52	51	62	66	70	52	51	50
Workers' compensation (medical) [5]	5,141	7,971	16,067	17,163	18,984	18,909	19,147	19,787
Defense Dept. hospital, medical	4,350	7,498	11,579	12,849	12,964	13,315	13,170	13,488
Maternal, child health programs	892	1,262	1,892	2,014	2,129	2,204	2,293	2,362
Public health activities	6,732	11,618	19,613	21,422	23,416	25,275	28,204	31,402
Veterans' hospital, medical care	5,934	8,713	11,424	12,367	13,206	14,299	15,291	15,618
Medical vocational rehabilitation	298	401	555	595	638	629	705	703
State and local hospitals [6]	5,589	7,030	11,346	11,049	11,114	12,440	12,329	12,322
Other [7]	3,059	3,263	5,009	5,710	6,192	6,532	7,002	7,511
Medical research	5,169	7,302	11,254	11,827	12,995	13,271	14,555	15,246
Medical facilities construction	2,014	2,569	3,022	2,981	3,541	3,840	4,100	4,476

[1] Change from immediate prior year. For explanation of average annual percent change, see Guide to Tabular Presentation. [2] Covers insurance benefits and amount retained by insurance companies for expenses, additions to reserves, and profits (net cost of insurance). [3] Represents expenditures for benefits and administrative cost from Federal hospital and medical insurance trust funds under old-age, survivors, disability, and health insurance programs; see text, section 12. [4] Payments made directly to suppliers of medical care (primarily Medicaid). [5] Includes medical benefits paid under public law by private insurance carriers, state governments, and self-insurers. [6] Expenditures not offset by other revenues. [7] Covers expenditures for Substance Abuse and Mental Health Services Administration, Indian Health Service; school health and other programs.

Source: U.S. Health Care Financing Administration, *Health Care Financing Review*, fall 1996.

Table 2.15 National health expenditures, by object: 1980–95. (In billions of dollars. Includes Puerto Rico and outlying areas)

OBJECT OF EXPENDITURE	1980	1985	1990	1991	1992	1993	1994	1995
Total	**247.2**	**428.2**	**697.5**	**761.7**	**834.2**	**892.1**	**937.1**	**988.5**
Spent by—								
Consumers	130.0	232.8	380.8	407.3	442.8	467.0	478.7	493.2
Government	104.8	174.3	284.3	320.3	355.4	386.5	419.9	456.4
Other [1]	12.5	21.1	32.3	34.1	36.0	38.5	38.6	38.9
Spent for—								
Health services and supplies	235.6	411.8	672.9	736.8	806.7	863.1	906.7	957.8
Personal health care expenses	217.0	376.4	614.7	676.6	740.5	786.9	827.9	878.8
Hospital care	102.7	168.3	256.4	282.3	305.4	323.3	335.0	350.1
Physician services	45.2	83.6	146.3	159.2	175.7	182.7	190.6	201.6
Dental services	13.3	21.7	31.6	33.3	37.0	39.2	42.1	45.8
Other professional services [2]	6.4	16.6	34.7	38.3	42.1	46.3	49.1	52.6
Home health care	2.4	5.6	13.1	16.1	19.6	23.0	26.3	28.6
Drugs/other medical nondurables	21.6	37.1	59.9	65.6	71.2	75.0	77.7	83.4
Vision products/other med. durables [3]	3.8	6.7	10.5	11.2	11.9	12.5	12.9	13.8
Nursing home care	17.6	30.7	50.9	57.2	62.3	67.0	72.4	77.9
Other health services	4.0	6.1	11.2	13.6	15.4	17.9	21.7	25.0
Net cost of insurance and admin. [4]	11.8	23.8	38.6	38.8	42.7	50.9	50.6	47.7
Government public health activities	6.7	11.6	19.6	21.4	23.4	25.3	28.2	31.4
Medical research	5.5	7.8	12.2	12.9	14.2	14.5	15.8	16.6
Medical facilities construction	6.2	8.5	12.3	12.0	13.4	14.5	14.6	14.0

[1] Includes nonpatient revenues, privately funded construction, and industrial inplant. [2] Includes services of registered and practical nurses in private duty, podiatrists, optometrists, physical therapists, clinical psychologists, chiropractors, naturopaths, and Christian Science practitioners. [3] Includes expenditures for eyeglasses, hearing aids, orthopedic appliances, artificial limbs, crutches, wheelchairs, etc. [4] Includes administrative expenses of federally financed health programs.

Source: U.S. Health Care Financing Administration, *Health Care Financing Review*, fall 1996.

Table 2.16   Health insurance coverage status, by selected characteristic: 1987–95. (Persons as of following year for coverage in the year shown. Government health insurance includes Medicare, Medicaid and military plans. Based on Current Population Survey)

CHARACTERISTIC	NUMBER (mil.)							PERCENT			
	Total persons	Covered by private or Government health insurance					Not covered by health insur-ance	Covered by private or Government health insurance			Not covered by health insur-ance
		Total [1]	Private		Government			Total [1]	Private	Medi-caid	
			Total	Group health [2]	Medi-care	Medi-caid					
1987	241.2	210.2	182.2	149.7	30.5	20.2	31.0	87.1	75.5	8.4	12.9
1988	243.7	211.0	182.0	150.9	30.9	20.7	32.7	86.6	74.7	8.5	13.4
1989	246.2	212.8	183.6	151.6	31.5	21.2	33.4	86.4	74.6	8.6	13.6
1990	248.9	214.2	182.1	150.2	32.3	24.3	34.7	86.1	73.2	9.7	13.9
1991	251.4	216.0	181.4	150.1	32.9	26.9	35.4	85.9	72.1	10.7	14.1
1992 [3]	256.8	218.2	181.5	148.8	33.2	29.4	38.6	85.0	70.7	11.5	15.0
1993 [3]	259.8	220.0	182.4	148.3	33.1	31.7	39.7	84.7	70.2	12.2	15.3
1994 [3]	262.1	222.4	184.3	159.6	33.9	31.6	39.7	84.8	70.3	12.1	15.2
1995, total [3][4]..	**264.3**	**223.7**	**185.9**	**161.5**	**34.7**	**31.9**	**40.6**	**84.6**	**70.3**	**12.1**	**15.4**
Age: Under 18 years.	71.1	61.4	47.0	43.8	0.3	16.5	9.8	86.2	66.1	23.2	13.8
18 to 24 years ...	24.8	17.8	15.0	12.5	0.1	3.0	7.0	71.8	60.2	12.1	28.2
25 to 34 years ...	40.9	31.6	27.9	26.0	0.4	3.5	9.4	77.1	68.3	8.5	22.9
35 to 44 years ...	43.1	35.9	32.8	30.6	0.8	2.9	7.1	83.4	76.2	6.6	16.6
45 to 54 years ...	31.6	27.4	25.3	23.3	0.9	1.8	4.2	86.7	80.0	5.6	13.3
55 to 64 years ...	21.1	18.3	16.1	14.1	1.7	1.4	2.8	86.7	76.5	6.7	13.3
65 years and over.	31.7	31.4	21.8	11.1	30.5	2.8	0.3	99.1	68.7	8.9	0.9
Sex: Male	129.1	107.5	91.3	80.7	14.9	13.4	21.6	83.2	70.7	10.4	16.8
Female	135.2	116.2	94.6	80.7	19.8	18.5	18.9	86.0	70.0	13.7	14.0
Race: White	218.4	187.3	161.3	139.2	30.6	20.5	31.1	85.8	73.8	9.4	14.2
Black	33.9	26.8	17.1	15.7	3.3	9.2	7.1	79.0	50.5	27.1	21.0
Hispanic origin [5]. ...	28.4	19.0	12.2	11.3	1.7	6.5	9.5	66.7	42.9	22.8	33.3

[1] Includes other Government insurance, not shown separately. Persons with coverage counted only once in total, even though they may have been covered by more that one type of policy.   [2] Related to employment of self or other family members. [3] Beginning 1992, data based on 1990 census adjusted population controls.   [4] Includes other races not shown separately. [5] Persons of Hispanic origin may be of any race.

Source: U.S. Bureau of the Census; "Health Insurance Coverage: 1995 - Table B;" published 26 September 1996; <http://www.census.gov/hhes/hlthins/cover95/c95tabb.html>; and unpublished data.

Table 2.17   Persons without health insurance coverage, by selected characteristic: 1989. (In per cent, except as indicated. Annual average of monthly figures. Based on Current Population Survey)

CHARACTERISTIC	Total	UNDER 65 YEARS OLD					65 years and over
		Total	Under 18 years	18 to 24 years	25 to 44 years	45 to 64 years	
All persons (1,000)	243,532	214,313	64,003	25,401	78,795	46,114	29,219
Persons not covered [1]	13.9	15.7	14.9	27.4	15.5	10.5	1.2
SEX							
Male	15.1	16.7	15.1	31.3	17.6	9.6	1.3
Female........................	12.7	14.6	14.7	23.7	13.6	11.2	1.2
RACE							
White........................	12.8	14.5	14.0	26.3	14.4	9.4	1.0
Black........................	20.2	21.9	18.9	34.3	22.5	17.5	2.5
Other........................	19.7	20.4	18.9	27.8	20.7	17.5	8.4
EDUCATION [2]							
Less than 12 years................	20.8	30.1	(X)	42.1	35.5	19.9	1.5
12 years......................	14.4	16.6	(X)	29.8	16.8	8.5	0.7
More than 12 years	8.4	9.2	(X)	16.0	9.0	5.8	1.3
EMPLOYMENT STATUS [2]							
Currently employed...............	13.9	14.3	(X)	26.6	13.6	9.0	1.5
Unemployed...................	38.3	39.2	(X)	44.5	40.8	26.5	(X)
Not in labor force................	10.8	18.5	(X)	26.0	21.2	12.8	1.2
FAMILY INCOME							
Less than $5,000................	27.1	31.3	25.5	27.3	42.4	35.5	1.5
$5,000 to $9,999	27.7	36.9	31.6	43.5	43.5	32.2	1.6
$10,000 to $19,999	24.3	30.1	30.2	37.5	32.0	21.3	1.1
$20,000 to $34,999	10.6	11.6	10.9	22.1	11.8	6.8	1.0
$35,000 to $49,999	5.8	6.0	4.0	18.4	5.8	3.9	0.8
$50,000 or more	3.6	3.7	2.3	12.9	3.7	1.9	1.6

X Not applicable.   [1] Excludes 9.7 million persons for whom insurance coverage was unknown. Includes persons whose demographic coverage was unknown.   [2] Excludes persons under 18 years old.
Source: U.S. National Center for Health Statistics, *Advance Data from Vital and Health Statistics*, No. 201, June 18, 1991.

2.5.5   THE FEDERAL BUDGET

Another key economic and political issue is the budget deficit. The following figure and table graphically illustrate the gap between the federal government's income and expenditure.

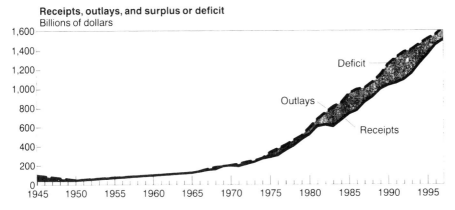

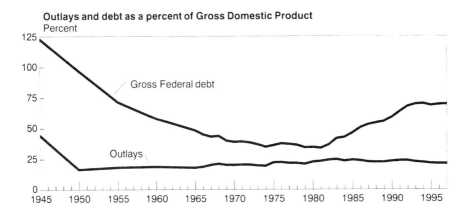

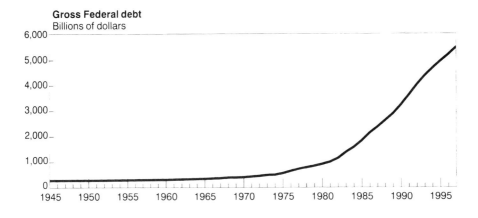

Source: Charts prepared by U.S. Bureau of the Census. For data, see table 515.

Figure 2.3   *Federal budget summary: 1945–97*

Table 2.18 Federal budget — summary: 1945–97. (In millions of dollars, except per cent. For fiscal years ending in year shown. The Balanced Budget and Emergency Deficit Control Act of 1985 put all the previously off-budget federal entities into the budget and moved Social Security off-budget. Minus sign indicates deficit or decrease)

YEAR	Receipts[1]	OUTLAYS[1] Total	OUTLAYS Human resources	OUTLAYS National defense	OUTLAYS Percent of GDP[2]	Surplus or deficit (-)	GROSS FEDERAL DEBT[3] Total	GFD Held by — Federal Gov't Account	GFD Held by — The public Total	GFD Held by public — Federal Reserve System	GFD As percent of GDP[2]	ANNUAL PERCENT CHANGE[4] Receipts	ANNUAL PERCENT CHANGE Outlays	ANNUAL PERCENT CHANGE Gross Federal debt[3]	Outlays, off-budget
1945	45,159	92,712	1,859	82,965	42.6	-47553	260,123	24,941	235,182	21,792	119.7	3.2	1.5	27.5	143
1950	39,443	42,562	14,221	13,724	15.6	-3119	256,853	37,830	219,023	18,331	94.2	0.1	9.6	1.7	524
1955	65,451	68,444	14,908	42,729	17.3	-2993	274,366	47,751	226,616	23,607	69.4	-6.0	-3.4	1.3	3,983
1960	92,492	92,191	26,184	48,130	17.8	301	290,525	53,686	236,840	26,523	56.1	16.7	0.1	1.1	10,850
1965	116,817	118,228	36,576	50,620	17.2	-1411	322,318	61,540	260,778	39,100	46.9	3.7	-0.3	2.0	16,529
1970	192,807	195,649	75,349	81,692	19.4	-2842	380,921	97,723	283,198	57,714	37.7	3.2	6.5	4.1	27,607
1973	230,799	245,707	119,522	76,681	18.8	-14908	466,291	125,381	340,910	75,181	35.7	11.3	6.5	7.0	45,589
1974	263,224	269,359	135,783	79,347	18.7	-6135	483,893	140,194	343,699	80,648	33.6	14.0	9.6	3.8	52,089
1975	279,090	332,332	173,245	86,509	21.4	-53242	541,925	147,225	394,700	84,993	34.9	6.0	23.4	12.0	60,440
1976	298,060	371,792	203,594	89,619	21.5	-73732	628,970	151,566	477,404	94,714	36.3	6.8	11.9	16.1	69,609
1976[5]	81,232	95,975	52,065	22,269	21.1	-14744	643,561	148,052	495,509	96,702	36.3	(X)	(X)	(X)	19,421
1977	355,559	409,218	221,895	97,241	20.8	-53659	706,398	157,295	549,103	105,004	35.8	19.3	10.1	12.3	80,716
1978	399,561	458,746	242,329	104,495	20.7	-59186	776,602	169,477	607,125	115,480	35.4	12.4	12.1	9.9	89,657
1979	463,302	504,032	267,574	116,342	20.2	-40729	829,470	189,162	640,308	115,594	35.1	16.0	9.8	6.8	99,978
1980	517,112	590,947	313,374	133,995	21.7	-73835	909,050	199,212	709,838	120,846	33.2	11.6	17.2	9.6	114,329
1981	599,272	678,249	362,022	157,513	22.2	-78976	994,845	209,507	785,338	124,466	32.6	15.9	14.8	9.4	135,196
1982	617,766	745,755	388,681	185,309	23.2	-127989	1,137,345	217,560	919,785	134,497	35.4	3.1	10.0	14.3	151,404
1983	600,562	808,380	426,003	209,903	23.6	-207818	1,371,710	240,114	1,131,596	155,527	40.4	-2.8	8.4	20.6	147,108
1984	666,499	851,888	432,042	227,413	22.3	-185388	1,564,657	264,159	1,300,498	155,122	41.0	11.0	5.4	14.1	165,813
1985	734,165	946,499	471,822	252,748	23.1	-212334	1,817,521	317,612	1,499,908	169,806	44.3	10.1	11.1	16.2	176,807
1986	769,260	990,505	481,594	273,375	22.6	-221245	2,120,629	383,919	1,736,709	190,855	48.5	4.8	4.6	16.7	183,498
1987	854,396	1,004,164	502,196	281,999	21.8	-149769	2,346,125	457,444	1,888,680	212,040	50.9	11.1	1.4	10.6	193,832
1988	909,303	1,064,489	533,404	290,361	21.5	-155187	2,601,307	550,507	2,050,799	229,218	52.5	6.4	6.0	10.9	202,691
1989	991,190	1,143,671	568,668	303,559	21.4	-152481	2,868,039	678,157	2,189,882	220,088	53.6	9.0	7.4	10.3	210,911
1990	1,031,969	1,253,163	619,329	299,331	22.0	-221194	3,206,564	795,841	2,410,722	234,410	56.4	4.1	9.6	11.8	225,065
1991	1,055,041	1,324,400	689,666	273,292	22.6	-269359	3,598,498	910,362	2,688,137	258,591	61.4	2.2	5.7	12.2	241,687
1992	1,091,279	1,381,681	772,440	298,350	22.5	-290402	4,002,136	1,003,302	2,998,834	296,397	65.1	3.4	4.3	11.2	252,339
1993	1,154,401	1,409,414	827,535	291,086	21.8	-255013	4,351,416	1,103,945	3,247,471	325,653	67.2	5.8	2.0	8.7	266,587
1994	1,258,627	1,461,731	869,414	281,642	21.1	-203104	4,643,705	1,211,588	3,432,117	355,150	68.0	9.0	3.7	6.7	279,372
1995	1,351,830	1,515,729	923,765	272,066	21.1	-163899	4,921,018	1,317,645	3,603,373	374,114	68.5	7.4	3.7	6.0	288,664
1996	1,426,775	1,572,411	969,942	265,556	21.4	-145636	5,207,298	1,438,614	3,768,684	(NA)	71.0	5.5	3.7	5.8	302,119
1997, est.	1,505,425	1,631,016	1,019,395	267,176	20.8	-125591	5,453,677	1,577,902	3,875,775	(NA)	69.4	5.5	3.7	4.7	315,002

NA Not available.   X Not applicable.   [1] Includes off-budget receipts and outlays.   [2] Gross domestic product as of fiscal year; for calendar year GDP, see section 14.   [3] See text, section 10, for discussion of debt concept.   [4] Change from previous year. For explanation of average annual percent see Guide to Tabular Presentation.   [5] Represents transition quarter, July-Sept.

Source: U.S. Office of Management and Budget, *Historical Tables*, annual.

2.5.6   TRADE AND AID

The relationship between the United States and the rest of the world is the principal concern of Chapter 4 of this book, and as indicated in that chapter the relationship has primarily been characterized by commerce. The figures and first two tables show recent patterns of trade and balance of trade with selected countries. Note the trade deficit with Japan. The final table shows grants and credits made to foreign countries between 1946 and 1994, reflected in this table is the United States' changed role in the world as a superpower after 1945. The Marshall Plan funding is clear in the 1946–55 grants to Western Europe, as is the support of American allies around the world. In addition the table shows that development and humanitarian aid has been provided for nearly every country in the world.

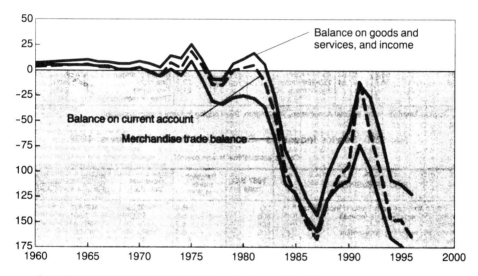

Source: Chart prepared by U.S. Bureau of the Census. For data, see table 1292.

Figure 2.4   *US international transaction balances: 1960–96*

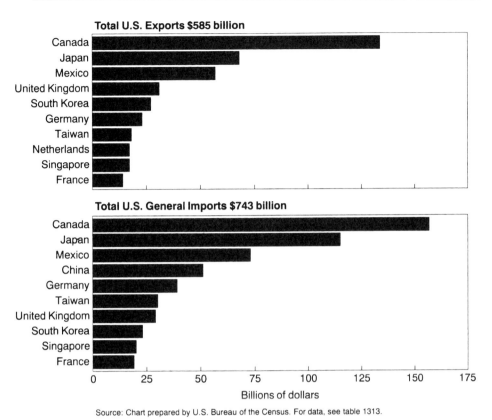

Total U.S. Exports $585 billion

Canada
Japan
Mexico
United Kingdom
South Korea
Germany
Taiwan
Netherlands
Singapore
France

Total U.S. General Imports $743 billion

Canada
Japan
Mexico
China
Germany
Taiwan
United Kingdom
South Korea
Singapore
France

0   25   50   75   100   125   150   175
Billions of dollars

Source: Chart prepared by U.S. Bureau of the Census. For data, see table 1313.

Figure 2.5   *Top purchasers of US exports and suppliers of US general imports: 1995*

Table 2.19   US balances on international transactions, by area and selected country: 1994–96. (In millions of dollars. Minus sign indicates debits)

AREA OR COUNTRY	1994, BALANCE ON—			1995, BALANCE ON—			1996, BALANCE ON—		
	Mer-chandise trade [1]	Goods, services, and income	Current account	Mer-chandise trade [1]	Goods, services, and income	Current account	Mer-chandise trade [1]	Goods, services, and income	Current account
All areas	**-166,121**	**-108,539**	**-148,405**	**-173,424**	**-113,079**	**-148,154**	**-187,674**	**-122,623**	**-165,095**
Western Europe.	-17,562	-21,979	-21,615	-15,208	-18,730	-18,051	-24,061	-27,766	-27,291
European Economic	-11,958	-18,548	-17,440	-12,711	-17,376	-15,993	-21,269	-26,559	-25,298
United Kingdom	1,112	-14,873	-13,641	1,291	-22,618	-21,394	1,485	-19,903	-18,697
Other Western Europe	-13,844	-7,501	-6,828	-11,537	1,090	1,991	-17,390	-6,478	-5,679
Eastern Europe	-481	-481	-4,181	-1,290	-989	-3,935	376	733	-2,364
Canada	-16,289	-5,610	-5,970	-20,502	-8,078	-8,443	-25,222	-12,014	-12,356
Latin America, other Western Hemisphere.	3,506	18,050	8,528	-8,783	1,891	-8,072	-13,836	-1,615	-12,261
Australia.	6,385	11,873	11,790	7,099	12,755	12,662	7,816	14,400	14,306
Japan [2]	-67,319	-64,500	-64,640	-60,351	-60,206	-60,334	-49,214	-49,163	-49,295
Other Asia and Africa	-74,450	-57,349	-73,467	-74,389	-52,790	-64,788	-83,535	-62,071	-79,189
International and unallocated . .	89	11,458	1,151	-	13,069	2,808	2	14,874	3,356

- Represents or rounds to zero.   [1] Adjusted to balance of payments basis; excludes exports under U.S. military sales contracts and imports under direct defense expenditures.   [2] Includes Ryukyu Islands.

Source: U.S. Bureau of Economic Analysis, *Survey of Current Business*, July 1996 and April 1997 issues. Major revisions to these data appear in the July 1997 issue of the *Survey of Current Business*.

Table 2.20 US international transactions, by type of transaction: 1980–96. (In millions of dollars. Minus sign indicates debits)

TYPE OF TRANSACTION	1980	1985	1988	1989	1990	1991	1992	1993	1994	1995	1996
Exports of goods and services [1]	344,440	382,747	560,233	641,659	697,083	717,726	736,704	762,851	840,006	969,189	1,032,478
Merchandise, excl. military [2][3]	224,250	215,915	320,230	362,120	389,307	416,913	440,352	456,832	502,463	575,940	611,669
Foods, feeds, and beverages	36,278	24,566	33,770	37,475	35,172	35,829	40,336	40,692	42,017	50,533	55,493
Industrial supplies and materials	72,088	61,159	90,019	99,826	105,503	109,826	109,592	111,870	121,552	146,375	147,660
Capital goods, except automotive	76,283	79,322	119,103	138,908	152,543	166,453	176,070	182,096	205,247	233,776	252,918
Automotive vehicles and parts [4]	17,443	24,945	33,397	34,888	36,465	40,008	47,027	52,534	57,777	61,827	64,460
Consumer goods (nonfood) [5]	17,751	14,593	26,981	37,317	43,719	46,858	51,424	54,655	59,981	64,425	70,160
Services	47,584	73,155	110,933	127,022	147,477	163,810	177,305	186,119	195,839	210,590	223,907
Transfers under U.S. military agency sales contracts	9,029	8,718	9,284	8,564	9,932	11,135	12,387	13,082	12,255	13,405	13,802
Travel	10,588	17,762	29,434	36,205	43,007	48,385	54,742	57,875	58,417	61,137	64,499
Passenger fares	2,591	4,411	8,976	10,657	15,298	15,854	16,618	16,611	17,083	18,534	19,579
Other transportation	11,618	14,674	19,811	21,106	22,745	23,331	23,691	23,894	25,861	28,063	29,115
Royalties and license fees	7,085	6,678	12,146	13,818	16,634	17,819	19,715	20,323	22,272	26,953	28,829
Other private services	6,276	20,035	[6]30,618	36,084	39,193	46,598	49,291	53,436	59,071	61,724	67,268
U.S. Government misc. services	398	878	664	587	668	690	861	899	880	775	815
Income on U.S. assets abroad	72,606	93,677	129,070	152,517	160,300	137,003	119,046	119,900	141,704	182,659	196,902
Direct investment	37,146	30,547	52,092	55,368	58,740	52,198	51,912	61,460	68,659	88,882	98,260
Other private receipts	32,898	57,631	70,275	91,496	91,048	76,781	60,020	53,332	68,946	89,064	94,078
U.S. Government receipts	2,562	5,499	6,703	5,653	10,512	8,023	7,114	5,108	4,099	4,713	4,564
Imports of goods, services and income	-333,774	-484,037	-662,403	-719,539	-756,522	-731,753	-763,773	-825,147	-948,544	-1,082,268	-1,155,101
Merchandise, excl. military [2][3]	-249,750	-338,088	-447,189	-477,365	-498,337	-490,981	-536,458	-589,441	-668,584	-749,364	-799,343
Foods, feeds, and beverages	-18,564	-21,850	-24,928	-24,898	-26,407	-26,205	-27,610	-27,866	-30,957	-33,176	-35,704
Industrial supplies and materials	-132,472	-114,008	-122,684	-135,363	-145,168	-132,963	-140,591	-152,437	-164,862	-183,818	-204,383
Capital goods, except automotive	-31,576	-61,287	-102,202	-112,156	-116,061	-120,802	-134,252	-152,305	-184,366	-221,431	-228,959
Automotive vehicles and parts [4]	-28,257	-64,905	-87,947	-87,356	-88,480	-85,696	-91,787	-102,420	-118,268	-124,773	-130,085
Consumer goods (nonfood) [5]	-34,268	-66,336	-96,425	-103,621	-105,053	-107,777	-122,656	-134,076	-146,358	-160,010	-171,118
Services	-41,491	-72,862	-99,491	-103,535	-118,783	-119,614	-119,464	-125,549	-134,097	-142,230	-150,440
Direct defense expenditures	-10,851	-13,108	-15,604	-15,313	-17,531	-16,409	-13,835	-12,202	-10,292	-9,820	-10,993
Travel	-10,397	-24,558	-32,114	-33,416	-37,349	-35,322	-38,552	-40,713	-43,782	-45,855	-48,712
Passenger Fares	-3,607	-6,444	-7,729	-8,249	-10,531	-10,012	-10,556	-11,313	-12,885	-14,313	-14,287
Other transportation	-11,790	-15,643	-20,969	-22,260	-25,168	-25,204	-25,459	-26,326	-27,983	-29,205	-29,100
Royalties and license fees	-724	-1,170	-2,601	-2,528	-3,135	-4,035	-5,074	-4,765	-5,518	-6,312	-7,036
Other private services	-2,909	-10,203	[6]-18,554	-19,998	-23,150	-26,516	-23,687	-27,897	-30,980	-33,970	-37,626
U.S. Government miscellaneous services	-1,214	-1,735	-1,921	-1,871	-1,919	-2,116	-2,301	-2,331	-2,657	-2,755	-2,686
Income on foreign assets in the United States	-42,532	-73,087	-115,722	-138,639	-139,402	-121,159	-107,851	-110,158	-145,863	-190,674	-205,318
Direct investment	-8,635	-7,213	-11,693	-6,507	-2,871	3,433	-317	-5,556	-21,230	-31,418	-33,817
Other private payments	-21,214	-42,745	-72,314	-93,768	-95,489	-83,063	-67,054	-63,041	-77,614	-97,977	-100,159
U.S. Government payments	-12,684	-23,129	-31,715	-38,364	-41,042	-41,529	-40,480	-41,561	-47,019	-61,279	-71,342
Unilateral transfers (excl. military grants, net	-8,349	-22,954	-26,266	-27,696	-35,219	4,510	-35,514	-37,640	-39,866	-35,075	-42,472
U.S. Government grants	-5,486	-11,268	-10,537	-10,911	-17,433	24,160	-15,799	-16,823	-15,816	-10,959	-14,634
U.S. Government pensions	-1,818	-2,138	-2,709	-2,744	-3,184	-3,730	-4,018	-4,081	-4,544	-3,420	-4,233
Private remittances and other transfers	-1,044	-9,549	-13,020	-14,041	-14,602	-15,920	-15,696	-16,736	-19,506	-20,696	-23,605

☆☆

Table 2.20 (continued)

TYPE OF TRANSACTION	1980	1985	1988	1989	1990	1991	1992	1993	1994	1995	1996
U.S. **assets abroad, net (increase/capital outflow (-))** ...	**-86,967**	**-39,889**	**-100,087**	**-168,744**	**-74,011**	**-57,881**	**-68,622**	**-194,609**	**-150,695**	**-307,856**	**-306,830**
U.S. official reserve assets, net ...	-8,155	-3,858	-3,912	-25,293	-2,158	5,763	3,901	-1,379	5,346	-9,742	6,668
Special drawing rights ...	-16	-897	127	-535	-192	-177	2,316	-537	-441	-808	370
Reserve position in the International Monetary Fund .	-1,667	908	1,025	471	731	-367	-2,692	-44	494	-2,466	-1,280
Foreign currencies ...	-6,472	-3,869	-5,064	-25,229	-2,697	6,307	4,277	-797	5,293	-6,468	7,578
U.S. Govt. assets, other than official reserve assets, net ...	-5,162	-2,821	2,967	1,259	2,307	2,911	-1,657	-342	-341	-280	-665
U.S. credits and other long-term assets ...	-9,860	-7,657	-7,680	-5,590	-8,430	-12,874	-7,398	-6,299	-5,208	-4,640	-4,909
Repayments on U.S. credits and other long-term assets ...	4,456	4,719	10,370	6,723	10,867	16,776	5,807	6,270	5,052	4,258	4,155
U.S. foreign currency holdings and U.S. short-term assets, net .	242	117	277	125	-130	-992	-66	-313	-185	102	89
U.S. private assets, net .	-73,651	-33,211	-99,141	-144,710	-74,160	-66,555	-70,866	-192,889	-155,700	-297,834	-312,833
Direct investments abroad ...	-19,222	-14,065	-16,175	-36,834	-29,950	-31,369	-42,640	-78,164	-54,465	-95,509	-88,304
Foreign securities ...	-3,568	-7,481	-7,846	-22,070	-28,765	-45,673	-49,166	-146,253	-60,270	-98,960	-104,533
U.S. claims on unaffiliated foreigners reported by U.S. nonbanking concerns ...	-4,023	-10,342	-21,193	-27,646	-27,824	11,097	45	1,581	-32,804	-34,219	-31,777
U.S. claims reported by U.S. banks, n.i.e.[8]	-46,838	-1,323	-53,927	-58,160	12,379	-610	20,895	29,947	-8,161	-69,146	-88,219
Foreign assets in the U.S., net (increase/capital inflow (+)) ...	**58,112**	**141,183**	**240,265**	**218,490**	**122,192**	**94,241**	**154,285**	**250,996**	**285,376**	**424,462**	**525,046**
Foreign official assets in the U.S. net .	15,497	-1,119	39,758	8,503	33,910	17,389	40,477	72,153	40,253	109,757	122,778
U.S. Government securities ...	11,895	-1,139	43,050	1,532	30,243	16,147	22,403	53,014	36,822	72,547	115,482
U.S. Treasury securities ...	9,708	-838	41,741	149	29,576	14,846	18,454	48,952	30,745	68,813	111,151
Other ...	2,187	-301	1,309	1,383	667	1,301	3,949	4,062	6,077	3,734	4,331
Other U.S. Government liabilities .	615	844	-467	160	1,868	1,367	2,191	1,713	2,344	1,082	1,404
U.S. liabilities reported by U.S. banks, n.i.e.[8]	-159	645	-319	4,976	3,385	-1,484	16,571	14,841	3,560	32,862	4,614
Other foreign official assets ...	3,145	-1,469	-2,506	1,835	-1,586	1,359	-688	2,585	-2,473	3,266	1,278
Other foreign assets in the United States, net .	42,615	142,301	200,507	209,987	88,282	76,853	113,808	178,843	245,123	314,705	402,268
Direct investments in the United States ...	16,918	20,010	57,278	67,736	47,915	22,004	17,600	43,022	49,760	60,236	83,950
U.S. Treasury securities ...	2,645	20,433	20,239	29,618	-2,534	18,826	37,131	24,381	34,225	99,340	153,784
U.S. securities other than U.S. Treasury securities ...	5,457	50,962	26,353	38,767	1,592	35,144	30,043	80,092	57,006	95,268	131,682
U.S. liabilities to unaffiliated foreigners reported by U.S. nonbanking concerns ...	6,852	9,851	32,893	22,086	45,133	-3,115	13,573	10,489	-7,710	34,578	34,410
U.S. liabilities reported by U.S. banks, n.i.e.[8]	10,743	41,045	63,744	51,780	-3,824	3,994	15,461	20,859	111,842	25,283	-1,558
Allocations of special drawing rights. ...	1,152	(X)	(X)	(X)	(X)	(X)	(X)	(X)	(X)	(X)	(X)
Statistical discrepancy ...	25,386	22,950	-11,743	55,830	46,476	-26,843	-23,080	43,550	13,724	31,548	-53,122
Balance on merchandise trade ...	-25,500	-122,173	-126,959	-115,245	-109,030	-74,068	-96,106	-132,609	-166,121	-173,424	-187,674
Balance on services ...	6,093	294	11,442	23,487	28,694	44,196	57,842	60,570	61,742	68,360	73,467
Balance on investment income ...	30,073	20,590	13,348	13,878	20,897	15,844	11,195	9,742	-4,159	-8,016	-8,416
Balance on goods, services, and income ...	10,666	-101,290	-102,170	-77,880	-59,439	-14,028	-27,069	-62,297	-108,539	-113,079	-122,623
Unilateral transfers, net ...	-8,349	-22,954	-26,266	-27,696	-35,219	4,510	-35,514	-37,640	-39,866	-35,075	-42,472
Balance on current account ...	2,317	-124,243	-128,436	-105,575	-94,657	-9,518	-62,583	-99,936	-148,405	-148,154	-165,095

- Represents zero.   NA Not available.   X Not applicable.   [1] Excludes transfers of goods and services under U.S. military grant programs.   [2] Excludes exports of goods under U.S. military agency sales contracts identified in Bureau of the Census export documents, excludes imports of goods under direct defense expenditures identified in Census import documents, and reflects various other adjustments (for valuation, coverage, and timing) of Census statistics to a balance of payments basis. [3] Includes other end-use items, not shown separately. [4] Includes engines. [5] Excludes automotive. [6] Break in series due to inclusion of new data. [7] Includes sales of foreign obligations to foreigners. [8] Not included elsewhere.

Source: U.S. Bureau of Economic Analysis, *Survey of Current Business*, July 1996 and April 1997 issues. Major revisions to these data appear in the July 1997 issue of the *Survey of Current Business*.

Table 2.21 US government foreign grants and credits, by type and country: 1946–94. (In millions of dollars. Negative figures occur when the total of grant returns, principal repayments, and/or foreign currencies disbursed by the US government exceeds new grants and new credits utilized and/or acquisitions of foreign currencies through new sales of farm products)

TYPE AND COUNTRY	1946-1955, total	1956-1965, total	1966-1975, total	1976-1985, total	1990	1991	1992	1993	1994, prel.
Total, net	51,509	49,723	70,355	104,153	14,280	-32,018	17,042	16,638	15,965
Investment in financial institutions . . .	635	655	2,719	10,432	1,301	1,498	1,419	1,132	1,417
Under assistance programs	50,875	49,067	67,636	93,720	12,979	-33,517	15,623	15,506	14,548
Western Europe.	33,067	6,752	1,004	1,612	-69	-5,985	324	124	166
Austria.	1,001	193	-19	34	-10	-19	-1	-1	-1
Belgium and Luxembourg	1,570	305	17	-46	-9	-3	-	-	-
Bosnia and Hercegovina.	-	-	-	-	-	-	40	30	50
Croatia	-	-	-	-	-	-	62	37	50
Denmark	596	276	64	-58	-	-	-	-	-
Finland	86	-26	-19	21	-8	-5	-5	-26	-1
France.	8,661	-171	-93	-222	-15	-8	-2	-2	-1
Germany	3,881	10	-117	-117	-338	-6,117	-	-1	-
Iceland	34	33	-8	-12	(Z)	-	-	-	-
Ireland.	146	-16	-51	7	2	-6	-6	-8	25
Italy	3,851	1,435	85	133	-30	-14	-	(Z)	-
Macedonia.	-	-	-	-	-	-	67	1	3
Netherlands	1,716	322	116	-180	-	-	-	-	-
Norway.	697	362	379	-257	-	-1	-15	-	-
Portugal.	248	241	34	1,003	56	44	159	53	115
Slovenia.	-	-	-	-	-	-	118	-6	-18
Spain	258	1,203	607	965	-122	-76	-104	-114	-55
Sweden.	107	-20	17	-1	-	-	-	-	-
United Kingdom.	7,458	105	-546	-964	-111	-113	-115	-118	-120
Yugoslavia.	1,356	1,151	84	174	-39	-58	-308	1	-1
Other [1] and unspecified	1,399	1,351	454	1,132	555	391	435	279	120
Eastern Europe	823	501	226	1,029	965	779	707	2,888	2,711
Albania	9	-	-	-	-	9	59	29	10
Armenia.	-	-	-	-	-	-	19	62	78
Belarus	-	-	-	-	-	-	27	74	36
Bulgaria	-	-	-	-	-	17	1	20	5
Czechoslovakia.	136	-	-	-5	(Z)	1	1	15	1
Czech Republic.	-	-	-	-	-	-	-	2	2
Estonia	-	-	-	-	-	-	21	1	(Z)
Georgia	-	-	-	-	-	-	5	72	53
Hungary.	18	5	-5	6	1	3	2	3	4
Kazakhstan	-	-	-	-	-	-	17	9	12
Kyrgyzstan	-	-	-	-	-	-	1	59	22
Latvia	-	-	-	-	-	-	21	1	2
Lithuania	-	-	-	-	-	-	21	24	15
Moldova.	-	-	-	-	-	-	9	25	22
Poland.	350	555	-75	1,017	919	646	57	21	5
Romania	-	-	92	55	64	39	10	14	9
Russia.	-	-	-	-	-	-	145	1,902	1,134
Soviet Union.	292	-59	214	-44	-30	3	-	5	-
Tajikistan	-	-	-	-	-	-	10	17	19
Turkmenistan	-	-	-	-	-	-	7	24	13
Ukraine	-	-	-	-	-	-	8	66	103
Other [2] and unspecified	17	(Z)	-	-	11	60	266	444	1,166
Near East and South Asia.	4,944	16,828	17,195	50,777	6,602	-24,672	7,493	7,631	7,060
Afghanistan	31	227	185	56	57	59	70	49	8
Bangladesh	-	-	701	1,670	175	168	154	109	176
Cyprus.	-	19	20	138	16	18	10	14	16
Egypt	41	1,009	271	13,600	4,976	2,508	2,537	2,760	2,236
Greece	2,026	1,281	905	362	282	-179	402	205	332
India	370	4,890	3,810	1,021	-8	100	78	54	32
Iran.	314	1,061	914	-847	-	-23	(Z)	-	-
Iraq [3].	13	81	-5	5	-7	365	119	115	135
Israel.	390	483	3,760	25,417	4,379	2,002	4,691	3,276	3,132
Jordan.	26	495	618	1,320	139	67	121	127	94
Kuwait	-	-	-	-	-2,506	-13,550	-2	-	-
Lebanon	15	78	90	233	8	5	11	7	5
Nepal	3	86	105	177	20	16	19	20	20
Oman	-	-	(Z)	79	4	3	13	24	1
Pakistan	189	3,092	2,048	1,971	526	346	123	-39	-162
Saudi Arabia.	12	35	23	-20	-1,614	-13,913	-1,328	-	-
Sri Lanka.	(Z)	89	153	512	72	109	53	77	34
Syria	1	57	15	262	(Z)	-	-	2	-
Turkey	1,295	3,020	2,703	3,760	367	798	300	629	226
United Arab Emirates	-	-	-	-	-361	-3,709	-	-	-
Yemen (Sanaa).	-	40	24	216	14	-	-	-	-
Yemen.	-	-	-	-	28	19	14	21	1
UNRWA [4].	131	274	296	596	7	76	69	140	7
Other and unspecified	85	510	559	248	27	43	41	43	765

See footnotes at end of table.

Table 2.21 (continued)

COUNTRY	1946-1955, total	1956-1965, total	1966-1975, total	1976-1985, total	1990	1991	1992	1993	1994, prel.
Africa	**147**	**2,272**	**3,610**	**11,066**	**1,841**	**1,483**	**1,624**	**1,773**	**1,861**
Algeria	1	135	263	345	59	-42	-14	-11	28
Angola	-	-	6	115	-15	-4	-20	8	37
Benin	-	7	12	44	5	10	17	12	16
Botswana	-	(Z)	35	169	17	11	8	15	14
Burkina	-	5	40	287	15	32	17	20	13
Burundi	-	4	5	62	18	6	16	19	36
Cameroon	-	16	50	150	42	57	42	23	14
Cape Verde	-	-	1	68	6	7	9	5	5
Chad	(Z)	5	20	145	24	26	26	22	9
Eritrea	-	-	-	-	-	-	-	4	19
Ethiopia	13	200	297	310	54	123	88	137	126
Ghana	(Z)	64	203	152	14	32	36	48	55
Guinea	-	58	68	74	15	22	21	34	33
Ivory Coast	-	14	57	57	25	58	46	21	38
Kenya	(Z)	34	76	549	110	87	90	79	40
Lesotho	-	(Z)	27	197	15	11	16	7	6
Liberia	24	139	86	459	31	64	40	29	42
Madagascar	(Z)	7	13	86	33	31	20	26	22
Malawi	-	5	30	56	34	48	47	41	33
Mali	-	12	58	199	31	44	31	37	30
Mauritania	-	1	20	161	11	6	3	7	2
Morocco	7	464	413	948	95	100	26	21	26
Mozambique	-	-	1	175	80	89	72	75	68
Niger	-	5	64	223	33	44	34	29	15
Nigeria	(Z)	87	284	267	156	34	31	18	52
Rwanda	-	2	13	91	13	27	10	32	271
Senegal	-	18	48	361	60	39	47	54	31
Sierra Leone	(Z)	22	36	85	2	10	16	8	7
Somalia	(Z)	42	47	582	77	11	337	506	24
South Africa	20	-101	-11	2	20	28	44	66	71
Sudan	-	86	52	1,358	145	113	32	35	44
Swaziland	-	(Z)	8	58	14	13	13	14	10
Tanzania	2	34	123	259	40	42	28	28	24
Togo	-	9	18	60	10	19	12	8	7
Tunisia	2	407	376	563	38	5	16	-4	1
Uganda	-	12	33	40	43	39	26	58	51
Zaire	(Z)	258	342	938	241	48	33	9	(Z)
Zambia	-	1	35	331	63	50	76	52	21
Zimbabwe	-	(Z)	(Z)	271	10	27	67	28	34
Other and unspecified	76	219	361	769	156	113	165	154	484
Far East and Pacific	**9,678**	**16,199**	**34,767**	**9,622**	**35**	**-8,991**	**777**	**-1**	**722**
Australia	-9	(Z)	276	-12	-34	-26	-18	-2	-1
Burma	25	134	43	31	1	-3	(Z)	-2	-2
Cambodia	28	327	1,760	87	5	6	14	29	16
China	-	-	-	49	71	55	31	14	6
Hong Kong	3	35	41	11	-8	-	-	1	1
Indonesia	246	501	1,390	1,661	46	23	82	-64	23
Japan and Ryukyu Islands	3,267	1,318	-345	-210	-635	-9,377	-30	-2	-1
South Korea	1,420	4,744	5,426	3,518	-192	-331	-133	-431	-55
Laos	37	647	1,868	8	(Z)	(Z)	1	(Z)	(Z)
Malaysia	1	30	86	39	-1	-2	(Z)	(Z)	1
Mongolia	-	-	-	-	-	17	2	36	17
New Zealand	3	2	95	-68	-2	-2	-1	-	-
Pacific Islands, Trust Territory of the [5]	28	89	488	1,260	221	178	204	152	317
Philippines	1,028	554	729	1,466	556	391	534	129	-53
Singapore	-	(Z)	78	110	(Z)	(Z)	(Z)	(Z)	(Z)
Taiwan	1,267	2,681	1,523	648	-7	-8	-7	-9	-8
Thailand	192	727	996	733	-19	49	44	84	245
Vietnam	244	3,566	19,720	18	2	1	2	2	-7
Other and unspecified	1,898	844	595	273	33	38	54	60	224
Western Hemisphere	1,248	5,181	6,816	9,847	2,003	2,014	2,465	673	798
Argentina	86	342	34	21	64	87	90	80	26
Bolivia	77	288	270	413	112	197	185	129	111
Brazil	509	1,400	1,518	399	260	-22	410	-188	-60
Canada	-1	4	272	317	-41	-50	-38	-41	-120
Chile	100	740	724	-565	-32	-40	-55	-39	-36
Colombia	43	446	846	298	-30	7	-78	-235	-8
Costa Rica	15	83	103	687	108	63	24	15	-7
Dominican Republic	2	184	360	550	27	25	3	163	9
Ecuador	32	131	144	153	61	26	30	17	19
El Salvador	3	56	93	1,681	303	308	278	212	87
Guatemala	23	146	160	270	96	82	109	74	51
Guyana	(Z)	7	71	36	42	11	9	6	8
Haiti	27	75	42	370	53	69	54	59	162
Honduras	6	53	113	801	223	193	130	92	49
Jamaica	16	3	120	643	108	109	84	34	99

See footnotes at end of table.

Table 2.21 (continued)

COUNTRY	1946-1955, total	1956-1965, total	1966-1975, total	1976-1985, total	1990	1991	1992	1993	1994, prel.
Western Hemisphere— Continued:									
Mexico	225	178	305	1,162	140	38	-110	-160	-231
Nicaragua	8	67	150	197	100	396	207	37	41
Panama	10	103	210	205	102	153	193	49	6
Paraguay	4	67	86	22	(Z)	1	(Z)	1	2
Peru	55	304	274	757	87	139	671	113	41
Trinidad and Tobago	-	35	21	151	5	5	-10	-11	-9
Uruguay	8	90	116	-9	-4	-5	2	-1	2
Venezuela	6	156	115	-35	-18	-14	-2	1	(Z)
Other [6] and unspecified	-6	224	671	1,325	237	236	280	266	557
Other international organizations and unspecified areas	969	1,335	4,018	9,768	1,603	1,855	2,234	2,419	1,230

Z Less than $500,000.   [1] Includes European Atomic Energy Community, European Coal and Steel Community, European Payments Union, European Productivity Agency, North Atlantic Treaty Organization, and Organization for European Economic Cooperation.   [2] Foreign assistance in 1989-94 to the countries of Eastern Europe and to the Newly Independent States of the former Soviet Union was reported primarily on a regional basis.   [3] Foreign assistance to Iraq in 1991-94 was direct humanitarian assistance to ethnic minorities of Northern Iraq after the conflict in the Persian Gulf.   [4] United Nations Relief and Works Agency for Palestine refugees.   [5] Excludes transactions with Commonwealth of the Northern Mariana Islands after October 1986; includes transactions with Federated States of Micronesia, Republic of the Marshall Islands, and Republic of Palau.   [6] Includes Andean Development Corporation, Caribbean Development Bank, Central American Bank for Economic Integration, Eastern Caribbean Central Bank, Inter-American Institute of Agricultural Science, Organizations of American States, and Pan American Health Organization.

Source: U.S. Bureau of Economic Analysis, press releases, and unpublished data.

DEMOCRACY

3.1 INTRODUCTION

The collection of documents in this chapter reflect an indication of the strength of the American commitment to democracy. Interestingly they also reveal the tensions that have existed and continue to exist in the American democratic tradition. The discourse of twentieth-century politics in the United States, on the whole, has celebrated democracy but marginalized these tensions. Although there have been alternative voices, such as the Students for a Democratic Society during the 1960s, they have been relatively few and without influence. Americans, and their political representatives, broadly speaking, have shared an unproblematic view of themselves as democrats and the United States as the pre-eminent democracy in the world. However, these tensions have been present from the foundation of the Republic and they cannot be concealed as is evident from the documents.

'We hold these truths to be self-evident', wrote Thomas Jefferson in the Declaration of Independence, 'that all men are created equal'. After the great battle of Gettysburg during the middle of the Civil War, Abraham Lincoln declared: 'Fourscore and seven years ago our fathers brought forth, on this continent, a new nation, conceived in Liberty, and dedicated to the proposition that all men are created equal.' The words of Lincoln and Jefferson are but two of innumerable testaments to the democratic ideal of equality, although few have been as eloquent or have captured the American imagination to quite the same extent. They are a very powerful expression of the centrality of equality and democracy to the political tradition in the United States. Yet at the precise moment that Jefferson was affirming his faith in the equality of all men, there were almost a million black slaves in the American colonies, some of whom, incidentally, belonged to Jefferson. Lincoln's words were delivered during a conflict when the nation had been split asunder over slavery. Although the Civil War resolved the question of legal servitude it did not resolve the inequality of Afro-Americans. Lincoln had no sympathy with slavery but neither did he view black Americans as his equals. This is not intended to suggest that Lincoln and Jefferson were less than honest or enthusiastic over their proclaimed belief in equality. It does indicate, however, that eighteenth- and nineteenth-century notions of equality and democracy were rather different from current understandings. They were far more exclusionary. Women as well as people of colour were not deemed to be full members of the polity or of civil society. Equality did not apply to them. The exclusion of Afro-Americans from the sentiments of the Declaration is evidence that their status has always been profoundly problematic and continues to be so in certain respects.

The Thirteenth, Fourteenth and Fifteenth Amendments to the Constitution of the United States ended slavery and established constitutional protections for the former slaves, but it did not provide equality, even the legal equality that these amendments were designed to achieve. Within a few years after the end of the Civil War, a variety of practices were introduced and put into operation to ensure the continued subordination of Afro-Americans. By the early decades of the twentieth century, the experience of most black Americans was defined by racial segregation and the indignity of being second class citizens. Some of the documents chronicle the successful struggle this century to achieve redress.

The 1896 Supreme Court decision in *Plessy v. Ferguson* set much of the scene for the civil rights struggle in the twentieth century legitimizing segregation through the principle of 'separate but equal' treatment of the races. President Truman's Executive Order of 1948 desegregating the armed forces was a milestone, although it is a striking reminder that the US military operated a system of racial separation in the war against Nazism and fascism. This apparent and manifest contradiction was one of the reasons that lay behind Truman's Executive Order. Similarly the opinion of Chief Justice Warren in *Brown v. Board of Education* is one of the most important reaffirmations of equality in American life, although it had to be made because equal treatment was being denied to black school children throughout most of the southern United States. Although *Brown* constitutionally prohibited the practice of racial segregation in public governmentally funded schools, several southern states refused to accept the decision and the enforcement of the judgement would take many years of contested litigation and several instances of severe public disorder. Moreover *Brown* only applied to education, and racial segregation was far more widespread. It was deeply embedded in the fabric of life in the southern United States. Virtually all services and activities in those states were provided on a racially segregated basis and these were not altered until the passage of the Civil Rights Act of 1964. Again the transition to integration was far from easy. Nor was it easy to obtain the passage of the Act. The Civil Rights movement had struggled long and hard to achieve this objective over several decades and against the bitter hostility of the white southern establishment. Martin Luther King's memorable speech delivered from the steps of the Lincoln Memorial in 1963 was one of the key defining moments of the Civil Rights movement and central to the passage of the Act. It is also noteworthy that President Lyndon Johnson's moving speech in 1965 and the passage of the Voting Rights Act, a vital reform and perhaps the most significant piece of civil rights legislation, was a recognition that as recently as the 1960s the most basic entitlement of a democracy, the right to vote, was denied to millions of Afro-Americans. In the middle of the Cold War — a conflict frequently characterized as a contest between the free world and totalitarianism — the disfranchisement of millions of black Americans was unacceptable. It is hardly surprising then that the voices of some Afro-Americans have not been entirely enthusiastic about the black experience in the US. Malcolm X is one of the most powerful of these voices.

The civil rights documents reveal the extent and the tenacity of discrimination against Afro-Americans, but they also demonstrate that reform can be achieved. The American political process has always possessed the capacity to adapt and to respond to the demands of the electorate. However, it has done so slowly, cautiously and incrementally. The political system does not act with speed and dispatch and of course it was not designed to do so, a fact which tells us a great deal about democracy in America. The American Constitution was designed to satisfy several objectives. The Founding Fathers — those remarkable men who met in Philadelphia in 1787 — wanted to create a political system that was based on consent, which permitted the representation of diverse opinions and interests, guaranteed political and other liberties and protected property rights. They also wanted to ensure that Americans had an effective national government, the absence of which might threaten the survival of the United States. This was not an easy task but they created a document, which in the words of William Gladstone was ' … the most wonderful work ever struck off at a given time by the brain and purpose of man'. The admiration is understandable and all the more noteworthy because the Founding Fathers were not statesmen/philosophers. They were politicians in a convention who had to compromise and arrive at arrangements if a Constitution which had broad approval was going to emerge. But despite the deals and agreements it is possible to detect some overriding concerns. The single most important of these concerns was the mistrust and fear of government. The Founding Fathers mistrusted the institutions of government and those who would seek to gain control over the levers of power because they would almost certainly misuse it. Government had to be controlled and the American Constitution was designed to achieve that objective through a complex and sophisticated set of arrangements. But who was most likely to abuse this power? Virtually everybody was the belief of the Founding Fathers, but the group that aroused the greatest concern, according to the 'father of the Constitution' James Madison, was the 'majority faction'. In *The Federalist* No.10, Madison outlines these concerns and his view was enormously influential. The Constitution that emerged sought to prevent or at least to make it as difficult as possible for the majority to rule. Of course this antipathy to majorities soon abated. The discourse of American politics within a few decades after 1787 became aggressively democratic and assertively populist, but the Constitution was not altered significantly and has continued to be essentially unchanged. The legacy of the intellectual climate of eighteenth-century America is still powerfully present and continues to have a significant impact on the conduct of politics and government in the United States.

One of the legacies has been the central role of the federal courts and the US Supreme Court in particular in the operation of the political system. The

judgement in *Brown v. Board of Education* was perhaps the single most important event in sounding the death-knell for racial segregation. The ending of
segregation, however welcome, should not disguise the fact that this key
decision was taken by judges and not by politicians and legislators. Of course
this conforms with the Madisonian view that politicians and the electorate
they represent are not to be trusted. Judges are far more trustworthy than
members of legislatures. Again it is a revealing fact about the democratic tradition in the United States that so many vital and central decisions are made
by the judiciary and not by the political representatives of the American people. *The United States v. Nixon* was also a landmark decision which had a very
dramatic and immediate impact. It set in train the events that led to the resignation of the President of the United States. The trail of the Watergate scandal, which started as a minor and inconsequential burglary, led inexorably to
the Oval Office of the White House. Perhaps on this occasion the Founding
Father's fears and mistrust of politicians proved to be fully justified.

President Nixon's speech at his first inauguration was in striking contrast to
his remarks on his departure in disgrace from the White House. The inaugural speech of any newly elected President provides a unique opportunity to
both reflect on the past and set the tone and the themes of the new administration. Nixon was given the opportunity to heal the bitter divisions that had
developed over the US involvement in Vietnam and certainly his inaugural
speech was conciliatory, but the atmosphere generated by the inaugural soon
dissipated and the Nixon White House always had a beleaguered feel to it
even when he was re-elected by a landslide in 1972. The most memorable
inaugurals of this century have successfully established the direction that the
new President was going to take. Observers of Franklin D. Roosevelt's first
inaugural claimed to have seen the nation's despondency and gloom lifting
visibly. The Great Depression, above all, had sapped the nation's morale but
in a remarkable speech Roosevelt generated hope and optimism. The
inaugural was followed by a flurry of activity and a blizzard of legislative
proposals to deal with the economic crisis. Some of the legislation worked
while others clearly failed, but Roosevelt had established that his administration was going to act and not merely respond to events. The inaugural speech
defined both the man and the administration. Similarly in 1961, John F.
Kennedy articulated the feeling that the United States was witnessing the
transfer of power between generations. Those who had commanded the
nation through the Second World War were giving way to the junior ranks.
This new generation was more assertive about the role of the United States in
the world and far more sanguine about the use of American power. The
Kennedy Administration both reflected and gave voice to this confidence,
which was evident in its conduct of foreign policy. Unfortunately, not all the
decisions taken in the 'one thousand days of Camelot' proved to be an
unqualified success. Jimmy Carter's 1977 inaugural address marked the beginning of an attempt to set a new political agenda which was not altogether
successful. The next striking inaugural address was delivered by Ronald
Reagan in 1981. Reagan gave notice that the next four years were going to be
a period of change. His first administration certainly altered the politics of
the United States. The move to détente with the Soviet bloc was halted and

the 'second Cold War' was started, although the Reagan years saw the beginning of the end of hostilities with the Soviet Union. Domestically there was a sharp change, if not in substance then certainly in attitude, toward 'big government'. Government, according to Reagan, was not the solution it was the problem, a theme taken up a few years later in the 'Contract with America'. Perhaps only the Republican administrations of the 1920s were quite so antipathetic towards government. Bill Clinton views the world very differently. However, his attempt to implement the programme outlined in his second inaugural was to be complicated by a scandal which would result in his trial by the Senate.

3.2   PRE-TWENTIETH CENTURY

3.2.1   THE DECLARATION OF INDEPENDENCE (1776)

The Declaration of Independence was approved by the Continental Congress on 4 July 1776. The Congress, set up in 1774, was made up of representatives of the thirteen colonies and its importance had increased as the relationship between Britain and the colonies deteriorated towards irreconcilable breakdown. By the time the Continental Congress formed a sub-committee to consider the issue of independence, fighting had already taken place and a 'Continental Army' had been formed under the command of George Washington. The sub-committee included Thomas Jefferson, John Adams and Benjamin Franklin.

Much of the text, which was drafted by Jefferson, is concerned with justifying the split from Britain, but of more lasting importance was the opening section establishing a framework of political philosophy and principles for the new republics. The Declaration established the independence of the thirteen states from each other as well as from Britain, and for over ten years they were united through mutual interest in a confederation, a period of considerable democratic experimentation.

When in the Course of human events, it becomes necessary for one people to dissolve the political bands which have connected them with another, and to assume among the powers of the earth, the separate and equal station to which the Laws of Nature and of Nature's God entitle them, a decent respect to the opinions of mankind requires that they should declare the causes which impel them to the separation. We hold these truths to be self-evident, that all men are created equal, that they are endowed by their Creator with certain unalienable Rights, that among these are Life, Liberty, and the pursuit of Happiness. That to secure these rights, Governments are instituted among Men, deriving their just powers from the consent of the governed. That whenever any Form of Government becomes destructive of these ends it is the Right of the People to alter or to abolish it, and to institute new Government, laying its foundation on such principles and organizing its powers in such form, as to them shall seem most likely to effect their Safety and Happiness. Prudence, indeed, will dictate that Governments long established should not be changed for light and transient causes; and accordingly all experience hath shewn, that man-kind are more disposed to suffer, while evils are sufferable, than to right themselves by abolishing the forms to which they are accustomed. But when a long train of abuses and usurpations, pursuing invariably the same Object evinces a design to reduce them under absolute Despotism, it is their right, it is their duty, to throw off such Government, and to provide new Guards for their future security. Such has been the patient sufferance of these Colonies; and such is now the necessity which constrains them to alter their former Systems of Government. The history of the present King of Great Britain is a history of repeated injuries and usurpations, all having in direct object the establishment of an absolute Tyranny over these States. To prove this, let Facts be submitted to a candid world. He has refused his Assent to Laws, the most wholesome and necessary for the public good. He has forbidden his Governors to pass Laws of immediate and pressing importance, unless suspended in their operation till his Assent should be obtained; and when so suspended, he has utterly neglected to attend to them. He has refused to pass other Laws for the accommodation of large districts of people, unless those people would relinquish the right of Representation in the Legislature, a right inestimable to them and formidable to tyrants only. He has called together legislative bodies at places unusual, uncomfortable, and distant from the depository of their public Records, for the sole purpose of fatiguing them into compliance with his measures. He has dissolved Representative Houses repeatedly, for opposing with manly firmness his invasions on the rights of the people. He has refused for a long time, after dissolutions, to cause others to be elected; whereby the Legislative powers, incapable of Annihilation, have returned to the People at large for their exercise; the State remaining in the mean time exposed to all the dangers of invasion from without, and convulsions within. He has endeavoured to prevent the population of these States; for that purpose obstructing the Laws for Naturalization of Foreigners; refusing to pass others to encourage their migrations hither, and raising the conditions of new Appropriations of Lands. He has obstructed the Administration of Justice, by refusing his Assent to Laws for establishing Judiciary powers. He has made Judges dependent on his Will alone, for the tenure of their offices, and the amount and payment of their salaries. He has erected a multitude of New Offices, and sent hither swarms of Officers to harrass our people, and eat out their substance. He has kept among us, in times of peace, standing Armies without the Consent of our legislatures. He has affected to render the Military independent of and superior to the Civil power. He has combined with others to subject us to a jurisdiction foreign to our constitution, and unacknowledged by our laws; giving his Assent to their Acts of pretended Legislation: For Quartering large bodies of armed troops among us: For protecting them, by a mock Trial, from punishment for any Murders which they should commit on the Inhabitants of these States: For cutting off our Trade with all parts of the world: For imposing Taxes on us without our Consent:

For depriving us in many cases of the benefits of Trial by Jury: For transporting us beyond Seas to be tried for pretended offences: For abolishing the free System of English Laws in a neighbouring Province, establishing therein an Arbitrary government, and enlarging its Boundaries so as to render it at once an example and fit instrument for introducing the same absolute rule into these Colonies: For taking away our Charters, abolishing our most valuable Laws, and altering fundamentally the Forms of our Governments: For suspending our own Legislatures, and declaring themselves invested with power to legislate for us in all cases whatsoever. He has abdicated Government here, by declaring us out of his Protection and waging War against us. He has plundered our seas, ravaged our Coasts, burnt our towns, and destroyed the Lives of our people. He is at this time transporting large Armies of foreign Mercenaries to compleat the works of death, desolation and tyranny, already begun with circumstances of Cruelty and perfidy scarcely paralleled in the most barbarous ages, and totally unworthy the Head of a civilized nation. He has constrained our fellow Citizens taken Captive on the high Seas to bear Arms against their Country, to become the executioners of their friends and Brethren, or to fall themselves by their Hands. He has excited domestic insurrections amongst us, and has endeavoured to bring on the inhabitants of our frontiers, the merciless Indian Savages, whose known rule of warfare, is an undistinguished destruction of all ages, sexes and conditions. In every stage of these Oppressions We have Petitioned for Redress in the most humble terms: Our repeated Petitions have been answered only by repeated injury. A Prince, whose character is thus marked by every act which may define a Tyrant, is unfit to be the ruler of a free people. Nor have We been wanting in attentions to our British brethren. We have warned them from time to time of attempts by their legislature to extend an unwarrantable jurisdiction over us. We have reminded them of the circumstances of our emigration and settlement here. We have appealed to their native justice and magnanimity, and we have conjured them by the ties of our common kindred to disavow these usurpations, which, would inevitably interrupt our connections and correspondence. They too have been deaf to the voice of Justice and of consanguinity. We must, therefore, acquiesce in the necessity, which denounces our Separation, and hold them, as we hold the rest of mankind, Enemies in War, in Peace Friends.

We, therefore, the Representatives of the United States of America, in General Congress, Assembled, appealing to the Supreme Judge of the world for the rectitude of our intentions, do, in the Name, and by Authority of the good People of these Colonies, solemnly publish and declare, That these United Colonies are, and of Right ought to be Free and Independent States; that they are Absolved from all Allegiance to the British Crown, and that all political connection between them and the State of Great Britain, is and ought to be totally dissolved; and that as Free and Independent States, they have full Power to levy War, conclude Peace, contract Alliances, establish Commerce, and to do all other Acts and Things which Independent States may of right do. And for the support of this Declaration, with a firm reliance on the protection of divine Providence, we mutually pledge to each other our Lives, our Fortunes and our sacred Honor.

John Hancock

Button Gwinnett	Benjamin Rush
Lyman Hall	Benja. Franklin
Geo Walton.	John Morton
Wm. Hooper	Geo Clymer
Joseph Hewes	Jas. Smith
John Penn	Geo. Taylor
Edward Rutledge.	James Wilson
Thos. Heyward Junr.	Geo. Ross
Thomas Lynch Junr.	Cæsar Rodney
Arthur Middleton	Geo Read
Samuel Chase	Tho M: Kean
Wm. Paca	Wm. Floyd
Thos. Stone	Phil. Livingston
Charles Carroll of Carrollton	Frans. Lewis
George Wythe	Lewis Morris
Richard Henry Lee	Richd. Stockton
Th: Jefferson	Jno Witherspoon
Benja. Harrison	Fras. Hopkinson
Thos. Nelson jr.	John Hart
Francis Lightfoot Lee	Abra Clark
Carter Braxton	Josiah Bartlett
Robt. Morris	Wm: Whipple
John Adams	Saml. Adams
Robt. Treat Paine	Roger Sherman
Elbridge Gerry	Saml. Huntington
Step. Hopkins	Wm. Williams
William Ellery	Oliver Wolcott
	Matthew Thornton

Source: Commager, H.S. (ed.) (1963) *Documents of American History* (7th edn), New York, Appleton Century Crofts, vol.1, p.100.

3.2.2   THE CONSTITUTION OF THE UNITED STATES OF AMERICA

The political experience of the newly independent states ushered in a widespread desire for a more stable and secure system of government. This desire culminated in a Federal Constitutional Convention which was held in Philadelphia in 1787. The delegates, later known as the Founding Fathers, produced a Constitution which was then ratified by the states. The Constitution established the United States of America as a federal republic and put in place its major institutions while laying down the nature of their powers and their relationships with each other and with the individual states. The underlying themes of these relationships involved a separation of power between the institutions, and a system of 'checks and balances' designed to prevent the concentration and abuse of that power.

Amendments to the Constitution

The Bill of Rights, 1791

The Constitutional Convention had left many dissatisfied by the absence of specific individual rights, not least because of recent experiences during the War of Independence and by events in Europe. The pressure for such rights to be included in the Constitution led the first Congress of the United States to adopt ten amendments to the Constitution in 1791. These amendments are collectively known as the Bill of Rights.

The Civil War amendments XIII–XV

The period between 1791 and 1865 saw only two amendments, largely technical concerning the judiciary and the method of presidential election. However, the Constitution had failed to deal with the paradox at the centre of the democratic experiment: slavery. This paradox was resolved by the Civil War (1861–5). The North's victory preserved and strengthened the Union and allowed the United States to move along a path which could now be presented as its destiny, most notably in Lincoln's Gettysburg Address. In the years that followed the Civil War the Constitution was amended to abolish slavery, to establish equal protection before the law, and to disqualify from government those who had rebelled against the Union (unless Congress saw fit to readmit them). It was also amended so that the vote can not be refused on the grounds of race or colour.

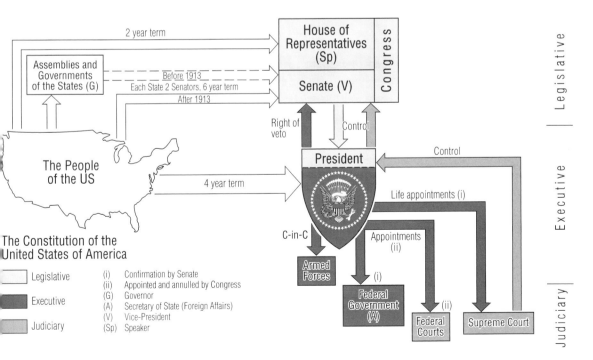

Figure 3.1 *Checks and balances of the US Constitution*

Twentieth-century amendments

Democratic development and experimentation have continued apace during the twentieth century with twelve amendments to date. The Nineteenth Amendment guaranteed women the vote in 1920, an essential feature of any democratic polity by modern standards. The voting age was lowered to eighteen and other amendments have modified the institutions of government (especially the presidency) and methods of representation. However, one constitutional experiment proved to be a dramatic failure; the Eighteenth Amendment of 1919 which made the manufacture, sale and transportation of alcoholic drinks illegal had an altogether different impact from its sponsors' intentions. Undermining of the law, a boost to organized crime, and a romanticizing of bootlegging-gangsters were among the consequences of prohibition. It was repealed by the Twenty-First Amendment in 1933.

We the people of the United States, in order to form a more perfect Union, establish Justice, insure domestic Tranquility, provide for the common defence, promote the general Welfare, and secure the Blessings of Liberty to ourselves and our Posterity, do ordain and establish this CONSTITUTION for the United States of America.

ARTICLE I

Section 1. All legislative Powers herein granted shall be vested in a Congress of the United States, which shall consist of a Senate and House of Representatives.

Section 2. The House of Representatives shall be composed of Members chosen every second Year by the People of the several States, and the Electors in each State shall have the Qualifications requisite for Electors of the most numerous Branch of the State Legislature.

No person shall be a Representative who shall not have attained to the Age of twenty-five Years, and been seven Years a Citizen of the United States, and who shall not, when elected, be an Inhabitant of that State in which he shall be chosen.

(Representatives and direct Taxes shall be apportioned among the several States which may be included within this Union, according to their respective Numbers, which shall be determined by adding to the whole Number of free Persons, including those bound to Service for a Term of Years, and excluding Indians not taxed, three-fifths of all other persons.[1]) The actual Enumeration shall be made within three Years after the first Meeting of Congress of the United States, and within every subsequent Term of ten Years, in such Manner as they shall by Law direct. The Number of Representatives shall not exceed one for every thirty thousand, but each State shall have at

[1] This provision was modified by the Sixteenth Amendment. The three-fifths reference to slaves was rendered obsolete by the Thirteenth and Fourteenth Amendments.

Least one Representative; and until such enumeration shall be made, the State of New Hampshire shall be entitled to chuse three, Massachusetts eight, Rhode Island and Providence Plantations one, Connecticut five, New York six, New Jersey four, Pennsylvania eight, Delaware one, Maryland six, Virginia ten, North Carolina five, South Carolina five, and Georgia three.

When vacancies happen in the Representation from any State, the Executive Authority thereof shall issue Writs of Election to fill such Vacancies.

The House of Representatives shall chuse their Speaker and other Officers; and shall have the sole Power of Impeachment.

Section 3. The Senate of the United States shall be composed of two Senators from each State, chosen by the Legislature thereof,[2] for six Years; and each Senator shall have one Vote.

Immediately after they shall be assembled in Consequence of the first Election, they shall be divided as equally as may be into three Classes. The Seats of the Senators of the first Class shall be vacated at the Expiration of the second Year, of the second Class at the Expiration of the fourth Year, and of the third Class at the Expiration of the sixth Year, so that one-third may be chosen every second Year; and if Vacancies happen by Resignation, or otherwise, during the Recess of the Legislature of any State, the Executive thereof may make temporary appointments until the next Meeting of the Legislature, which shall then fill such vacancies.

No person shall be a Senator who shall not have attained to the Age of thirty Years, and been nine Years a Citizen of the United States, and who shall not, when elected, be an Inhabitant of that State for which he shall be chosen.

The Vice President of the United States shall be President of the Senate, but shall have no Vote, unless they be equally divided.

The Senate shall chuse their other Officers, and also a President pro tempore, in the absence of the Vice President, or when he shall exercise the Office of President of the United States.

The Senate shall have the sole Power to try all Impeachments. When sitting for that Purpose, they shall be on Oath or Affirmation. When the President of the United States is tried, the Chief Justice shall preside: And no Person shall be convicted without the Concurrence of two-thirds of the Members present.

Judgment in Cases of Impeachment shall not extend further than to removal from Office, and disqualification to hold and enjoy any Office of honor, Trust or Profit under the United States: but the Party convicted shall nevertheless be liable and subject to Indictment, Trial, Judgment and Punishment, according to Law.

Section 4. The Times, Places and Manner of holding Elections for Senators and Representatives, shall be prescribed in each State by the Legislature thereof; but the Congress may at any time by law make or alter such Regulations, except as to the Places of chusing Senators.

---

[2]See the Seventeenth Amendment.

The Congress shall assemble at least once in every Year, and such Meeting shall be on the first Monday in December, unless they shall by Law appoint a different Day.[3]

Section 5. Each House shall be the Judge of the Elections, Returns and Qualifications of its own Members, and a Majority of each shall constitute a Quorum to do Business; but a smaller Number may adjourn from day to day, and may be authorized to compel the Attendance of absent Members, in such Manner, and under such Penalties as each House may provide.

Each House may determine the Rules of its Proceedings, punish its Members for disorderly Behaviour, and, with the Concurrence of two-thirds, expel a Member.

Each House shall keep a Journal of its Proceedings and from time to time publish the same, excepting such Parts as may in their Judgment require Secrecy; and the Yeas and Nays of the Members of either House on any question shall, at the Desire of one-fifth of those Present, be entered on the Journal.

Neither House, during the Session of Congress, shall, without the Consent of the other, adjourn for more than three days, not to any other Place than that in which the two Houses shall be sitting.

Section 6. The Senators and Representatives shall receive a Compensation for their Services, to be ascertained by Law, and paid out of the Treasury of the United States. They shall in all Cases, except Treason, Felony, and Breach of the Peace, be privileged from Arrest during their Attendance at the Session of their respective Houses, and in going to and returning from the same; and for any Speech or Debate in either House, they shall not be questioned in any other Place.

No Senator or Representative shall, during the Time for which he was elected, be appointed to any civil Office under the Authority of the United States, which shall have been created, or the Emoluments whereof shall have been increased during such time; and no Person holding any Office under the United States, shall be a Member of either House during his Continuance in Office.

Section 7. All Bills for raising Revenue shall originate in the House of Representatives; but the Senate may propose or concur with Amendments as on other Bills.

Every Bill which shall have passed the House of Representatives and the Senate, shall, before it become a Law, be presented to the President of the United States; if he approve he shall sign it, but if not he shall return it, with his Objections to that House in which it shall have originated, who shall enter the Objections at large on their Journal, and proceed to reconsider it. If after such Reconsideration two-thirds of that House shall agree to pass the Bill, it shall be sent, together with the Objections, to the other House, by which it shall likewise be reconsidered, and if approved by two-thirds of that House, it shall become a law. But in all such Cases the Votes of both Houses shall be determined by Yeas and Nays, and the Names of the

[3]See the Twentieth Amendment.

Persons voting for and against the Bill shall be entered on the Journal of each House respectively. If any Bill shall not be returned by the President within ten Days (Sundays excepted) after it shall have been presented to him, the Same shall be a Law, in like Manner as if he had signed it, unless the Congress by their Adjournment prevent its Return, in which Case it shall not be a Law.

Every Order, Resolution, or Vote to which the Concurrence of the Senate and House of Representatives may be necessary (except on a question of Adjournment) shall be presented to the President of the United States; and before the Same shall take Effect, shall be approved by him, or being disapproved by him, shall be repassed by two-thirds of the Senate and House of Representatives, according to the Rules and Limitations prescribed in the Case of a Bill.

Section 8. The Congress shall have Power To Lay and collect Taxes, Duties, Imposts and Excises, to pay the Debts and provide for the common Defence and general Welfare of the United States; but all Duties, Imposts and Excises shall be uniform throughout the United States;

To borrow money on the Credit of the United States;

To regulate Commerce with foreign Nations, and among the several States, and with the Indian Tribes;

To establish an uniform Rule of Naturalization, and uniform Laws on the subject of Bankruptcies throughout the United States;

To coin Money, regulate the Value thereof, and of foreign Coin, and fix the Standard of Weights and Measures;

To provide for the Punishment of counterfeiting the Securities and current Coin of the United States;

To establish Post Offices and post Roads;

To promote the Progress of Science and useful arts, by securing for limited Times to Authors and Inventors the exclusive Right to their respective Writings and Discoveries;

To constitute Tribunals inferior to the supreme Court;

To define and punish Piracies and Felonies committed on the high Seas, and Offences against the Law of Nations;

To declare War, grant Letters of Marque and Reprisal, and make Rules concerning Captures on Land and Water;

To raise and support Armies, but no Appropriation of Money to that Use shall be for a longer Term than two Years;

To provide and maintain a Navy;

To make Rules for the government and Regulation of the land and naval Forces;

To provide for calling forth the Militia to execute the Laws of the Union, suppress Insurrections and repel Invasions;

To provide for organizing, arming, and disciplining the Militia, and for governing such Part of them as may be employed in the Service of the United States, reserving to the States respectively, the Appointment of the Officers, and the Authority of training the Militia according to the discipline prescribed by Congress;

To exercise exclusive Legislation in all Cases whatsoever, over such District (not exceeding ten Miles square) as may, by Cession of particular States, and the acceptance of Congress, become the Seat of the Government of the United States, and to exercise like Authority over all Places purchased by the Consent of the Legislature of the State in which the Same shall be, for the Erection of Forts, Magazines, Arsenals, dock-Yards, and other needful Buildings; — And

To make all Laws which shall be necessary and proper for carrying into Execution the foregoing Powers, and all other Powers vested by this Constitution in the Government of the United States, or in any Department or Officer thereof.

Section 9. The Migration or Importation of such Persons as any of the States now existing shall think proper to admit, shall not be prohibited by the Congress prior to the Year one thousand eight hundred and eight, but a tax or duty may be imposed on such importation, not exceeding ten dollars for each Person.

The privilege of the Writ of Habeas Corpus shall not be suspended, unless when in Cases of Rebellion or Invasion the public Safety may require it.

No Bill of Attainder or ex post facto Law shall be passed.

No capitation, or other direct, Tax shall be laid, unless in Proportion to the Census or Enumeration herein before directed to be taken.[4]

No Tax or Duty shall be laid on Articles exported from any State.

No Preference shall be given by any Regulation of Commerce or Revenue to the Ports of one State over those of another: nor shall Vessels bound to, or from, one State, be obliged to enter, clear, or pay Duties in another.

No Money shall be drawn from the Treasury, but in consequence of Appropriations made by Law; and a regular Statement and Account of the Receipts and Expenditures of all public Money shall be published from time to time.

No Title of Nobility shall be granted by the United States: And no Person holding any Office of Profit or Trust under them, shall, without the Consent of the Congress, accept of any present, Emolument, Office, or Title, of any kind whatever, from any King, Prince, or foreign State.

Section 10. No State shall enter into any Treaty, Alliance, or Confederation; grant Letters of Marque and Reprisal; coin Money; emit Bills of Credit; make any Thing but gold and silver Coin a Tender in Payment of Debts; pass any Bill of Attainder, ex post facto Law, or Law impairing the Obligation of Contracts, or grant any Title of Nobility.

No State shall, without the Consent of the Congress, lay any Imposts or Duties on Imports or Exports, except what may be absolutely necessary for executing its inspection Laws: and the net Produce of all Duties and Imposts, laid by any State on Imports or Exports, shall be for the Use of the Treasury of the United States; and all such Laws shall be subject to the Revision and Control of the Congress.

[4]See the Sixteenth Amendment.

No State shall, without the Consent of Congress, lay any duty of Tonnage, keep Troops, or Ships of War in time of Peace, enter into any Agreement or Compact with another State, or with a foreign Power, or engage in War, unless actually invaded, or in such imminent Danger as will not admit of delay.

ARTICLE II

Section 1. The executive Power shall be vested in a President of the United States of America. He shall hold his Office during the Term of four Years, and, together with the Vice President, chosen for the same Term, be elected, as follows:

Each State shall appoint, in such Manner as the Legislation thereof may direct, a Number of Electors, equal to the whole number of Senators and Representatives to which the State may be entitled in the Congress: but no Senator or Representative, or Person holding an Office of Trust or Profit under the United States, shall be appointed an Elector.

The Electors shall meet in their respective States, and vote by Ballot for two persons, of whom one at least shall not be an Inhabitant of the same State with themselves. And they shall make a List of all the Persons voted for, and of the Number of Votes for each; which List they shall sign and certify, and transmit sealed to the Seat of the Government of the United States, directed to the President of the Senate. The President of the Senate shall, in the Presence of the Senate and House of Representatives, open all the Certificates, and the Votes shall then be counted. The Person having the greatest Number of Votes shall be the President, if such Number be a Majority of the whole Number of Electors appointed; and if there be more than one who have such Majority, and have an Equal Number of Votes, then the House of Representatives shall immediately chuse by Ballot one of them for President; and if no Person have a Majority, then from the five highest on the List the said House shall in like Manner chuse the President. But in chusing the President, the Votes shall be taken by States, the Representation from each State having one Vote; A quorum for this Purpose shall consist of a Member or Members from two-thirds of the States, and a Majority of all the States shall be necessary to a Choice. In every Case, after the Choice of the President, the Person having the greatest Number of Votes of the Electors shall be the Vice President. But if there should remain two or more who have equal Votes, the Senate shall chuse from them by Ballot the Vice President.[5]

The Congress may determine the Time of chusing the Electors, and the Day on which they shall give their Votes; which Day shall be the same throughout the United States.

No person except a natural born Citizen, or a Citizen of the United States, at the time of the Adoption of this Constitution, shall be eligible to the Office of President; neither shall any Person be eligible to that Office who

[5]This paragraph was superseded by the Twelfth Amendment.

shall not have attained to the Age of thirty-five Years, and been fourteen Years a Resident within the United States.

In Case of the Removal of the President from Office, or of his Death, Resignation, or Inability to discharge the Powers and Duties of the said Office, the same shall devolve on the Vice President, and the Congress may by Law provide for the Case of Removal, Death, Resignation or Inability, both of the President and Vice President, declaring what Officer shall then act as President, and such Officer shall act accordingly, until the Disability be removed, or a President shall be elected.

The President shall, at stated Times, receive for his Services, a Compensation, which shall neither be increased nor diminished during the Period for which he shall have been elected, and he shall not receive within that Period any other Emolument from the United States, or any of them.

Before he enter on the Execution of his Office, he shall take the following Oath or Affirmation: — 'I do solemnly swear (or affirm) that I will faithfully execute the Office of President of the United States, and will to the best of my Ability, preserve, protect and defend the Constitution of the United States.'

Section 2. The President shall be Commander in Chief of the Army and Navy of the United States, and of the Militia of the several States, when called into the actual Service of the United States; He may require the Opinion, in writing, of the principal officer in each of the executive Departments, upon any subject relating to the Duties of their respective Offices, and he shall have Power to Grant Reprieves and Pardons for Offences against the United States, except in Cases of Impeachment.

He shall have Power, by and with the Advice and Consent of the Senate, to make Treaties, provided two-thirds of the Senators present concur; and he shall nominate, and by and with the Advice and Consent of the Senate, shall appoint Ambassadors, other public Ministers and Consuls, Judges of the supreme Court, and all other Officers of the United States, whose Appointments are not herein otherwise provided for, and which shall be established by Law: but the Congress may by Law vest the Appointment of such inferior Officers, as they think proper, in the President alone, in the Courts of Law, or in the Heads of Departments.

The President shall have Power to fill up all Vacancies that may happen during the Recess of the Senate, by granting Commissions which shall expire at the End of their next Session.

Section 3. He shall from time to time give to the Congress Information of the State of the Union, and recommend to their Consideration such Measures as he shall judge necessary and expedient; he may, on extraordinary Occasions, convene both Houses, or either of them, and, in Cases of Disagreement between them, with Respect to the Time of Adjournment, he may adjourn them to such Time as he shall think proper; he shall receive Ambassadors and other public Ministers; he shall take Care that the Laws be faithfully executed, and shall Commission all the Officers of the United States.

Section 4. The President, Vice President and all civil Officers of the United States, shall be removed from Office on Impeachment for, and Conviction of, Treason, Bribery, or other high Crimes and Misdemeanors.

ARTICLE III

Section 1. The judicial Power of the United States, shall be vested in one supreme Court, and in such inferior Courts as the Congress may from time to time ordain and establish. The Judges, both of the supreme and inferior Courts, shall hold their offices during good Behaviour, and shall, at stated Times, receive for their Services, a Compensation, which shall not be diminished during their Continuance in Office.

Section 2. The judicial Power shall extend to all Cases, in Law and Equity, arising under this Constitution, the Laws of the United States and Treaties made, or which shall be made, under their Authority; — to all Cases affecting Ambassadors, other public Ministers and Consuls; — to all Cases of admiralty and maritime Jurisdiction; — to Controversies to which the United States shall be a Party; — to Controversies between two or more States; — between a State and Citizens of another State;[6] — between Citizens of different States, — between Citizens of the same State claiming Lands under Grants of different States, and between a State, or the Citizens thereof, and foreign States, Citizens or Subjects.

In all Cases affecting Ambassadors, other public Ministers and Consuls, and those in which a State shall be a Party, the supreme Court shall have original Jurisdiction.

In all the other Cases before mentioned, the supreme Court shall have appellate Jurisdiction, both as to Law and Fact, with such Exceptions, and under such Regulations as the Congress shall make.

The trial of all Crimes, except in Cases of Impeachment, shall be by Jury; and such Trial shall be held in the State where the said Crimes shall have been committed; but when not committed within any State, the Trial shall be at such Place or Places as the Congress may by Law have directed.

Section 3. Treason against the United States, shall consist only in levying War against them, or in adhering to their Enemies, giving them Aid and Comfort. No Person shall be convicted of Treason unless on the Testimony of two Witnesses to the same overt Act, or on Confession in open Court.

The Congress shall have power to declare the Punishment of Treason, but no Attainder of Treason shall work Corruption of Blood, or Forfeiture except during the Life of the Person attainted.

ARTICLE IV

Section 1. Full Faith and Credit shall be given in each State to the public Acts, Records, and judicial Proceedings of every other State. And the Congress may by general Laws prescribe the Manner in which such Acts, Records and Proceedings shall be proved, and the Effect thereof.

---

[6]See the Eleventh Amendment.

Section 2. The Citizens of each State shall be entitled to all Privileges and Immunities of Citizens in the several States.

A Person charged in any State with Treason, Felony, or other Crime, who shall flee from Justice, and be found in another State, shall on demand of the executive Authority of the State from which he fled, be delivered up, to be removed to the State having Jurisdiction of the Crime.

No Person held to Service or Labour in one State, under the Laws thereof, escaping into another, shall, in Consequence of any Law or Regulation therein, be discharged from such Service or Labour, but shall be delivered up on Claim of the Party to whom such Service or Labour may be due.[7]

Section 3. New States may be admitted by the Congress into this Union; but no new States shall be formed or erected within the Jurisdiction of any other State; nor any State be formed by the Junction of two or more States, or parts of States, without the Consent of the Legislatures of the States concerned as well as of the Congress.

The Congress shall have Power to dispose of and make all needful Rules and Regulations respecting the Territory or other Property belonging to the United States; and nothing in this Constitution shall be so construed as to Prejudice any Claims of the United States, or of any particular State.

Section 4. The United States shall guarantee to every State in this Union a Republican Form of Government, and shall protect each of them against Invasion; and on Application of the Legislature, or of the Executive (when the Legislature cannot be convened) against domestic Violence.

ARTICLE V

The Congress, whenever two-thirds of both Houses shall deem it necessary, shall propose Amendments to this Constitution, or, on the Application of the Legislatures of two-thirds of the several States, shall call a Convention for proposing Amendments, which, in either Case, shall be valid to all Intents and Purposes, as part of this Constitution, when ratified by the Legislatures of three-fourths of the several States, or by Conventions in three-fourths thereof, as the one or the other Mode of Ratification may be proposed by the Congress; Provided that no Amendment which may be made prior to the Year one thousand eight hundred and eight shall in any Manner affect the first and fourth Clauses in the Ninth Section of the first Article; and that no State, without its Consent, shall be deprived of its equal Suffrage in the Senate.

ARTICLE VI

All Debts contracted and Engagements entered into, before the Adoption of this Constitution, shall be as valid against the United States under this Constitution, as under the Confederation.

---

[7] Obsolete. See the Thirteenth Amendment.

This Constitution, and the Laws of the United States which shall be made in Pursuance thereof; and all Treaties made, or which shall be made, under the Authority of the United States, shall be the supreme Law of the Land; and the Judges in every State shall be bound thereby, any Thing in the Constitution or Laws of any State to the Contrary notwithstanding.

The Senators and Representatives before mentioned, and the Members of the several State Legislatures, and all executive and judicial Officers, both of the United States and of the several States, shall be bound by Oath or Affirmation, to support this Constitution; but no religious Test shall ever be required as a Qualification to any Office or public Trust under the United States.

ARTICLE VII

The Ratification of the Conventions of nine States, shall be sufficient for the Establishment of this Constitution between the States so ratifying the Same.

Done in Convention by the Unanimous Consent of the States present the Seventeenth Day of September in the Year of our Lord one thousand seven hundred and Eighty seven and of the Independence of the United States of America the Twelfth. In Witness whereof We have hereunto subscribed our Names.

Go. Washington — Presidt and deputy from Virginia

New Hampshire
John Langdon
Nicholas Gilman

Massachusetts
Nathaniel Gorham
Rufus King

Connecticut
Wm Saml Johnson
Roger Sherman

New York
Alexander Hamilton

New Jersey
Wil: Livingston
David Brearley
Wm Paterson
Jona: Dayton

Pennsylvania
B. Franklin
Thomas Mifflin
Robt Morris
Geo. Clymer
Thos. Fitzsimons
Jared Ingersoll
James Wilson
Gouv Morris

Delaware
Geo: Read
Gunning Bedford jun
John Dickinson
Richard Bassett
Jaco: Broom

Maryland
James McHenry
Dan of St Thos Jenifer
Danl Carroll

Virginia
John Blair
James Madison Jr

North Carolina
Wm Blount
Richd Dobbs Spaight
Hu Williamson

South Carolina
J. Rutledge
Charles Cotesworth Pinckney
Charles Pinckney
Pierce Butler

Georgia
William Few
Abr Baldwin

AMENDMENTS[8]

Amendment I

Congress shall make no law respecting an establishment of religion, or prohibiting the free exercise thereof; or abridging the freedom of speech, or of
the press; or the right of the people peaceably to assemble, and to petition
the Government for a redress of grievances.

Amendment II

A well regulated Militia, being necessary to the security of a free State, the
right of the people to keep and bear Arms, shall not be infringed.

Amendment III

No Soldier shall, in time of peace, be quartered in any house, without the
consent of the Owner, nor in time of war, but in a manner to be prescribed
by law.

Amendment IV

The right of the people to be secure in their persons, houses, papers, and
effects, against unreasonable searches and seizures, shall not be violated,
and no Warrants shall issue, but upon probable cause, supported by Oath or
affirmation, and particularly describing the place to be searched, and the
persons or things to be seized.

Amendment V

No person shall be held to answer for a capital, or otherwise infamous
crime, unless on a presentment or indictment of a Grand Jury, except in
cases arising in the land or naval forces, or in the Militia, when in actual
service in time of War or public danger; nor shall any person be subject for
the same offence to be twice put in jeopardy of life or limb; nor shall be
compelled in any criminal case to be a witness against himself, nor be
deprived of life, liberty, or property, without due process of law; nor shall
private property be taken for public use, without just compensation.

Amendment VI

In all criminal prosecutions, the accused shall enjoy the right to a speedy
and public trial, by an impartial jury of the State and district wherein the
crime shall have been committed, which district shall have been previously
ascertained by law, and to be informed of the nature and the cause of the
accusation; to be confronted with the witnesses against him; to have compulsory process for obtaining Witnesses in his favor, and to have the Assistance of Counsel for his defence.

[8]The first ten amendments were adopted in 1791.

Amendment VII

In suits at common law, where the value in controversy shall exceed twenty dollars, the right of trial by jury shall be preserved, and no fact tried by a jury, shall be otherwise re-examined in any Court of the United States, than according to the rules of the common law.

Amendment VIII

Excessive bail shall not be required, nor excessive fines imposed, nor cruel and unusual punishments inflicted.

Amendment IX

The enumeration in the Constitution, of certain rights, shall not be construed to deny or disparage others retained by the people.

Amendment X

The powers not delegated to the United States by the Constitution, nor prohibited by it to the States, are reserved to the States respectively, or to the people.

Amendment XI[9]

The Judicial power of the United States shall not be construed to extend to any suit in law or equity, commenced or prosecuted against one of the United States by Citizens of another State, or by Citizens or Subjects of any Foreign State.

Amendment XII[10]

The Electors shall meet in their respective states, and vote by ballot for President and Vice-President, one of whom, at least, shall not be an inhabitant of the same state with themselves; they shall name in their ballots the person voted for as President, and in distinct ballots the person voted for as Vice-President, and they shall make distinct lists of all persons voted for as President, and of all persons voted for as Vice-President, and of the number of votes for each, which lists they shall sign and certify, and transmit sealed to the seat of government of the United States, directed to the President of the Senate; — The President of the Senate shall, in the presence of the Senate and House of Representatives, open all the certificates and the votes shall then be counted; — The person having the greatest number of votes for President, shall be the President, if such a number be a majority of the whole number of Electors appointed; and if no person have such majority, then from the persons having the highest numbers not exceeding three on the list of those voted for as President, the House of Representatives shall

[9]Adopted in 1798.

[10]Adopted in 1804.

choose immediately, by ballot, the President. But in choosing the President, the votes shall be taken by states, the representation from each state having one vote; a quorum for this purpose shall consist of a member or members from two-thirds of the states, and a majority of all the states shall be necessary to a choice. And if the House of Representatives shall not choose a President whenever the right of choice shall devolve upon them, before the fourth day of March next following, then the Vice-President shall act as President, as in the case of the death or other constitutional disability of the President. The person having the greatest number of votes as Vice-President, shall be the Vice-President, if such number be a majority of the whole number of Electors appointed, and if no person have a majority, then from the two highest numbers on the list, the Senate shall choose the Vice-President; a quorum for the purpose shall consist of two-thirds of the whole number of Senators, and a majority of the whole number shall be necessary to a choice. But no person constitutionally ineligible to the office of President shall be eligible to that of Vice-President of the United States.

Amendment XIII[11]

Section 1. Neither slavery nor involuntary servitude, except as a punishment for crime whereof the party shall have been duly convicted, shall exist within the United States, or any place subject to their jurisdiction.

Section 2. Congress shall have power to enforce this article by appropriate legislation.

Amendment XIV[12]

Section 1. All persons born or naturalized in the United States, and subject to the jurisdiction thereof, are citizens of the United States and of the State wherein they reside. No State shall make or enforce any law which shall abridge the privileges or immunities of citizens of the United States; nor shall any State deprive any person of life, liberty, or property, without due process of law; nor deny to any person within its jurisdiction the equal protection of the laws.

Section 2. Representatives shall be apportioned among the several States according to their respective numbers, counting the whole number of persons in each State, excluding Indians not taxed. But when the right to vote at any election for the choice of electors for President and Vice President of the United States, Representatives in Congress, the Executive and Judicial officers of a State, or the members of the Legislature thereof, is denied to any of the male inhabitants of such State, being twenty-one years of age, and citizens of the United States, or in any way abridged, except for participation in rebellion, or other crime, the basis of representation therein shall be reduced in the proportion which the number of such male citizens shall

[11]Adopted in 1865.

[12]Adopted in 1868.

bear to the whole number of male citizens twenty-one years of age in such State.

Section 3. No person shall be a Senator or Representative in Congress, or elector of President and Vice President, or hold any office, civil or military, under the United States, or under any State, who, having previously taken an oath, as a member of Congress, or as an officer of the United States, or as a member of any State legislature, or as an executive or judicial officer of any State, to support the Constitution of the United States, shall have engaged in insurrection or rebellion against the same, or given aid or comfort to the enemies thereof. But Congress may by a vote of two-thirds of each House, remove such disability.

Section 4. The validity of the public debt of the United States, authorized by law, including debts incurred for payment of pensions and bounties for services in suppressing insurrection or rebellion, shall not be questioned. But neither the United States nor any State shall assume or pay any debt or obligation incurred in aid of insurrection or rebellion against the United States, or any claim for the loss or emancipation of any slave; but all such debts, obligations and claims shall be held illegal and void.

Section 5. The Congress shall have power to enforce, by appropriate legislation, the provisions of this article.

Amendment XV[13]

Section 1. The right of citizens of the United States to vote shall not be denied or abridged by the United States or by any State on account of race, color, or previous condition of servitude.

Section 2. The Congress shall have power to enforce this article by appropriate legislation.

Amendment XVI[14]

The Congress shall have power to lay and collect taxes on incomes, from whatever source derived, without apportionment among the several States, and without regard to any census or enumeration.

Amendment XVII[15]

The Senate of the United States shall be composed of two Senators from each State, elected by the people thereof, for six years, and each Senator shall have one vote. The electors in each State shall have the qualifications requisite for electors of the most numerous branch of the State legislatures.

[13]Adopted in 1870.

[14]Adopted in 1913.

[15]Adopted in 1913.

When vacancies happen in the representation of any State in the Senate, the executive authority of such State shall issue writs of election to fill such vacancies: Provided, That the legislature of any State may empower the executive thereof to make temporary appointments until the people fill the vacancies by election as the legislature may direct.

This amendment shall not be so construed as to affect the election or term of any Senator chosen before it becomes valid as part of the Constitution.

Amendment XVIII[16]

After one year from the ratification of this article, the manufacture, sale, or transportation of intoxicating liquors within, the importation thereof into, or the exportation thereof from the United States and all territory subject to the jurisdiction thereof for beverage purposes is hereby prohibited.

The Congress and the several States shall have concurrent power to enforce this article by appropriate legislation.

This article shall be inoperative unless it shall have been ratified as an amendment to the Constitution by the legislatures of the several States, as provided in the Constitution, within seven years from the date of the submission hereof to the States by the Congress.

Amendment XIX[17]

The right of Citizens of the United States to vote shall not be denied or abridged by the United States or by any States on account of sex.

The Congress shall have power, by appropriate legislation, to enforce the provisions of this article.

Amendment XX[18]

Section 1. The terms of the President and Vice-President shall end at noon on the twentieth day of January, and the terms of Senators and Representatives at noon on the third day of January, of the years in which such terms would have ended if this article had not been ratified; and the terms of their successors shall then begin.

Section 2. The Congress shall assemble at least once in every year, and such meeting shall begin at noon on the third day of January, unless they shall by law appoint a different day.

Section 3. If, at the time fixed for the beginning of the term of the President, the President-elect shall have died, the Vice-President-elect shall become President. If a President shall not have been chosen before the time fixed for the beginning of his term, or if the President-elect shall have failed to

[16]Adopted in 1919. Repealed by the Twenty-first Amendment.

[17]Adopted in 1920.

[18]Adopted in 1933.

qualify, then the Vice-President-elect shall act as President until a President shall have qualified; and the Congress may by law provide for the case wherein neither a President-elect nor a Vice-President-elect shall have qualified, declaring who shall then act as President, or the manner in which one who is to act shall be selected, and such person shall act accordingly until a President or Vice-President shall have qualified.

Section 4. The Congress may by law provide for the case of the death of any of the persons from whom the House of Representatives may choose a President whenever the right of choice shall have devolved upon them, and for the case of the death of any of the persons from whom the Senate may choose a Vice-President whenever the right of choice shall have devolved upon them.

Section 5. Sections 1 and 2 shall take effect on the 15th day of October following the ratification of this article.

Section 6. This article shall be inoperative unless it shall have been ratified as an amendment to the Constitution by the legislatures of three-fourths of the several States within seven years from the date of its submission.

Amendment XXI[19]

Section 1. The eighteenth article of amendment to the Constitution of the United States is hereby repealed.

Section 2. The transportation or importation into any State, Territory, or possession of the United States for delivery or use therein of intoxicating liquors, in violation of the laws thereof, is hereby prohibited.

Section 3. This article shall be inoperative unless it shall have been ratified as an amendment to the Constitution by conventions in the several States, as provided in the Constitution, within seven years from the date of the submission hereof to the States by the Congress.

Amendment XXII[20]

Section 1. No person shall be elected to the office of the President more than twice, and no person who has held the office of President, or acted as President, for more than two years of a term to which some other person was elected President shall be elected to the office of the President more than once. But this Article shall not apply to any person holding the office of President when this Article was proposed by the Congress, and shall not prevent any person who may be holding the office of President, or acting as President, during the term within which this Article becomes operative from holding the office of President or acting as President during the remainder of such term.

[19]Adopted in 1933.

[20]Adopted in 1951.

Section 2. This article shall be inoperative unless it shall have been ratified as an amendment to the Constitution by the Legislatures of three-fourths of the several States within seven years from the date of its submission to the States by the Congress.

Amendment XXIII[21]

Section 1. The District constituting the seat of Government of the United States shall appoint in such manner as the Congress may direct:

A number of electors of President and Vice President equal to the whole number of Senators and Representatives in Congress to which the District would be entitled if it were a State, but in no event more than the least populous State; they shall be in addition to those appointed by the States; but they shall be considered, for the purposes of the election of President and Vice President, to be electors appointed by a State; and they shall meet in the District and perform such duties as provided by the twelfth article of amendment.

Section 2. The Congress shall have power to enforce this article by appropriate legislation.

Amendment XXIV[22]

Section 1. The right of citizens of the United States to vote in any primary or other election for the President or Vice President, for electors for President or Vice President, or for Senator or Representative in Congress, shall not be denied or abridged by the United States or any State by reason of failure to pay any poll tax or other tax.

Section 2. The Congress shall have power to enforce this article by appropriate legislation.

Amendment XXV[23]

Section 1. In case of the removal of the President from office or of his death or resignation, the Vice President shall become President.

Section 2. Whenever there is a vacancy in the office of the Vice President, the President shall nominate a Vice President who shall take office upon confirmation by a majority vote of both Houses of Congress.

Section 3. Whenever the President transmits to the President pro tempore of the Senate and the Speaker of the House of Representatives his written declaration that he is unable to discharge the powers and duties of his office, and until he transmits to them a written declaration to the contrary,

[21] Adopted in 1961.

[22] Adopted in 1964.

[23] Adopted in 1967.

such powers and duties shall be discharged by the Vice President as Acting President.

Section 4. Whenever the Vice President and a majority of either the principal officers of the executive departments or of such other body as Congress may by law provide, transmit to the President pro tempore of the Senate and the Speaker of the House of Representatives their written declaration that the President is unable to discharge the powers and duties of his office, the Vice President shall immediately assume the powers and duties of the office as Acting President.

Thereafter, when the President transmits to the President pro tempore of the Senate and the Speaker of the House of Representatives his written declaration that no inability exists, he shall resume the powers and duties of his office unless the Vice President and a majority of either the principal officers of the executive department or of such other body as Congress may by law provide, transmit within four days to the President pro tempore of the Senate and the Speaker of the House of Representatives their written declaration that the President is unable to discharge the powers and duties of his office. Thereupon Congress shall decide the issue, assembling within forty-eight hours for that purpose if not in session. If the Congress, within twenty-one days after receipt of the latter written declaration, or, if Congress is not in session, within twenty-one days after Congress is required to assemble, determines by two-thirds vote of both Houses that the President is unable to discharge the powers and duties of his office, the Vice President shall continue to discharge the same as Acting President; otherwise, the President shall resume the powers and duties of his office.

Amendment XXVI[24]

Section 1. The right of citizens of the United States, who are eighteen years of age or older, to vote shall not be denied or abridged by the United States or any State on account of age.

Section 2. The Congress shall have power to enforce this article by appropriate legislation.

Amendment XXVII[25]

No law, varying the compensation for the services of Senators and Representatives, shall take effect, until an election of Representatives shall have intervened.

Source: White House Web Site, Electronic Publications. Available from: http://www.pub.whitehouse.gov/WH/Publications/html/Publications.html

[24]Adopted in 1971.

[25]Adopted in 1992.

3.2.3   NUMBER 10 OF *THE FEDERALIST PAPERS* (1787)

James Madison was a key figure in the movement for a federal system of government and played an important part as a delegate at the Constitutional Convention in drafting the Constitution. After the Convention Madison, Alexander Hamilton and John Jay worked to persuade the individual states to accept the Constitution and join the Union. They produced *The Federalist Papers*, a series of 85 political articles published in newspapers. Number 10, by Madison, emphasizes the danger of factions in government and the advantage of a Federal Union in controlling the effects of their 'mischiefs'. It was addressed to the people of the State of New York which joined the Union in December 1787.

To the People of the State of New York: Among the numerous advantages promised by a well constructed Union, none deserves to be more accurately developed than its tendency to break and control the violence of faction. The friend of popular governments never finds himself so much alarmed for their character and fate, as when he contemplates their propensity to this dangerous vice. He will not fail, therefore, to set a due value on any plan which, without violating the principles to which he is attached, provides a proper cure for it. The instability, injustice, and confusion introduced into the public councils, have, in truth, been the mortal diseases under which popular governments have everywhere perished; as they continue to be the favorite and fruitful topics from which the adversaries to liberty derive their most specious declamations. The valuable improvements made by the American constitutions on the popular models, both ancient and modern, cannot certainly be too much admired; but it would be an unwarrantable partiality, to contend that they have as effectually obviated the danger on this side, as was wished and expected. Complaints are everywhere heard from our most considerate and virtuous citizens, equally the friends of public and private faiths, and of public and personal liberty, that our governments are too unstable, that the public good is disregarded in the conflicts of rival parties, and that measures are too often decided, not according to the rules of justice and the rights of the minor party, but by the superior force of an interested and overbearing majority. However anxiously we may wish that these complaints had no foundation, the evidence of known facts will not permit us to deny that they are in some degree true. It will be found, indeed, on a candid review of our situation, that some of the distresses under which we labor have been erroneously charged on the operation of our governments; but it will be found, at the same time, that other causes will not alone account for many of our heaviest misfortunes; and particularly, for that prevailing and increasing distrust of public engagements, and alarm for private rights, which are echoed from one end of the continent to the other. These must be chiefly, if not wholly, effects of the unsteadiness and injustice with which a factious spirit has tainted our public administrations.

By a faction, I understand a number of citizens, whether amounting to a majority or minority of the whole, who are united and actuated by some common impulse of passion, or of interest, adverse to the rights of other citizens, or to the permanent and aggregate interests of the community.

There are two methods of curing the mischiefs of faction: the one, by removing its causes; the other, by controlling its effects.

There are again two methods of removing the causes of faction: the one, by destroying the liberty which is essential to its existence; the other, by giving to every citizen the same opinions, the same passions, and the same interests.

It could never be more truly said than of the first remedy, that it was worse than the disease. Liberty is to faction what air is to fire, an ailment without which it instantly expires. But it could not be less folly to abolish liberty, which is essential to political life, because it nourishes faction, than it would be to wish the annihilation of air, which is essential to animal life, because it imparts to fire its destructive agency.

The second expedient is as impracticable as the first would be unwise. As long as the reason of man continues fallible, and he is at liberty to exercise it, different opinions will be formed. As long as the connection subsists between his reason and his self-love, his opinions and his passion will have a reciprocal influence on each other, and the former will be objects to which the latter will attach themselves. The diversity in the faculties of men, from which the rights of property originate, is not less an insuperable obstacle to a uniformity of interests. The protection of these faculties is the first object of government. From the protection of different and unequal faculties of acquiring property, the possession of different degrees and kinds of property immediately results; and from the influence of these on the sentiments and views of the respective proprietors, ensues a division of the society into different interests and parties.

The latent causes of faction are thus sown in the nature of man; and we see them everywhere brought into different degrees of activity, according to the different circumstances of civil society. A zeal for different opinions concerning religion, concerning government, and many other points, as well of speculation as of practise; an attachment to different leaders ambitiously contending for pre-eminence and power; or to persons of other descriptions whose fortunes have been interesting to the human passions, have, in turn, divided mankind into parties, inflamed them with mutual animosity, and rendered them much more disposed to vex and oppress each other than to co-operate for their common good. So strong is this propensity of mankind to fall into mutual animosities, that where no substantial occasion presents itself, the most frivolous and fanciful distinctions have been sufficient to kindle their unfriendly passions and excite their most violent conflicts. But the most common and durable source of factions has been the various and unequal distribution of property. Those who hold and those who are without property have ever formed distinct interests in society. Those who are creditors, and those who are debtors, fall under a like discrimination. A landed interest, a manufacturing interest, a mercantile interest, a moneyed interest, with many lesser interests, grow up of necessity in civilized nations, and divide them into different classes, actuated by different sentiments and views. The regulation of these various and interfering interests forms the principal task of modern legislation, and involves the spirit of party and faction in the necessary and ordinary operations of the government.

No man is allowed to be a judge in his own cause, because his interest would certainly bias his judgment, and, not improbably, corrupt his integrity. With equal, nay with greater reason, a body of men are unfit to be both judges and parties at the same time; yet what are many of the most important acts of legislation, but so many judicial determinations, not indeed concerning the rights of single persons, but concerning the rights of large bodies of citizens? And what are the different classes of legislators but advocates and parties to the causes which they determine? Is a law proposed concerning private debts? It is a question to which the creditors are parties on one side and the debtors on the other. Justice ought to hold the balance between them. Yet the parties are, and must be, themselves the judges; and the most numerous party, or, in other words, the most powerful faction, must be expected to prevail. Shall domestic manufacturers be encouraged, and in what degree, by restrictions on foreign manufactures? These are questions which would be differently decided by the landed and the manufacturing classes, and probably be neither with a sole regard to justice and the public good. The apportionment of taxes on the various descriptions of property is an act which seems to require the most exact impartiality; yet there is, perhaps, no legislative act in which greater opportunity and temptation are given to a predominant party to trample on the rules of justice. Every shilling with which they overburden the interior number, is a shilling saved to their own pockets.

It is in vain to say that enlightened statesmen will be able to adjust these clashing interests, and render them all subservient to the public good. Enlightened statesmen will not always be at the helm. Nor, in many cases, can such an adjustment be made at all without taking into view indirect and remote considerations, which will rarely prevail over the immediate interest which one party may find in disregarding the rights of another or the good of the whole.

The inference to which we are brought is, that the *causes* of faction cannot be removed, and that relief is only to be sought in the means of controlling its *effects*.

If a faction consists of less than a majority, relief is supplied by the republican principle, which enables the majority to defeat its sinister view by regular vote. It may clog the administration, it may convulse the society, but it will be unable to execute and mask its violence under the forms of the Constitution. When a majority is included in a faction, the form of popular government, on the other hand, enables it to sacrifice to its ruling passion or interest both the public good and the rights of other citizens. To secure the public good and private rights against the danger of such a faction, and at the same time to preserve the spirit and the form of popular government, is then the great object to which our inquiries are directed. Let me add that it is the great desideratum by which this form of government can be rescued from the opprobrium under which it has so long labored, and be recommended to the esteem and adoption of mankind.

By what means is this object attainable? Evidently by one of two only. Either the existence of the same passion or interest in a majority at the same time must be prevented, or the majority, having such coexistent passion or interest, must be rendered, by their number and local situation, unable to concert and carry into effect schemes of oppression. If the impulse and the opportunity be suffered to coincide, we well know that neither moral nor religious motives can be relied on as an adequate control. They are not found to be such on the injustice and violence of individuals, and lose their efficacy in proportion to the number combined together, that is, in proportion as their efficacy becomes needful.

From this view of the subject it may be concluded that a pure democracy, by which I mean a society consisting of a small number of citizens, who assemble and administer the government in person, can admit of no cure for the mischiefs of faction. A common passion or interest will, in almost every case, be felt by a majority of the whole; a communication and concert result from the form of government itself; and there is nothing to check the inducements to sacrifice the weaker party or an obnoxious individual. Hence it is that such democracies have ever been spectacles of turbulence and contention; have ever been found incompatible with personal security or the rights of property; and have in general been as short in their lives as they have been violent in their deaths. Theoretic politicians, who have patronized this species of government, have erroneously supposed that by reducing mankind to a perfect equality in their political rights, they would, at the same time, be perfectly equalized and assimilated in their possessions, their opinions, and their passions.

A republic, by which I mean a government in which the scheme of representation takes place, opens a different prospect, and promises the cure for which we are seeking. Let me examine the points in which it varies from pure democracy, and we shall comprehend both the nature of the cure and the efficacy which it must derive from the Union.

The two great points of difference between a democracy and a republic are: first, the delegation of the government, in the latter, to a small number of citizens, elected by the rest; secondly, the greater number of citizens, and greater sphere of country, over which the latter may be extended.

The effect of the first difference is, on the one hand, to refine and enlarge the public views, by passing them through the medium of a chosen body of citizens, whose wisdom may best discern the true interests of their country, and whose patriotism and love of justice will be least likely to sacrifice it to temporary or partial consideration. Under such a regulation, it may well happen that the public voice, pronounced by the representatives of the people, will be more consonant to the public good than if pronounced by the people themselves, convened for the purpose. On the other hand, the effect may be inverted. Men of factious tempers, of local prejudices, or of sinister designs, may, by intrigue, by corruption, or by other means, first obtain the suffrages, and then betray the interests, of the people. The question resulting is, whether small or extensive republics are more favorable to the election of proper guardians of the public weal; and it is clearly decided in favor of the latter by two obvious considerations:

In the first place, it is to be remarked that, however small the republic may be, the representatives must be raised to a certain number, in order to guard against the cabals of a few; and that, however large it may be, they must be limited to a certain number, in order to guard against the confusion of a multitude. Hence, the number of representatives in the two cases not being in proportion to that of the two constituents, and being proportionally greater in the small republic, it follows that, if the proportion of fit characters be not less in the large than in the small republic, the former will present a greater option, and consequently a greater probability of a fit choice.

In the next place, as each representative will be chosen by a greater number of citizens in the large than in the small republic, it will be more difficult for unworthy candidates to practice with success the vicious arts by which elections are too often carried; and the suffrages of the people being more free, will be more likely to centre in men who possess the most attractive merit and the most diffusive and established characters.

It must be confessed that in this, as in most other cases, there is a mean, on both sides of which inconveniences will be found to lie. By enlarging too much the number of electors, you render the representative too little acquainted with all their local circumstances and lesser interests; as by reducing it too much, you render him unduly attached to these, and too little fit to comprehend and pursue great and national objects. The federal Constitution forms a happy combination in this respect; the great and aggregate interests being referred to the national, the local and particular to the State legislatures.

The other point of difference is, the greater number of citizens and extent of territory which may be brought within the compass of republican than of democratic government; and it is this circumstance principally which renders factious combinations less to be dreaded in the former than in the latter. The smaller the society, the fewer probably will be the distinct parties and interests composing it; the fewer the distinct parties and interests, the more frequently will a majority be found of the same party; and the smaller the number of individuals composing a majority, and the smaller the compass within which they are placed, the more easily will they concert and execute their plans of oppression. Extend the sphere, and take in a greater variety of parties and interests; you make it less probable that a majority of the whole will have a common motive to invade the rights of other citizens; or if such a common motive exists, it will be more difficult for all who feel it to discover their own strength, and to act in unison with each other. Besides other impediments, it may be remarked that, where there is a consciousness of unjust or dishonorable purposes, communication is always checked by distrust in proportion to the number whose concurrence is necessary.

Hence, it clearly appears, that the same advantage which a republic has over a democracy, in controlling the effects of faction, is enjoyed by a large over a small republic — is enjoyed by the Union over the States composing it. Does the advantage consist in the substitution of representatives whose enlightened views and virtuous sentiments render them superior to local prejudices and to schemes of injustice? It will not be denied that the representation of the Union will be most likely to possess these requisite endowments. Does it consist in the greater security afforded by a greater variety of parties, against the event of any one party being able to outnumber and oppress the rest? In an equal degree does the increased variety of parties comprised within the Union, increase this security. Does it, in fine, consist in the greater obstacles opposed to the concert and accomplishment of the secret wishes of an unjust and interested majority? Here, again, the extent of the Union gives it the most palpable advantage.

The influence of factious leaders may kindle a flame within their particular States, but will be unable to spread a general conflagration through the other States. A religious sect may degenerate into a political faction in a part of the Confederacy; but the variety of sects dispersed over the entire face of it must secure the national councils against any danger from that source. A rage for paper money, for an abolition of debts, for an equal division of property, or for any other improper or wicked project, will be less apt to pervade the whole body of the Union than a particular member of it; in the same proportion as such a malady is more likely to taint a particular county or district, than an entire State.

In the extent and proper structure of the Union, therefore, we behold a republican remedy for the diseases most incident to republican government. And according to the degree of pleasure and pride we feel in being republicans, ought to be our zeal in cherishing the spirit and supporting the character of Federalists.

Source: Encyclopaedia Britannica (1976) *The Annals of America, The Bicentennial Edition 1776–1976, Vol.3*, Chicago, Encyclopaedia Britannica, Inc., pp.216–20.

3.2.4   THE GETTYSBURG ADDRESS (1863)

In July 1863 the Confederate Army under Robert E. Lee, having
marched deep into Union territory, was defeated at Gettysburg, Pennsylvania and forced to retreat. Though nearly two years of hard fighting remained before the last Confederate forces surrendered, the Battle
of Gettysburg had been a decisive turning point in the Civil War. In
November of the same year President Lincoln attended the dedication
of a nearby cemetery for most of the 6,000 killed in the battle. His
address at the dedication reaffirmed the principles of the Founding
Fathers and emphasized his overriding war aim; the preservation of
the Union.

Fourscore and seven years ago our fathers brought forth, on this continent, a
new nation, conceived in Liberty, and dedicated to the proposition that all
men are created equal.

Now we are engaged in a great civil war, testing whether that nation, or any
nation so conceived, and so dedicated, can long endure. We are met on a
great battlefield of that war. We have come to dedicate a portion of that
field, as a final resting-place for those who have gave their lives, that that
nation might live. It is altogether fitting and proper that we should do this.

But, in a larger sense, we can not dedicate — we can not consecrate — we
can not hallow — this ground. The brave men, living and dead, who struggled here, have consecrated it far above our poor power to add or detract.
The world will little note, nor long remember what we say here, but it can
never forget what they did here. It is for us the living, rather, to be dedicated here to the unfinished work which they who fought here have thus far
so nobly advanced. It is rather for us to be here dedicated to the great task
remaining before us — that from these honored dead we take increased
devotion to that cause for which they have gave the last full measure of
devotion — that we here highly resolve that these dead shall not have died
in vain — that this nation, under God, shall have a new birth of freedom —
and that government of the people, by the people, for the people, shall not
perish from the earth.

Source: Commager, H.S. (ed.) (1963) *Documents of American History* (7th edn), New
York, Appleton Century Crofts, vol.1, p.428.

3.3   PRESIDENTIAL INAUGURALS

All presidential inaugurals mark a new beginning in the politics of the
nation to some extent, but perhaps the first four reproduced here have
more claim to significance than some others this century. While each

speech addresses the principal concerns of its time, all refer back to the founders of the nation and all seek the blessing of God.

Franklin D. Roosevelt's first address in 1933, drafted with his close adviser Professor Raymond Moley of Columbia University, proved to be a stirring call to action in the face of the Great Depression. It ushered in the policies of the New Deal and tied the economic well-being of citizens closer than ever before to America's democratic ideals.

The narrow victory of the youthful Democrat John F. Kennedy brought eight years of Republican presidency to an end. His inaugural address in 1961 included input from a variety of sources and personal advisers. The speech aimed to signal a new spirit and tone in government — and throughout society — from the energy and vitality of a new generation of twentieth-century Americans. This 'new spirit' was cut short by Kennedy's assassination one thousand days later.

Democrat Jimmy Carter's 1976 victory came in a period of malaise in the presidency. It followed the Watergate scandal, which brought Nixon's presidency to an end, and the presidency of Gerald Ford, who assumed the office after Nixon's resignation. However, President Carter's single term was not generally perceived as a success either.

Ronald Reagan's first term, which began in 1981, ended the period of malaise. Reagan's message was one of 'getting the state off the backs of the people' and allowing them to forge economic recovery and political renewal. It proved to be a popular message from a popular President.

With the election of President Bill Clinton the Reagan/Bush era came to an end after twelve years, when even foreign policy triumphs could not divert American public attention from domestic economic problems. The final inaugural included in this section opened the eventful second term of President Clinton.

3.3.1 FRANKLIN D. ROOSEVELT'S FIRST INAUGURAL ADDRESS (1933)

This is a day of national consecration.

I am certain that my fellow Americans expect that on my induction into the Presidency I will address them with a candor and a decision which the present situation of our Nation impels. This is pre-eminently the time to speak the truth, the whole truth, frankly and boldly. Nor need we shrink from honestly facing conditions in our country today. This great Nation will endure as it has endured, will revive and will prosper. So, first of all, let me assert my firm belief that the only thing we have to fear is fear itself — nameless, unreasoning, unjustified terror which paralyzes needed efforts to convert retreat into advance. In every dark hour of our national life a leadership of frankness and vigor has met with that understanding and support

Franklin D. Roosevelt's first inaugural address, March 1933

of the people themselves which is essential to victory. I am convinced that you will again give that support to leadership in these critical days.

In such a spirit on my part and on yours we face our common difficulties. They concern, thank God, only material things. Values have shrunken to fantastic levels; taxes have risen; our ability to pay has fallen; government of all kinds is faced by serious curtailment of income; the means of exchange are frozen in the currents of trade; the withered leaves of industrial enterprise lie on every side; farmers find no markets for their produce; the savings on many years in thousands of families are gone.

More important, a host of unemployed citizens face the grim problem of existence, and an equally great number toil with little return. Only a foolish optimist can deny the dark realities of the moment.

Yet our distress comes from no failure of substance. We are stricken by no plague of locusts. Compared with the perils which our forefathers conquered because they believed and were not afraid, we have still much to be thankful for. Nature still offers her bounty and human efforts have multiplied it. Plenty is at our doorstep, but a generous use of it languishes in the very sight of the supply. Primarily this is because rulers of the exchange of mankind's good have failed through their own stubbornness and their own incompetence, have admitted their failure, and have abdicated. Practices of the unscrupulous money changers stand indicted in the court of public opinion, rejected by the hearts and minds of men.

True they have tried, but their efforts have been cast in the pattern of an outworn tradition. Faced by failure of credit they have proposed only the lending of more money. Stripped of the lure of profit by which to induce our people to follow their false leadership, they have resorted to exhortations, pleading tearfully for restored confidence. They know only the rules of a generation of self-seekers. They have no vision, and when there is no vision the people perish.

The money changers have fled from their high seats in the temple of our civilization. We may now restore that temple to the ancient truths. The measure of the restoration lies in the extent to which we apply social values more noble than mere monetary profit.

Happiness lies not in the mere possession of money; it lies in the joy of achievement, in the thrill of creative effort. The joy and moral stimulation of work no longer must be forgotten in the mad chase of evanescent profits. These dark days will be worth all they cost us if they teach us that our true destiny is not to be ministered unto but to minister to ourselves and to our fellow men.

Recognition of the falsity of material wealth as the standard of success goes hand in hand with the abandonment of the false belief that public office and high political position are to be valued only by the standards or pride of place and personal profit; and there must be an end to a conduct in banking and in business which too often has given to a sacred trust the likeness of callous and selfish wrongdoing. Small wonder that confidence languishes, for it thrives only on honesty, on honor, on the sacredness of obligations, on faithful protection, on unselfish performance; without them it cannot live.

Restoration calls, however, not for changes in ethics alone. This Nation asks for action, and action now.

Our greatest primary task is to put people to work. This is no unsolvable problem if we face it wisely and courageously. It can be accomplished in part by direct recruiting by the Government itself, treating the task as we would treat the emergency of a war, but at the same time, through this employment, accomplishing greatly needed projects to stimulate and reorganize the use of our natural resources.

Hand in hand with this we must frankly recognize the overbalance of population in our industrial centers and, by engaging on a national scale in a redistribution, endeavor to provide a better use of the land for those best fitted for the land. The task can be helped by definite efforts to raise the values of agricultural products and with this the power to purchase the output of our cities. It can be helped by preventing realistically the tragedy of the growing loss through foreclosure of our small homes and our farms. It can be helped by insistence that the Federal, State, and local governments act forthwith on the demand that their cost be drastically reduced. It can be helped by the unifying of relief activities which today are often scattered, uneconomical, and unequal. It can be helped by national planning for and supervision of all forms of transportation and of communications and other utilities which have a definitely public character. There are many ways in which it can be helped, but it can never be helped merely by talking about it. We must act and act quickly.

Finally, in our progress toward a resumption of work we require two safeguards against a return of the evils of the old order: there must be a strict supervision of all banking and credits and investments, so that there will be an end to speculation with other people's money; and there must be provision for an adequate but sound currency.

These are the lines of attack. I shall presently urge upon a new Congress, in special session, detailed measures for their fulfilment, and I shall seek the immediate assistance of the several States.

Through this program of action we address ourselves to putting our own national house in order and making income balance outgo. Our international trade relations, though vastly important, are in point of time and necessity secondary to the establishment of a sound national economy. I favor as a practical policy the putting of first things first. I shall spare no effort to restore world trade by international economic readjustment, but the emergency at home cannot wait on that accomplishment.

The basic thought that guides these specific means of national recovery is not narrowly nationalistic. It is the insistence, as a first consideration, upon the interdependence of the various elements in and parts of the United States — a recognition of the old and permanently important manifestation of the American spirit of the pioneer. It is the way to recovery. It is the immediate way. It is the strongest assurance that the recovery will endure.

In the field of world policy I would dedicate this Nation to the policy of the good neighbor — the neighbor who resolutely respects himself and, because he does so, respects the rights of others — the neighbor who respects his obligations and respects the sanctity of his agreements in and with a world of neighbors.

If I read the temper of our people correctly, we now realize as we have never realized before our interdependence on each other; that we cannot merely take but we must give as well; that if we are to go forward, we must move as a trained and loyal army willing to sacrifice for the good of a common discipline, because without such discipline no progress is made, no leadership becomes effective. We are, I know, ready and willing to submit our lives and property to such discipline, because it makes possible a leadership which aims at a larger good. This I propose to offer, pledging that the larger purposes will bind upon us all as a sacred obligation with a unity of duty hitherto evoked only in time of armed strife.

With this pledge taken, I assume unhesitatingly the leadership of this great army of our people dedicated to a disciplined attack upon our common problems.

Action in this image and to this end is feasible under the form of govern-ment which we have inherited from our ancestors. Our Constitution is so simple and practical that it is possible always to meet extraordinary needs by changes in emphasis and arrangement without loss of essential form. That is why our constitutional system has proved itself the most superbly enduring political mechanism the modern world has produced. It has met every stress of vast expansion of territory, of foreign wars, of bitter internal strife, of world relations.

It is to be hoped that the normal balance of Executive and legislative auth-ority may be wholly adequate to meet the unprecedented task before us. But it may be that an unprecedented demand and need for undelayed action may call for temporary departure from that normal balance of public procedure.

I am prepared under my constitutional duty to recommend the measures that a stricken Nation in the midst of a stricken world may require. These measures, or such other measures as the Congress may build out of its experience and wisdom, I shall seek, within my constitutional authority, to bring to speedy adoption.

But in the event that the Congress shall fail to take one of these two courses, and in the event that the national emergency is still critical, I shall not evade the clear course of duty that will then confront me. I shall ask the Congress for the one remaining instrument to meet the crisis — broad Executive power to wage a war against the emergency, as great as the power that would be given to me if we were in fact invaded by a foreign foe.

For the trust reposed in me I will return the courage and the devotion that befit the time. I can do no less.

We face the arduous days that lie before us in the warm courage of national unity; with the clear consciousness of seeking old and precious moral values; with the clean satisfaction that comes from the stern performance of duty by old and young alike. We aim at the assurance of a rounded and permanent national life.

We do not distrust the future of essential democracy. The people of the United States have not failed. In their need they have registered a mandate that they want direct, vigorous action. They have asked for discipline and direction under leadership. They have made me the present instrument of their wishes. In the spirit of the gift I take it.

In this dedication of a Nation we humbly ask the blessing of God. May He protect each and every one of us. May He guide me in the days to come.

Source: Encyclopaedia Britannica (1976) *The Annals of America, The Bicentennial Edition 1776–1976, Vol.15*, Chicago, Encyclopaedia Britannica, Inc., pp.205–8.

3.3.2 JOHN F. KENNEDY'S INAUGURAL ADDRESS (1961)

We observe today not a victory of a party but a celebration of freedom — symbolizing an end as well as a beginning — signifying renewal as well as change. For I have sworn before you and Almighty God the same solemn oath our forebears prescribed nearly a century and three quarters ago.

The world is very different now. For man holds in his mortal hands the power to abolish all forms of human poverty and all forms of human life. And yet the same revolutionary beliefs for which our forebears fought are still at issue around the globe — the belief that the rights of man come not from the generosity of the state but from the hand of God.

We dare not forget today that we are the heirs of that first revolution. Let the word go forth from this time and place, to friend and foe alike, that the torch has been passed to a new generation of Americans — born in this century, tempered by war, disciplined by a hard and bitter peace, proud of our ancient heritage — and unwilling to witness or permit the slow undoing of those human rights to which this Nation has always been committed, and to which we are committed today at home and around the world.

Let every nation know, whether it wishes us well or ill, that we shall pay any price, bear any burden, meet any hardship, support any friend, oppose any foe to assure the survival and success of liberty.

This much we pledge — and more.

To those old allies whose cultural and spiritual origins we share, we pledge the loyalty of faithful friends. United, there is little we cannot do in a host of cooperative ventures. Divided, there is little we can do — for we dare not meet a powerful challenge at odds and split asunder.

To those new states whom we welcome to the ranks of the free, we pledge our word that one form of colonial control shall not have passed away merely to be replaced by a far more iron tyranny. We shall not always expect to find them supporting our view. But we shall always hope to find them strongly supporting their own freedom — and to remember that, in the past, those who foolishly sought power by riding the back of the tiger ended up inside.

To those peoples in the huts and villages of half the globe struggling to break the bonds of mass misery, we pledge our best efforts to help them help themselves, for whatever period is required — not because the Communists may be doing it, not because we seek their votes, but because it is right. If a free society cannot help the many who are poor, it cannot save the few who are rich.

To our sister republics south of our border, we offer a special pledge — to convert our good words into good deeds — in a new alliance for progress — to assist free men and free governments in casting off the chains of poverty. But this peaceful revolution of hope cannot become the prey of hostile powers. Let all our neighbors know that we shall join with them to oppose aggression or subversion anywhere in the Americas. And let every other power know that this hemisphere intends to remain the master of its own house.

To that world assembly of sovereign states, the United Nations, our last best hope in an age where the instruments of war have far outpaced the instruments of peace, we renew our pledge of support — to prevent it from becoming merely a forum for invective — to strengthen its shield of the new and the weak — and to enlarge the area in which its writ may run.

Finally, to those nations who would make themselves our adversary, we offer not a pledge but a request: that both sides begin anew the quest for peace, before the dark powers of destruction unleashed by science engulf all humanity in planned or accidental self-destruction.

We dare not tempt them with weakness. For only when our arms are sufficient beyond doubt can we be certain beyond doubt that they will never be employed.

But neither can two great and powerful groups of nations take comfort from our present course — both sides overburdened by the cost of modern weapons, both rightly alarmed by the steady spread of the deadly atom, yet both racing to alter that uncertain balance of terror that stays the hand of mankind's final war.

So let us begin anew — remembering on both sides that civility is not a sign of weakness, and sincerity is always subject to proof. Let us never negotiate out of fear. But let us never fear to negotiate.

Let both sides explore what problems unite us instead of belaboring those problems which divide us. Let both sides, for the first time, formulate serious and precise proposals for the inspection and control of arms — and bring the absolute power to destroy other nations under the absolute control of all nations.

Let both sides seek to invoke the wonders of science instead of its terrors. Together let us explore the stars, conquer the deserts, eradicate disease, tap the ocean depths and encourage the arts and commerce.

Let both sides unite to heed in all corners of the earth the command of Isaiah — to 'undo the heavy burdens and to let the oppressed go free'.

And if a beach-head of cooperation may push back the jungle of suspicion, let both sides join in a new endeavor; not a new balance of power, but a new world of law, where the strong are just and the weak secure and the peace preserved.

All this will not be finished in the first one hundred days. Nor will it be finished in the first one thousand days, nor in the life of this Administration, nor even perhaps in our life-time on this planet. But let us begin.

In your hands, my fellow citizens, more than mine, will rest the final success or failure of our course. Since this country was founded, each generation of Americans has been summoned to give testimony to its national loyalty. The graves of young Americans who answered the call to service surround the globe.

Now the trumpet summons us again — not as a call to bear arms, though arms we need — not as a call to battle, though embattled we are — but a call to bear the burden of a long twilight struggle, year in and year out, 'rejoicing in hope, patient in tribulation' — a struggle against the common enemies of man: tyranny, poverty, disease and war itself.

Can we forge against these enemies a grand and global alliance, North and South, East and West, that can assure a more fruitful life for all mankind? Will you join in that historic effort?

In the long history of the world, only a few generations have been granted the role of defending freedom in its hour of maximum danger. I do not shrink from this responsibility — I welcome it. I do not believe that any of us would exchange places with any other people or any other generation. The energy, the faith, the devotion which we bring to this endeavor will light our country and all who serve it — and the glow from that fire can truly light the world.

And so, my fellow Americans: Ask not what your country can do for you — ask what you can do for your country.

My fellow citizens of the world: Ask not what America will do for you, but what together we can do for the freedom of man.

Finally, whether you are citizens of America or citizens of the world, ask of us here the same high standards of strength and sacrifice which we ask of you. With a good conscience our only sure reward, with history the final judge of our deeds, let us go forth to lead the land we love, asking His blessing and His help, but knowing that here on earth God's work must truly be our own.

Source: Commager, H.S. (ed.) (1963) *Documents of American History* (7th edn), New York, Appleton Century Crofts, vol.2, p.688.

3.3.3 JIMMY CARTER'S INAUGURAL ADDRESS (1977)

For myself and for our Nation, I want to thank my predecessor for all he has done to heal our land.

In this outward and physical ceremony we attest once again to the inner and spiritual strength of our Nation. As my high school teacher, Miss Julia Coleman, used to say: 'We must adjust to changing times and still hold to unchanging principles.'

Here before me is the Bible used in the inauguration of our first President, in 1789, and I have just taken the oath of office on the Bible my mother gave me a few years ago, opened to a timeless admonition from the ancient prophet Micah: 'He hath showed thee, O man, what is good; and what doth the Lord require of thee, but to do justly, and to love mercy, and to walk humbly with thy God.' (Micah 6:8)

This inauguration ceremony marks a new beginning, a new dedication within our Government, and a new spirit among us all. A President may sense and proclaim that new spirit, but only a people can provide it.

Two centuries ago our Nation's birth was a milestone in the long quest for freedom, but the bold and brilliant dream which excited the founders of this Nation still awaits its consummation. I have no new dream to set forth today, but rather urge a fresh faith in the old dream.

Ours was the first society openly to define itself in terms of both spirituality and of human liberty. It is that unique self-definition which has given us an exceptional appeal, but it also imposes on us a special obligation, to take on those moral duties which, when assumed, seem invariably to be in our own best interests.

You have given me a great responsibility — to stay close to you, to be worthy of you, and to exemplify what you are. Let us create together a new national spirit of unity and trust. Your strength can compensate for my weakness, and your wisdom can help to minimize my mistakes.

Let us learn together and laugh together and work together and pray together, confident that in the end we will triumph together in the right.

The American dream endures. We must once again have full faith in our country and in one another. I believe America can be better. We can be even stronger than before.

Let our recent mistakes bring a resurgent commitment to the basic principles of our Nation, for we know that if we despise our own government we have no future. We recall in special times when we have stood briefly, but magnificently, united. In those times no prize was beyond our grasp.

But we cannot dwell upon remembered glory. We cannot afford to drift. We reject the prospect of failure or mediocrity or an inferior quality of life for any person. Our Government must at the same time be both competent and compassionate.

We have already found a high degree of personal liberty, and we are now struggling to enhance equality of opportunity. Our commitment to human rights must be absolute, our laws fair, our natural beauty preserved; the powerful must not persecute the weak, and human dignity must be enhanced.

We have learned that 'more' is not necessarily 'better', that even our great Nation has its recognized limits, and that we can neither answer all questions nor solve all problems. We cannot afford to do everything, nor can we afford to lack boldness as we meet the future. So, together, in a spirit of individual sacrifice for the common good, we must simply do our best.

Our Nation can be strong abroad only if it is strong at home. And we know that the best way to enhance freedom in other lands is to demonstrate here that our democratic system is worthy of emulation.

To be true to ourselves, we must be true to others. We will not behave in foreign places so as to violate our rules and standards here at home, for we know that the trust which our Nation earns is essential to our strength.

The world itself is now dominated by a new spirit. Peoples more numerous and more politically aware are craving and now demanding their place in the sun — not just for the benefit of their own physical condition, but for basic human rights.

The passion for freedom is on the rise. Tapping this new spirit, there can be no nobler nor more ambitious task for America to undertake on this day of a new beginning than to help shape a just and peaceful world that is truly humane.

We are a strong nation, and we will maintain strength so sufficient that it need not be proven in combat — a quiet strength based not merely on size of an arsenal, but on the nobility of ideas.

We will be ever vigilant and never vulnerable, and we will fight our wars against poverty, ignorance, and injustice — for those are the enemies against which our forces can be honorably marshaled.

We are a purely idealistic Nation, but let no one confuse our idealism with weakness.

Because we are free we can never be indifferent to the fate of freedom elsewhere. Our moral sense dictates a clearcut preference for these societies which share with us an abiding respect for individual human rights. We do not seek to intimidate, but it is clear that a world which others can dominate with impunity would be inhospitable to decency and a threat to the well-being of all people.

The world is still engaged in a massive armaments race designed to ensure continuing equivalent strength among potential adversaries. We pledge perseverance and wisdom in our efforts to limit the world's armaments to those necessary for each nation's own domestic safety. And we will move this year a step toward ultimate goal — the elimination of all nuclear weapons from this Earth. We urge all other people to join us, for success can mean life instead of death.

Within us, the people of the United States, there is evident a serious and purposeful rekindling of confidence. And I join in the hope that when my time as your President has ended, people might say this about our Nation:

> that we had remembered the words of Micah and renewed our search for humility, mercy, and justice;

that we had torn down the barriers that separated those of different race and region and religion, and where there had been mistrust, built unity, with a respect for diversity;

that we had found productive work for those able to perform it;

that we had strengthened the American family, which is the basis of our society;

that we had ensured respect for the law, and equal treatment under the law, for the weak and the powerful, for the rich and the poor;

and that we had enabled our people to be proud of their own Government once again.

I would hope that the nations of the world might say that we had built a lasting peace, built not on weapons of war but on international policies which reflect our own most precious values.

These are not just my goals, and they will not be my accomplishments, but the affirmation of our Nation's continuing moral strength and our belief in an undiminished, ever-expanding American dream.

Source: Jimmy Carter Library Web Site. Available from:
http://carterlibrary.galileo.peachnet.edu/inaugadd.htm

3.3.4   RONALD REAGAN'S FIRST INAUGURAL ADDRESS (1981)

To a few of us here today this is a solemn and most momentous occasion, and yet in the history of our nation it is a commonplace occurrence. The orderly transfer of authority as called for in the Constitution routinely takes place, as it has for almost two centuries, and few of us stop to think how unique we really are. In the eyes of many in the world, this every-four-year ceremony we accept as normal is nothing less than a miracle.

Mr President, I want our fellow citizens to know how much you did to carry on this tradition. By your gracious cooperation in the transition process, you have shown a watching world that we are a united people pledged to maintaining a political system which guarantees individual liberty to a greater degree than any other, and I thank you and your people for all your help in maintaining the continuity which is the bulwark of our republic.

The business of our nation goes forward. These United States are confronted with an economic affliction of great proportions. We suffer from the longest and one of the worst sustained inflations in our national history. It distorts our economic decisions, penalizes thrift, and crushes the struggling young and the fixed-income elderly alike. It threatens to shatter the lives of millions of our people.

Idle industries have cast workers into unemployment, human misery, and personal indignity. Those who do work are denied a fair return for their labor by a tax system which penalizes successful achievement and keeps us from maintaining full productivity.

But great as our tax burden is, it has not kept pace with public spending. For decades we have piled deficit upon deficit, mortgaging our future and our children's future for the temporary convenience of the present. To continue this long trend is to guarantee tremendous social, cultural, political, and economic upheavals.

You and I, as individuals, can, by borrowing, live beyond our means, but for only a limited period of time. Why, then, should we think that collectively, as a nation, we're not bound by that same limitation? We must act today in order to preserve tomorrow. And let there be no misunderstanding: We are going to begin to act, beginning today.

The economic ills we suffer have come upon us over several decades. They will not go away in days, weeks, or months, but they will go away. They will go away because we as Americans have the capacity now, as we've had in the past, to do whatever needs to be done to preserve this last and greatest bastion of freedom.

In this present crisis, government is not the solution to our problem; government is the problem. From time to time we've been tempted to believe that society has become too complex to be managed by self-rule, that government by an élite group is superior to government for, by, and of the people. Well, if no one among us is capable of governing himself, then who among us has the capacity to govern someone else? All of us together, in and out of government, must bear the burden. The solutions we seek must be equitable, with no one group singled out to pay a higher price.

We hear much of special interest groups. Well, our concern must be for a special interest group that has been too long neglected. It knows no sectional boundaries or ethnic and racial divisions, and it crosses political party lines. It is made up of men and women who raise our food, patrol our streets, man our mines and factories, teach our children, keep our homes, and heal us when we're sick — professionals, industrialists, shopkeepers, clerks, cabbies, and truck drivers. They are, in short, 'we the people', this breed called Americans.

Well, this administration's objective will be a healthy, vigorous, growing economy that provides equal opportunities for all Americans, with no barriers born of bigotry or discrimination. Putting America back to work means putting all Americans back to work. Ending inflation means freeing all Americans from the terror of runaway living costs. All must share in the productive work of this 'new beginning', and all must share in the bounty of a revived economy. With the idealism and fair play which are the core of our system and our strength, we can have a strong and prosperous America, at peace with itself and the world.

So, as we begin, let us take inventory. We are a nation that has a government — not the other way around. And this makes us special among the nations of the earth. Our government has no power except that granted it by the people. It is time to check and reverse the growth of government, which shows signs of having grown beyond the consent of the governed.

It is my intention to curb the size and influence of the federal establishment and to demand recognition of the distinction between the powers granted to the federal government and those reserved to the states or to the people. All of us need to be reminded that the federal government did not create the states; the states created the federal government.

Now, so there will be no misunderstanding, it's not my intention to do away with government. It is rather to make it work — work with us, not over us; to stand by our side, not ride on our back. Government can and must provide opportunity, not smother it; foster productivity, not stifle it.

If we look to the answer as to why for so many years we achieved so much, prospered as no other people on earth, it was because here in this land we unleashed the energy and individual genius of man to a greater extent than has ever been done before. Freedom and the dignity of the individual have been more available and assured here than in any other place on earth. The price for this freedom at times has been high, but we have never been unwilling to pay that price.

It is no coincidence that our present troubles parallel and are proportionate to the intervention and intrusion in our lives that result from unnecessary and excessive growth of government. It is time for us to realize that we're too great a nation to limit ourselves to small dreams. We're not, as some would have us believe, doomed to an inevitable decline. I do not believe in a fate that will fall on us no matter what we do. I do believe in a fate that will fall on us if we do nothing. So, with all the creative energy at our command, let us begin an era of national renewal. Let us review our determination, our courage, and our strength. And let us renew our faith and our hope.

We have every right to dream heroic dreams. Those who say that we're in a time when there are no heroes, they just don't know where to look. You can see heroes every day going in and out of factory gates. Others, a handful in number, produce enough food to feed all of us and then the world beyond. You meet heroes across a counter, and they're on both sides of that counter. There are entrepreneurs with faith in themselves and faith in an idea who create new jobs, new wealth and opportunity. They're individuals and families whose taxes support the government and whose voluntary gifts support church, charity, culture, art, and education. Their patriotism is quiet, but deep. Their values sustain our national life.

Now, I have used the words 'they' and 'their' in speaking of these heroes. I could say 'you' and 'your', because I'm addressing the heroes of whom I speak — you, the citizens of this blessed land. Your dreams, your hopes, your goals are going to be the dreams, the hopes, and the goals of this administration, so help me God.

We shall reflect the compassion that is so much a part of your makeup. How can we love our country and not love our countrymen; and loving them, reach out a hand when they fall, heal them when they're sick, and provide opportunity to make them self-sufficient so they will be equal in fact and not just in theory?

Can we solve the problems confronting us? Well, the answer is an unequivocal and emphatic 'yes'. To paraphrase Winston Churchill, I did not take the oath I've just taken with the intention of presiding over the dissolution of the world's strongest economy.

In the days ahead I will propose removing the roadblocks that have slowed our economy and reduced productivity. Steps will be taken aimed at restoring the balance between the various levels of government. Progress may be slow, measured in inches and feet, not miles, but we will progress. It is time to reawaken this industrial giant, to get government back within its means, and to lighten our punitive tax burden. And these will be our first priorities, and on these principles there will be no compromise.

On the eve of our struggle for independence a man who might have been one of the greatest among the Founding Fathers, Dr Joseph Warren, president of the Massachusetts Congress, said to his fellow Americans, 'Our country is in danger, but not to be despaired of ... On you depend the fortunes of America. You are to decide the important questions upon which rests the happiness and the liberty of millions yet unborn. Act worthy of yourselves.'

Well, I believe we, the Americans of today, are ready to act worthy of ourselves, ready to do what must be done to ensure happiness and liberty for ourselves, our children, and our children's children. And as we renew ourselves here in our own land, we will be seen as having greater strength throughout the world. We will again be the exemplar of freedom and a beacon of hope for those who do not now have freedom.

To those neighbors and allies who share our freedom, we will strengthen our historic ties and assure them of our support and firm commitment. We will match loyalty with loyalty. We will strive for mutually beneficial relations. We will not use our friendship to impose on their sovereignty, for our own sovereignty is not for sale.

As for the enemies of freedom, those who are potential adversaries, they will be reminded that peace is the highest aspiration of the American people. We will negotiate for it, sacrifice for it; we will not surrender for it, now or ever.

Our forbearance should never be misunderstood. Our reluctance for conflict should not be misjudged as a failure of will. When action is required to preserve our national security, we will act. We will maintain sufficient strength to prevail if need be, knowing that if we do so we have the best chance of never having to use that strength.

Above all, we must realize that no arsenal or no weapon in the arsenals of the world is so formidable as the will and moral courage of free men and women. It is a weapon our adversaries in today's world do not have. It is a weapon that we as Americans do have. Let that be understood by those who practice terrorism and prey upon their neighbors.

I'm told that tens of thousands of prayer meetings are being held on this day, and for that I'm deeply grateful. We are a nation under God, and I believe God intended for us to be free. It would be fitting and good, I think, if on each Inaugural Day in future years it should be declared a day of prayer.

This is the first time in our history that this ceremony has been held, as you've been told, on this West Front of the Capitol. Standing here, one faces a magnificent vista, opening up on this city's special beauty and history. At the end of this open mall are those shrines to the giants on whose shoulders we stand.

Directly in front of me, the monument to a monumental man, George Washington, father of our country. A man of humility who came to greatness reluctantly. He led America out of revolutionary victory into infant nationhood. Off to one side, the stately memorial to Thomas Jefferson. The Declaration of Independence flames with his eloquence. And then, beyond the Reflecting Pool, the dignified columns of the Lincoln Memorial. Whoever would understand in his heart the meaning of America will find it in the life of Abraham Lincoln.

Beyond those monuments to heroism is the Potomac River, and on the far shore the sloping hills of Arlington National Cemetery, with its row upon row of simple white markers bearing crosses or Stars of David. They add up to only a tiny fraction of the price that has been paid for our freedom.

Each one of those markers is a monument to the kind of hero I spoke of earlier. Their lives ended in places called Belleau Wood, the Argonne, Omaha Beach, Salerno, and halfway around the world on Guadalcanal, Tarawa, Pork Chop Hill, the Chosin Reservoir, and in a hundred rice paddies and jungles of a place called Vietnam.

Under one such marker lies a young man, Martin Treptow, who left his job in a small town barbershop in 1917 to go to France with the famed Rainbow Division. There, on the western front, he was killed trying to carry a message between battalions under heavy artillery fire.

We're told that on his body was found a diary. On the flyleaf under the heading 'My Pledge', he had written these words: 'America must win this war. Therefore I will work, I will save, I will sacrifice, I will endure, I will fight cheerfully and do my utmost, as if the issue of the whole struggle depended on me alone.'

The crisis we are facing today does not require of us the kind of sacrifice that Martin Treptow and so many thousands of others were called upon to make. It does require, however, our best effort and our willingness to believe in ourselves and to believe in our capacity to perform great deeds, to believe that together with God's help we can and will resolve the problems which now confront us.

And after all, why shouldn't we believe that? We are Americans.

God bless you, and thank you.

Source: Columbia University Bartleby Library Web Site. Available from: http://www.co.columbia.edu/acis/bartleby/inaugural/index.html

3.3.5 BILL CLINTON'S SECOND INAUGURAL ADDRESS (1997)

Bill Clinton being sworn in for a second term as President by US Supreme Court Chief Justice William Rehnquist, 20 January 1997

My fellow citizens:

At this last presidential inauguration of the 20th century, let us lift our eyes toward the challenges that await us in the next century. It is our great good fortune that time and chance have put us not only at the edge of a new century, in a new millennium, but on the edge of a bright new prospect in human affairs — a moment that will define our course, and our character, for decades to come. We must keep our old democracy forever young. Guided by the ancient vision of a promised land, let us set our sights upon a land of new promise.

The promise of America was born in the 18th century out of the bold conviction that we are all created equal. It was extended and preserved in the

19th century, when our nation spread across the continent, saved the union, and abolished the awful scourge of slavery.

Then, in turmoil and triumph, that promise exploded onto the world stage to make this the American Century.

And what a century it has been. America became the world's mightiest industrial power; saved the world from tyranny in two world wars and a long cold war; and time and again, reached out across the globe to millions who, like us, longed for the blessings of liberty.

Along the way, Americans produced a great middle class and security in old age; built unrivaled centers of learning and opened public schools to all; split the atom and explored the heavens; invented the computer and the microchip; and deepened the wellspring of justice by making a revolution in civil rights for African Americans and all minorities, and extending the circle of citizenship, opportunity and dignity to women.

Now, for the third time, a new century is upon us, and another time to choose. We began the 19th century with a choice, to spread our nation from coast to coast. We began the 20th century with a choice, to harness the Industrial Revolution to our values of free enterprise, conservation, and human decency. Those choices made all the difference. At the dawn of the 21st century a free people must now choose to shape the forces of the Information Age and the global society, to unleash the limitless potential of all our people, and, yes, to form a more perfect union.

When last we gathered, our march to this new future seemed less certain than it does today. We vowed then to set a clear course to renew our nation.

In these four years, we have been touched by tragedy, exhilarated by challenge, strengthened by achievement. America stands alone as the world's indispensable nation. Once again, our economy is the strongest on Earth. Once again, we are building stronger families, thriving communities, better educational opportunities, a cleaner environment. Problems that once seemed destined to deepen now bend to our efforts: our streets are safer and record numbers of our fellow citizens have moved from welfare to work.

And once again, we have resolved for our time a great debate over the role of government. Today we can declare: Government is not the problem, and government is not the solution. We — the American people — we are the solution. (Applause.) Our founders understood that well and gave us a democracy strong enough to endure for centuries, flexible enough to face our common challenges and advance our common dreams in each new day.

As times change, so government must change. We need a new government for a new century — humble enough not to try to solve all our problems for us, but strong enough to give us the tools to solve our problems for ourselves; a government that is smaller, lives within its means, and does more with less. Yet where it can stand up for our values and interests in the world, and where it can give Americans the power to make a real difference in their everyday lives, government should do more, not less. The preeminent mission of our new government is to give all Americans an opportunity — not a guarantee, but a real opportunity — to build better lives. (Applause.)

Beyond that, my fellow citizens, the future is up to us. Our founders taught us that the preservation of our liberty and our union depends upon responsible citizenship. And we need a new sense of responsibility for a new century. There is work to do, work that government alone cannot do: teaching children to read; hiring people off welfare rolls; coming out from behind locked doors and shuttered windows to help reclaim our streets from drugs and gangs and crime; taking time out of our own lives to serve others.

Each and every one of us, in our own way, must assume personal responsibility — not only for ourselves and our families, but for our neighbors and our nation. (Applause.) Our greatest responsibility is to embrace a new spirit of community for a new century. For any one of us to succeed, we must succeed as one America.

The challenge of our past remains the challenge of our future — will we be one nation, one people, with one common destiny, or not? Will we all come together, or come apart?

The divide of race has been America's constant curse. And each new wave of immigrants gives new targets to old prejudices. Prejudice and contempt, cloaked in the pretense of religious or political conviction are no different. (Applause.) These forces have nearly destroyed our nation in the past. They plague us still. They fuel the fanaticism of terror. And they torment the lives of millions in fractured nations all around the world.

These obsessions cripple both those who hate and, of course, those who are hated, robbing both of what they might become. We cannot, we will not, succumb to the dark impulses that lurk in the far regions of the soul everywhere. We shall overcome them. (Applause.) And we shall replace them with the generous spirit of a people who feel at home with one another.

Our rich texture of racial, religious and political diversity will be a Godsend in the 21st century. Great rewards will come to those who can live together, learn together, work together, forge new ties that bind together.

As this new era approaches we can already see its broad outlines. Ten years ago, the Internet was the mystical province of physicists; today, it is a commonplace encyclopedia for millions of schoolchildren. Scientists now are decoding the blueprint of human life. Cures for our most feared illnesses seem close at hand.

The world is no longer divided into two hostile camps. Instead, now we are building bonds with nations that once were our adversaries. Growing connections of commerce and culture give us a chance to lift the fortunes and spirits of people the world over. And for the very first time in all of history, more people on this planet live under democracy than dictatorship. (Applause.)

My fellow Americans, as we look back at this remarkable century, we may ask, can we hope not just to follow, but even to surpass the achievements of the 20th century in America and to avoid the awful bloodshed that stained its legacy? To that question, every American here and every American in our land today must answer a resounding 'Yes'. (Applause.)

This is the heart of our task. With a new vision of government, a new sense of responsibility, a new spirit of community, we will sustain America's journey. The promise we sought in a new land we will find again in a land of new promise. (Applause.)

In this new land, education will be every citizen's most prized possession. Our schools will have the highest standards in the world, igniting the spark of possibility in the eyes of every girl and every boy. And the doors of higher education will be open to all. The knowledge and power of the Information Age will be within reach not just of the few, but of every classroom, every library, every child. Parents and children will have time not only to work, but to read and play together. And the plans they make at their kitchen table will be those of a better home, a better job, the certain chance to go to college.

Our streets will echo again with the laughter of our children, because no one will try to shoot them or sell them drugs anymore. Everyone who can work, will work, with today's permanent under class part of tomorrow's growing middle class. New miracles of medicine at last will reach not only those who can claim care now, but the children and hardworking families too long denied.

We will stand mighty for peace and freedom, and maintain a strong defense against terror and destruction. Our children will sleep free from the threat of nuclear, chemical or biological weapons. Ports and airports, farms and factories will thrive with trade and innovation and ideas. And the world's great democracy will lead a whole world of democracies.

Our land of new promise will be a nation that meets its obligations — a nation that balances its budget, but never loses the balance of its values. (Applause.) A nation where our grandparents have secure retirement and health care, and their grandchildren know we have made the reforms necessary to sustain those benefits for their time. (Applause.) A nation that fortifies the world's most productive economy even as it protects the great natural bounty of our water, air, and majestic land.

And in this land of new promise, we will have reformed our politics so that the voice of the people will always speak louder than the din of narrow interests — regaining the participation and deserving the trust of all Americans. (Applause.)

Fellow citizens, let us build that America, a nation ever moving forward toward realizing the full potential of all its citizens. Prosperity and power — yes, they are important, and we must maintain them. But let us never forget: The greatest progress we have made, and the greatest progress we have yet to make, is in the human heart. In the end, all the world's wealth and a thousand armies are no match for the strength and decency of the human spirit. (Applause.)

Thirty-four years ago, the man whose life we celebrate today spoke to us down there, at the other end of this Mall, in words that moved the conscience of a nation. Like a prophet of old, he told of his dream that one day America would rise up and treat all its citizens as equals before the law and in the heart. Martin Luther King's dream was the American Dream. His quest is our quest: the ceaseless striving to live out our true creed. Our history has been built on such dreams and labors. And by our dreams and labors we will redeem the promise of America in the 21st century.

To that effort I pledge all my strength and every power of my office. I ask the members of Congress here to join in that pledge. The American people returned to office a President of one party and a Congress of another. Surely, they did not do this to advance the politics of petty bickering and extreme partisanship they plainly deplore. (Applause.) No, they call on us instead to be repairers of the breach, and to move on with America's mission.

America demands and deserves big things from us — and nothing big ever came from being small. (Applause.) Let us remember the timeless wisdom of Cardinal Bernardin, when facing the end of his own life. He said: 'It is wrong to waste the precious gift of time, on acrimony and division.'

Fellow citizens, we must not waste the previous gift of this time. For all of us are on that same journey of our lives, and our journey, too, will come to an end. But the journey of our America must go on.

And so, my fellow Americans, we must be strong, for there is much to dare. The demands of our time are great and they are different. Let us meet them with faith and courage, with patience and a grateful and happy heart. Let us shape the hope of this day into the noblest chapter in our history. Yes, let us build our bridge. (Applause.) A bridge wide enough and strong enough for every American to cross over to a blessed land of new promise.

May those generations whose faces we cannot yet see, whose names we may never know, say of us here that we led our beloved land into a new century with the American Dream alive for all her children; with the American promise of a more perfect union a reality for all her people; with America's bright flame of freedom spreading throughout all the world.

From the height of this place and the summit of this century, let us go forth. May God strengthen our hands for the good work ahead — and always, always bless our America. (Applause.)

Source: White House Web Site, Electronic Publications. Available from: http://www.pub.whitehouse.gov/WH/Publications/html/Publications.html

3.4   ELECTIONS AND GOVERNMENT

The following tables provide information on the changing party composition of the Congress since 1789, and details of presidential elections since 1936. The hold of the two party system this century is evident in the relative lack of success of third (minority) party presidential candidates. Also included is an official summary chart of the government of the United States as of July 1993.

Table 3.1 Presidents, elections and Congresses: 1789–1999

Year	President	Congress	House Majority party	House Minority party	Senate Majority party	Senate Minority party
1789–1797	George Washington	1st	38 Admin	26 Opp	17 Admin	9 Opp
		2nd	37 Fed	33 Dem-R	16 Fed	13 Dem-R
		3rd	57 Dem-R	48 Fed	17 Fed	13 Dem-R
		4th	54 Fed	52 Dem-R	19 Fed	13 Dem-R
1797–1801	John Adams	5th	58 Fed	48 Dem-R	20 Fed	12 Dem-R
		6th	64 Fed	42 Dem-R	19 Fed	13 Dem-R
1801–1809	Thomas Jefferson	7th	69 Dem-R	36 Fed	18 Dem-R	13 Fed
		8th	102 Dem-R	39 Fed	25 Dem-R	9 Fed
		9th	116 Dem-R	25 Fed	27 Dem-R	7 Fed
		10th	118 Dem-R	24 Fed	28 Dem-R	6 Fed
1809–1817	James Madison	11th	94 Dem-R	48 Fed	28 Dem-R	6 Fed
		12th	108 Dem-R	36 Fed	30 Dem-R	6 Fed
		13th	112 Dem-R	68 Fed	27 Dem-R	9 Fed
		14th	117 Dem-R	65 Fed	25 Dem-R	11 Fed
1817–1825	James Monroe	15th	141 Dem-R	42 Fed	34 Dem-R	10 Fed
		16th	156 Dem-R	27 Fed	35 Dem-R	7 Fed
		17th	158 Dem-R	25 Fed	44 Dem-R	4 Fed
		18th	187 Dem-R	26 Fed	44 Dem-R	4 Fed
1825–1829	John Quincy Adams	19th	105 Admin	97 Dem-J	26 Admin	20 Dem-J
		20th	119 Dem-J	94 Admin	28 Dem-J	20 Admin
1829–1837	Andrew Jackson	21st	139 Dem	74 Nat R	26 Dem	22 Nat R
		22nd	141 Dem	58 Nat R	25 Dem	21 Nat R
		23rd	147 Dem	53 AntiMas	20 Dem	20 Nat R
		24th	145 Dem	98 Whig	27 Dem	25 Whig
1837–1841	Martin Van Buren	25th	108 Dem	107 Whig	30 Dem	18 Whig
		26th	124 Dem	118 Whig	28 Dem	22 Whig
1841	William H. Harrison					
1841–1845	John Tyler	27th	133 Whig	102 Dem	28 Whig	22 Dem
		28th	142 Dem	79 Whig	28 Whig	25 Dem
1845–1849	James K. Polk	29th	143 Dem	77 Whig	31 Dem	25 Whig
		30th	115 Whig	108 Dem	36 Dem	21 Whig
1849–1850	Zachary Taylor	31st	112 Dem	109 Whig	35 Dem	25 Whig
1850–1853	Millard Fillmore	32nd	140 Dem	88 Whig	35 Dem	24 Whig
1853–1857	Franklin Pierce	33rd	159 Dem	71 Whig	38 Dem	22 Whig
		34th	108 Rep	83 Dem	40 Dem	15 Rep
1857–1861	James Buchanan	35th	118 Dem	92 Rep	36 Dem	20 Rep
		36th	114 Rep	92 Dem	36 Dem	26 Rep
1861–1865	Abraham Lincoln	37th	105 Rep	43 Dem	31 Rep	10 Dem
		38th	102 Rep	75 Dem	36 Rep	9 Dem

Table 3.1 **Presidents, elections and Congresses: 1789–1999 (continued)**

Year	President	Congress	House Majority party	House Minority party	Senate Majority party	Senate Minority party
1865–1869	Andrew Johnson	39th	149 Union	42 Dem	42 Union	10 Dem
		40th	143 Rep	49 Dem	42 Rep	11 Dem
1869–1877	Ulysses S. Grant	41st	149 Rep	63 Dem	56 Rep	11 Dem
		42nd	134 Rep	104 Dem	52 Rep	17 Dem
		43rd	194 Rep	92 Dem	49 Rep	19 Dem
		44th	169 Rep	109 Dem	45 Rep	29 Dem
1877–1881	Rutherford B. Hayes	45th	153 Dem	140 Rep	39 Rep	36 Dem
		46th	149 Dem	130 Rep	42 Dem	33 Rep
1881	James A. Garfield	47th	147 Rep	135 Dem	37 Rep	37 Dem
1881–1885	Chester A. Arthur	48th	197 Dem	118 Rep	38 Rep	36 Dem
1885–1889	Grover Cleveland	49th	183 Dem	140 Rep	43 Rep	34 Dem
		50th	169 Dem	152 Rep	39 Rep	37 Dem
1889–1893	Benjamin Harrison	51st	166 Rep	159 Dem	39 Rep	37 Dem
		52nd	235 Dem	88 Rep	47 Rep	39 Dem
1893–1897	Grover Cleveland	53rd	218 Dem	127 Rep	44 Dem	38 Rep
		54th	244 Rep	105 Dem	43 Rep	39 Dem
1897–1901	William McKinley	55th	204 Rep	113 Dem	47 Rep	34 Dem
		56th	185 Rep	163 Dem	53 Rep	26 Dem
1901–1909	Theodore Roosevelt	57th	197 Rep	151 Dem	55 Rep	31 Dem
		58th	208 Rep	178 Dem	57 Rep	33 Dem
		59th	250 Rep	136 Dem	57 Rep	33 Dem
		60th	222 Rep	164 Dem	61 Rep	31 Dem
1909–1913	William Howard Taft	61st	219 Rep	172 Dem	61 Rep	32 Dem
		62nd	228 Dem	161 Rep	51 Rep	41 Dem
1913–1921	Woodrow Wilson	63rd	291 Dem	127 Rep	51 Dem	44 Rep
		64th	230 Dem	196 Rep	56 Dem	40 Rep
		65th	216 Dem	210 Rep	53 Dem	42 Rep
		66th	240 Rep	190 Dem	49 Rep	47 Dem
1921–1923	William G. Harding	67th	301 Rep	131 Dem	59 Rep	37 Dem
1923–1929	Calvin Coolidge	68th	225 Rep	205 Dem	51 Rep	43 Dem
		69th	247 Rep	183 Dem	56 Rep	39 Dem
		70th	237 Rep	195 Dem	49 Rep	46 Dem
1929–1933	Herbert Hoover	71st	267 Rep	167 Dem	56 Rep	39 Dem
		72nd	220 Dem	214 Rep	48 Rep	47 Dem
1933–1945	Franklin D. Roosevelt	73rd	310 Dem	117 Rep	60 Dem	35 Rep
		74th	319 Dem	103 Rep	69 Dem	25 Rep
		75th	331 Dem	89 Rep	76 Dem	16 Rep
		76th	261 Dem	164 Rep	69 Dem	23 Rep
		77th	268 Dem	162 Rep	66 Dem	28 Rep
		78th	218 Dem	208 Rep	58 Dem	37 Rep

Table 3.1 Presidents, elections and Congresses: 1789–1999 (continued)

Year	President	Congress	House Majority party	House Minority party	Senate Majority party	Senate Minority party
1945–1953	Harry S. Truman	79th	242 Dem	190 Rep	56 Dem	38 Rep
		80th	245 Rep	188 Dem	51 Rep	45 Dem
		81st	263 Dem	171 Rep	54 Dem	42 Rep
		82nd	234 Dem	199 Rep	49 Dem	47 Rep
1953–1961	Dwight D. Eisenhower	83rd	221 Rep	211 Dem	48 Rep	47 Dem
		84th	232 Dem	203 Rep	48 Dem	47 Rep
		85th	233 Dem	200 Rep	49 Dem	47 Rep
		86th	283 Dem	153 Rep	64 Dem	34 Rep
1961–1963	John F. Kennedy	87th	263 Dem	174 Rep	65 Dem	35 Rep
1963–1969	Lyndon B. Johnson	88th	258 Dem	177 Rep	67 Dem	33 Rep
		89th	295 Dem	140 Rep	68 Dem	32 Rep
		90th	247 Dem	187 Rep	64 Dem	36 Rep
1969–1974	Richard M. Nixon	91st	243 Dem	192 Rep	57 Dem	43 Rep
		92nd	254 Dem	180 Rep	54 Dem	44 Rep
1974–1977	Gerald R. Ford	93rd	239 Dem	192 Rep	56 Dem	42 Rep
		94th	291 Dem	144 Rep	60 Dem	37 Rep
1977–1981	Jimmy Carter	95th	292 Dem	143 Rep	61 Dem	38 Rep
		96th	276 Dem	157 Rep	58 Dem	41 Rep
1981–1989	Ronald Reagan	97th	243 Dem	192 Rep	53 Rep	46 Dem
		98th	269 Dem	165 Rep	54 Rep	46 Dem
		99th	252 Dem	182 Rep	53 Rep	47 Dem
1989–1993	George Bush	100th	258 Dem	177 Rep	55 Dem	45 Rep
		101st	259 Dem	174 Rep	55 Dem	45 Rep
1993–	Bill Clinton	102nd	267 Dem	167 Rep	56 Dem	44 Rep
		103rd	258 Dem	176 Rep	57 Dem	43 Rep
		104th	230 Rep	204 Dem	52 Rep	48 Dem
		105th	227 Rep	207 Dem	52 Rep	48 Dem
		106th	228 Rep	206 Dem	55 Rep	45 Dem

Abbreviations:

Admin	= Administration supporters
AntiMas	= Anti-Masonic
Dem	= Democratic
Dem-R	= Democratic Republican
Fed	= Federalist
Dem-J	= Jacksonian Democrats
Nat R	= National Republican
Opp	= Opponents of administration
Rep	= Republican
Union	= Unionist

Source: The Office of the Clerk of the House Web Site. Available from: http://clerkweb.house.gov/; see also Maidment, R. and McGrew, T. (1991) *The American Political Process* (2nd edn), London, Sage in association with The Open University.

Table 3.2 Vote cast for President, by major political party: 1936–96. (Prior to 1960, excludes Alaska and Hawaii; prior to 1964, excludes DC. Vote cast for major party candidates include the votes of minor parties cast for those candidates)

YEAR	CANDIDATES FOR PRESIDENT		VOTE CAST FOR PRESIDENT						
	Democratic	Republican	Total popular vote [1] (1,000)	Democratic			Republican		
				Popular vote		Electoral vote	Popular vote		Electoral vote
				Number (1,000)	Percent		Number (1,000)	Percent	
1936	F. D. Roosevelt . .	Landon	45,655	27,757	60.8	523	16,684	36.5	8
1940	F. D. Roosevelt . .	Willkie	49,900	27,313	54.7	449	22,348	44.8	82
1944	F. D. Roosevelt . .	Dewey	47,977	25,613	53.4	432	22,018	45.9	99
1948	Truman	Dewey	48,794	24,179	49.6	303	21,991	45.1	189
1952	Stevenson	Eisenhower.	61,551	27,315	44.4	89	33,936	55.1	442
1956	Stevenson	Eisenhower.	62,027	26,023	42.0	73	35,590	57.4	457
1960	Kennedy	Nixon.	68,838	34,227	49.7	303	34,108	49.5	219
1964	Johnson.	Goldwater.	70,645	43,130	61.1	486	27,178	38.5	52
1968	Humphrey	Nixon.	73,212	31,275	42.7	191	31,785	43.4	301
1972	McGovern	Nixon.	77,719	29,170	37.5	17	47,170	60.7	520
1976	Carter	Ford	81,556	40,831	50.1	297	39,148	48.0	240
1980	Carter	Reagan	86,515	35,484	41.0	49	43,904	50.7	489
1984	Mondale.	Reagan	92,653	37,577	40.6	13	54,455	58.8	525
1988	Dukakis	Bush	91,595	41,809	45.6	111	48,886	53.4	426
1992	Clinton.	Bush	104,425	44,909	43.0	370	39,104	37.4	168
1996	Clinton.	Dole	96,273	47,401	49.2	379	39,197	40.7	159

[1] Include votes for minor party candidates, independents, unpledged electors, and scattered write-in votes.

Source: Congressional Quarterly, Inc., Washington, D.C.. *America at the Polls 2*, 1965, and *America Votes*, biennial, (copyright).

Table 3.3 Vote cast for leading minority party candidates for President: 1936–96. (See heading for Table 3.2)

YEAR	Candidate	Party	Popular vote (1,000)	Candidate	Party	Popular vote (1,000)
1936 . .	William Lemke	Union	892	Norman Thomas . . .	Socialist	188
1940 . .	Norman Thomas . . .	Socialist	116	Roger Babson	Prohibition	59
1944 . .	Norman Thomas . . .	Socialist	79	Claude Watson	Prohibition	75
1948 . .	Strom Thurmond . . .	States' Rights.	1,176	Henry Wallace	Progressive	1,157
1952 . .	Vincent Hallinan. . . .	Progressive	140	Stuart Hamblen	Prohibition	73
1956 . .	T. Coleman Andrews.	States' Rights.	111	Eric Hass	Socialist Labor	44
1960 . .	Eric Hass	Socialist Labor	48	Rutherford Decker . .	Prohibition	46
1964 . .	Eric Hass	Socialist Labor	45	Clifton DeBerry . . .	Socialist Workers	33
1968 . .	George Wallace	American Independent.	9,906	Henning Blomen . . .	Socialist Labor	53
1972 . .	John Schmitz.	American.	1,099	Benjamin Spock. . . .	People's	79
1976 . .	Eugene McCarthy . .	Independent	757	Roger McBride.	Libertarian.	173
1980 . .	John Anderson	Independent	5,720	Ed Clark	Libertarian.	921
1984 . .	David Bergland	Libertarian.	228	Lyndon H. LaRouche.	Independent	79
1988 . .	Ron Paul	Libertarian.	432	Lenora B. Fulani . . .	New Alliance	217
1992 . .	H. Ross Perot	Independent	19,742	Andre Marrou	Libertarian.	292
1996 . .	H. Ross Perot	Reform Party	8,085	Ralph Nader	Green.	685

Source: Congressional Quarterly, Inc. Washington, D.C., *America at the Polls 1920-1996*, 1997; and *America Votes*, biennial (copyright).

☆☆☆

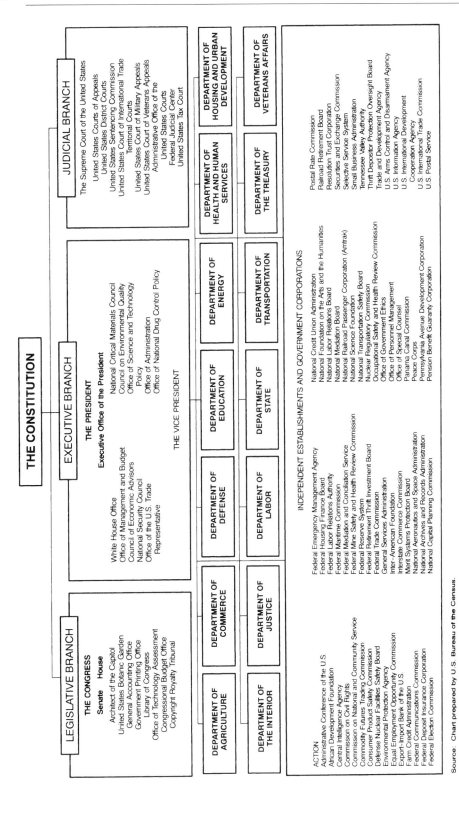

Source: Chart prepared by U.S. Bureau of the Census.

Figure 3.2 The government of the United States (as of July 1993)

3.5 CIVIL RIGHTS

3.5.1 *PLESSY v. FERGUSON* (1896)

The Supreme Court case of *Plessy v. Ferguson* was important in setting the scene for the struggle by Black Americans for Civil Rights in the twentieth century. The 1896 decision, which would not be overturned until 1954, meant that segregation, the provision of 'separate but equal accommodation', was constitutional. The case involved the segregation of railway carriages in Louisiana. Homer A. Plessy, who was part Negro and could pass for white, was arrested after sitting in a carriage provided for white people and refusing to move after he had made it known he was a Negro. The document includes an extract from the majority opinion from Mr Justice Brown, and part of the opinion of the one dissenting judge, Mr Justice Harlan.

Mr Justice Brown:

This case turns upon the constitutionality of an act of the General Assembly of the state of Louisiana, passed in 1890, providing for separate railway carriages for the white and colored races. […] The 1st Section of the statute enacts

> That all railway companies carrying passengers in their coaches in this state shall provide equal but separate accommodations for the white and colored races, by providing two or more passenger coaches for each passenger train, or by dividing the passenger coaches by a partition so as to secure separate accommodations: *Provided*, that this section shall not be construed to apply to street railroads. No person or persons, shall be admitted to occupy seats in coaches, other than, the ones, assigned, to them on account of the race they belong to. …

By the 2nd Section it was enacted

> That the officers of such passenger trains shall have power and are hereby required to assign each passenger to the coach or compartment used for the race to which such passenger belongs; any passenger insisting on going into a coach or compartment to which by race he does not belong shall be liable to a fine of $25, or, in lieu thereof, to imprisonment for a period of not more than twenty days in the parish prison; and any officer of any railroad insisting on assigning a passenger to a coach or compartment other than the one set aside for the race to which said passenger belongs shall be liable to a fine of $25, or, in lieu thereof, to imprisonment for a period of not more than twenty days in the parish prison; and should any passenger refuse to occupy the coach or compartment to which he

or she is assigned by the officer of such railway, said officer shall have power to refuse to carry such passenger on his train, and for such refusal neither he nor the railway company which he represents shall be liable for damages in any of the courts of this state. …

The constitutionality of this act is attacked upon the ground that it conflicts both with the Thirteenth Amendment of the Constitution, abolishing slavery, and the Fourteenth Amendment, which prohibits certain restrictive legislation on the part of the states.

1.   That it does not conflict with the Thirteenth Amendment, which abolished slavery and involuntary servitude except as a punishment for crime, is too clear for argument. […] A statute which implies merely a legal distinction between the white and colored races — a distinction which is founded in the color of the two races, and which must always exist so long as white men are distinguished from the other race by color — has no tendency to destroy the legal equality of the two races or reestablish a state of involuntary servitude. Indeed, we do not understand that the Thirteenth Amendment is strenuously relied upon by the plaintiff in error in this connection.

2.   By the Fourteenth Amendment, all persons born or naturalized in the United States and subject to the jurisdiction thereof are made citizens of the United States and of the state wherein they reside; and the states are forbidden from making or enforcing any law which shall abridge the privileges or immunities of citizens of the United States, or shall deprive any person of life, liberty, or property without due process of law, or deny to any person within their jurisdiction the equal protection of the laws.

The proper construction of this amendment was first called to the attention of this court in the *Slaughter-House Cases* […] which involved, however, not a question of race but one of exclusive privileges. The case did not call for any expression of opinion as to the exact rights it was intended to secure to the colored race, but it was said generally that its main purpose was to establish the citizenship of the Negro; to give definitions of citizenship of the United States and of the states, and to protect from the hostile legislation of the states the privileges and immunities of citizens of the United States as distinguished from those of citizens of the states.

The object of the amendment was undoubtedly to enforce the absolute equality of the two races before the law, but in the nature of things it could not have been intended to abolish distinctions based upon color, or to enforce social as distinguished from political equality, or a commingling of the two races upon terms unsatisfactory to either. Laws permitting, and even requiring, their separation in places where they are liable to be brought into contact do not necessarily imply the inferiority of either race to the other, and have been generally, if not universally, recognized as within the competency of the state legislatures in the exercise of their police power. The most common instance of this is connected with the establishment of separate schools for white and colored children, which has been held to be a valid exercise of the legislative power even by courts of states where the political rights of the colored race have been longest and most earnestly enforced. [...]

While we think the enforced separation of the races, as applied to the internal commerce of the state, neither abridges the privileges or immunities of the colored man, deprives him of his property without due process of law, nor denies him the equal protection of the laws, within the meaning of the Fourteenth Amendment, we are not prepared to say that the conductor, in assigning passengers to the coaches according to their race, does not act at his peril, or that the provision of the 2nd Section of the act, that denies to the passenger compensation in damages for a refusal to receive him into the coach in which he properly belongs, is a valid exercise of the legislative power. Indeed, we understand it to be conceded by the state's attorney, that such part of the act as exempts from liability the railway company and its officers is unconstitutional.

The power to assign to a particular coach obviously implies the power to determine to which race the passenger belongs, as well as the power to determine who, under the laws of the particular state, is to be deemed a white and who a colored person. This question, though indicated in the brief of the plaintiff in error, does not properly arise upon the record in this case, since the only issue made is as to the unconstitutionality of the act, so far as it requires the railway to provide separate accommodations and the conductor to assign passengers according to their race.

It is claimed by the plaintiff in error that, in any mixed community, the reputation of belonging to the dominant race, in this instance the white race, is *property*, in the same sense that a right of action, or of inheritance, is property. Conceding this to be so for the purposes of this case, we are unable to see how this statute deprives him of, or in any way affects, his right to such property. If he be a white man and assigned to a colored coach, he may have his action for damages against the company for being deprived of his so-called property. Upon the other hand, if he be a colored man and be so assigned, he has been deprived of no property since he is not lawfully entitled to the reputation of being a white man.

In this connection, it is also suggested by the learned counsel for the plaintiff in error that the same argument that will justify the state legislature in requiring railways to provide separate accommodations for the two races will also authorize them to require separate cars to be provided for people whose hair is of a certain color, or who are aliens, or who belong to certain nationalities, or to enact laws requiring colored people to walk upon one side of the street and white people upon the other, or requiring white men's houses to be painted white and colored men's black, or their vehicles or business signs to be of different colors, upon the theory that one side of the street is as good as the other, or that a house or vehicle of one color is as good as one of another color. The reply to all this is that every exercise of the police power must be reasonable and extend only to such laws as are enacted in good faith for the promotion for the public good and not for the annoyance or oppression of a particular class. [...]

So far, then, as a conflict with the Fourteenth Amendment is concerned, the case reduces itself to the question whether the statute of Louisiana is a reasonable regulation, and with respect to this there must necessarily be a large discretion on the part of the legislature. In determining the question of reasonableness, it is at liberty to act with reference to the established usages, customs, and traditions of the people, and with a view to the promotion of their comfort, and the preservation of the public peace and good order. Gauged by this standard, we cannot say that a law which authorizes or even requires the separation of the two races in public conveyances is unreasonable or more obnoxious to the Fourteenth Amendment than the acts of Congress requiring separate schools for colored children in the District of Columbia, the constitutionality of which does not seem to have been questioned, or the corresponding acts of state legislatures.

We consider the underlying fallacy of the plaintiff's argument to consist in the assumption that the enforced separation of the two races stamps the colored race with a badge of inferiority. If this be so, it is not by reason of anything found in the act, but solely because the colored race chooses to put that construction upon it. The argument necessarily assumes that if, as had been more than once the case, and is not unlikely to be so again, the colored race should become the dominant power in the state legislature and should enact a law in precisely similar terms, it would thereby relegate the white race to an inferior position. We imagine that the white race, at least, would not acquiesce in this assumption.

The argument also assumes that social prejudices may be overcome by legislation and that equal rights cannot be secured to the Negro except by an enforced commingling of the two races. We cannot accept this proposition. If the two races are to meet upon terms of social equality, it must be the result of natural affinities, a mutual appreciation of each other's merits, and a voluntary consent of individuals. As was said by the Court of Appeals of New York in *People v. Gallagher* […]

> This end can neither be accomplished nor promoted by laws which conflict with the general sentiment of the community upon whom they are designed to operate. When the government, therefore, has secured to each of its citizens equal rights before the law and equal opportunities for improvement and progress, it has accomplished the end for which it was organized and performed all of the functions respecting social advantages with which it is endowed.

Legislation is powerless to eradicate racial instincts or to abolish distinctions based upon physical differences, and the attempt to do so can only result in accentuating the difficulties of the present situation. If the civil and political rights of both races be equal, one cannot be inferior to the other civilly or politically. If one race be inferior to the other socially, the Constitution of the United States cannot put them upon the same plane.

It is true that the question of the proportion of colored blood necessary to constitute a colored person as distinguished from a white person is one upon which there is a difference of opinion in the different states, some holding that any visible admixture of black blood stamps the person as belonging to the colored race (*State v. Chavers*, 5 Jones, [N.C.] 1, p.11); others that it depends upon the preponderance of blood (*Gray v. State*, 4 Ohio, 354; *Monroe v. Collins*, 17 Ohio St. 665); and still others that the predominance of white blood must only be in the proportion of three-fourths (*People v. Dean*, 14 Michigan, 406; *Jones v. Commonwealth*, 80 Virginia, 538). But these are questions to be determined under the laws of each state and are not properly put in issue in this case. Under the allegations of his petition it may undoubtedly become a question of importance whether, under the laws of Louisiana, the petitioner belongs to the white or colored race.

The judgment of the court below is, therefore, *affirmed*.

[There was one dissenting opinion:]

Mr Justice Harlan:

In respect of civil rights, common to all citizens, the Constitution of the United States does not, I think, permit any public authority to know the race of those entitled to be protected in the enjoyment of such rights. Every true man has pride of race, and, under appropriate circumstances, when the rights of others, his equals before the law, are not to be affected, it is his privilege to express such pride and to take such action based upon it as to him seems proper. But I deny that any legislative body or judicial tribunal may have regard to the race of citizens when the civil rights of those citizens are involved. Indeed, such legislation as that here in question is inconsistent, not only with that equality of rights which pertains to citizenship, national and state, but with the personal liberty enjoyed by everyone within the United States.

The Thirteenth Amendment does not permit the withholding or the deprivation of any right necessarily inhering in freedom. It not only struck down the institution of slavery as previously existing in the United States but it prevents the imposition of any burdens or disabilities that constitute badges of slavery or servitude. It decreed universal civil freedom in this country. This Court has so adjudged. But that amendment having been found inadequate to the protection of the rights of those who had been in slavery, it was followed by the Fourteenth Amendment, which added greatly to the dignity and glory of American citizenship and to the security of personal liberty by declaring that 'all persons born or naturalized in the United States and subject to the jurisdiction thereof are citizens of the United States and of the state wherein they reside,' and that 'no state shall make or enforce any law which shall abridge the privileges or immunities of citizens of the United States; nor shall any state deprive any person of life, liberty, or property without due process of law, nor deny to any person within its jurisdiction the equal protection of the laws.'

These two amendments, if enforced according to their true intent and meaning, will protect all the civil rights that pertain to freedom and citizenship. Finally, and to the end that no citizen should be denied on account of his race the privilege of participating in the political control of his country, it was declared by the Fifteenth Amendment that 'the right of citizens of the United States to vote shall not be denied or abridged by the United States or by any state on account of race, color, or previous condition of servitude.'

These notable additions to the fundamental law were welcomed by the friends of liberty throughout the world. They removed the race line from our governmental systems. They had, as this Court has said, a common purpose; namely, to secure 'to a race recently emancipated, a race that through many generations have been held in slavery, all the civil rights that the superior race enjoy.' They declared, in legal effect, this Court has further said, 'that the law in the states shall be the same for the black as for the white; that all persons, whether colored or white, shall stand equal before the laws of the states, and, in regard to the colored race, for whose protection the amendment was primarily designed, that no discrimination shall be made against them by law because of their color.'

We also said: 'The words of the amendment, it is true, are prohibitory, but they contain a necessary implication of a positive immunity, or right, most valuable to the colored race — the right to exemption from unfriendly legislation against them distinctively as colored — exemption from legal discriminations, implying inferiority in civil society, lessening the security of their enjoyment of the rights which others enjoy, and discriminations which are steps toward reducing them to the condition of a subject race.' It was, consequently, adjudged that a state law that excluded citizens of the colored race from juries because of their race and however well-qualified in other respects to discharge the duties of jurymen was repugnant to the Fourteenth Amendment. […]

The decisions referred to show the scope of the recent amendments of the Constitution. They also show that it is not within the power of a state to prohibit colored citizens, because of their race, from participating as jurors in the administration of justice.

It was said in argument that the statute of Louisiana does not discriminate against either race, but prescribes a rule applicable alike to white and colored citizens. But this argument does not meet the difficulty. Everyone knows that the statute in question had its origin in the purpose, not so much to exclude white persons from railroad cars occupied by blacks as to exclude colored people from coaches occupied by or assigned to white persons. Railroad corporations of Louisiana did not make discrimination among whites in the matter of accommodation for travelers. The thing to accomplish was, under the guise of giving equal accommodation for whites and blacks, to compel the latter to keep to themselves while traveling in railroad passenger coaches. No one would be so wanting in candor as to assert the contrary.

The fundamental objection, therefore, to the statute is that it interferes with the personal freedom of citizens. 'Personal liberty,' it has been well said, 'consists in the power of locomotion, of changing situation, or removing one's person to whatsoever places one's own inclination may direct, without imprisonment or restraint, unless by due course of law.' […] If a white man and a black man choose to occupy the same public conveyance on a public highway, it is their right to do so, and no government proceeding alone on grounds of race can prevent it without infringing the personal liberty of each.

It is one thing for railroad carriers to furnish, or to be required by law to furnish, equal accommodations for all whom they are under a legal duty to carry. It is quite another thing for government to forbid citizens of the white and back races from traveling in the same public conveyance, and to punish officers of railroad companies for permitting persons of the two races to occupy the same passenger coach. If a state can prescribe, as a rule of civil conduct, that whites and blacks shall not travel as passengers in the same railroad coach, why may it not so regulate the use of the streets of its cities and towns as to compel white citizens to keep on one side of a street and black citizens to keep on the other?

Why may it not, upon like grounds, punish whites and blacks who ride together in street cars or in open vehicles on a public road or street? Why may it not require sheriffs to assign whites to one side of a courtroom and blacks to the other? And why may it not also prohibit the commingling of the two races in the galleries of legislative halls or in public assemblages convened for the consideration of the political questions of the day? Further, if this statute of Louisiana is consistent with the personal liberty of citizens, why may not the state require the separation in railroad coaches of native and naturalized citizens of the United States, or of Protestants and Roman Catholics?

[…]

I am of opinion that the statute of Louisiana is inconsistent with the personal liberty of citizens, white and black, in that state, and hostile to both the spirit and letter of the Constitution of the United States. If laws of like character should be enacted in the several states of the Union, the effect would be in the highest degree mischievous. Slavery, as an institution tolerated by law, would, it is true, have disappeared from our country, but there would remain a power in the states, by sinister legislation, to interfere with the full enjoyment of the blessings of freedom; to regulate civil rights, common to all citizens, upon the basis of race; and to place in a condition of legal inferiority a large body of American citizens now constituting a part of the political community called the People of the United States, for whom, and by whom through representatives, our government is administered. Such a system is inconsistent with the guarantee given by the Constitution to each state of a republican form of government and may be stricken down by Congressional action or by the courts in the discharge of their solemn duty to maintain the supreme law of the land, anything in the constitution or laws of any state to the contrary notwithstanding.

For the reasons stated, I am constrained to withhold my assent from the opinion and judgment of the majority.

Source: Encyclopaedia Britannica (1976) *The Annals of America, The Bicentennial Edition 1776–1976, Vol.2*, Chicago, Encyclopaedia Britannica, Inc., pp.92–100.

3.5.2   DESEGREGATION OF THE ARMED FORCES (1948)

Black Americans had been recruited to the armed forces of the United States since the Civil War, however, they had been organized in segregated military units. This Executive Order (number 9981) from President Truman was an important step in the struggle for civil rights. The implementation of the order was helped by the need for efficient use of personnel in the Korean War (1950–5).

Whereas it is essential that there be maintained in the armed services of the United States the highest standards of democracy, with equality of treatment and opportunity for all those who serve in our country's defense:

Now, therefore, by virtue of the authority vested in me as President of the Untied States, by the Constitution and the statutes of the United States, and as Commander in Chief of the armed services, it is hereby ordered as follows:

1   It is hereby declared to be the policy of the President that there shall be equality of treatment and opportunity for all persons in the armed services without regard to race, color, religion or national origin. This policy shall be put into effect as rapidly as possible, having due regard to the time required to effectuate any necessary changes without impairing efficiency or morale.

2   There shall be created in the National Military Establishment an advisory committee to be known as the President's Committee on Equality of Treatment and Opportunity in the Armed Services, which shall be composed of seven members to be designated by the President.

3   The Committee is authorized on behalf of the President to examine into the rules, procedures and practices of the armed services in order to determine in what respect such rules, procedures and practices may be altered or improved with a view to carrying out the policy of this order. The Committee shall confer and advise with the Secretary of Defense, the Secretary of the Army, the Secretary of the Navy, and the Secretary of the Air Force, and shall make such recommendations to the President and to said Secretaries as in the judgment of the Committee will effectuate the policy hereof.

4   All executive departments and agencies of the Federal Government are authorized and directed to cooperate with the Committee in its work, and to furnish the Committee such information or the services of such persons as the Committee may require in the performance of its duties.

5   When requested by the Committee to do so, persons in the armed services or in any of the executive departments and agencies of the Federal Government shall testify before the Committee and shall make available

for the use of the Committee such documents and other information as the Committee may require.

6   The Committee shall continue to exist until such time as the President shall terminate its existence by Executive Order.

Source: Encyclopaedia Britannica (1976) *The Annals of America, The Bicentennial Edition 1776–1976, Vol.16*, Chicago, Encyclopaedia Britannica, Inc., pp.513–14.

3.5.3   *BROWN v. BOARD OF EDUCATION OF TOPEKA* (1954)

The Supreme Court decision on *Brown v. Board of Education of Topeka* was a landmark decision for the Civil Rights movement. The issue was segregation and public education in the South where black and white children's segregation into different schools was widespread. This practice had been measured against the Fourteenth Amendment to the Constitution, passed after the Civil War, which required that a state should not 'deny to any person within its jurisdiction the equal protection of the laws'. The legality of segregation was based on the principle of 'separate but equal'; see *Plessy v. Ferguson*, Document 3.5.1. The argument put forward on this occasion by the National Association for the Advancement of Colored People (NAACP) was that, not withstanding the equality of resources provided for black and white schools (and there was considerable evidence that black schools were disadvantaged in resource allocation), the practice of segregation was inherently unequal and therefore unconstitutional. In 1954 the Supreme Court agreed. However, implementation would be complex and problematic and it is this issue which Questions 4 and 5 refer to in the last paragraph of the decision.

These cases come to us from the States of Kansas, South Carolina, Virginia, and Delaware. They are premised on different facts and different local conditions, but a common legal question justifies their consideration together in this consolidated opinion.

In each of the cases, minors of the Negro race, through their legal representatives, seek the aid of the courts in obtaining admission to the public schools of their community on a nonsegregated basis. In each instance, they had been denied admission to schools attended by white children under laws requiring or permitting segregation according to race. This segregation was alleged to deprive the plaintiffs of the equal protection of the laws under the Fourteenth Amendment. In each of the cases other than the Delaware case, a three-judge federal district court denied relief to the plaintiffs on the so-called 'separate but equal' doctrine announced by this Court in *Plessy* v. *Ferguson*, 163 U.S. 537. Under that doctrine, equality of treatment is accorded when the races are provided substantially equal facilities, even

(Left) Ten years after the landmark decision Linda Brown stands in front of Sumner School in Topeka, Kansas. Refusal of the school to admit Linda, then aged 9, in 1951, led to the suit whose name was given to several cases which reached the Supreme Court. The decision on 17 May 1954 came too late for Linda, but her two sisters attended Sumner School. (Right) NAACP attorneys George E.C. Hayes, Thurgood Marshall and James M. Nabrit celebrate the decision outside the Supreme Court

though these facilities be separate. In the Delaware case, the Supreme Court of Delaware adhered to that doctrine, but ordered that the plaintiffs be admitted to the white schools because of their superiority to the Negro schools.

The plaintiffs contend that segregated public schools are not 'equal' and cannot be made 'equal', and that hence they are deprived of the equal protection of the laws. Because of the obvious importance of the question presented, the Court took jurisdiction. Argument was heard in the 1952 Term, and reargument was heard this Term on certain questions propounded by the Court.

Reargument was largely devoted to the circumstances surrounding the adoption of the Fourteenth Amendment in 1868. It covered exhaustively consideration of the Amendment in Congress, ratification by the states, then existing practices in racial segregation, and the views of proponents and opponents of the Amendment. This discussion and our own investigation convince us that, although these sources cast some light, it is not enough to resolve the problem with which we are faced. At best, they are inconclusive. The most avid proponents of the post-War Amendments undoubtedly intended them to remove all legal distinctions among 'all persons born or naturalized in the United States.' Their opponents, just as certainly, were antagonistic to both the letter and the spirit of the Amendments and wished them to have the most limited effect. What others in Congress and the state legislatures had in mind cannot be determined with any degree of certainty.

An additional reason for the inconclusive nature of the Amendment's history, with respect to segregated schools, is the status of public education at that time. In the South, the movement toward free common schools, supported by general taxation, had not yet taken hold. Education of white children was largely in the hands of private groups. Education of Negroes was almost non-existent, and practically all of the race were illiterate. In fact, any education of Negroes was forbidden by law in some states. Today, in contrast, many Negroes have achieved outstanding success in the arts and sciences as well as in the business and professional world. It is true that public school education at the time of the Amendment had advanced further in the North, but the effect of the Amendment on Northern States was generally ignored in the congressional debates. Even in the North, the conditions of public education did not approximate those existing today. The curriculum was usually rudimentary; ungraded schools were common in rural areas; the school term was but three months a year in many states; and compulsory school attendance was virtually unknown. As a consequence, it is not surprising that there should be so little in the history of the Fourteenth Amendment relating to its intended effect on public education.

In the first cases in this Court construing the Fourteenth Amendment, decided shortly after its adoption, the Court interpreted it as proscribing all state-imposed discriminations against the Negro race. The doctrine of 'separate but equal' did not make its appearance in this Court until 1896 in the case of *Plessy* v. *Ferguson, supra,* involving not education but transportation. American courts have since labored with the doctrine for over half a century. In this Court, there have been six cases involving the 'separate but equal' doctrine in the field of public education. In *Cumming* v. *Board of Education of Richmond County,* 175 U.S. 528, and *Gong Lum* v. *Rice,* 275 U.S. 78, the validity of the doctrine itself was not challenged. In more recent cases, all on the graduate school level, inequality was found in that specific benefits enjoyed by white students were denied to Negro students of the same educational qualifications. *Missouri ex rel. Gaines* v. *Canada,* 305 U.S. 337; *Sipuel* v. *Board of Regents of University of Oklahoma,* 332 U.S. 631; *Sweatt* v. *Painter,* 339 U.S. 629; *McLaurin* v. *Oklahoma State Regents,* 339 U.S. 637. In none of these cases was it necessary to re-examine the doctrine to grant relief to the Negro plaintiff. And in *Sweatt* v. *Painter, supra,* the Court expressly reserved decision on the question whether *Plessy* v. *Ferguson* should be held inapplicable to public education.

In the instant cases, that question is directly presented. Here, unlike *Sweatt* v. *Painter,* there are findings below that the Negro and white schools involved have been equalized, or are being equalized, with respect to buildings, curricula, qualifications and salaries of teachers, and other 'tangible' factors. Our decision, therefore, cannot turn on merely a comparison of these tangible factors in the Negro and white schools involved in each of the cases. We must look instead to the effect of segregation itself on public education.

In approaching this problem, we cannot turn the clock back to 1868 when the Amendment was adopted, or even to 1896 when *Plessy* v. *Ferguson* was written. We must consider public education in the light of its full development and its present place in American life throughout the Nation. Only in this way can it be determined if segregation in public schools deprives these plaintiffs of the equal protection of the laws.

Today, education is perhaps the most important function of state and local governments. Compulsory school attendance laws and the great expenditures for education both demonstrate our recognition of the importance of education to our democratic society. It is required in the performance of our most basic public responsibilities, even service in the armed forces. It is the very foundation of good citizenship. Today it is a principal instrument in awakening the child to cultural values, in preparing him for later professional training, and in helping him to adjust normally to his environment. In these days, it is doubtful that any child may reasonably be expected to succeed in life if he is denied the opportunity of an education. Such an opportunity, where the state has undertaken to provide it, is a right which must be made available to all on equal terms.

We come then to the question presented: Does segregation of children in public schools solely on the basis of race, even though the physical facilities and other 'tangible' factors may be equal, deprive the children of the minority group of equal educational opportunities? We believe that it does.

In *Sweatt* v. *Painter, supra*, in finding that a segregated law school for Negroes could not provide them equal educational opportunities, this Court relied in large part on 'those qualities which are incapable of objective measurement but which make for greatness in a law school.' In *McLaurin* v. *Oklahoma State Regents, supra*, the Court, in requiring that a Negro admitted to a white graduate school be treated like all other students, again resorted to intangible considerations: ' … his ability to study, to engage in discussions and exchange views with other students, and, in general, to learn his profession.' Such considerations apply with added force to children in grade and high schools. To separate them from others of similar age and qualifications solely because of their race generates a feeling of inferiority as to their status in the community that may affect their hearts and minds in a way unlikely ever to be undone. The effect of this separation on their educational opportunities was well stated by a finding in the Kansas case by a court which nevertheless felt compelled to rule against the Negro plaintiffs:

> Segregation of white and colored children in public schools has a detrimental effect upon the colored children. The impact is greater when it has the sanction of the law; for the policy of separating the races is usually interpreted as denoting the inferiority of the negro group. A sense of inferiority affects the motivation of a child to learn. Segregation with the sanction of law, therefore, has a tendency to [retard] the educational and mental development of negro children and to deprive them of some of the benefits they would receive in a racial[ly] integrated school system.

Whatever may have been the extent of psychological knowledge at the time of *Plessy* v. *Ferguson*, this finding is amply supported by modern authority. Any language in *Plessy* v. *Ferguson* contrary to this finding is rejected.

We conclude that in the field of public education the doctrine of 'separate but equal' has no place. Separate educational facilities are inherently unequal. Therefore, we hold that the plaintiffs and others similarly situated for whom the actions have been brought are, by reason of the segregation complained of, deprived of the equal protection of the laws guaranteed by the Fourteenth Amendment. This disposition makes unnecessary any discussion whether such segregation also violates the Due Process Clause of the Fourteenth Amendment.

Because these are class actions, because of the wide applicability of this decision, and because of the great variety of local conditions, the formulation of decrees in these cases presents problems of considerable complexity. On reargument, the consideration of appropriate relief was necessarily subordinated to the primary question — the constitutionality of segregation in public education. We have now announced that such segregation is a denial of the equal protection of the laws. In order that we may have the full assistance of the parties in formulating decrees, the cases will be restored to the docket, and the parties are requested to present further argument on Questions 4 and 5 previously propounded by the Court for the reargument this Term. The Attorney General of the United States is again invited to participate. The Attorneys General of the states requiring or permitting segregation in public education will also be permitted to appear as *amici curiae* upon request to do so by September 5, 1954, and submission of briefs by October 1, 1954.

Source: Encyclopaedia Britannica (1976) *The Annals of America, The Bicentennial Edition 1776–1976, Vol.17*, Chicago, Encyclopaedia Britannica, Inc., pp.253–8.

3.5.4 MARTIN LUTHER KING, Jr.: 'I HAVE A DREAM' (1963)

The 'I have a dream' speech was the culmination of the Civil Rights movement 'March for Freedom', which ended with a mass rally in front of the Lincoln Memorial in Washington, DC on 28 August 1963. In the minds of many it has taken a place beside those documents which have mapped out the United States' route to a democratic destiny.

Five score years ago, a great American, in whose symbolic shadow we stand, signed the Emancipation Proclamation. This momentous decree came as a great beacon light of hope to millions of Negro slaves who had been seared in the flames of withering injustice. It came as a joyous daybreak to end the long night of captivity.

But one hundred years later, we must face the tragic fact the Negro is still not free. One hundred years later, the life of the Negro is still sadly crippled by the manacles of segregation and the chains of discrimination. One hundred

Dr Martin Luther King, Jr., Washington, DC, 28 August 1963

years later, the Negro lives on a lonely island of poverty in the midst of a vast ocean of material prosperity. One hundred years later, the Negro is still languished in the corners of American society and finds himself an exile in his own land. So we have come here today to dramatize an appalling condition.

In a sense we have come to our nation's Capital to cash a check. When the architects of our republic wrote the magnificent words of the Constitution and the Declaration of Independence, they were signing a promissory note to which every American was to fall heir. This note was a promise that all men would be guaranteed the unalienable rights of life, liberty, and the pursuit of happiness.

It is obvious today that America has defaulted on this promissory note inso-far as her citizens of color are concerned. Instead of honoring this sacred obligation, America has given the Negro people a bad check; a check which has come back marked 'insufficient funds'. But we refuse to believe that the bank of justice is bankrupt. We refuse to believe that there are insufficient funds in the great vaults of opportunity of this nation. So we have come to cash this check — a check that will give us upon demand the riches of freedom and the security of justice.

We have also come to this hallowed spot to remind America of the fierce urgency of *now*. This is no time to engage in the luxury of cooling off or to take the tranquilizing drug of gradualism. *Now* is the time to make real the promises of democracy. *Now* is the time to rise from the dark and desolate valley of segregation to the sunlit path of racial justice. *Now* is the time to open the doors of opportunity to all of God's children. *Now* is the time to lift our nation from the quicksands of racial injustice to the solid rock of brotherhood.

It would be fatal for the nation to overlook the urgency of the moment and to underestimate the determination of the Negro. This sweltering summer of the Negro's legitimate discontent will not pass until there is an invigorating autumn of freedom and equality. Nineteen sixty-three is not an end, but a beginning. Those who hope that the Negro needed to blow off steam and will now be content will have a rude awakening if the nation returns to business as usual. There will be neither rest nor tranquillity in America until the Negro is granted his citizenship rights. The whirlwinds of revolt will continue to shake the foundations of our nation until the bright day of justice emerges.

But there is something that I must say to my people who stand on the warm threshold which leads into the palace of justice. In the process of gaining our rightful place we must not be guilty of wrongful deeds. Let us not seek to satisfy our thirst for freedom by drinking from the cup of bitterness and hatred. We must forever conduct our struggle on the high plane of dignity and discipline. We must not allow our creative protest to degenerate into physical violence. Again and again we must rise to the majestic heights of meeting physical force with soul force.

The marvelous new militancy which has engulfed the Negro community must not lead us to a distrust of all white people, for many of our white brothers, as evidenced by their presence here today, have come to realize that their destiny is tied up with our destiny and their freedom is inextricably bound to our freedom. We cannot walk alone.

And as we walk, we must make the pledge that we shall march ahead. We cannot turn back. There are those who are asking the devotees of civil rights, 'When will you be satisfied?'

We can never be satisfied as long as the Negro is the victim of the unspeakable horrors of police brutality.

We can never be satisfied as long as our bodies, heavy with the fatigue of travel, cannot gain lodging in the motels of the highways and the hotels of the cities.

We cannot be satisfied as long as the Negro's basic mobility is from a smaller ghetto to a larger one.

We can never be satisfied as long as a Negro in Mississippi cannot vote and a Negro in New York believes he has nothing for which to vote.

No, no, we are not satisfied, and we will not be satisfied until justice rolls down like waters and righteousness like a mighty stream.

I am not unmindful that some of you have come here out of great trials and tribulations. Some of you have come fresh from narrow jail cells. Some of you have come from areas where your quest for freedom left you battered by the storms of persecution and staggered by the winds of police brutality. You have been veterans of creative suffering. Continue to work with the faith that unearned suffering is redemptive.

Go back to Mississippi, go back to Alabama, go back to South Carolina, go back to Georgia, go back to Louisiana, go back to the slums and ghettos of our Northern cities, knowing that somehow this situation can and will be changed. Let us not wallow in the valley of despair.

I say to you today, my friends, that in spite of the difficulties and frustrations of the moment I still have a dream. It is a dream deeply rooted in the American dream.

I have a dream that one day this nation will rise up and live out the true meaning of its creed: 'We hold these truths to be self-evident; that all men are created equal.'

I have a dream that one day on the red hills of Georgia the sons of former slaves and the sons of former slaveowners will be able to sit down together at the table of brotherhood.

I have a dream that one day even the state of Mississippi, a desert state sweltering with the heat of injustice and oppression, will be transformed into an oasis of freedom and justice.

I have a dream that my four little children will one day live in a nation where they will not be judged by the color of their skin but by the content of their character.

I have a dream today.

I have a dream that one day the state of Alabama, whose governor's lips are presently dripping with the words of interposition and nullification, will be transformed into a situation where little black boys and black girls will be able to join hands with little white boys and white girls and walk together as sisters and brothers.

I have a dream today.

I have a dream that one day every valley shall be exalted, every hill and mountain shall be made low, the rough places will be made plain, and the crooked places will be made straight, and the glory of the Lord shall be revealed, and all flesh shall see it together.

This is our hope. This is the faith with which I return to the South. With this faith we will be able to hew out of the mountain of despair a stone of hope. With this faith we will be able to transform the jangling discords of our nation into a beautiful symphony of brotherhood.

With this faith we will be able to work together, to pray together, to struggle together, to go to jail together, to stand up for freedom together, knowing that we will be free one day.

This will be the day when all of God's children will be able to sing with new meaning, 'My country 'tis of thee, sweet land of liberty, of thee I sing. Land where my fathers died, land of the Pilgrims' pride, from every mountainside, let freedom ring.'

And if America is to be a great nation, this must become true. So let freedom ring from the prodigious hilltops of New Hampshire. Let freedom ring from the mighty mountains of New York. Let freedom ring from the heightening Alleghenies of Pennsylvania!

Let freedom ring from the snowcapped Rockies of Colorado! Let freedom ring from the curvaceous peaks of California! But not only that; let freedom ring from Stone Mountain of Georgia! Let freedom ring from Lookout Mountain of Tennessee!

Let freedom ring from every hill and molehill of Mississippi. From every mountainside, let freedom ring.

When we let freedom ring, when we let it ring from every village and every hamlet, from every state and every city, we will be able to speed up that day when all of God's children, black men and white men, Jews and Gentiles, Protestants and Catholics, will be able to join hands and sing in the words of the old Negro spiritual, 'Free at last! Free at last! Thank God Almighty, we are free at last!'

Source: Encyclopaedia Britannica (1976) *The Annals of America, The Bicentennial Edition 1776–1976, Vol.18*, Chicago, Encyclopaedia Britannica, Inc., pp.156–9.

3.5.5 EXTRACT FROM THE AUTOBIOGRAPHY OF MALCOLM X (1965)

An alternative approach and reaction to the experiences of black Americans is clear in the autobiography of Malcolm X. The X represented his true African name which was unknown to him, he had abandoned his given family name which had its origin in slavery. Malcolm X's opinions, and religion, changed over time. The following extract represents his views shortly before his murder in 1965.

[…]

I must be honest. Negroes — Afro-Americans — showed no inclination to rush to the United Nations and demand justice for themselves here in America. I really had known in advance that they wouldn't. The American white man has so thoroughly brainwashed the black man to see himself as only a domestic 'civil rights' problem that it will probably take longer than I live before the Negro sees that the struggle of the American black man is international.

And I had known, too, that Negroes would not rush to follow me into the orthodox Islam which had given me the insight and perspective to see that the black men and white men truly could be brothers. America's Negroes — especially older Negroes — are too indelibly soaked in Christianity's double standard of oppression.

So, in the 'public invited' meetings which I began holding each Sunday afternoon or evening in Harlem's well-known Audubon Ballroom, as I addressed predominantly non-Muslim Negro audiences, I did not immediately attempt to press the Islamic religion, but instead to embrace all who sat before me:

' — not Muslim, nor Christian, Catholic, nor Protestant ... Baptist nor Methodist, Democrat nor Republican, Mason nor Elk! I mean the black people of America — and the black people all over this earth! Because it is as this collective mass of black people that we have been deprived not only of our civil rights, but even of our human rights, the right to human dignity ... '

On the streets, after my speeches, in the faces and the voices of the people I met — even those who would pump my hands and want my autograph — I would feel the wait-and-see attitude. I would feel — and I understood — their uncertainty about where I stood. Since the Civil War's 'freedom', the black man has gone down so many fruitless paths. His leaders, very largely, had failed him. The religion of Christianity had failed him. The black man was scarred, he was cautious, he was apprehensive.

[...]

My thinking had been opened up wide in Mecca. In the long letters I wrote to friends, I tried to convey to them my new insights into the American black man's struggle and his problems, as well as the depths of my search for truth and justice.

'I've had enough of someone else's propaganda', I had written to these friends. 'I'm for truth, no matter who tells it. I'm for justice, no matter who it is for or against. I'm a human being first and foremost, and as such I'm for whoever and whatever benefits humanity *as a whole*.'

Largely, the American white man's press refused to convey that I was now attempting to teach Negroes a new direction. With the 1964 'long, hot summer' steadily producing new incidents, I was constantly accused of 'stirring up Negroes'. Every time I had another radio or television microphone at my mouth, when I was asked about 'stirring up Negroes' or 'inciting violence', I'd get hot.

'It takes no one to stir up the sociological dynamite that stems from the unemployment, bad housing, and inferior education already in the ghettos. This explosively criminal condition has existed for so long, it needs no fuse; it fuses itself; it spontaneously combusts from within itself ... '

They called me 'the angriest Negro in America'. I wouldn't deny that charge. I spoke exactly as I felt. 'I *believe* in anger. The Bible says there is a *time* for anger.' They called me 'a teacher, a fomenter of violence'. I would say point blank, 'That is a lie. I'm not for wanton violence, I'm for justice. I feel that if white people were attacked by Negroes — if the forces of law prove unable, or inadequate, or reluctant to protect those whites from those Negroes — then those white people should protect and defend themselves from those Negroes, using arms if necessary. And I feel that when the law fails to protect Negroes from whites' attack, then those Negroes should use arms, if necessary, to defend themselves.'

'Malcolm X Advocates Armed Negroes!'

What was wrong with that? I'll tell you what was wrong. I was a black man talking about physical defense against the white man. The white man can lynch and burn and bomb and beat Negroes — that's all right: 'Have patience' … 'The customs are entrenched' … 'Things are getting better'.

Well, I believe it's a crime for anyone who is being brutalized to continue to accept that brutality without doing something to defend himself. If that's how 'Christian' philosophy is interpreted, if that's what Gandhian philosophy teaches, well, then, I will call them criminal philosophies.

I tried in every speech I made to clarify my new position regarding white people — 'I don't speak against the sincere, well-meaning, good white people. I have learned that there *are* some. I have learned that not all white people are racists. I am speaking against and my fight is against the white *racists*. I firmly believe that Negroes have the right to fight against these racists, by any means that are necessary.'

[…]

Source: Malcolm X (1968) *The Autobiography of Malcolm X*, London, Penguin, p.481.

3.5.6   VOTING RIGHTS: PRESIDENT JOHNSON'S SPEECH TO CONGRESS (1965)

Supreme Court rulings and even Amendments to the Constitution did not necessarily mean that legal rights would be implemented. In the face of deeply entrenched opposition, especially in parts of the South, many black Americans were effectively excluded from the democratic process. This exclusion was a source of much frustration and alienation from the conventional political system. In his speech to Congress, introducing the Voting Rights Bill, President Lyndon B. Johnson called for action by the federal government to guarantee that the rights of black Americans to register for the vote, and to vote at elections, should not be thwarted by bigotry. Large majorities in both Houses of Congress made the bill law, but its effectiveness could still be undermined by local conditions.

I speak tonight for the dignity of man and the destiny of democracy. I urge every member of both parties, Americans of all religions and of all colors, from every section of this country, to join me in that cause.

At times history and fate meet at a single time in a single place to shape a turning point in man's unending search for freedom. So it was at Lexington and Concord. So it was a century ago at Appomattox. So it was last week in Selma, Alabama.

There, long-suffering men and women peacefully protested the denial of their rights as Americans. Many were brutally assaulted. One good man, a man of God, was killed.

There is no cause for pride in what has happened in Selma. There is no cause for self-satisfaction in the long denial of equal rights of millions of Americans.

But there is cause for hope and for faith in our democracy in what is happening here tonight.

For the cries of pain and the hymns and protests of oppressed people, have summoned into convocation all the majesty of this great government of the greatest nation on earth.

Our mission is at once the oldest and the most basic of this country: to right wrong, to do justice, to serve man.

In our time we have come to live with the moments of great crisis. Our lives have been marked with debate about great issues, issues of war and peace, issues of prosperity and depression. But rarely in any time does an issue lay bare the secret heart of America itself. Rarely are we met with a challenge, not to our growth or abundance, or our welfare of our security, but rather to the values and the purposes and the meaning of our beloved nation.

The issue of equal rights for American Negroes is such an issue. And should we defeat every enemy, and should we double our wealth and conquer the stars and still be unequal to this issue, then we will have failed as a people and as a nation.

For with a country as with a person, 'What is a man profited, if he shall gain the whole world, and lose his own soul?'

There is no Negro problem. There is no Southern problem. There is no Northern problem. There is only an American problem. And we are met here tonight as Americans, not as Democrats or Republicans, we are met here as Americans to solve that problem.

This was the first nation in the history of the world to be founded with a purpose. The great phrases of that purpose still sound in every American heart, North and South: 'All men are created equal' — 'government by consent of the governed' — 'give me liberty or give me death.' Those are not just clever words. Those are not just empty theories. In their name Americans have fought and died for two centuries, and tonight around the world they stand there as guardians of our liberty, risking their lives.

Those words are a promise to every citizen that he shall share in the dignity of man. This dignity cannot be found in a man's possessions. It cannot be found in his power or in his position. It really rests on his right to be treated as a man equal in opportunity to all others. It says that he shall share in freedom, he shall choose his leaders, educate his children, provide for his family according to his ability and his merits as a human being.

To apply any other test — to deny a man his hopes because of his color or race, or his religion, or the place of his birth — is not only to do injustice, it is to deny America and to dishonor the dead who gave their lives for American freedom.

Our fathers believed that if this noble view of the rights of man was to flourish, it must be rooted in democracy. The most basic right of all was the right to choose your own leaders. The history of this country in large measure is the history of expansion of that right to all of our people.

Many of the issues of civil rights are very complex and most difficult. But about this there can and should be no argument. Every American citizen must have an equal right to vote. There is no reason which can excuse the denial of that right. There is no duty which weighs more heavily on us than the duty we have to ensure that right.

Yet the harsh fact is that in many places in this country men and women are kept from voting simply because they are Negroes.

Every device of which human ingenuity is capable has been used to deny this right. The Negro citizen may go to register only to be told that the day is wrong, or the hour is late, or the official in charge is absent. And if he persists and if he manages to present himself to the registrar, he may be disqualified because he did not spell out his middle name or because he abbreviated a word on the application. And if he manages to fill out an application he is given a test. The registrar is the sole judge of whether he passes this test. He may be asked to recite the entire Constitution, or explain the most complex provisions of state laws. And even a college degree cannot be used to prove that he can read and write.

For the fact is that the only way to pass these barriers is to show a white skin.

Experience has clearly shown that the existing process of law cannot overcome systematic and ingenious discrimination. No law that we now have on the books — and I have helped to put three of them there — can ensue the right to vote when local officials are determined to deny it.

In such a case our duty must be clear to all of us. The Constitution says that no person shall be kept from voting because of his race or his color. We have all sworn an oath before God to support and to defend that Constitution. We must now act in obedience to that oath.

Wednesday I will send to Congress a law designed to eliminate illegal barriers to the right to vote.

The broad principle of that bill will be in the hands of the Democratic and Republican leaders tomorrow. After they have reviewed it, it will come here formally as a bill. I am grateful for this opportunity to come here tonight at the invitation of the leadership to reason with my friends, to give them my views and to visit with my former colleagues.

I have had prepared a more comprehensive analysis of the legislation which I have intended to transmit to the clerks tomorrow, but which I will submit to the clerks tonight; but I want to really discuss with you now briefly the main proposals of this legislation.

This bill will strike down restrictions to voting in all elections — Federal, State, and local — which have been used to deny Negroes the right to vote.

This bill will establish a simple, uniform standard which cannot be used however ingenious the effort to flout our Constitution.

It will provide for citizens to be registered by officials of the United States government, if the state officials refuse to register them.

It will eliminate tedious, unnecessary lawsuits which delay the right to vote.

Finally, this legislation will ensure that properly registered individuals are not prohibited from voting.

I will welcome the suggestions from all of the members of Congress. I have no doubt that I will get some on ways and means to strengthen this law and to make it effective. But experience has plainly shown that this is the only path to carry out the command of the Constitution.

To those who seek to avoid action by their national government in their own communities, who want to and who seek to maintain purely local control over elections, the answer is simple.

Open your polling places to all your people.

Allow men and women to register and vote whatever the color of their skin.

Extend the rights of citizenship to every citizen of this land.

There is no constitutional issue here. The command of the Constitution is plain.

There is no moral issue. It is wrong to deny any of your fellow Americans the right to vote in this country.

There is no issue of states rights or national rights. There is only the struggle for human rights.

I have not the slightest doubt what will be your answer.

But the last time a President sent a civil rights bill to the Congress it contained a provision to protect voting rights in Federal elections. That civil rights bill was passed after eight long months of debate. And when that bill came to my desk from the Congress for my signature, the heart of the voting provision had been eliminated.

This time, on this issue, there must be no delay, or no hesitation or no compromise with our purpose.

We cannot, we must not refuse to protect the right of every American to vote in every election that he may desire to participate in. And we ought not, we must not wait another eight months before we get a bill. We have already waited a hundred years and more and the time for waiting is gone.

So I ask you to join me in working long hours, nights, and weekends if necessary, to pass this bill. And I don't make that request lightly. Far from the window where I sit with the problems of our country, I recognize that from outside this chamber is the outraged conscience of a nation, the grave concern of many nations and the harsh judgment of history on our acts.

But even if we pass this bill, the battle will not be over. What happened in Selma is part of a far larger movement which reaches into every section and state of America. It is the effort of American Negroes to secure for themselves the full blessings of American life.

Their cause must be our cause too. Because it is not just Negroes, but really it is all of us, who must overcome the crippling legacy of bigotry and injustice. And we shall overcome.

As a man whose roots go deeply into Southern soil I know how agonizing racial feelings are. I know how difficult it is to reshape the attitudes and the structure of our society.

But a century has passed, more than a hundred years, since the Negro was freed. And he is not fully free tonight.

It was more than a hundred years ago that Abraham Lincoln, the great President of the Northern party, signed the Emancipation Proclamation, but emancipation is a proclamation and not a fact.

A century has passed, more than a hundred years since equality was promised. And yet the Negro is not equal.

A century has passed since the day of promise. And the promise is unkept.

The time of justice has now come. I tell you that I believe sincerely that no force can hold it back. It is right in the eyes of man and God that it should come. And when it does, I think that day will brighten the lives of every American.

For Negroes are not the only victims. How many white children have gone uneducated, how many white families have lived in stark poverty, how many white lives have been scarred by fear because we wasted our energy and our substance to maintain the barrier of hatred and terror.

So I say to all of you here and to all in the nation tonight, that those who appeal to you to hold on to the past do so at the cost of denying you your future.

This great, rich, restless country can offer opportunity and education and hope to all — all black and white, all North and South, sharecropper, and city dweller. These are the enemies — poverty, ignorance, disease. They are enemies, not our fellow man, not our neighbor, and these enemies too, poverty, disease and ignorance, we shall overcome.

Now let none of us in any section look with prideful righteousness on the troubles in another section or the problems of our neighbors. There is really no part of America where the promise of equality has been fully kept. In Buffalo as well as in Birmingham, in Philadelphia as well as in Selma, Americans are struggling for the fruits of freedom.

This is one nation. What happens in Selma or in Cincinnati is a matter of legitimate concern to every American. But let each of us look within our own hearts and our own communities, and let each of us put our shoulder to the wheel to root out injustice wherever it exists.

As we meet here in this peaceful historic chamber tonight, men from the South, some of whom were at Iwo Jima, men from the North who have carried Old Glory to far corners of the world and brought it back without a stain on it, men from the East and West are all fighting together without regard to religion, or color, or region, in Vietnam, men from every region fought for us across the world twenty years ago. And now in these common dangers and these common sacrifices the South made its contribution of honor and gallantry no less than any other region of the great Republic. In some instances, a great many of them more. And I have not the slightest doubt that good men from everywhere in this country, from the Great Lakes to the Gulf of Mexico, from the Golden Gate to the harbors along the Atlantic, will rally now together in this cause to vindicate the freedom of all Americans. For all of us owe this duty; and I believe all of us will respond to it.

Your President makes that request of every American.

The real hero of this struggle is the American Negro. His actions and protests, his courage to risk safety and even to risk his life, have awakened the conscience of this nation. His demonstrations have been designed to call attention to injustice, designed to provoke change, designed to stir reform. He has called upon us to make good the promise of America. And who among us can say that we would have made the same progress were it not for his persistent bravery, and his faith in American democracy.

For at the real heart of battle for equality is a deep seated belief in the democratic process. Equality depends not on the force of arms or tear gas but depends upon the force of moral right — not on recourse to violence but on respect for law and order.

There have been many pressures upon your President and there will be others as the days come and go, but I pledge you tonight that we intend to fight this battle where it should be fought, in the courts, and in the Congress, and in the hearts of men.

We must preserve the right of free speech and the right of free assembly. But the right of free speech does not carry with it as has been said, the right to holler fire in a crowed theater. We must preserve the right to free assembly but free assembly does not carry with it the right to block public thorough-fares to traffic.

We do have a right to protest, and a right to march under conditions that do not infringe the Constitutional rights of our neigbors. I intend to protect all those rights as long as I am permitted to serve in this Office.

We will guard against violence, knowing it strikes from our hands the very weapons with which we seek progress — obedience to law, and belief in American values.

In Selma as elsewhere we seek and pray for peace. We seek order. We seek unity. But we will not accept the peace of stifled rights, or the order imposed by fear, or the unity that stifles protest. For peace cannot be pur-chased at the cost of liberty.

In Selma tonight — and we had a good day there — as in every city, we are working for just and peaceful settlement. We must all remember that after this speech I am making tonight, after the police and the FBI and the mar-shals have all gone, and after you have promptly passed this bill, the people of Selma and the other cities of the nation must still live and work together. And when the attention of the nation has gone elsewhere they must try to heal the wounds and to build a new community. This cannot be easily done on a battleground of violence as the history of the South itself shows. It is in recognition of this that men of both races have shown such an outstandingly impressive responsibility in recent days, last Tuesday, again today.

The bill that I am presenting to you will be known as a civil rights bill. But, in a larger sense, most of the program I am recommending is a civil right. Its object is to open the city of hope to all people of all races, because all Americans just must have the right to vote. And we are going to give them that right.

All Americans must have the privileges of citizenship regardless of race. And they are going to have those privileges of citizenship regardless of race.

But I would like to caution you and remind you that to exercise these privi-leges takes much more than just legal right. It requires a trained mind and a healthy body. It requires a decent home, and the chance to find a job, and the opportunity to escape from the clutches of poverty.

Of course people cannot contribute to the nation if they are never taught to read or write, if their bodies are stunted from hunger, if their sickness goes untended, if their life is spent in hopeless poverty just drawing a welfare check.

So we want to open the gates to opportunity. But we are also going to give all our people, black and white, the help that they need to walk through those gates.

My first job after college was as a teacher in Cotulla, Texas, in a small Mexican-American school. Few of them could speak English and I couldn't speak much Spanish. My students were poor and they often came to class without breakfast, hungry, and they knew even in their youth that pain of prejudice. They never seemed to know why people disliked them. But they knew it was so. Because I saw it in their eyes. I often walked home late in the afternoon after the classes were finished, wishing there was more that I could do. But all I knew was to teach them the little that I knew, hoping that it might help them against the hardships that lay ahead.

Somehow you never forget what poverty and hatred can do when you see its scars on the hopeful face of a young child.

I never thought then in 1928 that I would be standing here in 1965. It never even occurred to me in my fondest dreams that I might have the chance to help the sons and daughters of those students and to help people like them all over this country. But now I do have that chance and I let you in on a secret, I mean to use it. And I hope that you will use it with me.

This is the richest and most powerful country which ever occupied this globe. The might of past empires is little compared to ours.

But I do not want to be the President who built empires, or sought grandeur, or extended dominion. I want to be the President who educated young children to the wonders of their world. I want to be the President who helped to feed the hungry and to prepare them to be taxpayers instead of taxeaters. I want to be the President who helped the poor to find their own way and who protected the right of every citizen to vote in every election. I want to be the President who helped to end hatred among his fellow men and who prompted love among the people of all races and all regions and all parties. I want to be the President who helped to end war among the brothers of this earth.

And so at the request of your beloved Speaker and Senator from Montana, the Majority Leader, the Senator from Illinois, the Minority Leader, Mr McCulloch and other leaders of both parties, I came here tonight not as President Roosevelt came down one time in person to veto a bonus bill, not as President Truman came down one time to urge the passage of a railroad bill, but I came down here to ask you to share this task with me and to share it with the people that we both work for. I want this to be the Congress, Republicans and Democrats alike, which did all those things for all these people.

Beyond this great chamber, out yonder, the fifty states are the people we serve. Who can tell what deep unspoken hopes are in their hearts tonight as they sit there and listen. We all can guess, from our own lives, how difficult they often find their own pursuit of happiness. How many problems each little family has. They look most of all to themselves for their futures. But I think that they also look to each of us.

Above the pyramid on the great seal of the United States it says — in Latin — 'God has favored our undertaking'.

God will not favor everything that we do. It is rather our duty to divine His will. But I cannot help believing that He truly understands and that He really favors the undertaking that we begin here tonight.

Source: Hanover College, Indiana, Department of History Web Site. Available from: http://history.hanover.edu/20th/johnson.htm

3.6 INVESTIGATING THE PRESIDENT

3.6.1 *THE UNITED STATES v. RICHARD M. NIXON (1974)*

This ruling of the Supreme Court forced President Nixon to hand over more of the 'Watergate tapes' to the Special Prosecutor appointed by Nixon to investigate the Watergate affair. These tapes, secretly recorded on Nixon's orders, were of conversations and meetings held in the White House. The tapes implicated Nixon in the break-in to the Watergate Centre headquarters of his Democratic opponents in the 1972 presidential election, and the subsequent cover-up. After the ruling events moved rapidly towards the President's resignation in the face of imminent impeachment by Congress. The Supreme Court was concerned with the issues and legal precedents surrounding presidential privilege and the rule of law. While recognizing the many executive privileges accorded to the President, it effectively ruled that the President was not above the law.

These cases present for review the denial of a motion, filed on behalf of the President of the United States, in the case of *United States* v. *Mitchell et al.* (D.C. Crim. No. 74-110), to quash a third-party subpoena *duces tecum* issued by the United States District Court for the District of Columbia, pursuant to Fed. Rule Crim. Proc. 17 (c). The subpoena directed the President to produce certain tape recordings and documents relating to his conversations with aides and advisers. The court rejected the President's claims of absolute executive privilege, of lack of jurisdiction, and of failure to satisfy the requirements of Rule 17 (c). The President appealed to the Court of Appeals. We granted the United States' petition for certiorari before judgment, and also the President's responsive cross-petition for certiorari before judgment, because of the public importance of the issues presented and the need for their prompt resolution. […]

On March 1, 1974, a grand jury of the United States District Court for the District of Columbia returned an indictment charging seven named individuals with various offenses, including conspiracy to defraud the United States and to an unindicted co-conspirator. On April 18, 1974, upon motion of the Special Prosecutor, see n. 8, *infra*, a subpoena *duces tecum* was issued pursuant to Rule 17 (c) to the President by the United States District Court and made returnable on May 2, 1974. This subpoena required the production, in advance of the September 9 trial date, of certain tapes, memoranda, papers, transcripts, or other writings relating to certain precisely identified meetings between the President and others. The Special Prosecutor was able to fix the time, place and persons present at these discussions because the White House daily logs and appointment records had been delivered to him. On April 30, the President publicly released edited transcripts of 43 conversations; portions of 20 conversations subject to subpoena in the present case were included. On May 1, 1974, the President's counsel, filed a 'special appearance' and a motion to quash the subpoena, under Rule 17 (c). This motion was accompanied by a formal claim of privilege. At a subsequent hearing, further motions to expunge the grand jury's action naming the President as an unindicted co-conspirator and for protective orders against the disclosure of that information were filed or raised orally by counsel for the President.

On May 20, 1974, the District Court denied the motion to quash and the motions to expunge and for protective orders. […] It further ordered 'the President or any subordinate officer, official or employee with custody or control of the documents or objects subpoenaed', […] to deliver to the District Court, on or before May 31, 1974, the originals of all subpoenaed items, as well as an index and analysis of those items, together with tape copies of those portions of the subpoenaed recordings for which transcripts had been released to the public by the President on April 30, The District Court rejected jurisdictional challenges based on a contention that the dispute was nonjusticiable because it was between the Special Prosecutor and the Chief Executive and hence 'intra-executive' in character; it also rejected the contention that the judiciary was without authority to review an assertion of executive privilege by the President. The court's rejection of the first challenge was based on the authority and powers vested in the Special Prosecutor by the regulation promulgated by the Attorney General; the court concluded that a justiciable controversy was presented. The second challenge was held to be foreclosed by the decision in *Nixon* v. *Sirica*, — U.S. App. D.C. — , 487 F. 2d 700 (1973).

The District Court held that the judiciary, not the President, was the final arbiter of a claim of executive privilege. The court concluded that, under the circumstances of this case, the presumptive privilege was overcome by the Special Prosecutor's prima facie 'demonstration of need sufficiently compelling to warrant judicial examination in chambers … ' […]. The court held, finally, that the Special Prosecutor had satisfied the requirements of Rule 17 (c). The District Court stayed its order pending appellate review on condition that review was sought before 4 p.m., May 24. The court further provided that matters filed under seal remain under seal when transmitted as part of the record.

On May 24, 1974, the President filed a timely notice of appeal from the District Court order, and the certified record from the District Court was docketed in the United States Court of Appeals for the District of Columbia Circuit. On the same day, the President also filed a petition for writ of mandamus in the Court of Appeals seeking review of the District Court order.

Later on May 24, the Special Prosecutor also filed, in this Court, a petition for a writ of certiorari before judgment. On May 31, the petition was granted with an expedited briefing schedule. […] On June 6, the President filed, under seal, a cross-petition for writ of certiorari before judgment. This cross-petition was granted June 15, 1974, [...] and the case was set for argument on July 8, 1974.

[...]

II. JUSTICIABILITY

In the District Court, the President's counsel argued that the court lacked jurisdiction to issue the subpoena because the matter was an intra-branch dispute between a subordinate and superior officer of the Executive Branch and hence not subject to judicial resolution. That argument has been renewed in this Court with emphasis on the contention that the dispute does not present a 'case' or 'controversy' which can be adjudicated in the federal courts. The President's counsel argues that the federal courts should not intrude into areas committed to the other branches of Government. He views the present dispute as essentially a 'jurisdictional' dispute within the Executive Branch which he analogizes to a dispute between two congressional committees. Since the Executive Branch has exclusive authority and absolute discretion to decide whether to prosecute a case, [...] it is contended that a President's decision is final in determining what evidence is to be used in a given criminal case. Although his counsel concedes the President has delegated certain specific powers to the Special Prosecutor, he has not 'waived nor delegated to the Special Prosecutor the President's duty to claim privilege as to all materials ... which fall within the President's inherent authority to refuse to disclose to any executive officer.' Brief for the President 47. The Special Prosecutor's demand for the items therefore presents, in the view of the President's counsel, a political question under *Baker v. Carr,* 369 U.S. 186 (1962), since it involves a 'textually demonstrable' grant of power under Art. II.

The mere assertion of a claim of an 'intra-branch dispute', without more, has never operated to defeat federal jurisdiction; justiciability does not depend on such a surface inquiry. In *United States* v. *ICC,* 337 U.S. 426 (1949), the Court observed 'courts must look behind names that symbolize the parties to determine whether a justiciable case or controversy is presented.' *Id.,* at 430. [...]

Our starting point is the nature of the proceeding for which the evidence is sought — here a pending criminal prosecution. It is a judicial proceeding in a federal court alleging violation of federal laws and is brought in the name of the United States as sovereign. [...] Under the authority of Art. II § 2, Congress has vested in the Attorney General the power to conduct the criminal litigation of the United States Government. [...] It has also vested in him the power to appoint subordinate officers to assist him in the discharge of his duties. [...] Acting pursuant to those statutes, the Attorney General has delegated the authority to represent the United States in these particular matters to a Special Prosecutor with unique authority and tenure. The regulation gives the Special Prosecutor explicit power to contest the invocation of executive privilege in the process of seeking evidence deemed relevant to the performance of these specially delegated duties. [...]

So long as this regulation is extant it has the force of law. In *Accardi* v. *Shaughnessy*, 347 U.S. 260 (1953), regulations of the Attorney General delegated certain of his discretionary powers to the Board of Immigration Appeals and required that Board to exercise its own discretion on appeals in deportation cases. The Court held that so long as the Attorney General's regulations remained operative, he denied himself the authority to exercise the discretion delegated to the Board even though the original authority was his and he could reassert it by amending the regulations. […]

Here, as in *Accardi*, it is theoretically possible for the Attorney General to amend or revoke the regulation defining the Special Prosecutor's authority. But he has not done so. So long as this regulation remains in force the Executive Branch is bound by it, and indeed the United States as the sovereign composed of the three branches is bound to respect and to enforce it. Moreover, the delegation of authority to the Special Prosecutor in this case is not an ordinary delegation by the Attorney General to a subordinate officer: with the authorization of the President, the Acting Attorney General provided in the regulation that the Special Prosecutor was not to be removed without the 'consensus' of eight designated leaders of Congress. Note 8, *supra*.

The demands of and the resistance to the subpoena present an obvious controversy in the ordinary sense, but that alone is not sufficient to meet constitutional standards. In the constitutional sense, controversy means more than disagreement and conflict; rather it means the kind of controversy courts traditionally resolve. Here at issue is the production or nonproduction of specified evidence deemed by the Special Prosecutor to be relevant and admissible in a pending criminal case. It is sought by one official of the Government within the scope of his express authority; it is resisted by the Chief Executive on the ground of his duty to preserve the confidentiality of the communications of the President. Whatever the correct answer on the merits, these issues are 'of a type which are traditionally justiciable.' *United States* v. *ICC*, 337 U.S., at 430. The independent Special Prosecutor with his asserted need for the subpoenaed material in the underlying criminal prosecution is opposed by the President with his steadfast assertion of privilege against disclosure of the material. This setting assures there is 'that concrete adverseness which sharpens the presentation of issues upon which the court so largely depends for illumination of difficult constitutional questions.' *Baker* v. *Carr*, 369 U.S., at 204. Moreover, since the matter is one arising in the regular course of a federal criminal prosecution, it is within the traditional scope of Art. III power. *Id.*, at 198.

In light of the uniqueness of the setting in which the conflict arises, the fact that both parties are officers of the Executive Branch cannot be viewed as a barrier to justiciability. It would be inconsistent with the applicable law and regulation, and the unique facts of this case to conclude other than that the Special Prosecutor has standing to bring this action and that a justiciable controversy is presented for decision.

[…]

IV. THE CLAIM OF PRIVILEGE

A.

[...] we turn to the claim that the subpoena should be quashed because it demands 'confidential conversations between a President and his close advisors that it would be inconsistent with the public interest to produce.' App. 48a. The first contention is a broad claim that the separation of powers doctrine precludes judicial review of a President's claim of privilege. The second contention is that if he does not prevail on the claim of absolute privilege, the court should hold as a matter of constitutional law that the privilege prevails over the subpoena *duces tecum*.

In the performance of assigned constitutional duties each branch of the Government must initially interpret the Constitution, and the interpretation of its powers by any branch is due great respect from the others. The President's counsel, as we have noted, reads the Constitution as providing an absolute privilege of confidentiality for all presidential communications. Many decisions of this Court, however, have unequivocally reaffirmed the holding of *Marbury* v. *Madison*, 1 Cranch 137 (1803), that 'it is emphatically the province and duty of the judicial department to say what the law is.' *Id.*, at 177.

No holding of the Court has defined the scope of judicial power specifically relating to the enforcement of a subpoena for confidential presidential communications for use in a criminal prosecution, but other exercises of powers by the Executive Branch and the Legislative Branch have been found invalid as in conflict with the Constitution. *Powell* v. *McCormack, supra; Youngstown, supra.* In a series of cases, the Court interpreted the explicit immunity conferred by express provisions of the Constitution on Members of the House and Senate by the Speech or Debate Clause, U.S. Const. Art. I, § 6. [...] Since this Court has consistently exercised the power to construe and delineate claims arising under express powers, it must follow that the Court has authority to interpret claims with respect to powers alleged to derive from enumerated powers.

Our system of government 'requires that federal courts on occasion interpret the Constitution in a manner at variance with the construction given the document by another branch.' *Powell* v. *McCormack, supra*, 549. And in *Baker* v. *Carr*, 369 U.S., at 211, the Court stated:

> [d]eciding whether a matter has in any measure been committed by the Constitution to another branch of government, or whether the action of that branch exceeds whatever authority has been committed, is itself a delicate exercise in constitutional interpretation, and is a responsibility of this Court as ultimate interpreter of the Constitution.

Notwithstanding the deference each branch must accord the others, the 'judicial power of the United States' vested in the federal courts by Art. III, § 1 of the Constitution can no more be shared with the Executive Branch than the Chief Executive, for example, can share with the Judiciary the veto power, or the Congress share with the Judiciary the power to override a presidential veto. Any other conclusion would be contrary to the basic concept of separation of powers and the checks and balances that flow from the scheme of a tripartite government. The Federalist, No. 47, p. 313 (C.F. Mittel ed. 1938). We therefore reaffirm that it is 'emphatically the province and the duty' of this Court 'to say what the law is' with respect to the claim of privilege presented in this case. *Marbury* v. *Madison, supra,* at 177.

B.

In support of his claim of absolute privilege, the President's counsel urges two grounds one of which is common to all governments and one of which is peculiar to our system of separation of powers. The first ground is the valid need for protection of communications between high government officials and those who advise and assist them in the performance of their manifold duties; the importance of this confidentiality is too plain to require further discussion. Human experience teaches that those who expect public dissemination of their remarks may well temper candor with a concern for appearances and for their own interests to the detriment of the decision making process. Whatever the nature of the privilege of confidentiality of presidential communications in the exercise of Art. II powers the privilege can be said to derive from the supremacy of each branch within its own assigned area of constitutional duties. Certain powers and privileges flow from the nature of enumerated powers; the protection of the confidentiality of presidential communications has similar constitutional underpinnings.

The second ground asserted by the President's counsel in support of the claim of absolute privilege rests on the doctrine of separation of powers. Here it is argued that the independence of the Executive Branch within its own sphere, […] insulates a president from a judicial subpoena in an ongoing criminal prosecution, and thereby protects confidential presidential communications.

However, neither the doctrine of separation of powers, nor the need for confidentiality of high level communications, without more, can sustain an absolute, unqualified presidential privilege of immunity from judicial process under all circumstances. The President's need for complete candor and objectivity from advisers calls for great deference from the courts. However, when the privilege depends solely on the broad, undifferentiated claim of public interest in the confidentiality of such conversations, a confrontation with other values arises. Absent a claim of need to protect military, diplomatic or sensitive national security secrets, we find it difficult to accept the argument that even the very important interest in confidentiality of presidential communications is significantly diminished by production of such material for *in camera* inspection with all the protection that a district court will be obliged to provide.

The impediment that an absolute, unqualified privilege would place in the way of the primary constitutional duty of the Judicial Branch to do justice in criminal prosecutions would plainly conflict with the function of the courts under Art. III. In designing the structure of our Government and dividing and allocating the sovereign power among three coequal branches, the Framers of the Constitution sought to provide a comprehensive system, but the separate powers were not intended to operate with absolute independence.

> While the Constitution diffuses power the better to secure liberty, it also contemplates that practice will integrate the dispersed powers into a workable government. It enjoins upon its branches separateness but interdependence, autonomy but reciprocity.

> *Youngstown Sheet & Tube Co.* v. *Sawyer*, 343 U.S. 579, 635 (1952)
>
> (Jackson, J., concurring)

To read the Art. II powers of the President as providing an absolute privilege as against a subpoena essential to enforcement of criminal statutes on no more than a generalized claim of the public interest in confidentiality of nonmilitary and nondiplomatic discussions would upset the constitutional balance of 'a workable government' and gravely impair the role of the courts under Art. III.

C.

Since we conclude that the legitimate needs of the judicial process may outweigh presidential privilege, it is necessary to resolve those competing interests in a manner that preserves the essential functions of each branch. The right and indeed the duty to resolve that question does not free the judiciary from according high respect to the representations made on behalf of the President. [...]

The expectation of a President to the confidentiality of his conversations and correspondence, like the claim of confidentiality of judicial deliberations, for example, has all the values to which we accord deference for the privacy of all citizens and added to those values the necessity for protection of the public interest in candid, objective, and even blunt or harsh opinions in presidential decision making. A President and those who assist him must be free to explore alternatives in the process of shaping policies and making decisions and to do so in a way many would be unwilling to express except privately. These are the considerations justifying a presumptive privilege for presidential communications. The privilege is fundamental to the operation of government and inextricably rooted in the separation of powers under the Constitution. In *Nixon* v. *Sirica*,— U.S. App. D.C. — , 487 F. 2d 700 (1973), the Court of Appeals held that such presidential communications are 'presumptively privileged', *id.*, at 717, and this position is accepted by both parties in the present litigation. We agree with Mr Chief Justice Marshall's observation, therefore, that 'in no case of this kind would a court be required to proceed against the President as against an ordinary individual.' *United States* v. *Burr*, 25 Fed. Cas. 187, 191 (No. 14,694) (CCD Va. 1807).

But this presumptive privilege must be considered in light of our historic commitment to the rule of law. This is nowhere more profoundly manifest than in our view that 'the twofold aim [of criminal justice] is that guilt shall not escape or innocence suffer.' *Berger* v. *United States*, 295 U.S. 78, 88 (1935). We have elected to employ an adversary system of criminal justice in which the parties contest all issues before a court of law. The need to develop all relevant facts in the adversary system is both fundamental and comprehensive. The end of criminal justice would be defeated if judgments were to be founded on a partial or speculative presentation of the facts. The very integrity of the judicial system and public confidence in the system depend on full disclosure of all the facts, within the framework of the rules of evidence. To ensure that justice is done, it is imperative to the function of courts that compulsory process be available for the production of evidence needed either by the prosecution or by the defense.

Only recently the Court restated the ancient proposition of law, albeit in the context of a grand jury inquiry rather than a trial,

> that the public ... has a right to every man's evidence' except for those persons protected by a constitutional, common law, or statutory privilege, [...]

The privileges referred to by the Court are designed to protect weighty and legitimate competing interests. Thus, the Fifth Amendment to the Constitution provides that no man 'shall be compelled in any criminal case to be a witness against himself.' And, generally, an attorney or a priest may not be required to disclose what has been revealed in professional confidence. These and other interests are recognized in law by privileges against forced disclosure, established in the Constitution, by statute, or at common law. Whatever their origins, these exceptions to the demand for every man's evidence are not lightly created nor expansively construed, for they are in derogation of the search for truth.

In this case the President challenges a subpoena served on him as a third party requiring the production of materials for use in a criminal prosecution on the claim that he has a privilege against disclosure of confidential communications. He does not place his claim of privilege on the ground they are military or diplomatic secrets. As to these areas of Art. II duties the courts have traditionally shown the utmost deference to presidential responsibilities. In *C. & S. Air Lines* v. *Waterman Steamship Corp.*, 333 U.S. 103, 111 (1948), dealing with presidential authority involving foreign policy considerations, the Court said:

> The President, both as Commander-in-Chief and as the Nation's organ for foreign affairs, has available intelligence services whose reports are not and ought not to be published to the world. It would be intolerable that courts, without the relevant information, should review and perhaps nullify actions of the Executive taken on information properly held secret.

Id., at 111

In *United States* v. *Reynolds*, 345 U.S. 1 (1952), dealing with a claimant's demand for evidence in a damage case against the Government the Court said:

> It may be possible to satisfy the court, from all the circumstances of the case, that there is a reasonable danger that compulsion of the evidence will expose military matters which, in the interest of national security, should not be divulged. When this is the case, the occasion for the privilege is appropriate, and the court should not jeopardize the security which the privilege is meant to protect by insisting upon an examination of the evidence, even by the judge alone, in chambers.

No case of the Court, however, has extended this high degree of deference to a President's generalized interest in confidentiality. Nowhere in the Constitution, as we have noted earlier, is there any explicit reference to a privilege of confidentiality, yet to the extent this interest relates to the effective discharge of a President's powers, it is constitutionally based.

The right to the production of all evidence at a criminal trial similarly has constitutional dimensions. The Sixth Amendment explicitly confers upon every defendant in a criminal trial the right 'to be confronted with the witnesses against him' and 'to have compulsory process for obtaining witnesses in his favor.' Moreover, the Fifth Amendment also guarantees that no person shall be deprived of liberty without due process of law. It is the manifest duty of the courts to vindicate those guarantees and to accomplish that it is essential that all relevant and admissible evidence be produced.

In this case we must weigh the importance of the general privilege of confidentiality of presidential communications in performance of his responsibilities against the inroads of such a privilege on the fair administration of criminal justice. The interest in preserving confidentiality is weighty indeed and entitled to great respect. However we cannot conclude that advisers will be moved to temper the candor of their remarks by the infrequent occasions of disclosure because of the possibility that such conversations will be called for in the context of a criminal prosecution.

On the other hand, the allowance of the privilege to withhold evidence that is demonstrably relevant in a criminal trial would cut deeply into the guarantee of due process of law and gravely impair the basic function of the courts. A President's acknowledged need for confidentiality in the communications of his office is general in nature, whereas the constitutional need for production of relevant evidence in a criminal proceeding is specific and central to the fair adjudication of a particular criminal case in the administration of justice. Without access to specific facts a criminal prosecution may be totally frustrated. The President's broad interest in confidentiality of communications will not be vitiated by disclosure of a limited number of conversations preliminarily shown to have some bearing on the pending criminal cases.

We conclude that when the ground for asserting privilege as to subpoenaed materials sought for use in a criminal trial is based only on the generalized interest in confidentiality, it cannot prevail over the fundamental demands of due process of law in the fair administration of criminal justice. The generalized assertion of privilege must yield to the demonstrated, specific need for evidence in a pending criminal trial.

D.

We have earlier determined that the District Court did not err in authorizing the issuance of the subpoena. If a President concludes that compliance with a subpoena would be injurious to the public interest he may properly, as was done here, invoke a claim of privilege on the return of the subpoena. Upon receiving a claim of privilege from the Chief Executive, it became the further duty of the District Court to treat the subpoenaed material as presumptively privileged and to require the Special Prosecutor to demonstrate that the presidential material was 'essential to the justice of the [pending criminal] case.' *United States* v. *Burr, supra*, at 192. Here the District Court treated the material as presumptively privileged, proceeded to find that the Special Prosecutor had made a sufficient showing to rebut the presumption and ordered an *in camera* examination of the subpoenaed material. On the basis of our examination of the record we are unable to conclude that the District Court erred in ordering the inspection. Accordingly we affirm the order of the District Court that subpoenaed materials be transmitted to that court. […]

E.

[…] Mr Chief Justice Marshall sitting as a trial judge in the *Burr* case, *supra*, was extraordinarily careful to point out that:

> [I]n no case of this kind would a Court be required to proceed against the President as against an ordinary individual.

> *United States* v. *Burr*, 25 Fed. Cases 187, 191 (No. 14,694)

Marshall's statement cannot be read to mean in any sense that a President is above the law, but relates to the singularly unique role under Art. II of a President's communications and activities, related to the performance of duties under that Article. Moreover, a President's communications and activities encompass a vastly wider range of sensitive material than would be true of any 'ordinary individual'. It is therefore necessary in the public interest to afford presidential confidentiality the greatest protection consistent with the fair administration of justice. […]

Source: Cornell University Law School, NY, Legal Information Institute Web Site. Available from: http://www.law.cornell.edu/

3.6.2 IMPEACHING PRESIDENT CLINTON (1998)

The investigation by Independent Counsel Kenneth Starr and the reaction and response to his report came to dominate the second term of President Clinton. The Office of the Independent Counsel initially began an investigation into Whitewater — a failed land deal involving the President in his home state of Arkansas. However, the focus of the investigation moved to the relationship between the President and White House employee Monica Lewinsky. In 1994 Paula Jones filed a lawsuit against the President, alleging sexual harassment some years before while he was Governor of Arkansas. In connection with this case the President was required to provide certain information on alleged relationships with other women; he was asked about Monica Lewinsky, and denied having 'sexual relations' with her. Events unfolded through 1998, and following evidence given by Monica Lewinsky and others, the issue became one of perjury and witness tampering. The key question is whether such actions constitute 'high Crimes and Misdemeanors' — the requirement for impeachment (see Article II, Section 4 of the Constitution).

The documents reproduced here are an extract from the Referral to the House of Representatives submitted by the Office of the Independent Counsel (commonly known as the Starr Report); part of the initial response from the White House issued three days later; and the two Articles of the House of Representatives Resolution for impeachment which were passed on 19 December 1998. The vote was on clear Party lines and in the midst of a new crisis with Iraq. It was this Resolution which led to the President's trial by the Senate. Since the necessary two-thirds majority was not reached he was acquitted by the Senate.

REFERRAL TO THE UNITED STATES HOUSE OF REPRESENTATIVES

SUBMITTED BY THE OFFICE OF THE INDEPENDENT COUNSEL

September 9, 1998

Introduction

As required by Section 595(c) of Title 28 of the United States Code, the Office of the Independent Counsel ('OIC' or 'Office') hereby submits substantial and credible information that President William Jefferson Clinton committed acts that may constitute grounds for an impeachment.

The information reveals that President Clinton:

lied under oath at a civil deposition while he was a defendant in a sexual harassment lawsuit;

lied under oath to a grand jury;

attempted to influence the testimony of a potential witness who had direct knowledge of facts that would reveal the falsity of his deposition testimony;

attempted to obstruct justice by facilitating a witness's plan to refuse to comply with a subpoena;

attempted to obstruct justice by encouraging a witness to file an affidavit that the President knew would be false, and then by making use of that false affidavit at his own deposition;

lied to potential grand jury witnesses, knowing that they would repeat those lies before the grand jury; and

engaged in a pattern of conduct that was inconsistent with his constitutional duty to faithfully execute the laws.

The evidence shows that these acts, and others, were part of a pattern that began as an effort to prevent the disclosure of information about the President's relationship with a former White House intern and employee, Monica S. Lewinsky, and continued as an effort to prevent the information from being disclosed in an ongoing criminal investigation.

[...]

The significance of the evidence of wrongdoing

It is not the role of this Office to determine whether the President's actions warrant impeachment by the House and removal by the Senate; those judgments are, of course, constitutionally entrusted to the legislative branch. This Office is authorized, rather, to conduct criminal investigations and to seek criminal prosecutions for matters within its jurisdiction. In carrying out its investigation, however, this Office also has a statutory duty to disclose to Congress information that 'may constitute grounds for an impeachment,' a task that inevitably requires judgment about the seriousness of the acts revealed by the evidence.

From the beginning, this phase of the OIC's investigation has been criticized as an improper inquiry into the President's personal behavior; indeed, the President himself suggested that specific inquiries into his conduct were part of an effort to 'criminalize my private life.' The regrettable fact that the investigation has often required witnesses to discuss sensitive personal matters has fueled this perception.

All Americans, including the President, are entitled to enjoy a private family life, free from public or governmental scrutiny. But the privacy concerns raised in this case are subject to limits, three of which we briefly set forth here.

First. The first limit was imposed when the President was sued in federal court for alleged sexual harassment. The evidence in such litigation is often personal. At times, that evidence is highly embarrassing for both plaintiff and defendant. As Judge Wright noted at the President's January 1998 deposition, 'I have never had a sexual harassment case where there was not some embarrassment.' Nevertheless, Congress and the Supreme Court have concluded that embarrassment-related concerns must give way to the greater interest in allowing aggrieved parties to pursue their claims. Courts have long recognized the difficulties of proving sexual harassment in the workplace, inasmuch as improper or unlawful behavior often takes place in private. To excuse a party who lied or concealed evidence on the ground that the evidence covered only 'personal' or 'private' behavior would frustrate the goals that Congress and the courts have sought to achieve in enacting and interpreting the Nation's sexual harassment laws. That is particularly true when the conduct that is being concealed — sexual relations in the workplace between a high official and a young subordinate employee — itself conflicts with those goals.

Second. The second limit was imposed when Judge Wright required disclosure of the precise information that is in part the subject of this Referral. A federal judge specifically ordered the President, on more than one occasion, to provide the requested information about relationships with other women, including Monica Lewinsky. The fact that Judge Wright later determined that the evidence would not be admissible at trial, and still later granted judgment in the President's favor, does not change the President's legal duty at the time he testified. Like every litigant, the President was entitled to object to the discovery questions, and to seek guidance from the court if he thought those questions were improper. But having failed to convince the court that his objections were well founded, the President was duty bound to testify truthfully and fully. Perjury and attempts to obstruct the gathering of evidence can never be an acceptable response to a court order, regardless of the eventual course or outcome of the litigation.

The Supreme Court has spoken forcefully about perjury and other forms of obstruction of justice:

> In this constitutional process of securing a witness' testimony, perjury simply has no place whatever. Perjured testimony is an obvious and flagrant affront to the basic concepts of judicial proceedings. Effective restraints against this type of egregious offense are therefore imperative.

The insidious effects of perjury occur whether the case is civil or criminal. Only a few years ago, the Supreme Court considered a false statement made in a civil administrative proceeding: 'False testimony in a formal proceeding is intolerable. We must neither reward nor condone such a "flagrant affront" to the truth-seeking function of adversary proceedings. … Perjury should be severely sanctioned in appropriate cases.' Stated more simply, '[p]erjury is an obstruction of justice.'

Third. The third limit is unique to the President. 'The Presidency is more than an executive responsibility. It is the inspiring symbol of all that is highest in American purpose and ideals.' When he took the Oath of Office in 1993 and again in 1997, President Clinton swore that he would 'faithfully execute the Office of President.' As the head of the Executive Branch, the President has the constitutional duty to 'take Care that the Laws be faithfully executed.' The President gave his testimony in the *Jones* case under oath and in the presence of a federal judge, a member of a co-equal branch of government; he then testified before a federal grand jury, a body of citizens who had themselves taken an oath to seek the truth. In view of the enormous trust and responsibility attendant to his high Office, the President has a manifest duty to ensure that his conduct at all times complies with the law of the land.

In sum, perjury and acts that obstruct justice by any citizen — whether in a criminal case, a grand jury investigation, a congressional hearing, a civil trial, or civil discovery — are profoundly serious matters. When such acts are committed by the President of the United States, we believe those acts 'may constitute grounds for an impeachment.'

[...]

There is substantial and credible information that President Clinton committed acts that may constitute grounds for an impeachment

[...]

There is substantial and credible information supporting the following eleven possible grounds for impeachment:

1. President Clinton lied under oath in his civil case when he denied a sexual affair, a sexual relationship, or sexual relations with Monica Lewinsky.

2. President Clinton lied under oath to the grand jury about his sexual relationship with Ms Lewinsky.

3. In his civil deposition, to support his false statement about the sexual relationship, President Clinton also lied under oath about being alone with Ms Lewinsky and about the many gifts exchanged between Ms Lewinsky and him.

4. President Clinton lied under oath in his civil deposition about his discussions with Ms Lewinsky concerning her involvement in the *Jones* case.

5. During the *Jones* case, the President obstructed justice and had an understanding with Ms Lewinsky to jointly conceal the truth about their relationship by concealing gifts subpoenaed by Ms Jones's attorneys.

6. During the *Jones* case, the President obstructed justice and had an understanding with Ms Lewinsky to jointly conceal the truth of their relationship from the judicial process by a scheme that included the following means: (i) Both the President and Ms Lewinsky understood that they would lie under oath in the *Jones* case about their sexual relationship; (ii) the President suggested to Ms Lewinsky that she prepare an affidavit that, for the President's purposes, would memorialize her testimony under oath and could be used to prevent questioning of both of them about their relationship; (iii) Ms Lewinsky signed and filed the false

affidavit; (iv) the President used Ms Lewinsky's false affidavit at his deposition in an attempt to head off questions about Ms Lewinsky; and (v) when that failed, the President lied under oath at his civil deposition about the relationship with Ms Lewinsky.

7. President Clinton endeavored to obstruct justice by helping Ms Lewinsky obtain a job in New York at a time when she would have been a witness harmful to him were she to tell the truth in the *Jones* case.

8. President Clinton lied under oath in his civil deposition about his discussions with Vernon Jordan concerning Ms Lewinsky's involvement in the *Jones* case.

9. The President improperly tampered with a potential witness by attempting to corruptly influence the testimony of his personal secretary, Betty Currie, in the days after his civil deposition.

10. President Clinton endeavored to obstruct justice during the grand jury investigation by refusing to testify for seven months *and* lying to senior White House aides with knowledge that they would relay the President's false statements to the grand jury — and did thereby deceive, obstruct, and impede the grand jury.

11. President Clinton abused his constitutional authority by (i) lying to the public and the Congress in January 1998 about his relationship with Ms Lewinsky; (ii) promising at that time to cooperate fully with the grand jury investigation; (iii) later refusing six invitations to testify voluntarily to the grand jury; (iv) invoking Executive Privilege; (v) lying to the grand jury in August 1998; and (vi) lying again to the public and Congress on August 17, 1998 — all as part of an effort to hinder, impede, and deflect possible inquiry by the Congress of the United States.

[...]

Source: House of Representatives Judiciary Committee Web Site. Available from: http://www.house.gov/judiciary/icreport.htm

INITIAL RESPONSE TO REFERRAL OF THE OFFICE OF THE INDEPENDENT COUNSEL

David E. Kendall
Nicole K. Seligman
Emmet T. Flood
Max Stier
Glen Donath
Alicia L. Marti

Charles F.C. Ruff
Cheryl Mills
Lanny A. Breuer

Williams & Connolly
725 12th Street, N.W.
Washington, DC 20005

Office of the White House Counsel
The White House
Washington, DC 20005

September 12, 1998

On May 31, 1998, the spokesman for Independent Counsel Kenneth W. Starr declared that the Office's Monica Lewinsky investigation 'is not about sex. This case is about perjury, subornation of perjury, witness tampering, obstruction of justice. That is what this case is about.' Now that the 450-page Referral to the United States House of Representatives Pursuant to Title 28, United States Code § 595(c) (the 'Referral') is public, it is plain that 'sex' is precisely what this four-and-a-half year investigation has boiled down to. The Referral is so loaded with irrelevant and unnecessary graphic and salacious allegations that only one conclusion is possible: its principal purpose is to damage the President.

The President has acknowledged and apologized for an inappropriate sexual relationship with Ms Lewinsky, so there is no need to describe that relationship in ugly detail. No one denies that the relationship was wrong or that the President was responsible. The Referral's pious defense of its pornographic specificity is that, in the Independent Counsel's view:

> 'the details are crucial to an informed evaluation of the testimony, the credibility of witnesses, and the reliability of other evidence. Many of the details reveal highly personal information; many are sexually explicit. This is unfortunate, but it is essential.'

Narrative at 20. This statement is patently false. Any fair reader of the Referral will easily discern that many of the lurid allegations, which need not be recounted here, have no justification at all, even in terms of any OIC [Office of the Independent Counsel] legal theory. They plainly do not relate, even arguably, to activities which may be within the definition of 'sexual relations' in the President's *Jones* deposition, which is the excuse advanced by the OIC. They are simply part of a hit-and-run smear campaign, and their inclusion says volumes about the OIC's tactics and objectives.

Review of a prosecutor's case necessarily starts with an analysis of the charges, and that is what we offer here. This is necessarily a very preliminary response, offered on the basis of less than a day's analysis and without any access to the factual materials cited in the Referral.

Spectacularly absent from the Referral is any discussion of contradictory or exculpatory evidence or any evidence that would cast doubt on the credibility of the testimony the OIC cites (but does not explicitly quote). This is a failure of fundamental fairness which is highly prejudicial to the President and it is reason alone to withhold judgment on the Referral's allegations until all the prosecutors' evidence can be scrutinized — and then challenged, as necessary, by evidence from the President.

The real critique can occur only with access to the materials on which the prosecutors have ostensibly relied. Only at that time can contradictory evidence be identified and the context and consistency (or lack thereof) of the cited evidence be ascertained. Since we have not been given access to the transcripts and other materials compiled by the OIC, our inquiry is therefore necessarily limited. But even with this limited access, our preliminary review reaffirms how little this highly intrusive and disruptive investigation has in fact yielded. In instance after instance, the OIC's allegations fail to withstand scrutiny either as a factual matter, or a legal matter, or both. The Referral quickly emerges as a portrait of biased recounting, skewed analysis, and unconscionable overreaching.

In our Preliminary Memorandum, filed yesterday, at pages 3–12, we set forth at some length the various ways in which impeachable 'high Crimes and Misdemeanors' have been defined. Nothing in the Referral even approximates such conduct. In the English practice from which the Framers borrowed the phrase, 'High Crimes and Misdemeanors' denoted political offenses, the critical element of which was *injury to the state*. Impeachment was intended to redress public offenses committed by public officials in violation of the public trust and duties. Because presidential impeachment invalidates the will of the American people, it was designed to be justified for the gravest wrongs — offenses against the Constitution itself. In short, only 'serious assaults on the integrity of the processes of government,' and 'such crimes as would so stain a president as to make his continuance in office dangerous to the public order,' constitute impeachable offenses. The eleven supposed 'grounds for impeachment' set forth in the section of the Referral called 'Acts That May Constitute Grounds for an Impeachment' ('Acts') fall far short of that high standard, and their very allegation demeans the constitutional process. The document is at bottom overreaching in an extravagant effort to find a case where there is none.

[…]

Source: White House Web Site. Available from:
http://www.whitehouse.gov/WH/New/html/clinton9-12.html

IN THE HOUSE OF REPRESENTATIVES

December 15, 1998

Mr. HYDE submitted the following resolution; which was referred to the House Calendar and ordered to be printed.

RESOLUTION

Impeaching William Jefferson Clinton, President of the United States, for high crimes and misdemeanors.

> *Resolved*, That William Jefferson Clinton, President of the United States, is impeached for high crimes and misdemeanors, and that the following articles of impeachment be exhibited to the United States Senate:

> Articles of impeachment exhibited by the House of Representatives of the United States of America in the name of itself and of the people of the United States of America, against William Jefferson Clinton, President of the United States of America, in maintenance and support of its impeachment against him for high crimes and misdemeanors.

Article I

In his conduct while President of the United States, William Jefferson Clinton, in violation of his constitutional oath faithfully to execute the office of President of the United States and, to the best of his ability, preserve, protect, and defend the Constitution of the United States, and in violation of his constitutional duty to take care that the laws be faithfully executed, has willfully corrupted and manipulated the judicial process of the United States for his personal gain and exoneration, impeding the administration of justice, in that:

On August 17, 1998, William Jefferson Clinton swore to tell the truth, the whole truth, and nothing but the truth before a Federal grand jury of the United States. Contrary to that oath, William Jefferson Clinton willfully provided perjurious, false and misleading testimony to the grand jury concerning one or more of the following: (1) the nature and details of his relationship with a subordinate Government employee; (2) prior perjurious, false and misleading testimony he gave in a Federal civil rights action brought against him; (3) prior false and misleading statements he allowed his attorney to make to a Federal judge in that civil rights action; and (4) his corrupt efforts to influence the testimony of witnesses and to impede the discovery of evidence in that civil rights action.

In doing this, William Jefferson Clinton has undermined the integrity of his office, has brought disrepute on the Presidency, has betrayed his trust as President, and has acted in a manner subversive of the rule of law and justice, to the manifest injury of the people of the United States.

Wherefore, William Jefferson Clinton, by such conduct, warrants impeachment and trial, and removal from office and disqualification to hold and enjoy any office of honor, trust, or profit under the United States.

[…]

Article III

In his conduct while President of the United States, William Jefferson Clinton, in violation of his constitutional oath faithfully to execute the office of President of the United States and, to the best of his ability, preserve, protect, and defend the Constitution of the United States, and in violation of his constitutional duty to take care that the laws be faithfully executed, has prevented, obstructed, and impeded the administration of justice, and has to that end engaged personally, and through his subordinates and agents, in a course of conduct or scheme designed to delay, impede, cover up, and conceal the existence of evidence and testimony related to a Federal civil rights action brought against him in a duly instituted judicial proceeding.

The means used to implement this course of conduct or scheme included one or more of the following acts:

(1) On or about December 17, 1997, William Jefferson Clinton corruptly encouraged a witness in a Federal civil rights action brought against

him to execute a sworn affidavit in that proceeding that he knew to be perjurious, false and misleading.

(2) On or about December 17, 1997, William Jefferson Clinton corruptly encouraged a witness in a Federal civil rights action brought against him to give perjurious, false and misleading testimony if and when called to testify personally in that proceeding.

(3) On or about December 28, 1997, William Jefferson Clinton corruptly engaged in, encouraged, or supported a scheme to conceal evidence that had been subpoenaed in a Federal civil rights action brought against him.

(4) Beginning on or about December 7, 1997, and continuing through and including January 14, 1998, William Jefferson Clinton intensified and succeeded in an effort to secure job assistance to a witness in a Federal civil rights action brought against him in order to corruptly prevent the truthful testimony of that witness in that proceeding at a time when the truthful testimony of that witness would have been harmful to him.

(5) On January 17, 1998, at his deposition in a Federal civil rights action brought against him, William Jefferson Clinton corruptly allowed his attorney to make false and misleading statements to a Federal judge characterizing an affidavit, in order to prevent questioning deemed relevant by the judge. Such false and misleading statements were subsequently acknowledged by his attorney in a communication to that judge.

(6) On or about January 18 and January 20–21, 1998, William Jefferson Clinton related a false and misleading account of events relevant to a Federal civil rights action brought against him to a potential witness in that proceeding, in order to corruptly influence the testimony of that witness.

(7) On or about January 21, 23 and 26, 1998, William Jefferson Clinton made false and misleading statements to potential witnesses in a Federal grand jury proceeding in order to corruptly influence the testimony of those witnesses. The false and misleading statements made by William Jefferson Clinton were repeated by the witnesses to the grand jury, causing the grand jury to receive false and misleading information.

In all of this, William Jefferson Clinton has undermined the integrity of his office, has brought disrepute on the Presidency, has betrayed his trust as President, and has acted in a manner subversive of the rule of law and justice, to the manifest injury of the people of the United States.

Wherefore, William Jefferson Clinton, by such conduct, warrants impeachment and trial, and removal from office and disqualification to hold and enjoy any office of honor, trust, or profit under the United States.

[…]

Source: House of Representatives Judiciary Committee Web Site. Available from: http://www.house.gov/judiciary/hres581.html

3.7   NEW LEFT TO NEW RIGHT

The following two documents are included to give an impression of very different radical approaches to American society and government. One from the New Left of the 1960s, the other from the New Right of the 1980s and 1990s.

The new spirit of the early 1960s made its mark throughout the United States, not least among the country's students, where the radical but largely non-ideological New Left was making itself felt. Students for a Democratic Society reflected this movement and at its Port Huron, Michigan convention in 1962 it adopted a statement drafted by Tom Hayden and others, extracts of which are reproduced below.

The idealism and hope of the Port Huron Statement and the early 1960s was to give way to the period of bitter struggles over opposition to the war in Vietnam and civil rights. By the early 1970s the New Left was fragmented and disillusioned. Throughout the period the New Left was looked upon with suspicion and hostility by much of the media and the traditional political and business establishment.

The late 1970s and 1980s saw the rise of a more radical conservative New Right in the United States, reacting against what was seen as too liberal, intrusive and burdensome government. Leading elements of the Republican Party were at the forefront of this movement and although a Republican, Ronald Reagan, was elected President in 1980, there was still a clear Democratic Party majority in the Congress. The Contract with America was the 1994 election programme for the Republicans. The elections saw the Republicans gaining majority positions in both the House and Senate (see Table 3.1). From the start of the 104th Congress in January 1995 the Republicans moved rapidly to implement much of the programme outlined in the Contract, under the leadership of new House Speaker Newt Gingrich, the principal architect of the Contract. This was done in the face of some resistance from Democratic President Bill Clinton.

3.7.1   THE PORT HURON STATEMENT (1962)

We are people of this generation, bred in at least modest comfort, housed now in universities, looking uncomfortably to the world we inherit.

When we were kids the United States was the wealthiest and strongest country in the world: the only one with the atom bomb, the least scarred by modern war, an initiator of the United Nations that we thought would distribute Western influence throughout the world. Freedom and equality for each individual, government of, by, and for the people — these American values we found good, principles by which we could live as men. Many of us began maturing in complacency.

As we grew, however, our comfort was penetrated by events too troubling to dismiss. First, the permeating and victimizing fact of human degradation, symbolized by the Southern struggle against racial bigotry, compelled most of us from silence to activism. Second, the enclosing fact of the Cold War, symbolized by the presence of the Bomb, brought awareness that we ourselves, and our friends, and millions of abstract 'others' we knew more directly because of our common peril, might die at any time. We might deliberately ignore, or avoid, or fail to feel all other human problems, but not these two, for these were too immediate and crushing in their impact, too challenging in the demand that we as individuals take the responsibility for encounter and resolution.

While these and other problems either directly oppressed us or rankled our consciences and became our own subjective concerns, we began to see complicated and disturbing paradoxes in our surrounding America. The declaration 'all men are created equal ... ' rang hollow before the facts of Negro life in the South and the big cities of the North. The proclaimed peaceful intentions of the United States contradicted its economic and military investments in the Cold War status quo.

We witnessed, and continue to witness, other paradoxes. With nuclear energy whole cities can easily be powered, yet the dominant nation-states seem more likely to unleash destruction greater than that incurred in all wars of human history. Although our own technology is destroying old and creating new forms of social organization, men still tolerate meaningless work and idleness. While two-thirds of mankind suffers undernourishment, our own upper classes revel amidst superfluous abundance. Although world population is expected to double in forty years, the nations still tolerate anarchy as a major principle of international conduct and uncontrolled exploitation governs the sapping of the earth's physical resources. Although mankind desperately needs revolutionary leadership, America rests in national stalemate, its goals ambiguous and tradition-bound instead of informed and clear, its democratic system apathetic and manipulated rather than 'of, by, and for the people'.

Not only did tarnish appear on our image of American virtue, not only did disillusion occur when the hypocrisy of American ideals was discovered, but we began to sense that what we had originally seen as the American Golden Age was actually the decline of an era. The worldwide outbreak of revolution against colonialism and imperialism, the entrenchment of totalitarian states, the menace of war, overpopulation, international disorder, supertechnology — these trends were testing the tenacity of our own commitment to democracy and freedom and our abilities to visualize their application to a world in upheaval.

Our work is guided by the sense that we may be the last generation in the experiment with living. But we are a minority — the vast majority of our people regard the temporary equilibriums of our society and world as eternally-functional parts. In this is perhaps the outstanding paradox: we ourselves are imbued with urgency, yet the message of our society is that there is no viable alternative to the present. Beneath the reassuring tones of the politicians, beneath the common opinion that America will 'muddle through', beneath the stagnation of those who have closed their minds to the future, is the pervading feeling that there simply are no alternatives, that our times have witnessed the exhaustion not only of Utopias, but of any new departures as well. Feeling the press of complexity upon the emptiness of life, people are fearful of the thought that at any moment things might thrust out of control. They fear change itself, since change might smash whatever invisible framework seems to hold back chaos for them now. For most Americans, all crusades are suspect, threatening. The fact that each individual sees apathy in his fellows perpetuates the common reluctance to organize for change. The dominant institutions are complex enough to blunt the minds of their potential critics, and entrenched enough to swiftly dissipate or entirely repel the energies of protest and reform, thus limiting human expectancies. Then, too, we are a materially improved society, and by our own improvements we seem to have weakened the case for further change.

Some would have us believe that Americans feel contentment amidst prosperity — but might it not better be called a glaze above deeply-felt anxieties about their role in the new world? And if these anxieties produce a developed indifference to human affairs, do they not as well produce a yearning to believe there *is* an alternative to the present, that something *can* be done to change circumstances in the school, the workplaces, the bureaucracies, the government? It is to this latter yearning, at once the spark and engine of change, that we direct our present appeal. The search for truly democratic alternatives to the present, and a commitment to social experimentation with them, is a worthy and fulfilling human enterprise, one which moves us and, we hope, others today. On such a basis do we offer this document of our convictions and analysis: as an effort in understanding and changing the conditions of humanity in the late twentieth century, an effort rooted in the ancient, still unfulfilled conception of man attaining determining influence over his circumstances of life. […]

Making values explicit — an initial task in establishing alternatives — is an activity that has been devalued and corrupted. The conventional moral terms of the age, the politician moralities — 'free world', 'people's democracies' — reflect realities poorly, if at all, and seem to function more as ruling myths than as descriptive principles. But neither has our experience in the universities brought us moral enlightenment. Our professors and administrators sacrifice controversy to public relations; their curriculums change more slowly than the living events of the world; their skills and silence are purchased by investors in the arms race; passion is called unscholastic. The questions we might want raised — what is really important? can we live in a different and better way? if we wanted to change society, how would we do it? — are not thought to be questions of a 'fruitful, empirical nature', and thus are brushed aside.

Unlike youth in other countries we are used to moral leadership being exercised and moral dimensions being clarified by our elders. But today, for us, not even the liberal and socialist preachments of the past seem adequate to the forms of the present. Consider the old slogans: Capitalism Cannot Reform Itself, United Front Against Fascism, General Strike, All Out on May Day. Or, more recently, No Cooperation with Commies and Fellow Travellers, Ideologies Are Exhausted, Bipartisanship, No Utopias. These are incomplete, and there are few new prophets. It has been said that our liberal and socialist predecessors were plagued by vision without program, while our own generation is plagued by program without vision. All around us there is astute grasp of method, technique — the committee, the ad hoc group, the lobbyist, the hard and soft sell, the make, the projected image — but, if pressed critically, such expertise is incompetent to explain its implicit ideals. It is highly fashionable to identify oneself by old categories, or by naming a respected political figure, or by explaining 'how we would vote' on various issues.

Theoretic chaos has replaced the idealistic thinking of old — and, unable to reconstitute theoretic order, men have condemned idealism itself. Doubt has replaced hopefulness — and men act out a defeatism that is labelled realistic. The decline of utopia and hope is in fact one of the defining features of social life today. The reasons are various: the dreams of the older left were perverted by Stalinism and never recreated; the congressional stalemate makes men narrow their view of the possible; the specialization of human activity leaves little room for sweeping thought; the horrors of the twentieth century, symbolized in the gas-ovens and concentration camps and atom bombs, have blasted hopefulness. To be idealistic is to be considered apocalyptic, deluded. To have no serious aspirations, on the contrary, is to be 'tough-minded'.

In suggesting social goals and values, therefore, we are aware of entering a sphere of some disrepute. Perhaps matured by the past, we have no sure formulas, no closed theories — but that does not mean values are beyond discussion and tentative determination. A first task of any social movement is to convince people that the search for orienting theories and the creation of human values is complex but worthwhile. We are aware that to avoid platitudes we must analyze the concrete conditions of social order. But to direct such an analysis we must use the guideposts of basic principles. Our own social values involve conceptions of human beings, human relationships, and social systems.

We regard *men* as infinitely precious and possessed of unfulfilled capacities for reason, freedom, and love. In affirming these principles we are aware of countering perhaps the dominant conceptions of man in the twentieth century: that he is a thing to be manipulated, and that he is inherently incapable of directing his own affairs. We oppose the depersonalization that reduces human beings to the status of things — if anything, the brutalities of the twentieth century teach that means and ends are intimately related, that vague appeals to 'posterity' cannot justify the mutilations of the present. We oppose, too, the doctrine of human incompetence because it rests essentially on the modern fact that men have been 'competently' manipulated into incompetence — we see little reason why men cannot meet with increasing skill the complexities and responsibilities of their situation, if society is organized not for minority, but for majority, participation in decision-making.

Men have unrealized potential for self-cultivation, self-direction, self-understanding, and creativity. It is potential that we regard as crucial and to which we appeal, not to the human potentiality for violence, unreason, and submission to authority. The goal of man and society should be human independence: a concern not with image of popularity but with finding a meaning in life that is personally authentic; a quality of mind not compulsively driven by a sense of powerlessness, nor one which unthinkingly adopts status values, nor one which represses all threats to its habits, but one which has full, spontaneous access to present and past experiences, one which easily unites the fragmented parts of personal history, one which openly faces problems which are troubling and unresolved; one with an intuitive awareness of possibilities, an active sense of curiosity, an ability and willingness to learn.

This kind of independence does not mean egoistic individualism — the object is not to have one's way so much as it is to have a way that is one's own. Nor do we deify man — we merely have faith in his potential.

Human relationships should involve fraternity and honesty. Human interdependence is contemporary fact; human brotherhood must be willed however, as a condition of future survival and as the most appropriate form of social relations. Personal links between man and man are needed, especially to go beyond the partial and fragmentary bonds of function that bind men only as worker to worker, employer to employee, teacher to student, American to Russian.

Loneliness, estrangement, isolation describe the vast distance between man and man today. These dominant tendencies cannot be overcome by better personnel management, nor by improved gadgets, but only when a love of man overcomes the idolatrous worship of things by man.

As the individualism we affirm is not egoism, the selflessness we affirm is not self-elimination. On the contrary, we believe in generosity of a kind that imprints one's unique individual qualities in the relation to other men, and to all human activity. Further, to dislike isolation is not to favor the abolition of privacy; the latter differs from isolation in that it occurs or is abolished according to individual will. Finally, we would replace power and personal uniqueness rooted in possession, privilege, or circumstance by power and uniqueness rooted in love, reflectiveness, reason, and creativity.

As a *social system* we seek the establishment of a democracy of individual participation, governed by two central aims: that the individual share in those social decisions determining the quality and direction of his life; that society be organized to encourage independence in men and provide the media for their common participation.

In a participatory democracy, the political life would be based in several root principles:

- that decision-making of basic social consequence be carried on by public groupings;

- that politics be seen positively, as the art of collectively creating an acceptable pattern of social relations;

- that politics has the function of bringing people out of isolation and into community, thus being a necessary, though not sufficient, means of finding meaning in personal life;

- that the political order should serve to clarify problems in a way instrumental to their solution; it should provide outlets for the expression of personal grievance and aspiration; opposing views should be organized so as to illuminate choices and facilitate the attainment of goals; channels should be commonly available to relate men to knowledge and to power so that private problems — from bad recreation facilities to personal alienation — are formulated as general issues.

The economic sphere would have as its basis the principles:

- that work should involve incentives worthier than money or survival. It should be educative, not stultifying; creative, not mechanical; self-direct, not manipulated, encouraging independence, a respect for others, a sense of dignity and a willingness to accept social responsibility, since it is this experience that has crucial influence on habits, perceptions and individual ethics;

- that the economic experience is so personally decisive that the individual must share in its full determination;

- that the economy itself is of such social importance that its major resources and means of production should be open to democratic participation and subject to democratic social regulation.

Like the political and economic ones, major social institutions — cultural, education, rehabilitative, and others — should be generally organized with the well-being and dignity of man as the essential measure of success.

In social change or interchange, we find violence to be abhorrent because it requires generally the transformation of the target, be it a human being or a community of people, into a depersonalized object of hate. It is imperative that the means of violence be abolished and the institutions — local, national, international — that encourage nonviolence as a condition of conflict be developed.

These are our central values, in skeletal form. It remains vital to understand their denial or attainment in the context of the modern world.

Source: Griffith, R. (ed.) (1992) *Major Problems in American History Since 1945*, Lexington, Mass., D.C. Heath, p.447.

3.7.2 THE CONTRACT WITH AMERICA (1994)

by Rep. Newt Gingrich, Rep. Dick Armey, and the House Republicans

The Contract's Core Principles. The Contract with America is rooted in 3 core principles:

Accountability — The government is too big and spends too much, and Congress and unelected bureaucrats have become so entrenched to be unresponsive to the public they are supposed to serve. The GOP ['Grand Old Party'] contract restores accountability to government.

Responsibility — Bigger government and more federal programs usurp personal responsibility from families and individuals. The GOP contract restores a proper balance between government and personal responsibility.

Opportunity — The American Dream is out of the reach of too many families because of burdensome government regulations and harsh tax laws. The GOP contract restores the American dream.

THE CONTRACT

As Republican Members of the House of Representatives and as citizens seeking to join that body we propose not just to change its policies, but even more important, to restore the bonds of trust between the people and their elected representatives.

That is why, in this era of official evasion and posturing, we offer instead a detailed agenda for national renewal, a written commitment with no fine print.

This year's election offers the chance, after four decades of one-party control, to bring to the House a new majority that will transform the way Congress works. That historic change would be the end of government that is too big, too intrusive, and too easy with the public's money. It can be the beginning of a Congress that respects the values and shares the faith of the American family.

Like Lincoln, our first Republican president, we intend to act 'with firmness in the right, as God gives us to see the right.' To restore accountability to Congress. To end its cycle of scandal and disgrace. To make us all proud again of the way free people govern themselves.

On the first day of the 104th Congress, the new Republican majority will immediately pass the following major reforms, aimed at restoring the faith and trust of the American people in their government:

FIRST, require all laws that apply to the rest of the country also apply equally to the Congress;

SECOND, select a major, independent auditing firm to conduct a comprehensive audit of Congress for waste, fraud or abuse;

THIRD, cut the number of House committees, and cut committee staff by one-third;

FOURTH, limit the terms of all committee chairs;

FIFTH, ban the casting of proxy votes in committee;

SIXTH, require committee meetings to be open to the public;

SEVENTH, require a three-fifths majority vote to pass a tax increase;

EIGHTH, guarantee an honest accounting of our Federal Budget by implementing zero base-line budgeting.

Thereafter, within the first 100 days of the 104th Congress, we shall bring to the House Floor the following bills, each to be given full and open debate, each to be given a clear and fair vote and each to be immediately available this day for public inspection and scrutiny.

1. THE FISCAL RESPONSIBILITY ACT

   A balanced budget/tax limitation amendment and a legislative line-item veto to restore fiscal responsibility to an out-of-control Congress, requiring them to live under the same budget constraints as families and businesses.

2. THE TAKING BACK OF OUR STREETS ACT

   An anti-crime package including stronger truth-in-sentencing, 'good faith' exclusionary rule exemptions, effective death penalty provisions, and cuts in social spending from this summer's 'crime' bill to fund prison construction and additional law enforcement to keep people secure in their neighborhoods and kids safe in their schools.

3. THE PERSONAL RESPONSIBILITY ACT

   Discourage illegitimacy and teen pregnancy by prohibiting welfare to minor mothers and denying increased AFDC [Aid for Dependent Children] for additional children while on welfare, cut spending for welfare programs, and enact a tough two-years-and-out provision with work requirements to promote individual responsibility.

4. THE FAMILY REINFORCEMENT ACT

   Child support enforcement, tax incentives for adoption, strengthening rights of parents in their children's education, stronger child pornography laws, and an elderly dependent care tax credit to reinforce the central role of families in American society.

5. THE AMERICAN DREAM RESTORATION ACT

   A $500 per child tax credit, begin repeal of the marriage tax penalty, and creation of American Dream Savings Accounts to provide middle class tax relief.

6. THE NATIONAL SECURITY RESTORATION ACT

   No US troops under UN command and restoration of the essential parts of our national security funding to strengthen our national defense and maintain our credibility around the world.

7. THE SENIOR CITIZENS FAIRNESS ACT

Raise the Social Security earnings limit which currently forces seniors out of the work force, repeal the 1993 tax hikes on Social Security benefits and provide tax incentives for private long-term care insurance to let Older Americans keep more of what they have earned over the years.

8. THE JOB CREATION AND WAGE ENHANCEMENT ACT

Small business incentives, capital gains cut and indexation, neutral cost recovery, risk assessment/cost–benefit analysis, strengthening the Regulatory Flexibility Act and unfunded mandate reform to create jobs and raise worker wages.

9. THE COMMON SENSE LEGAL REFORM ACT

'Loser pays' laws, reasonable limits on punitive damages and reform of product liability laws to stem the endless tide of litigation.

10. THE CITIZEN LEGISLATURE ACT

A first-ever vote on term limits to replace career politicians with citizen legislators.

Further, we will instruct the House Budget Committee to report to the floor and we will work to enact additional budget savings, beyond the budget cuts specifically included in the legislation described above, to ensure that the Federal budget deficit will be less than it would have been without the enactment of these bills.

Respecting the judgment of our fellow citizens as we seek their mandate for reform, we hereby pledge our names to this Contract with America.

Source: House of Representatives Speaker News Web Site. Available from: http://speakernews.house.gov/contract.htm

EMPIRE

4.1 INTRODUCTION

The documents in this chapter chronicle the conduct of American foreign policy. They provide a fascinating portrait of how the United States both viewed the rest of the world and of its own role within the international community. Over the past one hundred years America's perception of the world has undergone a remarkable change as has the nation's attitude towards responding to developments in the rest of the globe. In many respects this has been unsurprising as the events of the twentieth century have been momentous for the entire world but in particular for the United States. The American intervention in the First World War, its central role in the Second World War, its leadership in the Cold War which ended in the disintegration of the Soviet Union, were extraordinary developments for a nation that until the twentieth century was wedded to the doctrine of isolationism. In addition there were the interventions in Korea and Vietnam, both of which were difficult and in the case of the latter appears to have left a permanent scar on the body politic. But whatever the difficulties, the United States embraced internationalism and a central role in the affairs of the globe with the attendant implications of an American empire. Nevertheless, and intriguingly, some of the views and instincts that were present at the creation of the Republic never disappeared entirely and have shown some indications of surfacing as the century draws to a close.

Nothing could have appeared more remote or indeed more unattractive than an American empire in 1796, the year of President George Washington's farewell address. Washington took the opportunity of his retirement from public life to speak to his fellow citizens of his concerns and offer his advice for the future. Washington's views, which he shared with the generation of Americans that had achieved independence, derived from a profound sense of America being a new society and a bold experiment. Americans were committed to republicanism, representative institutions and the common man, while the world beyond the shores of the United States was élitist, corrupt and unattractive. Europe, in particular, represented all that the United States had rejected and Americans only recently had fought a war to remove the corrupt practices and values of Europe from American soil. But unfortunately while American values were admirable and as a people Americans were more honest and straightforward, they were also far more innocent and consequently capable of being manipulated by the nations of Europe. Accordingly Washington's advice to his fellow citizens was to avoid foreign political entanglements as far as possible. Isolationism should be the 'great rule' of US foreign policy and this advice guided the conduct of policy until well into the twentieth century, although it should be noted that isolationism was reasonably flexible, as is evident from the Monroe Doctrine.

The Monroe Doctrine in many respects emerged from the same set of instincts and concerns as Washington's farewell address. Once again fear of Europe was at centre stage. The United States wished to protect itself against what it viewed as European incursions into the western hemisphere. But in order to do so the United States could not be rigidly isolationist and be exclusively absorbed with domestic concerns. If it wished to prevent the European colonization of the Americas the US would have to exert its power and influence beyond its borders and would need to modify a policy of rigid isolationism. The result was the Monroe Doctrine which set out the position that the United States would oppose the expansion of European power in the Americas. The western hemisphere was in effect declared to be an area of special concern to the United States and accordingly the US would be both interested and involved in the affairs of the area. Although the nations of Europe and indeed Latin America have continually rejected the claims of the Monroe Doctrine, it became one of the key constructs of American foreign policy towards the region. The historical importance of the Doctrine can be observed from the fact that it frequently has been cited by several Presidents during the twentieth century in explaining and justifying their policies towards Latin America.

For most of the century after the Monroe Doctrine, the United States conducted an isolationist foreign policy, staying aloof from the rest of the world with the exception of the Americas. However, this was not particularly difficult as the country was absorbed overwhelmingly with the westward expansion of the continent and the development of nationhood. The collective energy of Americans was channelled into domestic affairs and there were no perceived external threats, at least of any permanent significance. The world beyond the western hemisphere was not an American concern. The First World War saw the beginning of the end of this age of innocence. The United States felt that it could not avoid a reluctant and belated entry into this conflict because President Woodrow Wilson and the Congress believed that vital American interests were at stake. But as it became clear that Germany was going to be defeated, two issues arose. The first concerned the basis on which the war was going to end. What principles would govern the peace? Interestingly, the United States took a position that was distinctively different from its European allies. Accordingly, in 1918, President Wilson sought an agreement that was based on a set of ethical principles which could be applied universally. He wanted to move away from the world of power politics and national advantage, which to

American eyes had brought about the conflict in the first place. Wilson's fourteen points derived from an American tradition that gave primacy to ethics and morality in the conduct of foreign policy. Of course, it would be inaccurate to suggest that only ethical considerations had guided US foreign policy until 1918, the Monroe Doctrine provides evidence that the United States like any other nation has been very aware of its own interests and has sought to protect them. But perhaps what is different about the United States is the recurrent if not permanent tension between realpolitik and morality in the formation of foreign policy.

The second issue that had to be addressed in 1918 concerned the role that the United States was going to play in the international community. The view of President Wilson was that America had to modify its commitment to isolationism and participate more fully. However, the failure of Wilson to convince the other European nations to adopt the fourteen points, his consequent political weakness and the power of isolationist sentiment combined to defeat any major departure from traditional American foreign policy. The 1920s, with the election of Republican Presidents and a 'return to normalcy', saw a resumption of isolationism. The intervention in the First World War became a deviation from the norm. However, the war had substantially altered the globe and isolationism was both more difficult to maintain and justify. The United States had emerged from the war as a major force in the world on a par with Britain, France, and Germany. It now possessed the largest economy and it could only ignore the rest of the world at its peril. The onset of the Great Depression at the end of the 1920s and the rise of the Fascist dictatorships in Europe only increased the alarm of those in the United States who wished to see a reversal of isolationism. However, the electoral appeal of isolationism was still potent and although President Franklin D. Roosevelt, a Democrat elected in 1932, believed that American interests required a degree of involvement, he could only move with considerable caution.

The outbreak of the Second World War in Europe in 1939 and the military success of Nazi Germany brought these concerns to the fore. The Roosevelt Administration was in no doubt that a German victory would pose a profound danger to the US, but there was no broad consensus of support for American entry to the war. Indeed, during the 1940 presidential campaign when Roosevelt was elected for an unprecedented third term, he felt compelled to say that he did not wish to see the United States involved in the war. However, after the election, he felt able politically to make clear his opposition to Germany and his support for Britain. In 1941, both the Lend-Lease Act and the Atlantic Charter made it all but explicit where the Administration stood. Whether the United States would have entered the war without the attack on Pearl Harbor in December 1941 remains one of those intriguing historical questions. However, the Japanese action ended the debate over whether the US should enter the war. It also ended American isolationism.

The world at the end of 1945 was strikingly different from 1939. The great European powers were no longer great. Germany had been defeated, France was in urgent need of reconstruction and Britain was exhausted by the conflict. Admittedly the Soviet Union had emerged from the Second World War in a comparatively far more favourable position, but there can be little doubt that the United States was, by any measure, the most powerful nation in the world. It could not abdicate from the international community and there was little call for it to do so. President Roosevelt and his immediate successor, Harry S. Truman, as well as the Congress were all committed to the US playing a key role in the establishment of a world order after 1945. The precise definition of that role and the nature of the world order in 1945 and the years immediately after were unclear. Certainly in 1945, the Truman Administration did not envisage that the United States would be involved in a set of global military alliances or that there would be garrisons of American troops stationed overseas on an almost permanent basis. However, that was the position within a few years after the end of the war. The Cold War had begun.

This is not the occasion to discuss the origins of the Cold War. It has been, and continues to be, a subject of considerable scholarly debate, but it is not a matter of concern here. The documents in this book offer the perspective of successive US administrations. As far as the Truman Administration was concerned, the Soviet Union was a totalitarian regime with expansionist ambitions. It sought to create a Soviet empire and should it succeed it would pose as substantial a danger to the United States as had Nazi Germany. Accordingly it had to be resisted and in those immediate post-1945 years the American response to what it viewed as Soviet aggression and expansionism was established. The Truman Doctrine, the Marshall Plan and the formation of the North Atlantic Treaty Organization were among the most significant responses to the perceived Soviet threat. The Soviet Union and its allies needed to be 'contained'. Interestingly, this policy commanded very considerable support from both major parties and throughout the country. Indeed it would be true to say that apart from those who inhabited the fringes of political life, there was no important voice raised against the direction of US foreign policy after 1948 for almost 20 years.

The Cold War dominated American political life for the next four decades. Its impact was pervasive and profound. The United States policed the world or at least policed the western world. Apart from NATO, the nation entered into a series of other regional alliances, maintained for the first time in its history a permanent and large military establishment, entered two major wars in Korea and Vietnam, and launched a series of more limited military operations in the Middle East, South-East Asia and Latin America. The United States had become a truly global power with a range of commitments and actions that were similar in some respects to those of European nations that had developed colonial empires during the eighteenth and nineteenth centuries.

The Cold War also had its effect on domestic politics. The anti-communist hysteria of the late 1940s and early 1950s was destructive and unattractive. But perhaps other consequences were even more far reaching. The imperative of winning the Cold War took precedence over other issues such as civil rights as well as social and economic reform. Defence expenditures consumed a significantly large percentage of the national budget and perhaps of even greater significance was the increase in power of certain sectors of American society. President Eisenhower, a Republican, took the occasion of his farewell address from office in 1961 to raise his concern about the power of a large military establishment acting in concert with an industrial sector dependent on orders for military equipment. The military-industrial complex as it came to be known was felt by many to have too much influence on the making of public policy.

The impact of the Cold War even extended to American constitutional and political arrangements. This period saw a remarkable rise in presidential power. The balance between the Congress and the presidency was altered in favour of the latter. To a considerable extent this was due to the deference shown by the Congress to successive Presidents in the arena of foreign policy. It was only too anxious and willing to submit to presidential leadership. The Congress was prepared to give the President *carte blanche* in matters of national security. A notable example was the Gulf of Tonkin Resolution which was passed by the Congress in 1964. President Lyndon B. Johnson persuaded the Congress to pass the Resolution after a military incident in the Gulf of Tonkin. However, Johnson failed to disclose all the relevant information and at the very least misled the Congress about the full extent of American military operations in the area. The Congress in turn gave no indication of wishing to investigate the issue in any depth and in a sense failed to carry out its political obligation. It was an important failure because the Resolution provided the legal basis for the American military intervention in Vietnam; an intervention that was escalated sharply in 1965.

The episode in Vietnam and the failure of that policy was one of the watersheds in American history after 1945. The great post-Second World War consensus over foreign policy broke down and to some extent has never been reassembled. The assumption that the United States should police the world was widely challenged, although it was not replaced by any alternative world view that commanded widespread support. The Nixon Doctrine was one of several attempts to provide a coherent framework for the conduct of foreign policy, but the Republican Administration of President Richard M. Nixon was consumed and then destroyed by the domestic scandal of Watergate. The consequence was a period of drift and indecision by the United States, with the brief and weak presidencies of Gerald Ford, a Republican who succeeded Nixon on his resignation in 1975, and Jimmy Carter, a Democrat who defeated Ford in the presidential election of 1976. In addition, the Congress attempted to restore the balance of power in its relationship with the presidency. It became considerably more assertive, but more significantly passed the 'war-powers resolution' in 1973. The Act was designed to prevent the commitment of American military forces without congressional approval. A President can now only commit the armed forces in a national emergency and even then any such action has to gain congressional approval within 60 days. The Act substantially limited the freedom that all Presidents until 1973 had under their constitutional authority as Commander-in-Chief. In fact President Nixon vetoed the Act but the veto was overridden by the Congress.

The memory of Vietnam continues. Congress is not acquiescent in matters of foreign policy. Even during the eight years of the presidency of Republican Ronald Reagan, when leadership from the White House was more assertive, the Congress was not prepared to give the President all that he desired. However, this was a period of renewed antagonism with the Soviet Union which some scholars have labelled the Second Cold War. Certainly Reagan's characterization of the Soviet Union as an 'evil empire' and the dramatic increase in military expenditure during the 1980s sharply raised the tensions between the two nations. Ironically, by the end of the second Reagan Administration détente between the two countries had been established and the Cold War was at an end.

The post-Cold War world of the 1990s left the United States as the only superpower. The changing political, economic and security context in which the United States found itself caused policy makers to review and attempt to redefine America's role in a more uncertain world. How successful the process will be remains to be seen.

4.2   PRE-TWENTIETH CENTURY

4.2.1   GEORGE WASHINGTON'S FAREWELL ADDRESS (1796)

This address was published in the *Daily American Advertiser* on 19 September 1796 to mark the retirement of George Washington from public office after his second term as President. James Madison and Alexander Hamilton both contributed to the drafting and redrafting of the text, but the final version expressed Washington's concerns and advice for the new republic. In domestic affairs he warned Americans to beware of the dangers of the political factionism of party and the regional differences threatening the Union. However, his advice on foreign policy had a more lasting impact and contributed to the isolationism which was the major feature of that policy well into the twentieth century. He advised that a 'great rule' be adopted, that the United States in extending commercial relations to foreign nations should 'have with them as little *political* connection as possible'. Isolationism remains a powerful force in America's thinking on foreign relations.

[…]

I have already intimated to you the danger of parties in the State, with par-ticular reference to the founding of them on geographical discriminations. Let me now take a more comprehensive view, and warn you in the most solemn manner against the baneful effects of the spirit of party generally.

This spirit, unfortunately, is inseparable from our nature, having its root in the strongest passions of the human mind. It exists under different shapes in all governments, more or less stifled, controlled, or repressed; but in those of the popular form it is seen in its greatest rankness and is truly their worst enemy.

The alternate domination of one faction over another, sharpened by the spirit of revenge natural to party dissension, which in different ages and countries has perpetrated the most horrid enormities, is itself a frightful des-potism. But this leads at length to a more formal and permanent despotism. The disorders and miseries which result gradually incline the minds of men to seek security and repose in the absolute power of an individual, and sooner or later the chief of some prevailing faction, more able or more fortu-nate than his competitors, turns this disposition to the purposes of his own elevation on the ruins of public liberty.

Without looking forward to an extremity of this kind (which nevertheless ought not to be entirely out of sight), the common and continual mischiefs of the spirit of party are sufficient to make it the interest and duty of a wise people to discourage and restrain it.

It serves always to distract the public councils and enfeeble the public administration. It agitates the community with ill-founded jealousies and false alarms; kindles the animosity of one part against another; foments occasionally riot and insurrection. It opens the door to foreign influence and corruption, which find a facilitated access to the government itself through the channels of party passion. Thus the policy and the will of one country are subjected to the policy and will of another.

There is an opinion that parties in free countries are useful checks upon the administration of the government, and serve to keep alive the spirit of lib-erty. This within certain limits is probably true; and in governments of a monarchical cast patriotism may look with indulgence, if not with favor, upon the spirit of party. But in those of the popular character, in govern-ments purely elective, it is a spirit not to be encouraged. From their natural tendency it is certain there will always be enough of that spirit for every salutary purpose; and there being constant danger of excess, the effort ought to be by force of public opinion to mitigate and assuage it. A fire not to be quenched, it demands a uniform vigilance to prevent its bursting into a flame, lest, instead of warming, it should consume.

It is important, likewise, that the habits of thinking in a free country should inspire caution in those intrusted with its administration to confine them-selves within their respective constitutional spheres, avoiding in the exercise of the powers of one department to encroach upon another. The spirit of encroachment tends to consolidate the powers of all the departments in one, and thus to create, whatever the form of government, a real despotism. A just estimate of that love of power and proneness to abuse it which predominates in the human heart is sufficient to satisfy us of the truth of this position. The necessity of reciprocal checks in the exercise of political power, by dividing and distributing it into different depositories, and constituting each the guardian of the public weal against invasions by the others, has been evinced by experiments ancient and modern, some of them in our country and under our own eyes. To preserve them must be as necessary as to institute them. If in the opinion of the people the distribution or modification of the constitutional powers be in any particular wrong, let it be corrected by an amendment in the way which the Constitution designates. But let there be no change by usurpation; for though this in one instance may be the instrument of good, it is the customary weapon by which free governments are destroyed. The precedent must always greatly overbalance in permanent evil any partial or transient benefit which the use can at any time yield.

Of all the dispositions and habits which lead to political prosperity, religion and morality are indispensable supports. In vain would that man claim the tribute of patriotism who should labor to subvert these great pillars of human happiness — these firmest props of the duties of men and citizens. The mere politician, equally with the pious man, ought to respect and to cherish them. A volume could not trace all their connections with private and public felicity. Let it simply be asked, Where is the security for property, for reputation, for life, if the sense of religious obligation *desert* the oaths which are the instruments of investigation in courts of justice? And let us with caution indulge the supposition that morality can be maintained without religion. Whatever may be conceded to the influence of refined education on minds of peculiar structure, reason and experience both forbid us to expect that national morality can prevail in exclusion of religious principle.

It is substantially true that virtue or morality is a necessary spring of popular government. The rule indeed extends with more or less force to every species of free government. Who that is a sincere friend to it can look with indifference upon attempts to shake the foundation of the fabric? Promote, then, as an object of primary importance, institutions for the general diffusion of knowledge. In proportion as the structure of a government gives force to public opinion, it is essential that public opinion should be enlightened.

As a very important source of strength and security, cherish public credit. One method of preserving it is to use it as sparingly as possible, avoiding occasions of expense by cultivating peace, but remembering also that timely disbursements to prepare for danger frequently prevent much greater disbursements to repel it; avoiding likewise the accumulation of debt, not only by shunning occasions of expense, but by vigorous exertions in time of peace to discharge the debts which unavoidable wars have occasioned, not ungenerously throwing upon posterity the burthen which we ourselves ought to bear. The execution of these maxims belongs to your representatives; but it is necessary that public opinion should cooperate. To facilitate to them the performance of their duty it is essential that you should practically bear in mind that toward the payment of debts there must be revenue; that to have revenue there must be taxes; that no taxes can be devised which are not more or less inconvenient and unpleasant; that the intrinsic embarrassment inseparable from the selection of the proper objects (which is always a choice of difficulties), ought to be a decisive motive for a candid construction of the conduct of the Government in making it, and for a spirit of acquiescence in the measures for obtaining revenue which the public exigencies may at any time dictate.

Observe good faith and justice toward all nations. Cultivate peace and harmony with all. Religion and morality enjoin this conduct. And can it be that good policy does not equally enjoin it? It will be worthy of a free, enlightened, and at no distant period a great nation to give to mankind the magnanimous and too novel example of a people always guided by an exalted justice and benevolence. Who can doubt that in the course of time and things the fruits of such a plan would richly repay any temporary advantages which might be lost by a steady adherence to it? Can it be that Providence has not connected the permanent felicity of a nation with its virtue? The experiment, at least, is recommended by every sentiment which ennobles human nature. Alas! is it rendered impossible by its vices?

In the execution of such a plan nothing is more essential than that permanent, inveterate antipathies against particular nations and passionate attachments for others should be excluded, and that in place of them just and amicable feelings toward all should be cultivated. The nation which indulges toward another an habitual hatred or an habitual fondness is in some degree a slave. It is a slave to its animosity or to its affection, either of which is sufficient to lead it astray from its duty and its interest. Antipathy in one nation against another disposes each more readily to offer insult and injury, to lay hold of slight causes of umbrage, and to be haughty and intractable when accidental or trifling occasions of dispute occur.

Hence frequent collisions, obstinate, envenomed, and bloody contests. The nation prompted by ill will and resentment sometimes impels to war the government contrary to the best calculations of policy. The government sometimes participates in the national propensity, and adopts through passion what reason would reject. At other times it makes the animosity of the nation subservient to projects of hostility, instigated by pride, ambition, and other sinister and pernicious motives. The peace often, sometimes perhaps the liberty, of nations has been the victim.

So, likewise, a passionate attachment of one nation for another produces a variety of evils. Sympathy for the favorite nation, facilitating the illusion of an imaginary common interest in cases where no real common interest exists, and infusing into one the enmities of the other, betrays the former into a participation in the quarrels and wars of the latter without adequate inducement or justification. It leads also to concessions to the favorite nation of privileges denied to others, which is apt doubly to injure the nation making the concessions by unnecessarily parting with what ought to have been retained, and by exciting jealousy, ill-will, and a disposition to retaliate in the parties from whom equal privileges are withheld; and it gives to ambitious, corrupted, or deluded citizens (who devote themselves to the favorite nation) facility to betray or sacrifice the interests of their own country without odium, sometimes even with popularity, gilding with the appearances of a virtuous sense of obligation, a commendable deference for public opinion, or a laudable zeal for public good the base or foolish compliances of ambition, corruption, or infatuation.

As avenues to foreign influence in innumerable ways, such attachments are particularly alarming to the truly enlightened and independent patriot. How many opportunities do they afford to tamper with domestic factions, to practice the arts of seduction, to mislead public opinion, to influence or awe the public councils! Such an attachment of a small or weak toward a great and powerful nation dooms the former to be the satellite of the latter. Against the insidious wiles of foreign influence (I conjure you to believe me, fellow-citizens) the jealousy of a free people ought to be *constantly* awake, since history and experience prove that foreign influence is one of the most baneful foes of republican government. But that jealousy, to be useful, must be impartial, else it becomes the instrument of the very influence to be avoided, instead of a defense against it. Excessive partiality for one foreign nation and excessive dislike of another cause those whom they actuate to see danger only on one side, and serve to veil and even second the arts of influence on the other. Real patriots who may resist the intrigues of the favorite are liable to become suspected and odious, while its tools and dupes usurp the applause and confidence of the people to surrender their interests.

The great rule of conduct for us in regard to foreign nations is, in extending our commercial relations to have with them as little *political* connection as possible. So far as we have already formed engagements let them be fulfilled with perfect good faith. Here let us stop.

Europe has a set of primary interests which to us have none or a very remote relation. Hence she must be engaged in frequent controversies, the causes of which are essentially foreign to our concerns. Hence, therefore, it must be unwise in us to implicate ourselves by artificial ties in the ordinary vicissitudes of her politics or the ordinary combinations and collisions of her friendships or enmities.

Our detached and distant situation invites and enables us to pursue a different course. If we remain one people, under an efficient government, the period is not far off when we may defy material injury from external annoyance; when we may take such an attitude as will cause the neutrality we may at any time resolve upon to be scrupulously respected; when belligerent nations, under the impossibility of making acquisitions upon us, will not lightly hazard the giving us provocation; when we may choose peace or war, as our interest, guided by justice, shall counsel.

Why forego the advantages of so peculiar a situation? Why quit our own to stand upon foreign ground? Why, by interweaving our destiny with that of any part of Europe, entangle our peace and prosperity in the toils of European ambition, rivalship, interest, humor, or caprice?

It is our true policy to steer clear of permanent alliances with any portion of the foreign world, so far, I mean, as we are now at liberty to do it; for let me not be understood as capable of patronizing infidelity to existing engagements. I hold the maxim no less applicable to public than to private affairs that honesty is always the best policy. I repeat, therefore, let those engagements be observed in their genuine sense. But in my opinion it is unnecessary and would be unwise to extend them.

Taking care always to keep ourselves by suitable establishments on a respectable defensive posture, we may safely trust to temporary alliances for extraordinary emergencies.

Harmony, liberal intercourse with all nations are recommended by policy, humanity, and interest. But even our commercial policy should hold an equal and impartial hand, neither seeking nor granting exclusive favors or preferences; consulting the natural course of things; diffusing and diversifying by gentle means the streams of commerce, but forcing nothing; establishing with powers so disposed, in order to give trade a stable course, to define the rights of our merchants, and to enable the Government to support them, conventional rules of intercourse, the best that present circumstances and mutual opinion will permit, but temporary and liable to be from time to time abandoned or varied as experience and circumstance shall dictate; constantly keeping in view that it is folly in one nation to look for disinterested favors from another; that it must pay with a portion of its independence for whatever it may accept under that character; that by such acceptance it may place itself in the condition of having given equivalents for nominal favors, and yet of being reproached with ingratitude for not giving more. There can be no greater error than to expect or calculate upon real favors from nation to nation. It is an illusion which experience must cure, which a just pride ought to discard.

In offering to you, my countrymen, these counsels of an old and affectionate friend I dare not hope they will make the strong and lasting impression I could wish — that they will control the usual current of the passions or prevent our nation from running the course which has hitherto marked the destiny of nations. But if I may even flatter myself that they may be productive of some partial benefit, some occasional good — that they may now and then recur to moderate the fury of party spirit, to warn against the mischiefs of foreign intrigue, to guard against the impostures of pretended patriotism — this hope will be a full recompense for the solicitude for your welfare by which they have been dictated.

How far in the discharge of my official duties I have been guided by the principles which have been delineated the public records and other evidences of my conduct must witness to you and to the world. To myself, the assurance of my own conscience is that I have at least believed myself to be guided by them.

In relation to the still subsisting war in Europe my proclamation of the 22d of April, 1793, is the index to my plan. Sanctioned by your approving voice and by that of your representatives in both Houses of Congress, the spirit of that measure has continually governed me, uninfluenced by any attempts to deter or divert me from it.

After deliberate examination, with the aid of the best lights I could obtain, I was well satisfied that our country, under all the circumstances of the case, had a right to take, and was bound in duty and interest to take, a neutral position. Having taken it, I determined as far as should depend upon me to maintain it with moderation, perseverance, and firmness.

The considerations which respect the right to hold this conduct it is not necessary on this occasion to detail. I will only observe that, according to my understanding of the matter, that right, so far from being denied by any of the belligerent powers, has been virtually admitted by all.

The duty of holding a neutral conduct may be inferred, without anything more, from the obligation which justice and humanity impose on every nation, in cases in which it is free to act, to maintain inviolate the relations of peace and amity toward other nations.

The inducements of interest for observing that conduct will best be referred to your own reflections and experience. With me a predominant motive has been to endeavor to gain time to our country to settle and mature its yet recent institutions, and to progress without interruption to that degree of strength and consistency which is necessary to give it, humanly speaking, the command of its own fortunes.

Though in reviewing the incidents of my Administration I am unconscious of intentional error, I am nevertheless too sensible of my defects not to think it probable that I may have committed many errors. Whatever they may be, I fervently beseech the Almighty to avert or mitigate the evils to which they may tend. I shall also carry with me the hope that my country will never cease to view them with indulgence, and that, after forty-five years of my life dedicated to its service with an upright zeal, the faults of incompetent abilities will be consigned to oblivion, as myself must soon be to the mansions of rest.

Relying on its kindness in this as in other things, and actuated by that fervent love toward it which is so natural to a man who views in it the native soil of himself and his progenitors for several generations, I anticipate with pleasing expectation that retreat in which I promise myself to realize without alloy the sweet enjoyment of partaking in the midst of my fellow-citizens the benign influence of good laws under a free government — the ever-favorite object of my heart, and the happy reward, as I trust, of our mutual cares, labors, and dangers.

Source: University of Virginia, George Washington Papers Web Site. Available from: http://www.virginia.edu/gwpapers/seldoc.html

4.2.2 THE MONROE DOCTRINE (1823)

Though isolationist, the affairs of the rest of the American continents were seen by many as legitimate matters of interest and often concern to the United States. The basic foreign-policy principle of the Monroe Doctrine has been as relevant in the twentieth century as it was when President James Monroe addressed the Congress on 2 December 1823. The doctrine formulated between the President and Secretary of State John Quincy Adams made clear the US opposition to any overseas (especially European) political or colonizing involvement in any nation or part of the American continents. The principal causes for concern at the time were Russian claims to Alaska and the northern Pacific coast, and the possibility of Spain trying to reassert its authority over the newly independent states of Latin America. In the twentieth century the same doctrine held for Soviet involvement in Cuba and Central America.

[…] At the proposal of the Russian Imperial Government, made through the minister of the Emperor residing here, a full power and instructions have been transmitted to the minister of the United States at St. Petersburg to arrange by amicable negotiation the respective rights and interests of the two nations on the northwest coast of this continent. A similar proposal had been made by His Imperial Majesty to the Government of Great Britain, which has likewise been acceded to. The Government of the United States has been desirous by this friendly proceeding of manifesting the great value which they have invariably attached to the friendship of the Emperor and their solicitude to cultivate the best understanding with his Government. In the discussions to which this interest has given rise and in the arrangements by which they may terminate the occasion has been judged proper for asserting, as a principle in which the rights and interests of the United States are involved, that the American continents, by the free and independent condition which they have assumed and maintain, are henceforth not to be considered as subjects for future colonization by any European powers. […]

It was stated at the commencement of the last session that a great effort was then making in Spain and Portugal to improve the condition of the people of those countries, and that it appeared to be conducted with extraordinary moderation. It need scarcely be remarked that the result has been so far very different from what was then anticipated. Of events in that quarter of the globe, with which we have so much intercourse and from which we derive our origin, we have always been anxious and interested spectators. The citizens of the United States cherish sentiments the most friendly in favor of the liberty and happiness of their fellow-men on that side of the Atlantic. In the wars of the European powers in matters relating to themselves we have never taken any part, nor does it comport with our policy so to do. It is only when our rights are invaded or seriously menaced that we resent injuries or make preparation for our defense. With the movements in this hemisphere we are of necessity more immediately connected, and by causes which must be obvious to all enlightened and impartial observers. The political system of the allied powers is essentially different in this respect from that of America. This difference proceeds from that which exists in their respective Governments; and to the defense of our own, which has been achieved by the loss of so much blood and treasure, and matured by the wisdom of their most enlightened citizens, and under which we have enjoyed unexampled felicity, this whole nation is devoted. We owe it, therefore, to candor and to the amicable relations existing between the United States and those powers to declare that we should consider any attempt on their part to extend their system to any portion of this hemisphere as dangerous to our peace and safety. With the existing colonies or dependencies of any European power we have not interfered and shall not interfere. But with the Governments who have declared their independence and maintained it, and whose independence we have, on great consideration and on just principles, acknowledged, we could not view any interposition for the purpose of oppressing them, or controlling in any other manner their destiny, by any European power in any other light than as the manifestation of an unfriendly disposition toward the United States. In the war between those new Governments and Spain we declared our neutrality at the time of their recognition, and to this we have adhered, and shall continue to adhere, provided no change shall occur which, in the judgment of the competent authorities of this Government, shall make a corresponding change on the part of the United States indispensable to their security.

The late events in Spain and Portugal show that Europe is still unsettled. Of this important fact no stronger proof can be adduced than that the allied powers should have thought it proper, on any principle satisfactory to themselves, to have interposed by force in the internal concerns of Spain. To what extent such interposition may be carried, on the same principle, is a question in which all independent powers whose governments differ from theirs are interested, even those most remote, and surely none more so than the United States. Our policy in regard to Europe, which was adopted at an early stage of the wars which have so long agitated that quarter of the globe, nevertheless remains the same, which is, not to interfere in the internal concerns of any of its powers; to consider the government *de facto* as the legitimate government for us; to cultivate friendly relations with it, and to preserve those relations by a frank, firm, and manly policy, meeting in all instances the just claims of every power, submitting to injuries from none. But in regard to these continents circumstances are eminently and conspicuously different. It is impossible that the allied powers should extend their political system to any portion of either continent without endangering our peace and happiness; nor can anyone believe that our southern brethren, if left to themselves, would adopt it of their own accord. It is equally impossible, therefore, that we should behold such interposition in any form with indifference. If we look to the comparative strength and resources of Spain and those new Governments, and their distance from each other, it must be obvious that she can never subdue them. It is still the true policy of the United States to leave the parties to themselves, in the hope that other powers will pursue the same course.

Source: Commager, H.S. (ed.) (1963) *Documents of American History* (7th edn), New York, Appleton Century Crofts, vol.1, pp.235–7.

4.3   BETWEEN THE WORLD WARS

4.3.1   WILSON'S FOURTEEN POINTS (1918)

Isolation from the political affairs of Europe came to an end when the United States became involved, somewhat reluctantly, in the First World War. In an attempt to blockade Britain into submission Germany started a campaign of unrestricted submarine warfare against commercial shipping in the Atlantic. Conflict with neutral America became inevitable and the US declared war on Germany in April 1917. President Wilson was determined that America's war aims should be based on clearly defined principles and that those principles should form the basis of the settlement at the end of the war. The fourteen points were announced to the Congress on 8 January 1918. In the peace settlement Wilson was only partly successful in the face of pressure from the other Allied powers and domestic reluctance to get too involved.

Once more, as repeatedly before, the spokesmen of the Central Empires have indicated their desires to discuss the objects of the war and the possible bases of a general peace. Parleys have been in progress at Brest-Litovsk between representatives of the Central Powers to which the attention of all the belligerents has been invited for the purpose of ascertaining whether it may be possible to extend these parleys into a general conference with regard to terms of peace and settlement. The Russian representatives presented not only a perfectly definite statement of the principles upon which they would be willing to conclude peace but also an equally definite programme of the concrete application of these principles. The representatives of the Central Powers, on their part, presented an outline of settlement which, if much less definite, seemed susceptible of liberal interpretation until their specific programme of practical terms was added. That programme proposed no concessions at all either to the sovereignty of Russia or to the preferences of the populations with whose fortunes it dealt, but meant, in a word, that the Central Empires were to keep every foot of territory their armed forces had occupied, — every province, every city, every point of vantage, — as a permanent addition to their territories and their power. It is a reasonable conjecture that the general principles of settlement which they at first suggested originated with the more liberal statesmen of Germany and Austria, the men who have begun to feel the force of their own peoples' thought and purpose, while the concrete terms of actual settlement came from the military leaders who have no thought but to keep what they have got. The negotiations have been broken off. The Russian representatives were sincere and in earnest. They cannot entertain such proposals of conquest and domination.

The whole incident is full of significance. It is also full of perplexity. With whom are the Russian representatives dealing? For whom are the representatives of the Central Empires speaking? Are they speaking for the majorities of their respective parliaments or for the minority parties, that military and imperialistic minority which has so far dominated their whole policy and controlled the affairs of Turkey and of the Balkan states which have felt obliged to become their associates in this war? The Russian representatives have insisted, very justly, very wisely, and in the true spirit of modern democracy, that the conferences they have been holding with the Teutonic and Turkish statesmen should be held within open, not closed, doors, and all the world has been audience, as was desired. To whom have we been listening, then? To those who speak the spirit and intention of the Resolutions of the German Reichstag of the ninth of July last, the spirit and intention of the liberal leaders and parties of Germany, or to those who resist and defy that spirit and intention and insist upon conquest and subjugation? Or are we listening, in fact, to both, unreconciled and in open and hopeless contradiction? These are very serious and pregnant questions. Upon the answer to them depends the peace of the world.

But, whatever the results of the parleys at Brest-Litovsk, whatever the confusions of counsel and of purpose in the utterances of the spokesmen of the Central Empires, they have again attempted to acquaint the world with their objects in the war and have again challenged their adversaries to say what their objects are and what sort of settlement they would deem just and satisfactory. There is no good reason why that challenge should not be responded to, and responded to with the utmost candor. We did not wait for it. Not once, but again and again, we have laid out whole thought and purpose before the world, not in general terms only, but each time with sufficient definition to make it clear what sort of definitive terms of settlement must necessarily spring out of them. Within the last week Mr Lloyd George has spoken with admirable candor and in admirable spirit for the people and Government of Great Britain. There is no confusion of counsel among the adversaries of the Central Powers, no uncertainty of principle, no vagueness of detail. The only secrecy of counsel, the only lack of fearless frankness, the only failure to make definite statement of the objects of the war, lies with Germany and her Allies. The issues of life and death hang upon these definitions. No statesman who has the least conception of his responsibility ought for a moment to permit himself to continue this tragical and appalling outpouring of blood and treasure unless he is sure beyond a peradventure that the objects of the vital sacrifice are part and parcel of the very life of Society and that the people for whom he speaks think them right and imperative as he does.

There is, moreover, a voice calling for these definitions of principle and of purpose which is, it seems to me, more thrilling and more compelling than any of the many moving voices with which the troubled air of the world is filled. It is the voice of the Russian people. They are prostrate and all but helpless, it would seem, before the grim power of Germany, which has hitherto known no relenting and no pity. Their power, apparently, is shattered.

And yet their soul is not subservient. They will not yield either in principle or in action. Their conception of what is right, of what it is humane and honorable for them to accept, has been stated with a frankness, a largeness of view, a generosity of spirit, and a universal human sympathy which must challenge the admiration of every friend of mankind; and they have refused to compound their ideals or desert others that they themselves may be safe. They call to us to say what it is that we desire, in what, if in anything, our purpose and out spirit differ from theirs; and I believe that the people of the United States would wish me to respond, with utter simplicity and frankness. Whether their present leaders believe it or not, it is our heartfelt desire and hope that some way may be opened whereby we may be privileged to assist the people of Russia to attain their utmost hope of liberty and ordered peace.

It will be our wish and purpose that the processes of peace, when they are begun, shall be absolutely open and that they shall involve and permit henceforth no secret understandings of any kind. The day of conquest and aggrandizement is gone by; so is also the day of secret covenants entered into in the interest of particular governments and likely at some unlooked-for moment to upset the peace of the world. It is this happy fact, now clear to the view of every public man whose thoughts do not still linger in an age that is dead and gone, which makes it possible for every nation whose purposes are consistent with justice and the peace of the world to avow now or at any other time the objects it has in view.

We entered this war because violations of right had occurred which touched us to the quick and made the life of our own people impossible unless they were corrected and the world secured once for all against their recurrence. What we demand in this war, therefore, is nothing peculiar to ourselves. It is that the world be made fit and safe to live in; and particularly that it be made safe for every peace-loving nation which, like our own, wishes to live its own life, determine its own institutions, be assured of justice and fair dealing by the other peoples of the world as against force and selfish aggression. All the peoples of the world are in effect partners in this interest, and for our own part we see very clearly that unless justice be done to others it will not be done to us. The programme of the world's peace, therefore, is our programme; and that programme, the only possible programme, as we see it, is this:

I.   Open covenants of peace, openly arrived at, after which there shall be no private international understandings of any kind but diplomacy shall proceed always frankly and in the public view.

II. Absolute freedom of navigation upon the seas, outside territorial waters, alike in peace and in war, except as the seas may be closed in whole or in part by international action for the enforcement of international covenants.

III. The removal, so far as possible, of all economic barriers and the establishment of an equality of trade conditions among all the nations consenting to the peace and associating themselves for its maintenance.

IV. Adequate guarantees given and taken that national armaments will be reduced to the lowest point consistent with domestic safety.

V. A free, open-minded, and absolutely impartial adjustment of all colonial claims, based upon a strict observance of the principle that in determining all such questions of sovereignty the interests of the populations concerned must have equal weight with the equitable claims of the government whose title is to be determined.

VI. The evacuation of all Russian territory and such a settlement of all questions affecting Russia as will secure the best and freest cooperation of the other nations of the world in obtaining for her an unhampered and unembarrassed opportunity for the independent determination of her own political development and national policy and assure her of a sincere welcome into the society of free nations under institutions of her own choosing; and, more than a welcome, assistance also of every kind that she may need and may herself desire. The treatment accorded Russia by her sister nations in the months to come will be the acid test of their good will, of their comprehension of her needs as distinguished from their own interests, and of their intelligent and unselfish sympathy.

VII. Belgium, the whole world will agree, must be evacuated and restored, without any attempt to limit the sovereignty which she enjoys in common with all other free nations. No other single act will serve as this will serve to restore confidence among the nations in the laws which they have themselves set and determined for the government of their relations with one another. Without this healing act the whole structure and validity of international law is forever impaired.

VIII. All French territory should be freed and the invaded portions restored, and the wrong done to France by Prussia in 1871 in the matter of Alsace-Lorraine, which has unsettled the peace of the world for nearly fifty years, should be righted, in order that peace may once more be made secure in the interest of all.

IX. A readjustment of the frontiers of Italy should be effected along clearly recognizable lines of nationality.

X. The peoples of Austria-Hungary, whose place among the nations we wish to see safeguarded and assured, should be accorded the freest opportunity of autonomous development.

XI. Rumania, Serbia, and Montenegro should be evacuated; occupied territories restored; Serbia accorded free and secure access to the sea; and the relations of the several Balkan states to one another determined by friendly counsel along historically established lines of allegiance and nationality; and international guarantees of the political and economic independence and territorial integrity of the several Balkan states should be entered into.

XII. The Turkish portions of the present Ottoman Empire should be assured a secure sovereignty, but the other nationalities which are now under

Turkish rule should be assured an undoubted security of life and an absolutely unmolested opportunity of autonomous development, and the Dardanelles should be permanently opened as a free passage to the ships and commerce of all nations under international guarantees.

XIII. An independent Polish state should be erected which should include the territories inhabited by indisputably Polish populations, which should be assured a free and secure access to the sea, and whose political and economic independence and territorial integrity should be guaranteed by international covenant.

XIV. A general association of nations must be formed under specific covenants for the purpose of affording mutual guarantees of political independence and territorial integrity to great and small states alike.

In regard to these essential rectifications of wrong and assertions of right we feel ourselves to be intimate partners of all the governments and peoples associated together against the Imperialists. We cannot be separated in interest or divided in purpose. We stand together until the end.

For such arrangements and covenants we are willing to fight and to continue to fight until they are achieved; but only because we wish the right to prevail and desire a just and stable peace such as can be secured only by removing the chief provocations to war, which this programme does remove. We have no jealousy of German greatness, and there is nothing in this programme that impairs it. We grudge her no achievement or distinction of learning or of pacific enterprise such as have made her record very bright and very enviable. We do not wish to injure her or to block in any way her legitimate influence or power. We do not wish to fight her either with arms or with hostile arrangements of trade if she is willing to associate herself with us and the other peace-loving nations of the world in covenants of justice and law and fair dealing. We wish her only to accept a place of equality among the peoples of the world, — the new world in which we now live, — instead of a place of mastery.

Neither do we presume to suggest to her any alteration or modification of her institutions. But it is necessary, we must frankly say, and necessary as a preliminary to any intelligent dealings with her on our part, that we should know whom her spokesmen speak for when they speak to us, whether for the Reichstag majority or for the military party and the men whose creed is imperial domination.

We have spoken now, surely, in terms too concrete to admit of any further doubt or question. An evident principle runs through the whole programme I have outlined. It is the principle of justice to all peoples and nationalities, and their right to live on equal terms of liberty and safety with one another, whether they be strong or weak. Unless this principle be made its foundation no part of the structure of international justice can stand. The people of the United States could act upon no other principle; and to the vindication of this principle they are ready to devote their lives, their honor, and everything that they possess. The moral climax of this the culminating and final war for human liberty has come, and they are ready to put their own strength, their own highest purpose, their own integrity and devotion to the test.

Source: see also *Foreign Relations of the United States: 1918 Supplement 1* (1933) Washington D.C., pp.12–17; and Baker, R.S. and Dodd, W.E. (eds) (1925) *The Public Papers of Woodrow Wilson*, New York, Harper and Brothers, vol.V, pp.158–61.

4.3.2 THE LEND-LEASE ACT (1941)

Non-involvement in the political affairs of the rest of the world remained the dominant attitude in the United States for most of the inter-war period. However, many, including President Roosevelt, believed that vital American interests were at stake in the conflicts developing in Europe and the Far East. After the outbreak of war in Europe in 1939 and the fall of France in 1940, Roosevelt considered the defence of Britain to be vital to the interests of the United States. While the US remained technically neutral the Roosevelt Administration was able to exchange 50 destroyers for a number of British air and naval bases. Then, in March 1941, the Lend-Lease Act allowed the sale of war materials to any country whose defence the President considered would promote the defence of the US, and without the need for immediate payment.

Be it enacted by the Senate and House of Representatives of the United States of America in Congress assembled, That this Act may be cited as 'An Act to Promote the Defense of the United States'.

[…]

SEC. 2. AS USED IN THIS ACT —

(a)   The term 'defense article' means —

  (1) Any weapon, munition, aircraft, vessel, or boat;

  (2) Any machinery, facility, tool, material, or supply necessary for the manufacture, production, processing, repair, servicing, or operation of any article described in this subsection;

  (3) Any component material or part of or equipment for any article described in this subsection;

  (4) Any agricultural, industrial or other commodity or article for defense.

Such term 'defense article' includes any article described in this subsection: Manufactured or procured pursuant to section 3, or to which the United States or any foreign government has or hereafter acquires title, possession, or control.

(b)   The term 'defense information' means any plan, specification, design, prototype, or information pertaining to any defense article.

SEC. 3

(a)   Notwithstanding the provisions of any other law, the President may, from time to time, when he deems it in the interest of national defense, authorize the Secretary of War, the Secretary of the Navy, or the head of any other department or agency of the Government —

(1) To manufacture in arsenals, factories, and shipyards under their jurisdiction, or otherwise procure, to the extent to which funds are made available therefore, or contracts are authorized from time to time by the Congress, or both, any defense article for the government of any country whose defense the President deems vital to the defense of the United States.

(2) To sell, transfer title to, exchange, lease, lend, or otherwise dispose of, to any such government any defense article, but no defense article not manufactured or procured under paragraph (1) shall in any way be disposed of under this paragraph, except after consultation with the Chief of Staff of the Army or the Chief of Naval Operations of the Navy, or both. The value of defense articles disposed of in any way under authority of this paragraph, and procured from funds heretofore appropriated, shall not exceed $1,300,000,000. The value of such defense articles shall be determined by the head of the department or agency concerned or such other department, agency or officer as shall be designated in the manner provided in the rules and regulations issued hereunder. Defense articles procured from funds hereafter appropriated to any department or agency of the Government, other than from funds authorized to be appropriated under this Act, shall not be disposed of in any way under authority of this paragraph except to the extent hereafter authorized by the Congress in the Acts appropriating such funds or otherwise.

(3) To test, inspect, prove, repair, outfit, recondition, or otherwise to place in good working order, to the extent to which funds are made available therefor, or contracts are authorized from time to time by the Congress, or both, any defense article for any such government, or to procure any or all such services by private contract.

(4) To communicate to any such government any defense information, pertaining to any defense article furnished to such government under paragraph (2) of this subsection.

(5) To release for export any defense article disposed of in any way under this subsection to any such government.

(b)   The terms and conditions upon which any such foreign government receives any aid authorized under subsection (a) shall be those which the President deems satisfactory, and the benefit to the United States may be payment or repayment in kind or property, or any other direct or indirect benefit which the President deems satisfactory.

(c)   After June 30, 1943, or after the passage of a concurrent resolution by the two Houses before June 30, 1943, which declares that the powers conferred by or pursuant to subsection (a) are no longer necessary to promote the defense of the United States, neither the President nor the head of any department or agency shall exercise any of the powers conferred by or pursuant to subsection (a); except that until July 1, 1946, any of such powers may be exercised to the extent necessary to carry out a contract or agreement with such a foreign government made before July 1, 1943, or before the passage of such concurrent resolution, whichever is the earlier.

(d)   Nothing in this Act shall be construed to authorize or to permit the authorization of convoying vessels by naval vessels of the United States.

(e)   Nothing in this Act shall be construed to authorize or to permit the authorization of the entry of any American vessel into a combat area in violation of section 3 of the Neutrality Act of 1939.

SEC. 4

All contracts or agreements made for the disposition of any defense article or defense information pursuant to section 3 shall contain a clause by which the foreign government undertakes that it will not, without the consent of the President, transfer title to or possession of such defense article or defense information by gift, sale, or otherwise, or permit its use by anyone not an officer, employee, or agent of such foreign government.

SEC. 5

(a)   The Secretary of War, the Secretary of the Navy, or the head of any other department or agency of the Government involved shall, when any such defense article or defense information is exported, immediately inform the department or agency designated by the President to administer section 6 of the Act of July 2, 1940 (54 Stat. 714), of the quantities, character, value, terms of disposition, and destination of the article and information so exported.

(b)   The President from time to time, but not less frequently than once every ninety days, shall transmit to the Congress a report of operations under this Act except such information as he deems incompatible with the public interest to disclose. Reports provided for under this subsection shall be transmitted to the Secretary of the Senate or the Clerk of the House of Representatives, as the case may be, if the Senate or the House of Representatives, as the case may be, is not in session.

SEC. 6

(a)   There is hereby authorized to be appropriate from time to time, out of any money in the Treasury not otherwise appropriated, such amounts as may be necessary to carry out the provisions and accomplish the purposes of this Act.

(b)   All money and all property which is converted into money received under section 3 from any government shall, with the approval of the Director of the Budget, revert to the respective appropriation or appropriations out of which funds were expended with respect to the defense article or defense information for which such consideration is received, and shall be available for expenditure for the purpose for which such expended funds were appropriated by law, during the fiscal year in which such funds are received and the ensuing fiscal year; but in no event shall any funds so received be available for expenditure after June 30, 1946.

SEC. 7

The Secretary of War, the Secretary of the Navy, and the head of the department or agency shall in all contracts or agreements for the disposition of any defense article or defense information fully protect the rights of all citizens of the United States who have patent rights in and to any such article or information which is hereby authorized to be disposed of and the payments collected for royalties on such patents shall be paid to the owners and holders of such patents.

SEC. 8

The Secretaries of War and of the Navy are hereby authorized to purchase or otherwise acquire arms, ammunition, and implements of war produced within the jurisdiction of any country to which section 3 is applicable, whenever the President deems such purchase or acquisition to be necessary in the interests of the defense of the United States.

SEC. 9

The President may, from time to time, promulgate such rules and regulations as may be necessary and proper to carry out any of the provisions of this Act; and he may exercise any power or authority conferred on him by this Act through such department, agency, or officer as he shall direct.

SEC. 10

Nothing in this Act shall be construed to change existing law relating to the use of the land and naval forces of the United States, except insofar as such use relates to the manufacture, procurement, and repair of defense articles, the communication of information and other noncombatant purposes enumerated in this Act.

SEC. 11

If any provision of this Act or the application of such provision to any circumstance shall be held invalid, the validity of the remainder of the Act and the applicability of such provision to other circumstances shall not be affected thereby.

Source: Ferrell, R.H. (ed.) (1971) *America as a World Power 1872–1945*, Columbia, University of South Carolina Press.

4.3.3   THE ATLANTIC CHARTER (1941)

The attitude of the Roosevelt Administration to Nazi Germany was made very clear in a joint declaration of principles by the President and British Prime Minister Winston Churchill when they met in August 1941. The Charter effectively laid down America's war aims, a war the US was not yet involved in. Though America's direct entry into the conflict was becoming increasingly inevitable, the final decision for war was to be made elsewhere.

Joint declaration of the President of the United States of America and the Prime Minister, Mr Churchill, representing His Majesty's Government in the United Kingdom, being met together, deem it right to make known certain common principles in the national policies of their respective countries on which they base their hopes for a better future for the world.

First, their countries seek no aggrandizement, territorial or other;

Second, they desire to see no territorial changes that do not accord with the freely expressed wishes of the peoples concerned;

Third, they respect the right of all peoples to choose the form of government under which they will live; and they wish to see sovereign rights and self government restored to those who have been forcibly deprived of them;

Fourth, they will endeavor, with due respect for their existing obligations, to further the enjoyment by all States, great or small, victor or vanquished, of access, on equal terms, to the trade and to the raw materials of the world which are needed for their economic prosperity;

Fifth, they desire to bring about the fullest collaboration between all nations in the economic field with the object of securing, for all, improved labor standards, economic advancement and social security;

Sixth, after the final destruction of the Nazi tyranny, they hope to see established a peace which will afford to all nations the means of dwelling in safety within their own boundaries, and which will afford assurance that all the men in all the lands may live out their lives in freedom from fear and want;

Seventh, such a peace should enable all men to traverse the high seas and oceans without hindrance;

Eighth, they believe that all of the nations of the world, for realistic as well as spiritual reasons must come to the abandonment of the use of force. Since no future peace can be maintained if land, sea or air armaments continue to be employed by nations which threaten, or may threaten, aggression outside of their frontiers, they believe, pending the establishment of a wider and permanent system of general security, that the disarmament of such nations is essential. They will likewise aid and encourage all other practicable measures which will lighten for peace-loving peoples the crushing burden of armaments.

Source: Ferrell, R.H. (ed.) (1971) *America as a World Power 1872–1945*, Columbia, University of South Carolina Press.

4.3.4 THE DECLARATION OF WAR (1941)

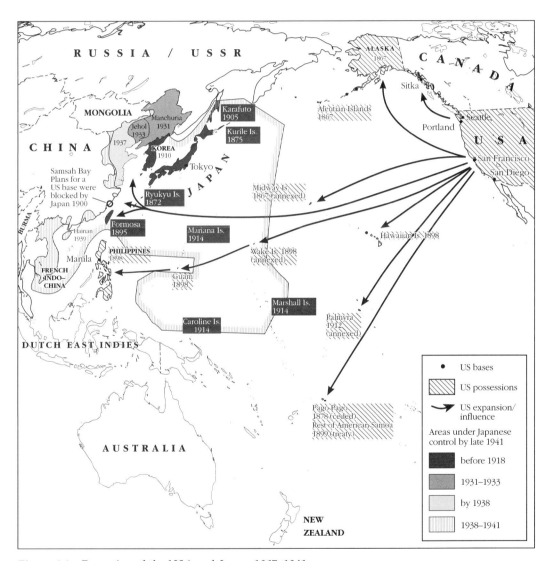

Figure 4.1 *Expansion of the USA and Japan, 1867–1941*

Source: Thomas, A. *et al.* (1994) *Third World Atlas* (2nd edn), Buckingham, Open University Press in association with The Open University, p.46; see also Eccleston *et al.* (1998) *The Asia-Pacific Profile*, London, Routledge in association with The Open University, Figure 4.

The United States and Japan had been rivals in the Pacific for some time (see Figure 4.1), but Japanese territorial and economic ambitions through the 1930s had resulted in a serious deterioration in relations. In 1941 America had cancelled trade agreements and imposed an oil and scrap metal embargo after Japan had occupied large parts of China and South-East Asia, but negotiations calling for a Japanese withdrawal failed. On 7 December 1941 the Japanese launched a surprise attack on the American Pacific Fleet at its Pearl Harbor base in Hawaii. The next day President Roosevelt made the following announcement to the Congress and asked that war be declared: the resolution for a state of war was promptly passed. The 8 December also saw Britain declare war on Japan, and on 11 December, Germany and Italy declared war against the United States. The area involved and the key events of the war in the Pacific are summarized in Figure 4.2.

USS West Virginia, Pearl Harbor, 7 December 1941

Yesterday, December 7, 1941 — a date which will live in infamy — the United States of America was suddenly and deliberately attacked by naval and air forces of the Empire of Japan.

The United States was at peace with that Nation and, at the solicitation of Japan, was still in conversation with its Government and its Emperor looking toward the maintenance of peace in the Pacific. Indeed, one hour after Japanese air squadrons had commenced bombing in Oahu, the Japanese Ambassador to the United States and his colleague delivered to the Secretary of State a formal reply to a recent American message. While this reply stated that it seemed useless to continue the existing diplomatic negotiations, it contained no threat or hint of war or armed attack.

It will be recorded that the distance of Hawaii from Japan makes it obvious that the attack was deliberately planned many days or even weeks ago. During the intervening time the Japanese Government has deliberately sought to deceive the United States by false statements and expressions of hope for continued peace.

The attack yesterday on the Hawaiian Islands has caused severe damage to American naval and military forces. Very many American lives have been lost. In addition American ships have been reported torpedoed on the high seas between San Francisco and Honolulu.

Yesterday the Japanese Government also launched an attack against Malaya.

Last night Japanese forces attacked Hong Kong.

Last night Japanese forces attacked Guam.

Last night Japanese forces attacked the Philippine Islands.

Last night the Japanese attacked Wake Island.

This morning the Japanese attacked Midway Island.

Japan has, therefore, undertaken a surprise offensive extending throughout the Pacific area. The facts of yesterday speak for themselves. The people of the United States have already formed their opinions and well understand the implications to the very life and safety of our Nation.

As Commander-in-Chief of the Army and Navy I have directed that all measures be taken for our defense.

Always will we remember the character of the onslaught against us.

No matter how long it may take us to overcome this premeditated invasion, the American people in their righteous might will win through to absolute victory.

I believe I interpret the will of the Congress and of the people when I assert that we will not only defend ourselves to the uttermost but will make very certain that this form of treachery shall never endanger us again.

Hostilities exist. There is no blinking at the fact that our people, our territory, and our interests are in grave danger.

With confidence in our armed forces — with the unbounded determination of our people — we will gain the inevitable triumph — so help us God.

I ask that the Congress declare that since the unprovoked and dastardly attack by Japan on Sunday, December seventh, a state of war has existed between the United States and the Japanese Empire.

Source: Ferrell, R.H. (ed.) (1971) *America as a World Power 1872–1945*, Columbia, University of South Carolina Press.

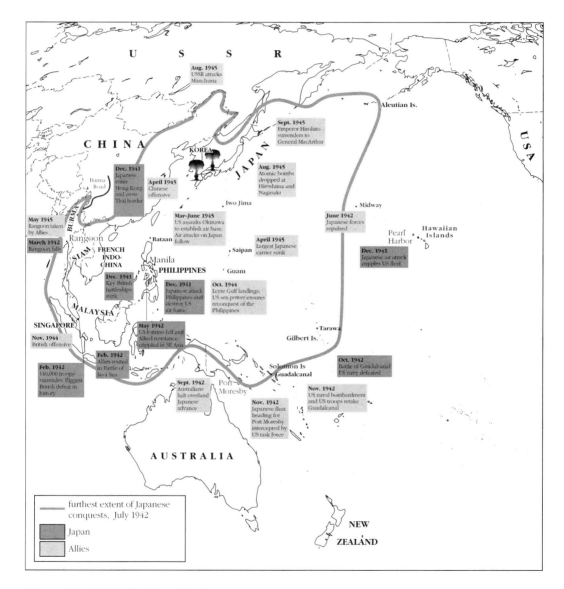

Figure 4.2 *The Pacific War, 1941–45*

Source: Burns, R. (ed.) (1991) *War in the Pacific, 1937–1945*, London, Bison; *The Times Atlas of World History* (1978) London, Times Books; see also Eccleston *et al.* (1998) *The Asia-Pacific Profile*, London, Routledge in association with The Open University, Figure 7.

4.4 THE COLD WAR ERA

4.4.1 THE TRUMAN DOCTRINE (1947)

> The wartime partnership between the United States and the Soviet Union soon turned to mistrust and suspicion when the war was over. In addition to the ideological issue, which had existed since the Russian revolution, much of the tension resulted from the actions of the two newly-emerged superpowers in relation to the liberated and defeated nations of Europe and the Far East. The wartime conferences of the 'Big Three' allies had agreed on certain levels of influence in these areas, but Britain was no longer in a position to play a major role and in 1947 announced it was withdrawing its support for the Greek government which faced a communist led rebellion. At the same time the Soviet Union was exerting pressure on Turkey in an attempt to gain more influence. On 12 March 1947 President Truman addressed Congress requesting aid for both Greece and Turkey.

Mr President, Mr Speaker, Members of the Congress of the United States:

The gravity of the situation which confronts the world today necessitates my appearance before a joint session of the Congress.

The foreign policy and the national security of this country are involved.

One aspect of the present situation, which I present to you at this time for your consideration and decision, concerns Greece and Turkey.

The United States has received from the Greek Government an urgent appeal for financial and economic assistance. Preliminary reports from the American Economic Mission now in Greece and reports from the American Ambassador in Greece corroborate the statement of the Greek Government that assistance is imperative if Greece is to survive as a free nation.

I do not believe that the American people and the Congress wish to turn a deaf ear to the appeal of the Greek Government.

Greece is not a rich country. Lack of sufficient natural resources has always forced the Greek people to work hard to make both ends meet. Since 1940, this industrious, peace loving country has suffered invasion, four years of cruel enemy occupation, and bitter internal strife.

When forces of liberation entered Greece they found that the retreating Germans had destroyed virtually all the railways, roads, port facilities, communications, and merchant marine. More than a thousand villages had been burned. Eighty-five percent of the children were tubercular. Livestock, poultry, and draft animals had almost disappeared. Inflation had wiped out practically all savings.

President Harry S. Truman, c. 1945

As a result of these tragic conditions, a militant minority, exploiting human want and misery, was able to create political chaos which, until now, has made economic recovery impossible. […]

The very existence of the Greek state is today threatened by the terrorist activities of several thousand armed men, led by Communists, who defy the government's authority at a number of points, particularly along the northern boundaries. A Commission appointed by the United Nations Security Council is at present investigating disturbed conditions in northern Greece and alleged border violations along the frontier between Greece on the one hand and Albania, Bulgaria, and Yugoslavia on the other.

Meanwhile, the Greek Government is unable to cope with the situation. The Greek army is small and poorly equipped. It needs supplies and equipment if it is to restore authority to the government throughout Greek territory.

Greece must have assistance if it is to become a self-supporting and self-respecting democracy. […]

No government is perfect. One of the chief virtues of a democracy, however, is that its defects are always visible and under democratic processes can be pointed out and corrected. The government of Greece is not perfect. Nevertheless it represents 85 percent of the members of the Greek Parliament who were chosen in an election last year. Foreign observers, including 692 Americans, considered this election to be a fair expression of the views of the Greek people.

The Greek Government has been operating in an atmosphere of chaos and extremism. It has made mistakes. The extension of aid by this country does not mean that the United States condones everything that the Greek Government has done or will do. We have condemned in the past, and we condemn now, extremist measures of the right or the left. We have in the past advised tolerance, and we advise tolerance now.

Greece's neighbor, Turkey, also deserves our attention.

The future of Turkey as an independent and economically sound state is clearly no less important to the freedom-loving peoples of the world than the future of Greece. The circumstances in which Turkey finds itself today are considerably different from those of Greece. Turkey has been spared the disasters that have beset Greece. And during the war, the United States and Great Britain furnished Turkey with material aid.

Nevertheless, Turkey now needs our support.

Since the war Turkey has sought additional financial assistance from Great Britain and the United States for the purpose of effecting that modernization necessary for the maintenance of its national integrity.

That integrity is essential to the preservation of order in the Middle East.

The British Government has informed us that, owing to its own difficulties, it can no longer extend financial or economic aid to Turkey.

As in the case of Greece, if Turkey is to have the assistance it needs, the United States must supply it. We are the only country able to provide that help.

I am fully aware of the broad implications involved if the United States extends assistance to Greece and Turkey, and I shall discuss these implications with you at this time.

One of the primary objectives of the foreign policy of the United States is the creation of conditions in which we and other nations will be able to work out a way of life free from coercion. This was a fundamental issue in the war with Germany and Japan. Our victory was won over countries which sought to impose their will, and their way of life, upon other nations.

To ensure the peaceful development of nations, free from coercion, the United States has taken a leading part in establishing the United Nations. The United Nations is designed to make possible lasting freedom and independence for all its members. We shall not realize our objectives, however, unless we are willing to help free peoples to maintain their free institutions and their national integrity against aggressive movements that seek to impose upon them totalitarian regimes. This is no more than a frank recognition that totalitarian regimes imposed upon free peoples, by direct or indirect aggression, undermine the foundations of international peace and hence the security of the United States.

The peoples of a number of countries of the world have recently had totalitarian regimes forced upon them against their will. The Government of the United States has made frequent protests against coercion and intimidation, in violation of the Yalta agreement, in Poland, Rumania, and Bulgaria. I must also state that in a number of other countries there have been similar developments.

At the present moment in world history nearly every nation must choose between alternative ways of life. The choice is too often not a free one.

One way of life is based upon the will of the majority, and is distinguished by free institutions, representative government, free elections, guarantees of individual liberty, freedom of speech and religion, and freedom from political oppression.

The second way of life is based upon the will of a minority forcibly imposed upon the majority. It relies upon terror and oppression, a controlled press and radio, fixed elections, and the suppression of personal freedoms.

I believe that it must be the policy of the United States to support free peoples who are resisting attempted subjugation by armed minorities or by outside pressures.

I believe that we must assist free peoples to work out their own destinies in their own way.

I believe that our help should be primarily through economic and financial aid which is essential to economic stability and orderly political processes.

The world is not static, and the *status quo* is not sacred. But we cannot allow changes in the *status quo* in violation of the Charter of the United Nations by such methods as coercion, or by such subterfuges as political infiltration. In helping free and independent nations to maintain their freedom, the United States will be giving effect to the principles of the Charter of the United Nations.

It is necessary only to glance at a map to realize that the survival and integrity of the Greek nation are of grave importance in a much wider situation. If Greece should fall under the control of an armed minority, the effect upon its neighbor, Turkey, would be immediate and serious. Confusion and disorder might well spread throughout the entire Middle East.

Moreover, the disappearance of Greece as an independent state would have a profound effect upon those countries in Europe whose peoples are struggling against great difficulties to maintain their freedoms and their independence while they repair the damages of war.

It would be an unspeakable tragedy if these countries, which have struggled so long against overwhelming odds, should lose that victory for which they sacrificed so much. Collapse of free institutions and loss of independence would be disastrous not only for them but for the world. Discouragement and possibly failure would quickly be the lot of neighboring peoples striving to maintain their freedom and independence.

Should we fail to aid Greece and Turkey in this fateful hour, the effect will be far reaching to the West as well as to the East. […]

Source: Griffith, R. (ed.) (1992) *Major Problems in American History Since 1945*, Lexington, Mass., D.C. Heath, p.111.

4.4.2   THE MARSHALL PLAN (1947)

The Marshall Plan was a response to the prospect of imminent economic collapse of the war-ravaged economies of Europe and the political dangers that would ensue. The Plan was announced by Secretary of State George C. Marshall at his honorary degree ceremony at Harvard University on 5 June 1947. It followed on from the approach taken in the Truman Doctrine and offered economic aid to all nations of Europe. The Soviet Union, and those nations of Eastern Europe increasingly under its influence and control, declined the offer. Western Europe accepted. The Plan was a great success and laid the foundations of Western Europe's post-war economic power, it also strengthened the political ties between Western Europe and the United States.

Secretary of State George Marshall, 5 June 1947

I need not tell you gentlemen that the world situation is very serious. That must be apparent to all intelligent people. I think one difficulty is that the problem is one of such enormous complexity that the very mass of facts presented to the public by press and radio make it exceedingly difficult for the man in the street to reach a clear appraisement of the situation. Furthermore, the people of this country are distant from the troubled areas of the earth and it is hard for them to comprehend the plight and consequent reactions of the long suffering peoples, and the effect of those reactions on their governments in connection with our efforts to promote peace in the world.

In considering the requirements for the rehabilitation of Europe, the physical loss of life, the visible destruction of cities, factories, mines, and railroads was correctly estimated, but it has become obvious during recent months that this visible destruction was probably less serious than the dislocation of the entire fabric of European economy. For the past 10 years conditions have been highly abnormal. The feverish preparation for war and the more feverish maintenance of the war effort engulfed all aspects of national economies. Machinery has fallen into disrepair or is entirely obsolete. Under the arbitrary and destructive Nazi rule, virtually every possible enterprise was geared into the German war machine. Long-standing commercial ties, private institutions, banks, insurance companies, and shipping companies disappeared, through loss of capital, absorption through nationalization, or by simple destruction. In many countries, confidence in the local currency has been severely shaken. The breakdown of the business structure of Europe during the war was complete. Recovery has been seriously retarded by the fact that two years after the close of hostilities a peace settlement with Germany and Austria has not been agreed upon. But even given a more prompt solution of these difficult problems, the rehabilitation of the economic structure of Europe quite evidently will require a much longer time and greater effort than had been foreseen.

There is a phase of this matter which is both interesting and serious. The farmer has always produced the foodstuffs to exchange with the city dweller for the other necessities of life. This division of labor is the basis of modern civilization. At the present time it is threatened with breakdown. The town and city industries are not producing adequate goods to exchange with the food-producing farmer. Raw materials and fuel are in short supply. Machinery is lacking or worn out. The farmer or the peasant cannot find the goods for sale which he desires to purchase. So the sale of his farm produce for money which he cannot use seems to him an unprofitable transaction. He, therefore, has withdrawn many fields from crop cultivation and is using them for grazing. He feeds more grain to stock and finds for himself and his family an ample supply of food, however short he may be on clothing and the other ordinary gadgets of civilization. Meanwhile people in the cities are short of food and fuel. So the governments are forced to use their foreign money and credits to procure these necessities abroad. This process exhausts funds which are urgently needed for reconstruction. Thus a very serious situation is rapidly developing which bodes no good for the world. The modern system of the division of labor upon which the exchange of products is based is in danger of breaking down.

The truth of the matter is that Europe's requirements for the next three or four years of foreign food and other essential products — principally from America — are so much greater than her present ability to pay that she must have substantial additional help or face economic, social, and political deterioration of a very grave character.

The remedy lies in breaking the vicious circle and restoring the confidence of the European people in the economic future of their own countries and of Europe as a whole. The manufacturer and the farmer throughout wide areas must be able and willing to exchange their products for currencies the continuing value of which is not open to question.

Aside from the demoralizing effect on the world at large and the possibilities of disturbances arising as a result of the desperation of the people concerned, the consequences to the economy of the United States should be apparent to all. It is logical that the United States should do whatever it is able to do to assist in the return of normal economic health in the world, without which there can be no political stability and no assured peace. Our policy is directed not against any country or doctrine but against hunger, poverty, desperation, and chaos. Its purpose should be the revival of a working economy in the world so as to permit the emergence of political and social conditions in which free institutions can exist. Such assistance, I am convinced, must not be on a piecemeal basis as various crises develop. Any assistance that this Government may render in the future should provide a cure rather than a mere palliative. Any government that is willing to assist in the task of recovery will find full cooperation, I am sure, on the part of the United States Government. Any government which maneuvers to block the recovery of other countries cannot expect help from us. Furthermore, governments, political parties, or groups which seek to perpetuate human misery in order to profit therefrom politically or otherwise will encounter the opposition of the United States.

It is already evident that, before the United States Government can proceed much further in its efforts to alleviate the situation and help start the European world on its way to recovery, there must be some agreement among the countries of Europe as to the requirements of the situation and the part those countries themselves will take in order to give proper effect to whatever action might be undertaken by this Government. It would be neither fitting nor efficacious for this Government to undertake to draw up unilaterally a program designed to place Europe on its feet economically. This is the business of the Europeans. The initiative, I think, must come from Europe. The role of this country should consist of friendly aid in the drafting of a European program so far as it may be practical for us to do so. The program should be a joint one, agreed to by a number, if not all, European nations.

An essential part of any successful action on the part of the United States is an understanding on the part of the people of America of the character of the problem and the remedies to be applied. Political passion and prejudice should have no part. With foresight, and a willingness on the part of our people to face up to the vast responsibility which history has clearly placed upon our country, the difficulties I have outlined can and will be overcome.

Source: Ferrell, R.H. (ed.) (1975) *America in a Divided World 1945–1972*, Columbia, University of South Carolina Press.

4.4.3 THE NORTH ATLANTIC TREATY ORGANIZATION (1949)

The nature of the relations between the United States and the Soviet Union and the political and economic division of Europe was soon reflected in the formation of military alliances, NATO and the Warsaw Pact. The NATO treaty came into effect on 24 August 1949 and included the US, the UK, Canada, France, Italy, Portugal, Belgium, Denmark, Norway, the Netherlands, Iceland and Luxembourg. Greece and Turkey joined in 1952, West Germany in 1955, and Spain in 1982. The terms of the treaty meant that an attack on one member was an attack on all. The United States had moved from isolationism to be part of a European peacetime military alliance.

In the post-Cold War world of 1993 a 'Partnership for Peace' was offered to the nations of Central and Eastern Europe, followed by full membership to certain countries in 1998 (see Sections 4.5.3 and 4.5.5). In 1994 NATO took its first military action when it enforced the United Nations 'no-fly zone' following the civil war in the former Yugoslavia by shooting down Serbian war planes.

The Parties to this Treaty reaffirm their faith in the purposes and principles of the Charter of the United Nations and their desire to live in peace with all peoples and all governments.

They are determined to safeguard the freedom, common heritage and civilization of their peoples, founded on the principles of democracy, individual liberty and the rule of law.

They seek to promote stability and well-being in the North Atlantic area.

They are resolved to unite their efforts for collective defense and for the preservation of peace and security.

They therefore agree to this North Atlantic Treaty:

ARTICLE 1

The Parties undertake, as set forth in the Charter of the United Nations, to settle any international disputes in which they may be involved by peaceful means in such a manner that international peace and security, and justice, are not endangered, and to refrain in their international relations from the threat or use of force in any manner inconsistent with the purposes of the United Nations.

ARTICLE 2

The Parties will contribute toward the further development of peaceful and friendly international relations by strengthening their free institutions, by bringing about a better understanding of the principles upon which these institutions are founded, and by promoting conditions of stability and well-being. They will seek to eliminate conflict in their international economic policies and will encourage economic collaboration between any or all of them.

ARTICLE 3

In order more effectively to achieve the objectives of this Treaty, the Parties, separately and jointly, by means of continuous and effective self-help and mutual aid, will maintain and develop their individual and collective capacity to resist armed attack.

ARTICLE 4

The Parties will consult together whenever, in the opinion of any of them, the territorial integrity, political independence or security of any of the Parties is threatened.

ARTICLE 5

The Parties agree that an armed attack against one or more of them in Europe or North America shall be considered an attack against them all; and consequently they agree that, if such an armed attack occurs, each of them, in exercise of the right of individual or collective self-defense recognized by Article 51 of the Charter of the United Nations, will assist the Party or Parties so attacked by taking forthwith, individually and in concert with the other Parties, such action as it deems necessary, including the use of armed force, to restore and maintain the security of the North Atlantic area.

Any such armed attack and all measures taken as a result thereof shall immediately be reported to the Security Council. Such measures shall be terminated when the Security Council has taken the measures necessary to restore and maintain international peace and security.

ARTICLE 6

For the purpose of Article 5 an armed attack on one or more of the Parties is deemed to include an armed attack on the territory of any of the Parties in Europe or North America, on the Algerian departments of France, on the occupation forces of any Party in Europe, on the islands under the jurisdiction of any Party in the North Atlantic area north of the Tropic of Cancer or on the vessels or aircraft in this area of any of the Parties.

ARTICLE 7

This Treaty does not affect, and shall not be interpreted as affecting, in any way the rights and obligations under the Charter of the Parties which are members of the United Nations, or the primary responsibility of the Security Council for the maintenance of international peace and security.

ARTICLE 8

Each Party declares that none of the international engagements now in force between it and any other of the Parties or any third state is in conflict with the provisions of this Treaty, and undertakes not to enter into any international engagement in conflict with this Treaty.

ARTICLE 9

The Parties hereby establish a council, on which each of them shall be represented, to consider matters concerning the implementation of this Treaty. The council shall be so organized as to be able to meet promptly at any time. The council shall set up such subsidiary bodies as may be necessary; in particular it shall establish immediately a defense committee which shall recommend measures for the implementation of Articles 3 and 5.

ARTICLE 10

The Parties may, by unanimous agreement, invite any other European state in a position to further the principles of this Treaty and to contribute to the security of the North Atlantic area to accede to this Treaty. Any state so invited may become a party to the Treaty by depositing its instrument of accession with the Government of the United States of America. The Government of the United States of America will inform each of the Parties of the deposit of each such instrument of accession.

ARTICLE 11

This Treaty shall be ratified and its provisions carried out by the Parties in accordance with their respective constitutional processes. The instruments of ratification shall be deposited as soon as possible with the Government of the United States of America, which will notify all the other signatories of each deposit. The Treaty shall enter into force between the states which have ratified it as soon as the ratifications of the majority of the signatories, including the ratifications of Belgium, Canada, France, Luxembourg, the Netherlands, the United Kingdom and the United States, have been deposited and shall come into effect with respect to other states on the date of the deposit of their ratifications.

ARTICLE 12

After the Treaty has been in force for ten years, or at any time thereafter, the Parties shall, if any of them so requests, consult together for the purpose of reviewing the Treaty, having regard for the factors then affecting peace and security in the North Atlantic area, including the development of universal as well as regional arrangements under the Charter of the United Nations for the maintenance of international peace and security.

ARTICLE 13

After the Treaty has been in force for twenty years, any Party may cease to be a party one year after its notice of denunciation has been given to the Government of the United States of America, which will inform the Governments of the other Parties of the deposit of each notice of denunciation.

ARTICLE 14

This Treaty, of which the English and French texts are equally authentic, shall be deposited in the archives of the Government of the United States of America. Duly certified copies thereof will be transmitted by that Government to the Governments of the other signatories.

Source: Ferrell, R.H. (ed.) (1975) *America in a Divided World 1945–1972*, Columbia, University of South Carolina Press.

4.4.4 NATIONAL SECURITY COUNCIL PAPER No.68 (1950)

Though top secret at the time and for many years afterwards, the National Security Council Paper No.68 is a central document in understanding the Cold War. Its analysis of Soviet intentions and capabilities set the tone and framework, at the highest levels, for US relations with the Soviet Union. The US reaction to the perceived Soviet threat was to be one of containment. The notion of rolling back the gains of communism was not actively pursued. The NSC Paper was drafted by Paul Nitze for the consideration of President Truman and senior members of his administration.

A REPORT TO THE NATIONAL SECURITY COUNCIL BY THE EXECUTIVE SECRETARY (LAY)

Washington, April 14, 1950

TOP SECRET

NSC 68

Note by the Executive Secretary to the National Security Council on United States Objectives and Programs for National Security

[...]

The enclosed letter by the President and the Report by the Secretaries of State and Defense referred to therein are transmitted herewith for consideration by the National Security Council, the Secretary of the Treasury, the

Economic Cooperation Administrator, the Director of the Bureau of the Budget, and the Chairman, Council of Economic Advisers, at the next regularly scheduled meeting of the Council on Thursday, April 20, 1950.

A proposed procedure for carrying out the President's directive as a matter of urgency is being circulated for concurrent consideration in the reference memorandum of April 14.

It is requested that this report be handled with special security precautions in accordance with the President's desire that no publicity be given this report or its contents without his approval.

JAMES S. LAY, JR.

[ENCLOSURE 1] THE PRESIDENT TO THE EXECUTIVE SECRETARY OF THE NATIONAL SECURITY COUNCIL (LAY)

Washington, April 12, 1950

TOP SECRET

Dear Mr Lay:

After consideration of the Report by the Secretaries of State and Defense, dated April 7, 1950, re-examining our objectives in peace and war and the effect of these objectives on our strategic plans, I have decided to refer that Report to the National Security Council for consideration, with the request that the National Security Council provide me with further information on the implications of the Conclusions contained therein. I am particularly anxious that the Council give me a clearer indication of the programs which are envisaged in the Report, including estimates of the probable cost of such programs.

Because of the effect of these Conclusions upon the budgetary and economic situation, it is my desire that the Economic Cooperation Administrator, the Director of the Bureau of the Budget, and the Chairman, Council of Economic Advisers, participate in the consideration of this Report by the Council, in addition to the regular participation of the Secretary of the Treasury.

Pending the urgent completion of this study, I am concerned that action on existing programs should not be postponed or delayed. In addition, it is my desire that no publicity be given to this Report or its contents without my approval.

   Sincerely yours,

HARRY S. TRUMAN

[ENCLOSURE 2] A REPORT TO THE PRESIDENT PURSUANT TO THE PRESIDENT'S DIRECTIVE OF JANUARY 31, 1950

[Washington,] April 7, 1950

TOP SECRET

Contents

TERMS OF REFERENCE

The following report is submitted in response to the President's directive of January 31 which reads:

> That the President direct the Secretary of State and the Secretary of Defense to undertake a reexamination of our objectives in peace and war and of the effect of these objectives on our strategic plans, in the light of the probable fission bomb capability and possible thermonuclear bomb capability of the Soviet Union.

The document which recommended that such a directive be issued[1] reads in part:

> It must be considered whether a decision to proceed with a program directed toward determining feasibility prejudges the more fundamental decisions (a) as to whether, in the event that a test of a thermonuclear weapon proves successful, such weapons should be stockpiled, or (b) if stockpiled, the conditions under which they might be used in war. If a test of a thermonuclear weapon proves successful, the pressures to produce and stockpile such weapons to be held for the same purposes for which fission bombs are then being held will be greatly increased. The question of use policy can be adequately assessed only as a part of a general reexamination of this country's strategic plans and its objectives in peace and war. Such reexamination would need to consider national policy not only with respect to possible thermonuclear weapons, but also with respect to fission weapons — viewed in the light of the probable fission bomb capability and the possible thermonuclear bomb capability of the Soviet Union. The moral, psychological, and political questions involved in this problem would need to be taken into account and be given due weight. The outcome of this reexamination would have a crucial bearing on the further question as to whether there should be a revision in the nature of the agreements, including the international control of atomic energy, which we have been seeking to reach with the U.S.S.R.

ANALYSIS

I.   Background of the Present Crisis

Within the past thirty-five years the world has experienced two global wars of tremendous violence. It has witnessed two revolutions — the Russian and the Chinese — of extreme scope and intensity. It has also seen the collapse of five empires — the Ottoman, the Austro-Hungarian, German, Italian and Japanese — and the drastic decline of two major imperial systems, the British and the French. During the span of one generation, the international

[1]A Report by the Special Committee of the National Security Council to President Truman on the Development of Thermonuclear Weapons, 31 January 1950.

distribution of power has been fundamentally altered. For several centuries it had proved impossible for any one nation to gain such preponderant strength that a coalition of other nations could not in time face it with greater strength. The international scene was marked by recurring periods of violence and war, but a system of sovereign and independent states was maintained, over which no state was able to achieve hegemony.

Two complex sets of factors have now basically altered this historical distribution of power. First, the defeat of Germany and Japan and the decline of the British and French Empires have interacted with the development of the United States and the Soviet Union in such a way that power has increasingly gravitated to these two centers. Second, the Soviet Union, unlike previous aspirants to hegemony, is animated by a new fanatic faith, antithetical to our own, and seeks to impose its absolute authority over the rest of the world. Conflict has, therefore, become endemic and is waged, on the part of the Soviet Union, by violent or non-violent methods in accordance with the dictates of expediency. With the development of increasingly terrifying weapons of mass destruction, every individual faces the ever-present possibility of annihilation should the conflict enter the phase of total war.

On the one hand, the people of the world yearn for relief from the anxiety arising from the risk of atomic war. On the other hand, any substantial further extension of the area under domination of the Kremlin would raise the possibility that no coalition adequate to confront the Kremlin with greater strength could be assembled. It is in this context that this Republic and its citizens in the ascendancy of their strength stand in their deepest peril.

The issues that face us are momentous, involving the fulfillment or destruction not only of this Republic but of civilization itself. They are issues which will not await our deliberations. With conscience and resolution this Government and the people it represents must now take new and fateful decisions.

II. Fundamental Purpose of the United States

The fundamental purpose of the United States is laid down in the Preamble to the Constitution: ' … to form a more perfect Union, establish Justice, insure domestic Tranquility, provide for the common defence, promote the general Welfare, and secure the Blessings of Liberty to ourselves and our Posterity.' In essence, the fundamental purpose is to assure the integrity and vitality of our free society, which is founded upon the dignity and worth of the individual.

Three realities emerge as a consequence of this purpose: Our determination to maintain the essential elements of individual freedom, as set forth in the Constitution and Bill of Rights; our determination to create conditions under which our free and democratic system can live and prosper; and our determination to fight if necessary to defend our way of life, for which as in the Declaration of Independence, 'with a firm reliance on the protection of Divine Providence, we mutually pledge to each other our lives, our Fortunes and our sacred Honor.'

III. Fundamental Design of the Kremlin

The fundamental design of those who control the Soviet Union and the international communist movement is to retain and solidify their absolute power, first in the Soviet Union and second in the areas now under their control. In the minds of the Soviet leaders, however, achievement of this design requires the dynamic extension of their authority and the ultimate elimination of any effective opposition to their authority.

The design, therefore, calls for the complete subversion or forcible destruction of the machinery of government and structure of society in the countries of the non-Soviet world and their replacement by an apparatus and structure subservient to and controlled from the Kremlin. To that end Soviet efforts are now directed toward the domination of the Eurasian land mass. The United States, as the principal center of power in the non-Soviet world and the bulwark of opposition to Soviet expansion, is the principal enemy whose integrity and vitality must be subverted or destroyed by one means or another if the Kremlin is to achieve its fundamental design.

IV. The Underlying Conflict in the Realm of Ideas and Values Between the U.S. Purpose and the Kremlin design

A. *Nature of conflict:*

The Kremlin regards the United States as the only major threat to the achievement of its fundamental design. There is a basic conflict between the idea of freedom under a government of laws, and the idea of slavery under the grim oligarchy of the Kremlin, which has come to a crisis with the polarization of power described in Section I, and the exclusive possession of atomic weapons by the two protagonists. The idea of freedom, moreover, is peculiarly and intolerably subversive of the idea of slavery. But the converse is not true. The implacable purpose of the slave state to eliminate the challenge of freedom has placed the two great powers at opposite poles. It is this fact which gives the present polarization of power the quality of crisis.

The free society values the individual as an end in himself, requiring of him only that measure of self discipline and self restraint which make the rights of each individual compatible with the rights of every other individual. The freedom of the individual has as its counterpart, therefore, the negative responsibility of the individual not to exercise his freedom in ways inconsistent with the freedom of other individuals and the positive responsibility to make constructive use of his freedom in the building of a just society.

From this idea of freedom with responsibility derives the marvelous diversity, the deep tolerance, the lawfulness of the free society. This is the explanation of the strength of free men. It constitutes the integrity and the vitality of a free and democratic system. The free society attempts to create and maintain an environment in which every individual has the opportunity to realize his creative powers. It also explains why the free society tolerates those within it who would use their freedom to destroy it. By the same token, in relations between nations, the prime reliance of the free society is on the strength and appeal of its idea, and it feels no compulsion sooner or later to bring all societies into conformity with it.

For the free society does not fear, it welcomes, diversity. It derives its strength from its hospitality even to antipathetic ideas. It is a market for free trade in ideas, secure in its faith that free men will take the best wares, and grow to a fuller and better realization of their powers in exercising their choice.

The idea of freedom is the most contagious idea in history, more contagious than the idea of submission to authority. For the breadth of freedom cannot be tolerated in a society which has come under the domination of an individual or group of individuals with a will to absolute power. Where the despot holds absolute power — the absolute power of the absolutely powerful will — all other wills must be subjugated in an act of willing submission, a degradation willed by the individual upon himself under the compulsion of a perverted faith. It is the first article of this faith that he finds and can only find the meaning of his existence in serving the ends of the system. The system becomes God, and submission to the will of God becomes submission to the will of the system. It is not enough to yield outwardly to the system — even Ghandian non-violence is not acceptable — for the spirit of resistance and the devotion to a higher authority might then remain, and the individual would not be wholly submissive.

The same compulsion which demands total power over all men within the Soviet state without a single exception, demands total power over all Communist Parties and all states under Soviet domination. Thus Stalin has said that the theory and tactics of Leninism as expounded by the Bolshevik party are mandatory for the proletarian parties of all countries. A true internationalist is defined as one who unhesitatingly upholds the position of the Soviet Union and in the satellite states true patriotism is love of the Soviet Union. By the same token the 'peace policy' of the Soviet Union, described at a Party Congress as 'a more advantageous form of fighting capitalism', is a device to divide and immobilize the non-Communist world, and the peace the Soviet Union seeks is the peace of total conformity to Soviet policy.

The antipathy of slavery to freedom explains the iron curtain, the isolation, the autarchy of the society whose end is absolute power. The existence and persistence of the idea of freedom is a permanent and continuous threat to the foundation of the slave society; and it therefore regards as intolerable the long continued existence of freedom in the world. What is new, what makes the continuing crisis, is the polarization of power which now inescapably confronts the slave society with the free.

The assault on free institutions is world-wide now, and in the context of the present polarization of power a defeat of free institutions anywhere is a defeat everywhere. The shock we sustained in the destruction of Czechoslovakia was not in the measure of Czechoslovakia's material importance to us. In a material sense, her capabilities were already at Soviet disposal. But when the integrity of Czechoslovak institutions was destroyed, it was in the intangible scale of values that we registered a loss more damaging than the material loss we had already suffered.

Thus unwillingly our free society finds itself mortally challenged by the Soviet system. No other value system is so wholly irreconcilable with ours, so implacable in its purpose to destroy ours, so capable of turning to its own uses the most dangerous and divisive trends in our own society, no other so skillfully and powerfully evokes the elements of irrationality in human nature everywhere, and no other has the support of a great and growing center of military power.

B. *Objectives:*

The objectives of a free society are determined by its fundamental values and by the necessity for maintaining the material environment in which they flourish. Logically and in fact, therefore, the Kremlin's challenge to the United States is directed not only to our values but to our physical capacity to protect their environment. It is a challenge which encompasses both peace and war and our objectives in peace and war must take account of it.

1. Thus we must make ourselves strong, both in the way in which we affirm our values in the conduct of our national life, and in the development of our military and economic strength.

2. We must lead in building a successfully functioning political and economic system in the free world. It is only by practical affirmation, abroad as well as at home, of our essential values, that we can preserve our own integrity, in which lies the real frustration of the Kremlin design.

3. But beyond thus affirming our values our policy and actions must be such as to foster a fundamental change in the nature of the Soviet system, a change toward which the frustration of the design is the first and perhaps the most important step. Clearly it will not only be less costly but more effective if this change occurs to a maximum extent as a result of internal forces in Soviet society.

In a shrinking world, which now faces the threat of atomic warfare, it is not an adequate objective merely to seek to check the Kremlin design, for the absence of order among nations is becoming less and less tolerable. This fact imposes on us, in our own interests, the responsibility of world leadership. It demands that we make the attempt, and accept the risks inherent in it, to bring about order and justice by means consistent with the principles of freedom and democracy. We should limit our requirement of the Soviet Union to its participation with other nations on the basis of equality and respect for the rights of others. Subject to this requirement, we must with our allies and the former subject peoples seek to create a world society based on the principle of consent. Its framework cannot be inflexible. It will consist of many national communities of great and varying abilities and resources, and hence of war potential. The seeds of conflicts will inevitably exist or will come into being. To acknowledge this is only to acknowledge the impossibility of a final solution. Not to acknowledge it can be fatally dangerous in a world in which there are no final solutions.

All these objectives of a free society are equally valid and necessary in peace and war. But every consideration of devotion to our fundamental values and to our national security demands that we seek to achieve them by the strategy of the cold war. It is only by developing the moral and material strength of the free world that the Soviet regime will become convinced of the falsity of its assumptions and that the pre-conditions for workable agreements can be created. By practically demonstrating the integrity and vitality of our system the free world widens the area of possible agreement and thus can hope gradually to bring about a Soviet acknowledgement of realities which in sum will eventually constitute a frustration of the Soviet design. Short of this, however, it might be possible to create a situation which will induce the Soviet Union to accommodate itself, with or without the conscious abandonment of its design, to coexistence on tolerable terms with the non-Soviet world. Such a development would be a triumph for the idea of freedom and democracy. It must be an immediate objective of United States policy.

There is no reason, in the event of war, for us to alter our over-all objectives. They do not include unconditional surrender, the subjugation of the Russian peoples or a Russia shorn of its economic potential. Such a course would irrevocably unite the Russian people behind the regime which enslaves them. Rather these objectives contemplate Soviet acceptance of the specific and limited conditions requisite to an international environment in which free institutions can flourish, and in which the Russian peoples will have a new chance to work out their own destiny. If we can make the Russian people our allies in the enterprise we will obviously have made our task easier and victory more certain.

The objectives outlined in NSC 20/4 (November 23, 1948) and quoted in Chapter X, are fully consistent with the objectives stated in this paper, and they remain valid. The growing intensity of the conflict which has been imposed upon us, however, requires the changes of emphasis and the additions that are apparent. Coupled with the probable fission bomb capability and possible thermonuclear bomb capability of the Soviet Union, the intensifying struggle requires us to face the fact that we can expect no lasting abatement of the crisis unless and until a change occurs in the nature of the Soviet system.

C. *Means:*

The free society is limited in its choice of means to achieve its ends.

Compulsion is the negation of freedom, except when it is used to enforce the rights common to all. The resort to force, internally or externally, is therefore a last resort for a free society. The act is permissible only when one individual or groups of individuals within it threaten the basic rights of other individuals or when another society seeks to impose its will upon it. The free society cherishes and protects as fundamental the rights of the minority against the will of a majority, because these rights are the inalienable rights of each and every individual.

The resort to force, to compulsion, to the imposition of its will is therefore a difficult and dangerous act for a free society, which is warranted only in the face of even greater dangers. The necessity of the act must be clear and compelling; the act must commend itself to the overwhelming majority as an inescapable exception to the basic idea of freedom; or the regenerative capacity of free men after the act has been performed will be endangered.

The Kremlin is able to select whatever means are expedient in seeking to carry out its fundamental design. Thus it can make the best of several possible worlds, conducting the struggle on those levels where it considers it profitable and enjoying the benefits of a pseudo-peace on those levels where it is not ready for a contest. At the ideological or psychological level, in the struggle for men's minds, the conflict is world-wide. At the political and economic level, within states and in the relations between states, the struggle for power is being intensified. And at the military level, the Kremlin has thus far been careful not to commit a technical breach of the peace, although using its vast forces to intimidate its neighbors, and to support an aggressive foreign policy, and not hesitating through its agents to resort to arms in favorable circumstances. The attempt to carry out its fundamental design is being pressed, therefore, with all means which are believed expedient in the present situation, and the Kremlin has inextricably engaged us in the conflict between its design and our purpose.

We have no such freedom of choice, and least of all in the use of force. Resort to war is not only a last resort for a free society, but it is also an act which cannot definitively end the fundamental conflict in the realm of ideas. The idea of slavery can only be overcome by the timely and persistent demonstration of the superiority of the idea of freedom. Military victory alone would only partially and perhaps only temporarily affect the fundamental conflict, for although the ability of the Kremlin to threaten our security might be for a time destroyed, the resurgence of totalitarian forces and the re-establishment of the Soviet system or its equivalent would not be long delayed unless great progress were made in the fundamental conflict.

Practical and ideological considerations therefore both impel us to the conclusion that we have no choice but to demonstrate the superiority of the idea of freedom by its constructive application, and to attempt to change the world situation by means short of war in such a way as to frustrate the Kremlin design and hasten the decay of the Soviet system.

For us the role of military power is to serve the national purpose by deterring an attack upon us while we seek by other means to create an environment in which our free society can flourish, and by fighting, if necessary, to defend the integrity and vitality of our free society and to defeat any aggressor. The Kremlin uses Soviet military power to back up and serve the Kremlin design. It does not hesitate to use military force aggressively if that course is expedient in the achievement of its design. The differences between our fundamental purpose and the Kremlin design, therefore, are reflected in our respective attitudes toward and use of military force.

Our free society, confronted by a threat to its basic values, naturally will take such action, including the use of military force, as may be required to protect those values. The integrity of our system will not be jeopardized by any measures, covert or overt, violent or non-violent, which serve the purposes of frustrating the Kremlin design, nor does the necessity for conducting ourselves so as to affirm our values in actions as well as words forbid such measures, provided only they are appropriately calculated to that end and are not so excessive or misdirected as to make us enemies of the people instead of the evil men who have enslaved them.

But if war comes, what is the role of force? Unless we so use it that the Russian people can perceive that our effort is directed against the regime and its power for aggression, and not against their own interests, we will unite the regime and the people in the kind of last ditch fight in which no underlying problems are solved, new ones are created, and where our basic principles are obscured and compromised. If we do not in the application of force demonstrate the nature of our objectives we will, in fact, have compromised from the outset our fundamental purpose. In the words of the Federalist (No.28) 'The means to be employed must be proportioned to the extent of the mischief.' The mischief may be a global war or it may be a Soviet campaign for limited objectives. In either case we should take no avoidable initiative which would cause it to become a war of annihilation, and if we have the forces to defeat a Soviet drive for limited objectives it may well be to our interest not to let it become a global war. Our aim in applying force must be to compel the acceptance of terms consistent with our objectives, and our capabilities for the application of force should, therefore, within the limits of what we can sustain over the long pull, be congruent to the range of tasks which we may encounter.

[...]

VI. U.S. Intentions and Capabilities — Actual and Potential

A. *Political and Psychological*

Our overall policy at the present time may be described as one designed to foster a world environment in which the American system can survive and flourish. It therefore rejects the concept of isolation and affirms the necessity of our positive participation in the world community.

This broad intention embraces two subsidiary policies. One is a policy which we would probably pursue even if there were no Soviet threat. It is a policy of attempting to develop a healthy international community. The other is the policy of 'containing' the Soviet system. These two policies are closely interrelated and interact on one another. Nevertheless, the distinction between them is basically valid and contributes to a clearer understanding of what we are tying to do.

The policy of striving to develop a healthy international community is the long-term constructive effort which we are engaged in. It was this policy which gave rise to our vigorous sponsorship of the United Nations. It is of course the principal reason for our long continuing endeavors to create and now develop the Inter-American system. It, as much as containment, underlay our efforts to rehabilitate Western Europe. Most of our international economic activities can likewise be explained in terms of this policy.

In a world of polarized power, the policies designed to develop a healthy international community are more than ever necessary to our own strength.

As for the policy of 'containment', it is one which seeks by all means short of war to (1) block further expansion of Soviet power, (2) expose the falsities of Soviet pretensions, (3) induce a retraction of the Kremlin's control and influence and (4) in general, so foster the seeds of destruction within the Soviet system that the Kremlin is brought at least to the point of modifying its behavior to conform to generally accepted international standards.

It was and continues to be cardinal in this policy that we possess superior overall power in ourselves or in dependable combination with other like-minded nations. One of the most important ingredients of power is military strength. In the concept of 'containment', the maintenance of a strong military posture is deemed to be essential for two reasons: (1) as an ultimate guarantee of our national security and (2) as an indispensable backdrop to the conduct of the policy of 'containment'. Without superior aggregate military strength, in being and readily mobilizable, a policy of 'containment' — which is in effect a policy of calculated and gradual coercion — is no more than a policy of bluff.

At the same time, it is essential to the successful conduct of a policy of 'containment' that we always leave open the possibility of negotiation with the U.S.S.R. A diplomatic freeze — and we are in one now — tends to defeat the very purposes of 'containment' because it raises tensions at the same time that it makes Soviet retractions and adjustments in the direction of moderated behavior more difficult. It also tends to inhibit our initiative and deprives us of opportunities for maintaining a moral ascendency in our struggle with the Soviet system.

In 'containment' it is desirable to exert pressure in a fashion which will avoid so far as possible directly challenging Soviet prestige, to keep open the possibility for the U.S.S.R. to retreat before pressure with a minimum loss of face and to secure political advantage from the failure of the Kremlin to yield or take advantage of the openings we leave it.

We have failed to implement adequately these two fundamental aspects of 'containment'. In the face of obviously mounting Soviet military strength ours has declined relatively. Partly as a byproduct of this, but also for other reasons, we now find ourselves at a diplomatic impasse with the Soviet Union, with the Kremlin growing bolder, with both of us holding on grimly to what we have and with ourselves facing difficult decisions.

[...]

IX. Possible Courses of Action

[...]

D. *The Remaining Course of Action — a Rapid Build-up of Political, Economic, and Military Strength in the Free World*

A more rapid build-up of political, economic, and military strength and thereby of confidence in the free world than is now contemplated is the only course which is consistent with progress toward achieving our fundamental purpose. The frustration of the Kremlin design requires the free world to develop a successfully functioning political and economic system and a vigorous political offensive against the Soviet Union. These, in turn, require an adequate military shield under which they can develop. It is necessary to have the military power to deter, if possible, Soviet expansion, and to defeat, if necessary, aggressive Soviet or Soviet-directed actions of a limited or total character. The potential strength of the free world is great; its ability to develop these military capabilities and its will to resist Soviet expansion will be determined by the wisdom and will with which it undertakes to meet its political and economic problems.

1. *Military aspects.* It has been indicated in Chapter VI that U.S. military capabilities are strategically more defensive in nature than offensive and are more potential than actual. It is evident, from an analysis of the past and of the trend of weapon development, that there is now and will be in the future no absolute defense. The history of war also indicates that a favorable decision can only be achieved through offensive action. Even a defensive strategy, if it is to be successful, calls not only for defensive forces to hold vital positions while mobilizing and preparing for the offensive, but also for offensive forces to attack the enemy and keep him off balance.

The two fundamental requirements which must be met by forces in being or readily available are support of foreign policy and protection against disaster. To meet the second requirement, the forces in being or readily available must be able, at a minimum, to perform certain basic tasks:

   a. To defend the Western Hemisphere and essential allied areas in order that their war-making capabilities can be developed;

   b. To provide and protect a mobilization base while the offensive forces required for victory are being built up;

   c. To conduct offensive operations to destroy vital elements of the Soviet war-making capacity, and to keep the enemy off balance until the full offensive strength of the United States and its allies can be brought to bear;

   d. To defend and maintain the lines of communication and base areas necessary to the execution of the above tasks; and

   e. To provide such aid to allies as is essential to the execution of their role in the above tasks.

In the broadest terms, the ability to perform these tasks requires a build-up of military strength by the United States and its allies to a point at which the combined strength will be superior for at least these tasks, both initially and throughout a war, to the forces that can be brought to bear by the Soviet Union and its satellites. In specific terms, it is not essential to match item for item with the Soviet Union, but to provide an adequate defense against air attack on the United States and Canada and an adequate defense against air and surface attack on the United Kingdom and Western Europe, Alaska, the Western Pacific, Africa, and the Near and Middle East, and on the long lines of communication to these areas. Furthermore, it is mandatory that in building up our strength, we enlarge upon our technical superiority by an accelerated exploitation of the scientific potential of the United States and our allies.

Forces of this size and character are necessary not only for protection against disaster but also to support our foreign policy. In fact, it can be argued that larger forces in being and readily available are necessary to inhibit a would-be aggressor than to provide the nucleus of strength and the mobilization base on which the tremendous forces required for victory can be built. For example, in both World Wars I and II the ultimate victors had the strength, in the end, to win though they had not had the strength in being or readily available to prevent the outbreak of war. In part, at least, this was because they had not had the military strength on which to base a strong foreign policy. At any rate, it is clear that a substantial and rapid building up of strength in the free world is necessary to support a firm policy intended to check and to roll back the Kremlin's drive for world domination.

Moreover, the United States and the other free countries do not now have the forces in being and readily available to defeat local Soviet moves with local action, but must accept reverses or make these local moves the occasion for war — for which we are not prepared. This situation makes for great uneasiness among our allies, particularly in Western Europe, for whom total war means, initially, Soviet occupation. Thus, unless our combined strength is rapidly increased, our allies will tend to become increasingly reluctant to support a firm foreign policy on our part and increasingly anxious to seek other solutions, even though they are aware that appeasement means defeat. An important advantage in adopting the fourth course of action lies in its psychological impact — the revival of confidence and hope in the future. It is recognized, of course, that any announcement of the recommended course of action could be exploited by the Soviet Union in its peace campaign and would have adverse psychological effects in certain parts of the free world until the necessary increase in strength had been achieved. Therefore, in any announcement of policy and in the character of the measures adopted, emphasis should be given to the essentially defensive character and care should be taken to minimize, so far as possible, unfavorable domestic and foreign reactions.

2.   *Political and economic aspects.* The immediate objectives — to the achievement of which such a build-up of strength is a necessary though not a sufficient condition — are a renewed initiative in the cold war and a situation to which the Kremlin would find it expedient to accommodate itself, first by relaxing tensions and pressures and then by gradual with-

drawal. The United States cannot alone provide the resources required for such a build-up of strength. The other free countries must carry their part of the burden, but their ability and determination to do it will depend on the action the United States takes to develop its own strength and on the adequacy of its foreign political and economic policies. Improvement in political and economic conditions in the free world, as has been emphasized above, is necessary as a basis for building up the will and the means to resist and for dynamically affirming the integrity and vitality of our free and democratic way of life on which our ultimate victory depends.

At the same time, we should take dynamic steps to reduce the power and influence of the Kremlin inside the Soviet Union and other areas under its control. The objective would be the establishment of friendly regimes not under Kremlin domination. Such action is essential to engage the Kremlin's attention, keep it off balance and force an increased expenditure of Soviet resources in counteractions. In other words, it would be the current Soviet cold war technique used against the Soviet Union.

A program for rapidly building up strength and improving political and economic conditions will place heavy demands on our courage and intelligence; it will be costly; it will be dangerous. But half-measures will be more costly and more dangerous, for they will be inadequate to prevent and may actually invite war. Budgetary considerations will need to be subordinated to the stark fact that our very independence as a nation may be at stake.

A comprehensive and decisive program to win the peace and frustrate the Kremlin design should be so designed that it can be sustained for as long as necessary to achieve our national objectives. It would probably involve:

(1) The development of an adequate political and economic framework for the achievement of our long-range objectives.

(2) A substantial increase in expenditures for military purposes adequate to meet the requirements for the tasks listed in Section D-1.

(3) A substantial increase in military assistance programs, designed to foster cooperative efforts, which will adequately and efficiently meet the requirements of our allies for the tasks referred to in Section D-1-*e*.

(4) Some increase in economic assistance programs and recognition of the need to continue these programs until their purposes have been accomplished.

(5) A concerted attack on the problem of the United States balance of payments, along the lines already approved by the President.

(6) Development of programs designed to build and maintain confidence among other peoples in our strength and resolution, and to wage overt psychological warfare calculated to encourage mass defections from Soviet allegiance and to frustrate the Kremlin design in other ways.

(7) Intensification of affirmative and timely measures and operations by covert means in the fields of economic warfare and political and psycho-

logical warfare with a view to fomenting and supporting unrest and revolt in selected strategic satellite countries.

(8) Development of internal security and civilian defense programs.

(9) Improvement and intensification of intelligence activities.

(10) Reduction of Federal expenditures for purposes other than defense and foreign assistance, if necessary by the deferment of certain desirable programs.

(11) Increased taxes.

Essential as prerequisites to the success of this program would be (*a*) consultations with Congressional leaders designed to make the program the object of non-partisan legislative support, and (*b*) a presentation to the public of a full explanation of the facts and implications of present international trends.

The program will be costly, but it is relevant to recall the disproportion between the potential capabilities of the Soviet and non-Soviet worlds (cf. Chapters V and VI). The Soviet Union is currently devoting about 40 percent of available resources (gross national product plus reparations, equal in 1949 to about $65 billion) to military expenditures (14 percent) and to investment (26 percent), much of which is in war-supporting industries. In an emergency the Soviet Union could increase the allocation of resources to these purposes to about 50 percent, or by one-fourth.

The United States is currently devoting about 22 percent of its gross national product ($255 billion in 1949) to military expenditures (6 percent), foreign assistance (2 percent), and investment (14 percent), a little of which is in war-supporting industries. (As was pointed out in Chapter V; the 'fighting value' obtained per dollar of expenditure by the Soviet Union considerably exceeds that obtained by the United States, primarily because of the extremely low military and civilian living standards in the Soviet Union.) In an emergency the United States could devote upward of 50 percent of its gross national product to these purposes (as it did during the last war), an increase of several times present expenditures for direct and indirect military purposes and foreign assistance.

From the point of view of the economy as a whole, the program might not result in a real decrease in the standard of living, for the economic effects of the program might be to increase the gross national product by more than the amount being absorbed for additional military and foreign assistance purposes. One of the most significant lessons of our World War II experience was that the American economy, when it operates at a level approaching full efficiency, can provide enormous resources for purposes other than civilian consumption while simultaneously providing a high standard of living. After allowing for price changes, personal consumption expenditures rose by about one-fifth between 1939 and 1944, even though the economy had in the meantime increased the amount of resources going into Government use by $60–$65 billion (in 1939 prices).

This comparison between the potentials of the Soviet Union and the United States also holds true for the Soviet world and the free world and is of fundamental importance in considering the courses of action open to the United States.

The comparison gives renewed emphasis to the fact that the problems faced by the free countries in their efforts to build a successfully functioning system lie not so much in the field of economics as in the field of politics. The building of such a system may require more rapid progress toward the closer association of the free countries in harmony with the concept of the United Nations. It is clear that our long-range objectives require a strengthened United Nations, or a successor organization, to which the world can look for the maintenance of peace and order in a system based on freedom and justice. It also seems clear that a unifying ideal of this kind might awaken and arouse the latent spiritual energies of free men everywhere and obtain their enthusiastic support for a positive program for peace going far beyond the frustration of the Kremlin design and opening vistas to the future that would outweigh short-run sacrifices.

The threat to the free world involved in the development of the Soviet Union's atomic and other capabilities will rise steadily and rather rapidly. For the time being, the United States possesses a marked atomic superiority over the Soviet Union which, together with the potential capabilities of the United States and other free countries in other forces and weapons, inhibits aggressive Soviet action. This provides an opportunity for the United States, in cooperation with other free countries, to launch a build-up of strength which will support a firm policy directed to the frustration of the Kremlin design. The immediate goal of our efforts to build a successfully functioning political and economic system in the free world backed by adequate military strength is to postpone and avert the disastrous situation which, in light of the Soviet Union's probable fission bomb capability and possible thermo-nuclear bomb capability, might arise in 1954 on a continuation of our present programs. By acting promptly and vigorously in such a way that this date is, so to speak, pushed into the future, we would permit time for the process of accommodation, withdrawal and frustration to produce the necessary changes in the Soviet system. Time is short, however, and the risks of war attendant upon a decision to build up strength will steadily increase the longer we defer it.

CONCLUSIONS AND RECOMMENDATIONS

Conclusions

The foregoing analysis indicates that the probable fission bomb capability and possible thermonuclear bomb capability of the Soviet Union have greatly intensified the Soviet threat to the security of the United States. This threat is of the same character as that described in NSC 20/4 (approved by the President on November 24, 1948) but is more immediate than had previously been estimated. In particular, the United States now faces the contingency that within the next four or five years the Soviet Union will possess the military capability of delivering a surprise atomic attack of such weight that the United States must have substantially increased general air, ground, and sea strength, atomic capabilities, and air and civilian defenses to deter war and to provide reasonable assurance in the event of war, that it could survive the initial blow and go on to the eventual attainment of its objectives. In return, this contingency requires the intensification of our efforts in the fields of intelligence and research and development.

Allowing for the immediacy of the danger, the following statement of Soviet threats, contained in NSC 20/4, remains valid:

14. The gravest threat to the security of the United States within the foreseeable future stems from the hostile designs and formidable power of the U.S.S.R., and from the nature of the Soviet system.

15. The political, economic, and psychological warfare which the U.S.S.R. is now waging has dangerous potentialities for weakening the relative world position of the United States and disrupting its traditional institutions by means short of war, unless sufficient resistance is encountered in the policies of this and other non-communist countries.

16. The risk of war with the U.S.S.R. is sufficient to warrant, in common prudence, timely and adequate preparation by the United States.

a. Even though present estimates indicate that the Soviet leaders probably do not intend deliberate armed action involving the United States at this time, the possibility of such deliberate resort to war cannot be ruled out.

b. Now and for the foreseeable future there is a continuing danger that war will arise either through Soviet miscalculation of the determination of the United States to use all the means at its command to safeguard its security, through Soviet misinterpretation of our intentions, or through U.S. miscalculation of Soviet reactions to measures which we might take.

17. Soviet domination of the potential power of Eurasia, whether achieved by armed aggression or by political and subversive means, would be strategically and politically unacceptable to the United States.

18. The capability of the United States either in peace or in the event of war to cope with threats to its security or to gain its objectives would be severely weakened by internal development, important among which are:

a. Serious espionage, subversion and sabotage, particularly by concerted and well-directed communist activity.

b. Prolonged or exaggerated economic instability.

c.   Internal political and social disunity.

d.   Inadequate or excessive armament or foreign aid expenditures.

e.   An excessive or wasteful usage of our resources in time of peace.

f.   Lessening of U.S. prestige and influence through vacillation or appeasement or lack of skill and imagination in the conduct of its foreign policy or by shirking world responsibilities.

g.   Development of a false sense of security through a deceptive change in Soviet tactics.

[…]

In the light of present and prospective Soviet atomic capabilities, the action which can be taken under present programs and plans, however, becomes dangerously inadequate, in both timing and scope, to accomplish the rapid progress toward the attainment of the United States political, economic, and military objectives which is now imperative.

A continuation of present trends would result in a serious decline in the strength of the free world relative to the Soviet Union and its satellites. This unfavorable trend arises from the inadequacy of current programs and plans rather than from any error in our objectives and aims. These trends lead in the direction of isolation, not by deliberate decision but by lack of the necessary basis for a vigorous initiative in the conflict with the Soviet Union.

Our position as the center of power in the free world places a heavy responsibility upon the United States for leadership. We must organize and enlist the energies and resources of the free world in a positive program for peace which will frustrate the Kremlin design for world domination by creating a situation in the free world to which the Kremlin will be compelled to adjust. Without such a cooperative effort, led by the United States, we will have to make gradual withdrawals under pressure until we discover one day that we have sacrificed positions of vital interest.

It is imperative that this trend be reversed by a much more rapid and concerted build-up of the actual strength of both the United States and the other nations of the free world. The analysis shows that this will be costly and will involve significant domestic financial and economic adjustments.

The execution of such a build-up, however, requires that the United States have an affirmative program beyond the solely defensive one of countering the threat posed by the Soviet Union. This program must light the path to peace and order among nations in a system based on freedom and justice, as contemplated in the Charter of the United Nations. Further, it must envisage the political and economic measures with which and the military shield behind which the free world can work to frustrate the Kremlin design by the strategy of the cold war; for every consideration of devotion to our fundamental values and to our national security demands that we achieve our objectives by the strategy of the cold war; building up our military strength in order that it may not have to be used. The only sure victory lies in the frustration of the Kremlin design by the steady development of the moral and material strength of the free world and its projection into the Soviet world in such a way as to bring about an internal change in the Soviet system. Such a positive program — harmonious with our fundamental national purpose and our objectives — is necessary if we are to regain and retain the initiative and to win and hold the necessary popular support and cooperation in the United States and the rest of the free world.

This program should include a plan for negotiation with the Soviet Union, developed and agreed with our allies and which is consonant with our objectives. The United States and its allies, particularly the United Kingdom and France, should always be ready to negotiate with the Soviet Union on terms consistent with our objectives. The present world situation, however, is one which militates against successful negotiations with the Kremlin — for the terms of agreements on important pending issues would reflect present realities and would therefore be unacceptable, if not disastrous, to the United States and the rest of the free world. After a decision and a start on building up the strength of the free world has been made, it might then be desirable for the United States to take an initiative in seeking negotiations in the hope that it might facilitate the process of accommodation by the Kremlin to the new situation. Failing that, the unwillingness of the Kremlin to accept equitable terms or its bad faith in observing them would assist in consolidating popular opinion in the free world in support of the measures necessary to sustain the build-up.

[...]

The whole success of the proposed program hangs ultimately on recognition by this Government, the American people, and all free peoples, that the cold war is in fact a real war in which the survival of the free world is at stake. Essential prerequisites to success are consultations with Congressional leaders designed to make the program the object of non-partisan legislative support, and a presentation to the public of a full explanation of the facts and implications of the present international situation. The prosecution of the program will require of us all the ingenuity, sacrifice, and unity demanded by the vital importance of the issue and the tenacity to persevere until our national objectives have been attained.

[...]

Source: *Naval War College Review* (1975) Newport RI, Naval War College Press, vol.XXVII, no.6/sequence no.255, pp.51–108.

4.4.5   PRESIDENT EISENHOWER'S FAREWELL ADDRESS (1961)

The Second World War and Cold War which followed it had an immense impact on American society, the period saw a rapid growth in the military capability of the United States and the arms industry which supplied it. Over the same period the technological revolution was transforming every facet of American life. Such developments created new sources of power and influence, and it is this that concerned President Eisenhower on leaving office. In his farewell address to the American people on 17 January 1961 he warned of the potential threat to American values and best interests of forces such as the 'military-industrial complex'.

My fellow Americans:

[...]

Until the latest of our world conflicts, the United States had no armaments industry. American makers of plowshares could, with time and as required, make swords as well. But now we can no longer risk emergency improvisation of national defense; we have been compelled to create a permanent armaments industry of vast proportions. Added to this, three and a half million men and women are directly engaged in the defense establishment. We annually spend on military security more than the net income of all United States corporations.

This conjunction of an immense military establishment and a large arms industry is new in the American experience. The total influence — economic, political, even spiritual — is felt in every city, every statehouse, every office of the federal government. We recognize the imperative need for this development. Yet we must not fail to comprehend its grave implications. Our toil, resources, and livelihood are all involved; so is the very structure of our society.

In the councils of government, we must guard against the acquisition of unwarranted influence, whether sought or unsought, by the military-industrial complex. The potential for the disastrous rise of misplaced power exists and will persist.

We must never let the weight of this combination endanger our liberties or democratic processes. We should take nothing for granted. Only an alert and knowledgeable citizenry can compel the proper meshing of the huge industrial and military machinery of defense with our peaceful methods and goals, so that security and liberty may prosper together.

Akin to, and largely responsible for the sweeping changes in our industrial-military posture, has been the technological revolution during recent decades.

In this revolution, research has become central; it also becomes more formalized, complex, and costly. A steadily increasing share is conducted for, by, or at the direction of, the federal government.

Today, the solitary inventor, tinkering in his shop, has been overshadowed by task forces of scientists in laboratories and testing fields. In the same fashion, the free university, historically the fountainhead of free ideas and scientific discovery, has experienced a revolution in the conduct of research. Partly because of the huge costs involved, a government contract becomes virtually a substitute for intellectual curiosity. For every old blackboard there are now hundreds of new electronic computers.

The prospect of domination of the nation's scholars by federal employment, project allocations, and the power of money is ever present — and is gravely to be regarded.

Yet, in holding scientific research and discovery in respect, as we should, we must also be alert to the equal and opposite danger that public policy could itself become the captive of a scientific-technological elite.

It is the task of statesmanship to mold, to balance, and to integrate these and other forces, new and old, within the principles of our democratic system — ever aiming toward the supreme goals of our free society.

Another factor in maintaining balance involves the element of time. As we peer into society's future, we — you and I, and our government — must avoid the impulse to live only for today, plundering, for our own ease and convenience, the precious resources of tomorrow. We cannot mortgage the material assets of our grandchildren without risking the loss also of their political and spiritual heritage. We want democracy to survive for all generations to come, not to become the insolvent phantom of tomorrow.

Down the long lane of the history yet to be written America knows that this world of ours, ever growing smaller, must avoid becoming a community of dreadful fear and hate, and be, instead, a proud confederation of mutual trust and respect.

Such a confederation must be one of equals. The weakest must come to the conference table with the same confidence as do we, protected as we are by our moral, economic, and military strength. That table, though scarred by many past frustrations, cannot be abandoned for the certain agony of the battlefield.

Disarmament, with mutual honor and confidence, is a continuing imperative. Together we must learn how to compose differences, not with arms, but with intellect and decent purpose. Because this need is so sharp and apparent I confess that I lay down my official responsibilities in this field with a definite sense of disappointment. As one who has witnessed the horror and the lingering sadness of war — as one who knows that another war could utterly destroy this civilization which has been so slowly and painfully built over thousands of years — I wish I could say tonight that a lasting peace is in sight.

Happily, I can say that war has been avoided. Steady progress toward our ultimate goal has been made. But, so much remains to be done. […]

Source: Encyclopaedia Britannica (1976) *The Annals of America, The Bicentennial Edition 1776–1976, Vol.18*, Chicago, Encyclopaedia Britannica, Inc., pp.1–5.

4.4.6 THE CUBAN MISSILE CRISIS: PRESIDENT KENNEDY'S SPEECH (1962)

The Cold War reached a crisis point over Cuba. After the 1959 revolution, which ousted the corrupt regime of Fulgencio Batista and brought a new government under Fidel Castro to power, relations between the United States and Castro turned sour as communist influence on his government eventually led to a one-party state. Under the Eisenhower Administration the Central Intelligence Agency had begun training a group of exiles for invasion and counter revolution. This operation was allowed to proceed under President Kennedy and ended in the disastrous Bay of Pigs invasion in 1961. Thereafter Soviet aid to Cuba increased, and included technical support for the construction of missile emplacements. These were spotted by US reconnaissance planes and Kennedy made the following televised speech on 22 October 1962. The crisis ended after seven tense days when the Soviet Union agreed to remove the missiles if the United States lifted the blockade ('quarantine') and promised not to invade the island.

President Kennedy addressing the American people on television and radio from the White House, 22 October 1962

Good evening, my fellow citizens. The Government, as promised, has maintained the closest surveillance of the Soviet military buildup on the island of Cuba. Within the past week unmistakable evidence has established the fact that a series of offensive missile sites is now in preparation on that imprisoned island. The purpose of these bases can be none other than to provide a nuclear strike capability against the Western Hemisphere.

Upon receiving the first preliminary hard information of this nature last Tuesday morning at 9:00 a.m., I directed that our surveillance be stepped up. And having now confirmed and completed our evaluation of the evidence and our decision on a course of action, this Government feels obliged to report this new crisis to you in fullest detail.

The characteristics of these new missile sites indicate two distinct types of installations. Several of them include medium-range ballistic missiles capable of carrying a nuclear warhead for a distance of more than 1,000 nautical miles. Each of these missiles, in short, is capable of striking Washington, DC, the Panama Canal, Cape Canaveral, Mexico City, or any other city in the southeastern part of the United States, in Central America, or in the Caribbean area.

Additional sites not yet completed appear to be designed for intermediate-range ballistic missiles capable of traveling more than twice as far — and thus capable of striking most of the major cities in the Western Hemisphere, ranging as far north as Hudson Bay, Canada, and as far south as Lima, Peru. In addition, jet bombers, capable of carrying nuclear weapons, are now being uncrated and assembled in Cuba, while the necessary air bases are being prepared.

This urgent transformation of Cuba into an important strategic base — by the presence of these large, long-range, and clearly offensive weapons of sudden mass destruction — constitutes an explicit threat to the peace and security of all the Americas, in flagrant and deliberate defiance of the Rio Pact of 1947, the traditions of this nation and hemisphere, the Joint Resolution of the 87th Congress, the Charter of the United Nations, and my own public warnings to the Soviets on September 4 and 13.

This action also contradicts the repeated assurances of Soviet spokesmen, both publicly and privately delivered, that the arms buildup in Cuba would retain its original defensive character and that the Soviet Union had no need or desire to station strategic missiles on the territory of any other nation.

The size of this undertaking makes clear that it has been planned for some months. Yet only last month, after I had made clear the distinction between any introduction of ground-to-ground missiles and the existence of defensive antiaircraft missiles, the Soviet Government publicly stated on September 11 that, and I quote, 'The armaments and military equipment sent to Cuba are designed exclusively for defensive purposes', and, and I quote the Soviet Government, 'There is no need for the Soviet Government to shift its weapons for a retaliatory blow to any other country, for instance Cuba', and that, and I quote the Government, 'The Soviet Union has so powerful rockets to carry these nuclear warheads that there is no need to search for sites for them beyond the boundaries of the Soviet Union'. That statement was false.

Only last Thursday, as evidence of this rapid offensive buildup was already in my hand, Soviet Foreign Minister Gromyko told me in my office that he was instructed to make it clear once again, as he said his Government had already done, that Soviet assistance to Cuba, and I quote, 'pursued solely the purpose of contributing to the defense capabilities of Cuba', that, and I quote him, 'training by Soviet specialists of Cuban nationals in handling defensive armaments was by no means offensive', and that 'if it were otherwise', Mr Gromyko went on, 'the Soviet Government would never become involved in rendering such assistance'. That statement also was false.

Neither the United States of America nor the world community of nations can tolerate deliberate deception and offensive threats on the part of any nation, large or small. We no longer live in a world where only the actual firing of weapons represents a sufficient challenge to a nation's security to constitute maximum peril. Nuclear weapons are so destructive and ballistic missiles are so swift that any substantially increased possibility of their use or any sudden change in their deployment may well be regarded as a definite threat to peace.

For many years both the Soviet Union and the United States, recognizing this fact, have deployed strategic nuclear weapons with great care, never upsetting the precarious *status quo* which insured that these weapons would not be used in the absence of some vital challenge. Our own strategic missiles have never been transferred to the territory of any other nation under a cloak of secrecy and deception; and our history, unlike that of the Soviets since the end of World War II, demonstrates that we have no desire to dominate or conquer any other nation or impose our system upon its people. Nevertheless, American citizens have become adjusted to living daily on the bull's eye of Soviet missiles located inside the USSR or in submarines.

In that sense missiles in Cuba add to an already clear and present danger — although it should be noted the nations of Latin America have never previously been subjected to a potential nuclear threat.

But this secret, swift, and extraordinary buildup of Communist missiles — in an area well known to have a special and historical relationship to the United States and the nations of the Western Hemisphere, in violation of Soviet assurances, and in defiance of American and hemispheric policy — this sudden, clandestine decision to station strategic weapons for the first time outside of Soviet soil — is a deliberately provocative and unjustified change in the *status quo* which cannot be accepted by this country if our courage and our commitments are ever to be trusted again by either friend or foe.

The 1930s taught us a clear lesson: Aggressive conduct, if allowed to grow unchecked and unchallenged, ultimately leads to war. This nation is opposed to war. We are also true to our word. Our unswerving objective, therefore, must be to prevent the use of these missiles against this or any other country and to secure their withdrawal or elimination from the Western Hemisphere.

Our policy has been one of patience and restraint, as befits a peaceful and powerful nation, which leads a worldwide alliance. We have been determined not to be diverted from our central concerns by mere irritants and fanatics. But now further action is required — and it is underway; and these actions may only be the beginning. We will not prematurely or unnecessarily risk the costs of worldwide nuclear war in which even the fruits of victory would be ashes in our mouth — but neither will we shrink from that risk at any time it must be faced.

Acting, therefore, in the defense of our own security and of the entire Western Hemisphere, and under the authority entrusted to me by the Constitution as endorsed by the resolution of the Congress, I have directed that the following *initial* steps be taken immediately:

First: To halt this offensive buildup, a strict quarantine on all offensive military equipment under shipment to Cuba is being initiated. All ships of any kind bound for Cuba from whatever nation or port will, if found to contain cargoes of offensive weapons, be turned back. This quarantine will be extended, if needed, to other types of cargo and carriers. We are not at this time, however, denying the necessities of life as the Soviets attempted to do in their Berlin blockade of 1948.

Second: I have directed the continued and increased close surveillance of Cuba and its military buildup. The Foreign Ministers of the OAS [Organization of American States] in their communique of October 3 rejected secrecy on such matters in this hemisphere. Should these offensive military preparations continue, thus increasing the threat to the hemisphere, further action will be justified. I have directed the Armed Forces to prepare for any eventualities; and I trust that, in the interest of both the Cuban people and the Soviet technicians at the sites, the hazards to all concerned of continuing this threat will be recognized.

Third: It shall be the policy of this nation to regard any nuclear missile launched from Cuba against any nation in the Western Hemisphere as an attack by the Soviet Union on the United States, requiring a full retaliatory response upon the Soviet Union.

Fourth: As a necessary military precaution I have reinforced our base at Guantanamo, evacuated today the dependents of our personnel there, and ordered additional military units to be on a standby alert basis.

Fifth: We are calling tonight for an immediate meeting of the Organ of Consultation, under the Organization of American States, to consider this threat to hemispheric security and to invoke articles 6 and 8 of the Rio Treaty in support of all necessary action. The United Nations Charter allows for regional security arrangements — and the nations of this hemisphere decided long ago against the military presence of outside powers. Our other allies around the world have also been alerted.

Sixth: Under the Charter of the United Nations, we are asking tonight that an emergency meeting of the Security Council be convoked without delay to take action against this latest Soviet threat to world peace. Our resolution will call for the prompt dismantling and withdrawal of all offensive weapons in Cuba, under the supervision of UN observers, before the quarantine can be lifted.

Seventh and finally: I call upon Chairman Khrushchev to halt and eliminate this clandestine, reckless, and provocative threat to world peace and to stable relations between our two nations. I call upon him further to abandon this course of world domination and to join in an historic effort to end the perilous arms race and transform the history of man. He has an opportunity now to move the world back from the abyss of destruction — by returning to his Government's own words that it had no need to station missiles outside its own territory, and withdrawing these weapons from Cuba — by refraining from any action which will widen or deepen the present crisis — and then by participating in a search for peaceful and permanent solutions.

This nation is prepared to present its case against the Soviet threat to peace, and our own proposals for a peaceful world, at any time and in any forum — in the OAS, in the United Nations, or in any other meeting that could be useful — without limiting our freedom of action.

We have in the past made strenuous efforts to limit the spread of nuclear weapons. We have proposed the elimination of all arms and military bases in a fair and effective disarmament treaty. We are prepared to discuss new proposals for the removal of tensions on both sides — including the possibilities of a genuinely independent Cuba, free to determine its own destiny. We have no wish to war with the Soviet Union, for we are a peaceful people who desire to live in peace with all other peoples.

But it is difficult to settle or even discuss these problems in an atmosphere of intimidation. That is why this latest Soviet threat — or any other threat which is made either independently or in response to our actions this week — must and will be met with determination. Any hostile move anywhere in the world against the safety and freedom of peoples to whom we are committed — including in particular the brave people of West Berlin — will be met by whatever action is needed.

Finally, I want to say a few words to the captive people of Cuba, to whom this speech is being directly carried by special radio facilities. I speak to you as a friend, as one who knows of your deep attachment to your fatherland, as one who shares your aspirations for liberty and justice for all. And I have watched and the American people have watched with deep sorrow how your nationalist revolution was betrayed and how your fatherland fell under foreign domination. Now your leaders are no longer Cuban leaders inspired by Cuban ideals. They are puppets and agents of an international conspiracy which has turned Cuba against your friends and neighbors in the Americas — and turned it into the first Latin American country to become a target for nuclear war, the first Latin American country to have these weapons on its soil.

These new weapons are not in your interest. They contribute nothing to your peace and well-being. They can only undermine it. But this country has no wish to cause you to suffer or to impose any system upon you. We know that your lives and land are being used as pawns by those who deny you freedom.

Many times in the past the Cuban people have risen to throw out tyrants who destroyed their liberty. And I have no doubt that most Cubans today look forward to the time when they will be truly free — free from foreign domination, free to choose their own leaders, free to select their own system, free to own their own land, free to speak and write and worship without fear or degradation. And then shall Cuba be welcomed back to the society of free nations and to the associations of this hemisphere.

My fellow citizens, let no one doubt that this is a difficult and dangerous effort on which we have set out. No one can foresee precisely what course it will take or what costs or casualties will be incurred. Many months of sacrifice and self-discipline lie ahead — months in which both our patience and our will will be tested, months in which many threats and denunciations will keep us aware of our dangers. But the greatest danger of all would be to do nothing.

The path we have chosen for the present is full of hazards, as all paths are; but it is the one most consistent with our character and courage as a nation and our commitments around the world. The cost of freedom is always high — but Americans have always paid it. And one path we shall never choose, and that is the path of surrender or submission.

Our goal is not the victory of might but the vindication of right — not peace at the expense of freedom, but both peace *and* freedom, here in this hemisphere and, we hope, around the world. God willing, that goal will be achieved.

Source: Ferrell, R.H. (ed.) (1975) *America in a Divided World 1945–1972*, Columbia, University of South Carolina Press.

4.4.7 PRESIDENT KENNEDY'S 'STRATEGY OF PEACE' SPEECH (1963)

In June of 1963 President Kennedy gave a speech at the American University outlining his views on the relationship with the Soviet Union, and his hopes and fears for the future. While more conciliatory in tone than the Cuban missile crisis speech, and acutely aware of the dangers and costs of the Cold War, the mistrust of the Soviet leadership is still very evident in the speech. Progress was made in some areas, the direct 'hot line' between Moscow and Washington was established and a partial nuclear test ban treaty was signed in August 1963.

[…] I have, therefore, chosen this time and place to discuss a topic on which ignorance too often abounds and the truth is too rarely perceived — and that is the most important topic on earth: peace.

What kind of peace do I mean and what kind of peace do we seek? Not a Pax Americana enforced on the world by American weapons of war. Not the peace of the grave or the security of the slave. I am talking about the genuine peace — the kind of peace that makes life on earth worth living — and the kind that enables men and nations to grow and to hope and build a better life for their children — not merely peace for Americans but peace for all men and women — not merely peace in our time but peace in all time.

I speak of peace because of the new face of war. Total war makes no sense in an age where great powers can maintain large and relatively invulnerable nuclear forces and refuse to surrender without resort to those forces. It makes no sense in an age when a single nuclear weapon contains almost ten times the explosive force delivered by all the Allied air forces in the second world war. It makes no sense in an age when the deadly poisons produced by a nuclear exchange would be carried by wind and water and soil and seed to the far corners of the globe and to generations yet unborn.

Today the expenditure of billions of dollars every year on weapons acquired for the purpose of making sure we never need them is essential to the keeping of peace. But surely the acquisition of such idle stockpiles — which can only destroy and can never create — is not the only, much less the most efficient, means of assuring peace.

I speak of peace, therefore, as the necessary rational end of rational men. I realize the pursuit of peace is not as dramatic as the pursuit of war — and frequently the words of the pursuer fall on deaf ears. But we have no more urgent task.

Some say that it is useless to speak of peace or world law or world disarmament — and that it will be useless until the leaders of the Soviet Union adopt a more enlightened attitude. I hope they do. I believe we can help them do it.

But I also believe that we must re-examine our own attitudes — as individuals and as a nation — for our attitude is as essential as theirs. And every graduate of this school, every thoughtful citizen who despairs of war and wishes to bring peace, should begin by looking inward — by examining his own attitude towards the course of the cold war and toward freedom and peace here at home.

First: Examine our attitude towards peace itself. Too many of us think it is impossible. Too many think it is unreal. But that is a dangerous, defeatist belief. It leads to the conclusion that war is inevitable — that mankind is doomed — that we are gripped by forces we cannot control.

We need not accept that view. Our problems are man-made. Therefore, they can be solved by man. And man can be as big as he wants. No problem of human destiny is beyond human beings. Man's reason and spirit have often solved the seemingly unsolvable — and we believe they can do it again.

I am not referring to the absolute infinite concepts of universal peace and goodwill of which some fantasies and fanatics dream. I do not deny the value of hopes and dreams but we merely invite discouragement and incredulity by making that our only and immediate goal.

Let us focus instead on a more practical, more attainable peace — based not on a sudden revolution in human nature but on a gradual evolution in human institutions — on a series of concrete actions and effective agreement which are in the interests of all concerned.

There is no single, simple key to this peace — no grand or magic formula to be adopted by one or two powers. Genuine peace must be the product of many nations, the sum of many acts. It must be dynamic, not static, changing to meet the challenge of each new generation. For peace is a process — a way of solving problems.

With such a peace, there will still be quarrels and conflicting interests, as there are within families and nations. World peace, like community peace, does not require that each man love his neighbor — it requires only that they live together with mutual tolerance, submitting their disputes to a just and peaceful settlement. And history teaches us that enmities between nations, as between individuals, do not last forever. However fixed our likes and dislikes may seem, the tide of time and events will often bring surprising changes in the relations between nations and neighbors.

So let us persevere. Peace need not be impracticable — and war need not be inevitable. By defining our goal more clearly — by making it seem more manageable and less remote — we can help all people to see it, to draw hope from it, and to move irresistibly towards it.

And second: Let us re-examine our attitude towards the Soviet Union. It is discouraging to think that their leaders may actually believe what their propagandists write.

It is discouraging to read a recent authoritative Soviet text on military strategy and find, on page after page, wholly baseless and incredible claims — such as the allegation that 'American imperialist circles are preparing to unleash different types of war ... that there is a very real threat of a preventative war being unleashed by American imperialists against the Soviet Union ... (and that) the political aims', and I quote, 'of the American imperialists are to enslave economically and politically the European and other capitalist countries ... (and) to achieve world domination ... by means of aggressive war.'

Truly, as it was written long ago: 'The wicked flee when no man pursueth.' Yet it is sad to read these Soviet statements — to realize the extent of the gulf between us. But it is also a warning — a warning to the American people not to fall into the same trap as the Soviets, not to see only a distorted and desperate view of the other side, not to see conflict as inevitable, accommodation as impossible and communication as nothing more than an exchange of threats.

No government or social system is so evil that its people must be considered as lacking in virtue. As Americans, we find Communism profoundly repugnant as a negation of personal freedom and dignity. But we can still hail the Russian people for their many achievements — in science and space, in economic and industrial growth, in culture, in acts of courage.

Among the many traits the peoples of our two countries have in common, none is stronger than our mutual abhorrence of war. Almost unique among the major world powers, we have never been at war with each other. And no nation in the history of battle ever suffered more than the Soviet Union in the second world war. At least 20,000,000 lost their lives. Countless millions of homes and families were burned or sacked. A third of the nation's territory, including two-thirds of its industrial base, was turned into a wasteland — a loss equivalent to the destruction of this country east of Chicago.

Today, should total war every break out again — no matter how — our two countries will be the primary targets. It is an ironic but accurate fact that the two strongest powers are the two in the most danger of devastation. All we have built, all we have worked for, would be destroyed in the first 24 hours. And even in the cold war — which brings burdens and dangers to so many countries, including this nation's closest allies — our two countries bear the heaviest burdens. For we are both devoting massive sums of money to weapons that could be better devoted to combat ignorance, poverty and disease.

We are both caught up in a vicious and dangerous cycle with suspicion on one side breeding suspicion on the other, and new weapons begetting counter-weapons.

In short, both the United States and its allies, and the Soviet Union and its allies, have a mutually deep interest in a just and genuine peace and in halting the arms race. Agreements to this end are in the interests of the Soviet Union as well as ours — and even the most hostile nations can be relied upon to accept and keep those treaty obligations and only those treaty obligations, which are in their own interest.

So, let us not be blind to our differences — but let us also direct attention to our common interests and the means by which those differences can be resolved. And if we cannot end now our differences, at least we can help make the world safe for diversity. For, in the final analysis, our most basic common link is that we all inhabit this small planet. We all breathe the same air. We all cherish our children's future. And we are all mortal.

Third: Let us re-examine our attitude towards the cold war, remembering we are not engaged in a debate, seeking to pile up debating points. We are not here distributing blame or pointing the finger of judgment. We must deal with the world as it is, and not as it might have been had the history of the last eighteen years been different.

We must, therefore, persevere in the search for peace in the hope that constructive changes within the Communist bloc might bring within reach solutions which now seem beyond us. We must conduct our affairs in such a way that it becomes in the Communists' interest to agree on a genuine peace. And above all, while defending our own vital interests, nuclear powers must avert those confrontations which bring an adversary to a choice of either a humiliating retreat or a nuclear war. To adopt that kind of course in the nuclear age would be evidence only of the bankruptcy of our policy — or of a collective death-wish for the world.

To secure these ends, America's weapons are non-provocative, carefully controlled, designed to deter and capable of selective use. Our military forces are committed to peace and disciplined in self-restraint. Our diplomats are instructed to avoid unnecessary irritants and purely rhetorical hostility.

For we can seek a relaxation of tensions without relaxing our guard. And, for our part, we do not need to use threats to prove that we are resolute. We do not need to jam foreign broadcasts out of fear our faith will be eroded. We are unwilling to impose our system on any unwilling people — but we are willing and able to engage in peaceful competition with any people on earth.

Meanwhile, we seek to strengthen the United Nations, to help solve its financial problems, to make it a more effective instrument for peace, to develop it into a genuine world security system — a system capable of resolving disputes on the basis of law, of insuring the security of the large and the small, and of creating conditions under which arms can finally be abolished.

At the same time we seek to keep peace inside the non-Communist world, where many nations, all of them our friends, are divided over issues which weaken Western unity, which invite Communist intervention, or which threaten to erupt into war.

Our efforts in West New Guinea, in the Congo, in the Middle East and the Indian subcontinent have been persistent and patient despite criticism from both sides. We have also tried to set an example for others — by seeking to adjust small but significant differences with our own closest neighbors in Mexico and Canada.

Speaking of other nations, I wish to make one point clear. We are bound to many nations by alliances. These alliances exist because our concern and theirs substantially overlap. Our commitment to defend Western Europe and West Berlin, for example, stands undiminished because of the identity of our vital interests. The United States will make no deal with the Soviet Union at the expense of other nations and other peoples, not merely because they are our partners, but also because their interests and ours converge.

Our interests converge, however, not only in defending the frontiers of freedom, but in pursuing the paths of peace.

It is our hope — and the purpose of allied policies — to convince the Soviet Union that she, too, should let each nation choose its own future, so long as that choice does not interfere with the choices of others. The communist drive to impose their political and economic system on others is the primary cause of world tension today. For there can be no doubt that, if all nations could refrain from interfering in the self-determination of others, the peace would be much more assured.

This will require a new effort to achieve world law — a new context for world discussions. It will require increased understanding between the Soviets and ourselves. And increased understanding will require increased contact and communication.

One step in this direction is the proposed arrangement for a direct line between Moscow and Washington, to avoid on each side the dangerous delays, misunderstanding, and misreadings of the other's actions which might occur in a time of crisis.

We have also been talking in Geneva about other first-step measures of arms control, designed to limit the intensity of the arms race and reduce the risks of accidental war.

Our primary long-range interest in Geneva, however, is general and complete disarmament — designed to take place by stages, permitting parallel political developments to build the new institutions of peace which would take the place of arms. The pursuit of disarmament has been an effort of this Government since the 1920s. It has been urgently sought by the past three Administrations. And however dim the prospects are today, we intend to continue this effort — to continue it in order that all countries, including our own, can better grasp what the problems and the possibilities of disarmament are.

The only major area of these negotiations where the end is in sight — yet where a fresh start is badly needed — is in a treaty to outlaw nuclear tests. The conclusion of such a treaty — so near and yet so far — would check the spiraling arms race in one of its most dangerous areas. It would place the nuclear powers in a position to deal more effectively with one of the greatest hazards which man faces in 1963 — the further spread of nuclear weapons. It would increase our security — it would decrease the prospects of war.

Surely this goal is sufficiently important to require our steady pursuit, yielding neither to the temptation to give up the whole effort nor the temptation to give up our insistence on vital and responsible safeguards.

I am taking this opportunity, therefore, to announce two important decisions in this regard:

First: Chairman Khrushchev, Prime Minister Macmillan and I have agreed that high-level discussions will shortly begin in Moscow towards early agreement on a comprehensive test ban treaty. Our hopes must be tempered with the caution of history — but with our hopes go the hopes of all mankind.

Second: To make clear our good faith and solemn convictions on the matter, I now declare that the United States does not propose to conduct nuclear tests in the atmosphere so long as other states do not do so. We will not be the first to resume. Such a declaration is no substitute for a formal binding treaty — but I hope it will help us achieve one. Nor would such a treaty be a substitute for disarmament — but I hope it will help us achieve it.

Finally, my fellow Americans, let us examine our attitude towards peace and freedom here at home. The quality and spirit of our own society must justify and support our efforts abroad. We must show it in the dedication of our own lives — as many of you who are graduating today will have an opportunity to do, by serving without pay in the Peace Corps abroad or in the proposed National Service Corps here at home.

But wherever we are, we must all, in our daily lives, live up to the age-old faith that peace and freedom walk together. In too many of our cities today, the peace is not secure because freedom is incomplete.

It is the responsibility of the executive branch at all levels of government — local, state and national — to provide and protect that freedom for all of our citizens by all means within our authority. It is the responsibility of the legislative branch at all levels, wherever the authority is not now adequate, to make it adequate. And it is the responsibility of all citizens in all sections of this country to respect the rights of others and respect the law of the land.

All this is not unrelated to world peace. 'When a man's ways please the Lord', the scriptures tell us, 'he maketh even his enemies to be at peace with him'. And is not peace, in the last analysis, basically a matter of human rights — the right to live out our lives without fear of devastation — the right to breathe air as nature provided it — the right of future generations to a healthy existence?

While we proceed to safeguard our national interests, let us also safeguard human interests. And the elimination of war and arms is clearly in the interest of both.

No treaty, however much it may be to the advantage of all, however tightly it may be worded, can provide absolute security against the risks of deception and evasion. But it can — if it is sufficiently effective in its enforcement and it is sufficiently in the interests of its signers — offer far more security and far fewer risks than an unabated, uncontrolled, unpredictable arms race.

The United States, as the world knows, will never start a war. We do not want a war. We do not now expect a war. This generation of Americans has already had enough — more than enough — of war and hate and oppression. We shall be prepared if others wish it. We shall be alert to try to stop it. But we shall also do our part to build a world of peace where the weak are safe and the strong are just.

We are not helpless before that task or hopeless of its success. Confident and unafraid, we labor on — not toward a strategy of annihilation but toward a strategy of peace. Thank you.

Source: John F. Kennedy Library and Museum, Web Site. Available from: http://www.cs.umb.edu/jfklibrary/index.htm

4.4.8   THE GULF OF TONKIN RESOLUTION (1964)

American involvement in the affairs of Indo-China began during the region's occupation by Japan in the Second World War and continued through the period in which France attempted to re-establish control over its pre-war colony. France had been defeated by 1955 and Indo-China had become the independent states of Cambodia, Laos and Vietnam. However, fighting continued, partly on ideological grounds, and Vietnam soon split into two. America provided substantial aid for anticommunist forces in the area, especially the South Vietnamese government in its struggle against Vietcong partisans supported by the communist led North. By the beginning of President Johnson's Administration in 1963 the United States had over 15,000 troops supporting South Vietnam, however, the military situation did not improve for the South. The Gulf of Tonkin Resolution of August 1964 followed an incident involving American destroyers off the coast of North Vietnam. This incident was used as a pretext to escalate the war by direct US air and naval attacks on North Vietnam. This continued until America had over 500,000 troops in Vietnam, over 50,000 of whom were killed. However, the military situation never improved and America began withdrawing in 1969, a withdrawal that was completed in 1973. The South fell to the communist forces in 1975.

Whereas naval units of the Communist regime in Vietnam, in violation of the principles of the Charter of the United Nations and of international law, have deliberately and repeatedly attacked United States naval vessels lawfully present in international waters, and have thereby created a serious threat to international peace; and

Whereas these attacks are part of a deliberate and systematic campaign of aggression that the Communist regime in North Vietnam has been waging against its neighbors and the nations joined with them in the collective defense of their freedom; and

Whereas the United States is assisting the peoples of southeast Asia to protect their freedom and has no territorial, military or political ambitions in that area, but desires only that these peoples should be left in peace to work out their own destinies in their own way: Now, therefore, be it

Resolved by the Senate and House of Representatives of the United States of America in Congress assembled, That the Congress approves and supports the determination of the President, as Commander in Chief, to take all necessary measures to repel any armed attack against the forces of the United States and to prevent further aggression.

Sec. 2. The United States regards as vital to its national interest and to world peace the maintenance of international peace and security in southeast Asia. Consonant with the Constitution of the United States and the Charter of the

United Nations and in accordance with its obligations under the Southeast Asia Collective Defense Treaty, the United States is, therefore, prepared, as the President determines, to take all necessary steps, including the use of armed force, to assist any member or protocol state of the Southeast Asia Collective Defense Treaty requesting assistance in defense of its freedom.

Sec. 3. This resolution shall expire when the President shall determine that the peace and security of the area is reasonably assured by international conditions created by action of the United Nations or otherwise, except that it may be terminated earlier by concurrent resolution of the Congress.

> The Congress was not told that the US naval vessels were involved in electronic intelligence gathering and that details of the incident were not as clear cut as had been suggested. The Resolution secured overwhelming support in the Congress. President Johnson signed it on 10 August 1964 and made the following statement.

My fellow Americans: One week ago, half a world away, our Nation was faced by the challenge of deliberate and unprovoked acts of aggression in southeast Asia.

The cause of peace clearly required that we respond with a prompt and unmistakable reply.

As Commander in Chief the responsibility was mine — and mine alone. I gave the orders for that reply, and it has been given.

But, as President, there rested upon me still another responsibility — the responsibility of submitting our course to the representatives of the people, for them to verify it or veto it.

I directed that to be done last Tuesday.

Within 24 hours the resolution before me now had been placed before each House of Congress. In each House the resolution was promptly examined in committee and reported for action.

In each House there followed free and serious debate.

In each House the resolution was passed on Friday last — with a total of 502 votes in support and 2 opposed.

Thus, today, our course is clearly known in every land.

There can be no mistake — no miscalculation — of where America stands or what this generation of Americans stand for.

The unanimity of the Congress reflects the unanimity of the country.

The resolution is short. It is straightforward. I hope that it will be read around the world.

The position of the United States is stated plainly. To any armed attack upon our forces, we shall reply.

To any in southeast Asia who ask our help in defending their freedom, we shall give it.

In that region there is nothing we covet, nothing we seek — no territory, no military position, no political ambition.

Our one desire — our one determination — is that the people of southeast Asia be left in peace to work out their own destinies in their own way.

This resolution stands squarely within the four corners of the Constitution of the United States. It is clearly consistent with the principles and purposes of the Charter of the United Nations.

This is another new page in the outstanding record of accomplishments the 88th Congress is writing.

Americans of all parties and philosophies can be justly proud — and justly grateful. Proud that democracy has once again demonstrated its capacity to act swiftly and decisively against aggressors. Grateful that there is in our National Government understanding, accord, and unity between the executive and legislative branches — without regard to partisanship.

This is a great strength that we must always preserve.

This resolution confirms and reinforces powers of the Presidency. I pledge to all Americans to use those powers with all the wisdom and judgment God grants to me.

It is everlastingly right that we should be resolute in reply to aggression and steadfast in support of our friends.

But it is everlastingly necessary that our actions should be careful and should be measured.

We are the most powerful of all nations — we must strive also to be the most responsible of nations.

So, in this spirit, and with this pledge, I now sign this resolution.

Source: Ferrell, R.H. (ed.) (1975) *America in a Divided World 1945–1972*, Columbia, University of South Carolina Press.

4.4.9   THE NIXON DOCTRINE (1969)

The Nixon Doctrine reflected a shift in emphasis in American support for its overseas allies. The doctrine emerged out of a number of statements by President Nixon and senior members of his administration, principally Nixon's statement to reporters on the Pacific island of Guam during his Asian tour of July 1969, extracts of which are reproduced below. The new emphasis was to be on the US helping its allies to help themselves more. In Vietnam this was linked to American withdrawal from direct involvement in the fighting while continuing to provide South Vietnamese allies with technical and economic aid.

> Another element of the doctrine, not addressed in the Guam statement, concerned America's desire for the increasingly prosperous European allies to contribute more towards the cost of their own security. The human and economic cost that the United States was prepared to bear in the Cold War had its limits.

[...]

I think what would be of greatest interest to you before we go to your questions is to give you the perspective that I have with regard to Asia and America's role in Asia.

[...]

The United States is going to be facing, we hope before too long — no one can say how long, but before too long — a major decision: What will be its role in Asia and in the Pacific after the end of the war in Vietnam? We will be facing that decision, but also the Asian nations will be wondering about what that decision is.

When I talked to Prime Minister Gorton [of Australia], for example, he indicated, in the conversations he had had with a number of Asian leaders, they all wondered whether the United States, because of its frustration over the war in Vietnam, because of its earlier frustration over the war in Korea — whether the United States would continue to play a significant role in Asia, or whether the United States, like the French before, and then the British, and, of course, the Dutch — whether we would withdraw from the Pacific and play a minor role.

This is a decision that will have to be made, of course, as the war comes to an end. But the time to develop the thinking which will go into that decision is now. I think that one of the weaknesses in American foreign policy is that too often we react rather precipitately to events as they occur. We fail to have the perspective and the long-range view which is essential for a policy that will be viable.

As I see it, even though the war in Vietnam has been, as we all know, a terribly frustrating one, and, as a result of that frustration, even though there would be a tendency for many Americans to say, 'After we are through with that, let's not become involved in Asia', I am convinced that the way to avoid becoming involved in another war in Asia is for the United States to continue to play a significant role.

I think the way that we could become involved would be to attempt withdrawal, because, whether we like it or not, geography makes us a Pacific power. And when we consider, for example, that Indonesia at its closest point is only 14 miles from the Philippines, when we consider that Guam, where we are presently standing, of course, is in the heart of Asia, when we consider the interests of the whole Pacific as they relate to Alaska and Hawaii, we can all realize this.

Also, as we look over the historical perspective, while World War II began in Europe, for the United States it began in the Pacific. It came from Asia. The Korean war came from Asia. The Vietnamese war came from Asia.

So, as we consider our past history, the United States' involvement in war so often has been tied to our Pacific policy, or our lack of a Pacific policy, as the case might be.

As we look at Asia today, we see that the major world power which adopts a very aggressive attitude and a belligerent attitude in its foreign policy, Communist China, of course, is in Asia, and we find that the two minor world powers — minor, although they do have significant strength as we have learned — that most greatly threaten the peace of the world, that adopt the most belligerent foreign policy, are in Asia, North Korea and, of course, North Vietnam.

When we consider those factors we, I think, realize that if we are thinking down the road, down the long road — not just 4 years, 5 years, but 10, 15 or 20 — that if we are going to have peace in the world, that potentially the greatest threat to that peace will be in the Pacific.

I do not mean to suggest that the Mid-east is not a potential threat to the peace of the world and that there are not problems in Latin America that concern us, or in Africa and, of course, over it all, we see the great potential conflict between the United States and the Soviet Union, the East–West conflict between the two super powers.

But as far as those other areas are concerned, the possibility of finding some kind of solution, I think, is potentially greater than it is in the Asian area.

Pursuing that line of reasoning a bit further then, I would like to put it in a more positive sense: When we look at the problems in Asia, the threat to peace that is presented by the growing power of Communist China, the belligerence of North Korea and North Vietnam, we should not let that obscure the great promise that is here.

As I have often said, the fastest rate of growth in the world is occurring in non-Communist Asia. Japan, in the last 10 years, has tripled its GNP [Gross National Product]; South Korea has doubled its GNP; Taiwan has doubled its GNP; Thailand has doubled its GNP. The same is true of Singapore and of Malaysia.

The record in some of the other countries is not as impressive. But consider the Philippines where there are very grave problems, as you will learn when you are there, political problems and others. One of the brighter spots is that when I was in the Philippines in 1953, it was a major importer of rice. Today, as a result of 'miracle rice', it no longer has to import it. Some progress is being made in an area like that.

When we look at India and Pakistan and the terribly difficult and traumatic experience they have had, because of their conflict with each other more than with the problems they have had from the outside, the picture tends to be rather black.

But India's rate of growth as a result of 2 good crop years, and a reasonably good one this year, has been at 6 per cent. If we can get the population problem — if they can — under better control the promise for the future, of course, is rather bright.

As far as Pakistan is concerned, they are emphasizing growth in manufacturing. They are growing at the rate of 10 per cent per year in manufacturing and from 1965 to 1970 their agricultural production will go up 21 per cent.

When you visit these two countries, even in the brief visits that we have, when you see the poverty which strikes you in the face, if you have not seen it before, with a tremendous impact, you will wonder whether there is a great deal to hope for. But all I can say is that having seen what it was in 1953 and seeing what it was again in 1967, the amount of progress that has taken place, even in those countries where the rate has not been as high as others, is a very, very formidable thing to see.

So, what I am trying to suggest is this: As we look at Asia, it poses, in my view, over the long haul, looking down to the end of the century, the greatest threat to the peace of the world, and, for that reason the United States should continue to play a significant role. It also poses, it seems to me, the greatest hope for progress in the world — progress in the world because of the ability, the resources, the ability of the people, the resources physically that are available in this part of the world. And for these reasons, I think we need policies that will see that we play a part and a part that is appropriate to the conditions that we will find.

Now, one other point I would make very briefly is that in terms of this situation as far as the role we should play, we must recognize that there are two great, new factors which you will see, incidentally, particularly when you arrive in the Philippines — something you will see there that we didn't see in 1953, to show you how quickly it has changed: a very great growth of nationalism, nationalism even in the Philippines, vis-à-vis the United States, as well as other countries in the world. And, also, at the same time that national pride is becoming a major factor, regional pride is becoming a major factor.

The second factor is one that is going to, I believe, have a major impact on the future of Asia, and it is something that we must take into account. Asians will say in every country that we visit that they do not want to be dictated to from the outside, Asia for the Asians. And that is what we want, and that is the role we should play. We should assist, but we should not dictate.

At this time, the political and economic plans that they are gradually developing are very hopeful. We will give assistance to those plans. We, of course, will keep the treaty commitments that we have.

But as far as our role is concerned, we must avoid that kind of policy that will make countries in Asia so dependent upon us that we are dragged into conflicts such as the one that we have in Vietnam.

This is going to be a difficult line to follow. It is one, however, that I think, with proper planning, we can develop.

Source: US President (1971) *Public Papers of the Presidents of the United States: Richard Nixon, 1969*, Washington, Government Printing Office, pp.544–56.

4.4.10   THE JAVITS ACT: 'WAR-POWERS RESOLUTION' (1973)

During the Vietnam War successive Presidents had effectively escalated the conflict at different stages through their own initiatives, with little or no consultation with the Congress. The powers of the President as Commander-in-Chief of the Armed Forces had been a cause of concern in certain quarters for some time and the defeat in Vietnam and the fall in presidential prestige as the Watergate scandal emerged allowed Congress to put a curb on them. President Nixon vetoed the Act, claiming it undermined America's ability to respond effectively to international crises, but his veto was overturned by Congress. The 'war-powers resolution' remains a source of tension between President and Congress.

SECTION 1

This joint resolution may be cited as the 'war-powers resolution'.

SECTION 2

(A)   It is the purpose of this joint resolution to fulfill the intent of the framers of the Constitution of the United States and insure that the collective judgment of both the Congress and the President will apply to the introduction of United States armed forces into hostilities, or into situations where imminent involvement in hostilities is clearly indicated by the circumstances, and to the continued use of such forces in hostilities or in such situations. […]

SECTION 4

(A)   In the absence of a declaration of war, in any case in which United States armed forces are introduced

(1) into hostilities or into situations where imminent involvement in hostilities is clearly indicated by the circumstances;

(2) into the territory, airspace or waters of a foreign nation, while equipped for combat, except for developments which relate solely to supply, replacement, repair, or training of such forces; or

(3) in numbers which substantially enlarge United States armed forces equipped for combat already located in a foreign nation; the President shall submit within 48 hours to the Speaker of the House of Representatives and to the President pro Tempore of the Senate a report, in writing, setting forth

(a) the circumstances necessitating the introduction of the United States armed forces;

(b) the Constitutional and legislative authority under which such introduction took place; and

(c) the estimated scope and duration of the hostilities or involvement.

(B)   The President shall provide such other information as the Congress may request in the fulfillment of its Constitutional responsibilities with respect to committing the nation to war and to the use of United States armed forces abroad.

(C)   Whenever United States armed forces are introduced into hostilities or into any situation described in subsection (A) of this section, the President shall, so long as such armed forces continue to be engaged in such hostilities or situation, report to the Congress periodically on the status of such hostilities or situation, but in no event shall he report to the Congress less often than once every six months.

SECTION 5

[…]

(B)   Within 60 calendar days after a report is submitted or is required to be submitted pursuant to Section 4 (A) (1), whichever is earlier, the President shall terminate any use of United States armed forces with respect to which such report was submitted (or required to be submitted), unless the Congress (1) has declared war or has enacted a specific authorization for such use of United States armed forces, (2) has extended by law such 60-day period, or (3) is physically unable to meet as a result of an armed attack upon the United States. Such 60-day period shall be extended for not more than an additional 30 days if the President determines and certifies to the Congress in writing that unavoidable military necessity respecting the safety of United States armed forces requires the continued use of such armed forces in the course of bringing about a prompt removal of such forces.

(C)   Notwithstanding subsection (B), at any time that United States armed forces are engaged in hostilities outside the territory of the United States, its possessions and territories without a declaration of war or specific statutory authorization, such forces shall be removed by the President if the Congress so directs by concurrent resolution.

Source: Ferrell, R.H. (ed.) (1975) *America in a Divided World 1945–1972*, Columbia, University of South Carolina Press.

4.4.11 PRESIDENT REAGAN: THE SOVIET UNION AS AN 'EVIL EMPIRE' (1983)

The nature of the relationship between the United States and the Soviet Union was to be transformed during Ronald Reagan's two terms as President. By the time Reagan left office in 1989 the dramatic changes in the Soviet Union under President Gorbachev meant the Cold War was all but over. Reagan's response to these changes had been positive and supportive. This was in stark contrast to the approach of the first Reagan Administration on coming to office in 1981. A hard line with the Soviet Union had been its policy, so much so that the worsening of relations became known as the Second Cold War (as distinct from the previous period of relative 'détente'). A key speech of this policy was given to the National Association of Evangelicals on 8 March 1983.

During my first press conference as President, in answer to a direct question, I pointed out that, as good Marxist-Leninists, the Soviet leaders have openly and publicly declared that the only morality they recognize is that which will further their cause, which is world revolution. I think I should point out I was only quoting Lenin, their guiding spirit, who said in 1920 that they repudiate all morality that proceeds from supernatural ideas — that's their name for religion — or ideas that are outside class conceptions. Morality is entirely subordinate to the interests of class war. And everything is moral that is necessary for the annihilation of the old, exploiting social order and for uniting the proletariat.

Well, I think the refusal of many influential people to accept this elementary fact of Soviet doctrine illustrates an historical reluctance to see totalitarian powers for what they are. We saw this phenomenon in the 1930s. We see it too often today.

This doesn't mean we should isolate ourselves and refuse to seek an understanding with them. I intend to do everything I can to persuade them of our peaceful intent, to remind them that it was the West that refused to use its nuclear monopoly in the forties and fifties for territorial gain and which now proposes 50-percent cut in strategic ballistic missiles and the elimination of an entire class of land-based, intermediate-range nuclear missiles.

At the same time, however, they must be made to understand we will never compromise our principles and standards. We will never give away our freedom. We will never abandon our belief in God. And we will never stop searching for a genuine peace. But we can assure none of these things America stands for through the so-called nuclear freeze solutions proposed by some.

The truth is that a freeze now would be a very dangerous fraud, for that is merely the illusion of peace. The reality is that we must find peace through strength.

I would agree to a freeze if only we could freeze the Soviets' global desires. A freeze at current levels of weapons would remove any incentive for the Soviets to negotiate seriously in Geneva and virtually end our chances to achieve the major arms reductions which we have proposed. Instead, they would achieve their objectives through the freeze.

A freeze would reward the Soviet Union for its enormous and unparalleled military buildup. It would prevent the essential and long overdue modernization of United States and allied defenses and would leave our aging forces increasingly vulnerable. And an honest freeze would require extensive prior negotiations on the systems and numbers to be limited and on the measures to ensure effective verification and compliance. And the kind of a freeze that has been suggested would be virtually impossible to verify. Such a major effort would divert us completely from our current negotiations on achieving substantial reductions.

A number of years ago, I heard a young father, a very prominent young man in the entertainment world, addressing a tremendous gathering in California. It was during the time of the cold war, and communism and our own way of life were very much on people's minds. And he was speaking to that subject. And suddenly, though, I heard him saying, 'I love my little girls more than anything — ' And I said to myself, 'Oh, no, don't. You can't — don't say that.' But I had underestimated him. He went on: 'I would rather see my little girls die now, still believing in God, than have them grow up under communism and one day die no longer believing in God.'

There were thousands of young people in that audience. They came to their feet with shouts of joy. They had instantly recognized the profound truth in what he had said, with regard to the physical and the soul and what was truly important.

Yes, let us pray for the salvation of all of those who live in that totalitarian darkness — pray they will discover the joy of knowing God. But until they do, let us be aware that while they preach the supremacy of the state, declare its omnipotence over individual man, and predict its eventual domination of all peoples on the Earth, they are the focus of evil in the modern world.

It was C.S. Lewis who, in his unforgettable 'Screwtape Letters', wrote: 'The greatest evil is not done now in those sordid "dens of crime" that Dickens loved to paint. It is not even done in concentration camps and labor camps. In those we see its final result. But it is conceived and ordered (moved, seconded, carried and minuted) in clear, carpeted, warmed, and well-lighted offices, by quiet men with white collars and cut fingernails and smooth-shaven cheeks who do not need to raise their voice.'

Well, because these 'quiet men' do not 'raise their voices', because they sometimes speak in soothing tones of brotherhood and peace, because, like other dictators before them, they're always making 'their final territorial demand', some would have us accept them at their word and accommodate ourselves to their aggressive impulses. But if history teaches anything, it teaches that simple-minded appeasement or wishful thinking about our adversaries is folly. It means the betrayal of our past, the squandering of our freedom.

So, I urge you to speak out against those who would place the United States in a position of military and moral inferiority. You know, I've always believed that old Screwtape reserved his best efforts for those of you in the church. So, in your discussions of the nuclear freeze proposals, I urge you to beware the temptation of pride — the temptation of blithely declaring your- selves about it all and label both sides equally at fault, to ignore the facts of history and the aggressive impulses of an evil empire, to simply call the arms race a giant misunderstanding and thereby remove yourself from the struggle between right and wrong and good and evil.

I ask you to resist the attempts of those who would have you withhold your support for our efforts, this administration's efforts, to keep America strong and free, while we negotiate real and verifiable reductions in the world's nuclear arsenals and one day, with God's help, their total elimination.

While America's military strength is important, let me add here that I've always maintained that the struggle now going on for the world will never be decided by bombs or rockets, by armies or military might. The real crisis we face today is a spiritual one; at root, it is a test of moral will and faith.

Whittaker Chambers, the man whose own religious conversion made him a witness to one of the terrible traumas of our time, the Hiss-Chambers case, wrote that the crisis of the Western World exists to the degree in which the West is indifferent to God, the degree to which it collaborates in com- munism's attempt to make man stand alone without God. And then he said, for Marxism-Leninism is actually the second oldest faith, first proclaimed in the Garden of Eden with the words of temptation, 'Ye shall be as gods.'

The Western World can answer this challenge, he wrote, 'but only provided that its faith in God and the freedom He enjoins is as great as communism's faith in Man.'

I believe we shall rise to the challenge. I believe that communism is another sad, bizarre chapter in human history whose last pages even now are being written. I believe this because the source of our strength in the quest for human freedom is not material, but spiritual. And because it knows no limi- tation, it must terrify and ultimately triumph over those who would enslave their fellow man. For in the words of Isaiah: 'He giveth power to the faint; and to them that have no might He increased strength ... But they that wait upon the Lord shall renew their strength; they shall mount up with wings as eagles; they shall run, and not be weary ... '

Yes, change your world. One of our Founding Fathers, Thomas Paine, said, 'We have it within our power to begin the world over again.' We can do it, doing together what no one church could do by itself.

God bless you, and thank you very much.

Source: Griffith, R. (ed.) (1992) *Major Problems in American History Since 1945*, Lexington, Mass., D.C. Heath, p.690.

4.5 POST-COLD WAR

4.5.1 PRESIDENT BUSH PROCLAIMS A NEW WORLD ORDER (1990)

The end of the Cold War ushered in a period of co-operation between the United States and the Soviet Union, bilaterally and within the context of the United Nations. However, it also allowed long-standing antagonisms, suppressed in the climate of the Cold War, to re-emerge into open conflicts. One of the first major tests of the hoped for 'new world order' was the 1990–1 Gulf War. On 11 September 1990, the month after the Iraqi invasion of Kuwait, President Bush spoke before a special Joint Session of Congress and on television to the American people. The Iraqi armed forces were defeated and driven out of Kuwait, but Saddam Hussein remained in power. Tension between the United States and Iraq resulted in air strikes on a number of occasions throughout the 1990s.

We gather tonight, witness to events in the Persian Gulf as significant as they are tragic. In the early morning hours of August 2nd, following negotiations and promises by Iraq's dictator Saddam Hussein not to use force, a powerful Iraqi army invaded its trusting and much weaker neighbor, Kuwait. Within 3 days, 120,000 Iraqi troops with 850 tanks had poured into Kuwait and moved south to threaten Saudi Arabia. It was then that I decided to check that aggression.

At this moment, our brave servicemen and women stand watch in that distant desert and on distant seas, side-by-side with the forces of more than 20 other nations.

Tonight, I want to talk to you about what's at stake — what we must do together to defend civilized values around the world and maintain our economic strength at home.

THE OBJECTIVES AND GOALS

Our objectives in the Persian Gulf are clear; our goals defined and familiar.

- Iraq must withdraw from Kuwait completely, immediately, and without condition.

- Kuwait's legitimate government must be restored.

- The security and stability of the Persian Gulf must be assured.

- American citizens abroad must be protected.

These goals are not ours alone. They have been endorsed by the UN Security Council five times in as many weeks. Most countries share our concern for principle, and many have a stake in the stability of the Persian Gulf. This is not, as Saddam Hussein would have it, the United States against Iraq. It is Iraq against the world.

We stand today at a unique and extraordinary moment. The crisis in the Persian Gulf, as grave as it is, also offers a rare opportunity to move toward a historic period of cooperation. Out of these troubled times, our fifth objective — a new world order — can emerge; a new era — freer from the threat of terror, stronger in the pursuit of justice, and more secure in the quest for peace, an era in which the nations of the world, East and West, North and South, can prosper and live in harmony.

A hundred generations have searched for this elusive path to peace, while a thousand wars raged across the span of human endeavor. Today, that new world is struggling to be born, a world quite different from the one we have known, a world where the rule of law supplants the rule of the jungle, a world in which nations recognize the shared responsibility for freedom and justice, a world where the strong respect the rights of the weak.

This is the vision that I shared with President Gorbachev in Helsinki. He and other leaders from Europe, the gulf, and around the world understand that how we manage this crisis today could shape the future for generations to come.

The test we face is great — and so are the stakes. This is the first assault on the new world that we seek, the first test of our mettle. Had we not responded to this first provocation with clarity of purpose, if we do not continue to demonstrate our determination, it would be a signal to actual and potential despots around the world.

America and the world must defend common vital interests. And we will. America and the world must support the rule of law. And we will. America and the world must stand up to aggression. And we will. And one thing more; in the pursuit of these goals, America will not be intimidated.

Vital issues of principle are at stake. Saddam Hussein is literally trying to wipe a country off the face of the earth. We do not exaggerate. Nor do we exaggerate when we say Saddam Hussein will fail.

Vital economic interests are at risk as well. Iraq itself controls some 10% of the world's proven oil reserves. Iraq plus Kuwait controls twice that. An Iraq permitted to swallow Kuwait would have the economic and military power, as well as the arrogance, to intimidate and coerce its neighbors — neighbors that control the lion's share of the world's remaining oil reserves. We cannot permit a resource so vital to be dominated by one so ruthless. And we won't.

Recent events have surely proven that there is no substitute for American leadership. In the face of tyranny, let no one doubt American credibility and reliability. Let no one doubt our staying power. We will stand by our friends. One way or another, the leader of Iraq must learn this fundamental truth.

Our interest, our involvement in the gulf is not transitory. It predated Saddam Hussein's aggression and will survive it. Long after all our troops come home — and we all hope it is soon, very soon — there will be a lasting role for the United States in assisting the nations of the Persian Gulf. Our role then — to deter future aggression. Our role is to help our friends in their own self-defense, and, something else, to curb the proliferation of chemical, biological, ballistic missile, and, above all, nuclear technologies.

Let me also make clear that the United States has no quarrel with the Iraqi people. Our quarrel is with Iraq's dictator and with his aggression. Iraq will not be permitted to annex Kuwait. That is not a threat; that is not a boast; that is just the way it is going to be.

Source: Griffith, R. (ed.) (1992) *Major Problems in American History Since 1945*, Lexington, Mass., D.C. Heath, p.703.

4.5.2 THE PARIS JOINT DECLARATION (1990)

The transformation of the Soviet Union begun under Mikhail Gorbachev, and the response of the United States, brought the Cold War period to a close and this Declaration formally marked its end. It was signed by twenty-two nations, including the United States and the Soviet Union, at the Paris Conference on Security and Co-operation in Europe in November 1990. The Conference also produced the Treaty on Conventional Armed Forces in Europe and the Charter of Paris for a New Europe. However, new and resurgent security issues would soon replace the Cold War division of Europe.

The Heads of State or Government of Belgium, Bulgaria, Canada, the Czech and Slovak Federal Republic, Denmark, France, Germany, Greece, Hungary, Iceland, Italy, Luxembourg, the Netherlands, Norway, Poland, Portugal, Romania, Spain, Turkey, the Union of Soviet Socialist Republics, the United Kingdom and the United States of America

— greatly welcoming the historic changes in Europe

— gratified by the growing implementation throughout Europe of a common commitment to pluralist democracy, the rule of law and human rights, which are essential to lasting security on the continent,

— affirming the end of the era of division and confrontation which has lasted for more than four decades, the improvement in relations among their countries and the contribution this makes to the security of all,

— confident that the signature of the Treaty on Conventional Armed Forces in Europe represents a major contribution to the common objective of increased security and stability in Europe, and

— convinced that these developments must form part of a continuing process of co-operation in building the structures of a more united continent,

Issue the following Declaration:

1.   The signatories solemnly declare that, in the new era of European relations which is beginning, they are no longer adversaries, will build new partnerships and extend to each other the hand of friendship.

2.   They recall their obligations under the Charter of the United Nations and reaffirm all of their commitments under the Helsinki Final Act. They stress that all of the ten Helsinki Principles are of primary significance and that, accordingly, they will be equally and unreservedly applied, each of them being interpreted taking into account the others. In that context, they affirm their obligation and commitment to refrain from the threat or use of force against the territorial integrity or the political independence of any State, from seeking to change existing borders by threat or use of force, and from acting in any other manner inconsistent with the principles and purposes of those documents. None of their weapons will ever be used except in self-defence or otherwise in accordance with the Charter of the United Nations.

3.   They recognize that security is indivisible and that the security of each of their countries is inextricably linked to the security of all States participating in the Conference on Security and Co-operation in Europe [CSCE].

4.   They undertake to maintain only such military capabilities as are necessary to prevent war and provide for effective defence. They will bear in mind the relationship between military capabilities and doctrines.

5.   They reaffirm that every State has the right to be or not to be a party to a treaty of alliance.

6.   They note with approval the intensification of political and military contacts among them to promote mutual understanding and confidence. They welcome in this context the positive responses made to recent proposals for new regular diplomatic liaison.

7.   They declare their determination to contribute actively to conventional, nuclear and chemical arms control and disarmament agreements which enhance security and stability for all. In particular, they call for the early entry into force of the Treaty on Conventional Armed Forces in Europe and commit themselves to continue the process of strengthening peace in Europe through conventional arms control within the framework of the CSCE. They welcome the prospect of new negotiations between the United States and the Soviet Union on the reduction of their short-range nuclear forces.

8.   They welcome the contribution that confidence- and security-building measures [CSBMs] have made to lessening tensions and fully support the further development of such measures. They reaffirm the importance of the 'Open Skies' initiative and their determination to bring the negotiations to a successful conclusion as soon as possible.

9.   They pledge to work together with the other CSCE participating States to strengthen the CSCE process so that it can make an even greater contribution to security and stability in Europe. They recognize in particular the need to enhance political consultations among CSCE participants and to develop other CSCE mechanisms. They are convinced that the Treaty on Conventional Armed Forces in Europe and agreement on a substantial new set of CSBMs, together with new patterns of co-operation in the framework of the CSCE, will lead to increased security and thus to enduring peace and stability in Europe.

10.   They believe that the preceding points reflect the deep longing of their peoples for close co-operation and mutual understanding and declare that they will work steadily for the further development of their relations in accordance with the present Declaration as well as with the principles set forth in the Helsinki Final Act.

The original of this Declaration of which the English, French, German, Italian, Russian and Spanish texts are equally authentic will be transmitted to the Government of France which will retain it in its archives. The Government of France is requested to transmit the text of the Declaration to the Secretary-General of the United Nations, with a view to its circulation to all the members of the organization as an official document of the United Nations, indicating that it is not eligible for registration under Article 102 of the Charter of the United Nations. Each of the signatory States will receive from the Government of France a true copy of this Declaration.

In witness whereof the undersigned High Representatives have subscribed their signatures below.

Source: USIA Information Agency Web Site, Archives. Available from: http://www.usia.gov/usis.html

4.5.3   PARTNERSHIP FOR PEACE (1994)

The following declaration by NATO heads of government, made in January 1994, includes the 'Partnership for Peace' initiative towards the new democracies of Central and Eastern Europe. It also strongly reaffirms the importance to all NATO members of the continuing involvement of the United States in the security concerns of Europe. The declaration addresses the principal concern of the time, the conflict in former Yugoslavia, and indicates what were thought to be some of the potential sources of instability and conflict in the future.

1.   We, the Heads of State and Government of the member countries of the North Atlantic Alliance, have gathered in Brussels to renew our Alliance in light of the historic transformations affecting the entire continent of Europe. We welcome the new climate of cooperation that has emerged in Europe with the end of the period of global confrontation embodied in the Cold

War. However, we must also note that other causes of instability, tension and conflict have emerged. We therefore confirm the enduring validity and indispensability of our Alliance. It is based on a strong transatlantic link, the expression of a shared destiny. It reflects a European Security and Defence Identity gradually emerging as the expression of a mature Europe. It is reaching out to establish new patterns of cooperation throughout Europe. It rests, as also reflected in Article 2 of the Washington Treaty, upon close collaboration in all fields.

Building on our decisions in London and Rome and on our new Strategic Concept, we are undertaking initiatives designed to contribute to lasting peace, stability, and well-being in the whole of Europe, which has always been our Alliance's fundamental goal. We have agreed:

— to adapt further the Alliance's political and military structures to reflect both the full spectrum of its roles and the development of the emerging European Security and Defence Identity, and endorse the concept of Combined Joint Task Forces;

— to reaffirm that the Alliance remains open to the membership of other European countries;

— to launch a major initiative through a Partnership for Peace, in which we invite Partners to join us in new political and military efforts to work alongside the Alliance;

— to intensify our efforts against the proliferation of weapons of mass destruction and their means of delivery.

2.   We reaffirm our strong commitment to the transatlantic link, which is the bedrock of NATO. The continued substantial presence of United States forces in Europe is a fundamentally important aspect of that link. All our countries wish to continue the direct involvement of the United States and Canada in the security of Europe. We note that this is also the expressed wish of the new democracies of the East, which see in the transatlantic link an irreplaceable pledge of security and stability for Europe as a whole. The fuller integration of the countries of Central and Eastern Europe and of the former Soviet Union into a Europe whole and free cannot be successful without the strong and active participation of all Allies on both sides of the Atlantic.

3.   Today, we confirm and renew this link between North America and a Europe developing a Common Foreign and Security Policy and taking on greater responsibility on defence matters. We welcome the entry into force of the Treaty of Maastricht and the launching of the European Union, which will strengthen the European pillar of the Alliance and allow it to make a more coherent contribution to the security of all the Allies. We reaffirm that the Alliance is the essential forum for consultation among its members and the venue for agreement on policies bearing on the security and defence commitments of Allies under the Washington Treaty.

4.   We give our full support to the development of a European Security and Defence Identity which, as called for in the Maastricht Treaty, in the longer term perspective of a common defence policy within the European Union, might in time lead to a common defence compatible with that of the Atlantic Alliance. The emergence of a European Security and Defence Identity will strengthen the European pillar of the Alliance while reinforcing the transatlantic link and will enable European Allies to take greater responsibility for their common security and defence. The Alliance and the European Union share common strategic interests.

5.   We support strengthening the European pillar of the Alliance through the Western European Union, which is being developed as the defence component of the European Union. The Alliance's organization and resources will be adjusted so as to facilitate this. We welcome the close and growing cooperation between NATO and the WEU that has been achieved on the basis of agreed principles of complementarity and transparency. In future contingencies, NATO and the WEU will consult, including as necessary through joint Council meetings, on how to address such contingencies.

6.   We therefore stand ready to make collective assets of the Alliance available, on the basis of consultations in the North Atlantic Council, for WEU operations undertaken by the European Allies in pursuit of their Common Foreign and Security Policy. We support the development of separable but not separate capabilities which could respond to European requirements and contribute to Alliance security. Better European coordination and planning will also strengthen the European pillar and the Alliance itself. Integrated and multinational European structures, as they are further developed in the context of an emerging European Security and Defence Identity, will also increasingly have a similarly important role to play in enhancing the Allies' ability to work together in the common defence and other tasks.

7.   In pursuit of our common transatlantic security requirements, NATO increasingly will be called upon to undertake missions in addition to the traditional and fundamental task of collective defence of its members, which remains a core function. We reaffirm our offer to support, on a case by case basis in accordance with our own procedures, peacekeeping and other operations under the authority of the UN Security Council or the responsibility of the CSCE [Conference for Security and Cooperation in Europe], including by making available Alliance resources and expertise. Participation in any such operation or mission will remain subject to decisions of member states in accordance with national constitutions.

8.   Against this background, NATO must continue the adaptation of its command and force structure in line with requirements for flexible and timely responses contained in the Alliance's Strategic Concept. We also will need to strengthen the European pillar of the Alliance by facilitating the use of our military capabilities for NATO and European/WEU operations, and assist participation of non-NATO partners in joint peacekeeping operations and other contingencies as envisaged under the Partnership for Peace.

9.   Therefore, we direct the North Atlantic Council in Permanent Session, with the advice of the NATO Military Authorities, to examine how the Alliance's political and military structures and procedures might be developed and adapted to conduct more efficiently and flexibly the Alliance's missions, including peacekeeping, as well as to improve cooperation with the WEU and to reflect the emerging European Security and Defence Identity. As part of this process, we endorse the concept of Combined Joint Task Forces as a means to facilitate contingency operations, including operations with participating nations outside the Alliance. We have directed the North Atlantic Council, with the advice of the NATO Military Authorities, to develop this concept and establish the necessary capabilities. The Council, with the advice of the NATO Military Authorities, and in coordination with the WEU, will work on implementation in a manner that provides separable but not separate military capabilities that could be employed by NATO or the WEU. The North Atlantic Council in Permanent Session will report on the implementation of these decisions to Ministers at their next regular meeting in June 1994.

10.   Our own security is inseparably linked to that of all other states in Europe. The consolidation and preservation throughout the continent of democratic societies and their freedom from any form of coercion or intimidation are therefore of direct and material concern to us, as they are all other CSCE states under the commitments of the Helsinki Final Act and the Charter of Paris. We remain deeply committed to further strengthening the CSCE, which is the only organization comprising all European and North American countries, as an instrument of preventive diplomacy, conflict prevention, cooperative security, and the advancement of democracy and human rights. We actively support the efforts to enhance the operational capabilities of the CSCE for early warning, conflict prevention, and crisis management.

11.   As part of our overall effort to promote preventive diplomacy, we welcome the European Union proposal for a Pact on Stability in Europe, will contribute to its elaboration, and look forward to the opening conference which will take place in Paris in the Spring.

12.   Building on the close and long-standing partnership among the North American and European Allies, we are committed to enhancing security and stability in the whole of Europe. We therefore wish to strengthen ties with the democratic states to our East. We reaffirm that the Alliance, as provided for in Article 10 of the Washington Treaty, remains open to membership of other European states in a position to further the principles of the Treaty and to contribute to the security of the North Atlantic area. We expect and would welcome NATO expansion that would reach to democratic states to our East, as part of an evolutionary process, taking into account political and security developments in the whole of Europe.

13.   We have decided to launch an immediate and practical programme that will transform the relationship between NATO and participating states. This new programme goes beyond dialogue and cooperation to forge a real

partnership — a Partnership for Peace. We invite the other states participating in the North Atlantic Cooperation Council, and other CSCE countries able and willing to contribute to this programme, to join with us in this Partnership. Active participation in the Partnership for Peace will play an important role in the evolutionary process of the expansion of NATO.

14.   The Partnership for Peace, which will operate under the authority of the North Atlantic Council, will forge new security relationships between the North Atlantic Alliance and its Partners for Peace. Partner states will be invited by the North Atlantic Council to participate in political and military bodies at NATO Headquarters with respect to Partnership activities. The Partnership will expand and intensify political and military cooperation throughout Europe, increase stability, diminish threats to peace, and build strengthened relationships by promoting the spirit of practical cooperation and commitment to democratic principles that underpin our Alliance. NATO will consult with any active participant in the Partnership if that partner perceives a direct threat to its territorial integrity, political independence, or security. At a pace and scope determined by the capacity and desire of the individual participating states, we will work in concrete ways towards transparency in defence budgeting, promoting democratic control of defence ministries, joint planning, joint military exercises, and creating an ability to operate with NATO forces in such fields as peacekeeping, search and rescue and humanitarian operations, and others as may be agreed.

15.   To promote closer military cooperation and interoperability, we will propose, within the Partnership framework, peacekeeping field exercises beginning in 1994. To coordinate joint military activities within the Partnership, we will invite states participating in the Partnership to send permanent liaison officers to NATO Headquarters and a separate Partnership Coordination Cell at Mons (Belgium) that would, under the authority of the North Atlantic Council, carry out the military planning necessary to implement the Partnership programmes.

16.   Since its inception two years ago, the North Atlantic Cooperation Council has greatly expanded the depth and scope of its activities. We will continue to work with all our NACC partners to build cooperative relationships across the entire spectrum of the Alliance's activities. With the expansion of NACC activities and the establishment of the Partnership for Peace, we have decided to offer permanent facilities at NATO Headquarters for personnel from NACC countries and other Partnership for Peace participants in order to improve our working relationships and facilitate closer cooperation.

17.   Proliferation of weapons of mass destruction and their delivery means constitutes a threat to international security and is a matter of concern to NATO. We have decided to intensify and expand NATO's political and defence efforts against proliferation, taking into account the work already underway in other international fora and institutions. In this regard, we direct that work begin immediately in appropriate fora of the Alliance to develop an overall policy framework to consider how to reinforce ongoing

prevention efforts and how to reduce the proliferation threat and protect against it.

18.   We attach crucial importance to the full and timely implementation of existing arms control and disarmament agreements as well as to achieving further progress on key issues of arms control and disarmament, such as:

— the indefinite and unconditional extension of the Treaty on Non-Proliferation of Nuclear Weapons, and work towards an enhanced verification regime;

— the early entry into force of the Convention on Chemical Weapons and new measures to strengthen the Biological Weapons Convention;

— the negotiation of a universal and verifiable Comprehensive Test Ban Treaty;

— issues on the agenda of the CSCE Forum for Security Cooperation;

— ensuring the integrity of the CFE [Conventional Forces in Europe] Treaty and full compliance with all its provisions.

19.   We condemn all acts of international terrorism. They constitute flagrant violations of human dignity and rights and are a threat to the conduct of normal international relations. In accordance with our national legislation, we stress the need for the most effective cooperation possible to prevent and suppress this scourge.

20.   We reaffirm our support for political and economic reform in Russia and welcome the adoption of a new constitution and the holding of democratic parliamentary elections by the people of the Russian Federation. This is a major step forward in the establishment of a framework for the development of durable democratic institutions. We further welcome the Russian government's firm commitment to democratic and market reform and to a reformist foreign policy. These are important for security and stability in Europe. We believe that an independent, democratic, stable and nuclear-weapons-free Ukraine would likewise contribute to security and stability. We will continue to encourage and support the reform processes in both countries and to develop cooperation with them, as with other countries in Central and Eastern Europe.

21.   The situation in Southern Caucasus continues to be of special concern. We condemn the use of force for territorial gains. Respect for the territorial integrity, independence and sovereignty of Armenia, Azerbaijan and Georgia is essential to the establishment of peace, stability and cooperation in the region. We call upon all states to join international efforts under the aegis of the United Nations and the CSCE aimed at solving existing problems.

22.   We reiterate our conviction that security in Europe is greatly affected by security in the Mediterranean. We strongly welcome the agreements recently concluded in the Middle East peace process which offer an historic opportunity for a peaceful and lasting settlement in the area. This much-awaited breakthrough has had a positive impact on the overall situation in

the Mediterranean, thus opening the way to consider measures to promote dialogue, understanding and confidence-building between the countries in the region. We direct the Council in Permanent Session to continue to review the overall situation, and we encourage all efforts conducive to strengthening regional stability.

23.   As members of the Alliance, we deplore the continuing conflict in the former Yugoslavia. We continue to believe that the conflict in Bosnia must be settled at the negotiating table and not on the battlefield. Only the parties can bring peace to the former Yugoslavia. Only they can agree to lay down their arms and end the violence which for these many months has only served to demonstrate that no side can prevail in its pursuit of military victory.

24.   We are united in supporting the efforts of the United Nations and the European Union to secure a negotiated settlement of the conflict in Bosnia, agreeable to all parties, and we commend the European Union Action Plan of 22 November 1993 to secure such a negotiated settlement. We reaffirm our determination to contribute to the implementation of a viable settlement reached in good faith. We commend the front-line states for their key role in enforcing sanctions against those who continue to promote violence and aggression. We welcome the cooperation between NATO and the WEU in maintaining sanctions enforcement in the Adriatic.

25.   We denounce the violations by the parties of the agreements they have already signed to implement a ceasefire and to permit the unimpeded delivery of humanitarian assistance to the victims of this terrible conflict. This situation cannot be tolerated. We urge all the parties to respect their agreements. We are determined to eliminate obstacles to the accomplishment of the UNPROFOR [United Nations Protection Force] mandate. We will continue operations to enforce the No-Fly Zone over Bosnia. We call for the full implementation of the UNSC [United Nations Security Council] Resolutions regarding the reinforcement of UNPROFOR. We reaffirm our readiness, under the authority of the United Nations Security Council and in accordance with the Alliance decisions of 2 and 9 August 1993, to carry out air strikes in order to prevent the strangulation of Sarajevo, the safe areas and other threatened areas in Bosnia-Herzegovina. In this context, we urge the UNPROFOR authorities to draw up urgently plans to ensure that the blocked rotation of the UNPROFOR contingent in Srebrenica can take place and to examine how the airport at Tuzla can be opened for humanitarian relief purposes.

26.   The past five years have brought historic opportunities as well as new uncertainties and instabilities to Europe. Our Alliance has moved to adapt itself to the new circumstances, and today we have taken decisions in key areas. We have given our full support to the development of a European Security and Defence Identity. We have endorsed the concept of Combined Joint Task Forces as a means to adapt the Alliance to its future tasks. We have opened a new perspective of progressively closer relationships with the countries of Central and Eastern Europe and of the former Soviet Union.

In doing all this, we have renewed our Alliance as a joint endeavour of a North America and Europe permanently committed to their common and indivisible security. The challenges we face are many and serious. The decisions we have taken today will better enable us to meet them.

Source: NATO Web Site, Press Releases 1994. Available from: http://www.nato.int/docu/pr/pr94.htm

4.5.4 A NEW ATLANTIC COMMUNITY FOR THE TWENTY-FIRST CENTURY (1996)

With the changing global and European economic and security context, the United States sought to redefine its relationship with Europe in the late 1990s. There was a shift in emphasis towards partnership, consultation and multilateral action. In Stuttgart, Germany, Secretary of State Warren Christopher outlined the idea of a 'New Atlantic Community for the Twenty-first Century'. The speech marked the anniversary of Secretary of State James Byrnes's speech in the same place 50 years before which had pledged America's continuing political and military role in Europe after the Second World War.

Secretary of State Warren Christopher in Stuttgart, September 6, 1996.

[...]

In just a few years, we will begin a new century. Let me share with you the vision that President Clinton and I have for the United States and Europe in the next century. It is a vision for a New Atlantic Community. This community will build on the institutions our predecessors created, but, it will transcend the artificial boundaries of Cold War Europe. It will give North America a deeper partnership with a broader, more integrated Europe on this continent and around the world. It carries forward the principles that Secretary Byrnes set forth 50 years ago today.

As the next century dawns on this New Atlantic Community, our joint efforts will have made us confident that the democratic revolutions of 1989 will endure, confident that wars like the one in Bosnia can be prevented, and confident that every new democracy, large and small, can take its rightful place in a new Europe. In this New Atlantic Community, the United States will be fully engaged, in partnership with our friends and allies — and in a more effective European Union that is taking in new members. In this Community, NATO will remain the central pillar of our security engagement. It will be a new NATO, adapted to meet emerging challenges, with the full participation of all current Allies and several new members from the east. NATO's Partnership for Peace and the OSCE [Organization for Security and Co-operation in Europe] will give us the tools to prevent conflict and assure freedom for all of our citizens. In our vision for this New Atlantic Community, a democratic Russia will be a full partner. Our economies will be increasingly integrated and thriving. Europe and America will be taking joint action against the global threats we can only overcome by working together.

This is the kind of vision that gave our partnership strength and our people hope in the darkest, most dangerous days of the past century. Ten years ago, it was still a dream. Ten years from now, the opportunity may be lost. But I believe we can realize it if we meet four challenges together in the final years of this current century.

The first challenge is to build a secure and integrated Europe, to erase the Cold War's outdated frontiers forever. The new democracies of central Europe and the New Independent States want to be our partners. It is in our interest to help them assume our shared responsibilities. It is in our interest to extend to them the same structure of values and institutions that enabled Western Europe to overcome its own legacy of conflict and division. It is certainly in Germany's interest to work with us and our other Allies in this task, for it can make Germany's eastern border what its western border has long been: a gateway, and not a barrier.

[…]

Thanks to the Partnership for Peace, we can now form the first truly Europe-wide military coalitions, in which soldiers from Russia and America, Poland and Ukraine, Germany and Lithuania train side by side, ready to deploy at a moment's notice to protect our security. To this end, we should expand the Partnership's mandate beyond its current missions. We should involve our Partners in the Partnership for Peace in the planning as well as the execution of NATO's missions. We should give them a stronger voice by forming an Atlantic Partnership Council. In all of these ways, NATO gives us a foundation to build our New Atlantic Community — one in which all of Europe and North America work together to build lasting security.

The Organization for Security and Cooperation in Europe is essential to this evolving community. That is evident from its important and courageous missions in Bosnia, Chechnya, and the Baltics. The Helsinki principles — respect for an open society and the rule of law — provided the guidepost for all we accomplished in the last decade and they also shape our vision for the future. At the OSCE summit this December in Lisbon, we should build on these principles to define our security cooperation for the next century. In Lisbon, our leaders should take practical steps, such as launching negotiations to adapt the CFE [Conventional Forces in Europe] treaty to Europe's new security landscape.

Closer political cooperation in the European Union, and its coming enlargement, will contribute to the security and prosperity of the New Atlantic Community and strengthen the partnership between Europe and the United

States. President Clinton has been a strong supporter of deeper European integration, reaffirming the commitment made in earlier years by President John Kennedy.

[…]

The vision I have outlined here today for the New Atlantic Community can only succeed if we recognize Russia's vital role in the New Atlantic Community. For most of this century fear, tyranny, and self-isolation kept Russia from the European mainstream. But now, new patterns of trust and cooperation are taking hold. The Russian people are building a new society on a foundation of democratic and free market ideals. Though their struggle is far from complete, as the assault on Chechnya has demonstrated, the Russian people have rejected a return to the past and vindicated our confidence in their democracy — the same kind of confidence that Secretary Byrnes expressed from this platform 50 years ago. Now, an integrated, democratic Russia can participate in the construction of an integrated, democratic Europe.

Today, I want to say this to the Russian people: We welcome you as our full partners in building a new Europe that is free of tyranny, division, and war. We want to work with you to bring Russia into the family of market democracies. We want you to have a stake and a role in the institutions of European security and economic cooperation. That is why we seek a fundamentally new relationship between Russia and the new NATO. Such a relationship, I am confident, is possible. It is important to all of us. And we are determined to make it happen.

[…]

Our second challenge in building a New Atlantic Community is to promote prosperity among our nations and to extend it globally. The United States and Europe have built the largest economic relationship in the world. It supports over 14 million jobs on both sides of the Atlantic.

We must move toward a free and open Transatlantic Marketplace, as the United States and the EU foreshadowed in their summit meeting last December. As barriers fall and momentum builds, the boundaries of what seems feasible will certainly expand. We are already at a stage when we can realistically discuss the true integration of the economies of Europe and North America. We should now pursue practical steps toward even more visionary goals, such as reducing regulatory barriers.

Our vision for open trade and investment in the New Atlantic Community must be as broad as our vision of that community itself. In other words, it must extend to central Europe and the New Independent States, including Russia. President Yeltsin, for example, has made it a priority to open Russia to foreign investment and President Clinton is personally committed to encourage that goal. We strongly support Russia's entry into the WTO on appropriate commercial terms. We understand that Europe's new democracies, for all of those new democracies, stability depends on prosperity — and on our willingness to open Western markets to their products.

That is one reason we strongly support an expansive program for the enlargement of the European Union. The prospect of EU membership will help lock in democratic and market reforms in central and eastern Europe. It sets the stage for a true single European market. We believe that it should move forward swiftly.

Together, we also have a responsibility to ensure that the international economic system and its institutions are fit and ready for the 21st Century. We have already worked together to reform the International Monetary Fund and the World Bank. We completed the Uruguay Round and created the World Trade Organization. At the WTO's first ministerial meeting this December in Singapore, we should push to complete the Uruguay Round's unfinished business and begin to set priorities for the next century. We must also do our part to ensure that the world's poorest nations benefit from open markets. All this is a task for the United States and Europe.

Our New Atlantic Community will only be secure if we also work together to meet the threats that transcend our frontiers – threats like terrorism, nuclear proliferation, crime, drugs, disease, and damage to the environment. The danger posed by these threats is as great as any that we faced during the Cold War. Meeting these threats is our third challenge for the waning years of this century […].

Source: USIA Information Agency Web Site, Archives. Available from: http://www.usia.gov/usis.html

4.5.5 REMARKS BY THE PRESIDENT ON THE NATIONAL INTEREST FOR ENLARGING NATO (1998)

A new relationship with Europe required existing organizations such as NATO to adapt and to reflect new circumstances and challenges. Part of the adaptation involved the enlargement of the alliance. In 1997 NATO had agreed to recommend the entry of Poland, Hungary and the Czech Republic to its member nations. President Clinton made the following remarks on what he saw as American interests in NATO enlargement in an effort to gain support in the Senate for the ratification process. Poland, Hungary and the Czech Republic became full members of NATO in 1999.

Thank you. Thank you very much, Secretary Albright, General Shelton, General Sandler, Mr Berger, Senator Roth, to the members and representatives of the Joint Chiefs, members of the diplomatic corps, and other interested citizens, many of whom have held high positions in the national security apparatus of this country and the military of our country. We're grateful for everyone's presence here today.

I especially want to thank the members of the Senate who are here. I thank Senator Roth, the chairman of the NATO observer group, Senator Moynihan, Senator Smith, Senator Levin, Senator Lugar, Senator Robb, and Senator Thurmond. Your leadership and that of Senators Lott, Daschle, Helms and Biden and others in this chamber has truly, as the Secretary of State said, made this debate a model of bipartisan dialogue and action.

The Senate has held more than a dozen hearings on this matter. We have worked very closely with the Senate NATO observer group. And I must say, I was essentially gratified when the Senate Foreign Relations Committee voted 16 to 2 in support of enlargement.

Now, in the coming days the full Senate will act on this matter of critical importance to our national security. The admission of Poland, Hungary, and the Czech Republic to NATO will be a very important milestone in building the kind of world we want in the 21st century.

As has been said, I first proposed NATO enlargement four years ago, when General Joulwan was our commander in Brussels. Many times since, I've had the opportunity to speak on this issue. Now a final decision is at hand, and now it is important that all the American people focus on this matter closely. For this is one of those rare moments when we have within our grasp the opportunity to actually shape the future, to make the new century safer and more secure and less unstable than the one we are leaving.

We can truly be present at a new creation. When President Truman signed the North Atlantic Treaty 49 years ago next month, he expressed the goal of its founders in typically simple and straightforward language: to preserve their present peaceful situation and to protect it in the future. The dream of the generation that founded NATO was of a Europe whole and free. But the Europe of their time was lamentably divided by the Iron Curtain. Our generation can realize their dream. It is our opportunity and responsibility to do so, to create a new Europe undivided, democratic, and at peace for the very first time in all history.

Forging a new NATO in the 21st century will help to fulfil the commitment and the struggle that many of you in this room engaged in over the last 50 years. NATO can do for Europe's east what it did for Europe's west — protect new democracies against aggression, prevent a return to local rivalries, create the conditions in which prosperity can flourish.

In January of 1994, on my first trip to Europe for the NATO summit, we did take the lead in proposing a new NATO for a new era. First, by strengthening our Alliance to preserve its core mission of self-defense, while preparing it to take on the new challenges to our security and to Europe's stability. Second, by reaching out to new partners and taking in new members from among Europe's emerging democracies. And third, by forging a strong and cooperative relationship between NATO and Russia.

Over the past four years, persistently and pragmatically, we have put this strategy into place. NATO has shifted to smaller, more flexible forces better prepared to provide for our defense in this new era, but also trained and equipped for other contingencies. Its military power remains so unquestioned that it was the only force capable of stopping the fighting in Bosnia. NATO signed the Founding Act with Moscow, joining Russia and history's most successful alliance in common cause for a peaceful, democratic, undivided Europe. We signed a charter to build cooperation between NATO and Ukraine. We created the Partnership for Peace as a path to full NATO membership for some, and a strong and lasting link to the Alliance for others.

Today, the Partnership for Peace has exceeded its mission beyond the wildest dreams of those of us who started it. It has more than three dozen members.

Now we're on the threshold of bringing new members into NATO. The Alliance's enlargement will make America safer by making NATO stronger, adding new forces and new allies that can share our security burdens. Let me be very clear: NATO's core mission will remain the same — the defense of the territory of its members. The addition of new members will strengthen and enhance that mission. In pursuing enlargement, we have made sure not to alter NATO's core function or its ability to defend America and Europe's security.

Now I urge this Senate to do the same, and in particular not to impose new constraints on NATO's freedom of action, its military decision-making, or its ability to respond quickly and effectively to whatever challenges may arise. NATO's existing treaty and the way it makes defense and security decisions have served our nation's security well for half a century.

In the same way, the addition of these new members will help NATO meet new challenges to our security. In Bosnia, for example, Polish, Czech, and Hungarian soldiers serve alongside our own with skill and professionalism. Remember, this was one of the largest, single operational deployments of American troops in Europe since World War II. It was staged from a base in Taszar, Hungary. It simply would not have happened as swiftly, smoothly, or safely without the active help and support of Hungary.

As we look toward the 21st century, we're looking at other new security challenges as well — the spread of weapons of mass destruction and ballistic missile technology, terrorism and the potential for hi-tech attacks on our information systems. NATO must be prepared to meet and defeat this new generation of threats, to act flexibly and decisively under American leadership. With three new members in our ranks, NATO will be better able to meet those goals as well.

Enlargement also will help to make Europe more stable. Already, the very prospect of membership has encouraged nations throughout the region to accelerate reforms, resolve disputes, and improve cooperation.

Now, let me emphasize what I've said many times before and what all NATO allies have committed to: NATO's first new members should not be its last. Keeping the doors open to all of Europe's new democracies will help to ensure that enlargement benefits the security of the entire region, not just the first three new members.

At last summer's summit in Madrid, NATO agreed to examine the process of enlargement at our next summit in 1999. Neither NATO nor my administration has made any decisions or any commitments about when the next invitations for membership should be extended, or to whom. I have consulted broadly with Congress on decisions about the admissions of the first three members. I pledge to do the same before any future decisions are made. And of course any new members would also require the advice and the consent of the United States Senate.

For these reasons, I urge in the strongest terms the Senate to reject any effort to impose an artificial pause on the process of enlargement. Such a mandate is unnecessary and, I believe, unwise. If NATO is to remain strong, America's freedom to lead it must be unfettered and our freedom to co-operate with our other partners in NATO must remain unfettered. A unilateral freeze on enlargement would reduce our own country's flexibility and, perhaps even more important, our leverage, our ability to influence our partners. It would fracture NATO's open-door consensus, it would undermine further reforms in Europe's democracies, it would draw a new and potentially destabilizing line, at least temporarily, in Europe.

There are other steps we must take to prevent that division from re-emerging. We must continue to strengthen the partnership for peace with our many friends in Europe. We need to give even more practical expression to the agreements between NATO and Russia, and NATO and Ukraine, turning words into deeds. With Russia and other countries, we must continue to reduce our nuclear stockpiles — and we thank you, Senator Lugar, for your leadership on that — to combat the dangers of proliferation, to lower conventional arms ceilings all across Europe. And all of us together must help the Bosnian people to finish the job of bringing a lasting peace to their country. If you think about where we were just a year ago in Bosnia, not to mention two years ago, not to mention 1995, no one could have believed we would be here today.

It would not have happened had it not been for NATO, the Partnership for Peace allies, the Russians, all of those who have come together and joined hands to end the bloodiest conflict in Europe since the second world war.

Now we have to finish what America started four years ago, welcoming Hungary, Poland and the Czech Republic into our Alliance. If you look around at who is in the room today, you can see that they are more than willing to be a good partner. They will make NATO stronger; they will make Europe safer; and in so doing, they will make America and our young people more secure. They will make it less likely that the men and women in uniform who serve under General Shelton and the other generals here, and their successors in the 21st century, will have to fight and die because of problems in Europe.

A new NATO can extend the blessings of freedom and security in a new century. With the help of our allies, the support of the Senate, the strength of our continued commitment, we can bring Europe together — not by force of arms, but by possibilities of peace. That is the promise of this moment. And we must seize it.

Thank you very much.

Source: US State Department Web Site, NATO Enlargement Page. Available from: http://www.state.gov/www/regions/eur/natoindex_html

ASPECTS OF THE UNITED STATES IN MAPS AND STATISTICS

5.1 INTRODUCTION

This chapter is designed to provide a portrait of a number of aspects of the United States of America through statistical data, maps and diagrams. There can be few nations that can match the United States for the public availability of information. The federal government publishes a wealth of data from a variety of public and private sources including the regular national census, and most of the material in this section is taken from this source.

The information selected is intended to provide some basic facts and figures as well as insights into a number of specific areas. While most of the tables and diagrams include historical information there is a deliberate emphasis on the period since the Second World War and specifically on recent data and trends.

The tables have been reproduced from *The American Almanac 1992–1993* and *1996–1997* and references in some of the footnotes refer to this publication. *The Almanac* is published by The Reference Press and based on the *Statistical Abstract of the United States: 1992*. Tables from the *Statistical Abstract of the United States: 1997* have also been used. The *Statistical Abstract* is compiled by the US Bureau of the Census and has been published annually since 1880 by the Government Printing Office.

In several of the tables data are broken down by region, the composition of these regions is shown in the map at the end of this chapter, the map also indicates sub-regions and the standard abbreviation for each of the 50 states.

5.2 POPULATION

This section gives some basic data of the population, its growth, distribution and ethnic composition. It also charts, through tables and maps, the growth of the United States by area, and the accession of the states.

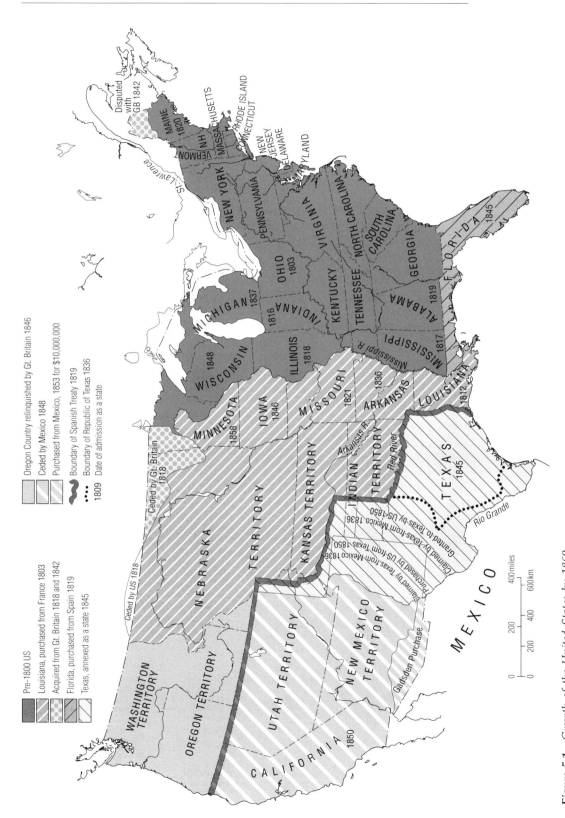

Figure 5.1 *Growth of the United States by 1860*

Source: see also The Open University (1984) A317 *Themes in British and American History*, Milton Keynes, The Open University, p.11.

Order of admission	State	Date of admission	Order of admission	State	Date of admission
1	Delaware	7 December 1787	26	Michigan	26 January 1837
2	Pennsylvania	12 December 1787	27	Florida	3 March 1845
3	New Jersey	18 December 1787	28	Texas	29 December 1845
4	Georgia	2 January 1788	29	Iowa	28 December 1846
5	Connecticut	9 January 1788	30	Wisconsin	29 May 1848
6	Massachusetts	7 February 1788	31	California	9 September 1850
7	Maryland	28 April 1788	32	Minnesota	11 May 1858
8	South Carolina	23 May 1788	33	Oregon	14 February 1859
9	New Hampshire	21 June 1788	34	Kansas	29 January 1861
10	Virginia	25 June 1788	35	West Virginia	20 June 1863
11	New York	26 July 1788	36	Nevada	31 October 1864
12	North Carolina	21 November 1789	37	Nebraska	1 March 1867
13	Rhode Island	29 May 1790	38	Colorado	1 August 1876
14	Vermont	4 March 1791	39	North Dakota	2 November 1889
15	Kentucky	1 June 1792	40	South Dakota	2 November 1889
16	Tennessee	1 June 1796	41	Montana	8 November 1889
17	Ohio	1 March 1803	42	Washington	11 November 1889
18	Louisiana	30 April 1812	43	Idaho	3 July 1890
19	Indiana	11 December 1816	44	Wyoming	10 July 1890
20	Mississippi	10 December 1817	45	Utah	4 January 1896
21	Illinois	3 December 1818	46	Oklahoma	16 November 1907
22	Alabama	14 December 1819	47	New Mexico	6 January 1912
23	Maine	15 March 1820	48	Arizona	14 February 1912
24	Missouri	10 August 1821	49	Alaska	3 January 1959
25	Arkansas	15 June 1836	50	Hawaii	21 August 1959

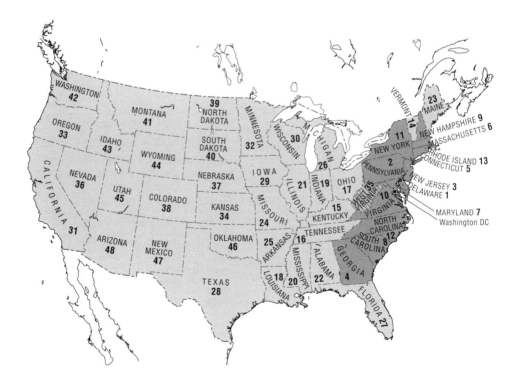

Figure 5.2   *Admission of states. The 13 original states are shaded darker*

Source: see also The Open University (1984) *A317 Themes in British and American History,* Milton Keynes, The Open University, p.14.

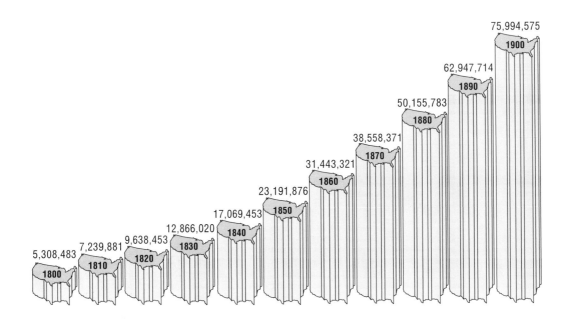

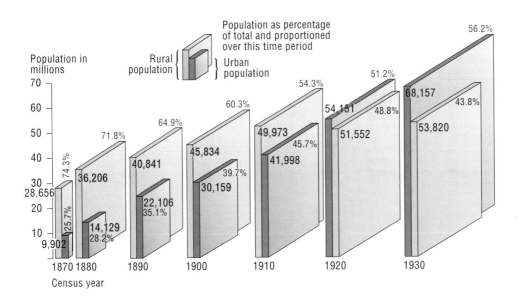

Figure 5.3 US population growth (top) and urban and rural population growth (bottom). Note the change from a rural to an urban majority between 1910 and 1920

Source: see also The Open University (1984) *A317 Themes in British and American History*, Milton Keynes, The Open University, p.14.

Table 5.1   Population and area: 1790–1990. (Area figures represent area on indicated date including in some cases considerable areas not then organized or settled, and not covered by the census. Total area figures for 1790–1970 have been recalculated on the basis of the remeasurement of States and counties for the 1980 census, but not on the basis of the 1990 census. The land and water area figures for past censuses have not been adjusted and are not strictly comparable with the total area data for comparable dates because the land areas were derived from different base data, and these values are know to have changed with the construction of reservoirs, draining of lakes, etc. Density figures are based on land area measurements as reported in earlier censuses)

CENSUS DATE	RESIDENT POPULATION				AREA (square miles)		
	Number	Per square mile of land area	Increase over preceding census		Total	Land	Water
			Number	Percent			
CONTERMINOUS U.S. [1]							
1790 (Aug. 2)	3,929,214	4.5	(X)	(X)	891,364	864,746	24,065
1800 (Aug. 4)	5,308,483	6.1	1,379,269	35.1	891,364	864,746	24,065
1810 (Aug. 6)	7,239,881	4.3	1,931,398	36.4	1,722,685	1,681,828	34,175
1820 (Aug. 7)	9,638,453	5.5	2,398,572	33.1	1,792,552	1,749,462	38,544
1830 (June 1)	12,866,020	7.4	3,227,567	33.5	1,792,552	1,749,462	38,544
1840 (June 1)	17,069,453	9.8	4,203,433	32.7	1,792,552	1,749,462	38,544
1850 (June 1)	23,191,876	7.9	6,122,423	35.9	2,991,655	2,940,042	52,705
1860 (June 1)	31,443,321	10.6	8,251,445	35.6	3,021,295	2,969,640	52,747
1870 (June 1)	[2]39,818,449	[2]13.4	8,375,128	26.6	3,021,295	2,969,640	52,747
1880 (June 1)	50,155,783	16.9	10,337,334	26.0	3,021,295	2,969,640	52,747
1890 (June 1)	62,947,714	21.2	12,791,931	25.5	3,021,295	2,969,640	52,747
1900 (June 1)	75,994,575	25.6	13,046,861	20.7	3,021,295	2,969,834	52,553
1910 (Apr. 15)	91,972,266	31.0	15,977,691	21.0	3,021,295	2,969,565	52,822
1920 (Jan. 1).	105,710,620	35.6	13,738,354	14.9	3,021,295	2,969,451	52,936
1930 (Apr. 1).	122,775,046	41.2	17,064,426	16.1	3,021,295	2,977,128	45,259
1940 (Apr. 1).	131,669,275	44.2	8,894,229	7.2	3,021,295	2,977,128	45,259
1950 (Apr. 1).	150,697,361	50.7	19,028,086	14.5	3,021,295	2,974,726	47,661
1960 (Apr. 1).	178,464,236	60.1	27,766,875	18.4	3,021,295	2,968,054	54,207
UNITED STATES							
1950 (Apr. 1).	151,325,798	42.6	19,161,229	14.5	3,618,770	3,552,206	63,005
1960 (Apr. 1).	179,323,175	50.6	27,997,377	18.5	3,618,770	3,540,911	74,212
1970 (Apr. 1).	[3]203,302,031	[3]57.4	23,978,856	13.4	3,618,770	[3]3,540,023	[3]78,444
1980 (Apr. 1).	[4]226,542,199	64.0	23,240,168	11.4	3,618,770	3,539,289	79,481
1990 (Apr. 1).	[5]248,718,301	70.3	22,176,102	9.8	[6]3,717,796	[6]3,536,278	[6][7]181,518

X Not applicable.   [1] Excludes Alaska and Hawaii.   [2] Revised to include adjustments for underenumeration in southern States; unrevised number is 38,558,371 (13.0 per square mile).   [3] Figures corrected after 1970 final reports were issued. [4] Total population count has been revised since the 1980 census publications. Numbers by age, race, Hispanic origin, and sex have not been corrected.   [5] The April 1, 1990, census count includes count question resolution corrections processed through December 1994, and does not include adjustments for census coverage errors.   [6] Data reflect corrections made after publication of the results.   [7] Comprises Great Lakes, inland, and coastal water. Data for prior years cover inland water only. For further explanation, see table 367.

Source: U.S. Bureau of the Census, *1990 Census of Population and Housing, Population and Housing Unit Counts* (CPH-2); 1990 Census of Population and Housing Listing (1990 CPH-L-157); and unpublished data.

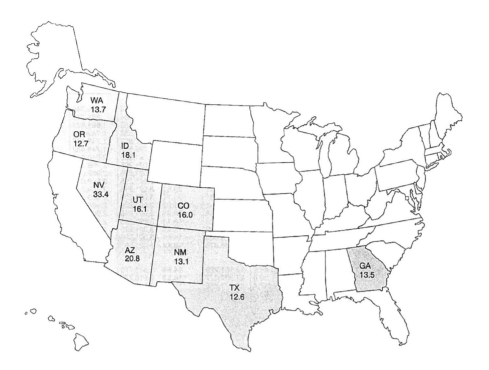

Figure 5.4 *Ten fastest growing states, per cent population change: 1990–96*

Source: US Bureau of the Census, *Statistical Abstract of the United States: 1997,* Government Printing Office, Figure 1.1.

Table 5.2 Population: 1900–91. (In thousands, except per cent. Estimates as of 1 July. Prior to 1940, excludes Alaska and Hawaii. Total population includes Armed Forces abroad; civilian population excludes Armed Forces)

YEAR	Resident population	YEAR	TOTAL Population	TOTAL Per cent change	Resident population	Civilian population	YEAR	TOTAL Population	TOTAL Per cent change	Resident population	Civilian population
1900....	76,094	1952...	157,553	1.73	156,393	153,892	1972...	209,896	1.08	209,284	207,511
1905....	83,822	1953...	160,184	1.67	158,956	156,595	1973...	211,909	0.96	211,357	209,600
1910....	92,407	1954...	163,026	1.77	161,884	159,695	1974...	213,854	0.92	213,342	211,636
1915....	100,546	1955...	165,931	1.78	165,069	162,967	1975...	215,973	0.99	215,465	213,789
1920....	106,461	1956...	168,903	1.79	168,088	166,055	1976...	218,035	0.95	217,563	215,894
1925....	115,829	1957...	171,984	1.82	171,187	169,110	1977...	220,239	1.01	219,760	218,106
1930....	123,077	1958...	174,882	1.68	174,149	172,226	1978...	222,585	1.06	222,095	220,467
1935....	127,250	1959...	177,830	1.69	177,135	175,277	1979...	225,055	1.11	224,567	222,969
1940....	132,457	1960...	180,671	1.60	179,979	178,140	1980...	227,722	1.18	227,220	225,616
1941....	133,669	1961...	183,691	1.67	182,992	181,143	1981...	229,958	0.98	229,457	227,809
1942....	134,617	1962...	186,538	1.55	185,771	183,677	1982...	232,192	0.97	231,669	229,999
1943....	135,107	1963...	189,242	1.45	188,483	186,493	1983...	234,321	0.92	233,806	232,111
1944....	133,915	1964...	191,889	1.40	191,141	189,141	1984...	236,370	0.87	235,847	234,131
1945....	133,434	1965...	194,303	1.26	193,526	191,605	1985...	238,492	0.90	237,950	236,245
1946....	140,686	1966...	196,560	1.16	195,576	193,420	1986...	240,680	0.92	240,162	238,441
1947....	144,083	1967...	198,712	1.09	197,457	195,264	1987...	242,836	0.90	242,321	240,582
1948....	146,730	1968...	200,706	1.00	199,399	197,113	1988...	245,057	0.91	244,534	242,852
1949....	149,304	1969...	202,677	0.98	201,385	199,145	1989...	247,343	0.93	246,820	245,132
1950....	152,271	1970...	205,052	1.17	203,984	201,895	1990...	249,924	1.04	249,415	247,775
1951....	153,982	1971...	207,661	1.27	206,827	204,866	1991...	252,688	1.11	252,177	250,566

Source: U.S. Bureau of the Census, *Current Population Reports,* series P-25, Nos. 311, 1045, and 1083.

Table 5.3   Centre of population: 1790–1990. ('Centre of population' is that point at which an imaginary flat, weightless, and rigid map of the US would balance if weights of identical value were placed on it so that each weight represented the location of one person on the date of the census)

YEAR	North latitude			West longitude			Approximate location
	°	′	″	°	′	″	
1790 (August 2)	39	16	30	76	11	12	23 miles east of Baltimore, MD
1850 (June 1)	38	59	0	81	19	0	23 miles southeast of Parkersburg, WV
1900 (June 1)	39	9	36	85	48	54	6 miles southeast of Columbus, IN
1950 (April 1)	38	50	21	88	9	33	8 miles north–northwest of Olney, Richland County, IL
1960 (April 1)	38	35	58	89	12	35	In Clinton Co. about 6 1/2 miles northwest of Centralia, IL
1970 (April 1)	38	27	47	89	42	22	5.3 miles east–southeast of the Mascoutah City Hall in St. Clair County, IL
1980 (April 1)	38	8	13	90	34	26	1/4 mile west of De Soto in Jefferson County, MO
1990 (April 1)	37	52	20	91	12	55	9.7 miles southeast of Steelville, MO

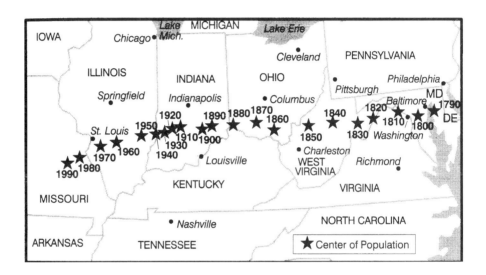

Table 5.4   US population abroad, by selected area: 1992. (In thousands. As of 3 June. Data compiled as part of non-combatant personnel evacuation requirements report)

AREA	Total[1]	Resident U.S. citizen	U.S. tourists	AREA	Total[1]	Resident U.S. citizen	U.S. tourists
Total[2]	**14,285**	**6,269**	**6,674**	Italy	155	102	28
Argentina	38	13	25	Japan	142	38	13
Australia	75	65	8	Jerusalem	28	26	2
Belgium	42	24	7	Martinique	221	(Z)	221
Brazil	46	34	11	Mexico	802	495	300
Canada	1,561	278	1,281	Netherlands	35	22	5
Costa Rica	31	25	4	Panama	36	8	1
Dominican Republic	97	87	9	Philippines	147	119	(Z)
Egypt	21	13	2	Portugal	47	31	12
France	224	126	91	Saudi Arabia	42	31	7
Germany	513	107	208	South Korea	72	8	38
Greece	70	38	30	Spain	60	27	31
Hong Kong	27	21	5	Switzerland	32	27	4
Ireland	71	43	28	United Kingdom	414	213	162
Israel	137	124	12	Venezuela	50	24	26

Z Less than 500. [1]Includes Dept. of Defense noncombatant employees, other U.S. government employees, and dependents of U.S. military and civilian employees, not shown separately. [2]Includes other areas not shown separately.
Source: U.S. Dept. of State, unpublished data.

Table 5.5 Immigration: 1820–1990. (In thousands, except rate. For fiscal years ending in year shown, except as noted. For 1820–67, alien passengers arriving; 1868–91 and 1895–7, immigrants arriving; 1892–4 and 1898 to the present, immigrants admitted. Rates based on Bureau of the Census estimates as of 1 July for resident population to 1929, and for total population thereafter (excluding Alaska and Hawaii prior to 1959). Population estimates for 1980–9 reflect revisions based on the 1990 Census of Population)

PERIOD	Number	Rate [1]	PERIOD OR YEAR	Number	Rate [1]	YEAR	Number	Rate [1]
1820 to 1990....	**56,994**	**3.4**	1911 to 1920	5,736	5.7	1981	597	2.6
1820 to 1830 [2]	152	1.2	1921 to 1930	4,107	3.5	1982	594	2.6
1831 to 1840 [3]	599	3.9	1931 to 1940	528	0.4	1983	560	2.4
1841 to 1850 [4]	1,713	8.4	1941 to 1950	1,035	0.7	1984	544	2.3
1851 to 1860 [4]	2,598	9.3	1951 to 1960	2,515	1.5	1985	570	2.4
1861 to 1870 [5]	2,315	6.4	1961 to 1970	3,322	1.7	1986	602	2.5
1871 to 1880	2,812	6.2	1971 to 1980	4,493	2.1	1987	602	2.5
1881 to 1890	5,247	9.2	1981 to 1990	7,338	3.1	1988	643	2.6
1891 to 1900	3,688	5.3	1970	373	1.8	1989 [6]	1,091	4.4
1901 to 1910	8,795	10.4	1980	531	2.3	1990 [6]	1,536	6.1

[1] Annual rate per 1,000 U.S. population. Rate computed by dividing sum of annual immigration totals by sum of annual U.S. population totals for same number of years. [2] Oct. 1, 1819, to Sept. 30, 1830. [3] Oct. 1, 1830, to Dec. 31, 1840. [4] Calendar years. [5] Jan. 1, 1861, to June 30, 1870. [6] Includes persons who were granted permanent residence under the legalization program of the Immigration Reform and Control Act of 1986.

Table 5.6 Immigrants, by country of birth: 1981–95. (In thousands. For fiscal years ending in year shown)

COUNTRY OF BIRTH	1981-90, total	1991-93, total	1994	1995	COUNTRY OF BIRTH	1981-90, total	1991-93, total	1994	1995
All countries	**7,338.1**	**3,705.4**	**804.4**	**720.5**	Syria.	20.6	8.7	2.4	2.4
Europe [1]	**705.6**	**438.9**	**160.9**	**128.2**	Taiwan	([3])	43.9	10.0	9.4
France	23.1	8.6	2.7	2.5	Thailand	64.4	21.1	5.5	5.1
Germany.	70.1	23.7	7.0	6.2	Turkey	20.9	7.2	1.8	2.9
Greece	29.1	5.8	1.4	1.3	Vietnam	401.4	192.7	41.3	41.8
Ireland	32.8	30.6	17.3	5.3	**North America** [1]	**3,125.0**	**1,896.4**	**272.2**	**231.5**
Italy	32.9	7.7	2.3	2.2	Canada	119.2	45.9	16.1	12.9
Poland	97.4	72.5	28.0	13.8	Mexico	1,653.3	1,286.5	111.4	89.9
Portugal	40.0	9.4	2.2	2.6	Caribbean [1]	892.7	337.0	104.8	96.8
Romania	38.9	20.2	3.4	4.9	Cuba.	159.2	35.8	14.7	17.9
Soviet Union, former [2] .	84.0	159.2	63.4	54.5	Dominican				
Armenia.	(NA)	(NA)	4.0	2.0	Republic.	251.8	128.8	51.2	38.5
Azerbaijan	(NA)	(NA)	3.8	1.9	Haiti	140.2	68.6	13.3	14.0
Belarus	(NA)	(NA)	5.4	3.8	Jamaica.	213.8	60.0	14.3	16.4
Moldova.	(NA)	(NA)	2.3	1.9	Trinidad and				
Russia.	(NA)	(NA)	15.2	14.6	Tobago	39.5	22.0	6.3	5.4
Ukraine	(NA)	(NA)	21.0	17.4	Central America [1]	458.7	226.8	39.9	31.8
Uzbekistan	(NA)	(NA)	3.4	3.6	El Salvador	214.6	100.4	17.6	11.7
United Kingdom	142.1	52.7	16.3	12.4	Guatemala	87.9	47.9	7.4	6.2
Yugoslavia.	19.2	8.1	3.4	8.3	Honduras	49.5	29.1	5.3	5.5
Asia [1]	**2,817.4**	**1,073.5**	**292.6**	**267.9**	Nicaragua	44.1	33.9	5.3	4.4
Afghanistan	26.6	8.5	2.3	1.4	Panama.	29.0	9.7	2.4	2.2
Bangladesh	15.2	17.7	3.4	6.1	**South America** [1]	**455.9**	**189.2**	**47.4**	**45.7**
Cambodia	116.6	7.5	1.4	1.5	Argentina	25.7	10.6	2.3	1.8
China	[3]388.8	137.5	54.0	35.5	Brazil	23.7	17.5	4.5	4.6
Hong Kong	63.0	30.0	7.7	7.2	Chile.	23.4	6.6	1.6	1.5
India	261.9	121.9	34.9	34.7	Colombia	124.4	45.7	10.8	10.8
Iran	154.8	47.6	11.4	9.2	Ecuador	56.0	24.6	5.9	6.4
Iraq	19.6	9.7	6.0	5.6	Guyana	95.4	29.1	7.7	7.4
Israel	36.3	13.8	3.4	2.5	Peru	64.4	36.6	9.2	8.1
Japan	43.2	23.0	6.1	4.8	Venezuela	17.9	7.7	2.4	2.6
Jordan	32.6	13.0	4.0	3.6	**Africa** [1]	**192.3**	**91.0**	**26.7**	**42.5**
Korea	338.8	63.9	16.0	16.0	Egypt	31.4	12.7	3.4	5.6
Laos	145.6	25.9	5.1	3.9	Ethiopia	27.2	15.0	3.9	7.0
Lebanon	41.6	17.3	4.3	3.9	Nigeria	35.3	16.9	4.0	6.8
Pakistan	61.3	39.5	8.7	9.8	South Africa	15.7	6.6	2.1	2.6
Philippines	495.3	188.1	53.5	51.0	Other countries [4]	41.9	16.4	4.6	4.7

NA Not available. [1] Includes countries not shown separately. [2] Includes other republics and unknown republics, not shown separately. [3] Data for Taiwan included with China. [4] Includes Australia, New Zealand, and unknown countries.
Source of tables 7 and 8: U.S. Immigration and Naturalization Service, *Statistical Yearbook*, annual; and releases.

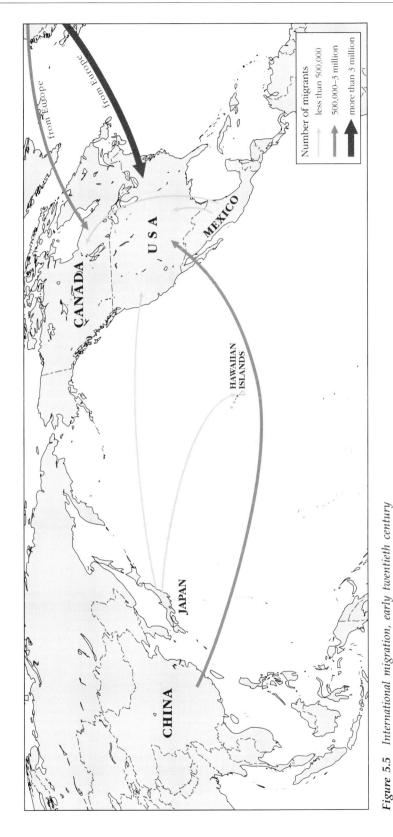

Figure 5.5 International migration, early twentieth century

Source: Segal, A. (1993) *An Atlas of International Migration*, London, Hans Zell; Lewis, W.A. (1978) *Growth and Fluctuations 1870–1913*, London, Allen & Unwin; see also Eccleston et al. (1998) *The Asia-Pacific Profile*, London, Routledge in association with The Open University, Figure 19.

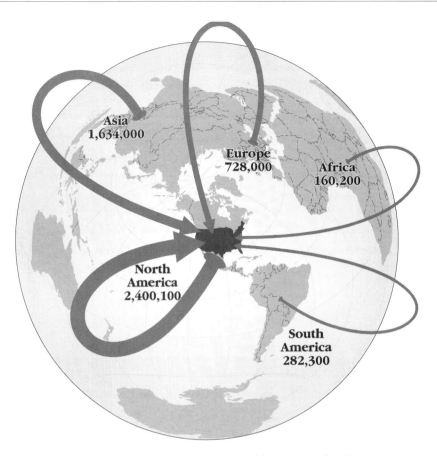

Figure 5.6 *Immigrants to the US, by region of birth: totals for the period 1991–95*

Source: US Bureau of the Census, *Statistical Abstract of the United States: 1997*, Government Printing Office, Table 8.

Table 5.7   Immigrants admitted, by leading country of birth and metropolitan area of intended residence: 1990. (For year ending 30 September. Includes Puerto Rico. Includes new arrivals and persons adjusting their status. MSA — metropolitan statistical area; PMSA — primary metropolitan statistical area; and NECMA — New England county metropolitan area as defined by US Office of Management and Budget, 30 June 1986)

METROPOLITAN AREA OF INTENDED RESIDENCE	Total [1]	Mexico	El Salvador	Philippines	Vietnam [2]	Dominican Republic	Guatemala	Korea	China: Mainland	India
Total [3]	1,536,483	679,068	80,173	63,756	48,662	42,195	32,303	32,301	31,815	30,667
Los Angeles-Long Beach, CA PMSA	374,773	231,267	42,172	11,644	4,745	86	18,446	6,059	3,525	1,440
New York, NY PMSA	164,330	6,436	2,853	4,750	1,155	25,430	1,895	3,586	9,030	3,530
Chicago, IL PMSA	73,107	41,848	631	2,655	742	70	1,839	1,238	802	3,024
Anaheim-Santa Ana, CA PMSA. . .	65,367	44,414	2,026	1,407	4,950	13	1,060	1,219	459	667
Houston, TX PMSA.	58,208	34,973	9,285	677	2,014	48	988	263	473	854
Miami-Hialeah, FL PMSA.	37,677	1,273	706	292	56	1,342	650	64	157	139
San Diego, CA MSA	37,208	25,540	226	3,539	1,575	13	190	205	278	114
Riverside-San Bernardino, CA PMSA	35,616	27,159	998	1,224	505	2	581	373	136	269
Washington, DC-MD-VA MSA. . . .	32,705	1,056	4,956	1,228	2,188	277	620	1,940	802	1,465
San Francisco, CA PMSA	29,144	7,060	2,871	3,574	1,459	6	686	358	3,782	248
Dallas, TX PMSA	28,533	19,391	1,595	270	1,015	15	377	391	248	523
San Jose, CA PMSA.	26,250	10,766	654	2,440	3,881	14	148	516	963	816
Oakland, CA PMSA	20,894	6,884	643	2,678	1,040	5	157	401	1,506	769
Boston-Lawrence-Salem-Lowell-Brockton, MA NECMA	20,776	215	698	246	1,435	2,093	494	241	1,115	501
Newark, NJ PMSA.	16,089	127	521	883	197	538	235	195	226	813
Nassau-Suffolk, NY PMSA.	14,823	262	2,643	424	94	829	365	389	394	807
Phoenix, AZ MSA.	14,714	10,726	206	211	692	5	198	146	176	130
El Paso, TX MSA.	14,476	14,009	25	33	5	1	15	59	18	20
Bergen-Passaic, NJ PMSA.	13,144	665	275	724	15	1,480	85	727	161	790
Philadelphia, PA-NJ PMSA.	11,440	382	64	577	1,228	126	37	909	439	931
Fresno, CA MSA	11,193	8,066	175	156	74	-	55	28	75	280
McAllen-Edinburg-Mission, TX MSA	9,937	9,719	29	10	-	2	27	7	2	1
Jersey City, NJ PMSA.	9,921	155	636	889	61	1,153	173	160	156	612
Fort Lauderdale-Hollywood-Pompano Beach, FL PMSA	9,906	349	112	127	87	111	67	58	92	145
Fort Worth-Arlington, TX PMSA . .	9,736	6,805	182	82	635	5	56	82	68	200
Oxnard-Ventura, CA PMSA	9,508	7,251	195	548	80	3	124	103	54	93
Sacramento, CA MSA.	8,933	3,378	137	602	604	4	43	222	307	172
San Antonio, TX MSA.	8,668	7,304	103	139	99	13	95	104	47	43
Atlanta, GA MSA	8,079	1,363	180	151	923	31	52	430	132	319
Seattle, WA MSA	7,335	573	61	1,025	1,083	2	26	542	403	153
Bakersfield, CA MSA	7,246	6,094	194	344	10	-	63	39	17	83
Detroit, MI PMSA	7,199	309	14	398	146	12	10	280	172	552
Honolulu, HI MSA.	6,706	44	6	3,051	537	-	-	678	511	16
Salinas-Seaside-Monterey, CA MSA	6,695	5,570	119	292	66	1	13	106	33	24
Middlesex-Somerset-Hunterdon, NJ PMSA.	6,414	177	68	433	46	636	51	205	222	1,093
San Juan, PR PMSA.	6,181	41	22	11	1	5,171	7	4	55	5
Brownsville-Harlingen, TX MSA. . .	6,175	5,883	75	38	-	-	22	1	6	1
Visalia-Tulare-Porterville, CA MSA.	5,925	4,846	62	175	3	-	20	11	10	56
Denver, CO PMSA	5,509	2,967	36	148	364	3	32	202	110	77
Santa Barbara-Santa Maria-Lompoc, CA MSA	5,489	4,483	43	178	28	1	127	49	24	27
Stockton, CA MSA	5,463	2,886	33	490	292	-	16	16	64	87
Minneapolis-St. Paul, MN-WI MSA.	5,439	193	15	156	559	6	15	246	106	145
Austin, TX MSA	5,044	3,496	183	37	195	1	27	70	60	53
West Palm Beach-Boca Raton-Delray Beach, FL MSA.	5,012	599	67	75	40	42	58	25	36	86
Las Vegas, NV MSA	4,986	2,607	250	413	132	7	67	148	105	33
Tampa-St. Petersburg-Clearwater, FL MSA.	4,721	913	36	166	418	37	35	88	40	91
Bridgeport-Stamford-Norwalk-Danbury, CT NECMA	4,507	111	62	77	146	123	92	44	69	207
Portland, OR PMSA	4,493	1,071	39	147	654	1	33	283	190	50
Santa Cruz, CA MSA	4,396	3,963	31	69	15	3	7	8	44	11
Tucson, AZ MSA	4,232	3,338	34	50	159	-	19	36	41	23
Modesto, CA MSA	4,062	2,869	36	62	34	2	22	26	20	98
Baltimore, MD MSA	3,732	99	38	223	108	21	13	544	122	221
Merced, CA MSA	3,696	2,755	37	47	1	-	8	9	10	118
Hartford-New Britain-Middletown-Bristol, CT NECMA	3,673	35	17	55	223	47	11	66	68	151
Lake County, IL PMSA	3,587	2,429	98	157	4	-	45	94	24	126
Providence-Pawtucket-Woonsocket, RI NECMA	3,566	75	35	88	33	539	259	36	73	45
Vallejo-Fairfield-Napa, CA PMSA. .	3,510	1,756	99	983	61	1	22	45	24	80
Orlando, FL MSA	3,445	318	49	134	259	92	22	69	30	99
Aurora-Elgin, IL PMSA.	3,085	2,601	15	37	15	4	17	25	4	51
Albuquerque, NM MSA	2,878	2,264	27	35	154	1	34	38	27	35
Oklahoma City, OK MSA	2,741	1,391	5	55	364	1	39	78	31	51
Laredo, TX MSA	2,557	2,498	11	1	-	-	19	1	-	5

- Represents zero.   [1] Includes other countries, not shown separately.   [2] Data for immigrants admitted under the legalization program are not available separately for Vietnam and thus not included in this column.   [3] Includes other metropolitan areas, not shown separately.

Source: U.S. Immigration and Naturalization Service, *Statistical Yearbook*, annual.

Table 5.8 Resident population — selected characteristics, 1790–1996, and projections 2000–2050. (In thousands)

DATE	SEX		RACE					Hispanic origin [1]
	Male	Female	White	Black	Other			
					Total	American Indian, Eskimo, Aleut	Asian and Pacific Islanders	
1790 (Aug. 2) [2]	(NA)	(NA)	3,172	757	(NA)	(NA)	(NA)	(NA)
1800 (Aug. 4) [2]	(NA)	(NA)	4,306	1,002	(NA)	(NA)	(NA)	(NA)
1850 (June 1) [2]	11,838	11,354	19,553	3,639	(NA)	(NA)	(NA)	(NA)
1900 (June 1) [2]	38,816	37,178	66,809	8,834	351	(NA)	(NA)	(NA)
1910 (Apr. 15) [2]	47,332	44,640	81,732	9,828	413	(NA)	(NA)	(NA)
1920 (Jan. 1) [2]	53,900	51,810	94,821	10,463	427	(NA)	(NA)	(NA)
1930 (Apr. 1) [2]	62,137	60,638	110,287	11,891	597	(NA)	(NA)	(NA)
1940 (Apr. 1) [2]	66,062	65,608	118,215	12,866	589	(NA)	(NA)	(NA)
1950 (Apr. 1) [2]	74,833	75,864	134,942	15,042	713	(NA)	(NA)	(NA)
1950 (Apr. 1)	75,187	76,139	135,150	15,045	1,131	(NA)	(NA)	(NA)
1960 (Apr. 1)	88,331	90,992	158,832	18,872	1,620	(NA)	(NA)	(NA)
1970 (Apr. 1) [3] [5] . . .	98,926	104,309	178,098	22,581	2,557	(NA)	(NA)	(NA)
1980 (Apr. 1) [4] [5] . . .	110,053	116,493	194,713	26,683	5,150	1,420	3,729	14,609
1990 (Apr. 1) [4] [6] . . .	121,244	127,474	208,710	30,486	9,523	2,065	7,458	22,354
1991 (July 1) [7]	122,984	129,122	210,979	31,107	10,020	2,110	7,911	23,416
1992 (July 1) [7]	124,511	130,500	212,910	31,654	10,448	2,147	8,300	24,349
1993 (July 1) [7]	125,938	131,858	214,760	32,168	10,867	2,184	8,683	25,326
1994 (July 1) [7]	127,261	133,111	216,480	32,647	11,245	2,220	9,025	26,300
1995 (July 1) [7]	128,569	134,321	218,149	33,095	11,646	2,254	9,392	27,277
1996 (July 1) [7]	129,810	135,474	219,749	33,503	12,032	2,288	9,743	28,269
2000 (July 1) [8]	134,181	140,453	225,532	35,454	13,647	2,402	11,245	31,366
2005 (July 1) [8]	139,785	146,196	232,463	37,734	15,784	2,572	13,212	36,057
2010 (July 1) [8]	145,584	152,132	239,588	40,109	18,019	2,754	15,265	41,139
2015 (July 1) [8]	151,750	158,383	247,193	42,586	20,355	2,941	17,413	46,705
2020 (July 1) [8]	158,021	164,721	254,887	45,075	22,780	3,129	19,651	52,652
2025 (July 1) [8]	164,119	170,931	262,227	47,539	25,284	3,319	21,965	58,930
2050 (July 1) [8]	193,234	200,696	294,615	60,592	38,724	4,371	34,352	96,508

NA Not available. [1] Persons of Hispanic origin may be of any race. [2] Excludes Alaska and Hawaii. [3] The revised 1970 resident population count is 203,302,031; which incorporates changes due to errors found after tabulations were completed. The race and sex data shown here reflect the official 1970 census count. [4] The race data shown have been modified; see text, section 1, for explanation. [5] See footnote 4, table 1. [6] The April 1, 1990, census count (248,718,291) includes count question resolution corrections processed through March 1994 and does not include adjustments for census coverage errors. [7] Estimated. [8] Middle series projection; see table 3.

Table 5.9 Resident population, by region, race, and Hispanic origin: 1990. (As of 1 April)

RACE AND HISPANIC ORIGIN	POPULATION (1,000)					PERCENT DISTRIBUTION				
	United States	North-east	Midwest	South	West	United States	North-east	Midwest	South	West
Total	**248,710**	**50,809**	**59,669**	**85,446**	**52,786**	**100.0**	**20.4**	**24.0**	**34.4**	**21.2**
White	199,686	42,069	52,018	65,582	40,017	100.0	21.1	26.0	32.8	20.0
Black	29,986	5,613	5,716	15,829	2,828	100.0	18.7	19.1	52.8	9.4
American Indian, Eskimo, Aleut	1,959	125	338	563	933	100.0	6.4	17.2	28.7	47.6
American Indian	1,878	122	334	557	866	100.0	6.5	17.8	29.7	46.1
Eskimo	57	2	2	3	51	100.0	2.9	3.5	4.9	88.8
Aleut	24	2	2	3	17	100.0	8.1	8.1	11.5	72.3
Asian or Pacific Islander [1] .	7,274	1,335	768	1,122	4,048	100.0	18.4	10.6	15.4	55.7
Chinese	1,645	445	133	204	863	100.0	27.0	8.1	12.4	52.4
Filipino	1,407	143	113	159	991	100.0	10.2	8.1	11.3	70.5
Japanese	848	74	63	67	643	100.0	8.8	7.5	7.9	75.9
Asian Indian	815	285	146	196	189	100.0	35.0	17.9	24.0	23.1
Korean	799	182	109	153	355	100.0	22.8	13.7	19.2	44.4
Vietnamese	615	61	52	169	334	100.0	9.8	8.5	27.4	54.3
Laotian	149	16	28	29	76	100.0	10.7	18.6	19.6	51.0
Cambodian	147	30	13	19	85	100.0	20.5	8.8	13.1	57.7
Thai	91	12	13	24	43	100.0	12.9	14.2	26.0	46.8
Hmong	90	2	37	2	50	100.0	1.9	41.3	1.8	55.0
Pakistani	81	28	15	22	17	100.0	34.3	18.9	26.5	20.4
Hawaiian	211	4	6	12	189	100.0	2.0	2.6	5.8	89.6
Samoan	63	2	2	4	55	100.0	2.4	3.6	6.4	87.6
Guamanian	49	4	3	8	34	100.0	7.3	6.4	16.8	69.5
Other races	9,805	1,667	829	2,350	4,960	100.0	17.0	8.5	24.0	50.6
Hispanic origin [2]	22,354	3,754	1,727	6,767	10,106	100.0	16.8	7.7	30.3	45.2
Mexican	13,496	175	1,153	4,344	7,824	100.0	1.3	8.5	32.2	58.0
Puerto Rican	2,728	1,872	258	406	192	100.0	68.6	9.4	14.9	7.0
Cuban	1,044	184	37	735	88	100.0	17.6	3.5	70.5	8.5
Other Hispanic	5,086	1,524	279	1,282	2,002	100.0	30.0	5.5	25.2	39.4
Not of Hispanic origin	226,356	47,055	57,942	78,679	42,680	100.0	20.8	25.6	34.8	18.9

[1] Includes other Asian and Pacific Islander races not shown separately. [2] Persons of Hispanic origin may be of any race.

Source: U.S. Bureau of the Census, press release CB91-216.

Table 5.10   Largest metropolitan areas — racial and Hispanic origin populations: 1990. (As of 1 April. Areas as defined by US Office of Management and Budget, 30 June 1990)

METROPOLITAN AREA [1]	Total population (1,000)	PERCENT OF TOTAL METROPOLITAN POPULATION			
		Black	American Indian, Eskimo, Aleut	Asian and Pacific Islander	Hispanic origin [2]
New York-Northern New Jersey-Long Island, NY-NJ-CT CMSA	18,087	18.2	0.3	4.8	15.4
Los Angeles-Anaheim-Riverside, CA CMSA	14,532	8.5	0.6	9.2	32.9
Chicago-Gary-Lake County, IL-IN-WI CMSA	8,066	19.2	0.2	3.2	11.1
San Francisco-Oakland-San Jose, CA CMSA	6,253	8.6	0.7	14.8	15.5
Philadelphia-Wilmington-Trenton, PA-NJ-DE-MD CMSA	5,899	18.7	0.2	2.1	3.8
Detroit-Ann Arbor, MI CMSA	4,665	20.9	0.4	1.5	1.9
Boston-Lawrence-Salem, MA-NH CMSA	4,172	5.7	0.2	2.9	4.6
Washington, DC-MD-VA MSA	3,924	26.6	0.3	5.2	5.7
Dallas-Fort Worth, TX CMSA	3,885	14.3	0.5	2.5	13.4
Houston-Galveston-Brazoria, TX CMSA	3,711	17.9	0.3	3.6	20.8
Miami-Fort Lauderdale, FL CMSA	3,193	18.5	0.2	1.4	33.3
Atlanta, GA MSA	2,834	26.0	0.2	1.8	2.0
Cleveland-Akron-Lorain, OH CMSA	2,760	16.0	0.2	1.0	1.9
Seattle-Tacoma, WA CMSA	2,559	4.8	1.3	6.4	3.0
San Diego, CA MSA	2,498	6.4	0.8	7.9	20.4
Minneapolis-St. Paul, MN-WI MSA	2,464	3.6	1.0	2.6	1.5
St. Louis, MO-IL MSA	2,444	17.3	0.2	1.0	1.1
Baltimore, MD MSA	2,382	25.9	0.3	1.8	1.3
Pittsburgh-Beaver Valley, PA CMSA	2,243	8.0	0.1	0.7	0.6
Phoenix, AZ MSA	2,122	3.5	1.8	1.7	16.3
Tampa-St. Petersburg-Clearwater, FL MSA	2,068	9.0	0.3	1.1	6.7
Denver-Boulder, CO CMSA	1,848	5.3	0.8	2.3	12.2
Cincinnati-Hamilton, OH-KY-IN CMSA	1,744	11.7	0.1	0.8	0.5
Milwaukee-Racine, WI CMSA	1,607	13.3	0.5	1.2	3.8
Kansas City, MO-KS MSA	1,566	12.8	0.5	1.1	2.9
Sacramento, CA MSA	1,481	6.9	1.1	7.7	11.6
Portland-Vancouver, OR-WA CMSA	1,478	2.8	0.9	3.5	3.4
Norfolk-Virginia Beach-Newport News, VA MSA	1,396	28.5	0.3	2.5	2.3
Columbus, OH MSA	1,377	12.0	-0.2	1.5	0.8
San Antonio, TX MSA	1,302	6.8	0.4	1.2	47.6
Indianapolis, IN MSA	1,250	13.8	0.2	0.8	0.9
New Orleans, LA MSA	1,239	34.7	0.3	1.7	4.3
Buffalo-Niagara Falls, NY CMSA	1,189	10.3	0.6	0.9	2.0
Charlotte-Gastonia-Rock Hill, NC-SC MSA	1,162	19.9	0.4	1.0	0.9
Providence-Pawtucket-Fall River, RI-MA CMSA	1,142	3.3	0.3	1.8	4.2
Hartford-New Britain-Middletown, CT CMSA	1,086	8.7	0.2	1.5	7.0
Orlando, FL MSA	1,073	12.4	0.3	1.9	9.0
Salt Lake City-Ogden, UT MSA	1,072	1.0	0.8	2.4	5.8
Rochester, NY MSA	1,002	9.4	0.3	1.4	3.1
Nashville, TN MSA	985	15.5	0.2	1.0	0.8
Memphis, TN-AR-MS MSA	982	40.6	0.2	0.8	0.8
Oklahoma City, OK MSA	959	10.5	4.8	1.9	3.6
Louisville, KY-IN MSA	953	13.1	0.2	0.6	0.6
Dayton-Springfield, OH MSA	951	13.3	0.2	1.0	0.8
Greensboro—Winston-Salem—High Point, NC MSA	942	19.3	0.3	0.7	0.8
Birmingham, AL MSA	908	27.1	0.2	0.4	0.4
Jacksonville, FL MSA	907	20.0	0.3	1.7	2.5
Albany-Schenectady-Troy, NY MSA	874	4.7	0.2	1.2	1.8
Richmond-Petersburg, VA MSA	866	29.2	0.3	1.4	1.1
West Palm Beach-Boca Raton-Delray Beach, FL MSA	864	12.5	0.1	1.0	7.7
Honolulu, HI MSA	836	3.1	0.4	63.0	6.8
Austin, TX MSA	782	9.2	0.4	2.4	20.5
Las Vegas, NV MSA	741	9.5	0.9	3.5	11.2
Raleigh-Durham, NC MSA	735	24.9	0.3	1.9	1.2
Scranton—Wilkes-Barre, PA MSA	734	1.0	0.1	0.5	0.8
Tulsa, OK MSA	709	8.2	6.8	0.9	2.1
Grand Rapids, MI MSA	688	6.0	0.5	1.1	3.3
Allentown-Bethlehem, PA-NJ MSA	687	2.0	0.1	1.1	4.2
Fresno, CA MSA	667	5.0	1.1	8.6	35.5
Tucson, AZ MSA	667	3.1	3.0	1.8	24.5
Syracuse, NY MSA	660	5.9	0.6	1.2	1.4
Greenville-Spartanburg, SC MSA	641	17.4	0.1	0.7	0.8
Omaha, NE-IA MSA	618	8.3	0.5	1.0	2.6
Toledo, OH MSA	614	11.4	0.2	1.0	3.3
Knoxville, TN MSA	605	6.0	0.2	0.8	0.5
El Paso, TX MSA	592	3.7	0.4	1.1	69.6
Harrisburg-Lebanon-Carlisle, PA MSA	588	6.7	0.1	1.1	1.7
Bakersfield, CA MSA	543	5.5	1.3	3.0	28.0
New Haven-Meriden, CT MSA	530	12.1	0.2	1.6	6.2
Springfield, MA MSA	530	6.6	0.2	1.0	9.0
Baton Rouge, LA MSA	528	29.6	0.2	1.1	1.4
Little Rock-North Little Rock, AR MSA	513	19.9	0.4	0.7	0.8
Charleston, SC MSA	507	30.2	0.3	1.2	1.5
Youngstown-Warren, OH MSA	493	11.1	0.2	0.4	1.5
Wichita, KS MSA	485	7.6	1.1	1.9	4.1

[1] Metropolitan areas are shown in rank order of total population of consolidated metropolitan statistical areas (CMSA) and metropolitan statistical areas (MSA).   [2] Persons of Hispanic origin may be of any race.

Source: U.S. Bureau of the Census, press release CB91-229.

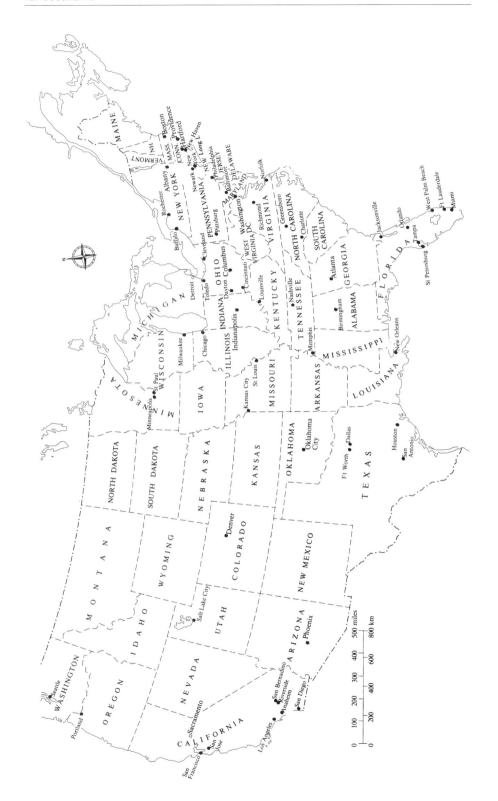

Figure 5.7 50 largest metropolitan areas, 1990

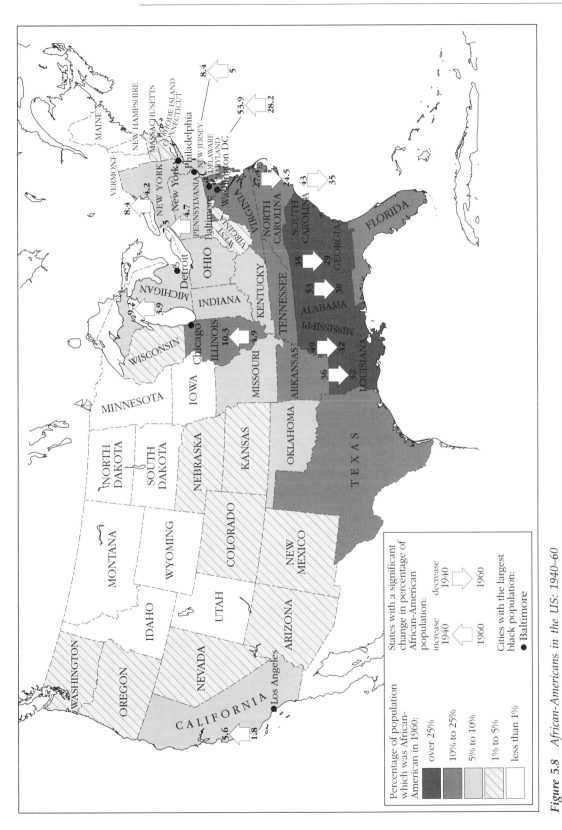

Figure 5.8 *African-Americans in the US: 1940–60*

Source: adapted from Gilbert, M. (1993) *The Dent Atlas of American History*, 3rd edn, London, Routledge; see also Potter *et al.* (1997) *Democratization*, Cambridge, Polity Press in association with The Open University, Map 5.1.

5.3   RELIGION

With around 60 per cent of the population currently belonging to religious bodies, religion has an important place in the culture and life of the US. The biggest religious grouping is 'Protestant' Christianity, however, there are a large number of individual churches, with complex histories, that come under this heading. The largest single religious group is the Roman Catholic Church. For the most part the Roman Catholic Church has maintained its position with the descendants of immigrants from Roman Catholic areas of Europe. The following tables show the size and diversity of religious bodies.

Table 5.11   Religious preference, church membership and attendance: 1957–90.
(In per cent. Covers civilian non-institutional population, 18 years old and over. Data represent averages of the combined results of several surveys during year. Data are subject to sampling variability)

YEAR	RELIGIOUS PREFERENCE					Church/ synagogue members	Persons attending church/ synagogue [1]	AGE AND REGION	Church/ synagogue members, 1990
	Protestant	Catholic	Jewish	Other	None				
1957	66	26	3	1	3	[2]73	47	18-29 years old. . . .	57
1967	67	25	3	3	2	[3]73	43	30-49 years old. . . .	63
1975	62	27	2	4	6	71	41	50 years and over . .	74
1980	61	28	2	2	7	69	40	East [4]	65
1985	57	28	2	4	9	71	42	Midwest [5]	70
1989	56	28	2	4	10	69	43	South [6]	70
1990	56	25	2	6	11	65	40	West [7]	54

[1] Persons who attended a church or synagogue in the last seven days.   [2] 1952 data.   [3] 1965 data.   [4] ME, NH, RI, NY, CT, VT, MA, NJ, PA, WV, DE, MD, and DC.   [5] OH, IN, IL, MI, MN, WI, IA, ND, SD, KS, NE, and MO.   [6] KY, TN, VA, NC, SC, GA, FL, AL, MS, TX, AR, OK, and LA.   [7] AZ, NM, CO, NV, MT, ID, WY, UT, CA, WA, OR, AK, and HI.
Source: Princeton Religion Research Center, Princeton, NJ, "Emerging Trends," periodical. Based on surveys conducted by The Gallup Organization, Inc.

Table 5.12   Religious bodies — church membership, 1960–89, and number of churches, 1989. (Membership in thousands, except as indicated)

RELIGIOUS BODY	MEMBERSHIP						Number of churches, 1989
	1960	1970	1975	1980	1985	1989	
Total	**114,449**	**131,045**	**131,013**	**134,817**	**142,926**	**147,607**	**350,337**
Members as percent of population [1]	64	63	61	59	60	60	(X)
Average members per local church	359	399	393	401	413	421	(X)
Buddhist Churches of America	20	100	60	60	100	19	67
Eastern Churches.	2,699	3,850	3,696	3,823	4,026	4,057	1,705
Jews [2]	5,367	5,870	6,115	5,920	5,835	5,944	3,416
Old Catholic, Polish National Catholic, and Armenian Churches.	590	848	846	924	1,024	980	442
The Roman Catholic Church	42,105	48,215	48,882	50,450	52,655	57,020	23,500
Protestants [3]	[4]63,669	71,713	71,043	73,479	79,096	79,387	320,039
Miscellaneous [5]	([4])	449	372	161	191	200	1,168

X Not applicable.   [1] Based on Bureau of the Census estimated total population as of July 1. Estimates for 1980's reflect results of 1990 census.   [2] Estimates of the Jewish community including those identified with Orthodox, Conservative and Reformed synagogues or temples.   [3] Includes nonprotestant bodies such as "Latter-day Saints" and "Jehovah's Witnesses."   [4] Data for "Miscellaneous" included with Protestants.   [5] Includes non-Christian bodies such as "Spiritualists," "Ethical Culture Movement," and "Unitarian-Universalists."
Source: National Council of the Churches of Christ in the United States of America, New York, NY, *Yearbook of American and Canadian Churches*, annual, (copyright).

Table 5.13   Religious bodies — selected data. (Includes the self-reported membership of religious bodies with 60,000 or more as reported to the Yearbook of American and Canadian Churches. Groups may be excluded if they do not supply information. The data are not standardized so comparisons between groups are difficult. The definition of 'church member' is determined by the religious body)

RELIGIOUS BODY	Year reported	Churches reported	Member-ship (1,000)	Pastors serving parishes [1]
African Methodist Episcopal Church [2]	1991	8,000	3,500	(NA)
African Methodist Episcopal Zion Church	1996	3,098	1,231	2,571
American Baptist Association	1986	1,705	250	1,740
American Baptist Churches in the U.S.A.	1995	5,823	1,517	4,974
Antiochian Orthodox Christian Archdiocese of North America, The	1995	184	300	200
Armenian Apostolic Church of America	1995	28	180	23
Assemblies of God	1995	11,823	2,388	17,693
Baptist Bible Fellowship International, The	1995	3,600	1,500	(NA)
Baptist General Conference	1995	857	135	(NA)
Baptist Missionary Association of America	1995	1,355	231	1,300
Buddhist [3]	1990	(NA)	401	(NA)
Christian and Missionary Alliance, The	1995	1,957	307	1,578
Christian Brethren (a.k.a. Plymouth Brethren)	1994	1,150	98	500
Christian Church (Disciples of Christ)	1995	4,036	930	4,010
Christian Churches and Churches of Christ	1988	5,579	1,071	5,525
Christian Congregation, Inc., The	1995	1,431	113	1,427
Christian Methodist Episcopal Church	1983	2,340	719	2,340
Christian Reformed Church in North America	1996	716	207	666
Church of God (Anderson, IN)	1995	2,307	224	3,011
Church of God (Cleveland, TN)	1995	6,060	753	3,121
Church of God in Christ, The	1991	15,300	5,500	28,988
Church of God of Prophecy, The	1995	1,961	73	8,636
Church of Jesus Christ of Latter-day Saints, The	1995	10,417	4,712	31,251
Church of the Brethren	1995	1,114	143	844
Church of the Nazarene	1995	5,135	602	5,111
Churches of Christ	1995	13,020	1,655	10,000
Conservative Baptist Association of America	1992	1,084	200	(NA)
Coptic Orthodox Church	1992	85	180	65
Cumberland Presbyterian Church	1995	783	88	(NA)
Diocese of the Armenian Church of America	1991	72	414	49
Episcopal Church, The	1995	7,415	2,537	8,037
Evangelical Covenant Church, The	1995	(NA)	91	(NA)
Evangelical Free Church of America	1996	1,224	243	1,936
Evangelical Lutheran Church in America	1995	10,955	5,190	9,819
Free Methodist Church of North America	1995	1,068	75	(NA)
Full Gospel Fellowship of Churches & Ministers International	1995	650	195	725
General Association of Regular Baptist Churches	1994	1,458	136	(NA)
General Baptists (General Association of)	1990	876	74	1,384
Grace Gospel Fellowship	1992	128	60	160
Greek Orthodox Archdiocese of North and South America	1977	532	1,950	610
Hindu [3]	1990	(NA)	227	(NA)
Independent Fundamental Churches of America	1995	670	70	(NA)
International Church of the Foursquare Gospel	1995	1,742	227	(NA)
International Council of Community Churches	1995	517	250	491
International Pentecostal Holiness Church	1995	1,653	157	(NA)
Jehovah's Witnesses	1995	10,541	966	(NA)
Jewish [3]	1990	(NA)	3,137	(NA)
Lutheran Church - Missouri Synod, The	1995	6,154	2,595	5,287
Mennonite Church	1995	986	91	1,350
Muslim / Islamic [3]	1990	(NA)	527	(NA)
National Association of Congregational Christian Churches	1995	426	70	600
National Association of Free Will Baptists	1995	2,491	214	2,800
National Baptist Convention of America, Inc.	1987	2,500	3,500	8,000
National Baptist Convention, U.S.A., Inc.	1992	33,000	8,200	32,832
National Missionary Baptist Convention of America	1992	(NA)	2,500	(NA)
Old Order Amish Church	1993	898	81	3,592
Orthodox Church in America	1995	600	2,000	650
Pentecostal Assemblies of the World	1994	1,760	1,000	4,262
Pentecostal Church of God, Inc.	1995	1,224	119	(NA)
Polish National Catholic Church of North America	1960	162	282	141
Presbyterian Church in America	1995	1,299	268	1,522
Presbyterian Church (U.S.A.)	1995	11,361	3,669	9,588
Progressive National Baptist Convention, Inc.	1995	2,000	2,500	(NA)
Reformed Church in America	1995	908	306	855
Reorganized Church of Jesus Christ of Latter-day Saints	1995	1,160	178	16,671
Roman Catholic Church, The	1995	19,726	60,280	(NA)
Romanian Orthodox Episcopate of America	1995	37	65	37
Salvation Army, The	1995	1,264	453	3,645
Serbian Orthodox Church in the U.S.A. and Canada	1986	68	67	60
Seventh-day Adventist Church	1995	4,297	791	2,307
Southern Baptist Convention	1995	40,039	15,663	38,123
Unitarian Universalist [3]	1990	(NA)	502	(NA)
United Church of Christ	1995	6,145	1,472	4,439
United Methodist Church, The	1995	36,361	8,539	19,560
Wesleyan Church (USA), The	1995	1,624	116	1,785
Wisconsin Evangelical Lutheran Synod	1995	1,252	412	1,198

NA Not available.   [1] Does not include retired clergy or clergy not working with congregations.   [2] Figures obtained from the *Directory of African American Religious Bodies, 1991.*   [3] Figures obtained from the National Survey of Religious Identification, a survey conducted by the City University of New York in 1990 and published in *One Nation Under God: Religion in Contemporary American Society,* by Barry Kosmin and Seymour Lachman (1993).

Source: Kenneth B. Bedell, editor, *Yearbook of American and Canadian Churches,* annual (copyright).

5.4 EDUCATION

The following tables and figures have been selected to provide a summary of education in the United States. The first four concentrate on how much education selected groups have received in recent times, in terms of enrolment and years of school completed, and High School dropout rates. The others examine higher education since the 1970s, again by enrolment but also by income and expenditure, and field of study. Note the improved levels of participation over the years of women and minority ethnic groups, and the recent changes in the fields of study, for example the rapid expansion of computer and information sciences.

Table 5.14　School enrolment: 1965–2006 (In thousands)

YEAR	TOTAL	ALL LEVELS		K THROUGH GRADE 8		GRADES 9 THROUGH 12		COLLEGE	
		Public	Private	Public	Private	Public	Private	Public	Private
1965	54,394	46,143	8,251	30,563	4,900	11,610	1,400	3,970	1,951
1970	59,838	52,322	7,516	32,558	4,052	13,336	1,311	6,428	2,153
1975	61,004	53,654	7,350	30,515	3,700	14,304	1,300	8,835	2,350
1980	58,305	50,335	7,971	27,647	3,992	13,231	1,339	9,457	2,640
1981	57,916	49,691	8,225	27,280	4,100	12,764	1,400	9,647	2,725
1982	57,591	49,262	8,330	27,161	4,200	12,405	1,400	9,696	2,730
1983	57,432	48,935	8,497	26,981	4,315	12,271	1,400	9,683	2,782
1984	57,150	48,686	8,465	26,905	4,300	12,304	1,400	9,477	2,765
1985	57,226	48,901	8,325	27,034	4,195	12,388	1,362	9,479	2,768
1986	57,709	49,467	8,242	27,420	4,116	12,333	1,336	9,714	2,790
1987	58,254	49,982	8,272	27,933	4,232	12,076	1,247	9,973	2,793
1988	58,485	50,349	8,136	28,501	4,036	11,687	1,206	10,161	2,894
1989	59,436	51,120	8,316	29,152	4,162	11,390	1,193	10,578	2,961
1990	60,267	52,061	8,206	29,878	4,095	11,338	1,137	10,845	2,974
1991	61,605	53,357	8,248	30,506	4,074	11,541	1,125	11,310	3,049
1992	62,686	54,208	8,478	31,088	4,212	11,735	1,163	11,385	3,103
1993	63,241	54,654	8,587	31,504	4,280	11,961	1,191	11,189	3,116
1994, prel. [1]	63,984	55,242	8,741	31,894	4,360	12,214	1,236	11,134	3,145
1995, est. [1]	64,623	55,753	8,869	32,085	4,431	12,576	1,269	11,092	3,169
1996, proj.	66,081	57,140	8,942	32,837	4,493	13,049	1,304	11,254	3,145
1997, proj.	66,996	57,930	9,067	33,226	4,547	13,299	1,329	11,405	3,191
1998, proj.	67,807	58,615	9,192	33,522	4,587	13,466	1,346	11,627	3,259
1999, proj.	68,570	59,251	9,319	33,692	4,610	13,673	1,367	11,886	3,342
2000, proj.	69,165	59,747	9,418	33,852	4,632	13,804	1,380	12,091	3,406
2001, proj.	69,604	60,116	9,488	34,029	4,656	13,862	1,386	12,225	3,446
2002, proj.	69,966	60,421	9,545	34,098	4,666	14,004	1,400	12,319	3,479
2003, proj.	70,244	60,654	9,589	34,065	4,661	14,169	1,416	12,420	3,512
2004, proj.	70,527	60,896	9,631	33,882	4,636	14,483	1,448	12,531	3,547
2005, proj.	70,816	61,144	9,672	33,680	4,609	14,818	1,481	12,646	3,582
2006, proj.	71,004	61,296	9,707	33,507	4,585	15,021	1,501	12,768	3,621

[1] College data are preliminary.

Source: U.S. National Center for Education Statistics, *Digest of Education Statistics*, annual, and *Projections of Education Statistics*, annual.

K is kindergarten; grades 1–8: Elementary School; grades 9–12: High School.

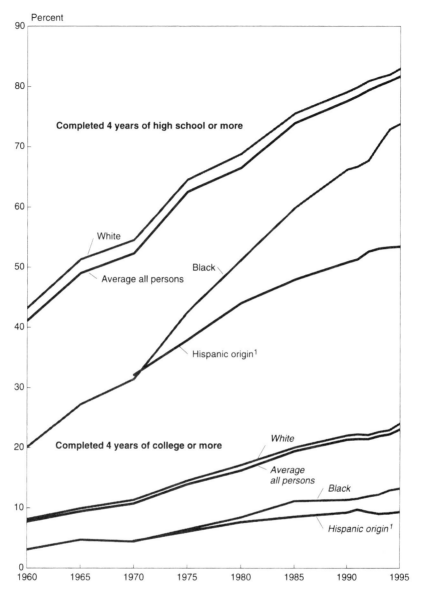

Figure 5.9 *Educational attainment by race and Hispanic origin: 1960–95.*
(For persons 25 years old and over)

[1] Persons of Hispanic origin may be of any race. Data for 1960 and 1965 not available for persons of Hispanic origin.

Source: US Bureau of the Census, *Statistical Abstract of the United States: 1997*, Government Printing Office, Figure 4.1.

Table 5.15 Educational attainment, by race, Hispanic origin, and sex: 1960–96.
(In per cent. For persons 25 years old and over. 1960, 1970, and 1980 as of 1 April and based on sample data from the censuses of population. Other years as of March and based on Current Population Survey)

YEAR	ALL RACES [1]		WHITE		BLACK		ASIAN AND PACIFIC ISLANDER		HISPANIC [2]	
	Male	Female	Male	Female	Male	Female	Male	Female	Male	Female
COMPLETED 4 YEARS OF HIGH SCHOOL OR MORE										
1960	39.5	42.5	41.6	44.7	18.2	21.8	(NA)	(NA)	(NA)	(NA)
1965	48.0	49.9	50.2	52.2	25.8	28.4	(NA)	(NA)	(NA)	(NA)
1970	51.9	52.8	54.0	55.0	30.1	32.5	(NA)	(NA)	37.9	34.2
1975	63.1	62.1	65.0	64.1	41.6	43.3	(NA)	(NA)	39.5	36.7
1980	67.3	65.8	69.6	68.1	50.8	51.5	(NA)	(NA)	67.3	65.8
1985	74.4	73.5	76.0	75.1	58.4	60.8	(NA)	(NA)	48.5	47.4
1990	77.7'	77.5	79.1	79.0	65.8	66.5	84.0	77.2	50.3	51.3
1993 [3]	80.5	80.0	81.8	81.3	69.6	71.1	(NA)	(NA)	52.9	53.2
1994 [3]	81.0	80.7	82.1	81.9	71.7	73.8	(NA)	(NA)	53.4	53.2
1995 [3]	81.7	81.6	83.0	83.0	73.4	74.1	(NA)	(NA)	52.9	53.8
1996 [3]	81.9	81.6	82.7	82.8	74.3	74.2	(NA)	(NA)	53.0	53.3
COMPLETED 4 YEARS OF COLLEGE OR MORE										
1960	9.7	5.8	10.3	6.0	2.8	3.3	(NA)	(NA)	(NA)	(NA)
1965	12.0	7.1	12.7	7.3	4.9	4.5	(NA)	(NA)	(NA)	(NA)
1970	13.5	8.1	14.4	8.4	4.2	4.6	(NA)	(NA)	7.8	4.3
1975	17.6	10.6	18.4	11.0	6.7	6.2	(NA)	(NA)	8.3	4.6
1980	20.1	12.8	21.3	13.3	8.4	8.3	(NA)	(NA)	9.4	6.0
1985	23.1	16.0	24.0	16.3	11.2	11.0	(NA)	(NA)	9.7	7.3
1990	24.4	18.4	25.3	19.0	11.9	10.8	44.9	35.4	9.8	8.7
1993 [3]	24.8	19.2	25.7	19.7	11.9	12.4	(NA)	(NA)	9.5	8.5
1994 [3]	25.1	19.6	26.1	20.0	12.8	13.0	(NA)	(NA)	9.6	8.6
1995 [3]	26.0	20.2	27.2	21.0	13.6	12.9	(NA)	(NA)	10.1	8.4
1996 [3]	26.0	21.4	26.9	21.8	12.4	14.6	(NA)	(NA)	10.3	8.3

NA Not available. [1] Includes other races, not shown separately. [2] Persons of Hispanic origin may be of any race. [3] Beginning 1993, persons high school graduates and those with a BA degree or higher.

Source: U.S. Bureau of the Census, *U.S. Census of Population, 1960, 1970, and 1980, vol.1;* and *Current Population Reports* P20-459, P20-493, P20-475, P20-489, P20-493; and unpublished data.

Table 5.16 High School dropouts, by race and Hispanic origin: 1975–95.
(In per cent. As of October)

ITEM	1975	1980	1985	1987 [1]	1988	1989	1990	1991	1992	1993	1994	1995
EVENT DROPOUTS [2]												
Total [3]	5.8	6.0	5.2	4.1	4.8	4.5	4.0	4.0	4.3	4.2	5.0	5.4
White	5.4	5.6	4.8	3.7	4.7	3.9	3.8	3.7	4.1	4.1	4.7	5.1
Male	5.0	6.4	4.9	4.1	5.1	4.1	4.1	3.6	3.8	4.1	4.6	5.4
Female	5.8	4.9	4.7	3.4	4.3	3.8	3.5	3.8	4.4	4.1	4.9	4.8
Black	8.7	8.3	7.7	6.4	6.3	7.7	5.1	6.2	4.9	5.4	6.2	6.1
Male	8.3	8.0	8.3	6.2	6.7	6.9	4.1	5.5	3.3	5.7	6.5	7.9
Female	9.0	8.5	7.2	6.4	6.0	8.6	6.0	7.0	6.7	5.0	5.7	4.4
Hispanic [4]	10.9	11.5	9.7	5.6	10.5	7.7	8.0	7.3	7.9	5.4	9.2	11.6
Male	10.1	16.9	9.3	5.0	12.3	7.6	8.7	10.4	5.8	5.7	8.4	10.9
Female	11.6	6.9	9.8	6.2	8.4	7.7	7.2	4.8	8.6	5.0	10.1	12.5
STATUS DROPOUTS [5]												
Total [3]	15.6	15.6	13.9	14.5	14.6	14.4	13.6	14.2	12.7	12.7	13.3	13.9
White	13.9	14.4	13.5	14.2	14.2	14.1	13.5	14.2	12.2	12.2	12.7	13.6
Male	13.5	15.7	14.7	15.1	15.4	15.4	15.4	14.2	13.3	13.0	13.6	14.3
Female	14.2	13.2	12.3	13.2	13.0	12.8	12.8	13.1	11.1	11.5	11.7	13.0
Black	27.3	23.5	17.6	17.0	17.7	16.4	15.1	15.6	16.3	16.4	15.5	14.4
Male	27.8	26.0	18.8	18.7	18.9	18.6	13.6	15.4	15.5	15.6	17.5	14.2
Female	26.9	21.5	16.6	15.4	16.6	14.5	16.2	15.8	17.1	17.2	13.7	14.6
Hispanic [4]	34.9	40.3	31.5	32.8	39.6	37.7	37.3	39.6	33.9	32.7	34.7	34.7
Male	32.6	42.6	35.8	34.5	40.2	40.3	39.8	44.4	38.4	34.7	36.1	34.2
Female	36.8	38.1	27.0	30.8	38.8	35.0	34.5	34.5	29.6	31.0	33.1	35.4

[1] Beginning 1987 reflects new editing procedures for cases with missing data on school enrollment. [2] Percent of students who drop out in a single year without completing high school. For grades 10 to 12. [3] Includes other races, not shown separately. [4] Persons of Hispanic origin may be of any race. [5] Percent of the population who have not completed high school and are not enrolled, regardless of when they dropped out. For persons 18 to 24 years old.

Source: U.S. Bureau of the Census, *Current Population Reports,* P20-492.

Table 5.17   Higher education — summary: 1970–95. (Institutions, staff, and enrolment as of autumn. Finances for fiscal year ending in the following year. Covers universities, colleges, professional schools, junior and teachers colleges, both publicly and privately controlled, regular session. Includes estimates for institutions not reporting)

ITEM	Unit	1970	1980	1985	1990	1991	1992	1993	1994, est.	1995, est.
ALL INSTITUTIONS										
Number of institutions [1]	Number .	2,556	3,231	3,340	3,559	3,601	3,638	3,632	3,688	3,706
4-year	Number .	1,665	1,957	2,029	2,141	2,157	2,169	2,190	2,215	2,244
2-year	Number .	891	1,274	1,311	1,418	1,444	1,469	1,442	1,473	1,462
Instructional staff—										
(Lecturer or above) [2]	1,000 . . .	474	686	715	817	826	877	915	915	910
Percent full-time	Percent .	78	66	64	61	65	(NA)	60	(NA)	(NA)
Total enrollment [3]	1,000 . . .	8,581	12,097	12,247	13,819	14,359	14,486	14,305	14,279	14,262
Male	1,000 . . .	5,044	5,874	5,818	6,284	6,502	6,524	6,427	6,372	6,343
Female	1,000 . . .	3,537	6,223	6,429	7,535	7,857	7,963	7,877	7,907	7,919
4-year institutions	1,000 . . .	6,262	7,571	7,716	8,579	8,707	8,765	8,739	8,749	8,769
2-year institutions	1,000 . . .	2,319	4,526	4,531	5,240	5,652	5,722	5,566	5,530	5,493
Full-time	1,000 . . .	5,816	7,098	7,075	7,821	8,115	8,162	8,128	8,138	8,129
Part-time	1,000 . . .	2,765	4,999	5,172	5,998	6,244	6,325	6,177	6,141	6,133
Public	1,000 . . .	6,428	9,457	9,479	10,845	11,310	11,385	11,189	11,134	11,092
Private	1,000 . . .	2,153	2,640	2,768	2,974	3,049	3,102	3,116	3,145	3,169
Undergraduate [4]	1,000 . . .	7,376	10,475	10,597	11,959	12,439	12,538	12,324	12,263	12,232
Men	1,000 . . .	4,254	5,000	4,962	5,380	5,571	5,583	5,484	5,422	5,401
Women	1,000 . . .	3,122	5,475	5,635	6,579	6,868	6,955	6,840	6,840	6,831
First-time freshmen	1,000 . . .	2,063	2,588	2,292	2,257	2,278	2,184	2,161	2,133	2,169
First professional	1,000 . . .	173	278	274	273	281	281	292	295	298
Men	1,000 . . .	159	199	180	167	170	169	173	174	174
Women	1,000 . . .	15	78	94	107	111	112	120	121	124
Graduate [4]	1,000 . . .	1,031	1,343	1,376	1,586	1,639	1,669	1,688	1,721	1,732
Men	1,000 . . .	630	675	677	737	761	772	771	776	768
Women	1,000 . . .	400	670	700	849	878	896	917	946	965
Current funds revenues [5]	Mil. dol .	23,879	65,585	100,438	149,766	161,396	170,881	179,227	(NA)	(NA)
Tuition and fees	Mil. dol .	5,021	13,773	23,117	37,434	41,559	45,346	48,647	(NA)	(NA)
Federal government	Mil. dol .	4,190	9,748	12,705	18,236	19,833	21,015	22,076	(NA)	(NA)
State government	Mil. dol .	6,503	20,106	29,912	39,481	40,587	41,248	41,910	(NA)	(NA)
Auxiliary enterprises	Mil. dol .	3,125	7,287	10,674	14,903	15,759	16,663	17,538	(NA)	(NA)
Plant funds [6]	Mil. dol .	(NA)	4,774	7,713	(NA)	(NA)	(NA)	(NA)	(NA)	(NA)
Increase in fund balance [7] . . .	Mil. dol .	498	2,793	7,239	(NA)	(NA)	(NA)	(NA)	(NA)	(NA)
Current funds expenditures [5] .	Mil. dol .	23,375	64,053	97,536	146,088	156,189	165,241	173,351	(NA)	(NA)
Educational and general [8] . . .	Mil. dol .	17,616	50,074	76,128	114,140	121,567	128,978	136,024	(NA)	(NA)
Auxiliary enterprises [9]	Mil. dol .	2,988	7,288	10,528	14,272	14,966	15,562	16,429	(NA)	(NA)
Gross addition to plant value . . .	Mil. dol .	4,165	6,471	10,149	19,672	(NA)	(NA)	(NA)	(NA)	(NA)
Value of plant	Mil. dol .	46,054	88,761	122,261	190,355	(NA)	(NA)	(NA)	(NA)	(NA)
Endowment (market value)	Mil. dol .	13,714	23,465	50,281	72,049	(NA)	(NA)	(NA)	(NA)	(NA)
2-YEAR INSTITUTIONS										
Number of institutions [1] [10] . . .	Number .	891	1,274	1,311	1,418	1,444	1,469	1,442	1,473	1,462
Public	Number .	654	945	932	972	999	1,024	1,021	1,036	1,047
Private	Number .	237	329	379	446	445	445	421	437	415
Instructional staff—										
(Lecturer or above) [2]	1,000 . . .	92	192	211	(NA)	235	(NA)	290	(NA)	(NA)
Enrollment [3] [4]	1,000 . . .	2,319	4,526	4,531	5,240	5,652	5,722	5,566	5,530	5,493
Public	1,000 . . .	2,195	4,329	4,270	4,996	5,405	5,485	5,337	5,308	5,278
Private	1,000 . . .	124	198	261	244	247	238	229	221	215
Male	1,000 . . .	1,375	2,047	2,002	2,233	2,402	2,413	2,345	2,323	2,329
Female	1,000 . . .	945	2,479	2,529	3,007	3,250	3,309	3,220	3,207	3,164
Current funds revenue [5]	Mil. dol .	2,504	8,505	12,293	18,021	19,695	20,805	21,961	(NA)	(NA)
Tuition and fees	Mil. dol .	413	1,618	2,618	4,029	4,649	5,218	5,594	(NA)	(NA)
State government	Mil. dol .	926	3,961	5,659	8,001	8,537	8,647	8,730	(NA)	(NA)
Local government	Mil. dol .	701	1,623	2,027	3,044	3,259	3,524	3,936	(NA)	(NA)
Current funds expenditures . .	Mil. dol .	2,327	8,212	11,976	17,494	18,814	19,941	21,187	(NA)	(NA)
Education and general [8]	Mil. dol .	2,073	7,608	11,118	16,270	17,462	18,578	19,763	(NA)	(NA)
Instruction	Mil. dol .	1,205	3,764	5,398	7,903	8,547	9,018	9,476	(NA)	(NA)

NA Not available.   [1] Beginning 1980, number of institutions includes count of branch campuses. Due to revised survey procedures, data beginning 1990 are not comparable with previous years.   [2] Due to revised survey methods, data beginning 1990 not comparable with previous years.   [3] Beginning 1980, branch campuses counted according to actual status, e.g., 2-year branch in 2-year category; previously a 2-year branch included in university category.   [4] Includes unclassified students. (Students taking courses for credit, but are not candidates for degrees.)   [5] Includes items not shown separately.   [6] Annual net increase in plant funds.   [7] Includes endowment, and, beginning 1980, annuity and student loans.   [8] Data for 1970 are not strictly comparable with later years.   [9] Includes activities.   [10] Beginning 1980, includes schools accredited by the National Association of Trade and Technical Schools.

Source: U.S. National Center for Education Statistics, *Digest of Education Statistics*, annual; *Projections of Education Statistics*, annual; and unpublished data.

Table 5.18   College enrolment, by sex, age, race, and Hispanic origin: 1975–95.
(In thousands. As of October for civilian non-institutional population, 14 years old and over. Based on Current Population Survey)

CHARACTERISTIC	1975	1980	1985	1988 [1]	1989	1990	1991	1992	1993	1994	1995
Total [2]	10,880	11,387	12,524	13,116	13,180	13,621	14,057	14,035	13,898	15,022	14,715
Male [3]	5,911	5,430	5,906	5,950	5,950	6,192	6,439	6,192	6,324	6,764	6,703
18 to 24 years	3,693	3,604	3,749	3,770	3,717	3,922	3,954	3,912	3,994	4,152	4,089
25 to 34 years	1,521	1,325	1,464	1,395	1,443	1,412	1,605	1,392	1,406	1,589	1,561
35 years old and over . .	569	405	561	727	716	772	832	789	873	958	985
Female [3]	4,969	5,957	6,618	7,166	7,231	7,429	7,618	7,844	7,574	8,258	8,013
18 to 24 years	3,243	3,625	3,788	4,021	4,085	4,042	4,218	4,429	4,199	4,576	4,452
25 to 34 years	947	1,378	1,599	1,568	1,639	1,749	1,680	1,732	1,688	1,830	1,788
35 years old and over . .	614	802	1,100	1,452	1,396	1,546	1,636	1,636	1,575	1,766	1,684
White [3]	9,546	9,925	10,781	11,140	11,243	11,488	11,686	11,710	11,434	12,222	12,021
18 to 24 years	6,116	6,334	6,500	6,659	6,631	6,635	6,813	6,916	6,763	7,118	7,011
25 to 34 years	2,147	2,328	2,604	2,448	2,597	2,698	2,661	2,582	2,505	2,735	2,686
35 years old and over . .	1,031	1,051	1,448	1,896	1,868	2,023	2,107	2,053	2,068	2,267	2,208
Male	5,263	4,804	5,103	5,078	5,136	5,235	5,304	5,210	5,222	5,524	5,535
Female	4,284	5,121	5,679	6,063	6,107	6,253	6,382	6,499	6,212	6,698	6,486
Black [3]	1,099	1,163	1,263	1,321	1,287	1,393	1,477	1,424	1,545	1,800	1,772
18 to 24 years	665	688	734	752	835	894	828	886	861	1,001	988
25 to 34 years	248	289	295	330	275	258	373	302	386	440	426
35 years old and over . .	152	156	213	206	146	207	257	208	284	323	334
Male	523	476	552	494	480	587	629	527	636	745	710
Female	577	686	712	827	807	807	848	897	909	1,054	1,062
Hispanic origin [3][4]	411	443	580	747	754	748	830	918	995	1,187	1,207
18 to 24 years	295	315	375	450	453	435	516	586	602	662	745
25 to 34 years	103	118	189	191	170	168	196	214	249	312	250
35 years old and over . .	(NA)	(NA)	(NA)	93	114	130	109	102	129	205	193
Male	218	222	279	355	353	364	347	388	442	529	568
Female	193	221	299	391	401	384	483	530	553	659	639

NA Not available.   [1] Beginning 1988, based on a revised edit and tabulation package.   [2] Includes other races not shown separately.   [3] Includes persons 14 to 17 years old, not shown separately.   [4] Persons of Hispanic origin may be of any race.

Source: U.S. Bureau of the Census, *Current Population Reports*, P20-492; and earlier reports.

Table 5.19   Bachelor's degrees earned, by field: 1971–94

FIELD OF STUDY	1971	1980	1985	1990	1994	PERCENT FEMALE 1971	PERCENT FEMALE 1994
Total	839,730	929,417	979,477	1,051,344	1,169,275	43.4	54.5
Agriculture and natural resources	12,672	22,802	18,107	12,900	18,070	4.2	35.0
Architecture and environmental design	5,570	9,132	9,325	9,364	8,975	11.9	35.8
Area, ethnic and cultural studies	2,582	2,840	2,985	4,613	5,573	52.4	64.9
Biological sciences/life sciences	35,743	46,370	38,445	37,204	51,383	29.1	51.2
Business and management	114,729	184,867	232,636	248,698	246,654	9.1	47.6
Communications [1]	10,802	28,616	42,002	51,308	51,827	35.3	58.8
Computer and information sciences	2,388	11,154	38,878	27,257	24,200	13.6	28.4
Education	176,307	118,038	88,072	105,112	107,600	74.5	77.3
Engineering [1]	50,046	68,893	95,828	81,322	78,225	0.8	14.9
English language and literature/letters	64,342	32,541	33,218	47,519	53,924	65.6	65.8
Foreign languages	20,536	12,089	10,827	12,386	14,378	74.0	70.1
Health sciences	25,226	63,920	64,422	58,302	74,421	77.1	82.4
Home economics	11,167	18,411	15,157	14,491	15,522	97.3	87.5
Law	545	683	1,157	1,592	2,171	5.0	70.2
Liberal/general studies	7,481	23,196	21,818	27,985	33,397	33.6	60.7
Library and archival sciences	1,013	398	197	77	62	92.0	91.9
Mathematics	24,937	11,872	15,861	15,176	14,396	37.9	46.3
Military technologies	357	38	299	196	19	0.3	15.8
Multi/interdisciplinary studies	6,286	11,277	12,978	16,267	25,167	22.8	64.0
Parks and recreation	1,621	5,753	4,725	4,582	11,470	34.7	49.2
Philosophy, religion, and theology	11,890	13,276	12,447	12,068	12,980	25.5	30.9
Physical sciences [1]	21,412	23,410	23,704	16,066	18,400	13.8	33.6
Protective services	2,045	15,015	12,510	15,354	23,009	9.2	38.4
Psychology	38,187	42,093	39,900	53,952	69,259	44.4	73.1
Public affairs	5,466	16,644	11,754	13,908	17,815	68.4	78.0
Social sciences [2]	155,324	103,662	91,570	118,083	133,680	36.8	46.1
Visual and performing arts	30,394	40,892	38,140	39,934	49,053	59.7	60.2
Unclassified	662	1,535	2,515	5,628	7,645	0.9	29.0

[1] Includes technologies.   [2] Includes history.
Source: U.S. National Center for Education Statistics, *Digest of Education Statistics*, annual.

5.5 LEISURE

The following tables indicate many of the wide variety of activities Americans participate in during their leisure time. For the most part the United States is a sporting nation which takes its recreational time very seriously.

Table 5.20   Selected spectator sports: 1985–95

SPORT	Unit	1985	1987	1990	1991	1992	1993	1994	1995
Baseball, major leagues: [1]									
Attendance	1,000	47,742	53,182	55,512	57,820	56,852	71,237	50,010	51,288
Regular season	1,000	46,824	52,011	54,824	56,814	55,873	70,257	50,010	50,469
National League	1,000	22,292	24,734	24,492	24,696	24,113	36,924	25,808	25,110
American League	1,000	24,532	27,277	30,332	32,118	31,760	33,333	24,202	25,359
Playoffs	1,000	591	784	479	633	668	636	(X)	533
World Series	1,000	327	387	209	373	311	344	(X)	286
Players' salaries: [2]									
Average	$1,000	371	412	598	851	1,029	1,076	1,168	1,111
Basketball: [3][4]									
NCAA—Men's college:									
Teams	Number	753	760	767	796	813	831	858	868
Attendance	1,000	26,584	26,798	28,741	29,250	29,378	28,527	28,390	28,548
NCAA—Women's college:									
Teams	Number	746	756	782	806	815	826	859	864
Attendance	1,000	2,072	2,156	2,777	3,013	3,397	4,193	4,557	4,962
Pro: [5]									
Teams	Number	23	23	27	27	27	27	27	27
Attendance, total [6]	1,000	11,534	13,190	18,586	18,009	18,609	19,120	19,350	19,883
Regular season	1,000	10,506	12,065	17,369	16,876	17,367	17,778	17,984	18,516
Average per game	Number	11,141	12,795	15,690	15,245	15,689	16,060	16,246	16,727
Playoffs	1,000	985	1,091	1,203	1,109	1,228	1,338	1,349	1,347
Players' salaries:									
Average	$1,000	325	440	817	989	1,202	1,348	1,700	(NA)
Football:									
NCAA College: [4]									
Teams	Number	509	507	533	548	552	560	568	565
Attendance	1,000	34,952	35,008	35,330	35,528	35,225	34,871	36,460	35,638
National Football League: [7]									
Teams	Number	28	28	28	28	28	28	(NA)	(NA)
Attendance, total [8]	1,000	14,058	[9]15,180	17,666	17,752	17,784	14,772	(NA)	(NA)
Regular season	1,000	13,345	[9]11,406	13,960	13,841	13,829	13,967	(NA)	(NA)
Average per game	Number	59,567	[9]54,315	62,321	61,792	61,736	62,352	(NA)	(NA)
Postseason games [10]	1,000	711	656	848	813	815	805	(NA)	(NA)
Players' salaries: [11]									
Average	$1,000	194	203	352	415	645	683	637	714
Median base salary	$1,000	140	175	236	250	325	330	325	335
National Hockey league: [12]									
Regular season attendance	1,000	11,621	12,118	12,344	12,770	13,917	15,714	(NA)	15,658
Playoffs attendance	1,000	1,153	1,337	1,442	1,328	1,346	1,440	(NA)	1,447
Horseracing: [13][14]									
Racing days	Number	13,745	14,208	13,841	(NA)	13,644	13,237	13,082	(NA)
Attendance	1,000	73,346	70,105	63,803	(NA)	49,275	45,688	42,065	(NA)
Pari-mutuel turnover	Mil. dol	12,222	13,122	7,162	14,094	14,078	13,718	14,143	(NA)
Revenue to government	Mil. dol	625	608	611	624	491.3	473	453	(NA)
Greyhound: [13]									
Total performances	Number	9,590	11,156	14,915	(NA)	17,528	17,976	17,035	(NA)
Attendance	1,000	23,853	26,215	28,660	(NA)	28,003	(NA)	(NA)	(NA)
Pari-mutuel turnover	Mil. dol	2,702	3,193	3,422	3,422	3,306	3,255	2,948	(NA)
Revenue to government	Mil. dol	201	221	235	(NA)	204.2	194.9	183.0	(NA)
Jai alai: [13]									
Total performances	Number	2,736	2,906	3,620	3,619	3,288	3,200	3,146	(NA)
Games played	Number	32,260	38,476	(NA)	(NA)	45,067	43,056	42,607	(NA)
Attendance	1,000	4,722	6,816	5,329	(NA)	4,634	4,194	3,684	(NA)
Pari-mutuel turnover	Mil. dol	664.0	707.5	545.5	(NA)	425.9	384.2	330.7	(NA)
Revenue to government	Mil. dol	50	51	39	39	30	27	22	(NA)
Professional rodeo: [15]									
Rodeos	Number	617	637	754	798	791	791	782	739
Performances	Number	1,887	1,832	2,159	2,241	2,269	2,269	2,245	2,217
Members	Number	5,239	5,342	5,693	5,748	5,760	5,760	6,415	6,894
Permit-holders (rookies)	Number	2,534	2,746	3,290	3,006	2,888	2,888	3,346	3,835

NA Not available.   X Not applicable. [1] Source: The National League of Professional Baseball Clubs, New York, NY, *National League Green Book;* and The American League of Professional Baseball Clubs, New York, NY, *American League Red Book.* [2] Source: Major League Baseball Players Association, New York, NY.   [3] Season ending in year shown.   [4] Source: National Collegiate Athletic Assn., Overland Park, KS. For women's attendance total, excludes double-headers with men's teams. [5] Source: National Basketball Assn., New York, NY.   [6] Includes All-Star game, not shown separately.   [7] Source: National Football League, New York, NY.   [8] 1987 through 1992 includes preseason attendance, not shown separately.   [9] Season was interrupted by a strike.   [10] Includes Pro Bowl, a nonchampionship game and Super Bowl.   [11] Source: National Football League Players Association, Washington, DC.   [12] For season beginning in year shown. Source: National Hockey League, Montreal, Quebec.   [13] Source: Association of Racing Commissioners International, Inc., Lexington, KY.   [14] Includes thoroughbred, harness, quarter horse, and fairs.   [15] Source: Professional Rodeo Cowboys Association, Colorado Springs, CO., *Official Professional Rodeo Media Guide,* annual, (copyright).

Source: Compiled from sources listed in footnotes.

Table 5.21 Selected recreational activities: 1975–95

ACTIVITY	Unit	1975	1980	1985	1990	1992	1993	1994	1995
Softball, amateur: [1]									
Total participants [2]	Million..	26	30	41	41	41	42	42	42
Youth participants	1,000..	450	650	712	1,100	1,207	1,208	1,209	1,350
Adult teams [3]	1,000..	66	110	152	188	202	200	196	187
Youth teams [3]	1,000..	9	18	31	46	57	62	68	74
Golfers (one round or more) [4][5]	1,000..	13,036	15,112	17,520	27,800	24,800	24,600	24,300	25,000
Golf rounds played [5]	1,000..	308,562	357,701	414,777	502,000	505,400	498,600	464,800	490,200
Golf facilities	Number.	11,370	12,005	12,346	12,846	13,210	13,439	13,683	14,074
Classification:									
Private	Number.	4,770	4,839	4,861	4,810	4,568	4,492	4,367	4,324
Daily fee	Number.	5,014	5,372	5,573	6,024	6,552	6,803	7,126	7,491
Municipal	Number.	1,586	1,794	1,912	2,012	2,090	2,144	2,190	2,259
Tennis: [6]									
Players	1,000..	[7]34,000	(NA)	13,000	21,000	22,630	21,500	16,500	17,820
Courts	1,000..	130	(NA)	220	220	230	230	240	240
Indoor	1,000..	8	(NA)	14	14	14	14	15	15
Tenpin bowling: [8]									
Participants, total	Million..	62.5	72.0	67.0	71.0	82.0	79.0	79.0	79.0
Male	Million..	29.9	34.0	32.0	35.4	40.2	36.3	36.3	36.3
Female	Million..	32.6	38.0	35.0	35.6	41.8	42.6	42.3	42.3
Establishments	Number.	8,577	8,591	8,275	7,611	7,395	7,250	7,183	7,049
Lanes	1,000..	141	154	155	148	144	143	142	139
Membership, total [9]	1,000..	8,751	9,664	8,064	6,588	5,873	5,599	5,201	4,925
American Bowling Congress	1,000..	4,300	4,688	3,657	3,036	2,712	2,576	2,455	2,370
Women's Bowling Congress	1,000..	3.692	4,187	3,714	2,859	2,523	2,403	2,191	2,036
Young American Bowling Alliance [10]	1,000..	759	789	693	693	638	620	555	519
Motion picture theaters [11]	1,000..	15	18	21	24	26	26	26	28
Four-wall	1,000..	11	14	18	23	25	25	26	27
Drive-in	1,000..	4	4	3	1	1	1	(Z)	1
Receipts, box office	Mil. dol..	2,115	2,749	3,749	5,022	4,871	5,154	5,396	5,494
Admission, average price	Dollars	2.05	2.69	3.55	4.23	4.15	4.14	4.18	4.35
Attendance	Million..	1,033	1,022	1,056	1,187	1,173	1,244	1,292	1,263
Boating: [12]									
Recreational boats owned	Million..	9.7	11.8	13.8	16.0	16.2	16.2	16.6	17.1
Outboard boats	Million..	5.7	6.8	7.4	7.9	7.7	7.7	7.9	7.8
Inboard boats	Million..	0.8	1.2	1.4	2.2	2.5	2.7	2.9	2.6
Sailboats	Million..	0.8	1.0	1.2	1.3	1.3	1.3	1.3	1.4
Canoes	Million..	2.4	1.3	1.8	2.3	2.4	2.4	2.4	2.3
Rowboats and other	Million..	([13])	1.5	1.8	2.3	2.3	2.1	2.1	3.0
Expenditures, total [14]	Bil. dol..	4.8	7.4	13.3	13.7	10.3	11.3	14.1	17.2
Outboard motors in use	1,000..	7,649	8,241	9,733	11,524	12,000	12,240	12,511	12,819
Motors sold	1,000..	435	315	392	352	272	283	317	308
Value, retail	Mil. dol..	411	554	1,319	1,546	1,268	1,364	1,793	1,882
Outboard boats sold	1,000..	328	290	305	227	192	205	231	215
Value, retail	Mil. dol..	263	408	759	978	839	914	1,426	1,362
Inboard/outdrive boats sold	1,000..	70	56	115	97	75	75	94	95
Value, retail	Mil. dol..	420	616	1,663	1,794	1,239	1,244	1,791	1,925
Inboard cruisers sold	1,000..	6.5	5.3	12.2	7.5	3.5	3.4	5.4	5.3
Value, retail	Mil. dol..	256	457	1,341	1,383	621	655	1,170	1,215

NA Not available.　Z Fewer than 500.　[1] Source: Amateur Softball Association, Oklahoma City, OK.　[2] Amateur Softball Association teams and other amateur softball teams.　[3] Amateur Softball Association teams only.　[4] Source: National Golf Foundation, Jupiter, FL.　[5] Prior to 1990, for persons 5 years of age and over; thereafter for persons 12 years of age and over.　[6] Source: Tennis Industry Association, White Plains, NY. Players for persons 12 years old and over who played at least once.　[7] 1974 data.　[8] For season ending in year shown. Persons 5 years old and over. Source: Bowling Headquarters, Greendale, WI.　[9] Membership totals are for U.S., Canada and for U.S. military personnel worldwide.　[10] Prior to 1985, represents American Jr. Bowling Congress and ABC/WIBC Collegiate Division.　[11] Source: Motion Picture Association of America, Inc., Encino, CA. Prior to 1975, figures represent theaters; thereafter, screens.　[12] Source: National Marine Manufacturers Association, Chicago, IL.　[13] Included in canoes.　[14] Represents estimated expenditures for new and used boats, motors, accessories, safety equipment, fuel, insurance, docking, maintenance, storage, repairs, and other expenses.

Source: Compiled from sources listed in footnotes.

Table 5.22 Participation in selected sports activities: 1995. (In thousands, except rank. For persons 7 years of age or older. Except as indicated, a participant plays a sport more than once in the year. Based on a sampling of 15,000 households)

ACTIVITY	ALL PERSONS Number	Rank	SEX Male	Female	AGE 7-11 years	12-17 years	18-24 years	25-34 years	35-44 years	45-54 years	55-64 years	65 years and over	HOUSEHOLD INCOME (dol.) Under 15,000	15,000-24,999	25,000-34,999	35,000-49,999	50,000-74,999	75,000 and over
Total	**235,460**	(X)	**114,348**	**121,114**	**18,898**	**22,154**	**25,467**	**41,670**	**42,149**	**30,224**	**21,241**	**33,659**	**46,429**	**36,325**	**34,260**	**41,588**	**47,424**	**29,435**
Number participated in:																		
Aerobic exercising[1]	23,052	12	4,302	18,750	784	1,553	4,120	6,522	4,587	2,872	1,164	1,450	3,043	2,895	2,974	4,159	5,626	4,356
Backpacking[2]	10,244	23	6,413	3,831	980	1,724	1,461	2,627	2,065	914	299	175	1,779	1,389	1,435	2,069	1,997	1,575
Badminton	5,758	28	2,541	3,217	890	1,255	777	1,055	1,137	508	85	51	795	1,027	932	1,224	1,200	581
Baseball	15,728	17	12,087	3,642	5,443	4,547	1,499	1,911	1,474	539	207	107	2,204	2,095	2,453	3,249	3,527	2,199
Basketball	30,098	9	20,918	9,180	6,315	8,720	4,707	5,331	3,389	1,038	413	184	4,594	3,765	4,246	5,569	7,593	4,331
Bicycle riding[1]	56,308	3	29,830	26,478	12,796	10,152	5,018	9,694	8,550	4,455	2,710	2,933	8,763	8,074	8,567	10,382	11,975	8,547
Billiards	31,108	8	19,364	11,744	1,465	3,744	7,547	9,189	5,228	2,426	913	597	5,067	5,086	4,553	6,446	6,112	3,844
Bowling	41,898	6	21,142	20,756	4,951	5,850	7,174	9,492	7,078	3,535	1,776	2,043	5,817	6,494	6,409	8,164	9,891	5,123
Calisthenics[1]	9,339	24	4,042	5,298	1,218	1,578	1,096	1,669	1,397	989	468	924	1,096	1,426	1,549	1,536	2,159	1,572
Camping[3]	42,818	5	22,835	19,983	5,379	5,707	5,482	9,061	8,619	4,337	2,504	1,729	6,218	6,518	6,696	9,380	9,417	4,588
Exercise walking[1]	70,268	1	25,097	45,171	2,176	3,503	6,241	13,294	14,180	11,626	8,286	10,961	12,143	10,543	10,121	12,322	14,906	10,233
Exercising with equipment[1]	44,328	4	20,583	23,745	722	3,357	5,899	10,599	9,773	7,084	3,380	3,515	4,550	5,408	5,693	8,223	11,723	8,732
Fishing—fresh water	39,282	7	26,444	12,838	4,621	4,363	4,430	7,961	7,782	4,919	2,703	2,502	7,051	5,715	6,474	8,186	7,814	4,042
Fishing—salt water	10,717	22	7,685	3,032	687	1,059	1,189	2,152	2,268	1,668	819	874	1,738	1,391	1,367	2,263	2,387	1,571
Football—tackle	8,270	27	7,366	904	1,623	3,579	1,383	1,029	384	137	47	88	1,402	1,147	1,431	1,493	1,824	974
Football—touch	12,095	19	9,796	2,299	2,956	3,803	2,086	1,898	917	255	127	53	1,941	1,855	1,717	2,312	2,720	1,549
Golf	23,959	11	18,016	5,943	866	2,020	2,451	5,697	4,921	3,675	1,823	2,506	1,580	2,020	3,170	4,101	7,106	5,981
Hiking	25,047	10	13,848	11,199	2,696	3,098	2,926	5,704	5,244	3,044	1,354	980	3,702	3,408	3,316	4,784	5,646	4,191
Hunting with firearms	16,253	16	13,968	2,285	555	1,898	2,312	4,246	3,497	1,983	988	775	2,503	2,585	2,828	3,608	3,098	1,630
Martial arts	4,549	30	2,912	1,637	1,317	822	621	786	538	242	152	71	931	718	623	821	792	664
Racquetball	4,699	29	3,343	1,356	150	425	1,135	1,543	791	485	103	66	514	590	643	813	1,299	839
Running/jogging[1]	20,635	13	11,874	8,761	2,037	3,594	3,703	5,008	3,215	1,960	616	503	2,486	2,569	2,650	3,840	5,101	3,989
Skiing—alpine/downhill	9,267	26	5,623	3,638	615	1,558	1,588	2,393	1,638	877	389	203	597	637	786	1,575	2,677	2,990
Skiing—cross country	3,428	31	1,757	1,672	288	438	443	557	801	479	298	125	509	203	374	464	963	914
Soccer	11,976	20	7,691	4,285	5,054	3,487	1,258	946	838	218	85	88	1,384	1,359	1,626	2,190	3,144	2,272
Softball	17,611	15	10,007	7,604	2,513	3,877	2,465	4,615	2,734	907	222	279	2,050	2,390	3,025	3,693	4,279	2,174
Swimming	61,531	2	28,944	32,587	11,255	10,098	6,860	10,809	10,905	5,172	3,110	3,322	8,258	7,763	8,468	11,695	14,492	10,855
Table tennis	9,274	25	5,474	3,799	1,087	2,165	1,341	1,782	1,664	699	255	280	1,012	1,170	1,212	1,986	2,315	1,579
Target shooting	11,193	21	9,019	2,174	720	1,450	1,632	3,084	2,270	1,207	565	267	1,570	1,730	1,964	2,540	2,123	1,267
Tennis	12,571	18	6,813	5,758	1,157	2,250	2,479	2,720	2,102	1,073	512	278	1,414	1,502	1,335	2,045	3,210	3,065
Volleyball	17,957	14	8,772	9,184	2,003	4,290	3,429	4,172	2,728	968	294	73	2,586	2,336	2,622	3,759	4,229	2,425

X Not applicable.   [1] Participant engaged in activity at least six times in the year.   [2] Includes wilderness camping.   [3] Vacation/overnight.

Source: National Sporting Goods Association, Mt. Prospect, IL, *Sports Participation in 1995: Series I* (copyright).

5.6 CRIME

For many the United States is synonymous with crime, and there are indeed very real problems. However, the image of crime in the media and in 'entertainment' can result in a rather distorted picture. The following tables include information on a wide range of crimes, their number, rate, and an indication of who the victims of crime are: crime is more likely to happen to a black male than to anyone else. The rate of crimes per 1,000 persons should be noted which puts them in a proper perspective, as should the differing levels of victimization for different groups.

Table 5.23 Murder — circumstances and weapons used or cause of death: 1980–95. (Based solely on police investigation)

CHARACTERISTIC	1980	1990	1994	1995	CHARACTERISTIC	1980	1990	1994	1995
Murders, total	21,860	20,273	22,084	20,220	Other motives	20.6	19.4	23.1	23.9
Percent distribution . . .	100.0	100.0	100.0	100.0	Unknown	15.1	24.8	28.1	28.9
CIRCUMSTANCES					TYPE OF WEAPON OR CAUSE OF DEATH				
Felonies, total	17.7	20.8	18.4	17.7	Guns	62.4	64.3	70.0	68.2
Robbery	10.8	9.2	9.4	9.3	Handguns	45.8	49.8	57.8	55.8
Narcotics	1.7	6.7	5.6	5.1	Cutting or stabbing . . .	19.3	17.4	12.7	12.6
Sex offenses	1.5	1.1	0.6	0.6	Blunt objects [1]	5.0	5.4	4.1	4.5
Other felonies	3.7	3.7	2.8	2.8	Personal weapons [2] . . .	5.9	5.5	5.3	5.9
Suspected felonies . . .	6.7	0.7	0.6	0.6	Strangulations,				
Argument, total	39.9	34.4	29.8	29.0	asphyxiations	2.3	2.0	1.8	1.9
Property or money . .	2.6	2.5	1.8	1.7	Fire	1.3	1.4	0.9	0.8
Romantic triangle . . .	2.3	2.0	1.7	1.4	All other [3]	3.8	4.0	5.2	6.1
Other arguments . . .	35.0	29.8	26.3	25.9					

[1] Refers to club, hammer, etc.   [2] Hands, fists, feet, etc.   [3] Includes poison, drowning, explosives, narcotics, and unknown.
Source: U.S. Federal Bureau of Investigation, *Crime in the United States*, annual.

Table 5.24 Homicide victims, by race and sex: 1970–95. (Rates per 100,000 resident population in specified group. Excludes deaths to non-residents of the US. Beginning 1980, deaths classified according to the ninth revision of the *International Classification of Diseases*; for earlier years, classified according to revision in use at the time)

YEAR	HOMICIDE VICTIMS					HOMICIDE RATE [2]				
	Total [1]	White		Black		Total [1]	White		Black	
		Male	Female	Male	Female		Male	Female	Male	Female
1970	16,848	5,865	1,938	7,265	1,569	8.3	6.8	2.1	67.6	13.3
1980	24,278	10,381	3,177	8,385	1,898	10.7	10.9	3.2	66.6	13.5
1981	23,646	9,941	3,125	8,312	1,825	10.3	10.4	3.1	64.8	12.7
1982	22,358	9,260	3,179	7,730	1,743	9.6	9.6	3.1	59.1	12.0
1983	20,191	8,355	2,880	6,822	1,672	8.6	8.6	2.8	51.4	11.3
1984	19,796	8,171	2,956	6,563	1,677	8.4	8.3	2.9	48.7	11.2
1985	19,893	8,122	3,041	6,616	1,666	8.3	8.2	2.9	48.4	11.0
1986	21,731	8,567	3,123	7,634	1,861	9.0	8.6	3.0	55.0	12.1
1987	21,103	7,979	3,149	7,518	1,969	8.7	7.9	3.0	53.3	12.6
1988	22,032	7,994	3,072	8,314	2,089	9.0	7.9	2.9	58.0	13.2
1989	22,909	8,337	2,971	8,888	2,074	9.2	8.2	2.8	61.1	12.9
1990	24,932	9,147	3,006	9,981	2,163	10.0	9.0	2.8	69.2	13.5
1991	26,513	9,581	3,201	10,628	2,330	10.5	9.3	3.0	72.0	14.2
1992	25,488	9,456	3,012	10,131	2,187	10.0	9.1	2.8	67.5	13.1
1993	26,009	9,054	3,232	10,640	2,297	10.1	8.6	3.0	69.7	13.6
1994	24,926	9,055	2,921	10,083	2,124	9.6	8.5	2.6	65.1	12.4
1995	21,577	(NA)	(NA)	(NA)	(NA)	8.2	(NA)	(NA)	(NA)	(NA)

NA Not available.   [1] Includes races not shown separately.   [2] Rate based on enumerated population figures as of April 1 for 1970, 1980, and 1990; July 1 estimates for other years.
Source: U.S. National Center for Health Statistics, *Vital Statistics of the United States*, annual, and unpublished data.

Table 5.25   Robbery and property crimes, by type and selected characteristic: 1980–95

ITEM	NUMBER OF OFFENSES (1,000)				RATE PER 100,000 INHABITANTS				AVERAGE VALUE LOST (dol.)	
	1980	1990	1994	1995	1980	1990	1994	1995	1994	1995
Robbery, total [1]	**566**	**639**	**620**	**581**	**251.1**	**257.0**	**237.7**	**220.9**	**801**	**873**
Type of crime:										
Street or highway	293	359	338	315	130.1	144.2	129.7	120.0	651	645
Commercial house	78	73	76	71	34.6	29.5	29.2	27.2	1,229	1,351
Gas station	23	18	13	13	10.4	7.1	5.2	5.1	450	959
Convenience store	38	39	32	30	17.0	15.6	12.2	11.4	387	400
Residence	60	62	67	63	26.8	25.1	25.9	24.0	1,041	1,082
Bank	8	9	9	9	3.8	3.8	3.4	3.5	3,551	4,015
Weapon used:										
Firearm	228	234	257	238	101.3	94.1	98.8	90.6	(NA)	(NA)
Knife or cutting instrument	73	76	59	53	32.3	30.7	22.5	20.1	(NA)	(NA)
Other dangerous weapon	51	61	60	53	22.8	24.5	22.9	20.2	(NA)	(NA)
Strongarm	214	268	243	236	94.8	107.7	93.5	90.0	(NA)	(NA)
Burglary, total	**3,795**	**3,074**	**2,712**	**2,595**	**1,684.1**	**1,235.9**	**1,041.8**	**987.6**	**1,311**	**1,259**
Forcible entry	2,789	2,150	1,822	1,737	1,237.5	864.5	700.0	661.2	(NA)	(NA)
Unlawful entry	711	678	677	657	315.6	272.8	260.1	250.1	(NA)	(NA)
Attempted forcible entry	295	245	213	201	131.0	98.7	81.7	76.4	(NA)	(NA)
Residence	2,525	2,033	1,814	1,736	1,120.6	817.4	696.7	660.6	1,296	1,211
Nonresidence	1,270	1,041	898	859	563.5	418.5	345.1	327.0	1,341	1,257
Occurred during the night	1,508	1,135	957	905	669.0	456.4	367.7	344.4	(NA)	(NA)
Occurred during the day	1,263	1,151	1,049	1,000	560.3	462.8	402.7	380.5	(NA)	(NA)
Larceny-theft, total	**7,137**	**7,946**	**7,876**	**8,001**	**3,167.0**	**3,194.8**	**3,025.4**	**3,044.9**	**505**	**535**
Pocket picking	85	81	64	51	37.9	32.4	24.5	19.4	428	350
Purse snatching	107	82	60	51	47.5	32.8	23.2	19.5	279	279
Shoplifting	773	1,291	1,178	1,205	343.0	519.1	452.4	458.4	133	108
From motor vehicles	1,231	1,744	1,865	1,940	546.4	701.3	716.4	738.5	542	531
Motor vehicle accessories	1,366	1,185	1,014	964	606.2	476.3	389.4	367.0	312	329
Bicycles	715	443	496	501	317.5	178.2	190.7	190.5	252	286
From buildings	1,187	1,118	1,027	1,004	526.9	449.4	394.3	382.1	851	891
From coin-operated machines	58	63	53	50	25.8	25.4	20.4	18.9	228	283
Other	1,613	1,940	2,120	2,235	715.7	780.0	814.2	850.5	680	770
Motor vehicles, total [2]	**1,132**	**1,636**	**1,539**	**1,473**	**502.2**	**657.8**	**591.2**	**560.5**	**4,940**	**5,129**
Automobiles	845	1,304	1,216	1,154	374.8	524.3	467.2	439.2	(NA)	(NA)
Trucks and buses	149	238	239	240	66.1	95.5	92.0	91.2	(NA)	(NA)

NA Not available.   [1] Includes other crimes not shown separately.   [2] Includes other types of motor vehicles not shown separately.

Source: U.S. Federal Bureau of Investigation, *Population-at-Risk Rates and Selected Crime Indicators*, annual.

Table 5.26   Number and rate of victimizations for crimes against persons and households, by type: 1973–90. (Data based on National Crime Survey)

YEAR	PERSONAL SECTOR								HOUSEHOLD SECTOR			
	Total	Violent crimes						Larce-ny— theft	Total	Bur-glary	Lar-ceny	Motor vehi-cle theft
		Total	Rape	Rob-bery	Assault							
					Total	Aggra-vated	Simple					
NUMBER (1,000)												
1973	20,322	5,351	156	1,108	4,087	1,655	2,432	14,971	15,340	6,459	7,537	1,344
1975	21,867	5,573	154	1,147	4,272	1,631	2,641	16,294	17,400	6,744	9,223	1,433
1980	21,430	6,130	174	1,209	4,747	1,707	3,041	15,300	18,821	6,973	10,468	1,381
1985	19,296	5,823	138	985	4,699	1,605	3,094	13,474	15,568	5,594	8,703	1,270
1986	18,751	5,515	130	1,009	4,376	1,543	2,833	13,235	15,368	5,557	8,455	1,356
1987	19,371	5,796	148	1,046	4,602	1,587	3,014	13,575	15,966	5,705	8,788	1,473
1988	19,966	5,910	127	1,048	4,734	1,741	2,993	14,056	15,830	5,777	8,419	1,634
1989	19,691	5,861	135	1,092	4,634	1,665	2,969	13,829	16,128	5,352	8,955	1,820
1990	18,984	6,009	130	1,150	4,729	1,601	3,128	12,975	15,419	5,148	8,304	1,968
RATE [1]												
1973	123.6	32.6	1.0	6.7	24.9	10.1	14.8	91.1	217.8	91.7	107.0	19.1
1975	128.9	32.8	0.9	6.8	25.2	9.6	15.6	96.0	236.5	91.7	125.4	19.5
1980	116.3	33.3	0.9	6.6	25.8	9.3	16.5	83.0	227.4	84.3	126.5	16.7
1985	99.4	30.0	0.7	5.1	24.2	8.3	15.9	69.4	174.4	62.7	97.5	14.2
1986	95.6	28.1	0.7	5.1	22.3	7.9	14.4	67.5	170.0	61.5	93.5	15.0
1987	98.0	29.3	0.8	5.3	23.3	8.0	15.2	68.7	173.9	62.1	95.7	16.0
1988	100.1	29.6	0.6	5.3	23.7	8.7	15.0	70.5	169.6	61.9	90.2	17.5
1989	97.8	29.1	0.7	5.4	23.0	8.3	14.7	68.7	169.9	56.4	94.4	19.2
1990	93.4	29.6	0.6	5.7	23.3	7.9	15.4	63.8	161.0	53.8	86.7	20.5

- Represents zero or rounds to zero.   [1] Rate per 1,000 persons, 12 years old and over; and per 1,000 households.

Source: U.S. Bureau of Justice Statistics, *Criminal Victimization in the United States*, annual.

Table 5.27   Victimization rates for crimes against persons: 1973–90. (Rates per 1,000 persons, 12 years old and over. Includes attempted crimes. Data based on National Crime Survey. Totals exclude personal larceny)

YEAR	Total [1]	White	Black	His-panic [2]	MALE			FEMALE			VICTIM-OFFENDER RELATIONSHIP	
					White	Black	His-panic [2]	White	Black	His-panic [2]	Stranger	Non-stranger
1973	33	32	42	36	43	53	53	21	32	22	22	11
1980	33	32	41	40	43	53	54	22	31	27	21	12
1981	35	33	50	39	44	61	53	23	40	26	23	12
1982	34	33	44	40	42	57	49	25	33	32	22	12
1983	31	30	41	38	39	50	48	21	33	29	18	13
1984	31	30	41	35	38	51	45	22	33	26	17	14
1985	30	29	38	30	38	47	33	21	31	27	18	12
1986	28	28	33	27	35	39	39	21	29	15	16	12
1987	29	28	42	39	36	52	44	20	34	35	17	13
1988	30	28	40	35	34	47	(NA)	22	35	(NA)	18	12
1989	29	28	36	39	35	50	50	22	25	28	18	12
1990	30	28	40	37	36	53	50	21	28	25	18	12

NA Not available.   [1] Includes races not shown separately.   [2] Hispanic persons may be of any race.

Table 5.28   Crime incidents, by place and time of occurrence and injury: 1990

INCIDENT CHARACTERISTICS	Rape	ROBBERY			ASSAULT			Per-sonal larceny with contact
		Total	Comple-ted	At-tempted	Total	Aggravat-ed	Simple assault	
Incidents, total	124,480	1,036,840	724,950	311,890	4,089,660	1,282,850	2,806,810	632,010
PERCENT DISTRIBUTION								
Place of occurrence	100.0	100.0	100.0	100.0	100.0	100.0	100.0	100.0
Inside own home.	35.0	9.4	10.8	6.3	13.4	11.8	14.1	[1]1.8
Near own home, on the street near home	[1]12.3	7.4	6.5	9.4	11.9	12.2	11.8	.6.4
Friend's, relative's, or neighbor's home . .	[1]10.5	4.8	4.3	.6.1	8.2	10.1	7.3	[1]1.7
Inside commercial property	9.4	4.9	6.4	[1]1.5	13.7	11.9	14.5	26.5
In parking lot or garage	3.4	12.7	11.4	15.8	7.9	9.6	7.1	6.5
Inside school, on school property	0.0	4.8	4.0	6.7	11.4	6.2	13.8	.5.4
In park, field, or playground	[1]0.5	.3	3.3	[1]2.5	4	4.8	3.6	[1]0.8
On street not near own or friend's home .	.17.9	41.2	42.8	37.3	20.0	22.1	19.1	23.0
Other	[1]11.0	11.7	10.6	14.5	9.6	11.2	8.7	27.8
Time of occurrence:								
Daytime (6 a.m. to 6 p.m.)	27.0	44.0	42.5	47.5	48.6	41.7	51.7	65.6
Nighttime	73.0	54.4	57.0	51.9	51.0	57.8	47.9	31.8
Percent of incidents:								
Involving the presence of a weapon	17.2	49.6	50.5	47.5	28.8	91.8	(X)	(X)
Resulting in victim injury	(NA)	34.5	35.7	31.6	33.0	39.2	29.8	(X)

NA Not available.   X Not applicable.   [1] Estimate based on about ten or fewer sample cases.
Source of tables 296 and 297: U.S. Bureau of Justice Statistics, *Criminal Victimization in the United States*, annual.

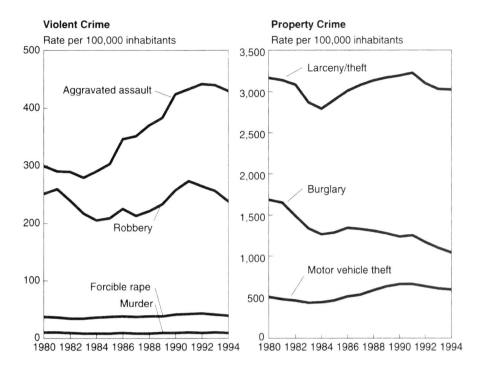

Figure 5.10   *Violent and property crime rates: 1980–94*

Source: US Bureau of the Census, *Statistical Abstract of the United States: 1997,*
Government Printing Office, Figure 5.1.

UNITED STATES CENSUS DIVISIONS AND REGIONS

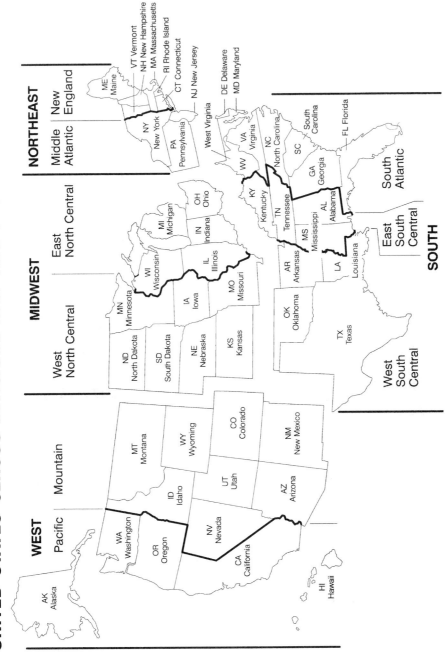

Source: US Bureau of the Census, *Statistical Abstract of the United States: 1997*, Government Printing Office.

ACKNOWLEDGEMENTS

Grateful acknowledgement is made to the following sources for permission to reproduce material in this book.

PHOTOGRAPHS

pp.15 and 94: Culver Pictures; p.22: © Mansell/Katz Pictures; p.31: MGM/Courtesy Kobal; p.38: United Artists/Courtesy Kobal; p.58: Courtesy of Ball State University; p.89: Courtesy of Henry Ford Museum and Greenfield Village; p.122: Department of Foreign Affairs and Trade, Australia; p.210: UPI/Bettmann; p.224: Tim Clary/Popperfoto/ASP; pp.243 (both), 247, 314 and 349: AP/Wide World Photos; pp.318 and 321: Popperfoto.

FIGURE

Figure 5.8: adapted from Gilbert, M. (1993) *The Dent Atlas of American History*, 3rd edn, Dent, © 1968, 1985 and 1993 by Martin Gilbert by permission of Routledge.

TEXT

Excerpt from 'One Culture and the New Sensibility', from *Against Interpretation* by Susan Sontag. Copyright © 1965, 1966 and copyright renewed © 1994 by Susan Sontag. Reprinted by permission of Farrar, Straus & Giroux, Inc. Also by permission of Aitken, Stone and Wiley; F. Scott Fitzgerald: *The Crack-Up*. Copyright 1945 by New Directions Publishing Corp. Reprinted by permission of New Directions Publishing Corp, and Harold Ober Associates Incorporated; All lines from 'A Supermarket in California' from *Collected Poems 1947–1980* by Allen Ginsberg. Copyright © 1955 by Allen Ginsberg. Copyright Renewed. Reprinted by permission of HarperCollins Publishers, Inc. Also reprinted by permission of Penguin Books from 'A Supermarket in California' from *Collected Poems 1947–1980* by Allen Ginsberg (Viking, 1985), © Allen Ginsberg 1956, 1984; Extract from Moley, R. (1971) *The Hay's Office*, by permission of Jerome S. Ozer (Publisher); 'The Age of Play', 'Confessions of an Automobilist', 'Confessions of a Ford Dealer' and 'Brokers and Suckers' from Mowry, George E., *The Twenties, Fords, Flappers and Fanatics*, © 1963, Reprinted by permission of Prentice-Hall, Englewood Cliffs, NJ; Extract from 'The Miracle of America', advertising pamphlet of the Advertising Council, USA (1948); Reprinted with the permission of Macmillan Publishing Company from *The Other America: Poverty in the United States*, by Michael Harrington. Copyright © 1962, 1969, 1981 by Michael Harrington; Excerpts from 'Why do they work so hard' and 'Inventions re-making leisure' in *Middletown, a Study in American Culture*, by Robert S. Lynd and Helen M. Lynd, copyright 1929, by Harcourt Brace & Company and renewed 1957, by Robert S. Lynd and Helen M. Lynd, reprinted by permission of the publisher; Bee, J.D. 'Eros and Thanatos: an analysis of the

INDEX